AF693298

ILLINOIS EVIDENCE

Illinois Rules of Evidence, Statutes, and Constitution
A Compendium for Criminal Litigation

This book is dedicated to Chief Justice Thomas R. Fitzgerald (ret.), whose vision and leadership led to the codification of the new Illinois Rules of Evidence.

ILLINOIS EVIDENCE

Illinois Rules of Evidence, Statutes, and Constitution
A Compendium for Criminal Litigation

Ralph Ruebner and Katarina Durcova

VANDEPLAS PUBLISHING, LLC

UNITED STATES OF AMERICA

Illinois Evidence: Illinois Rules of Evidence, Statutes, and Constitution
A Compendium for Criminal Litigation

Ruebner, Ralph and Durcova, Katarina

Published by:

Vandeplas Publishing, LLC – November 2012

801 International Parkway, 5th Floor
Lake Mary, FL. 32746
USA

www.vandeplaspublishing.com

Copyright © 2012 by Ralph Ruebner and Katarina Durcova
All rights reserved.
No part of this book may be reproduced, stored in a retrieval system, or transmitted by any means, electronic, mechanical, photocopying, recording, or otherwise, without written permission from the authors.

ISBN 978-1-60042-183-9

Contents

About the Author

Ralph Ruebner is a Professor of Law and the Associate Dean for Academic Affairs at The John Marshall Law School. He has taught evidence, criminal procedure, and international human rights law. He previously served as the Executive Director of the John Marshall Law School Criminal Justice Clinic and as the Deputy State Appellate Defender in both the First and Second Appellate Districts in Illinois. He is a 1969 graduate of the American University Washington College of Law.

About the Co-author

Katarina Durcova is a Staff Attorney at the Criminal Division of the Circuit Court of Cook County. She is a 2011 graduate of The John Marshall Law School and was a John Marshall Law School Library Research Fellow. She previously worked as a judicial extern for Justice Margaret O'Mara Frossard (ret.) at the First District of the Illinois Appellate Court and as a summer law clerk in the Pre-Trial Chamber of the International Criminal Tribunal for the former Yugoslavia in the Hague, the Netherlands.

Acknowledgments

The authors wish to acknowledge the generosity of Professor Michael H. Graham and Justice Gino L. DiVito (ret.), in permitting us to use their publications as supporting authorities in our Author's Commentary sections in this book. Professor Graham is the Advisor to the Special Supreme Court Committee on Evidence and is the author of GRAHAM'S HANDBOOK OF ILLINOIS EVIDENCE (10th ed. 2010). Justice DiVito is a member of the Special Supreme Court Committee on Evidence and is the author of *The Illinois Rules of Evidence: A Color-Coded Guide Containing the New Rules, the Committee's General and Specific Comments, a Comparison with the Federal Rules of Evidence, and Additional Commentary (Including the Federal Rules of Evidence as Amended Effective December 1, 2011)* (Jan. 1, 2012), http://www.tdrlawfirm.com/assets/downloads/Illinois_Rules_of_Evidence_Color-Coded_Guide.pdf. It has been a great honor for me to serve with them on this committee as its Reporter.

The authors wish to thank John Marshall Law School Dean John E. Corkery and Professor June H. Liebert, Director of the John Marshall Law School Library, for establishing the Library Fellows Program that enabled Katarina Durcova to work on this project. We extend a very special thank you to Ms. Raizel Liebler, the Research Services Librarian at The John Marshall Law School, for her guidance and support of the Library Fellows Program and the creation of this book. The authors also wish to thank Brittany Flaherty Theis, Esquire, and Jessica Kull, Esquire, for their research assistance.

Ralph Ruebner
Chicago
October 2012

Table of Authorities

Robert P. Burns, *A Wistful Retrospective on Wigmore and His Prescriptions for Illinois Evidence Law*, 100 NW. U. L. REV. 131 (2006).

Edward K. Cheng & Albert H. Yoon, *Does* Frye *or* Daubert *Matter? A Study of Scientific Admissibility Standards*, 91 VA. L. REV. 471 (2005).

Comments, *A Symposium on the Uniform Rules of Evidence and Illinois Evidence Law, Confidential Privileges*, 49 N.W. L. REV. 481 (1954).

Gino L. DiVito, *The Illinois Rules of Evidence: A Color-Coded Guide Containing the New Rules, the Committee's General and Specific Comments, a Comparison with the Federal Rules of Evidence, and Additional Commentary (Including the Federal Rules of Evidence as Amended Effective December 1, 2011)* (Jan. 1, 2012), http://www.tdrlawfirm.com/assets/downloads/Illinois_Rules_of_Evidence_Color-Coded_Guide.pdf.

HON. GEORGE FIEDLER, THE ILLINOIS LAW COURTS IN THREE CENTURIES: 1673-1973 (1973).

MICHAEL H. GRAHAM, GRAHAM'S HANDBOOK OF ILLINOIS EVIDENCE (10th ed. 2010).

Michael H. Graham, *Prior Inconsistent Statements—Impeachment and Substantive Admissibility: An Analysis of the Effect of Adopting the Proposed Illinois Rules of Evidence*, 1978 U. ILL. L. F. 329 (1978).

ROBERT S. HUNTER, TRIAL HANDBOOK FOR ILLINOIS LAWYERS (5th ed. 1983).

ILLINOIS COURTS: A HISTORY OF ILLINOIS JUDICIAL SYSTEMS, http://www.state.il.us/court/General/ History.asp (last visited Feb. 29, 2012).

Michael N. Kennedy, *Escaping the Fishbowl: A Proposal to Fortify the Deliberative Process*, 99 NW. U. L. REV. 1769 (2005).

STEPHEN A. SALTZBURG ET AL., 1 FEDERAL RULES OF EVIDENCE MANUAL (7th ed. 1998).

WILLIAM A. SCHROEDER, 11 ILL. PRAC., COURTROOM HANDBOOK ON ILLINOIS EVIDENCE (2010).

Ralph Slovenko, *Psychiatry and a Second Look at the Medical Privilege*, 6 WAYNE L. REV. 175 (1959-1960).

Robert A. Weninger, *Amended Federal Rule of Evidence 408: Trapping the Unwary*, 26 REV. LITIG. 401 (2007).

John H. Wigmore, *Some Evidence Statutes That Illinois Ought to Have*, 1 ILL. L. R. 9 (1906-1907).

MARK E. WOJCIK, ILLINOIS LEGAL RESEARCH (2d ed. 2009).

CHARLES ALAN WRIGHT & KENNETH W. GRAHAM, 23 FEDERAL PRACTICE & PROCEDURE, EVIDENCE (1999) (Current through the 2011 Supplement).

Introduction

The year 2012 marks 300 years since the introduction of European law in this part of our country that eventually became the State of Illinois. First came the customary law of Paris and the French civil law, then the Quebec Act of 1774, followed by the Northwest Ordinance of 1787 and the English common law, the Territory of Illinois law in 1809, and statehood in 1818. *See* HON. GEORGE FIEDLER, THE ILLINOIS LAW COURTS IN THREE CENTURIES: 1673-1973, 6-7, 16, 45, 99, 153 (1973); ILLINOIS COURTS: A HISTORY OF ILLINOIS JUDICIAL SYSTEMS, http://www.state.il.us/court/General/History.asp (last visited Feb. 29, 2012); MARK E. WOJCIK, ILLINOIS LEGAL RESEARCH 23-25 (2d ed. 2009). The first act under the new state constitution was the adoption of "the common law of England as the law of Illinois." WOJCIK, ILLINOIS LEGAL RESEARCH at 28-29; *see* Laws of the State of Illinois, p. 3, § 1 (1st Gen. Assemb., 2d Session, 1819) (stating that "the common law of England, all statutes or acts of the British Parliament made in aid of the common law prior to the fourth year of the reign of King James the I . . . shall be the rule of decision, and shall be considered as full force, until repealed by legislative authority"); 5 ILCS 50/1; Torres v. Walsh, 98 Ill. 2d 338 (1983).

The development of the rules of evidence followed quickly, a shared responsibility of the legislature and the Illinois Supreme Court. The first evidence statute was enacted in 1819. It addressed the authentication of federal, state and territorial law and certification of judicial records and proceedings of the courts of the United States. Laws of the State of Illinois, pp. 30-31, §§ 1-2 (1st Gen. Assemb., 2d Sess., 1819). Some of the earliest Illinois Supreme Court opinions establishing evidence rules were Sawyer v. Stephenson, 1 Ill. 24 (1820) (allowing limited impeachment of jury verdict with juror affidavit), and Mason v. Wash, 1 Ill. 39 (1822) (rejecting judicial notice of laws of other states). The law of evidence continued its development over the years as a joint venture of the General Assembly and the Supreme Court. For example, in 1827, the Fifth General Assembly enacted a law that required in civil cases the production of books and writings in possession by the parties to the litigation. The Revised Code of Laws of Illinois, Practice, p. 313, § 10 (5th Gen. Assemb., 1827). The Fifth General Assembly also enacted a statute that allowed a party to read land records in evidence. The Revised Code of Laws of Illinois, Conveyances, p. 102, § 17 (5th Gen. Assemb., 1827).

In 1836, the Illinois Supreme Court recognized the hearsay rule in Jones v. Doe *ex dem.* Bramblet, 2 Ill. 276 (1836) (declarations of third persons are not admissible in evidence), and in 1849 it ruled that evidence of general moral character was inadmissible to impeach the testimony of a witness in Frye v. President, etc., of Bank of Ill., to Use of Hardin, 11 Ill. 367 (1849) (only impeachment by evidence of "general character of the witness for truth and veracity" is proper). In 1854, the Illinois Supreme Court recognized the now discredited *res gestae* exception to the hearsay rule. *See* Brennan v. People, 15 Ill. 511 (1854) (finding *res gestae* to be relevant evidence on the issue of intent); Lander v. People, 104 Ill. 248, 256 (1882) (*res gestae* describes many "spontaneous exclamation[s]" relating to or explaining a startling or exciting event); *see also* People v. Dennis, 181 Ill. 2d 87 (1998) (noting that "Illinois has abandoned the concept of *res gestae* as amorphous, having been applied indiscriminately and inhibiting any reasonable analysis"); WILLIAM A. SCHROEDER, 11 ILL. PRAC., COURTROOM HANDBOOK ON ILLINOIS EVIDENCE § 803(0):1 (2010). In 1855, the Illinois Supreme Court recognized the past recollection recorded and dying declarations exceptions to the hearsay rule. See Iglehart v. Jernegan, 16 Ill. 513 (1855) (past recollection recorded); Starkey v. People, 17 Ill. 17 (1855) (noting that dying declarations are "statements of the deceased as to the cause of the injury from which death finally results, . . . admitted in evidence [as] an exception in the law of evidence"). The Illinois Supreme Court also recognized the then-existing state of mind exception to the hearsay rule in 1859. See Jumpertz v. People, 21 Ill. 375 (1859) (noting that evidence of victim's acts and declarations was admissible to show victim's state of mind).

Illinois adhered to the common law "voucher rule," which prohibited a party from impeaching its own witness. See Rockwood v. Poundstone, 38 Ill. 199, 201 (1865) (noting that "a party after producing and examining a witness, can not prove him to be of such a general bad character as would render him unworthy of credit" but rather it may call another witness to "disprove . . . facts" presented by the first witness); Chicago City Ry. Co. v. Gregory, 221 Ill. 591 (1906) (noting, that "[t]he law is well settled that a party to a suit cannot impeach a witness voluntarily called by him"). The Illinois legislature enacted the Statute of 1867, creating a legislative exception to the adverse party witness rule in civil cases. Public Laws of the State of Illinois, p. 185, § 6 (25th Gen. Assemb., 1867) (Springfield: Baker, Bailhache & Co.). Years later the legislature enacted an exception to the "voucher rule" in civil cases by allowing for impeachment of an adverse party's witness by a prior inconsistent statement. ILL. REV. STAT. 1977, ch. 110, § 60 (now 735 ILCS 5/2-1102). Illinois Supreme Court Rule 238 initially followed the "voucher rule" and did not allow the impeachment of a witness by the calling party. ILL. REV. STAT. 1967, ch. 110A, § 238. It subsequently abolished the "voucher rule" by amendment in 1982. ILL. SUP. CT. R. 238. The amended Illinois Supreme Court Rule 238 "liberalized" trial practice to allow a party to impeach its own witness. People v. Tate, 87 Ill. 2d 134 (1981). Illinois Supreme Court Rule 238(a) states that "[t]he credibility of a witness may be attacked by any party, including the party calling the witness."

Other examples of the collaboration between the Illinois Supreme Court and the legislature in creating evidentiary principles can be seen in the development of the rules governing witness disqualification and impeachment of a witness by a prior conviction. Historically, a witness was disqualified from testifying in civil and criminal cases by reason of a prior conviction for an "infamous" crime. The Public and General Statute Laws of the State of Illinois, Criminal Code, Third Div. § 15, at 201 (Stephen F. Gale, 1839); ILL. REV. STAT. 1874, p. 394, § 279 (the "infamous" crimes included "murder, rape, kidnapping, willful and corrupt perjury or subornation of perjury, arson, burglary, robbery, sodomy, . . . incest, larceny, forgery, counterfeiting, or bigamy"); Bartholomew v. People, 104 Ill. 601 (1882) (noting that "[u]nder the common law, persons convicted of crimes which rendered them infamous were excluded from being witnesses"). Certain misdemeanors designated as "*crimen falsi*" were considered infamous crimes "along with treason and any felony." People v. Spates, 77 Ill. 2d 193, 201-202 (1979). *Crimen falsi* included offenses "which injuriously affect[ed] the administration of public justice, such as perjury, subornation of perjury, suppression of testimony by bribery or conspiracy to procure the absence of a witness, or to accuse one wrongfully of a crime, or barratry, or the like." *Id.* at 201. The legislature subsequently amended the criminal code to eliminate witness disqualification by reason of conviction. ILL. REV. STAT. 1874, Div. 42, p. 410, § 6; 725 ILCS 5/115-16; Bartholomew v. People, 104 Ill. 601 (1882) (noting that legislature "remove[d] the common law disability"). The fact of conviction was admissible, however, to "affect" the credibility of the witness. ILL. REV. STAT. 1874, Div. 42, p. 410, § 6 (stating that "[n]o person shall be disqualified as a witness in a criminal case or proceeding by reason of his interest in the event of the same, as a party or otherwise, or by reason of his having been convicted of any crime, but such interest or conviction may be shown for the purpose of affecting his credibility"); Public Laws of the State of Illinois, p. 183, § 1 (25th Gen. Assemb., 1867) (Springfield: Baker, Bailhache & Co.); ILL. REV. STAT. 1967, ch. 38, § 155-1. In 1971, the Illinois Supreme Court interpreted the statute and decided to adopt the draft of Federal Rule of Evidence 609 in what came to be known as the *Montgomery* Rule. People v. Montgomery, 47 Ill. 2d 510 (1971). The *Montgomery* rule allows a party to impeach the credibility of a witness by a prior qualifying conviction in criminal as well as civil cases. *Montgomery*, 47 Ill. 2d at 517; Knowles v. Panopoulos, 66 Ill. 2d 585 (1977). A court will admit a qualifying conviction unless it "determines that the probative value of the evidence of the crime is substantially outweighed by the danger of unfair prejudice." *Montgomery*, 47 Ill. 2d at 516-17. Pursuant to the *Montgomery* rule, the admissibility of a prior conviction is entirely in the judge's discretion. *Id.* at 515.

The legislature together with the Supreme Court also created a business records exception to the hearsay rule. In 1867, the General Assembly enacted a law that allowed admissibility of business records in civil cases. Public Laws of the State of Illinois, Witnesses, p. 184, § 3 (25th Gen. Assemb., 1867) (Springfield: Baker, Bailhache & Co.). The admissibility of business records in civil cases subsequently came to be regulated by Illinois Supreme Court Rule 236(a) in 1967. ILL. REV. STAT. 1967, ch. 110A, § 236. Admissibility of business records in criminal cases was also codified in 1967 by 725 ILCS 5/115-5. Laws of the State of Illinois p. 2838, § 1 (75th Gen. Assemb., 1967). The legislature and the Supreme Court also developed special rules for the admissibility of medical and hospital records. Generally, medical and hospital records are not admissible as business records in a criminal trial. 725 ILCS 5/115-5(c)(1). Pursuant to 625 ILCS 5/11-501.4, enacted in 1987, however, "the results of blood or urine tests performed for the purpose of determining the content of alcohol, other drugs, or both, in an individual's blood or urine . . . [during] medical treatment in a hospital emergency room for injuries resulting from a motor vehicle accident" are admissible. Laws of the State of Illinois p. 4636 (85th Gen. Assemb., 1987); ILL. REV. STAT. 1991, ch. 95 1/2, § 11-501.4; People v. Jung, 192 Ill. 2d 1 (2000). Police accident reports are inadmissible in civil cases as records made in the regular course of business pursuant to Illinois Supreme Court Rule 236(b). ILL. R. EVID. Committee Commentary § 5, pg. 6-7. ILL. SUP. CT. R. 236(b). In criminal cases, statements contained in documents "made by anyone during an investigation of an alleged offense or during any investigation relating to pending or anticipated litigation of any kind" are inadmissible pursuant to 725 ILCS 5/115-5(c)(2). ILL. R. EVID. Committee Commentary § 5, pg. 6-7. Statements contained in police reports, however, may be used for impeachment purposes and may qualify for admissibility as past recollection recorded statements. *See* People v. Williams, 159 Ill. App. 3d 527 (1st Dist. 1987) (police dispatch card admissible to impeach defendant's testimony about time he had called police); People v. Strausberger, 151 Ill. App. 3d 832 (2d Dist. 1987) (admitting police accident report under past recollection recorded exception in a reckless homicide prosecution to establish why officer concluded that defendant was intoxicated on the night of the accident).

Current Illinois Supreme Court Rule 1 recognizes that the Supreme Court Rules apply in civil and criminal proceedings "together with the Civil Practice Law and the Code of Criminal Procedure." The new Illinois Rule of Evidence 101 reinforces the authority of the two branches to develop the laws of evidence but establishes the supremacy of the Illinois Supreme Court: "A statutory rule of evidence is effective unless in conflict with a rule or a decision of the Illinois Supreme Court." ILL. R. EVID. 101; *see also* Preface to the Final Draft of the Illinois Supreme Court Committee on Proposed Illinois Rules of Evidence iii-iv (July 18, 1977) (noting that "[t]he Illinois Supreme Court, under our present system of common law rules of evidence, is the final authority as to what the law of evidence is").

Codification of Illinois evidence was a quest for more than 100 years. *See* Robert P. Burns, *A Wistful Retrospective on Wigmore and His Prescriptions for Illinois Evidence Law*, 100 NW. U. L. REV. 131, 136-37 (2006). However, Professor and Dean of the Northwestern

University Law School, John H. Wigmore, writing in 1906 cautioned against wholesale rejection of the common law basis of Illinois evidence: "Remove not the ancient landmark, which thy fathers have set." John H. Wigmore, *Some Evidence Statutes that Illinois Ought to Have*, 1 ILL. L. R. 9, 9 (1906-1907). Dean Wigmore explained that "[o]f the pure common law rules . . . probably more remain untouched in Illinois today than in England. This, on the whole, is as it should be."

Dean Wigmore was not totally opposed to legislative efforts to modernize Illinois evidence. He stated that "not all change is dangerous; only a change untested by experience. If experience has elsewhere already tested and approved a change, then let us have it, by all means." Wigmore, 1 ILL. L. R. at 9. Dean Wigmore favored that certain statutory provisions enacted in England, Canada and other states be adopted by the Illinois legislature. For instance, he believed in the adoption of the rule allowing a party to impeach its own witness by self-contradiction. *Id.* at 9. He was also a proponent of the abolition of the rule in Queen's Case. Queen Caroline's Case, 2 Br. & B. 284, 129 Eng. Rep. 976 (1820); Wigmore, 1 ILL. L. R. at 9-10. The rule in Queen's Case required the cross-examiner to show the witness his or her written statement before examining the witness about its contents. People v. Moses, 11 Ill. 2d 84 (1957); People v. Perri, 381 Ill. 244 (1942). Dean Wigmore criticized the rule, stating that "if the witness had lied, and was ready to lie again, this gave him full warning and every chance to evade detection." *Id.* at 10. He noted that "[t]his rule did as much to blunt a legitimate cross-examination as any one rule could do." *Id.* He also believed that there was a need for the adoption of a rule allowing depositions in criminal cases, and the enactment of a hearsay exception allowing certain declarations of a deceased person. *Id.* at 10-11. He also urged the adoption of statutory provisions that would allow admissibility of certified copies of public or official documents in evidence. *Id.* at 11-12. He sought to expand pretrial discovery in civil and criminal trials beyond books or writings to include chattels—real or personal. *Id.* at 12. Dean Wigmore encouraged the adoption of a rule that would allow a cross-examiner to question a witness beyond the scope of direct examination as to any facts that are material to the issues on trial, and the enactment of a provision that would allow comparison of handwriting samples. *Id.* at 13.

The debate on modernizing Illinois evidence rules continued, and in 1971 it focused on hearsay and the Illinois "orthodox rule." The orthodox rule stood for the proposition that unless a prior inconsistent statement of a witness fell within a hearsay exception, it could not be introduced to prove the truth of the matter asserted. People v. Collins, 49 Ill. 2d 179, 194-95 (1971); Michael H. Graham, *Prior Inconsistent Statements—Impeachment and Substantive Admissibility: An Analysis of the Effect of Adopting the Proposed Illinois Rules of Evidence*, 1978 U. ILL. L. F. 329, 332 (1978). While a prior inconsistent statement could not be used substantively, it could be used as impeachment evidence to establish that the witness was untrustworthy. *Collins*, 49 Ill. 2d at 194-95; Graham, *Prior Inconsistent Statements*, 1978 U. ILL. L. F. at 332. Justice Schaefer explained in *Collins* that prior inconsistent statements, especially when used in criminal cases,

> are often highly incriminating and are usually made outside the presence of the defendant. To give these statements substantive value would allow an accused to be convicted on extrajudicial statements of witnesses—a practice that runs counter to the notions of fairness on which our legal system is founded.
>
> *Collins*, 49 Ill. 2d at 194.

The Illinois Supreme Court in *Collins* expressed its unwillingness "to adopt a rule which permits the substantive use of prior out-of-court statements of witnesses," and retained the orthodox rule. *Id.* at 198. Yet, shortly after the *Collins* decision, the Illinois Supreme Court established a committee to consider whether Illinois courts should depart from the "orthodox rule." Graham, *Prior Inconsistent Statements*, 1978 U. ILL. L. F. at 334. The majority of the committee decided against the modification of the orthodox rule because "there was no compelling need to change it." *Id.* at 334-35. The committee reasoned that "the rule work[ed] well and . . . a jury [was] able to consider prior statements admitted for impeachment purposes solely on the issue of credibility"; there were adequate remedies protecting the proponent from a witness that testified "in a manner contrary to the proponent's expectations"; "extrajudicial statements [were] inherently unreliable"; and witnesses often did not read signed statements. *Id.* at 334-35. The committee also noted that "even prior testimonial statements should be excluded" because "grand jury testimony is not subject to cross-examination," and abandonment of the orthodox rule "would turn discovery depositions into evidence depositions" and "turn preliminary hearings in criminal cases into extended adversary proceedings." *Id.* at 335. The Illinois Supreme Court subsequently confirmed the orthodox rule's validity in People v. Powell, 53 Ill. 2d 465 (1973), rejecting the defendant's request to admit a prior inconsistent statement as substantive evidence. Subsequent legislative action helped change the rule. In 1984, the legislature enacted 725 ILCS 5/115-10.1, which allows admissibility of some prior inconsistent statements as substantive evidence in criminal trials.

On November 10, 1975, the Illinois Supreme Court established the Illinois Supreme Court Committee on Rules of Evidence in an attempt to "review [] the Rules of Evidence applicable in Illinois courts and suggest [] such revisions as may be deemed desirable." Rex Carr, *Memorandum to the Illinois Supreme Court Committee on Proposed Illinois Rules of Evidence* (July 18, 1977). Mr. Rex Carr was the Chairman of the Committee; Professor Michael H. Graham, an Advisor to the current Special Supreme Court Committee on Evidence, was the Reporter; and the Honorable Gino L. DiVito, a member of the current Special Supreme Court Committee on Evidence, was a member of this committee as well. The Committee issued a report in 1977 in which it recommended that Illinois codify the rules of evidence using the Federal Rules of Evidence almost exclusively as a model. 1977 ILLINOIS SUPREME COURT COMMITTEE ON RULES OF EVIDENCE (Proposed Final Draft, July 18, 1977). The Committee's rationale for the codification of the rules of evidence was to promote efficiency of trials, to state rules "clearly and simply," to "improve the law of evidence," to facilitate future changes in evidence law, to reduce litigation by minimizing evidentiary trial errors, and to create "[u]niformity among jurisdictions." *Id.* at i-v. Mr. Lyle W. Allen drafted the minority report of the 1977 Committee, in which he argued that the proposed rules were "inadequate to the task for which they [were] purportedly recommended." *Id.* at xi. He explained that Illinois law was not "settled," and that adoption of the code therefore did not "codify established doctrines of evidence." *Id.* at viii, x, xi, 69.

There were a number of areas of contention in the 1977 report. One, for example, involved the proposed Illinois Rule of Evidence 301, pertaining to the nature of presumptions in civil cases. *Id.* at 14. The majority report urged the Committee to adopt the common law rule, which was consistent with Federal Rule of Evidence 301, and which did not require the "the burden of persuasion [to] shift," but rather allowed it to remain with the party who initially had it. *Id.* at 14-15. The proposed rule was based on the "bursting bubble" theory, which the majority of the Committee explained as follows:

> When fact A is established, fact B must be assumed until the opponent introduces evidence sufficient to support a finding by the trier of fact of the nonexistence of the presumed fact. Upon introduction of such evidence the presumption is overcome and disappears. However, any inference from fact A to fact B remains.
> *Id.* at 15.

The minority of the Committee argued that the "bursting bubble" theory caused the presumption to disappear "without regard to whether anyone believe[d] the evidence contrary to the presumed fact." *Id.* at 18. The minority contended that the "bursting bubble" theory had been "abrogated for a presumption based on a rational inference: the doctrine of res ipsa loquitur." *Id.* at 18. The majority disagreed, explaining that the proposed rule was consistent with the doctrine of *res ipsa loquitur*, noting that "the inference, or presumption, [would] not simply vanish or disappear when contrary evidence appear[ed], but [would] remain[] to be considered with all the other evidence in the case and must be weighed by the jury against the direct evidence offered by the party charged." *Id.* at 14. The minority argued that the majority position conflicted with and would "effectively negate []" various statutes that created presumptions and some that shifted the burden of proof. *Id.* at 18. The majority of the Committee disagreed with this contention, noting that the proposed rule gave "the legislature the option to shift the burden of persuasion if it" so desired. *Id.* at 14.

The minority of the Committee also opposed the majority's deletion of the words "considerations of undue delay, waste of time" as provided in Federal Rule of Evidence 403. *Id.* at 28. The majority's proposal excluded relevant evidence only on grounds of prejudice or confusion. *Id.* The minority argued that the language of Federal Rule of Evidence 403 should be reinstated "to permit the court to exercise its discretion to prevent undue delay and waste of time." *Id.*

The 1977 Committee members also disagreed about methods of proving a character trait. The majority proposed that only reputation evidence could be used to prove character. *Id.* at 30-31. The minority of the Committee supported the use of opinion testimony as well as reputation testimony to prove character, as consistent with Federal Rule of Evidence 405. *Id.* Another point of contention was the proposed Illinois Rule of Evidence 407 on subsequent remedial measures. The majority recommended that the Committee adopt language similar to the Federal Rule of Evidence 407, which excluded evidence of subsequent remedial measures to prove culpable or negligent conduct. *Id.* at 33. By urging the adoption of Federal Rule of Evidence 407, the majority report sought to "encourag[e] people to take, or at least not discourag[e] them from taking, steps in furtherance of added safety." *Id.* The minority opposed the adoption of Federal Rule of Evidence 407, noting that the reasons behind the rule "no longer ha[d] validity" because most defendants were insured and required to correct known defective conditions. *Id.* at 34.

The members of the 1977 Committee also disagreed about the proposed Illinois Rule of Evidence 408, dealing with the admissibility of evidence pertaining to compromise and offers to compromise. *Id.* at 35. The minority report urged the adoption of language similar to Federal Rule of Evidence 408, including the last sentence pertaining to admissibility of evidence that is offered for another purpose, which the majority report excluded as "unnecessary." *Id.* at 35.

The Committee also expressed concerns with the Supreme Court's authority to supersede legislatively created privileges. Nonetheless it went on to propose Illinois Rules of Evidence 502, 503, and 504, dealing with the lawyer-client privilege, trade secrets, and the informant's privilege, respectively. *Id.* at 46-54. Other areas of contention included the proposed Illinois Rules of Evidence 608 and 609. The minority of the Committee sought to allow opinion as well as reputation evidence to attack or support the credibility of a witness in the proposed Illinois Rule of Evidence 608(a). The majority of the Committee departed from Illinois common law and the federal standard in its proposed Illinois Rule of Evidence 609. *Id.* at 69. The minority report observed that the majority's proposal "present[ed] a standard totally opposite that established in [People v. Montgomery, 47 Ill. 2d 510 (1970)]," in that it required proof that probative value of evidence of a prior conviction substantially outweigh its prejudicial effect. *Id.* at 69. The minority also noted that the proposed rule disfavored the use of evidence of prior conviction to impeach and eliminated the court's exercise of discretion. *Id.* at 69. The majority of the Committee opposed the adoption of Federal Rule of Evidence 614 dealing with the authority of the trial judge to call and interrogate witnesses and instead encouraged a case-by-case development of the doctrine. *Id.* at 76. The minority disagreed, noting that "failure to recommend adoption of Federal Rule [of Evidence] 614 [could] result in undue curtailment of the judicial authority." *Id.* at 77. The 1977 Committee reserved for another day proposed Illinois Rule of Evidence 706 on the question of the appointment of a court's own expert. *Id.* at 86. The majority report "modeled" proposed Illinois Rules of Evidence 803(6) and 803(8) on Illinois Supreme Court Rule 236(a) and (b). *Id.* at 101-102. The minority of the Committee urged the adoption of Federal Rules of Evidence 803(6) and 803(8) "because of [the] breadth and the certainty of admissibility [they] provide[d]." *Id.* at 101-102. The Committee unanimously adopted Federal Rules of Evidence 702, 703, 704, and 705, governing testimony of expert witnesses and eliminated "the [Illinois common law] requirement[s] of a hypothetical question" and "preliminary disclosure of underlying facts and data." *Id.* at 79-85. The report, however, made radical changes to the hearsay rule by re-defining what is hearsay. For example, the minority urged the adoption of Federal Rule of Evidence 801(d)(1)(A), and rejected the majority's proposal which eliminated admissibility of grand jury testimony where a party was not afforded the right of contemporaneous cross-examination. *Id.* at 91. The minority argued that grand jury testimony should not be considered hearsay and should be admissible as substantive evidence whenever a witness' trial testimony was inconsistent with prior grand jury testimony. *Id.* There appears to be no formal record why the Illinois Supreme Court rejected the 1977 report, although Justice Gino L. DiVito (ret.) recalls that the Supreme Court had issued an order stating that it "had decided not to adopt codified rules of evidence at the present time."

On November 24, 2008, the Illinois Supreme Court announced the creation of a Special Supreme Court Committee on Illinois Evidence. The Honorable Donald C. Hudson served as the Committee's Chair and the Honorable Warren D. Wolfson (ret.) served as the Committee's Vice-Chair. Professor Michael H. Graham, who previously acted as a Reporter on the 1977 Committee, served as an Advisor. The author served as the Reporter. The Honorable Gino L. DiVito (ret.), who previously served on the 1977 Committee also served as a member of the current Committee. Other members of the Committee included the Honorable Robert L. Carter, the Honorable Tom Cross, an Illinois State Representative, the Honorable John J. Cullerton, President of the Illinois State Senate, the Honorable Nathaniel R. Howse, Jr., the Honorable Heidi Ladd, Eileen Letts, Esquire, Shannon M. McNulty, Esquire, Robert Neirynck, Esquire, the Honorable Dennis J. Porter, Solicitor General Michael Scodro, Todd Smith, Esquire, Brian K. Trentman, Esquire, Michael J. Warner, Esquire, and the Honorable Arthur J. Wilhelmi of the Illinois State Senate. The Supreme Court "charged [the Committee] with codifying the law of evidence in the state of Illinois" from "rules of evidence [that were] dispersed throughout case law, statutes and Illinois Supreme Court rules." ILL. R. EVID. Committee Commentary p. 1. After the Committee presented its proposal for the codification of Illinois evidence rules to the Illinois Supreme Court, the Supreme Court invited written comments from the bar and scheduled public hearings in Chicago on May 18, 2010, and in Springfield on May 20, 2010. Thereafter, the Committee reconvened and revised and submitted a final set of evidence rules to the Supreme Court. On September 27, 2010, the Supreme Court approved and promulgated the Committee's proposals as the first codified set of Illinois Rules of Evidence, effective January 1, 2011.

As noted in Illinois Rule of Evidence 1102, the Illinois Rules of Evidence are modeled on, but are not wholly identical to the Federal Rules of Evidence. Under the new Illinois Rules of Evidence there are 14 instances of "modernization" amounting to a substantive change in Illinois law. ILL. R. EVID. Committee Commentary § 3, p. 2-4. The Committee also provided commentary for five of the rules and reserved three rules for later development. ILL. R. EVID. Committee Commentary p. 1; ILL. R. EVID. 101, 404, 405, 609, and 702. The

Committee reserved Illinois Rule of Evidence 407 because of a lack of unity in the appellate court's interpretation of a "core issue" pertaining to subsequent remedial measures in products liability cases. ILL. R. EVID. Committee Commentary § 1, pg. 1. The Committee also reserved Illinois Rules of Evidence 803(1) and 803(18) "because Illinois common law does not recognize either a present sense impression or a learned treatise hearsay exception." ILL. R. EVID. Committee Commentary § 1, pg. 1.

The Committee also made several major substantive changes to Illinois law. For instance, the Committee altered the prior Illinois rule that only allowed proof of character by reputation and not by opinion testimony. Illinois Rule of Evidence 405 now allows opinion as well as reputation testimony to prove character where such evidence is admissible, and Illinois Rule of Evidence 608 does likewise when proving character for truthfulness. ILL. R. EVID. Committee Commentary § 4, pg. 4-5. The Committee also recommended a change to the Illinois common law to allow habit evidence "whether corroborated or not and regardless of the presence of eyewitnesses" pursuant to Illinois Rule of Evidence 406. ILL. R. EVID. Committee Commentary § 3, p. 2. Before the enactment of the Illinois Rules of Evidence, a party's out-of-court admission was considered hearsay but admissible substantively as an exception to the hearsay rule. *In re* Estate of Rennick, 181 Ill. 2d 395, 406 (1998) ("An admission by a party is substantive evidence admissible as an exception to the rule excluding hearsay."). Pursuant to Illinois Rule of Evidence 801(d)(2), such admissions are now considered "not hearsay." ILL. R. EVID. Committee Commentary § 3, pg. 2-3. Adoption of Illinois Rule of Evidence 803(3), pertaining to statements of then-existing mental, emotional, or physical condition, eliminated the common law requirements of unavailability of the declarant and "reasonable probability" of the statement's truthfulness. ILL. R. EVID. Committee Commentary § 4, pg. 5. Illinois Rule of Evidence 803(3) "permits admissibility of declarations of intent to do an act as evidence to establish intent and as evidence to prove the doing of the intended act regardless of the availability of the declarant and without the court finding a reasonable probability that the statement is truthful." ILL. R. EVID. Committee Commentary § 4, pg. 6. The Committee chose not to articulate the scope of privileges in Illinois Rule of Evidence 501, instead stating that privileges "shall be governed by the principles of the common law as they may be interpreted by Illinois courts in the light of reason and experience. ILL. R. EVID. 501. The Committee invited the General Assembly to continue to develop evidence law, emphasizing that the Illinois Rules of Evidence were not "intended to preclude the Illinois legislature from acting in the future with respect to the law of evidence in a manner that will not be in conflict with the Illinois Rules of Evidence, as reflected in Rule 101." ILL. R. EVID. Committee Commentary pg. 1.

The Committee explained that it "drafted the Illinois Rules of Evidence in accordance with the following principles":

> **(1) Codification:** With the exception of the two areas discussed below under "Recommendations," the Committee incorporated into the Illinois Rules of Evidence the current law of evidence in Illinois whenever the Illinois Supreme Court or the Illinois Appellate Court had clearly spoken on a principle of evidentiary law within the last 50 or so years. Thus, Rule 702 retains the *Frye* standard for expert opinion evidence pursuant to the holding in Donaldson v. Central Illinois Public Service Co., 199 Ill. 2d 63, 767 N.E.2d 314 (2002). The Committee reserved Rule 407, related to subsequent remedial measures, because Appellate Court opinions are sufficiently in conflict concerning a core issue that is now under review by the Supreme Court. Also reserved are Rules 803(1) and 803(18), because Illinois common law does not recognize either a present sense impression or a learned treatise hearsay exception.
>
> **(2) Statute Validity:** The Committee believes it avoided affecting the validity of existing statutes promulgated by the Illinois legislature. There is a possible conflict between Rule

609(d) and section 5-150(1)(c) of the Juvenile Court Act (705 ILCS 405/5-150(1)(c)) with respect to the use of juvenile adjudications for impeachment purposes. That possible conflict, however, is not the result of promulgation of Rule 609(d) because that rule simply codifies the Illinois Supreme Court's adoption of the 1971 draft of Fed. R. Evid. 609 in *People v. Montgomery*, 47 Ill. 2d 510, 268 N.E.2d 695 (1971). As noted in the Comment to Rule 609(d), the present codification is not intended to resolve the issue concerning the effect of the statute. Moreover, the Illinois Rules of Evidence permit the Illinois legislature to act in the future with respect to the law of evidence as long as the particular legislative enactment is not in conflict with an Illinois Supreme Court rule or an Illinois Supreme Court decision. See ILL. R. EVID. 101.

(3) Modernization: Where there was no conflict with statutes or recent Illinois Supreme Court or Illinois Appellate Court decisions, and where it was determined to be beneficial and uniformly or almost uniformly accepted elsewhere, the Committee incorporated into the Illinois Rules of Evidence uncontroversial developments with respect to the law of evidence as reflected in the Federal Rules of Evidence and the 44 surveyed jurisdictions. The 14 instances of modernization of note are as follows:

(1) **Rule 106. Remainder of or Related Writings or Recorded Statements.** Rule 106 permits the admission contemporaneously of any other part of a writing or recording or any other writing or recording which "ought in fairness" be considered at the same time. Prior Illinois law appears to have limited the concept of completeness to other parts of the same writing or recording or an addendum thereto. The "ought in fairness" requirement allows admissibility of statements made under separate circumstances.

(2) **Rule 406. Habit; Routine Practice.** Rule 406 confirms the clear direction of prior Illinois law that evidence of the habit of a person or of the routine practice of an organization, whether corroborated or not and regardless of the presence of eyewitnesses, is relevant to prove that the conduct of the person or organization on a particular occasion was in conformity with the habit or routine practice.

(3) **Rule 408. Compromise and Offers to Compromise.** Prior Illinois law did not preclude admissibility of statements made in compromise negotiations unless stated hypothetically. Because they were considered a trap for the unwary, Rule 408 makes such statements inadmissible without requiring the presence of qualifying language.

(4) **Rule 613(a). Examining Witness Concerning Prior Statement.** Rule 613(a) provides that a prior inconsistent statement need not be shown to a witness prior to cross-examination thereon. Illinois Central Railroad v. Wade, 206 Ill. 523, 69 N.E. 565 (1903), was to the contrary.

(5) **Rule 801(d). Statements Which Are Not Hearsay.** Rule 801(d)(1)(A) codifies an Illinois statute (725 ILCS 5/115-10.1) that applies only in criminal cases. It makes admissible as "not hearsay" (rather than as a hearsay exception) a prior inconsistent statement of a declarant who testifies at a trial or a hearing and is subject to cross-examination, when the prior inconsistent statement was given under oath at a trial, hearing, or other proceeding, or in a deposition, or under other specified circumstances. The rule does not apply in civil cases. Rule 801(d)(1)(B) also codifies an Illinois statute (725 ILCS 5/115-12). It makes admissible as "not hearsay" a declarant's prior statement of identification of a person made after perceiving that person, when the declarant testifies at a trial or hearing in a criminal case and is subject to cross-examination concerning the statement. Rule 801(d)(2) provides substantive admissibility, as "not hearsay," for admissions of a party opponent.

(6) **Rule 801(d)(2)(D). Statement by a Party's Agent or Servant.** Rule 801(d)(2)(D) confirms the clear direction of prior Illinois law that a statement by a party's agent or servant concerning a matter within the scope of the agency or employment, made during the existence of the relationship, constitutes an admission of a party-opponent.

(7) **Rule 803(13). Family Records.** The requirement that the declarant be unavailable and that the statement be made before the controversy or a motive to misrepresent arose, Sugrue v. Crilley, 329 Ill. 458, 160 N.E. 847 (1928), have been eliminated.

(8) **Rule 803(14), (15), (19), (20) and (23).** With respect to records of or statements in documents affecting an interest in property, reputation concerning personal or family history, and concerning boundaries or general history, and judgments as to personal, family or general history or boundaries, Illinois law in each area was sparse or nonexistent.

(9) **Rules 803(16) and 901(b)(8). Statements in Ancient Documents.** The 30-year limitation to real property, Reuter v. Stuckart, 181 Ill. 529, 54 N.E. 1014 (1899), is relaxed in favor of 20 years without subject matter restriction.

(10) **Rule 804(b)(3). Statement Against Interest.** Rule 804(b)(3) makes applicable to the prosecution as well as the defense the requirement that in a criminal case a statement tending to expose the declarant to criminal liability is not admissible as a hearsay exception unless corroborating circumstances clearly indicate the trustworthiness of the statement.

(11) **Rule 806. Attacking and Supporting Credibility of Declarant.** Rule 806 dispenses with the requirement of an opportunity to deny or explain an inconsistent statement or conduct of an out-of-court declarant under all circumstances when a hearsay statement is involved. Whether Illinois law had already dispensed with the requirement with respect to a deposition was unclear.

(12) **Rule 902(11). Certified Records of Regularly Conducted Activity.** Self-authentication of business records is provided by Rule 902(11), following the model of Fed. R. Evid. 902(11) and 902(12) and 18 U.S.C. 3505.

(13) **Rule 1004. Admissibility of Other Evidence of Contents.** Rule 1004 does not recognize degrees of secondary evidence previously recognized in Illinois. Illinois Land & Loan Co. v. Bonner, 75 Ill. 315 (1874). In addition, it is no longer necessary to show that reasonable efforts were employed beyond available judicial process or procedure to obtain an original possessed by a third party. Prussing v. Jackson, 208 Ill. 85, 69 N.E. 771 (1904).

(14) **Rule 1007. Testimony or Written Admission of Party.** The Rule 1007 provision that testimony or a written admission may be employed to prove the contents of a document appears never before to have been the law in Illinois. Bryan v. Smith, 3 Ill. 47 (1839)."

(4) Recommendations: The Committee recommended to the Illinois Supreme Court a limited number of changes to Illinois evidence law (1) where the particularized evidentiary principle was neither addressed by statute nor specifically addressed in a comprehensive manner within recent history by the Illinois Supreme Court and (2) where prior Illinois law simply did not properly reflect evidentiary policy considerations or raised practical application problems when considered in light of modern developments and evidence rules adopted elsewhere with respect to the identical issue. The Committee identified, and the Illinois Supreme Court approved, recommendations in only two areas:

(a) Opinion testimony is added to reputation testimony as a method of proof in Rule 405, when character evidence is admissible, and in Rule 608 with respect to character for truthfulness:

Rule 405.

METHODS OF PROVING CHARACTER

(a) Reputation or Opinion. In all cases in which evidence of character or a trait of character of a person is admissible, proof may be made by testimony as to reputation, or by testimony in the form of an opinion.

(b) Specific Instances of Conduct.

(1) In cases in which character or a trait of character of a person is an essential element of a charge, claim, or defense, proof may also be made of specific instances of that person's conduct; and

(2) In criminal homicide or battery cases when the accused raises the theory of self-defense and there is conflicting evidence as to whether the alleged victim was the aggressor, proof may also be made of specific instances of the alleged victim's prior violent conduct.

Rule 608.

EVIDENCE OF CHARACTER WITNESS

The credibility of a witness may be attacked or supported by evidence in the form of opinion or reputation, but subject to these limitations: (1) the evidence may refer only to character for truthfulness or untruthfulness, and (2) evidence of truthful character is admissible only after the character of the witness for truthfulness has been attacked by opinion or reputation evidence or otherwise.

(b) Rule 803(3) eliminates the requirements currently existing in Illinois law, that do not exist in any other jurisdiction, with respect to statements of then existing mental, emotional, or physical condition, that the statement be made by a declarant found unavailable to testify, and that the trial court find that there is a "reasonable probability" that the statement is truthful:

Rule 803.

HEARSAY EXCEPTIONS;
AVAILABILITY OF DECLARANT IMMATERIAL

The following are not excluded by the hearsay rule, even though the declarant is available as a witness:

***

(3) Then Existing Mental, Emotional, or Physical Condition. A statement of the declarant's then existing state of mind, emotion, sensation, or physical condition (such as intent, plan, motive, design, mental feeling, pain, and bodily health), but not including:

(A) a statement of memory or belief to prove the fact remembered or believed unless it relates to the execution, revocation, identification, or terms of declarant's will; or

(B) a statement of declarant's then existing state of mind, emotion, sensation, or physical condition to prove the state of mind, emotion, sensation, or physical condition of another declarant at that time or at any other time when such state of the other declarant is an issue in the action.

The initial reference in Illinois to "unavailability" and "reasonable probability" occurred in People v. Reddock, 13 Ill. App. 3d 296, 300 N.E.2d 31 (1973), adopting the position taken by the North Carolina Supreme Court in State v. Vestal, 278 N.C. 561, 180 S.E.2d 755 (1971), when dealing with statements of intent by a declarant to prove conduct by the declarant consistent with that intent. Subsequent cases simply incorporated the two qualifications without analysis, evaluation, critique, or discussion. No reference has been made to the fact that the two requirements were initially adopted solely to deal with the Mutual Life Ins. v. Hillmon, 145 U.S. 285 (1892), issue as to whether a statement of an out of court declarant expressing her intent to perform a future act was admissible as evidence to prove the doing of the intended act. Interestingly, the North Carolina version of Rule 803(3) in the North Carolina Rules of Evidence is in substance the same as Rule 803(3), i.e., neither a requirement of "unavailability" nor "reasonable probability" is included.

Rule 803(3) permits admissibility of declarations of intent to do an act as evidence to establish intent and as evidence to prove the doing of the intended act regardless of the availability of the declarant and without the court finding a reasonable probability that the statement is truthful. Consistent with prior Illinois law, Rule 803(3)(B) provides that the hearsay exception for admissibility of a statement of intent as tending to prove the doing of the act intended applies only to the statements of intent by a declarant to prove her future conduct, not the future conduct of another person.

(5) Structural Change: A hearsay exception in Illinois with respect to both business and public records is recognized in civil cases by Illinois Supreme Court Rule 236, excluding police accident reports, and in criminal cases by section 115 of the Code of Criminal Procedure (725 ILCS 5/115), excluding medical records and police investigative records. The Illinois Rules of Evidence in Rule 803(6), records of regularly conducted activity (i.e., business records), and in Rule 803(8), public records and reports, while retaining the exclusions described above, removes the difference between civil and criminal business and public records in favor of the traditional and otherwise uniformly accepted division between business records, Rule 803(6), and public records and reports, Rule 803(8), both applicable in civil and criminal cases.

Rule 803(6)-(10).

**HEARSAY EXCEPTIONS;
AVAILABILITY OF DECLARANT IMMATERIAL**

The following are not excluded by the hearsay rule, even though the declarant is available as a witness:

***

(6) Records of regularly conducted activity. A memorandum, report, record, or data compilation, in any form, of acts, events, conditions, opinions, or diagnoses, made at or near the time by, or from information transmitted by, a person with knowledge, if kept in the course of a regularly conducted business activity, and if it was the regular practice of that business activity to make the memorandum, report, record or data compilation, all as shown by the testimony of the custodian or other qualified witness, or by certification that complies with Rule 902(11), unless the source of information or the method or circumstances of preparation indicate lack of trustworthiness, but not including in criminal cases medical records. The term "business" as used in this paragraph includes business, institution, association, profession, occupation, and calling of every kind, whether or not conducted for profit.

(7) Absence of Entry in Records Kept in Accordance With the Provisions of Paragraph (6). Evidence that a matter is not included in the memoranda reports, records, or data compilations, in any form, kept in accordance with the provisions of paragraph (6), to prove the nonoccurrence or nonexistence of the matter, if the matter was of a kind of which a memorandum, report, record, or data compilation was regularly made and preserved, unless the sources of information or other circumstances indicate lack of trustworthiness.

(8) Public records and reports. Records, reports, statements, or data compilations, in any form, of public offices or agencies, setting forth (A) the activities of the office or agency, or (B) matters observed pursuant to duty imposed by law as to which matters there was a duty to report, excluding, however, police accident reports and in criminal cases medical records and matters observed by police officers and other law enforcement personnel, unless the sources of information or other circumstances indicate lack of trustworthiness.

(9) Records of Vital Statistics. Facts contained in records or data compilations, in any form, of births, fetal deaths, deaths, or marriages, if the report thereof was made to a public office pursuant to requirements of law.

(10) Absence of Public Record or Entry. To prove the absence of a record, report, statement, or data compilation, in any form, or the nonoccurrence or nonexistence of a matter of which a record, report, statement, or data compilation, in any form, was regularly made and preserved by a public office or agency, evidence in the form of a certification in accordance with Rule 902, or testimony, that diligent search failed to disclose the record, report, statement, or data compilation, or entry.

(6) Referenced Statutes: Numerous existing statutes, the validity of which are not affected by promulgation of the Illinois Rules of Evidence, ILL. R. EVID. 101, relate in one form or another to the law of evidence. The Committee felt it was inappropriate, unnecessary and unwise to refer specifically to the abundance of statutory authority in an Appendix or otherwise. Reference is, however, made in the body of the text of the Illinois Rules of Evidence to certain statutes by citation or verbatim incorporation. Such references and the reasons therefor are as follows:

(1) Rule 404(a)(2): Character testimony of the alleged victim offered by the accused is specifically made subject to the limitations on character evidence contained in the rape shield statute, 725 ILCS 5/115-7.

(2) Rule 404(b): The bar to evidence of other crimes, wrongs, or acts to prove character to show conformity is made subject to the provisions of 725 ILCS 5/115-7.3, dealing with enumerated sex-related offenses, along with 725 ILCS 5/115-7.4 and 725 ILCS 5/115-20, dealing with domestic violence and other enumerated offenses, all of which allow admissibility of other crimes, wrongs, or acts under certain circumstances.

(3) Rule 409: The parallel protection afforded by 735 ILCS 5/8-1901 with respect to payment of medical or similar expenses is specifically referenced in Rule 409 to preclude any possibility of conflict.

(4) Rule 611(c): 735 ILCS 5/2-1102 provides a definition of adverse party or agent with respect to hostile witnesses as to whom interrogation may be by leading questions.

(5) Rule 801(d)(1): The provisions of 725 ILCS 5/115-10.1, dealing with prior inconsistent statements in a criminal case, are incorporated nearly verbatim in Rule

801(d)(1)(A) in the interests of completeness and convenience. Similar treatment is given to prior statements of identification, 725 ILCS 5/115-12, in Rule 801(d)(1)(B).

(6) Rule 803(4)(B): 725 ILCS 5/115-13, dealing with statements by the victim to medical personnel in sexual abuse prosecutions, is included verbatim in recognition that the statute admits statements to examining physicians while the generally applicable provisions of Rule 803(4)(A) do not.

(7) Redundancy: Where redundancy exists between a rule contained in the Illinois Rules of Evidence and another Illinois Supreme Court rule, reference should be made solely to the appropriate Illinois rule of evidence.
ILL. R. EVID. Committee Commentary § 1-7, pp. 1-9.

Chapter 1

- **Article I – General Provisions**
  - **Rule 1102. Title**
  - **Introductory Principles**
    - **Rule 101. Scope**
    - **Rule 1101. Applicability of Rules**
    - **Rule 102. Purpose and Construction**
    - **Rule 103. Rulings on Evidence**
    - **Rule 104. Preliminary Questions**
    - **Rule 1008. Functions of Court and Jury**
    - **Rule 105. Limited Admissibility**
    - **Rule 106. Remainder of or Related Writings or Recorded Statements**
- **Article II – Judicial Notice**
  - **Rule 201. Judicial Notice of Adjudicative Facts**
- **Evidence Principles Not Addressed by the Illinois Rules of Evidence**
  - **Burdens of Proof**
  - **Stipulations**
  - **Inferences and Presumptions in Criminal Cases**
  - **Curative Admissibility**
- **Article III – Presumptions in Civil Actions and Proceedings**
  - **Rule 301. Presumptions in General in Civil Actions and Proceedings**

Chapter 1

Article I – General Provisions

Rule 1102. Title

These rules may be known and cited as the Illinois Rules of Evidence.

Adopted September 27, 2010, eff. January 1, 2011.

Introductory Principles

Rule 101. Scope

These rules govern proceedings in the courts of Illinois to the extent and with the exceptions stated in Rule 1101. A statutory rule of evidence is effective unless in conflict with a rule or a decision of the Illinois Supreme Court.

Adopted September 27, 2010, eff. January 1, 2011.

Official Comment

Rule 101 provides that a statutory rule of evidence is effective unless in conflict with an Illinois Supreme Court rule or decision. There is no current statutory rule of evidence that is in conflict with a rule contained in the Illinois Rules of Evidence, with the possible exception of the statute discussed in the commentary to Rule 609(d) below.

Rule 1101. Applicability of Rules

(a) Except as otherwise provided in paragraphs (b) and (c), these rules govern proceedings in the courts of Illinois.

(b) **Rules Inapplicable.** These rules (other than with respect to privileges) do not apply in the following situations:

(1) **Preliminary Questions of Fact.** The determination of questions of fact preliminary to admissibility of evidence when the issue is to be determined by the court under Rule 104.

(2) **Grand Jury.** Proceedings before grand juries.

(3) **Miscellaneous Proceedings.** Proceedings for extradition or rendition; preliminary examinations in criminal cases; sentencing, or granting or revoking probation, conditional discharge or supervision; issuance of warrants for arrest, criminal summonses, and search warrants; and proceedings with respect to release on bail or otherwise, and contempt proceedings in which the court may act summarily.

(c) **Small Claims Actions.** These rules apply to small claims actions, subject to the application of Supreme Court Rule 286(b).

Adopted September 27, 2010, eff. January 1, 2011.

Rule 102. Purpose and Construction

These rules shall be construed to secure fairness in administration, elimination of unjustifiable expense and delay, and promotion of growth and development of the law of evidence to the end that the truth may be ascertained and proceedings justly determined.

Adopted September 27, 2010, eff. January 1, 2011.

Rule 103. Rulings on Evidence

(a) Effect of Erroneous Ruling. Error may not be predicated upon a ruling which admits or excludes evidence unless a substantial right of the party is affected, and

(1) **Objection.** In case the ruling is one admitting evidence, a timely objection or motion to strike appears of record, stating the specific ground of objection, if the specific ground was not apparent from the context; or

(2) **Offer of Proof.** In case the ruling is one excluding evidence, the substance of the evidence was made known to the court by offer or was apparent from the context within which questions were asked.

(b) Record of Offer and Ruling. The court may add any other or further statement which shows the character of the evidence, the form in which it was offered, the objection made, and the ruling thereon. It may direct the making of an offer in question and answer form.

(c) Hearing of Jury. In jury cases, proceedings shall be conducted, to the extent practicable, so as to prevent inadmissible evidence from being suggested to the jury by any means, such as making statements or offers of proof or asking questions in the hearing of the jury.

(d) Plain Error. Nothing in this rule precludes taking notice of plain errors affecting substantial rights although they were not brought to the attention of the court.

Adopted September 27, 2010, eff. January 1, 2011.

AUTHOR'S COMMENTARY

The Illinois Rules of Evidence are consistent with Illinois common law principles. To preserve an error for review, a party must object at trial and file a posttrial motion. People v. Woods, 214 Ill. 2d 455 (2005). An objection is the most common method of excluding evidence, including testimony. The main purpose of an objection is to alert the trial judge why the evidence should not be admitted. People v. Cloutier, 178 Ill. 2d 141 (1997). Additionally, it allows the proponent an opportunity to seek the admissibility of the evidence in a proper way. It also preserves an alleged error concerning the admissibility of the evidence for appellate review. *Id.*

When a party objects to the admissibility of evidence or when an objection is sustained, the proponent of the evidence should make an offer of proof by explicitly stating what the evidence would reveal. People v. Andrews, 146 Ill. 2d 413 (1992). An offer of proof preserves the issue for appeal and enables the appellate court to review the propriety of the trial court's ruling. Unlike the Federal Rule of Evidence 103, the Illinois Rule of Evidence 103 requires a party to renew an objection or make an offer of proof to preserve an alleged error for appellate review. *See* Gino L. DiVito, *The Illinois Rules of Evidence: A Color-Coded Guide Containing the New Rules, the Committee's General and Specific Comments, a Comparison with the Federal Rules of Evidence, and Additional Commentary* (*Including the Federal Rules of Evidence as Amended Effective December 1, 2011*) (Jan. 1, 2012), at 13, http://www.tdrlawfirm.com/assets/downloads/Illinois_Rules_of_Evidence_Color-Coded_Guide.pdf [hereinafter DiVito, *Color-Coded Guide*]. In criminal cases, however, "the standard for renewal of an objection [. . .] may be more liberal." DiVito, *Color-Coded Guide*, at 13 (citing People v. Williams, 161 Ill. 2d 1 (1994)).

Parties may also make use of motions *in limine* to settle evidentiary disputes before trial. People v. Harvey, 211 Ill. 2d 368 (2004). Such motions should be encouraged because they streamline trial proceedings and reduce the possibility of trial errors. People v. Williams, 188 Ill. 2d 365 (1999). A motion *in limine* facilitates the authority of a trial judge to exclude collateral and extraneous evidence that may mislead or prejudice the jury. *Id.*

Evidentiary rulings are generally reviewed for abuse of discretion. People v. Becker, 239 Ill. 2d 215 (2010). The defendant must raise all alleged errors on appeal or they will be deemed waived. People v. Taylor, 2011 IL 110067. The plain error doctrine allows review of an unpreserved error when evidence is closely balanced or error was serious and prejudicial to the defendant. People v. Herron, 215 Ill. 2d 167 (2005).

RELEVANT ILLINOIS SUPREME COURT RULES

Illinois Supreme Court Rule 451

Rule 451. Instructions

(c) Section 2-1107 of the Code of Civil Procedure to Govern. Except as otherwise provided in these rules, instructions in criminal cases shall be tendered, settled, and given in accordance with section 2-1107 of the Code of Civil Procedure, but substantial defects are not waived by failure to make timely objections thereto if the interests of justice require. The court shall instruct the jury after the arguments are completed, or, in its discretion, at the close of all the evidence.

> Amended June 19, 1968, effective January 1, 1969; amended February 19, 1982, effective April 1, 1982; amended May 28, 1982, effective July 1, 1982; amended May 20, 1997, effective July 1, 1997; amended February 10, 2006, effective July 1, 2006.

Illinois Supreme Court Rule 615

Rule 615. The Cause on Appeal

(a) Insubstantial and Substantial Errors on Appeal. Any error, defect, irregularity, or variance which does not affect substantial rights shall be disregarded. Plain errors or defects affecting substantial rights may be noticed although they were not brought to the attention of the trial court.

(b) Powers of the Reviewing Court. On appeal the reviewing court may:

(1) reverse, affirm, or modify the judgment or order from which the appeal is taken;
(2) set aside, affirm, or modify any or all of the proceedings subsequent to or dependent upon the judgment or order from which the appeal is taken;
(3) reduce the degree of the offense of which the appellant was convicted;
(4) reduce the punishment imposed by the trial court; or
(5) order a new trial.

> **Committee Comments**
> This is section 121-9 of the Code of Criminal Procedure of 1963 without change in substance.

PRIOR ILLINOIS CASE LAW

1. Defendant Preserves Error for Appellate Review by Objecting at Trial and Raising the Issue in a Post-trial Motion

People v. Woods, 214 Ill. 2d 455 (2005)

Defendant was convicted of possession of a controlled substance. The police recovered heroin from underneath a vehicle near him during his arrest. At trial defendant failed to object to the admissibility of the controlled substance evidence and in fact stipulated to a chemist's testimony that the substance recovered was heroin. On appeal he contended for the first time that the state failed to prove him guilty beyond a reasonable doubt because it failed to show a sufficient chain of custody for the heroin recovered during the arrest. The appellate court found that the chain of custody was insufficient and that the evidence did not sustain the conviction. On appeal to the Illinois Supreme Court, state argued that defendant waived the challenge as to the custody of the narcotics because he failed to object at trial and in his post-trial motion. The Supreme Court noted that

> [o]rdinarily, a defendant must both specifically object at trial and raise the specific issue again in a posttrial motion to preserve any alleged error for review. People v. Enoch, 122 Ill. 2d 176, 186 (1988). If a defendant fails to satisfy either prong of this test, his challenge is considered waived on appeal. *Enoch*, 122 Ill. 2d at 186.

The Supreme Court emphasized that this rule is especially relevant where defendant challenges the admissibility rather than the sufficiency of the evidence. The Supreme Court emphasized that the defendant did not challenge the sufficiency of the evidence, for had he done so, his claim would not have been subject to the waiver rule and could have been raised for the first time on direct appeal. The Supreme Court explained that challenge to the adequacy in the chain of custody merely constitutes "an evidentiary issue that is generally subject to waiver on review if not preserved by defendant's making a specific objection at trial and including this specific claim in his or her posttrial motion." The Supreme Court concluded that the error here did not rise to the level of plain error because the defendant not only failed to object to the admissibility of the challenged evidence at trial, he also affirmatively waived his challenge by stipulating to testimony that the substance was heroin.

2. Party Must Present a Contemporaneous Objection or Waive the Issue
People v. Cloutier, 178 Ill. 2d 141 (1997)

Defendant contended that the state made improper remarks during closing argument of the aggravation/mitigation stage at his sentencing hearing. The state argued that defendant waived the issues when he failed to object to the remarks. Defendant claimed, however, that he "was excused from objecting" because of the trial court's consistent overruling of his objections throughout the hearing. The Illinois Supreme Court disagreed, noting that

> [d]efendant cite[d] no authority that one may dispense with contemporaneous objections and assert error on appeal merely because he or she has suffered adverse rulings on other unrelated objections. Contemporaneous objections will often enable the trial court to cure error, thereby avoiding the possible need to retry the defendant. Obviously, the requirement of a contemporaneous objection promotes judicial economy and the swift and fair administration of justice. We are hesitant to undermine these objectives by allowing a criminal defendant to base his choice whether to object not on the merits of the objection but on a general appraisal of the trial court's inclinations. Hence we agree with the State that these claims of error are waived.

But see People v. Sullivan, 72 Ill. 2d 36 (1978) (finding no waiver in defendant's failure to object to prosecutor's argument because the error was so serious as to prejudice the right to fair trial).

3. Objection Must Be Timely and State the Specific Grounds on Which It Is Based
People v. Jackson, 84 Ill. 2d 350 (1981)

Defendant was convicted of armed robbery and aggravated kidnapping. The appellate court reversed his conviction finding plain error due to improper remarks by the state during closing argument. Defense counsel failed to object to all of the improper remarks but did make a general objection to the closing statement. Counsel also failed to state any grounds for it and did not request a ruling on the objection; rather, counsel said he was "just objecting." The Illinois Supreme Court noted that

> it is well settled that, when a defendant fails to make a timely objection at trial or in the post-trial motion, irregularities in the closing argument complained of on review are ordinarily deemed waived. People v. Precup, 73 Ill. 2d 7 (1978); People v. Killebrew, 55 Ill. 2d 337 (1973); People v. Pearson, 52 Ill. 2d 260 (1972); People v. Winters, 29 Ill. 2d 74 (1963). Timely and specific objection at trial affords the court an opportunity to prevent most errors by sustaining the objection or instructing the jury to disregard the answer or remark. People v. Carlson, 79 Ill. 2d 564 (1980); People v. Baptist, 76 Ill. 2d 19 (1979). And specific references in post-trial motions to the reasons why a trial judge's actions or rulings were wrong enables him to reconsider their propriety in a less pressured environment. If an egregious error has actually occurred, the judge can order a new trial, thus avoiding the delay and expense of appellate review.

Defendant argued that although he failed to properly object to the prosecutor's comments, they were "so seriously prejudicial" as to constitute plain error. The Supreme Court noted that courts will only invoke the plain error doctrine where the evidence is closely balanced and it is "plainly apparent from the record that an error affecting substantial rights was committed." Here, the Supreme Court did not find that a plain error occurred because the evidence was not closely balanced. The Supreme Court concluded that even if the prosecutor's remarks were erroneous, "the verdict in this case could not have been otherwise had the improper remarks not been made."

4. General Objection Will Be Treated As One Directed at the Relevancy of the Evidence
People v. Ervin, 342 Ill. 421 (1930)

Defendant was convicted of embezzlement. Defendant, who was a clerk of a circuit court, argued that the money he allegedly embezzled belonged to him and not to the county. On direct examination defense counsel repeatedly questioned him about his intentions with respect to the fees which he failed to report. The state generally objected to this line of questioning and the objections were sustained. The Illinois Supreme Court noted that although some of the questions posed to the defendant were improper, the state failed to state the specific grounds for the objections. The Supreme Court explained that "[a] general objection only goes to the competency, relevancy, and materiality of the evidence sought to be introduced," and concluded that the trial court should have permitted the defendant to testify as to his intention in not recording the money he took because his intent was relevant to disproving the charge of embezzlement.

5. On Appeal, Objecting Party Will Not Be Allowed to Advance a Different Basis for Objecting to the Admissibility of Evidence
People v. Taylor, 2011 IL 110067

Defendant, a night security guard, was convicted of misdemeanor theft after he was caught stealing money from a high school principal's office. After some money went missing from the principal's desk, a police officer set up a surveillance camera in the office. The surveillance video showed defendant taking the cash. The police officer then copied the video onto a VHS tape. Defendant filed a motion *in limine* to exclude the video as evidence at trial but the trial court denied his motion. Defendant further argued at trial that

> (1) there was a 30-second jump with no explanation; (2) the camera was not working properly; (3) the evidence did not show [the police officer] was competent to operate the equipment; and (4) the State failed to preserve the recording without changes, additions or deletions as shown by the 30-second jump.

On appeal, the defendant challenged the admissibility of the VHS tape on different grounds, including that

> (1) the VHS tape was a duplicate recording; (2) the State failed to explain the process used to create the duplicate, (3) the State failed to show a chain of custody, and (4) the State failed to preserve the original recording.

The state argued that defendant was precluded from arguing these separate grounds on appeal because he did not object on these grounds at trial or in his post-trial motion. The Illinois Supreme Court agreed, concluding that the defendant could not advance a different theory of objection on appeal from that advanced at trial.

See also People v. Killebrew, 55 Ill. 2d 337 (1973) (finding waiver of objection to suggestiveness of photographs where defendant only objected at trial on foundation grounds).

6. Party May Object to an Answer It Elicited During Examination of a Witness Claiming Answer Is Not Responsive

People v. Fritz, 84 Ill. 2d 72 (1981)

Defendant was charged with indecent liberties with a child while he and his wife lived with a married couple and their children. Defendant's wife was babysitting the children on the night when the alleged crime happened. The defendant came into one child's room at 8 o'clock that evening and committed the acts with which he was charged.

Defendant's wife testified at trial. On direct examination, defense counsel asked the wife about defendant's whereabouts on the night the crime occurred. In her response she stated that her husband left the house that afternoon around 2 o'clock, said that he was going to work, and that she did not see him again until midnight. State objected to the wife's answer on the basis that she was presenting an alibi defense of which state was never notified. Defense moved to have the statement stricken. The trial court did not strike the statement and recessed. During recess, the trial court permitted state to cross-examine the wife about her statement while a court reporter took notes. The state later used her answers to impeach her at trial. The Illinois Supreme Court found that the wife

> could not competently testify as to the defendant's presence at any place except the apartment, since that is where she was" on the evening the crime allegedly took place. [. . .] Therefore, [her] volunteered, unresponsive statement that defendant told her he was going to work cannot be considered as evidence of an alibi: first, because it was volunteered; second, because [she] did not know whether defendant was actually going to work; and third because [she] was present at the scene of the alleged offense, not elsewhere.
>
> We think that the foregoing testimony, adduced due to [the wife's] volunteered remark which should have been stricken, is extremely prejudicial to the defendant. The defendant did not intend to produce evidence that he was at work at the time in question. It is the duty of the court to strike nonresponsive answers to questions, when a proper motion to do so is made. (Math v. Chicago City Ry. Co. (1909), 243 Ill. 114, 122, 90 N.E. 235.) Thus, the testimony elicited by the State put the defendant in the position of rebutting evidence which would not have been admitted if the motion to strike had been granted.

7. Trial Court Is Generally Not Required to Exclude Evidence *Sua Sponte If* Defendant Fails to Object

People v. Williams, 28 Ill. 2d 114 (1963)

Defendant was charged with armed robbery of a gas station attendant. Defense counsel moved to suppress an alleged confession by the defendant. The trial court did not rule on this motion because state noted that it would not use the confession at trial. During cross-examination by assistant public defender representing a co-defendant, a police officer made a reference to the confession. No defense motion to strike the answer was made at the time, but defense counsel moved for a mistrial at the close of state's case. The trial court denied the motion for mistrial. The Illinois Supreme Court found that defendant waived his objection by not raising it at trial and that

> [o]ne who fails to object to the admissibility of evidence waives his right to complain of the admission of that evidence. People v. Luckett, 24 Ill. 2d 550 (1962); People v. Trefonas, 9 Ill. 2d 92 (1956). The court is not required 'to exclude or stop the introduction of improper evidence where the defendant makes no objection, does not move to exclude it or does not disclaim the answers.' People v. Henry, 3 Ill. 2d 609, 614 (1954). The defendant suggests that he did not object to the admission of [the officer's] testimony because 'he did not want to get into this hassle in front of the jury.' But his attorney had the right to argue his objection out of the presence of the jury, and he did, in fact, exercise this right several times during the course of the trial. We are of the opinion that [defendant] received a fair trial.

8. Although Defendant Generally Cannot Object on Appeal to Evidence He or She Introduced, Where Motion to Exclude Evidence Is Denied Defendant May Preemptively Disclose the Evidence to Minimize Its Prejudicial Effect

People v. Spates, 77 Ill. 2d 193 (1979)

Defense counsel made a motion *in limine* prior to trial to exclude defendant's prior misdemeanor theft conviction as impeachment evidence. This motion was denied. In his own testimony, defendant disclosed his prior conviction on direct examination, but sought review of the trial court's ruling on his *in limine* motion on appeal. The Illinois Supreme Court determined defendant had preserved this issue for appeal. The Supreme Court stated a

> party waives the right to raise as error action taken by the court at the instance of that party; it is quite another matter when, after an exclusionary motion is denied, the party himself raises a matter so as to lessen its impact, when the party knows that if he does not raise it, the opponent will. The difference is that, in the first instance, the request and the subsequent assertion of error are inconsistent with one another. In the second instance the aim is consistent: once the motion to exclude the matter is denied, the party must try to limit the effect the matter will have on the trier of fact. He has not waived the issue by raising it; he has merely tried to ensure that it does the least damage to his witness' credibility. Under the precise facts presented herein, that is what the defendant has done. Therefore the defendant has properly preserved this issue for review.

9. Where Defendant's Motion to Exclude Evidence of Prior Juvenile Adjudication Is Denied and Defendant Is Impeached with Such Evidence Without Opening the Door, the Error Is Reversible

People v. Villa, 2011 IL 110777

Defendant was charged with aggravated battery with a firearm and aggravated discharge of a firearm. He gave signed inculpatory statements to interrogating police officers after he was arrested. Defendant subsequently recanted his statements. He filed a motion *in limine* prior to trial to bar state from using his juvenile adjudication for burglary as impeachment evidence. The trial court denied defendant's motion and permitted state to use the prior juvenile adjudication for impeachment purposes.

Defendant testified at trial that he did not commit the crime. He was asked why he gave a statement to the police admitting that he participated in it. Defendant responded that he had "never been in a situation like this before," that he had never been in prison and that he was scared. Defendant explained that he had never been arrested, interrogated, or charged as an adult. State challenged defendant's testimony and he further clarified that he had been interviewed by the same police officers before but that he was a juvenile at that time. Defendant distinguished the two police encounters and noted that he was previously interviewed as a juvenile and had never before been charged as an adult. The state offered a certified copy of defendant's juvenile adjudication and repeatedly argued during trial and in closing argument that this adjudication indicated that "defendant's trial testimony was not truthful."

The Illinois Supreme Court found that the trial court erred in allowing state to impeach defendant with his prior juvenile adjudication. It observed that defendant had not opened the door to such evidence by stating that he had never been arrested or charged as an adult before and had never been in prison. The Supreme Court noted that the state conceded that defendant had never been imprisoned. The Supreme Court explained that defendant also had not preemptively introduced his prior adjudication to lessen its prejudicial impact on the trier of fact. The Supreme Court also noted that defendant was not attempting to mislead the jury. Although the state was permitted to cross-examine defendant about prior police questioning, the Supreme Court found that state was prohibited from disclosing his prior criminal history. The Supreme Court observed that there was very little evidence of defendant's guilt and his credibility was crucial to a determination of his guilt. The court concluded that the evidentiary error in admitting his prior juvenile adjudication was therefore not harmless beyond a reasonable doubt.

10. Trial Court Must Allow a Party to Make an Offer of Proof and Refusal Is Generally Reversible Error

People v. Thompkins, 181 Ill. 2d 1 (1998)

Defendant was convicted of two murders. He filed a post-conviction petition alleging ineffective assistance of counsel at sentencing because counsel allegedly failed to present mitigating evidence on his behalf. The Illinois Supreme Court directed the trial court to conduct an evidentiary hearing. At that hearing he sought to introduce the testimony of various expert witnesses but the trial court found that the testimony would be of no assistance in the determination of the cause. He subsequently filed a motion for reconsideration or, in the alternative, leave to make offers of proof. The court denied defendant's request to make offers of proof of three out of four experts. The court admitted only an affidavit of mitigation specialist but refused to allow the expert to provide a live offer of proof although he was already on the stand. Defendant also made an offer of proof of his attorney on direct appeal, but the trial judge left the courtroom during this offer of proof. The trial court concluded that defendant had not been denied effective assistance of counsel at sentencing and affirmed defendant's sentence.

The Illinois Supreme Court found that the trial court abused its discretion in refusing to allow defendant to make offers of proof, leaving the courtroom during the offer of proof, and in striking other offers of proof from the record. The Supreme Court explained that

> [t]rial courts are required to permit counsel to make offers of proof, and a refusal to permit an offer generally is error. People v. Stefanov, 93 Ill. App. 3d 85, 87-88 (1st Dist. 1981); *In re*

Estate of Undziakiewicz, 54 Ill. App. 2d 382, 385 (1st Dist. 1964); M. GRAHAM, CLEARY & GRAHAM'S HANDBOOK OF ILLINOIS EVIDENCE § 103.7, at 24 (6th ed. 1994) (hereinafter GRAHAM); *cf.* J. STRONG, MCCORMICK ON EVIDENCE § 51, at 195 n. 7 (4th ed. 1992) (hereinafter MCCORMICK) (federal rule similar). An adequate offer of proof is the key to preserving a trial court's error in excluding evidence. People v. Andrews, 146 Ill. 2d 413, 420-21 (1992). The two primary functions of an offer of proof are to disclose to the trial judge and opposing counsel the nature of the offered evidence, enabling them to take appropriate action, and to provide the reviewing court with a record to determine whether exclusion of the evidence was erroneous and harmful. People v. Sanchez, 131 Ill. 2d 417, 425 (1989); *see Andrews*, 146 Ill. 2d at 421; GRAHAM § 103.7, at 21; *cf.* MCCORMICK § 51, at 196 n.8 (federal rule similar). Illinois courts of review have not hesitated to remand cases for new trials where circuit judges have mishandled attempts by defendants to make offers of proof on excluded evidence.

11. An Offer of Proof Is Not Required Where the Purpose of Evidence Is Clear and Evidence Is Relevant
People v. Lynch, 104 Ill. 2d 194 (1984)

Defendant shot the victim and claimed self-defense. He was convicted of voluntary manslaughter. Defendant sought to introduce the victim's three prior convictions for battery at trial. He intended to show that he acted reasonably in self-defense in light of the circumstances. The trial court excluded the evidence as irrelevant because defendant did not know about the victim's prior convictions when he shot him. The appellate court determined that defendant could not challenge the exclusion of the prior convictions because he had failed to make an offer of proof. The Illinois Supreme Court disagreed, observing that

> [t]he requirement of an offer of proof is not a formalistic ritual, but an aid to justice; where justice is not served, no such requirement will be enforced. For example, no offer is required if there was no practical opportunity to make one because of the trial court's hostility. Giddings v. Williams, 336 Ill. 482, 489-90 (1929). Similarly, if a question shows the purpose and materiality of the evidence, is in a proper form, and clearly admits of a favorable answer, the proponent need not make a formal offer of what the answer would be, unless the trial court asks for one. People v. Moretti, 6 Ill. 2d 494, 520-21 (1955); Hartnett v. Boston Store, 265 Ill. 331, 337 (1914). An offer of proof need not provide all the detail of the evidence itself, nor need the proponent expressly point out the natural inferences to be drawn from the proffered evidence. Bartholow v. Davies, 276 Ill. 505, 515 (1916). The appellate court's ruling would be correct in this case, therefore, only if a reviewing court could not fairly determine from the whole record whether excluding the battery convictions was reversible error.

The Supreme Court concluded that the defendant could challenge the exclusion of victim's prior convictions for battery in the absence of an offer of proof because the convictions could have been proved and they were "competent evidence to prove that [the victim] was an aggressive and violent man."

12. Party Need Not Provide Offer of Proof, Unless Directed by the Court, Where Question Shows Purpose and Materiality of Evidence
People v. Moretti, 6 Ill. 2d 494 (1955)

During a murder trial, defense counsel sought to establish that the victim was the aggressor by questioning a witness about the character and habits of the victim. Trial judge and counsel retired from the presence of the jury and defense counsel submitted a list of proposed questions. The court sustained objections to each question and witness was excused.

Defendant claimed proffered evidence was erroneously excluded and state countered that the claim was not preserved for review because no offer of proof was made. The Illinois Supreme Court held that where a question itself "shows the purpose and materiality of the evidence, and it is in proper form and clearly admits of an answer relative to the issues, the party by whom the question is propounded is not bound to state the facts proposed to be proved by the answer unless the court requires so to do."

13. Offer of Proof Must Explicitly State What the Excluded Evidence Would Reveal If Purpose, Content, and Basis of Offered Evidence Are Not Clear
People v. Andrews, 146 Ill. 2d 413 (1992)

Defendant was tried twice on charges of murder and armed robbery. The first trial resulted in mistrial after a hung jury, but he was convicted during the second trial. Defendant claimed racial discrimination in the selection of jurors pursuant to Batson v. Kentucky, 476 U.S. 79 (1986). The trial court conducted a *Batson* hearing during which it excluded certain testimony offered by the defendant. Defendant contended that the trial court erred in excluding testimony of his attorney who intended to testify about a conversation she had with members of the hung jury after mistrial was declared in the first trial. The state objected to this line of questioning. Defendant subsequently made an offer of proof indicating that the testimony would have shown state's attorney's reasoning during selection of the jury in the second trial. Defendant sought to show that if the state's attorney was present during a particular conversation, he would have had motive to discriminate on racial grounds against certain jurors. The Illinois Supreme Court noted that

> [w]here an objection is sustained to the offered testimony of a witness, an adequate offer of proof is made if counsel makes known to the trial court, with particularity, the substance of the witness' anticipated answer. M. GRAHAM, CLEARY & GRAHAM'S HANDBOOK OF ILLINOIS EVIDENCE § 103.7, at 21 (5th ed. 1990).) An offer of proof that merely summarizes the witness' testimony in a conclusory manner is inadequate. Mulhern v. Talk of the Town, Inc., 138 Ill. App. 3d 829, 834 (2d Dist. 1985). Neither will the unsupported speculation of counsel as to what the witness would say suffice. Yassin by Yassin v. Certified Grocers of Illinois, Inc., 150 Ill. App. 3d 1052, 1066 (1st Dist. 1986). Rather, in making the offer of proof, counsel must explicitly state what the excluded testimony would reveal and may not merely allude to what might be divulged by the testimony. People v. Brown, 104 Ill. App. 3d 1110, 1119 (1st Dist. 1982). The offer serves no purpose if it does not demonstrate, both to the trial court and to reviewing courts, the admissibility of the testimony which was foreclosed by the sustained objection. People *ex rel.* Fahner v. Hedrich, 108 Ill. App. 3d 83, 91 (2d Dist. 1982).

The Supreme Court concluded that the defense counsel failed to make a sufficient offer of proof because it was impossible to determine whether the excluded evidence was relevant to the issues in the case. Counsel did not provide any specifics about the content of the alleged conversation and the offer "amounted to no more than mere speculation as to what she believed the relevancy of the testimony might be, without any reference to what the testimony would actually consist of. Such speculation is not sufficient to preserve the issue for review."

For other cases discussing this topic, see:

People v. Peeples, 155 Ill. 2d 422 (1993) (finding that defendant's failure to make an offer of proof prevented review of any alleged error in trial court's exclusion of venirepersons' testimony about how each was assigned to the courthouse).

People v. Gacy, 103 Ill. 2d 1 (1984) (finding that where no offer of proof was made concerning testimony of defense experts as to statements made by defendant, it was impossible to determine the adverse effect of any possible error in trial court's exclusion of such evidence).

14. Entire Offer of Proof May Be Rejected If It Includes both Admissible and Inadmissible Testimony
People v. Duarte, 79 Ill. App. 3d 110 (1st Dist. 1979)

Defendant and co-defendant were jointly tried for murder and convicted. At trial, defendant called a police officer to testify that he overheard a certain conversation between co-defendant and another person in co-defendant's cell. Co-defendant's counsel objected to this line of questioning because the other person in the cell was co-defendant's attorney and the conversation was protected by the attorney-client privilege. The trial court sustained the objection but accepted an offer of proof stating that if the officer were allowed to testify, he would say that co-defendant confessed to the crime and stated that the other person "didn't have anything to do with" the murder. It was unclear whether the other person mentioned by co-defendant was the defendant or a third party. Defendant argued on appeal that the trial court erred in excluding the officer's testimony.

The First District of the Illinois Appellate Court acknowledged that offers of proof are often made by the attorney's recitation of the testimony he or she expects to elicit. The court suggested, however, that this method be used only when the witness is unavailable and the offer is sufficiently specific because the expected testimony might be entirely different from the actual testimony of the witness and this method deprives opposing counsel of the opportunity to cross-examine the witness. The court further observed that defendant failed to show how the officer's testimony was material and relevant to the case. Even if defendant had established the statement's relevancy certain portions of the proffered testimony were inadmissible hearsay. The court noted that "[w]here [. . .] admissible and inadmissible testimony are included in an offer of proof, the entire offer may be rejected."

15. Motions *in Limine* Raise Evidentiary Claims Prior to Trial and Are Reviewed for Abuse of Discretion
People v. Harvey, 211 Ill. 2d 368 (2004)

State moved *in limine* to exclude certain evidence introduced by defendant at trial. Defendant sought to show that a witness had motive to lie about the events surrounding commission of the crime. The trial court granted the state's motion, reasoning that the proffered evidence was not relevant to the crimes charged. Defendant argued on appeal that the trial court abused its discretion in excluding the evidence. The Illinois Supreme Court disagreed, noting that

> [g]enerally, evidentiary motions, such as motions *in limine*, are directed to the trial court's discretion, and reviewing courts will not disturb a trial court's evidentiary ruling absent an abuse of discretion. People v. Jackson, 182 Ill. 2d 30, 78-79 (1998). Relevant evidence is evidence having any tendency to make the existence of any fact that is of consequence to the determination of the action more probable than it would be without the evidence. People v. Lewis, 165 Ill. 2d 305, 329 (1995). A trial court may reject offered evidence on grounds of irrelevancy if it has little probative value due to its remoteness, uncertainty, or possibly unfair prejudicial nature. People v. Ward, 101 Ill. 2d 443, 455 (1984).

See also People v. Nelson, 235 Ill. 2d 386 (2009) (finding no abuse of discretion where trial court excluded evidence that was too remote and speculative).

16. Trial Court's Ruling on a Motion *in Limine* Which Has the Effect to Suppress State's Evidence Can Be Challenged in an Interlocutory Appeal
People v. Drum, 194 Ill. 2d 485 (2000)

Defendant, his brother and a friend were charged with first degree murder and were tried separately. The brother and friend each testified at their own trials and although they admitted to participating in the murder, they each claimed that defendant was the primary perpetrator. Although they were the only witnesses to the crime beside defendant, they "indicated that they did not intend to testify at defendant's trial." In a pretrial motion *in limine*, state sought to admit their prior testimony at defendant's trial. Trial court denied state's motion. State brought an interlocutory appeal and the appellate court found that it did not have jurisdiction to consider the ruling. The Illinois Supreme Court disagreed, noting that state should be allowed "to bring an interlocutory appeal from a pretrial evidentiary ruling that has the substantive effect of suppressing evidence." The Supreme Court observed that the ruling on the motion *in limine* had the effect of suppressing evidence because it prevented the trier of fact from considering the prior testimony of two witnesses. It concluded that the state was entitled to bring an interlocutory appeal from the order denying the motion *in limine*.

17. Motions *in Limine* May Help Reduce Possibility of Trial Errors by Excluding Evidence That May Be Prejudicial
People v. Williams, 188 Ill. 2d 365 (1999)

Defendant pleaded guilty to an attempted murder. The victim later died and defendant was charged with his murder. The trial court granted defendant's motion *in limine* to bar state from using his prior guilty plea in the attempted murder case as evidence in the murder prosecution. The trial court explained that defendant was never advised that his guilty plea could be used in a subsequent murder prosecution and was therefore unknowingly made. The appellate court affirmed the trial court's holding. The Illinois Supreme Court reviewed the ruling for abuse of discretion, noting that

> [a] motion *in limine* is a pretrial motion that seeks an order excluding inadmissible evidence and prohibiting questions concerning such evidence, without the necessity of having the questions asked and objections thereto made in front of the jury. Thus, the *in limine* order will protect the movant from whatever prejudicial impact the mere asking of the questions and the making of the objections may have upon a jury.

The Supreme Court reversed the lower courts' findings, noting that defendant was advised of all direct consequences of his guilty plea. It explained that direct consequences of a plea are "only those consequences of the sentence that the trial judge can impose," and that "a guilty plea is not invalid for failure of a trial court to warn a defendant of its possible effect on future criminal liability."

18. Trial Court Should Rule on Defendant's Motion *in Limine* to Bar Prior Convictions Before Defendant Testifies Unless There Is Compelling Reason to Delay Ruling
People v. Patrick, 233 Ill. 2d 62 (2009)

The Illinois Supreme Court recognized that a defendant's decision to testify is generally made only after the strength of the state's evidence is fully and properly evaluated. The Supreme Court noted that the defendant benefits from an early ruling on the admissibility of prior convictions evidence by being able to make strategic decisions about his defense.

Here, the trial court denied defendant's motion *in limine*, seeking to bar the state from presenting evidence of his prior convictions for possession of a controlled substance. The defendant argued self-defense and the Supreme Court emphasized that it was important for him to know whether his prior convictions could be used for impeachment before he took the stand. Moreover, state repeatedly argued that the jury should not believe "a three-time convicted felon." The Supreme Court held that, unless some compelling reason to delay the ruling exists, the trial court should rule on a defendant's motion to bar prior convictions before the defendant testifies. The Supreme Court further explained that situations requiring the defendant to testify prior to the court making its decision would be exceedingly rare. The court found that the trial court here did not articulate any justification for delaying the ruling, and its decision was "arbitrary and without reason." The Supreme Court held that the trial court's failure to rule on the motion *in limine* on the admissibility of prior convictions, when it had sufficient information to make the ruling, constituted an abuse of discretion.

See also Luce v. United States, 469 U.S. 38 (1984) (holding that defendant preserves a claim of improper impeachment with a prior conviction for review only if he or she testifies).

19. Trial Court's Withholding of Ruling on Defendant's Motion *in Limine* Does Not Require Reversal If Defendant Does Not Testify at Trial
People v. Averett, 237 Ill. 2d 1 (2010)

The Illinois Supreme Court considered whether defendants were entitled to relief even though they did not testify because the trial court had a "blanket policy" of deferring rulings on motions *in limine*, before defendants testified.

The Supreme Court observed that defendants were not prevented from testifying at trial by the trial court's policy, and noted that defendants may be "required to weigh the possibility of being impeached with their prior convictions along with other factors in determining whether to testify. The defendants' constitutional right to testify was not violated by any deterrent effect on their testimony due to the risk of being impeached with their prior convictions."

The Supreme Court further noted that courts cannot speculate on the possible testimony the defendants could have offered had they testified at trial. The Supreme Court concluded that the defendants' decision not to testify rendered this issue unreviewable.

20. Evidentiary Rulings Are Generally Reviewed for an Abuse of Discretion
People v. Becker, 239 Ill. 2d 215 (2010)

Defendant was charged with predatory criminal sexual assault of a child and criminal sexual assault for the alleged sexual assault of his three-year-old daughter. Prior to trial state sought to introduce various hearsay statements made by the victim to her mother, to a detective and to her mother in front of her mother's friend pursuant to 725 ILCS 5/115-10. At the section 115-10 hearing, the victim's mother testified that after visiting her father the child noted that he hurt her "front bottom" and later asked about "dad's special blue microphone." Detective testified that the child also made similar allegations but that there were inconsistencies in her account that he failed to clarify. A defense expert specializing in child psychology then testified. The expert had not interviewed the child but concluded upon review of the evidence that the child's accounts of the events may have been improperly "influenced" by suggestive questioning by the mother and the police detective. The expert concluded that there was no reason for her to interview the victim because her memory had been so tainted by the suggestive interview techniques as to preclude the elicitation of any "clean evidence." The expert also noted that if the victim were to testify, her testimony would not be reliable. The trial court excluded the expert's testimony and admitted the hearsay statements. The Illinois Supreme Court explained the

> basic standards of review applicable to evidentiary issues. The admission of evidence is within the sound discretion of a trial court, and a reviewing court will not reverse the trial court absent a showing of an abuse of that discretion. Snelson v. Kamm, 204 Ill. 2d 1, 24 (2003); People v. Hall, 195 Ill. 2d 1, 20-21 (2000). An abuse of discretion occurs where the trial court's decision

> is arbitrary, fanciful or unreasonable (People v. Illgen, 145 Ill. 2d 353, 364 (1991)) or where no reasonable person would agree with the position adopted by the trial court (Schwartz v. Cortelloni, 177 Ill. 2d 166, 176 (1997); *Illgen*, 145 Ill. 2d at 364). Decisions of whether to admit expert testimony are reviewed using this same abuse of discretion standard. *Snelson*, 204 Ill. 2d at 24; People v. Reid, 179 Ill. 2d 297, 313 (1997).

The Supreme Court concluded that the trial court did not abuse its discretion in excluding the expert's testimony. The Supreme Court observed that "it is generally improper to ask one witness to comment directly on the credibility of another witness . . . as '[q]uestions of credibility are to be resolved by the trier of fact.'" The Supreme Court also explained that the expert's testimony was not "beyond the ken of the average juror," and that its prejudicial impact would have outweighed any probative value of her testimony.

For other cases discussing the application of this standard of review, see:

- People v. Taylor, 2011 IL 110067 (reviewing trial court's decision to admit VHS tape for abuse of discretion and noting that the same standard governs admissibility of photographic evidence).
- People v. Garcia, 97 Ill. 2d 58 (1983) (reviewing trial court's determination of witness competency for abuse of discretion).
- People v. Blakes, 63 Ill. 2d 354 (1976) (reviewing trial court's limitation of scope of cross-examination for abuse of discretion).
- People v. Cross, 40 Ill. 2d 85 (1968) (reviewing trial court's decision to reopen a case for further evidence for abuse of discretion).

21. Reviewing Court Must Be Convinced Beyond a Reasonable Doubt That Error Is Harmless Where Claimed Error Impacts a Federal Constitutional Right

People v. McClanahan, 191 Ill. 2d 127 (2000)

Defendant was charged with the unlawful possession of less than 15 grams of cocaine. He challenged the constitutionality of 725 ILCS 5/115-15 that allows admissibility of laboratory reports without the testimony of the laboratory technician who conducted the analysis of the illegal substance. The Illinois Supreme Court explained that although a constitutional error may not automatically warrant reversal,

> before a constitutional error can be held to be harmless, the reviewing court must be able to declare beyond a reasonable doubt that the error did not contribute to the finding of guilt. People v. Smith, 38 Ill. 2d 13, 15 (1967). The burden of proof is on the State to show beyond a reasonable doubt that the constitutional error did not affect the outcome of the proceeding. Chapman v. California, 386 U.S. 18, 24 (1967); People v. Simms, 121 Ill. 2d 259 (1988).

The Supreme Court found that the statute was unconstitutional because it did not require state to show how the analysis was conducted or the qualifications of the technician who conducted the analysis. Moreover, the statute placed the burden of requesting the technician to testify on defendant within a specified amount of time and therefore required defendant to take affirmative steps to safeguard his or her confrontation rights. The Supreme Court explained that

> [t]he right of a defendant to be confronted with the witnesses against him is guaranteed by the Constitution and arises automatically at the initiation of the adversary process. Taylor v. Illinois, 484 U.S. 400, 410 (1988). Subsection (c) of section 115-15 impermissibly requires the defendant to take affirmative action to secure a right that he has already been constitutionally guaranteed or be deemed to have waived that right. We are unaware of any authority that

> permits the legislature to make a defendant's confrontation rights contingent upon action by the defendant, and the State has not argued that such authority exists.

The Supreme Court concluded that the state failed to show beyond a reasonable doubt that the error did not contribute to the guilty verdict and remanded the case for a new trial.

But see People v. Wrice, 2012 IL 111860 (holding that "use of a defendant's physically coerced confession as substantive evidence of his [or her] guilt is never harmless error").

22. Plain Error Doctrine Allows Review of an Unpreserved Error When Evidence Is Closely Balanced or Error Was Serious and Prejudicial to the Defendant
People v. Herron, 215 Ill. 2d 167 (2005)

Defendant appealed his first degree murder and armed robbery convictions claiming the trial court improperly instructed the jury about eyewitness identification testimony. The Illinois Supreme Court addressed the issue under the plain error doctrine, despite defendant's failure to object to the instruction at trial. The Supreme Court noted that in Illinois, a reviewing court may consider a forfeited issue when the evidence is so close that the jury's verdict may have resulted from the error regardless of the seriousness of the error, or the error is so serious that the defendant was denied a substantial right regardless of the closeness of the evidence.

In reviewing the history of the plain error doctrine, the Supreme Court noted the change from concern over the quality of defendant's representation to a broader concern with the overall fairness of the trial. The Supreme Court explained that the plain error doctrine is a limited exception to the general waiver rule, the purpose of which "is to protect the rights of the defendant and the integrity and reputation of the judicial process." To avoid convicting an innocent person and to maintain the integrity of the judicial process and the fairness of a criminal trial, the doctrine has two prongs. The plain error doctrine

> bypasses normal forfeiture principles and allows a reviewing court to consider unpreserved error when either (1) the evidence is close, regardless of the seriousness of the error, or (2) the error is serious, regardless of the closeness of the evidence. In the first instance, the defendant must prove "prejudicial error." That is, the defendant must show both that there was plain error and that the evidence was so closely balanced that the error alone severely threatened to tip the scales of justice against him. The State, of course, can respond by arguing that the evidence was not closely balanced, but rather strongly weighted against the defendant. In the second instance, the defendant must prove there was plain error and that the error was so serious that it affected the fairness of the defendant's trial and challenged the integrity of the judicial process. People v. Keene, 169 Ill. 2d 1, 17 (1995). Prejudice to the defendant is presumed because of the importance of the right involved, "*regardless* of the strength of the evidence." (Emphasis in original.) People v. Blue, 189 Ill. 2d 99, 138 (2000). In both instances, the burden of persuasion remains with the defendant.

The Illinois Supreme Court further noted that

> a jury instruction error rises to the level of plain error only when it 'creates a serious risk that the jurors incorrectly convicted the defendant because they did not understand the applicable law, so as to severely threaten the fairness of the trial.' [. . .] The defendant need not prove that the error in the instruction actually misled the jury. If the defendant carries the burden of persuasion and convinces a reviewing court that there was error and that the evidence was closely balanced, the case is not cloaked with a presumption of prejudice. The error is actually prejudicial, not presumptively prejudicial. We deal with probabilities, not certainties; we deal

> with risks and threats to the defendant's rights. When there is error in a close case, we choose to err on the side of fairness, so as not to convict an innocent person.

Here, the court held that because the verdict may have been different with a different instruction the appellate court correctly reversed defendant's convictions and remanded the case for a new trial.

23. To Satisfy the First Prong of Plain Error Analysis Defendant Must Show That Evidence Was Closely Balanced

People v. Naylor, 229 Ill. 2d 584 (2008)

Defendant was convicted of possession of heroin with intent to deliver and delivery of heroin at a bench trial. Defendant testified at trial and denied that he sold drugs on the day he was arrested. The state introduced and the trial court admitted the defendant's prior conviction of aggravated battery as impeachment evidence. The defendant was tried 13 years and 8 months after his battery conviction but was charged with the present offense only 9 years and 3 months after the prior conviction. The state failed to present evidence as to the date of the defendant's release from confinement on the battery conviction. Although defendant objected at trial to the admissibility of this conviction, he failed to include the issue in his post-trial motion. The appellate court used the date of conviction until the date of the new trial as the relevant time period and found that the battery conviction fell outside of the 10-year limit. The appellate court concluded that defendant was improperly impeached with the prior conviction and concluded that plain error occurred.

The Illinois Supreme Court found that the trial court erred in setting *Montgomery*'s end date as the date the defendant allegedly committed the charged offense. Although defendant forfeited the issue, the Supreme Court reviewed his claim for plain error. The Supreme Court concluded that

> [i]n this case, [. . .] the trial court considered defendant's prior conviction to fall within *Montgomery's* 10-year time limit. Indeed, the court actively participated with the State in searching for the erroneous date. We must conclude that the trial court improperly considered this incompetent evidence and, consequently, committed reversible error.
>
> ***
>
> Having concluded that the trial court committed reversible error, we must next determine whether the evidence presented at defendant's trial was closely balanced. "When error occurs in a close case, we will opt to 'err on the side of fairness, so as not to convict an innocent person.' "

The Supreme Court considered that defendant's case hinged on the credibility of witnesses and specifically his own credibility. He and the arresting police officers supplied two different accounts of the events but no extrinsic evidence was available to corroborate either version of the events. The Supreme Court observed that only moments after defendant's prior conviction was admitted as impeachment, the trial court stated that it believed the officers' version. The Supreme Court concluded that the evidence was closely balanced and that plain error occurred.

See also People v. Piatkowski, 225 Ill. 2d 551 (2007) (finding plain error on basis of first prong where trial court gave an internally inconsistent jury instruction).

24. To Satisfy the Second Prong of Plain Error Review Defendant Must Show That the Error Was So Serious as to Affect Fairness of Trial and Challenge Integrity of Judicial Process Regardless of Closeness of Evidence

People v. Walker, 232 Ill. 2d 113 (2009)

Defendant contended that the trial court abused its discretion in refusing to grant a continuance where defense counsel was unprepared to try his double murder case. The Illinois Supreme Court found that defendant forfeited this issue by not preserving it in a post-trial motion, and considered whether the issue was reviewable as plain error. The Supreme Court explained that

> [t]he plain-error doctrine is a limited and narrow exception to the general rule of procedural default (Naylor, 229 Ill. 2d 584, 593 (2008)) and allows a reviewing court to consider unpreserved error when one of two conditions is met:
>
>> "(1) a clear and obvious error occurs and the evidence is so closely balanced that the error alone threatened to tip the scales of justice against the defendant, regardless of the seriousness of the error, or (2) a clear or obvious error occurs and that error is so serious that it affected the fairness of the defendant's trial and challenged the integrity of the judicial process, regardless of the closeness of the evidence." People v. Piatkowski, 225 Ill. 2d 551, 565 (2007).
>
> Under both prongs of the plain-error doctrine, the burden of persuasion remains with defendant. *Naylor*, 229 Ill. 2d at 593. If a defendant fails to satisfy this burden, the result is that the "procedural default must be honored." People v. Keene, 169 Ill. 2d 1, 17 (1995). The initial step in conducting plain-error analysis is to determine whether error occurred at all. People v. Hudson, 228 Ill. 2d 181, 191 (2008). This requires us to conduct a substantive review of the issue. People v. Johnson, 208 Ill. 2d 53, 64 (2003).

The Supreme Court found that granting or denial of a continuance is reviewed for abuse of discretion and defendant's conviction will be reversed if it is found that his rights to a fair trial were prejudiced. The Supreme Court observed that the trial court "mechanically" denied defendant's motion for continuance without consideration of any relevant circumstances and pertinent factors. The Supreme Court concluded that the trial court abused its discretion and that its error was "so serious as to affect the fairness of defendant's trial and challenged the integrity of the judicial process, regardless of the closeness of the evidence."

25. Defendant's Failure to Meet His or Her Burden Under Both Prongs of Plain-Error Review

People v. Adams, 2012 IL 111168

Defendant was charged with possession of a controlled substance. At trial, the arresting officers testified that they found cocaine in one of defendant's pockets. Defendant, however, testified that the drugs were found on the ground near him and that he told the police at the time of the arrest that he had not dropped any drugs. In its closing argument, the state argued that if the jury believed the defendant, then it also had "to believe that [the arresting officer was] risking his credibility, his job, and his freedom over 0.8 grams of cocaine." Although the Illinois Supreme Court found that the prosecutor's remarks were improper because a "prosecutor [may not] argue assumptions or facts not based upon evidence in the case," it held that defendant failed to establish that the prosecutor's remarks amounted to plain error. The Supreme Court explained that

> plain-error doctrine permits a court of review to consider error that has been forfeited when either

> "(1) the evidence is close, regardless of the seriousness of the error, or (2) the error is serious, regardless of the closeness of the evidence. In the first instance, the defendant must prove 'prejudicial error.' That is, the defendant must show both that there was plain error and that the evidence was so closely balanced that the error alone severely threatened to tip the scales of justice against him. The State, of course, can respond by arguing that the evidence was not closely balanced, but rather strongly weighted against the defendant. In the second instance, the defendant must prove there was plain error and that the error was so serious that it affected the fairness of the defendant's trial and challenged the integrity of the judicial process. [Citation.] Prejudice to the defendant is presumed because of the importance of the right involved, 'regardless of the strength of the evidence.' (Emphasis in original.) [Citation.] In both instances, the burden of persuasion remains with the defendant." People v. Herron, 215 Ill. 2d 167, 187 (2005).

The Supreme Court observed that defendant failed to meet the closely balanced prong of plain error review because it found, after a "commonsense assessment" of the evidence, that "defendant's explanation of events, though not logically impossible, was highly improbable." Defendant claimed that the cocaine "was sitting in a parking lot [. . .] unsecured in any way" and that he coincidentally parked his car next to it. Defendant alleged that the arresting police officer "conspired [. . .] to attribute the drugs to defendant." The Supreme Court concluded that the prosecutor's statements did not "severely threaten to tip the scales of justice against" the accused because they "were not of a sort likely to inflame the passions of the jury" as the jury was informed that it should consider them only in evaluating the "believability of the witnesses."

The Supreme Court also determined that defendant failed to establish the fundamental fairness prong of plain error review because the error was not "so serious that it affected the fairness of [his] trial and challenged the integrity of the judicial process." Although the Supreme Court found that the prosecutorial remarks were improper, it did not find them serious enough for plain error review under the fundamental fairness prong.

See also People v. Lewis, 234 Ill. 2d 32 (2009) (holding that imposition of a street-value fine without a sufficient evidentiary basis to determine the value of the controlled substance was reviewable as plain error).

26. Plain Error Review Is Inappropriate Where the Record Is Not Fully and Fairly Developed for Resolution of the Issue as a Result of a Tactical Decision by Defense Counsel and Where Resolution of the Issue Would Not Affect the Outcome of the Prosecution

People v. White, 2011 IL 109689

Defendant was convicted of first degree murder. He argued on appeal that he had been denied his sixth amendment right to counsel. At defendant's lineup, the police prevented his attorney from observing the witnesses. Defendant failed to raise this issue at trial. The appellate court considered defendant's argument under plain error review after it found that the evidence was closely balanced. The appellate court concluded that "a total prohibition of defense counsel from observing the moment of identification was a violation of the accused's sixth amendment right to effective assistance of counsel, but [that] defendant's sixth amendment right to counsel had not attached at the time the lineup was conducted."

The Illinois Supreme Court affirmed the appellate court although it found it "unnecessary" and "inappropriate" for the appellate court to address defendant's constitutional argument. The Supreme Court found that the evidence was not closely balanced and that the appellate court erred in conducting plain error review. The Supreme Court observed that defendant failed to show prejudice under the closely-balanced-evidence prong, and that the evidence was "heavily" weighed in the state's favor. It pointed out that defense counsel made a tactical decision to not develop the record on this issue. The Supreme Court noted that

> [i]t was only because of the appellate court's first determination, an assessment that the evidence was closely balanced, that the appellate court addressed either of the issues now in controversy. It was only because the appellate court decided to address the lineup procedure—which it found violative of defendant's right to counsel—before it even considered whether a right to counsel existed, that the propriety of the lineup procedure was even reached. In view of this sequence of events, we believe it appropriate to caution courts of review—particularly when constitutional issues are involved—that they are not free rangers riding about the legal landscape looking for law to make. Judicial restraint is a principle of review that the justices of the Supreme Court strive to observe.
>
> ***
>
> We do not, and should not, manufacture reasons to address issues—constitutional or otherwise—where the record has not been fully and fairly developed for that purpose and where resolution of the issues is unnecessary. Certainly, it is a fundamental rule of judicial restraint that a court not reach constitutional questions in advance of the necessity of deciding them. *See* Nw. Austin Mun. Util. Dist. No. One v. Holder, 557 U.S. 193 (2009); Three Affiliated Tribes of the Fort Berthold Reservation v. Wold Engineering, P.C., 467 U.S. 138, 157-58 (1984). Where the only basis proffered for plain-error review is a claim that the evidence is closely balanced, an assessment of the impact of an alleged evidentiary error is readily made after reading the record. When it is clear that the alleged error would not have affected the outcome of the case, a court of review need not engage in the meaningless endeavor of determining whether error occurred.

Rule 104. Preliminary Questions

(a) Questions of Admissibility Generally. Preliminary questions concerning the qualification of a person to be a witness, the existence of a privilege, or the admissibility of evidence shall be determined by the court, subject to the provisions of subdivision (b). In making its determination, the court is not bound by the rules of evidence except those with respect to privileges.

(b) Relevancy Conditioned on Fact. When the relevancy of evidence depends upon the fulfillment of a condition of fact, the court shall admit it upon, or subject to, the introduction of evidence sufficient to support a finding of the fulfillment of the condition.

(c) Hearing of Jury. Hearings on the admissibility of confessions shall in all cases be conducted out of the hearing of the jury. Hearings on other preliminary matters shall be so conducted when the interests of justice require, or when an accused is a witness and so requests.

(d) Testimony by Accused. The accused does not, by testifying upon a preliminary matter, become subject to cross-examination as to other issues in the case.

(e) Weight and Credibility. This rule does not limit the right of a party to introduce before the jury evidence relevant to weight or credibility.

Adopted September 27, 2010, eff. January 1, 2011.

Rule 1008. Functions of Court and Jury

When the admissibility of other evidence of contents of writings, recordings, or photographs under these rules depends upon the fulfillment of a condition of fact, the question whether the condition has been fulfilled is ordinarily for the court to determine in accordance with the provisions of Rule 104(a). However, when an issue is raised (a) whether the asserted writing ever existed, or (b) whether another writing, recording, or photograph produced at the trial is the original, or (c) whether other evidence of contents correctly reflects the contents, the issue is for the trier of fact to determine as in the case of other issues of fact.

Adopted September 27, 2010, eff. January 1, 2011.

AUTHOR'S COMMENTARY

A jury trial delineates clear lines of responsibility between the judge and the jury. The judge rules on the admissibility of the evidence; the jury weighs it. People v. Taylor, 2011 IL 110067; People v. Boclair, 129 Ill. 2d 458 (1989). The judge determines questions of law; the jury finds and determines the facts. It is the jury's function to determine the credibility of the witnesses, weigh their testimony, and draw reasonable inferences from the evidence. 725 ILCS 5/115-4.

A judge may be called on to rule on the admissibility of evidence in a number of different ways: pretrial motions to suppress evidence, motions *in limine*, objections, motions to strike, and motions for mistrial. In ruling on the admissibility of evidence, the judge may be guided by preliminary evidentiary hearings or arguments of law presented by counsel. Pursuant to Illinois Rule of Evidence 104 and Illinois common law, in evaluating preliminary questions pertaining to the admissibility of evidence, a trial court is not bound by the rules of evidence unless it is ruling on issues that pertain to privileges. People v. Patterson, 192 Ill. 2d 93 (2000). Illinois Rule 104(a) is identical to Federal Rule of Evidence 104(a), in effect prior to its stylistic amendment on December 1, 2011, except that it substitutes "the court" for "it." Gino L. DiVito, *The Illinois Rules of Evidence: A Color-Coded Guide Containing the New Rules, the Committee's General and Specific Comments, a Comparison with the Federal Rules of Evidence, and Additional Commentary (Including the Federal Rules of Evidence as Amended Effective December 1, 2011)* (Jan. 1, 2012), at 16-17, http://www.tdrlawfirm.com/assets/downloads/Illinois_Rules_of_Evidence_Color-Coded_Guide.pdf.

The judge enjoys wide discretion in the manner he or she accomplishes the task of ruling on preliminary questions. A judge can hold a separate hearing out of the jury's presence or receive evidence conditionally in the jury's presence and then rule on its admissibility. If the judge rules against admissibility, it will strike the evidence and admonish the jury to disregard it. However, where there is an objection to the admissibility of a confession, the judge must hold the preliminary examination out of the jury's presence. People v. Caldwell, 39 Ill. 2d 346 (1968). With respect to all other preliminary matters, the judge may hold a preliminary examination out of the presence of the jury if "the interests of justice require," or on request of a testifying defendant. ILL. R. EVID. 104(c).

The first Illinois Supreme Court case to consider the application of Illinois Rule of Evidence 104 is People v. Taylor, 2011 IL 110067, and is discussed below.

RELEVANT STATUTORY AUTHORITY

Trial by Court and Jury: 725 ILCS 5/115-4

§ 115-4. Trial by Court and Jury.

(a) Questions of law shall be decided by the court and questions of fact by the jury.

***

(h) A trial by the court and jury shall be conducted in the presence of the defendant unless he waives the right to be present.

(i) After arguments of counsel the court shall instruct the jury as to the law.
Effective January 1, 1990.

ILLINOIS CASE LAW UNDER THE NEW ILLINOIS RULES OF EVIDENCE

1. Admissibility of Evidence Is Within the Discretion of the Trial Court

People v. Taylor, 2011 IL 110067

Defendant was caught stealing money out of a high school principal's office after a police officer installed a surveillance camera there. The police officer testified at defendant's bench trial regarding the surveillance equipment. He conceded that he "only recently begun using such equipment" and that he set the camera up according to instructions supplied by the camera's manufacturer. After the camera recorded defendant's actions, the officer copied the content of the video surveillance onto a VHS tape and locked it in his office desk. Defendant filed a motion *in limine* to exclude evidence of the tape. Defendant argued that the tape should be excluded because it contained a "30-second skip." The trial court denied defendant's motion. At trial, defendant objected to insufficient foundation for admissibility of the video and ultimately trial court found that the state had laid sufficient foundation and admitted the tape in evidence. The first segment of the video showed a man enter the principal's office, open a desk drawer and remove a pouch containing money. The second segment recorded 30 seconds after the first segment ended showed the man still crouched behind the desk and then leaving. Defense counsel again objected, noting that the state failed to explain the 30-second skip on the tape. The officer explained that the camera stops recording when it does not sense motion and then starts recording again as soon as it senses motion. The trial court convicted defendant of misdemeanor theft and subsequently denied his motion to reconsider.

The Illinois Supreme Court reviewed the trial court's decision to admit the VHS tape under an abuse of discretion standard, noting that "[u]nder this standard, an abuse occurs when the trial court's ruling is fanciful, unreasonable or when no reasonable person would adopt the trial court's view." In considering the admissibility of the tape, the Supreme Court noted that

> [m]ost jurisdictions now allow photographs and videotapes to be introduced as substantive evidence so long as a proper foundation is laid. *Id.* Such evidence is generally admitted under the "silent witness" theory. (citation omitted). Under this theory, a witness need not testify to the accuracy of the image depicted in the photographic or videotape evidence if the accuracy of the process that produced the evidence is established with an adequate foundation. In such a case, the evidence is "received as a so-called silent witness or as a witness which 'speaks for itself.'" The silent witness theory was originally utilized in Illinois and elsewhere in connection with the admissibility of X rays. *See* Stevens v. Illinois Central R.R. Co., 306 Ill. 370, 375 (1922). The majority of cases now involve automatic cameras or surveillance systems where videotapes, CDs or DVDs are made from the system and sought to be admitted.
>
> ***
>
> Most jurisdictions point out that the circumstances of each case and, thus, the requirements to guarantee the genuineness of the evidence, will always differ.

The Supreme Court indicated that the appellate court considered six different factors, including the device's capability to record, the operator's ability, proper operation of the device, chain of custody, identification of what the tape depicted and explanation of the copying process. The Supreme Court emphasized that although these factors may be relevant, each case must be approached on an individual basis with the "dispositive issue in every case [being] the accuracy and reliability of the process that produced the recording." Specifically, the Supreme Court observed that the appellate court erred in not considering a police report that discussed the copying process. The appellate court found that the copying process was insufficiently explained and that therefore the tape was inadmissible. The Supreme Court disagreed and explained that

> [i]t is widely recognized that when the trial court addresses preliminary questions, like the admissibility of evidence, it is not constrained by the usual rules of evidence. RALPH RUEBNER, ILLINOIS CRIMINAL TRIAL EVIDENCE 3 (4th ed. 2001); 11 ILL. PRAC., COURTROOM HANDBOOK ON ILLINOIS EVIDENCE § 104.1 (2001). *See also* ILL. R. EVID. 104(a) ("Preliminary questions concerning *** the admissibility of evidence shall be determined by the court, subject to the provisions of subdivision (b). In making its determination, the court is not bound by the rules of evidence except those with respect to privileges."). What this means is: "the court may consider hearsay or other evidence that would not be admissible if offered to the jury." Lorraine v. Markel Am. Ins. Co., 241 F.R.D. 534, 539 (D. Md. 2007); JACK B. WEINSTEIN & MARGARET A. BERGER, WEINSTEIN'S FEDERAL EVIDENCE § 901.06(1)(c)(iii) (2d ed. 1997) ("Rule 104(a) provides that inadmissible evidence may be considered in determining preliminary questions of admissibility."). Thus, the appellate court should have considered the report in determining the admissibility of the videotape and erred when it said there was no explanation of the copying process.

The Supreme Court concluded that the totality of circumstances indicated that the state laid sufficient foundation for admissibility of the tape by showing that the camera was able to record and was operating properly.

PRIOR ILLINOIS CASE LAW

1. Jury Assesses the Credibility of Witnesses and Weighs the Evidence

People v. Boclair, 129 Ill. 2d 458 (1989)

Defendant was convicted of murder and conspiracy and was sentenced to death in a separate sentencing hearing. On appeal to the Illinois Supreme Court, the convictions were affirmed but the death sentence vacated and the cause remanded for a new sentencing hearing. In upholding that guilty verdict the Supreme Court determined that the jury's verdict was not so unsatisfactory, unreasonable or improbable as to raise a reasonable doubt of defendant's guilt, stating that

> [t]he purpose of a jury is to make available the commonsense judgment of the community as a hedge against the overzealous or mistaken prosecutor. Taylor v. Louisiana, 419 U.S. 522, 530 (1975). It is the jury's duty to assess the credibility of witnesses and to weigh the evidence in determining a defendant's guilt or innocence. (citation omitted). That determination is entitled to great deference, and when the sufficiency of the evidence is challenged we will not retry the defendant, although it is our duty to set aside a conviction when the evidence raises a reasonable doubt of defendant's guilt. People v. Sanchez, 115 Ill. 2d 238, 260 (1986); People v. Collins, 106 Ill. 2d 237, 261 (1985). On review, 'the relevant question is whether, after reviewing the evidence in the light most favorable to the prosecution, *any* rational trier of fact could have found the essential elements of the crime beyond a reasonable doubt.' (Emphasis in original.) *Collins*, 106 Ill. 2d at 261.

2. Trial Court Determines Preliminary Questions Concerning Admissibility of Evidence without Regard to Rules of Evidence Except for Matters Pertaining to Privileges
People v. Patterson, 192 Ill. 2d 93 (2000)

Defendant was convicted of two murders. He filed a post-conviction petition in which he contended that his confession to the murders was coerced, relying on a report finding abuse of arrestees at the police station at that time was "systemic." Trial court held a suppression hearing and subsequently dismissed defendant's petition, finding that "nexus" between the allegation of torture and the defendant was "highly tenuous at best." Defendant appealed.

On appeal, defendant argued that his attorney was ineffective in his presentation of certain hearsay evidence during the suppression hearing. The attorney sought to introduce etchings that defendant made into a bench in the interrogation room after police questioned him. The etchings stated that police threatened, slapped, and suffocated the person who wrote them and that his or her confession to murder was false. The attorney argued that the etchings were admissible under various exceptions to the hearsay rule. Defendant claimed that his attorney should have argued that the etchings were admissible at pretrial hearings where the trial court determines admissibility of evidence. The Illinois Supreme Court noted that

> hearsay evidence is admissible during a motion to suppress, even though it is not admissible at trial. People v. Lesure, 271 Ill. App. 3d 679, 680 (1st Dist. 1995). Moreover, federal law supports defendant's argument. Federal Rule of Evidence 104(a) provides, in relevant part, "Preliminary questions concerning *** the admissibility of evidence shall be determined by the court ***. *In making its determination it is not bound by the rules of evidence except those with respect to privileges*." (Emphasis added.) FED. R. EVID. 104(a). The Supreme Court has explained that no automatic rule precludes the admission of hearsay when a trial court is determining the admissibility of evidence. United States v. Matlock, 415 U.S. 164 (1974); *see also* United States v. Bolin, 514 F.2d 554, 557 (7th Cir. 1975) (holding that "it is clear that hearsay evidence is admissible in a hearing on a motion to suppress").

3. Trial Court Need Not Conduct a Preliminary Inquiry into the Reliability of an Eyewitness Identification When It Was Not Procured Under Suggestive Circumstances Arranged by Law Enforcement
Perry v. New Hampshire, 132 S. Ct. 716 (2012)

Defendant was charged with theft by unauthorized taking and criminal mischief. A witness who observed a man breaking into cars in the parking lot outside of her kitchen window called the police. One police officer arrived at the scene and saw defendant holding two car stereos in his hand. The witness who saw the theft alerted the owner of the vehicle. The owner then came to the parking lot and spoke with the police officer. The owner told the police officer that he heard about the crime from the witness. The officer then left defendant standing in the parking lot with another officer and went to the witness' apartment to question her. The officer asked for a specific description of the perpetrator and the witness said that the man she saw breaking into the vehicle was "standing in the parking lot, next to the police officer." Police subsequently arrested defendant. Approximately one month after defendant's arrest, the police showed the witness a photographic array containing defendant's picture. The witness, however, was unable to identify the defendant. Defendant moved to suppress the witness' earlier identification, alleging that it violated his due process rights as it constituted a "one person showup." The trial court denied defendant's motion, concluding that the jury could properly determine the reliability of the witness' testimony. After an unsuccessful appeal to the state supreme court, the United States Supreme Court granted certiorari to determine "whether the Due Process Clause requires a trial judge to conduct a preliminary assessment of the reliability of an eyewitness identification made under suggestive circumstances not arranged by the police." Defendant contended that trial court should "prescreen eyewitness evidence for reliability any time an identification is made under suggestive circumstances." The Supreme Court disagreed, explaining that defendant did not allege any improper conduct by the police. The Supreme Court noted that

> [a] primary aim of excluding identification evidence obtained under unnecessarily suggestive circumstances [. . .] is to deter law enforcement use of improper lineups, showups, and photo arrays in the first place. [citation omitted]. Alerted to the prospect that identification evidence improperly obtained may be excluded, [. . .] police officers will "guard against unnecessarily suggestive procedures." [citation omitted]. This deterrence rationale is inapposite in cases, like [defendant's], in which the police engaged in no improper conduct.

Defendant contended that eyewitness identifications are "a uniquely unreliable form of evidence," but the Supreme Court noted "that the potential unreliability of a type of evidence does not alone render its introduction at [. . .] trial fundamentally unfair." The Supreme Court explained that

> [t]he fallibility of eyewitness evidence does not, without the taint of improper state conduct, warrant a due process rule requiring a trial court to screen such evidence for reliability before allowing the jury to assess its creditworthiness.
>
> Our unwillingness to enlarge the domain of due process as [defendant] and the dissent urge rests, in large part, on our recognition that the jury, not the judge, traditionally determines the reliability of evidence. [citation omitted]. We also take account of other safeguards built into our adversary system that caution juries against placing undue weight on eyewitness testimony of questionable reliability. These protections include the defendant's Sixth Amendment right to confront the eyewitness. *See* Maryland v. Craig, 497 U.S. 836, 845 (1990). Another is the defendant's right to the effective assistance of an attorney, who can expose the flaws in the eyewitness' testimony during cross-examination and focus the jury's attention on the fallibility of such testimony during opening and closing arguments. Eyewitness-specific jury instructions, which many federal and state courts have adopted, likewise warn the jury to take care in appraising identification evidence. [citations omitted]. The constitutional requirement that the government prove the defendant's guilt beyond a reasonable doubt also impedes convictions based on dubious identification evidence.
>
> ***
>
> State and federal rules of evidence, moreover, permit trial judges to exclude relevant evidence if its probative value is substantially outweighed by its prejudicial impact or potential for misleading the jury. *See, e.g.*, FED. RULE EVID. 403. In appropriate cases, some States also permit defendants to present expert testimony on the hazards of eyewitness identification evidence.

The Supreme Court observed that the witness testified about the limitations at play in her identification of the defendant, such as the distance between her window and where defendant stood, that it was late at night and that a van partly obstructed her view. She was also unable to describe defendant's features and could not pick him out of a photograph array. The Supreme Court therefore concluded that the introduction of the witness' identification without a preliminary assessment of its reliability by the trial judge did not prejudice defendant. The Supreme Court held that "the Due Process Clause does not require a preliminary judicial inquiry into the reliability of an eyewitness identification when the identification was not procured under unnecessarily suggestive circumstances arranged by law enforcement."

4. When Defendant Objects to Admissibility of a Confession as Involuntary, Trial Court Has Duty to Conduct Determination of Voluntariness of the Confession Outside of the Presence of the Jury

People v. Caldwell, 39 Ill. 2d 346 (1968)

Defendant was convicted of murder. His confession was admitted at trial and the jury was allowed to view the written confession during deliberations. In his appeal to the Illinois Supreme Court, defendant for the first time contended that although he signed the confession he was unable to read it and did not know what it said because the lighting was insufficient and he could not read. Defendant requested the Illinois Supreme Court to remand the case for a hearing to determine whether his confession was improperly admitted at trial. The Supreme Court noted that an

> objection during a criminal trial that no proper foundation has been laid for the admission of a defendant's statement is sufficient to require the trial judge to suspend the jury proceedings and conduct a hearing on the voluntariness of a confession offered by the prosecution for admission. People v. Thigpen, 33 Ill. 2d 595 (1966); People v. Taylor, 33 Ill. 2d 417 (1965); People v. Jackson, 31 Ill. 2d 408 (1964).
>
> ***
>
> The rule adopted in Jackson v. Denno, 378 U.S. 368 (1964), which requires that an initial judicial determination of the voluntariness of a defendant's confession be made outside the presence of the jury when objection is made to its admission, has long been the law in this State. *See* People v. Fox, 319 Ill. 606, 616-619 (1925). We have said that 'a confession may be challenged either by preliminary hearing on a motion to suppress (People v. Spencer, 27 Ill. 2d 320 (1963)) or by appropriate objection thereto at the trial (People v. Wagoner, 8 Ill. 2d 188 (1956)), and failure to pursue one of these devices ordinarily precludes consideration of the matter on appeal. People v. Williams, 26 Ill. 2d 190, 192 (1962); People v. Jones, 31 Ill. 2d 42, 50 (1964); People v. Taylor, 33 Ill. 2d 417 (1965). When a defense objection to a confession is made in apt time our procedure provides an appropriate avenue by which knowledge of the existence of a confession can be kept from the jury until its voluntariness has been determined.

The Supreme Court, however, found that defendant failed to properly object to the admissibility of the confession at trial and did not raise this issue in the appellate court. During trial, defendant merely objected generally at the close of state's case to the lack of foundation for admissibility of the weapon and the confession, but failed to advance specific objections to the evidence. The Supreme Court observed that the general objection to the weapon and to the confession was insufficient to state the grounds upon which the objection was based. The Supreme Court concluded that the trial court and the state could not have known that the defendant, by stating such a general objection, was requesting a hearing outside the presence of the jury with respect to the confession.

5. Defendant Cannot Challenge Trial Court's Answers to Jury's Questions When Defendant Fails to Object and Acquiesces

People v. Reid, 136 Ill. 2d 27 (1990)

Defendant was found guilty of armed robbery and murder. The defendant claimed the trial court erred in its responses to questions raised by the jury during its deliberations. The Illinois Supreme Court shed light on the range of permissible responses, explaining that there is a "duty to instruct the jury where clarification is requested, the original instructions are incomplete, and the jurors are manifestly confused," and that there are circumstances where "a circuit court has the duty to answer a jury's questions even if the jury received proper instructions." But trial courts may decline to answer where the instructions are "readily understandable and sufficiently explain the relevant law," or an answer by the court would cause the court to "express an opinion which would probably direct a verdict one way or the other," or if the jury's question is ambiguous and would require discussion of the facts that risks an expression of the trial court's opinion on evidence. Here, the judge consulted both sets of counsel prior to telling the jury to reach a verdict based on the instructions it had received. Since defendant did not object at the time, the issue was waived. Additionally, the defendant failed to show how the court's failure to directly answer the jury's question prejudiced him.

6. Defendant Has a Constitutional Right to Participate in Fashioning a Response to Inquiries Made by Jury, but Jury Verdict Will Not Be Set Aside If No Injury or Prejudice Resulted from *Ex Parte* Communication with Jury

People v. Childs, 159 Ill. 2d 217 (1994)

The state petitioned the Illinois Supreme Court to review the appellate court's holding that the trial court's *ex parte* instruction to the jury was reversible error. The Supreme Court affirmed the appellate court because

> an *ex parte* communication between a judge and a jury deprives a defendant of his constitutional rights to be present at and to participate for his protection in a critical stage of trial [and] the burden is on the State to prove beyond a reasonable doubt that the error was harmless.

The jury is entitled to have its explicit legal questions answered, and the defendant has a right to be informed of the questions posed by the jury and to be given an opportunity to participate in fashioning an appropriate response. The Supreme Court further noted, however, that

> a jury verdict will not be set aside where it is apparent that no injury or prejudice resulted from a communication to the jury either by the trial court or a third person outside the presence of the defendant and his counsel. People v. Brothers, 347 Ill. 530, 548 (1932); People v. Tilley, 411 Ill. 473, 478 (1952); People v. Mills, 40 Ill. 2d 4, 14 (1968); People v. Walker, 91 Ill. 2d 502, 516, (1982). Where it is established that an error of constitutional magnitude has occurred, the burden is on the one gaining advantage from the error, rather than the one claiming prejudice, to prove that the error did not contribute to the verdict but, rather, that it was harmless beyond a reasonable doubt. Chapman v. California, 386 U.S. 18, 23-24 (1967); People v. Bracey, 51 Ill. 2d 514, 519-20 (1972).

Here, the defendant shot and killed a security guard of a convenience store during an armed robbery. Defendant claimed that the shooting was accidental and that the guard brandished a weapon first. The trial court instructed the jury to decide whether defendant was "Guilty of Murder," "Guilty of Voluntary Manslaughter," "Guilty of Involuntary Manslaughter," and "Not Guilty of The Murder, Voluntary Manslaughter and Involuntary Manslaughter of [the victim]." The trial court also provided "Guilty of Armed Robbery" and "Not Guilty of Armed Robbery" verdict forms. The trial court did not instruct the jury as to felony murder. The jurors were confused about the instruction and asked the judge whether "the defendant [can] be guilty of armed robbery and voluntary or involuntary manslaughter or must murder be the only option with armed robbery?" The judge refused to clarify and simply instructed them to keep deliberating pursuant to the instructions. Defense counsel objected to the judge's answer to the jury's question. The Supreme Court noted that the jurors were confused and may have believed that they had to find defendant guilty or not guilty of all three offenses. The jurors found defendant guilty of murder and armed robbery. The Supreme Court noted that the jury asked an explicit question about a substantive legal issue and that the defendant was prejudiced by the trial court's answer. It also concluded that the state failed to show that the error was harmless beyond a reasonable doubt.

Rule 105. Limited Admissibility

When evidence which is admissible as to one party or for one purpose but not admissible as to another party or for another purpose is admitted, the court, upon request, shall restrict the evidence to its proper purpose or scope and instruct the jury accordingly.

Adopted September 27, 2010, eff. January 1, 2011.

AUTHOR'S COMMENTARY

Evidence that is admissible for one purpose should not be excluded because it may be inadmissible for another purpose. People v. Monroe, 66 Ill. 2d 317 (1977). The prejudicial effect, if any, resulting from the use of such evidence can be mitigated by giving the jury a limiting instruction. This instruction should inform the jury that it is to consider the particular evidence only for the limited purpose for which it is offered and admitted. People v. Heard, 187 Ill. 2d 36 (1999). It is the duty of the party against whom it is admitted to request a limiting instruction. People v. Robinson, 121 Ill. App. 3d 1003 (1st Dist. 1984). If the opponent fails to make such a request, it will ordinarily not be permitted to claim on appeal that the evidence had a prejudicial effect. People v. Gacho, 122 Ill. 2d 221 (1988). Illinois Rule of Evidence 105 differs from Federal Rule of Evidence 105, in effect prior to its stylistic amendment on December 1, 2011, in that it states that a "court, upon request, shall restrict the evidence to its proper *purpose* or scope," (emphasis added), whereas the Federal Rule states only that a "court, upon request, shall restrict the evidence to its proper scope." The Special Supreme Court Committee on Illinois Evidence added this distinction for purposes of "clarity." Gino L. DiVito, *The Illinois Rules of Evidence: A Color-Coded Guide Containing the New Rules, the Committee's General and Specific Comments, a Comparison with the Federal Rules of Evidence, and Additional Commentary* (*Including the Federal Rules of Evidence as Amended Effective December 1, 2011*) (Jan. 1, 2012), at 21, http://www.tdrlawfirm.com/assets/downloads/Illinois_Rules_of_Evidence_Color-Coded_Guide.pdf.

PRIOR ILLINOIS CASE LAW

1. Evidence Inadmissible for One Purpose May Be Admissible for Another
People v. Monroe, 66 Ill. 2d 317 (1977)

Defendant was convicted of delivery of a controlled substance (LSD) to an undercover special agent. Defendant argued, and the appellate court agreed, that the special agent's testimony that he had previously purchased drugs from the state's witness who introduced the special agent to the defendant was inadmissible. The appellate court found that the evidence was so prejudicial to defendant as to deprive him of the right to a fair trial. The Illinois Supreme Court held this testimony was relevant in that it explained why the special agent asked whether defendant had LSD for sale, and where more could be purchased. The probative value of this evidence outweighed its prejudicial effect. The Supreme Court reasoned that "evidence admissible for one purpose cannot be excluded for the reason that it would not be admitted for another purpose, and that the party against whom it is admitted may tender instructions appropriately limiting the purpose for which it may be considered."

2. Limiting Instructions Inform Jury to Consider Particular Evidence Only for the Limited Purpose for Which It Is Offered and Admitted
People v. Heard, 187 Ill. 2d 36 (1999)

Defendant was charged with first degree murder, home invasion, residential burglary and burglary in the murders of his ex-girlfriend, her new boyfriend and two of their friends. State introduced prior-crimes evidence showing "several violent episodes" between defendant and his ex-girlfriend. Defendant argued on appeal that introduction of this evidence was prejudicial and deprived him of a fair trial. The Illinois Supreme Court disagreed, noting:

> Defendant argues that a proper limiting instruction must accompany the admission of other-crimes evidence in order to ensure that the jury at no time uses the evidence for the improper purpose of forming a negative opinion of the defendant. We do not agree. The better practice may be for trial courts to instruct the jury, not only at the close of the case, but also at the time other-crimes evidence is admitted, of the limited purpose for which it may consider the other-crimes evidence. See People v. Denny, 241 Ill. App. 3d 345, 360-61 (1993); Illinois Pattern Jury Instructions, Criminal, No. 3.14, Committee Note (3d ed. Supp. 1996). The trial court's failure to do so, however, does not mandate reversal.

The Supreme Court concluded that the trial court properly gave a limiting instruction pertaining to the other-crimes evidence by instructing the jury that the evidence was admissible for the limited purpose of establishing defendant's motive and intent to harm the victims but not to show his propensity to commit violent crimes.

3. If Party Fails to Request a Limiting Instruction, It Waives Any Challenge as to the Prejudicial Effect of That Particular Evidence
People v. Gacho, 122 Ill. 2d 221 (1988)

Defendant was convicted of murder, aggravated kidnapping and armed robbery. State impeached a defense witness with prior inconsistent statements. Defendant failed to tender a limiting instruction that would inform the jury to consider these prior statements only for purposes of impeachment and not as substantive evidence. Defendant argued on appeal that it was error for the trial court to not tender such instruction. The Illinois Supreme Court refused to consider his argument. The Supreme Court found that defendant waived his claim because he had failed to tender a limiting instruction and did not raise the claim in his motion for a new trial.

4. Defense Counsel's Failure to Request a Limiting Instruction Requiring Jury to Consider Accomplice's Acquittal of the Charged Crime Only for Credibility Determination and Not in Determining Defendant's Guilt Is Not Ineffective Assistance Where Overwhelming Evidence of Defendant's Guilt Exists
Berghuis v. Thompkins, 130 S. Ct. 2250 (2010)

Defendant was implicated in a shooting death after he and two other men opened fire on the victim out of their vehicle. His defense at trial was that one of the other accomplices was the shooter. The accomplice testified at defendant's trial that he was merely the driver during the shooting and that he did not see who fired the shots. He also testified that he was previously acquitted of murder and assault charges arising from the incident. Defense counsel failed to object to this testimony or to request a limiting instruction informing the jury that it could only consider the evidence of accomplice's acquittal to determine his credibility, and not to establish the defendant's guilt. Defendant was convicted and filed a motion for a new trial where he claimed that his counsel was ineffective in failing to request a limiting instruction pertaining to the outcome of the accomplice's trial. The trial court denied his motion, reasoning that counsel's failure to request the instruction was not prejudicial to defendant. The state appellate court affirmed the trial court's ruling. The state supreme court denied discretionary review and defendant filed a petition for a writ of habeas corpus in the United

States District Court for the Eastern District of Michigan. The District Court also rejected defendant's claim. The United States Court of Appeals for the Sixth Circuit reversed, finding that the state court unreasonably applied clearly established federal law by rejecting defendant's ineffective assistance of counsel claim. The court explained that had a limiting instruction been given, there was a reasonable probability that the outcome of defendant's trial would have been different because defendant's primary strategy at trial was to shift blame to the accomplice.

The United States Supreme Court granted certiorari and explained that

> [t]o establish ineffective assistance of counsel, a defendant "must show both deficient performance and prejudice." [citation omitted] To establish prejudice, a "defendant must show that there is a reasonable probability that, but for counsel's unprofessional errors, the result of the proceeding would have been different." Strickland v. Washington, 466 U.S. 668, 694 (1984). In assessing prejudice, courts "must consider the totality of the evidence before the judge or jury." *Id.*, at 695.

The Supreme Court reversed the Sixth Circuit's decision, noting that

> [i]t seems doubtful that failure to request the instruction about the earlier acquittal or conviction was deficient representation; but on the assumption that it was, on this record [defendant] cannot show prejudice. The record establishes that it was not reasonably likely that the instruction would have made any difference in light of all the other evidence of guilt. The surviving victim [. . .] identified [defendant] as the shooter, and the identification was supported by a photograph taken from a surveillance camera. [. . .] The jury, moreover, was capable of assessing [the accomplice's] credibility, as it was instructed to do. The jury in [defendant's] case could have concluded that the earlier jury in [the accomplice's] case made a mistake, or alternatively, that [the accomplice] was not in fact guilty of the crime for which he had been charged. There was ample evidence in the record to support [defendant's] guilt under either theory, and his jury was instructed to weigh all of the evidence in determining whether there was guilt beyond a reasonable doubt. Under our *de novo* review of this record, [defendant] cannot show prejudice.

5. Limiting Instruction Is Inadequate to Ensure That Jury Only Considers Evidence for Its Proper Purpose Where There Is No Proper Purpose for Admissibility of the Evidence
People v. Cruz, 162 Ill. 2d 314 (1994)

Defendant and co-defendant were tried together and convicted of kidnapping, rape, and murder of a 10-year-old victim. Defendant's cousin testified for the state and denied making several prior inconsistent statements. The state impeached her testimony with a statement she had previously made to the police that she had seen a third person with defendant and co-defendant on the day of the murder. She further stated that defendant had visited her one evening, was very upset and told her he was in trouble. She denied making these statements and state impeached her with testimony of two additional witnesses. The state then attempted to use the impeachment evidence as substantive evidence in its closing argument. Although the trial court gave limiting instructions with respect to the evidence, the Illinois Supreme Court found that this was a fundamental error that could not be corrected with limiting instructions. The Supreme Court observed that the state could not impeach the witness because her statements were "entirely neutral" and did not affirmatively damage the state's case. The Supreme Court explained that

> [t]o reduce the risk that a jury might consider a prior inconsistent statement as independent evidence with substantive character, the jury should be cautioned and properly instructed to limit its consideration of the statement to its narrow purpose. People v. Bradford, 106 Ill. 2d

> 492, 501(1985) (citing cases). Even with instruction, however, such errors have been considered grounds for reversal. *See* People v. Bailey, 60 Ill. 2d 37, 44 (1975) (finding error, despite jury instruction, where prosecution attempted to improperly impart substantive character to impeached witness' prior inconsistent statements). And where Illinois courts have ruled that improper impeachment as well as improper substantive use of that evidence occurred, our courts have reversed without even considering the possible curative effect of jury instructions. *See* People v. Weaver, 92 Ill. 2d 545 (1982); *see also* People v. Johnson, 138 Ill. App. 3d 980 (5th Dist. 1985); *accord* People v. Kimbrough, 131 Ill. App. 2d 36 (1st Dist. 1970).

The present case concerns both improper impeachment and an attempt to substantively use the impeachment evidence during closing argument. Under such circumstances, limiting instructions were inadequate to ensure that the jury considered the evidence for any proper purpose because there was none. The instructions here could not cure this fundamental error.

See also Bruton v. United States, 391 U.S. 123 (1968) (finding that limiting instructions are not adequate to prevent jury from using improperly admitted evidence to determine defendant's guilt where co-defendant's confession implicating defendant is admitted at a joint trial);

And see People v. Williams, 182 Ill. 2d 171 (1998) (limiting instruction is insufficient to cure prejudice of non-testifying co-defendant's statement implicating defendant where statements were not cleansed of all references to non-declaring defendant);

But see Richardson v. Marsh, 481 U.S. 200 (1987) (limiting instruction directing jury to not use non-testifying co-defendant's confession against defendant is proper to safeguard defendant's rights where confession was redacted to eliminate all references to the defendant).

Rule 106. Remainder of or Related Writings or Recorded Statements

When a writing or recorded statement or part thereof is introduced by a party, an adverse party may require the introduction at that time of any other part or any other writing or recorded statement which ought in fairness to be considered contemporaneously with it.

Adopted September 27, 2010, eff. January 1, 2011.

Committee Commentary

Rule 106 permits the admission contemporaneously of any other part of a writing or recording or any other writing or recording which "ought in fairness" be considered at the same time. Prior Illinois law appears to have limited the concept of completeness to other parts of the same writing or recording or an addendum thereto. The "ought in fairness" requirement allows admissibility of statements made under separate circumstances.

ILL. R. EVID. Committee Commentary § 3(1), pg. 2.

AUTHOR'S COMMENTARY

Prior to the enactment of Illinois Rule of Evidence 106, Illinois common law "limited the concept of completeness to other parts of the *same* writing or recording or an addendum thereto." ILL. R. EVID. Committee Commentary § 3(1), pg. 2 (emphasis added); *see* People v. Patterson, 154 Ill. 2d 414 (1992). The completeness doctrine stood for the proposition that where a witness testified as to a portion of a writing or recording, the opponent could then bring out the remainder of the same writing or recording on cross-examination of the witness. People v. Williams, 109 Ill. 2d 327 (1985). Illinois Rule of Evidence 106 has adopted the language of the Federal Rule of Evidence 106 effective prior to its stylistic amendment on December 1, 2011, and now allows a party to introduce even "statements made under separate circumstances" to complete the testimony of a witness. ILL. R. EVID. Committee Commentary § 3(1), pg. 2; Gino L. DiVito, *The Illinois Rules of Evidence: A Color-Coded Guide Containing the New Rules, the Committee's General and Specific Comments, a Comparison with the Federal Rules of Evidence, and Additional Commentary (Including the Federal Rules of Evidence as Amended Effective December 1, 2011)* (Jan. 1, 2012), at 22, http://www.tdrlawfirm.com/assets/downloads/Illinois_Rules_of_Evidence_Color-Coded_Guide.pdf.

Prior Illinois common law evidence rules required a party seeking the introduction of the remainder of a writing or recording to show that it would be unduly prejudiced if the remainder is not entered into evidence. People v. Manning, 182 Ill. 2d 193 (1998). Rule 106 does not explicitly address this requirement and merely states that a remainder of a writing or recording will be admitted pursuant to the doctrine if fairness requires such a result. ILL. R. EVID. 106. Professor Graham has interpreted this requirement as stating that in order to invoke the doctrine a party must show that the jury would be misled if the remainder of the recording or writing is not introduced in evidence. MICHAEL H. GRAHAM, GRAHAM'S HANDBOOK OF ILLINOIS EVIDENCE § 106.2 (10th ed. 2010).

The purpose of the completeness doctrine is to promote the fairness of a trial and to ensure that the jury or judge in a bench trial is not left with half-truths or disguised evidence. The doctrine, however, is not an automatic right to introduce evidence that is otherwise inadmissible.

PRIOR ILLINOIS CASE LAW

1. Party Urging Admissibility of Evidence Pursuant to the Completeness Doctrine Must Specify the Portion of Statement or Recording That Must Be Admitted to Prevent Misleading the Jury

People v. Olinger, 112 Ill. 2d 324 (1986)

Defendant was sentenced to death after being convicted of murders of three people, armed robbery, armed violence, and conspiracy. On appeal, defendant claimed the trial court improperly precluded him from introducing exculpatory portions of statements he made to the police officer who testified for the state. The state introduced defendant's statement that he had participated in a burglary during which he stole various guns. Defendant sought to disclose the rest of his statement where he claimed that a third person stole the gun used to murder the victims during the burglary. Defendant contended that the trial court erred in not allowing this statement into evidence because it gave the jury the "mistaken impression" that he had admitted to taking the murder weapon. The Supreme Court disagreed, noting that a "defendant has no right to introduce portions of a statement which are not necessary to enable the jury to properly evaluate the portions introduced by the State." The Supreme Court observed that, in effect, the defendant was attempting to introduce his own exculpatory statements without having to take the stand and being subjected to impeachment.

Even if defendant's argument had merit, the Illinois Supreme Court refused to consider it because defendant failed to raise this argument at trial and only made a general request to have "*all* exculpatory portions of the statements" admitted. The Supreme Court explained that defendant must specify the portion of the statement necessary to prevent the jury from receiving a misleading impression as to the nature of the statement. The Supreme Court concluded that a trial court need not "*sua sponte* scrutinize the proffered statements to determine if there may be a rationale to admit some small portion thereof."

2. Evidence Introduced Pursuant to the Completeness Doctrine Must Be Relevant

People v. Williams, 109 Ill. 2d 327 (1985)

Defendant was charged with murder and theft. Defendant appealed his convictions and argued that the trial court erred in refusing to admit his two audio recorded statements into evidence. Two officers testified at trial about the content of the audio recordings. They each interviewed the defendant and were present when he gave his audio recorded statements. Defendant offered the recordings in evidence but the trial court refused to admit them indicating that they were merely cumulative evidence of the officers' testimony. The Illinois Supreme Court noted that the completeness doctrine stands for the

> general evidentiary principle that 'if one party introduces part of an utterance or writing the opposing party may introduce the remainder or so much thereof as is required to place that part originally offered in proper context so that a correct and true meaning is conveyed to the jury.' Lawson v. G.D. Searle & Co., 64 Ill. 2d 543, 556 (1976). See MCCORMICK, EVIDENCE sec. 56 (3d ed. 1984); CLEARY & GRAHAM, ILLINOIS EVIDENCE secs. 106.1, 106.2 (3d ed. 1979); 2 GARD, ILLINOIS EVIDENCE, Rule 15:31 (1979); 4 CALLAGHAN'S ILLINOIS EVIDENCE secs. 5.25, 5.26 (1964); 29 Am. Jur. 2d Evidence secs. 535, 599 (1967); *see also* FED. R. EVID. 106. ***
>
> [T]he right to bring out all of a conversation is not absolute, but depends upon the *relevancy* of the additional parts of the conversation the party wishes to introduce. [emphasis in original]

The Supreme Court found that although the defendant had an opportunity to cross-examine the officers extensively about the audio recordings, the actual tape recording had "independent relevance." The recordings could have shown that officers mischaracterized defendant's statements, may have revealed any inconsistencies between the officers' testimonies, and would have shown defendant's "demeanor and voice inflections." The Supreme Court concluded that the recordings should have been admitted pursuant to the doctrine of completeness.

3. Rule of Completeness Was Designed to Prevent Any Prejudice to a Party Resulting from Opponent Introducing Only an Incomplete Excerpt of the Evidence
Beech Aircraft Corp. v. Rainey, 488 U.S. 153 (1988)

Two Navy pilots were involved in a plane crash while flying a training aircraft. The spouses of the deceased pilots brought a product liability suit against the plane's manufacturer. A Navy report analyzing the possible causes of the crash indicated that although the cause was "almost impossible to determine," pilot error may have been to blame and technical issues with the craft could not be ruled out. The trial court admitted into evidence only the portion of the report pertaining to pilot error but excluded the portion indicating that a cause was not possible to determine and that technical problems may have been a factor.

The husband of one of the deceased pilots conducted an independent investigation and sent a letter to the Navy officer who conducted the initial report. The letter indicated that the most probable cause of the crash was a technical malfunction. The husband testified at trial but was prevented from testifying about the cause of the accident. He intended to show that the Navy's report's conclusions were inconsistent with eyewitness observations of the accident and also to rebut evidence gleaned out of a portion of his letter that indicated that his wife tried to cancel the flight because the other pilot was tired on the day of the accident.

The United States Supreme Court found that it was error to restrict the cross-examination of the husband and prevent him from presenting "a more complete picture" of what his letter contained. The Supreme Court explained that

> The common-law "rule of completeness," which underlies Federal Rule of Evidence 106, was designed to prevent exactly the type of prejudice of which [the husband] complains. In its aspect relevant to this litigation, the rule of completeness was stated succinctly by Wigmore:

> "[T]he opponent, against whom a part of an utterance has been put in, may in his turn complement it by putting in the remainder, in order to secure for the tribunal a complete understanding of the total tenor and effect of the utterance." 7 J. WIGMORE, EVIDENCE IN TRIALS AT COMMON LAW § 2113, p. 653 (J. Chadbourn rev. 1978).

The Supreme Court concluded that

> [i]n proposing Rule 106, the Advisory Committee stressed that it 'does not in any way circumscribe the right of the adversary to develop the matter on cross-examination or as part of his own case.' Advisory Committee's Notes on Fed. Rule Evid. 106, 28 U.S.C. App., p. 682. We take this to be a reaffirmation of the obvious: that when one party has made use of a portion of a document, such that misunderstanding or distortion can be averted only through presentation of another portion, the material required for completeness is *ipso facto* relevant and therefore admissible.

Article II – Judicial Notice

Rule 201. Judicial Notice of Adjudicative Facts

(a) Scope of Rule. This rule governs only judicial notice of adjudicative facts.

(b) Kinds of Facts. A judicially noticed fact must be one not subject to reasonable dispute in that it is either (1) generally known within the territorial jurisdiction of the trial court or (2) capable of accurate and ready determination by resort to sources whose accuracy cannot reasonably be questioned.

(c) When Discretionary. A court may take judicial notice, whether requested or not.

(d) When Mandatory. A court shall take judicial notice if requested by a party and supplied with the necessary information.

(e) Opportunity to Be Heard. A party is entitled upon timely request to an opportunity to be heard as to the propriety of taking judicial notice and the tenor of the matter noticed. In the absence of prior notification, the request may be made after judicial notice has been taken.

(f) Time of Taking Notice. Judicial notice may be taken at any stage of the proceeding.

(g) Informing the Jury. In a civil action or proceeding, the court shall inform the jury to accept as conclusive any fact judicially noticed. In a criminal case, the court shall inform the jury that it may, but is not required to, accept as conclusive any fact judicially noticed.

Adopted September 27, 2010, eff. January 1, 2011.

AUTHOR'S COMMENTARY

Judicial notice is a method of proof of adjudicative facts without the need for formal proof. The court may recognize certain facts as true. Judicial notice generally involves relatively unimportant evidentiary issues that have a high likelihood of truth, independent of the particular litigation at hand.

Prior to the enactment of the Illinois Rules of Evidence, it was "not entirely clear" when it was mandatory for a judge to take notice of a judicial fact and when a judge could take *sua sponte* judicial notice of a fact without a party's request. ROBERT S. HUNTER, TRIAL HANDBOOK FOR ILLINOIS LAWYERS § 45.3 (5th ed. 1983). Some courts approvingly cited Federal Rule of Evidence 201, but "refused to adopt it categorically." HUNTER at § 45.3, citing People v. Davis, 65 Ill. 2d 157 (1976); *see also*, People v. Speight, 153 Ill. 2d 365 (1992) (noting that the Illinois Supreme Court "previously considered [Federal Rule of

Evidence] 201, and decided not to adopt it"). The new Illinois Rule of Evidence 201 is modeled after Federal Rule of Evidence 201, in effect prior to its stylistic amendment on December 1, 2011, except that Illinois Rule of Evidence 201(g) has substituted "inform" and "informing" for "instruct" and "instructing." *See* Gino L. DiVito, *The Illinois Rules of Evidence: A Color-Coded Guide Containing the New Rules, the Committee's General and Specific Comments, a Comparison with the Federal Rules of Evidence, and Additional Commentary (Including the Federal Rules of Evidence as Amended Effective December 1, 2011)* (Jan. 1, 2012), at 23-25, http://www.tdrlawfirm.com/assets/downloads/Illinois_Rules_of_Evidence_Color-Coded_Guide.pdf.

Now, a court may take judicial notice *sua sponte* pursuant to Illinois Rule of Evidence 201(c). If, however, a party requests the court to take judicial notice of an adjudicative fact, the party must provide the court with the necessary information pursuant to Illinois Rule of Evidence 201(d). If a party makes a request for judicial notice and supplies the necessary materials to support its request, the court is required to take judicial notice. Pursuant to Illinois Rule of Evidence 201(g), the court in a criminal case is required to "inform the jury that it may, but is not required to, accept as conclusive" a judicially noticed fact.

PRIOR ILLINOIS CASE LAW

1. Courts May Take Judicial Notice of Matters That Are Commonly Known, or of Matters Not Commonly Known That Are Readily Verifiable from Sources of Indisputable Accuracy

People v. Fisher, 184 Ill. 2d 441 (1998)

Two defendants were separately arrested for driving under the influence of alcohol. At the time of arrest, both defendants had previous DUI convictions and refused to submit to blood alcohol content testing. Pursuant to 625 ILCS 5/6-208.1(a)(3), a driver who is not a first-time offender and who refuses to submit to BAC testing will have his or her driving privileges automatically suspended for two years. Section 6-208.1(a)(3) applied only to drivers who were 21 years of age or older. Drivers who were younger and received a summary suspension could receive hardship relief, but older drivers could not. Defendants argued on appeal that the provision violated equal protection of the law on basis of age in that younger drivers who had previous DUI convictions were more dangerous than drivers who were over 21 years old. Defendants presented no supporting evidence for this claim and requested that the court take judicial notice of the fact that drivers under 21 years of age pose a greater risk to highway safety than drivers over the age of 21. The Illinois Supreme Court refused to take judicial notice of this fact. It noted that

> [c]ourts may take judicial notice of matters which are commonly known, or, if not commonly known, are readily verifiable from sources of indisputable accuracy. Murdy v. Edgar, 103 Ill. 2d 384, 394 (1984). A cursory examination of relevant, if not indisputable, authority reveals that it is impossible to readily confirm that non-first offenders under the age of 21 pose the greater risk to highway safety.

For additional cases discussing judicial notice, see:

- People v. Hammond, 2011 IL 110044 (finding that it is proper for the Supreme Court to take judicial notice of the circuit court's rules).
- People v. Deleon, 227 Ill. 2d 322 (2008) (taking judicial notice of the distance between two locations due to the accuracy with which it can be determined).

People v. McKown, 226 Ill. 2d 245 (2007) (finding that trial court erred in taking judicial notice that the Horizontal Gaze Nystagmus test is generally accepted as an indicator of alcohol impairment because admissibility of such evidence varied greatly between states).

People v. Whitfield, 228 Ill. 2d 502 (2007) (Supreme Court taking judicial notice of parties' arguments raised in their briefs in the appellate court).

People v. Rivera, 221 Ill. 2d 481 (2006) (Supreme Court taking judicial notice that the original trial judge retired).

People v. Lewis, 223 Ill. 2d 393 (2006) (noting that trial court took judicial notice that defendant received several traffic tickets in Bloomington although his alibi witnesses claimed he was in Milwaukee during that time period).

People v. Knight, 75 Ill. 2d 291 (1979) (finding that trial court may properly take judicial notice of matters of record in its own proceedings).

People v. Tassone, 41 Ill. 2d 7 (1968) (taking judicial notice of a commonly known fact that stolen truck was valued at more than $150, noting that "judicial notice may be taken of the fact that property has some value, although . . . reluctant to take notice of any specific value").

People v. Robinson, 14 Ill. 2d 325 (1958) (taking judicial notice that heroin, even when found in a compound, is a derivative of opium).

People v. Duyvejonck, 337 Ill. 636 (1929) (taking judicial notice of the calendar and the fact that December 1, 1928, was Saturday and December 11 was Tuesday).

People v. Bucciferro, 37 Ill. App. 3d 211 (1st Dist. 1976) (taking judicial notice of geographical fact that a city is located in a certain county for purposes of establishing venue).

2. Trial Court Shall Take Judicial Notice If Properly Requested by a Party and May Take Judicial Notice *Sua Sponte* Whether Requested to or Not

People v. Barham, 337 Ill. App. 3d 1121 (5th Dist. 2003)

The Fifth District of the Illinois Appellate Court has noted that

> [a] court is not required to take judicial notice Judicial notice without a proper request to do so. People v. Varnado, 66 Ill. App. 3d 413, 419 (1st Dist. 1978). "A party desiring to have a fact judicially noticed should bring the matter to the attention of the court, on the record. If he does not, the court of review will not ordinarily judicially notice such fact." People v. Clifton, 11 Ill. App. 3d 112, 114 (3d Dist. 1973).
>
> In rare instances, a trial judge may take judicial notice, *sua sponte*, of facts, as long as the judge makes clear during the course of the trial and not after the evidence is closed what facts and sources are included in the *sua sponte* notice. *See* People v. Rotkvich, 256 Ill. App. 3d 124, 130 (1st Dist. 1993); People v. Speight, 222 Ill. App. 3d 766, 772 (1st Dist. 1991), *rev'd on other grounds*, 153 Ill. 2d 365 (1992). It is well-established that concepts of fair play require that all parties to an action be given a fair opportunity to confront and to rebut any evidence which might be damaging to their position. *See* Drovers National Bank of Chicago v. Great Southwest Fire Insurance Co., 55 Ill. App. 3d 953, 957 (1st Dist. 1977). A party has the same right to rebut evidence admitted by *sua sponte* judicial notice as it does to rebut evidence introduced by the opposing party.

Here, the defendant was convicted of reckless homicide following a bench trial. Defendant was driving a car that crashed into an embankment killing the passenger. A state trooper and a project engineer testified for the prosecution about the speed of the vehicle before and during the accident. The state trooper testified that the vehicle was traveling at approximate speed of

73 miles per hour right before the crash and about 50 miles per hour upon impact. The engineer testified that the vehicle recorded the speed at which it was traveling and that it showed defendant driving at speed of 76 miles per hour before the crash and 52 miles per hour during impact. The state offered no evidence to show the speed limit on the stretch of highway where the accident occurred. State suggested that the trial court could have taken *sua sponte* judicial notice of the fact that the maximum speed of "section 11-601(d) of the Illinois Vehicle Code (625 ILCS 5/11-601(d) (West 2000)) which provides that the maximum speed for passenger vehicles traveling on two-lane highways in Illinois is 55 miles per hour." The Fifth District noted that

> [a] reviewing court will not take judicial notice of critical evidentiary material that was not presented to and not considered by the fact finder during its deliberations. *See* Vulcan Materials Co. v. Bee Construction, 96 Ill. 2d 159 (1983); Ashland Savings & Loan Ass'n v. Aetna Insurance Co., 18 Ill. App. 3d 70, 78 (1974). Judicial notice cannot be extended to permit the introduction of new factual evidence not presented to the trial court. [. . .] We decline to take judicial notice of a material fact that was not considered by the fact finder and that defendant had no opportunity to rebut.

Evidence Principles Not Addressed by the Illinois Rules of Evidence

Burdens of Proof

Author's Commentary

In a criminal trial, the prosecutor has the ultimate burden of persuasion to prove the guilt of the accused under the constitutionally mandated quantum of proof beyond a reasonable doubt. Sullivan v. Louisiana, 508 U.S. 275 (1993). The burden of proof generally never shifts to the defendant. People v. Corbishly, 327 Ill. 312 (1927). However, when presenting an insanity defense, the defendant must rebut the presumption of sanity and prove his or her insanity by clear and convincing evidence. People v. Bellmyer, 199 Ill. 2d 529 (2002).

The defendant bears the burden of producing or going forward with evidence if he or she raises an affirmative defense to the charge. People v. Placek, 184 Ill. 2d 370 (1998). For all defenses other than insanity, the defendant must produce some evidence or point to the prosecutor's evidence that tends to raise an affirmative defense. *Id.* The burden is then on the prosecutor to rebut the affirmative defense beyond a reasonable doubt, except in the case of an insanity defense. *Id.*; 720 ILCS 5/6-2.

Relevant Statutory Authority

Trial by Court and Jury: 725 ILCS 5/115-4

§ 115-4. Trial by Court and Jury. (a) Questions of law shall be decided by the court and questions of fact by the jury.

***

(j) Unless the affirmative defense of insanity has been presented during the trial, the jury shall return a general verdict as to each offense charged. When the affirmative defense of insanity has been presented during the trial, the court shall provide the jury not only with general verdict forms but also with a special verdict form of not guilty by reason of insanity, as to each offense charged, and in such event the court shall separately instruct the jury that a special verdict of not guilty by reason of insanity may be returned instead of a general verdict but such special verdict requires a unanimous finding by the jury that the defendant committed the acts charged but at the time of the commission of those acts the defendant was insane. In the event of a verdict of not guilty by reason of insanity, a hearing shall be held pursuant to the Mental Health and Developmental Disabilities Code to determine whether the defendant is subject to involuntary admission. When the affirmative defense of insanity has been presented during the trial, the court, where warranted by the evidence, shall also provide the jury with a special verdict form of guilty but mentally ill, as to each offense charged and shall separately instruct the jury that a special verdict of guilty but mentally ill may be returned instead of a general verdict, but that such special verdict requires a unanimous finding by the jury that: (1) the State has proven beyond a reasonable doubt that the defendant is guilty of the offense charged; and (2) the defendant has failed to prove his insanity as required in subsection (b) of Section 3-2 of the Criminal Code of 1961, as amended, and subsections (a), (b) and (e) of Section 6-2 of the Criminal Code of 1961, as amended; and (3) the defendant has proven by a preponderance of the evidence that he was mentally ill, as defined in subsections (c) and (d) of Section 6-2 of the Criminal Code of 1961, as amended, at the time of the offense.

(k) When, at the close of the State's evidence or at the close of all of the evidence, the evidence is insufficient to support a finding or verdict of guilty the court may and on motion of the defendant shall make a finding or direct the jury to return a verdict of not guilty, enter a judgment of acquittal and discharge the defendant.

***

(o) A defendant tried by the court and jury shall only be found guilty, guilty but mentally ill, not guilty or not guilty by reason of insanity, upon the unanimous verdict of the jury.

Effective January 1, 1990.

Sexually Dangerous Persons Act: 725 ILCS 205/3.01

Civil Nature of the Proceedings; burden of proof; procedure.

§ 3.01. The proceedings under this Act shall be civil in nature, however, the burden of proof required to commit a defendant to confinement as a sexually dangerous person shall be the standard of proof required in a criminal proceedings of proof beyond a reasonable doubt. The provisions of the Civil Practice Law, and all existing and future amendments of that Law and modifications thereof and the Supreme Court Rules now or hereafter adopted in relation to that Law shall apply to all proceedings hereunder except as otherwise provided in this Act.

Affirmative Defense: 720 ILCS 5/3-2

§ 3-2. Affirmative defense.

(a) "Affirmative defense" means that unless the State's evidence raises the issue involving the alleged defense, the defendant, to raise the issue, must present some evidence thereon.

(b) If the issue involved in an affirmative defense, other than insanity, is raised then the State must sustain the burden of proving the defendant guilty beyond a reasonable doubt as to that issue together with all the other elements of the offense. If the affirmative defense of insanity is raised, the defendant bears the burden of proving by clear and convincing evidence his insanity at the time of the offense.

Effective June 19, 1998.

Defense of Insanity: 720 ILCS 5/6-2

§ 6-2. Insanity.

(a) A person is not criminally responsible for conduct if at the time of such conduct, as a result of mental disease or mental defect, he lacks substantial capacity to appreciate the criminality of his conduct.

(b) The terms "mental disease or mental defect" do not include an abnormality manifested only by repeated criminal or otherwise antisocial conduct.

(c) A person who, at the time of the commission of a criminal offense, was not insane but was suffering from a mental illness, is not relieved of criminal responsibility for his conduct and may be found guilty but mentally ill.

(d) For purposes of this Section, "mental illness" or "mentally ill" means a substantial disorder of thought, mood, or behavior which afflicted a person at the time of the commission of the offense and which impaired that person's judgment, but not to the extent that he is unable to appreciate the wrongfulness of his behavior.

(e) When the defense of insanity has been presented during the trial, the burden of proof is on the defendant to prove by clear and convincing evidence that the defendant is not guilty by reason of insanity. However, the burden of proof remains on the State to prove beyond a reasonable doubt each of the elements of each of the offenses charged, and, in a jury trial where the insanity defense has been presented, the jury must be instructed that it may not consider whether the defendant has met his burden of proving that he is not guilty by reason of insanity until and unless it has first determined that the State has proven the defendant guilty beyond a reasonable doubt of the offense with which he is charged.

Effective June 19, 1998.

Motion to Suppress Confession: 725 ILCS 5/114-11

§ 114-11. Motion to Suppress Confession.

(a) Prior to the trial of any criminal case a defendant may move to suppress as evidence any confession given by him on the ground that it was not voluntary.

(b) The motion shall be in writing and state facts showing wherein the confession is involuntary.

(c) If the allegations of the motion state facts which, if true, show that the confession was not voluntarily made the court shall conduct a hearing into the merits of the motion.

(d) The burden of going forward with the evidence and the burden of proving that a confession was voluntary shall be on the State. Objection to the failure of the State to call all material witnesses on the issue of whether the confession was voluntary must be made in the trial court.

(e) The motion shall be made only before a court with jurisdiction to try the offense.

(f) The issue of the admissibility of the confession shall not be submitted to the jury. The circumstances surrounding the making of the confession may be submitted to the jury as bearing upon the credibility or the weight to be given to the confession.

(g) The motion shall be made before trial unless opportunity therefor did not exist or the defendant was not aware of the grounds for the motion. If the motion is made during trial, and the court determines that the motion is not untimely, and the court conducts a hearing on the merits and enters an order suppressing the confession, the court shall terminate the trial with respect to every defendant who was a party to the hearing and who was within the scope of the order of suppression, without further proceedings, unless the State files a written notice that there will be no interlocutory appeal from such order of suppression. In the event of such termination, the court shall proceed with the trial of other defendants not thus affected. Such termination of trial shall be proper and shall not bar subsequent prosecution of the identical charges and defendants; however, if after such termination the State fails to prosecute the interlocutory appeal until a determination of the merits of the appeal by the reviewing court, the termination shall be improper within the meaning of subparagraph (a)(3) of Section 3-4 of the "Criminal Code of 1961," approved July 28, 1961, as amended, and subsequent prosecution of such defendants upon such charges shall be barred.

Effective August 28, 1969.

PRIOR ILLINOIS CASE LAW

1. In a Criminal Trial of Felony or Misdemeanor, the State Has the Burden of Proof to Show Each Element of the Crime Charged Beyond a Reasonable Doubt

Sullivan v. Louisiana, 508 U.S. 275 (1993)

Defendant was charged with first-degree murder during the commission of an armed robbery. The jury instruction given by the trial court failed to clearly indicate to the jury that the prosecution bears the burden of proof on all elements of the charged crime. The United States Supreme Court found the jury instruction unconstitutional, noting that

> [t]he prosecution bears the burden of proving all elements of the offense charged, (citations omitted) and must persuade the factfinder "beyond a reasonable doubt" of the facts necessary to establish each of those elements. (citations omitted). This beyond-a-reasonable-doubt requirement, which was adhered to by virtually all common-law jurisdictions, applies in state as well as federal proceedings.

The Supreme Court observed that the requirement that the defendant be proven guilty beyond a reasonable doubt and the right to a jury verdict are interrelated. The fifth and sixth amendments mandate a jury verdict be based on proof beyond a reasonable doubt.

2. Prosecutor Must Establish *Corpus Delicti* by Evidence Independent of Defendant's Confession to Sustain the Burden of Proof Beyond a Reasonable Doubt

People v. Sargent, 239 Ill. 2d 166 (2010)

Defendant was convicted of predatory criminal sexual assault of one of his minor stepsons and three counts of predatory criminal sexual assault and two counts of aggravated criminal sexual abuse of a younger stepson. After police officers interrogated him, defendant gave a videotaped confession. At trial, defendant repudiated his confession, claiming that he only confessed because he felt intimidated by the police. Defendant argued on appeal that his convictions on two of the three counts of predatory criminal sexual assault and two counts of aggravated criminal sexual abuse of the younger stepson should be overturned because the state failed to prove the *corpus delicti* of the crimes. He contended that his convictions were based only on the repudiated confession and that such evidence alone was not enough to prove him guilty of the crime beyond a reasonable doubt. The Illinois Supreme Court noted that

> [u]nder the law of Illinois, proof of an offense requires proof of two distinct propositions or facts beyond a reasonable doubt: (1) that a crime occurred, i.e., the *corpus delicti*; and (2) that the crime was committed by the person charged. People v. Lambert, 104 Ill. 2d 375, 378 (1984), quoting People v. Kirilenko, 1 Ill. 2d 90, 94 (1953). In many cases, and this is one, a defendant's confession may be integral to proving the *corpus delicti*. It is well established, however, that proof of the *corpus delicti* may not rest exclusively on a defendant's

> extrajudicial confession, admission, or other statement. People v. Furby, 138 Ill. 2d 434, 446 (1990). Where a defendant's confession is part of the proof of the *corpus delicti*, the prosecution must also adduce corroborating evidence independent of the defendant's own statement. People v. Cloutier, 156 Ill. 2d 483, 503 (1993). If a confession is not corroborated in this way, a conviction based on the confession cannot be sustained. People v. Willingham, 89 Ill. 2d 352, 358-59 (1982).
>
> The corroboration requirement stems from an historical mistrust of extrajudicial confessions. *Furby*, 138 Ill. 2d at 447. Two reasons are commonly advanced for this mistrust: (1) confessions are unreliable if coerced, and (2) for various psychological reasons, persons "confess" to crimes either that have never occurred or for which they are not legally responsible. People v. Dalton, 91 Ill. 2d 22, 29-30 (1982).

The Supreme Court explained that although the corroborating evidence must tend to show that the crime occurred, it "need not by itself, prove the existence of the crime beyond a reasonable doubt." The Supreme Court explained that where a defendant confessed to multiple crimes, corroborating evidence must show that defendant committed each offense. The Supreme Court reversed several of defendant's convictions because there was no independent corroborating evidence to support them.

3. Circumstantial Evidence Is Sufficient to Sustain a Conviction If It Proves Beyond a Reasonable Doubt the Elements of the Offense Charged
People v. Campbell, 146 Ill. 2d 363 (1992)

Defendant was convicted of residential burglary at a bench trial after muddy shoeprints were found at the victim's home and several items were missing. Shoe recovered from defendant had a unique matching pattern to shoe prints found at the scene of the crime. The Illinois Supreme Court noted that shoeprint evidence is circumstantial evidence, and that

> '[c]ircumstantial evidence is the proof of facts or circumstances which gives rise to a reasonable inference of other facts which tend to establish the guilt or innocence of a defendant.' People v. Jones, 105 Ill. 2d 342, 355 (1985); People v. Rhodes, 85 Ill. 2d 241, 249 (1981). Circumstantial evidence is sufficient to sustain a conviction if it satisfies proof beyond a reasonable doubt of the elements of the crime charged. See People v. Brown, 27 Ill. 2d 23 (1963).
>
> 'It is not necessary, however, that the jury be satisfied beyond a reasonable doubt as to each link in the chain of circumstances. It is sufficient if all the evidence taken together satisfies the jury beyond a reasonable doubt of the accused's guilt.' *Jones*, 105 Ill. 2d at 350, citing People v. Foster, 76 Ill. 2d 365, 374 (1979). Further, in weighing evidence, the trier of fact is not required to disregard inferences which flow normally from evidence before it (People v. Kelley, 29 Ill. 2d 53, 59 (1963)), nor need it search out all possible explanations consistent with innocence and raise them to a level of reasonable doubt. *Rhodes*, 85 Ill. 2d at 249.

The Supreme Court observed that the police retrieved the shoe from defendant, indicating that he "owned and had exclusive possession over the shoe." The Supreme Court noted that the trial court properly inferred from this evidence that defendant alone owned and possessed the shoe because defendant failed to contradict such inference. Defendant alleged that the shoeprint evidence was inadmissible because the forensic expert found only six points of similarity between his shoe and the shoeprint recovered from the crime scene. The Supreme Court disagreed, noting that "even one individual characteristic, depending on the nature and uniqueness, could be enough for a valid comparison." Defendant further argued that the shoeprint expert "ignored" dissimilarities. The Supreme Court indicated that although the expert was unclear about dissimilarities, any lack of similarity between the shoeprints goes to the weight of the evidence and is an issue for the trier of fact to decide. The Supreme Court concluded that there were "sufficient attendant circumstances" showing that the shoeprint was made at the time of the commission of the offense. It held that shoeprint evidence alone may be adequate to sustain a conviction if it proves beyond a reasonable doubt the elements of the offense charged. Here, the Supreme Court found that the shoeprint evidence together with evidence of opportunity and flight sustained defendant's conviction.

See also People v. Rhodes, 85 Ill. 2d 241 (1981) (holding fingerprint evidence found at the crime scene to be sufficient circumstantial evidence to support defendant's conviction for burglary beyond a reasonable doubt).

4. Although Commitment Proceedings Are Civil in Nature, an Accused May Be Committed Only If It Is Established Beyond a Reasonable Doubt That He or She Is a Sexually Dangerous Person
People v. Masterson, 2011 IL 110072

Defendant was declared a sexually dangerous person after a finding that he was a pedophile who was likely to reoffend unless he was committed. He challenged the constitutionality of the Sexually Dangerous Persons Act, 725 ILCS 205/0.01 (SDPA), claiming that it denied him equal protection of the law "by failing to provide him with the option to retain an independent psychiatrist to defend against commitment proceedings, an option afforded similarly situated individuals subject to commitment proceedings under the Sexually Violent Persons Commitment Act, 725 ILCS 207/1 ["SVPA"]." The Illinois Supreme Court disagreed. It explained that a "party challenging the constitutionality of [a] statute has the burden to prove its invalidity" and that defendant failed to do so. The Supreme Court found that defendant was not an individual similarly situation to persons committed under the SVPA, and that therefore his constitutional challenged failed.

The Supreme Court observed that pursuant to the SDPA, a prosecutor may request the commitment of an accused instead of proceeding with a criminal prosecution "when a person believed to be sexually dangerous is charged with a criminal offense." The Supreme Court noted that although the SDPA commitment proceedings "are civil in nature, [. . .] the State must prove sexual dangerousness beyond a reasonable doubt." Moreover, "to satisfy due process, the trier of fact in an SDPA proceeding must make an express finding that it is substantially probable the respondent would engage in the commission of sex offenses in the future if not confined." The Illinois Supreme Court distinguished the SDPA from the SVPA in the following manner:

> The SDPA is concerned with individuals who have been charged with any type of criminal offense and suffer from a mental disorder predisposing them to commit sex crimes. The SVPA, in contrast, is limited to persons with mental disorders who have been convicted of serious and violent sex offenses, and are facing potential release or discharge from state custody but continue to pose a risk to commit additional sex crimes. Put simply, the SDPA and the SVPA address two groups of individuals in completely different situations.

The Supreme Court found that defendant had not been charged with a violent sex crime as required under the SVPA and was therefore not similarly situated to individuals committed under the SVPA.

5. To Raise an Affirmative Defense, Defendant Bears the Burden of Producing Some Evidence That Tends to Raise the Defense
People v. Placek, 184 Ill. 2d 370 (1998)

Defendant was convicted of delivery of a controlled substance and possession of a controlled substance with intent to deliver after he sold cocaine to an undercover police officer. Defendant contended on appeal that the state failed to prove him guilty beyond a reasonable doubt because the evidence at trial showed that he was entrapped by the police. Defendant testified at trial that he was a dealer of auto parts and that he only agreed to sell cocaine to the undercover police officer so that the undercover officer would continue supplying him with auto parts. The Illinois Supreme Court observed that

> [o]nce a defendant presents some evidence to support an entrapment defense, the State bears the burden to rebut the entrapment defense beyond a reasonable doubt, in addition to proving all other elements of the crime. People v. Tipton, 78 Ill. 2d 477, 487 (1980). The question of whether the defendant was entrapped is to be resolved by the trier of fact. *See Tipton*, 78 Ill. 2d at 487. Following a conviction, a reviewing court must affirm where, after reviewing the evidence in the light most favorable to the prosecution, any rational trier of fact could have found the essential elements of the crime beyond a reasonable doubt. *See* People v. Campbell, 146 Ill. 2d 363, 374-75, (1992); *Tipton*, 78 Ill. 2d at 487.

The Supreme Court found that the evidence did not support an entrapment defense because it showed that defendant initiated discussions about drugs with the undercover police officer. Moreover, the Supreme Court observed that defendant was familiar with illegal substances, arranged the time and place for their exchange and set their price, and was therefore "predisposed to commit a drug-related offense."

6. State Bears the Burden of Proof as to the Voluntariness of a Confession by a Preponderance of the Evidence

People v. Richardson, 234 Ill. 2d 233 (2009)

Defendant was charged with first degree murder of his 11-month-old daughter. The police arrested defendant and placed him in custody. Before defendant was brought to the police station he "had no marks on his face." While in custody, defendant "received a black eye." Defendant subsequently gave an incriminating statement to the police. Prior to trial, defense filed a motion to suppress the statement claiming physical and mental coercion. Defendant alleged in his motion that the police threatened and choked him until he "passed out and hit his face and head." The Illinois Supreme Court noted that

> [w]here a defendant challenges the admissibility of an inculpatory statement through a motion to suppress, the State bears the burden of proving, by a preponderance of the evidence, that the statement was voluntary. 725 ILCS 5/114-11(d) (West 2000); People v. Slater, 228 Ill. 2d 137, 160 (2008); People v. Wilson, 116 Ill. 2d 29, 38 (1987); People v. King, 109 Ill. 2d 514, 525 (1986). The State carries the initial burden of making a *prima facie* case that the statement was voluntary. Once the State makes its *prima facie* case, the burden shifts to the defense to produce some evidence that the confession was involuntary (People v. Patterson, 154 Ill. 2d 414, 445 (1992)), and the burden reverts to the State only upon such production by the defense. *See* People v. Lopez, 114 Ill. App. 3d 1018, 1024 (1st Dist. 1983) (and cases cited therein); People v. Slaughter, 59 Ill. App. 3d 159, 161 (1978). However: "This court has held that when it is evident that a defendant has been injured while in police custody, the State must show, by clear and convincing evidence, that the injuries were not inflicted as a means of producing the confession." *Wilson*, 116 Ill. 2d at 40. [. . .] Ultimately, the constitutional test for the admission of a confession into evidence remains whether the confession was voluntary.

Here, the Supreme Court found that it was undisputed that defendant received a black eye while in police custody. The state was required to prove that the injury was "not inflicted as a means of producing [defendant's] inculpatory statement." The interviewing officers who testified at trial generally denied that they injured defendant and denied knowledge of how defendant came to be injured. An assistant state's attorney testified that defendant told him the individual who hurt him was not one of the interviewing officers but rather one of the guards who placed him in the interrogation room. Defendant also allegedly stated that the injury had nothing to do with his inculpatory statement. Based on this evidence, the Supreme Court concluded that the state showed by clear and convincing evidence the manner of the injury and that therefore his inculpatory statement was unrelated to his injury. The Supreme Court explained that a "confession is not rendered inadmissible as a matter of law because of an assault upon the defendant which occurred prior to, disconnected with, and apparently unrelated to the subsequent confession."

7. Where Defendant Raises an Insanity Defense, State Must Prove Beyond a Reasonable Doubt That Defendant Committed the Charged Offense and Defendant Must then Prove by Clear and Convincing Evidence That He or She Is Not Guilty by Reason of Insanity
People v. Bellmyer, 199 Ill. 2d 529 (2002)

Defendant was charged with first degree murder. He raised the affirmative defense of insanity. The parties presented stipulated evidence in a bench trial and the court found that the evidence was insufficient to determine whether defendant was insane. Defendant moved to dismiss the charges based on double jeopardy. Trial court denied his motion and conducted a trial. Defendant filed an interlocutory appeal to the appellate court and the appellate court found that double jeopardy barred a second trial. The Supreme Court reversed, noting that

> [a] stipulated bench trial is not tantamount to a guilty plea if the defendant presented and preserved a defense. People v. Horton, 143 Ill. 2d 11, 20, 22 (1991); accord 2 R. RUEBNER, ILLINOIS CRIMINAL PROCEDURE § 5.46, at 170 (3d ed. 1999). However, when a defendant in a stipulated bench trial stipulates not only to the evidence, but also to the sufficiency of the evidence to convict, the proceeding is tantamount to a guilty plea. *Horton*, 143 Ill. 2d at 22.
>
> When a defendant raises an insanity defense, the State must prove beyond a reasonable doubt that defendant committed the charged offense. The defendant then carries the burden of proving by clear and convincing evidence that he or she is not guilty by reason of insanity. 720 ILCS 5/6-2(e) (West 1998); accord 2 R. RUEBNER, ILLINOIS CRIMINAL PROCEDURE § 5.29, at 105-06 (3d ed. 1999); 6 L. PIECZYNSKI, ILLINOIS PRACTICE § 24.14, at 127 (1989). "When the defense can successfully show that the accused was insane at the time of the offense, the accused is relieved of any criminal responsibility even though the defense admits that the accused is the offending actor." 2 R. RUEBNER, ILLINOIS CRIMINAL PROCEDURE § 5.29, at 100 (3d ed. 1999).

The Illinois Supreme Court observed that defendant sought a finding of not guilty due to insanity and that the trial court had to determine his guilt or innocence. The Supreme Court noted that the parties never stipulated to the sufficiency of the evidence on the issue of insanity. The Supreme Court concluded that the defendant was not subject to double jeopardy and that the trial court should have rendered a judgment because the parties produced evidence from experts who all believed that defendant was insane.

See also People v. Smith, 195 Ill. 2d 179 (2000) (finding that trial counsel was not ineffective in failing to raise insanity defense although defendant had 'borderline personality disorder' where evidence that defendant tricked the victim by pretending to be his brother and concealed evidence of the murder would not have indicated to a reasonable attorney that an insanity defense was viable).

8. Judgment Finding Defendant Not Guilty by Reason of Insanity Is Equivalent to an Acquittal

People v. Harrison, 226 Ill. 2d 427 (2007)

Defendant was charged with murder. He pleaded not guilty and raised the defense of insanity. He was found not guilty by reason of insanity (NGRI). Defendant was subsequently sent to an inpatient mental health facility and committed to the custody of the Department of Human Services. He appealed, contending that his trial counsel was ineffective in failing to move to suppress his confession after he was found insane, and that state failed to prove him guilty beyond a reasonable doubt. The appellate court refused to consider his appeal, noting that defendant had been acquitted. Defendant contended that the appellate court erred in not accepting his appeal, arguing that an "NGRI judgment is actually a finding of guilty but insane and therefore should not be treated substantively as an acquittal barring appellate review." The Illinois Supreme Court disagreed, noting that

> [a] finding of NGRI is substantively different from a finding of guilty but mentally ill (GBMI).
>
> The Criminal Code of 1961 provides that a person who, at the time of the offense, "was not insane but was suffering from a mental illness, is not relieved of criminal responsibility *** and may be found guilty but mentally ill." 720 ILCS 5/6-2(c) (West 2002). This court has held that a defendant found guilty but mentally ill is "no less guilty than one who is guilty and not mentally ill; unlike insanity, a GBMI finding or plea does not relieve an offender of criminal responsibility for his conduct." People v. Crews, 122 Ill. 2d 266, 278 (1988). On the other hand, the legislature has provided that "[a] person *is not criminally responsible* for conduct if at the time of such conduct, as a result of mental disease or mental defect, he lacks substantial capacity to appreciate the criminality of his conduct." (Emphasis added.) 720 ILCS 5/6-2(a) (West 2002).
>
> The finding of NGRI is incompatible with guilt of the crime charged because the trial court expressly found [defendant] was unable to appreciate the criminality of his conduct. Accordingly, defendant's argument that an NGRI judgment is really a finding of "guilty but insane" is totally unsupported by the relevant statutory provisions and case law.

9. Defendant May Enter a Plea of Guilty but Mentally Ill If He or She Establishes Mental Illness by Preponderance of the Evidence

People v. Urdiales, 225 Ill. 2d 354 (2007)

Defendant was charged with murder. He entered a plea of guilty but mentally ill. The state disputed that defendant had a mental illness and the trial court rejected the guilty but mentally ill plea and defense of insanity at a bench trial. Defendant argued on appeal that the trial court abused its discretion in rejecting his plea of guilty but mentally ill. Both parties presented evidence pertaining to defendant's mental health via the testimony of various experts. All of the experts disagreed in the primary diagnosis of defendant. Evidence was introduced that defendant had previously murdered eight women and attempted to murder another. The trial court found that defendant had not established that he had a mental illness or that he was insane by a preponderance of the evidence. The Illinois Supreme Court noted that

> [t]he burden is on the defendant to prove, by a preponderance of the evidence, that he was mentally ill, as defined in subsections (c) and (d) of section 6-2. 725 ILCS 5/115-3(c)(3), 115-4(j) (West 2004); People v. Lantz, 186 Ill. 2d 243, 254 (1999). When a trier of fact finds a defendant guilty but mentally ill, that verdict does not relieve a defendant of criminal responsibility. People v. Johnson, 146 Ill. 2d 109, 131 (1991). A defendant who has been found guilty but mentally ill is subject to any sentence that could have been imposed upon a

> defendant who had been convicted of the same offense without a finding of mental illness, including the death penalty. *Johnson*, 146 Ill. 2d at 131-32. Indeed, the only discernible difference between the two verdicts is that, upon a finding of guilty but mentally ill, the Department of Corrections must "cause periodic inquiry and examination to be made concerning the nature, extent, continuance, and treatment of the defendant's mental illness" and provide "such psychiatric, psychological, or other counseling and treatment for the defendant as it determines necessary." 730 ILCS 5/5-2-6(b) (West 2004); *see* People v. Morris, 237 Ill. App. 3d 140, 145 (1992). As is the case when a defendant raises a defense of insanity, for which a defendant also bears the burden of proof, the existence of "mental illness," as defined in section 6-2, is a question of fact; thus, the trial court's resolution of that issue will not be overturned unless it is contrary to the manifest weight of the evidence. *See Johnson*, 146 Ill. 2d at 128-29.

The Illinois Supreme Court found that the trial court's finding that defendant failed to show that he was mentally ill as defined in section 6-2 was not against the manifest weight of the evidence. The Supreme Court observed that expert witnesses failed to agree with respect to defendant's diagnosis, that defendant functioned well in society and that he had the ability to carefully plan, carry out and cover up the murder.

10. Where Defendant Has Raised *Bona Fide* Doubt as to His Fitness to Stand Trial, State Must Show by Preponderance of Evidence That Defendant Is Fit
People v. McCullum, 66 Ill. 2d 306 (1977)

The Illinois Supreme Court declared a statute unconstitutional to the extent that it placed the burden of proving unfitness to stand trial on the defendant. The Supreme Court explained that

> [t]he concept of fitness to stand trial is grounded on the notion that it is fundamental to an adversary system of justice. Drope v. Missouri, 420 U.S. 162, 171-72 (1975). Fundamental fairness dictates that, where a defendant has raised a *[b]ona fide* doubt as to his fitness to stand trial, the State, as a matter of due process, should bear the ultimate burden of proving defendant's fitness to stand trial.

The state must prove defendant's fitness by a preponderance of the evidence.

See also People v. Johnson, 191 Ill. 2d 257 (2000) (finding that same burden of proof applies at a hearing to determine defendant's fitness to proceed with a post-conviction petition).

11. To Sustain a Conviction Based on a Guilty Plea, the Record Must Contain Basis from Which Trial Court Could Reasonably Reach the Conclusion That Defendant Actually Committed the Offense to Which Defendant Pleaded Guilty
People v. Barker, 83 Ill. 2d 319 (1980)

Defendant pleaded guilty to attempted murder. The trial court admonished defendant and the prosecutor recited the factual basis for the plea. After defendant agreed to the plea, the trial court found a factual basis for it and determined that the plea was voluntary. The Illinois Supreme Court held that to sustain a conviction on a guilty plea, the entire record of the proceedings must establish a factual basis for the plea. The Supreme Court found that a factual basis was established here and explained that

> the quantum of proof necessary to establish a factual basis for the plea is less than that necessary to sustain a conviction after a full trial [citations omitted]. All that is required to appear on the record is a basis from which the judge could reasonably reach the conclusion that

> the defendant actually committed the acts with the intent (if any) required to constitute the offense to which the defendant is pleading guilty.

12. The State Must Prove the Charge of Delinquency Beyond a Reasonable Doubt Where the Acts of the Alleged Delinquent Conduct Would Amount to a Crime If Charged Against an Adult
In re Urbasek, 38 Ill. 2d 535 (1967)

A juvenile stabbed an 11-year-old girl to death and was charged with her murder. The Illinois Supreme Court held that to sustain an adjudication of delinquency, the prosecutor must prove the charge beyond a reasonable doubt. This strict standard of proof is constitutionally mandated. The Illinois Supreme Court explained that

> it would not be consonant with due process or equal protection to grant allegedly delinquent juveniles the same procedural rights that protect adults charged with crimes, while depriving these rights of their full efficacy by allowing a finding of delinquency upon a lesser standard of proof than that required to sustain a criminal conviction. Since the same or even greater curtailment of freedom may attach to a finding of delinquency than results from a criminal conviction, we cannot say that it is constitutionally permissible to deprive the minor of the benefit of the standard of proof distilled by centuries of experience as a safeguard for adults.

13. State Must Prove Violation of Probation by a Preponderance of the Evidence
People v. Colon, 225 Ill. 2d 125 (2007)

Defendant pleaded guilty to aggravated unlawful use of a weapon and was granted probation. The state consequently charged defendant with unlawful use of a weapon by a felon and filed a petition to revoke his probation. Defendant claimed that the state failed to show that he violated his probation because the evidence was insufficient to show that he was in possession of firearm ammunition at the time he was arrested. A police officer testified that he saw defendant with a gun and that he subsequently fled. As defendant was running, the officer saw him release the magazine. The officer retrieved the magazine. No gun was found on the defendant when he was subsequently arrested. Defendant argued on appeal that there was no evidence that the magazine contained live ammunition. The Illinois Supreme Court noted that "to demonstrate that defendant violated a condition of his probation, the State had to show by a preponderance of the evidence that, while on probation, defendant knowingly possessed firearm ammunition as a felon." The Supreme Court disagreed with defendant's claim, noting that the evidence established that the ammunition was live. The Supreme Court concluded that the trial court's finding that defendant violated his probation was not against the manifest weight of the evidence.

Stipulations

Author's Commentary

Parties may waive formal proof of a fact in issue by agreeing to its truth. People v. Hawkins, 27 Ill. 2d 339 (1963). This shortcut to proof is a stipulation. While the parties may stipulate to evidence, they cannot stipulate to legal conclusions. People v. Lewis, 103 Ill. 2d 111 (1984). The parties cannot stipulate to the truth of facts that are otherwise inadmissible as a matter of law. People v. Baynes, 88 Ill. 2d 225 (1981).

PRIOR ILLINOIS CASE LAW

1. Defendant May Waive Formal Proof of a Fact in Issue by Agreeing to Its Truth

People v. Hawkins, 27 Ill. 2d 339 (1963)

Defendant was convicted of larceny of a motor vehicle. He claimed that state produced no evidence to show that the car was stolen. The Illinois Supreme Court disagreed, observing that defense stipulated to the vehicle owner's testimony indicating that his vehicle was missing from its usual parking spot. The Supreme Court explained that

> [a]n accused, by stipulation may waive the necessity of proof of all or part of the case which the People have alleged against him, and having done so, he cannot complain of the evidence which he has stipulated into the record. People v. Hare, 25 Ill. 2d 321 (1962); People v. Polk, 19 Ill. 2d 310 (1960). Although the defendant contends that the stipulation was inadequate to prove that the car belonged to [the victim], it is apparent that the stipulation, together with statements of counsel and of the defendant, shows that it was the understanding of the court, of counsel and of the defendant that the car which he was driving was that of [the victim]. No other facts or circumstances were shown which could have left in the mind of the court a reasonable doubt as to the defendant's guilt.

2. Generally, Once Defendant Enters a Stipulation He or She May Not Challenge Agreed Facts

People v. Baynes, 88 Ill. 2d 225 (1981)

Defendant was charged with burglary and misdemeanor theft. Defendant took a polygraph examination and its results were entered into evidence pursuant to a stipulation by the parties. Defendant did not object to the admissibility of this evidence at trial or in a post-trial motion and the state argued that he had waived his objection. The Illinois Supreme Court observed that

> [a] written and signed stipulation of the defendant and State's Attorney would normally foreclose review. People v. Pierce, 387 Ill. 608, 614 (1944); People v. Malin, 372 Ill. 422, 423 (1939). Parties who agree to certain terms are estopped from later objecting to the terms of that agreement. Generally, neither can complain of evidence stipulated into the record. People v. Polk, 19 Ill. 2d 310, 315 (1960).

This case, however, was different. The Supreme Court found that polygraph evidence is generally inadmissible and that a stipulation may not make inadmissible evidence admissible.

3. Name and Nature of Prior Offense Is Not Admissible Where Defendant Offers to Stipulate to the Nature of the Prior Crime

People v. Walker, 211 Ill. 2d 317 (2004)

Defendant was charged with possession of a weapon by a felon and unlawful sale of firearms. In a motion *in limine*, the defense objected to the disclosure of a prior conviction for possession of a controlled substance and offered to stipulate to a felony conviction. The state refused the stipulation. The defense was concerned that the jury would use the evidence to view the defendant as a drug dealer. In the opening statement, the prosecutor stated, "Ladies and gentlemen, this case is about a drug deal gone bad and a man who is willing to take any step possible to make sure that he got paid for the drugs he sold. That man is the defendant." The trial judge allowed the prosecutor to publish a certificate of the defendant's conviction over objection. The appellate court held this to be reversible error.

The Illinois Supreme Court affirmed the appellate court and found that to prove a violation of the unlawful possession of a weapon by a felon statute prosecutor must establish that defendant is a felon but need not prove the specific prior felony conviction. The Supreme Court held that requiring the specific name and nature of the prior felony to be identified at trial was unnecessary and prejudicial where defendant stipulated to his felon status. The court reviewed Old Chief v. United States, 519 U.S. 172 (1997) where the United States Supreme Court held that it is an abuse of discretion to admit the name and nature of defendant's prior offense when he or she offers to stipulate to a prior conviction. The court noted that although the United States Supreme Court decision in *Old Chief* was not binding since it was based on a federal statute, its reasoning was nonetheless persuasive. The court explained that

> the admission of a defendant's record of conviction creates a risk that he will be unfairly prejudiced. Moreover, because the only purpose for admitting a defendant's prior-conviction record is to establish felon status, the name and nature of the prior convictions is unnecessary surplusage without any evidentiary significance. Thus, a defendant's record of conviction has "discounted" probative value. On the other hand, the defendant's admission or stipulation is conclusive evidence of felon status which presents little or no risk of unfair prejudice. On balance, then, the probative value of the record of conviction is outweighed by the risk of unfair prejudice and the trial court should require the prosecution to meet its evidentiary obligation of proving felon status by using an admission or stipulation if one is offered by the defendant. We conclude, therefore, that when proving felon status is the only purpose for admitting evidence of a defendant's prior convictions, and the defendant offers to stipulate or admit to his prior felon status, a trial court abuses its discretion when it admits the defendant's record of conviction, thus informing the jury of the name and nature of the defendant's prior convictions.

But see People v. Nicholls, 42 Ill. 2d 91 (1969) (noting that state is not barred from proving a fact because defendant offers to stipulate; and finding that despite defendant's stipulation to content of photographs depicting victim's body, such photographs were admissible to show nature and extent of wounds and to corroborate defendant's confession).

4. Defendant May Waive His or Her Sixth Amendment Right to Confrontation by Stipulating to Admissibility of Unavailable Witness' Out-of-Court Statement
People v. Campbell, 208 Ill. 2d 203 (2003)

Defendant was charged with burglary after he entered a house occupied by two college roommates. The roommates were going out of town later that day for the spring break. A police officer testified at trial that burglaries increase significantly during times like spring break when most students leave town. On the day in question one occupant of the roommates' house was upstairs and the other was asleep on the couch downstairs. Defendant loudly knocked on the door for about two minutes. The upstairs occupant eventually came downstairs and saw defendant leaving the house. The state intended to call both roommates to testify at defendant's trial, but the roommate who was downstairs during the incident was unavailable. His testimony was material to the state's case because only he saw the defendant walk into his house and could testify as to whether defendant entered "without authority." State offered to stipulate to the unavailable witness' testimony and defense counsel agreed. The witness' stipulated testimony was that on the day in question he was asleep on the couch of his living room. He was awakened by loud knocking on the front door. He then heard the front door open and saw the defendant walk into the house. The defendant asked the witness if he had a room available for rent, after which the witness called the police and identified the defendant as the individual who entered his house without permission.

On appeal, defendant claimed that his attorney stipulated to the unavailable witness' testimony without his knowing consent and denied him the right to confront witnesses against him. In agreement with a majority of federal and state courts, the Illinois Supreme Court held that

> counsel in a criminal case may waive his client's sixth amendment right of confrontation by stipulating to the admission of evidence as long as the defendant does not object to or dissent from his attorney's decision, and where the decision to stipulate is a matter of legitimate trial tactics or prudent trial strategy. Where the stipulation includes a statement that the evidence is sufficient to convict the defendant or where the State's entire case is to be presented by stipulation, we find that a defendant must be personally admonished about the stipulation and must personally agree to the stipulation.

Defendant argued that without his attorney's stipulation to the key witness' testimony he could not have been convicted of the charged offense. Specifically, he argued that "defense counsel cannot stipulate to facts which establish the guilt of the accused because the constitutional right implicated in that situation is the right of a defendant in a criminal case to plead not guilty." The Supreme Court did not find that the stipulation impacted defendant's fundamental rights or that it established defendant's guilt. Rather, it found that defense counsel used the stipulation strategically to explain that defendant's mindset was innocent when he entered the house because he was looking for a room to rent. The Supreme Court concluded that without the stipulation the defendant lacked an innocent explanation for his entry into the house and that defense counsel's decision to stipulate to the evidence was therefore a matter of trial strategy.

See also People v. Phillips, 217 Ill. 2d 270 (2005) (finding that where defendant fails to object to a stipulation and defense counsel stipulates as a matter of trial strategy, defendant's right to confrontation is not violated).

5. Where a Stipulation Is Tantamount to a Guilty Plea, Defendant Must Receive Personal Admonishment and Must Indicated That He or She Agrees to Its Entry
People v. Clendenin, 238 Ill. 2d 302 (2010)

Defendant was charged with unlawful possession of child pornography after his girlfriend found computer disks containing what she believed was child pornography at his home and turned them over to the police. The parties agreed to a stipulated bench trial. They entered a stipulation that in response to a police officer's question about how many disks contained child pornography, defendant responded "not many." Defendant did not stipulate to the sufficiency of the evidence and indeed objected to it twice and filed a motion to suppress evidence seized from his home and the statements he gave to the police. The stipulation "explicitly stated that it did not concede the sufficiency of the evidence to support a conviction." The trial court found defendant guilty and he appealed his conviction. Defendant contended that the stipulation amounted to a guilty plea and that he should have received personal admonishment and agreed to its entry. The Illinois Supreme Court disagreed, noting that

> this case does not present the circumstance where the stipulation was tantamount to a guilty plea, which would remove it from the ambit of the [People v. Campbell, 208 Ill. 2d 203 (2003)], general rule. As we have repeatedly held, a stipulation is tantamount to a guilty plea—and therefore requires a defendant's personal admonishment and agreement—in only two instances: (1) the State's entire case is to be presented by stipulation and the defendant does not present or preserve a defense; or (2) the stipulation includes a statement that the evidence is sufficient to convict the defendant. [citation omitted].

> Applying this rule to the instant appeal, it is clear that neither instance is met. Although the State's entire case was presented by stipulation, defense counsel adequately preserved a defense by preserving the suppression issue for appellate review. The stipulation twice objected to evidence and testimony "on the same grounds presented" in the earlier suppression motion, twice requested the circuit court to reverse its denial of the suppression motion, and objected to all evidence seized from defendant's home and his statements to police "as the illegal fruit of the unlawful search and seizure of the computer disk delivered to the police by [defendant's girlfriend]." Moreover, the stipulation explicitly stated that it did not concede the sufficiency of the evidence to support a conviction. Accordingly, the stipulation was not tantamount to a guilty plea requiring that defendant receive personal admonishments and that he agree to its entry.

The Supreme Court concluded that the defense counsel validly waived defendant's right to confrontation by entering into the stipulation as a matter of trial strategy and that defendant did not object to the stipulation.

Inferences and Presumptions in Criminal Cases

AUTHOR'S COMMENTARY

An inference is a process of reasoning, not an evidentiary device, which allows the trier of fact to draw logical and reasonable conclusions from the evidence in finding the existence of one fact from proof of another fact. The trier of fact may accept or reject an inferred fact even in the absence of contradictory evidence. An inference carries no legal consequences whatsoever for the opposing party, and it is not required to produce any evidence to the contrary. People v. Bormet, 142 Ill. App. 3d 422 (1st Dist. 1986). A presumption, on the other hand, "is a legal device that either permits or requires the trier of fact to assume the existence of an ultimate fact, after establishing certain predicate facts." People v. Woodrum, 223 Ill. 2d 286, 308 (2006).

There are two types of presumptions: permissive and mandatory. A permissive presumption (usually incorrectly labeled as an inference) allows the trier of fact to presume the existence of an ultimate fact from proof of other facts. People v. Hester, 131 Ill. 2d 91 (1989). The trier of fact may accept or reject it, but if it accepts the presumed fact, the burden of production, but not the burden of persuasion, shifts to the opposing party to rebut the presumed fact by contradictory evidence. *Id.* A mandatory presumption is one that requires the fact finder to accept the presumed fact. *Id.* The fact finder is not free to reject it. The constitutional validity of such a presumption is measured by the most stringent standard of proof, which is proof beyond a reasonable doubt. People v. Housby, 84 Ill. 2d 415 (1981).

PRIOR ILLINOIS CASE LAW

1. Trier of Fact May Not Reject a Mandatory Presumption upon Proof of the Basic Fact, but May Accept or Reject a Permissive Presumption
People v. Hester, 131 Ill. 2d 91 (1989)

Defendant was charged and convicted of reckless homicide and driving under the influence of alcohol. At trial, the jury was instructed, in part, that it "*may* presume the defendant was under the influence of intoxicating liquor" if it found her breath was .10 percent or more by weight of alcohol based on the expert testimony. The appellate court reversed and remanded the case on the basis of improper jury instructions. It found that the substitution of the word "may" for "shall" resulted in "judicial legislation," and that the instruction contained a mandatory presumption although the jury was not instructed to find beyond a reasonable doubt that defendant's breath was .10 percent or more before it could rely on the presumption.

The Illinois Supreme Court disagreed and affirmed the circuit court's judgment. The Supreme Court explained that

> [i]t is a well-settled principle that an accused may only be convicted of a criminal offense by proof establishing her guilt beyond a reasonable doubt. In establishing an accused's guilt, the State may be entitled to rely upon presumptions or inferences. [citations omitted]
>
> It has been recognized that inferences and presumptions play a vital role in the expeditious resolution of factual questions, with the value of the presumption or inference resting on the strength of the connection between the elemental or ultimate fact presumed or inferred and the basic or evidentiary fact. In criminal cases, the use of a presumption or inference must not invade the territory of the fact finder to determine the existence of the ultimate or elemental fact beyond a reasonable doubt. [citations omitted]
>
> Presumptions are separated into two groups: mandatory and permissive. It must be determined into what group the presumption contained in the jury instruction at issue here falls. Sandstrom v. Montana, 442 U.S. 510, 514 (1979).
>
> A mandatory presumption is one where the fact finder is not free to reject the proffered presumption. A mandatory presumption may be conclusive, that is, "an irrebuttable direction" (*Sandstrom*, 442 U.S. at 517; People v. Housby, 84 Ill. 2d 415, 420 (1981)), or it may shift the burden of proof. "[I]t tells the trier that he or they *must* find the elemental fact upon proof of the basic fact, at least unless the defendant has come forward with some evidence to rebut the presumed connection between the two facts." (Emphasis in original.) [citations omitted]. A presumption, however, may not shift the burden of persuasion to the defendant; that burden must remain with the State. Francis v. Franklin, 471 U.S. 307 (1985); *Sandstrom*, 442 U.S. at 517-24; People v. Ziltz, 98 Ill. 2d 38, 44 (1983). The validity of a mandatory presumption is subject to a "beyond a reasonable doubt" test. Ulster County Court v. Allen, 442 U.S. 140, 165 (1979).
>
> A permissive presumption, on the other hand, is one where the fact finder is free to accept or reject the suggested presumption. *Allen*, 442 U.S. at 157. It places no burden on the defendant and "affects the application of the 'beyond a reasonable doubt' standard only if, under the facts of the case, there is no rational way the trier could make the connection permitted by the inference." *Allen*, 442 U.S. at 157. *See also Sandstrom*, 442 U.S. at 514-15; *Housby*, 84 Ill. 2d at 432-33; People v. Elliott, 143 Ill. App. 3d 72, 77 (1986). The validity of a permissive presumption is subject to a less stringent test: there must be a rational connection between the facts proved and the facts presumed, and the ultimate fact must be "more likely than not to flow" from the basic fact. *Housby*, 84 Ill. 2d at 420-21, quoting *Allen*, 442 U.S. at 165. *See also Francis*, 471 U.S. at 314-15. Nevertheless, the inference must be supported by corroborating evidence of guilt; if there is no corroborating evidence, the "leap from the proved fact to the presumed element" must still be proved beyond a reasonable doubt. *Housby*, 84 Ill. 2d at 421, citing *Allen*, 442 U.S. at 167.

In determining whether the instruction contained a permissive or a mandatory presumption the Supreme Court considered its text and "the way in which a reasonable juror could have interpreted the instruction." The Supreme Court observed that a juror was not required to draw the conclusion merely based on the fact that her blood alcohol level was .10 percent or more. The jurors were free to accept or reject such presumption. The Supreme Court noted that "common sense, experience, and scientific testing" have shown that there is a rational relationship between a blood alcohol level of .10 percent or more and being under the influence of alcohol. The Supreme Court concluded that the instruction taken as a whole was permissive and that defendant had not been deprived of due process of law.

2. An Unconstitutional Application of a Mandatory Presumption Can Be Harmless Error
People v. Woodrum, 223 Ill. 2d 286 (2006)

Defendant appealed his conviction of child abduction following a bench trial claiming that the child abduction statute created an unconstitutional mandatory presumption. The statute stated that "the luring or attempted luring of a child under the age of 16 into a motor vehicle, building, housetrailer, or dwelling place without the consent of the parent or lawful custodian of the child shall be *prima facie* evidence of other than a lawful purpose." 720 ILCS 5/10-5(b)(10).

The Illinois Supreme Court found that the statute created a mandatory presumption because it shifted the burden of proof to the defendant by presuming that defendant had unlawful purpose in luring a child into a vehicle or house. The Supreme Court explained that

> [a] mandatory presumption [. . .] requires the fact finder to accept the presumption. *Jordan*, 218 Ill. 2d at 265, citing *Pomykala*, 203 Ill. 2d at 203; Watts, 181 Ill. 2d at 141-42. Mandatory presumptions have been classified as conclusive or rebuttable. *Pomykala*, 203 Ill. 2d at 203; *Watts*, 181 Ill. 2d at 142. The Supreme Court has held that mandatory conclusive presumptions are unconstitutional because they conflict with the presumption of innocence. *See* Sandstrom v. Montana, 442 U.S. 510, 521-23 (1979). In *Sandstrom*, the Supreme Court further held that mandatory rebuttable presumptions shifting the burden of persuasion to a defendant are *per se* unconstitutional, as they relieve the State of the burden of proving each element of the offense beyond a reasonable doubt. *Sandstrom*, 442 U.S. at 524. This court has held that mandatory rebuttable presumptions shifting the burden of production to a defendant are also unconstitutional because they could, in effect, require a trial court to direct a verdict against a defendant on an element proved by the presumption. *Jordan*, 218 Ill. 2d at 266, quoting *Watts*, 181 Ill. 2d at 147. Thus, under Illinois law, all mandatory presumptions are *per se* unconstitutional. *Pomykala*, 203 Ill. 2d at 204.

Here, however, the Supreme Court held the application of the presumption was harmless error because the record established the trial court also relied on the defendant's statement, videotapes, and the defendant's conduct to determine whether he acted with other than a lawful purpose.

3. Presumptions and Inferences May Raise Due Process Concerns Because They Are Evidentiary Substitutes for Facts Inferred
People v. Housby, 84 Ill. 2d 415 (1981)

At trial, defendant was convicted of burglary and theft. The trial court instructed the jury that if it found "that the defendant had exclusive possession of recently stolen property, and there was no reasonable explanation of his possession, you may infer that the defendant obtained possession of the property by burglary." Defendant argued that the instruction "diluted" the state's burden to prove him guilty of burglary beyond a reasonable doubt.

The Illinois Supreme Court acknowledged that presumptions and inferences frequently raise due process concerns because they are "evidentiary substitutes for the facts inferred" and take the place of strict proof of the elements of the offense. The Supreme Court noted with respect to mandatory presumptions that "[w]hen the fact finder is compelled to rely upon the presumption, the inferred fact must flow beyond a reasonable doubt from the established fact." Regarding permissive presumptions, however, there need only be a "'rational connection' between the basic facts that the prosecution proved and the ultimate fact presumed, and the latter is 'more likely than not to flow from' the former." The Supreme Court noted that the "less stringent" test for permissive presumptions is

> supplemented with the requirement that the inference be supported by corroborating evidence of guilt. [. . .] But, where the permissive inference stands unsupported by corroborating circumstances, the lead from the proved fact to the presumed element must satisfy the higher standard proof beyond a reasonable doubt for there is nothing else on which to rest the fact finder's verdict of guilt.

The Supreme Court found that past Illinois decisions did not satisfy these tests, noting that

> [t]o the extent that past Illinois decisions have held that exclusive and unexplained possession of recently stolen property is sufficient, standing alone and without corroborating evidence of guilt, for conviction of burglary, those decisions [. . .] can no longer be applied, even when the inference is regarded as permissive. The presumption standing alone does not prove burglary beyond a reasonable doubt. The person in exclusive possession may be the burglar, to be sure, but he might also be a receiver of stolen property, guilty of theft but not burglary, an innocent purchaser without knowledge that the item is stolen, or even an innocent victim of circumstances.

Here, the Supreme Court found that the evidence against the defendant was "entirely circumstantial." Defendant was seen with recently stolen property and on the farm from which the property was stolen around the time it was taken. The Supreme Court found that the evidence established a rational connection between defendant's possession of the items and his participation in the burglary. The Supreme Court then evaluated whether the presumed fact more likely than not flowed from the proven facts. It observed that defendant was in possession of the stolen items three hours after they were taken from their owner. Defendant testified at trial that he was only helping his friend move some items that he recently bought and claimed that he was at home during the time of the burglary. His alibi was confirmed by his wife and brother-in-law. The Supreme Court, however, found that defendant volunteered the use of a truck that did not belong to him to pick up the items, he did not ask for money for the transportation, and did not doubt the "questionable circumstances" under which his friend came to possess the items. The Supreme Court indicated that these corroborating circumstances made it unlikely that defendant was merely "an innocent victim of circumstances," and concluded that "it was more likely than not" that defendant obtained possession over the items by burglary.

Curative Admissibility

Author's Commentary

The rule of curative admissibility permits a party to introduce evidence that is ordinarily inadmissible in order to explain or rebut improper evidence that was first introduced by the other party. The purpose of the rule is to eliminate the possibility that a jury would draw erroneous inferences from the evidence to the detriment of the party against whom the evidence was originally admitted. It is an equitable principle that attempts to cure the conduct of the party that first introduced the inadmissible evidence and who has opened the door to the opponent. People v. Manning, 182 Ill. 2d 193 (1998). The rule should limit the admissibility of the otherwise inadmissible evidence to the extent that it is necessary to shield a party from undue prejudice. *Id.*

PRIOR ILLINOIS CASE LAW

1. When Defense Counsel Opens the Door to Inadmissible Evidence on Cross-Examination, the Doctrine of Curative Admissibility Permits the State to Question Witness on Redirect Examination to Clarify or Explain

People v. Manning, 182 Ill. 2d 193 (1998)

Defendant was convicted by a jury of first degree murder and armed robbery. The appellate court reversed the convictions and remanded the case for a new trial, and the Illinois Supreme Court agreed. On appeal, the state conceded that the victim's out-of-court statement was inadmissible hearsay but invoked the doctrine of curative admissibility to argue that defense counsel's cross-examination of the victim's wife "opened the door" to the otherwise barred evidence.

The Illinois Supreme Court explained that in a criminal case "where the door to a particular subject is opened by defense counsel on cross-examination, the State may, on redirect, question the witness to clarify or explain the matters brought out during, or to remove or correct unfavorable inferences left by, the previous cross-examination." The doctrine of curative admissibility, however, does not allow "a party to introduce inadmissible evidence merely because the opponent brought out some new evidence on the same subject. The rule is merely protective and goes only as far as is necessary to shield a party from adverse inferences."

2. Where Witness Testimony Is Competent to Develop Proponent's Theory, Content of the Same Conversation on the Same Subject Is Likewise Competent for Opponent's Use in Rebuttal

People v. Kalpak, 10 Ill. 2d 411 (1957)

Two defendants were charged with the crime of abortion. The woman seeking an abortion was introduced by one defendant to "doc" who was later identified as the second defendant. The woman was brought to the "doc" and he performed an abortion. Her water broke after the alleged treatment and she started experiencing severe pain due to an infection. She subsequently went to the emergency room where she was examined by a physician. At trial, over defendant's objection, the prosecution elicited testimony of a conversation between the woman and her physician regarding previous treatment. The physician testified that she told him that a third party had previously treated her. He concluded that this treatment could have resulted in her water breaking. The Illinois Supreme Court concluded that the trial court erroneously admitted this testimony over defendant's objection. On cross-examination, however, defense counsel asked similarly improper questions of the doctor regarding the content of the same conversation. Specifically, defense inquired whether the woman told her physician that her water broke the night before she came to the emergency room. Defense further questioned the doctor whether it was possible that it was the water break that caused her pain and infection. The Supreme Court explained that

> [t]he admission of this evidence would likewise have been improper if offered by the People on direct examination; however, it was not error to admit it on cross-examination since the People had utilized that part of the conversation which was favorable to develop their theory of the case. The People induced the court to admit incompetent evidence and could not complain that the defendants availed themselves of similar evidence within the field of inquiry. 1 WIGMORE, EVIDENCE, sec. 15; MCCORMICK ON EVIDENCE, sec. 57; Jones v. Sanitary District, 265 Ill. 98 (1914). Nor was it error to permit the doctor to testify in rebuttal that instrumentation might have caused the breaking of the water bag, since on cross-examination he had been asked whether the breaking of the water bag might have caused the infection, and

both theories had been developed from information obtained from parts of the same conversation. If a witness testifies to part of a conversation on behalf of one party, the other is entitled to show all that was said in that conversation on the same subject. Scott v. People, 141 Ill. 195 (1892). If it was competent for the defendants to develop their defense from a statement made by [the woman] to her physician, it was likewise competent for the People to utilize information given by her in the same conversation on the same subject tending to rebut the defendants' case. In view of the curative admissibility of the evidence elicited by the defendants on cross-examination, we find no reversible error in the trial court's evidentiary ruling to which error is assigned.

Article III – Presumptions in Civil Actions and Proceedings

Note: Article III, Rule 301 will not be addressed within this book as it is not relevant to Illinois criminal evidence.

Rule 301. Presumptions in General in Civil Actions and Proceedings

In all civil actions and proceedings not otherwise provided for by rule, statute or court decision, a presumption imposes on the party against whom it is directed the burden of going forward with evidence to rebut or meet the presumption, but does not shift to such party the burden of proof in the sense of the risk of nonpersuasion, which remains throughout the trial upon the party on whom it was originally cast.

Adopted September 27, 2010, eff. January 1, 2011.

Chapter 2

Chapter 2

Article IV – Relevancy and Its Limits

Definition

Rule 401. Definition of "Relevant Evidence"

"Relevant evidence" means evidence having any tendency to make the existence of any fact that is of consequence to the determination of the action more probable or less probable than it would be without the evidence.

Adopted September 27, 2010, eff. January 1, 2011.

AUTHOR'S COMMENTARY

The Illinois Supreme Court previously adopted the definition of "relevancy" as found in Federal Rule of Evidence 401 in People v. Monroe, 66 Ill. 2d 317 (1977). The new Illinois Rule of Evidence 401 is identical to the Federal Rule of Evidence 401, in effect prior to its stylistic amendment on December 1, 2011. *See* Gino L. DiVito, *The Illinois Rules of Evidence: A Color-Coded Guide Containing the New Rules, the Committee's General and Specific Comments, a Comparison with the Federal Rules of Evidence, and Additional Commentary* (*Including the Federal Rules of Evidence as Amended Effective December 1, 2011*) (Jan. 1, 2012), at 29, http://www.tdrlawfirm.com/assets/downloads/Illinois_Rules_of_Evidence_Color-Coded_Guide.pdf.

PRIOR ILLINOIS CASE LAW

1. Adoption of the Federal Rules' Definition of Relevancy in Illinois
People v. Monroe, 66 Ill. 2d 317 (1977)

The Illinois Supreme Court adopted the definition of relevancy found in the Federal Rule of Evidence 401. The court found that an undercover police officer's testimony about his prior purchases of a controlled substance from a third party was relevant at defendant's trial because the third party's information ultimately led the officer to purchase drugs from the defendant.

Defendant was charged with delivery of a controlled substance. An undercover police officer testified at trial that he had asked a third party from whom he had previously bought LSD where he could purchase some more. The third party told the officer that he could buy some LSD at a nearby tavern. The third party entered the tavern and returned a short time later. He told the undercover officer that his source was not present at the tavern, but that the bartender would sell the LSD to him. The third party then introduced the officer to the defendant who was tending the bar. Defendant challenged admissibility of this evidence on appeal and the appellate court found that the officer's testimony pertaining to the third party's past sales of LSD to him was irrelevant and prejudicial to the defendant. On review to the Illinois Supreme Court, the state contended that the evidence was properly admitted as "relevant background information." The Supreme Court agreed and explained that

> [i]n deciding whether the evidence was admissible we are mindful that 'The basic principle that animates our law of evidence is that what is relevant is admissible. Exceptions to that principle must justify themselves.' People *ex rel.* Noren v. Dempsey, 10 Ill. 2d 288, 293 (1957). 'Relevancy is established where a fact offered tends to prove a fact in controversy or

renders a matter in issue more or less probable.' Marut v. Costello, 34 Ill. 2d 125, 128 (1965). A definition of 'relevant evidence,' fairly simple of application, is to be found in Rule 401 of the Federal Rules of Evidence, which provides: 'Relevant evidence' means evidence having any tendency to make the existence of any fact that is of consequence to the determination of the action more probable or less probable than it would be without the evidence.' The notes of the Advisory Committee state:

> 'Problems of relevancy call for an answer to the question whether an item of evidence, when tested by the processes of legal reasoning, possesses sufficient probative value to justify receiving it in evidence.
>
> ***
>
> Relevancy is not an inherent characteristic of any item of evidence but exists only as a relation between an item of evidence and a matter properly provable in the case. Does the item of evidence tend to prove the matter sought to be proved? Whether the relationship exists depends upon principles evolved by experience or science, applied logically to the situation at hand.
>
> ***
>
> The fact to be proved may be ultimate, intermediate, or evidentiary; it matters not, so long as it is of consequence in the determination of the action. ***

The Supreme Court concluded that the officer's testimony was "relevant background information" as it helped explain why the officer would ask the third party whether it had LSD for sale and where he could purchase some more of it.

Standards of Admissibility

Rule 402. Relevant Evidence Generally Admissible; Irrelevant Evidence Inadmissible

All relevant evidence is admissible, except as otherwise provided by law. Evidence which is not relevant is not admissible.

Adopted September 27, 2010, eff. January 1, 2011.

AUTHOR'S COMMENTARY

Illinois Rule of Evidence 402 is nearly identical to Federal Rule of Evidence 402 in effect prior to its stylistic amendment on December 1, 2011, except that Illinois Rule of Evidence 402 does not contain the specific exceptions noted in the Federal Rule of Evidence, such as those provided by the United States Constitution, federal statutes, federal evidentiary rules and other rules prescribed by the United States Supreme Court. *See* Gino L. DiVito, *The Illinois Rules of Evidence: A Color-Coded Guide Containing the New Rules, the Committee's General and Specific Comments, a Comparison with the Federal Rules of Evidence, and Additional Commentary* (*Including the Federal Rules of Evidence as Amended Effective December 1, 2011*) (Jan. 1, 2012), at 29, http://www.tdrlawfirm.com/assets/downloads/Illinois_Rules_of_Evidence_Color-Coded_Guide.pdf. Illinois Rule of Evidence 402 provides that "[a]ll relevant evidence is admissible, except as otherwise provided by *law*" (emphasis added).

Rule 403. Exclusion of Relevant Evidence on Grounds of Prejudice, Confusion, or Waste of Time

Although relevant, evidence may be excluded if its probative value is substantially outweighed by the danger of unfair prejudice, confusion of the issues, or misleading the jury, or by considerations of undue delay, waste of time, or needless presentation of cumulative evidence. Adopted September 27, 2010, eff. January 1, 2011.

AUTHOR'S COMMENTARY

Illinois Rule of Evidence 403 mirrors Federal Rule of Evidence 403, in effect prior to its stylistic amendment on December 1, 2011, and provides for exclusion of relevant evidence if "its probative value is substantially outweighed by the danger of unfair prejudice." *See* Gino L. DiVito, *The Illinois Rules of Evidence: A Color-Coded Guide Containing the New Rules, the Committee's General and Specific Comments, a Comparison with the Federal Rules of Evidence, and Additional Commentary* (*Including the Federal Rules of Evidence as Amended Effective December 1, 2011*) (Jan. 1, 2012), at 30, http://www.tdrlawfirm.com/assets/downloads/Illinois_Rules_of_Evidence_Color-Coded_Guide.pdf.

ILLINOIS CASE LAW UNDER THE NEW ILLINOIS RULES OF EVIDENCE

Evidence of a Video Recording of a Traffic Stop Is Relevant and Discoverable in Misdemeanor DUI Prosecutions

People v. Kladis, 2011 IL 110920

Defendant was arrested for a misdemeanor DUI and prior to trial requested that the state produce the arresting officer and any video tapes of her while she was in custody. State produced the officer at defendant's first hearing but did not have a copy of the videotape from the arresting officer's car. The state promised to have the videotape ready by the next court date. Instead of producing the videotape at the next court date, however, the state indicated that the video recording had been destroyed by the police department prior to the defendant's first hearing pursuant to a departmental policy. The trial court imposed sanctions on the state and prohibited it from introducing evidence pertaining to the content of the destroyed videotape. The trial court, however, allowed relevant evidence of defendant's conduct before the video started recording and after it had stopped. The state contended on appeal that the trial court's ruling "substantially impaired its ability to prosecute defendant," but the appellate court affirmed the trial court's decision. On review to the Illinois Supreme Court the state claimed that it had no obligation to tender the recording and that the trial court therefore erred in imposing sanctions. The state relied on People v. Schmidt, 56 Ill. 2d 572 (1974), arguing that video recordings are not discoverable because the Supreme Court in *Schmidt* set out a "rigid list" of items that are discoverable, including a list of witnesses, exculpatory evidence, any confession by the defendant and a "Driving While Intoxicated Arrest Report" in a misdemeanor DUI case. The Supreme Court explained that the state interpreted *Schmidt* too narrowly. It explained that it

> previously held that pretrial discovery "presupposes a range of relevance and materiality which includes not only what is admissible at the trial, but also that which leads to what is admissible." Krupp v. Chicago Transit Authority, 8 Ill. 2d 37, 41 (1956). The State overlooks the nature and relevancy of these discovery items, instead focusing on the incorrect concept that *Schmidt* set forth a rigid list which it believes should remain static and not take into account the fundamental changes which have occurred in law and society since that ruling.
>
> Relevancy is "determined by reference to the issues, for generally, something is relevant if it tends to prove or disprove something in issue." Bauter v. Reding, 68 Ill. App. 3d 171, 175 (1979). In the nearly four decades since we decided *Schmidt*, video recordings made by in-squad car cameras in misdemeanor DUI cases have become as relevant to the issue of proving or disproving guilt as the materials specifically mentioned in *Schmidt*. As such, allowing their discovery furthers the objectives of pretrial discovery to "enhance the truth-seeking process, to

> enable attorneys to better prepare for trial, to eliminate surprise and to promote an expeditious and final determination of controversies in accordance with the substantive rights of the parties." D.C. v. S.A., 178 Ill. 2d 551, 561 (1997).
>
> Since the time of *Schmidt*, the use of video recordings as evidence at trial has become a common practice to allow a defendant the opportunity to present an effective defense and to further the truth-seeking process. We recently reaffirmed the general admissibility of such evidence (People v. Taylor, 2011 IL 110067), and courts across the country are increasingly relying on video recordings to present an objective view of the facts in a case.
>
> ***
>
> In sum, we conclude that the routine video recording of traffic stops has now become an integral part of those encounters, objectively documenting what takes place by capturing the conduct and the words of both parties. We therefore hold that this important and relevant evidence falls within the scope of materials held to be discoverable under *Schmidt*. We therefore clarify that under *Schmidt*, these video recordings are discoverable in misdemeanor DUI cases.

The state argued that making video recordings discoverable in misdemeanor DUI prosecutions would be "unduly burdensome" and could "delay the judicial process." The Illinois Supreme Court disagreed, noting that

> [t]he video recording is relevant and admissible evidence because it reveals what transpired during the traffic stop which serves to further the truth-seeking function of a trial. This evidence may be helpful to both the defendant and the State. Indeed, the flow of cases actually going to trial may be eased upon allowing defendants and their counsel to review these recordings: those which reflect events favorable to the State may result in defendants willing to enter pleas which they otherwise may not have contemplated. This also advances the purpose of our DUI statutes to ensure that our roads remain safe from impaired drivers.
>
> ***
>
> In sum, we hold that the trial court did not abuse its discretion in finding that the video recording of defendant's stop and arrest was subject to discovery in her misdemeanor DUI case and that the State committed a discovery violation by allowing the destruction of the recording.

PRIOR ILLINOIS CASE LAW

1. Admissibility of Relevant Evidence Generally

People v. Mertz, 218 Ill. 2d 1 (2005)

The trial judge may exclude relevant evidence if he or she weighs the probative nature of the evidence and its prejudicial effect and determines that the probative value of the evidence is substantially outweighed by the danger of unfair prejudice. Relevant evidence that is merely cumulative in nature may be excluded, and evidence that is remote or collateral should be excluded. Evidence that tends to confuse or mislead the jury or wastes time may be excluded. These rules of admissibility are equally designed for both jury and bench trials.

Defendant was convicted of first degree murder, home invasion and aggravated criminal sexual assault; the death penalty was imposed. The Illinois Supreme Court held that defendant's admission to friends of prior involvement in an uncharged arson and murder was relevant and reliable. The court found that defendant's motive for making such an admission was a matter for the jury because there was no evidence of prompting or delusions. Cross examination is the best tool to determine reliability, and no testimony was developed through cross examination that any witness was promised leniency or favorable treatment in exchange for testimony. The court held that defendant's Internet viewing of sexually explicit sites, nude photos of his girlfriends, his e-mail address, his tattoos, the books he possessed, his possession of guns, and his "political" statements, while protected under the First Amendment, may be considered at sentencing because it is relevant and reliable.

The Illinois Supreme Court also found that admission of cumulative testimony of a "profiler" who compared the crime scene of the charged offense with the crime scene of the uncharged offenses was harmless error because other reliable evidence linked the defendant to the charged crime.

2. Testimony Regarding Police Investigation and Defendant's Flight Is Admissible
People v. Hanson, 238 Ill. 2d 74 (2010)

Detective was allowed to testify at trial regarding a conversation he had with defendant's sister in which she told the detective that she thought defendant was involved in the killings of his parents, sister and brother-in-law. Defendant argued that the testimony was improper and irrelevant opinion evidence. The court found the detective's testimony relevant and admitted it "to demonstrate the course of the criminal investigation . . . and [to provide] context for defendant's subsequent flight from police."

3. Evidence of Defendant's Burglary Technique Employed in Other Crimes Is Admissible
People v. Adkins, 239 Ill. 2d 1 (2010)

Murder defendant argued that his videotaped confession detailing his regular residential burglary techniques was irrelevant and prejudicial. The Illinois Supreme Court found that the evidence was not unduly prejudicial to the defendant because it supported the defense theory that defendant burglarized the victim's apartment but that he left the apartment before the victim was murdered.

> *See also* People v. Wheeler, 226 Ill. 2d 92 (2007) (finding no error in the exclusion of speculative evidence showing that victim was to testify against a gang leader to suggest that the gang leader and not the defendant killed the victim).

4. Evidence of Polygraph Results Is Inadmissible in Illinois Due to Its Great Potential to Confuse and Prejudice the Jury
People v. Baynes, 88 Ill. 2d 225 (1981)

Polygraph results are inadmissible to prove either the guilt or the innocence of the accused even when the parties stipulate to the results or the polygraph procedures are valid. Two general factors contribute to the unreliability of polygraph evidence: the disputed scientific reliability of the machine itself and the varying expertise of the examiners. With respect to the unreliability of the machine, the court stated that the "process has not reached a level of sophistication that makes it generally more probative than prejudicial." In this regard, the court reasoned that "[t]he polygraph's attempts to measure automatic physiological responses are influenced by variables which are not a function of the subject's guilt or innocence" and that the results "are subject to conscious and unconscious manipulation." Other factors that can influence the reliability of the results include:

> [C]omplicat[ion] by the tension of the subject . . . , his [or her] spontaneous autonomic activity. . . . abnormal blood pressure, heart and respiratory irregularities, fatigue, intoxication, rationalization, extreme nervousness, meditative abstraction, controlled breathing, instrument discomfort, uncomfortable room temperature, obesity, hidden muscular contractions, self-inflicted pain, mental incompetence psychopathy or schizophrenia, ingestion of a sedative, an

attempt to suppress a cough, fear induced by suspicion or accusation, or lack of fear of detection.

As to the examiner, the court noted that the competence of the results depended on the examiner's interpretations and in turn on his or her qualifications. It concluded that the results were in essence the subjective opinion of the examiner. Ultimately, in rejecting the admissibility of polygraph evidence, the court stated that "[n]o other form of evidence is as likely to be considered as completely determinative of guilt or innocence as a polygraph examination."

The court further noted that polygraph evidence has the potential to confuse and prejudice the jury, raising the "significant risk the jury will regard such evidence as conclusive. . . . A potential trial by polygraph is an unwarranted intrusion into the jury function. It is questionable whether any jury would follow limiting instructions because the polygraph evidence 'is likely to be shrouded with an aura of near infallibility, akin to the ancient oracle of Delphi.'"

5. Polygraph Evidence May Not Be Considered "By Any Participant in the Trial Process"
People v. Yarbrough, 93 Ill. 2d 421 (1982)

The trial court made references to defendant's polygraph examination and its results in considering defendant's post-trial motion for a new trial and appeal bond. The Illinois Supreme Court found that the trial court erred in making such references because "polygraph evidence is not reliable enough to be given consideration in any manner . . . by any participant in the trial process . . . be it judge or jury." The Supreme Court concluded that the defendant had the right to have his post-trial motions considered without a consideration of whether he had taken a polygraph exam and whether he had passed such an exam.

6. A Witness Should Not Be Identified as a Polygraph Examiner
People v. Nicholls, 44 Ill. 2d 533 (1970)

Defendant took a polygraph examination before confessing. The trial court barred defendant from identifying a witness as a polygraph examiner. Defendant sought to show that, as a polygraph examiner, the witness was a professional extractor of confessions and therefore his testimony should be considered suspect. The Supreme Court held that the trial court properly barred such testimony, as all evidence relating to a polygraph examination is inadmissible in Illinois, and the jury is sufficiently capable of judging the witness' credibility.

7. Statements Connected to Polygraph Examination May Be Admitted for the Limited Purpose of Determining Credibility and Reliability of Defendant's Confession
People v. Melock, 149 Ill. 2d 423 (1992)

Polygraph evidence may be admitted for the limited purpose of determining the credibility and reliability of a confession. The defendant sought to introduce evidence of the facts and circumstances of his polygraph examination. The trial court barred its admission. In deciding whether such evidence is admissible, the Supreme Court reviewed the law of other jurisdictions, federal law, as well as several Illinois cases. The court first noted that some jurisdictions depart from a "*per se*" rule barring admissibility and allow limited use of such evidence to determine the voluntariness of confessions. Similarly, federal courts allow evidence of polygraph examinations for the purpose of establishing the circumstances leading up to confessions. Moreover, Illinois courts have admitted polygraph evidence for the purpose of showing why defendants had confessed. The Supreme Court also noted that in Illinois only the trial judge determines the voluntariness of a confession, not the jury. The jury decides the credibility of a confession.

The court concluded that when the accused is denied the right to present such evidence, he or she is deprived of a fundamental right to have a fair opportunity to present a defense. The right to present a defense includes the right to controvert the state's proof, particularly regarding a confession. The probative value of evidence concerning the circumstances of a confession outweighs the prejudicial effect of polygraph evidence. Nonetheless, the court limited its holding. First, the trial judge has to give a limiting instruction to the jury stating that the evidence is only to be used in determining the credibility and reliability of a confession. Second, the state is not allowed to produce the results of a polygraph examination nor any specific questions that had been asked. Finally, the court expressly stated that it was not announcing a general rule on the admissibility of polygraph evidence. The court remained firm that the details and results of a polygraph are inadmissible.

8. Defendant Entitled to Controvert State's Proof of Voluntary Confession Through Examination of Circumstances Surrounding Polygraph Examination
People v. Lettrich, 413 Ill. 172 (1952)

Defendant was taken into custody for a murder of a young girl and was subjected to a polygraph test four times after being held at the police station for three days. Defendant testified that officers threatened him until he confessed to the crime. The defendant repudiated his confession, but the trial court found that the confession had been made voluntarily. There was no evidence linking defendant to the crime other than the allegedly coerced confession. The trial court refused to allow the key witness who gave defendant the polygraph test to be fully cross-examined by the defendant, unduly restricting defendant's cross-examination of the witness. The Illinois Supreme Court stated that the defendant "should have been permitted to show all the circumstances surrounding his questioning . . . including the nature and extent of the questioning." Moreover, "'justice requires that the jury consider every circumstance which reflects upon the reliability of that confession.'" The Supreme Court thus found that the trial court's improper limitations on defendant's cross-examination of the witness, along with other trial court errors and prosecutor's improper remarks warranted a new trial.

9. Judge Must Instruct Jury to Only Consider Polygraph Evidence for the Limited Purpose of Determining Credibility of Confession
People v. Triplett, 37 Ill. 2d 234 (1967)

If in the course of admitting a confession that occurred prior to or after a polygraph examination, evidence of the polygraph test is revealed, the judge must instruct the jury on the limited purpose of that evidence, namely that the use of the polygraph is a relevant circumstance that the jury may take into account in weighing the credibility of the confession.

Here, the defendant confessed shortly after taking a polygraph test. The trial court repeatedly overruled defense objections to the admissibility of evidence of the polygraph test. The appellate court affirmed, noting that the evidence of the polygraph test was admitted for the limited issue of voluntariness of defendant's confession. The Supreme Court reversed because there was no evidence that the trial court gave a limiting instruction, and stated that "the fact that the confession followed a polygraph examination is a relevant circumstance and that is the fact of the examination, rather than its result, that is significant."

10. Polygraph Evidence May Be Admitted as a "Shield" Against Defendant's Allegations of Coercion; Opening the Door to Such Evidence
People v. Jefferson, 184 Ill. 2d 486 (1998)

The Illinois Supreme Court extended the holding of People v. Melock, 149 Ill. 2d 423 (1992), to allow the state to present evidence of the circumstances surrounding the confession, including polygraph evidence, to rebut the defendant's claim of coercion. Defendant argued that the prosecution impermissibly alluded to polygraph evidence by referring to a witness as a "technician." The court noted the general rule that it is improper to identify a witness as a polygraph examiner, but here the prosecution was careful not to make a reference to the polygraph examination and its evidence was "sufficiently vague" so as to not lead "the jurors to any improper speculation."

The court further found that evidence that the defendant had agreed to take a polygraph examination and then confessed was admissible for the limited purpose of showing why she agreed to speak to the police. Prior to the admissibility of the polygraph evidence, the defendant testified that she had confessed because the police had promised her that if she gave a statement she would be released from custody to see her child who had only hours to live. The Supreme Court reasoned that her testimony opened the door to the use of the polygraph agreement for a limited purpose to establish an alternative explanation for her confession. Had the evidence not been allowed, the trier of fact would have been misled by her testimony concerning the circumstances that preceded her confession.

See also People v. Logan, 2011 IL App (1st) 093582 (admitting polygraph evidence as a "shield" against a witness who claimed that her grand jury testimony was coerced).

11. Polygraph Evidence May Not Be Used by the Prosecution in Its Case-in-Chief as a "Sword"

People v. Jackson, 202 Ill. 2d 361 (2002)

The prosecution cannot offer evidence of a witness' polygraph examination in its direct examination of the witness. In a bench trial, the defendant was charged and convicted with first degree murder of a female shopper in a store and attempt armed robbery. After arrest, defendant's co-offender first denied any involvement in the crime. Later, when confronted with the results of his polygraph test, the co-offender confessed in a recorded statement and named the defendant as the shooter. Later, the co-offender pleaded guilty.

On direct examination, the co-offender contradicted his confession, insisting that neither he nor the defendant was in the store on the day of the murder and that neither one had a plan to rob the store. The prosecutor then asked the witness whether he had taken a polygraph test before confessing. The defense objected but the prosecutor countered that the evidence was admissible to show a "course of conduct" leading up to the witness giving a confession to the police. The judge allowed the testimony "for a limited purpose," but did not explain what that purpose was. The witness then admitted that after he was confronted with negative polygraph test results he confessed and implicated the defendant. The Supreme Court reversed applying the plain error doctrine. The state argued that the evidence was proper to establish the sequence of events leading to the witness giving a confession because he stated on direct examination that his confession was obtained by the use of threats and false promises from the police and the assistant state's attorney who was present. The Supreme Court found that the state "attempted to use the evidence as a sword to advance its own case." The Supreme Court concluded that the admissibility of the polygraph evidence was reversible error.

12. Evidence of Polygraph Examination Is Inadmissible Even If Not Prejudicial

People v. Gard, 158 Ill. 2d 191 (1994)

Evidence that co-defendant and an eyewitness had taken polygraph examinations was referred to abundantly during trial. The court found plain error to admit evidence of the examinations because even though the evidence did not prejudice the defendant, the court reasoned that polygraph evidence is generally unreliable and repugnant to the integrity of the judicial process.

13. Photographs Are Admissible to Corroborate Testimony If Relevant and Not Prejudicial
People v. Chapman, 194 Ill. 2d 186 (2000)

"If photographs are relevant to prove facts at issue, they are admissible and may be shown to the jury unless the prejudicial nature of the photographs outweighs their probative value." Photographs are generally admissible to illustrate or corroborate the testimony of a witness if they tend to establish a fact in issue. For example, in a homicide prosecution, photographs are admissible to explain the cause of death, the amount of force used, or the condition of the crime scene, and to corroborate the expert testimony of a pathologist. Photographs may be admitted to show the time or the manner of a homicidal death and the condition of the victim's body; to contradict the defendant's version of the incident; to assist the jury in understanding medical testimony; and to prove the identity of the victim. Photographs are admissible to explain or corroborate testimony, and they may not be excluded merely on the basis that they are cumulative in nature. In fact, "[i]f photographs could aid the jury in understanding testimony, they may be admitted even if cumulative of that testimony." A trial judge may exercise wide discretion in admitting or excluding photographs subject to an abuse of discretion standard. However, if the photographs are not probative of a material fact but merely serve to inflame and prejudice the jury, they should not be admitted.

Here, the court allowed photographs depicting the victims' decomposed bodies to explain investigator's testimony regarding recovery of the bodies from the water. The court also allowed several photographs of the victims' bodies that were "least graphic" to be shown to the jury during deliberations because they were relevant to the issues in the case, and their probative value was not substantially outweighed by prejudice to the defendant.

14. Photographs May Be Used Substantively
People v. Normand, 215 Ill. 2d 539 (2005)

The Illinois Supreme Court found that photographs depicting pornographic images of children were "themselves the evidence of defendant's offense" in a child pornography prosecution. Defendant argued that the photographs were insufficient evidence to sustain his conviction because the state did not prove that actual children were used in making the computer images. The court disagreed, finding that the trier of fact was "capable of determining whether real children were used in pornographic images simply by viewing the images themselves." The court held that "any trier of fact could [have] conclude[d] beyond a reasonable doubt that the photographs depicted actual children, and that defendant knowingly possessed the images."

15. Even "Gruesome" Photographs May Be Admitted If Sufficiently Probative
People v. Terrell, 185 Ill. 2d 467 (1998)

The trial court admitted "gruesome" photographs depicting the autopsy of the victim. Defendant argued that they were improperly admitted as they were "disgusting and any probative value they had was outweighed by their potentially prejudicial effect." The Illinois Supreme Court disagreed, reasoning that "if a photograph has sufficient probative value, it may be admitted in spite of its gruesome or disgusting nature." The photographs in this case were highly relevant to show that the victim's death resulted from exceptionally heinous and brutal behavior and depicted the nature and extent of victim's injuries as well as the amount of force applied to cause such injuries.

For recent appellate court decisions discussing admissibility of photograph evidence, see:

People v. Richardson, 401 Ill. App. 3d 45 (1st Dist. 2010) (finding that trial court did not abuse its discretion in admitting 27 autopsy photographs of minor victim).
People v. Pelo, 404 Ill. App. 3d 839 (4th Dist. 2010) (finding graphic pornographic photographs relevant and probative where defendant emulated such images during assaults).

16. Demonstrative Evidence Is Admissible to Explain Testimony as Long as It Is Not Unduly Prejudicial
People v. Williams, 161 Ill. 2d 1 (1994)

While demonstrative evidence is not inherently probative of a fact in issue, it is admissible to help explain the testimony of a witness to the jury. "However, an exhibit which merely summarizes clearly understandable testimony and thereby serves only to memorialize particular evidence should be disallowed." The state constructed an eight-foot chart of defendant's criminal background during closing argument even though evidence of his prior offenses was introduced through witness testimony at trial. The Illinois Supreme Court found the admissibility of the chart "unfairly memorialized and unduly emphasized the evidence in aggravation," finding that the presentation of the chart was prejudicial error.

17. Demonstrative Evidence Is Not Admissible If Offered for the Principal Purpose of Prejudicing the Jury
People v. Blue, 189 Ill. 2d 99 (2000)

During trial for murder of a police officer, the state offered and the court allowed evidence of a headless mannequin wearing the "bloodied and brain splattered uniform" of the victim officer. On appeal, the defendant argued that it was an abuse of discretion for the court to allow the dressed mannequin into evidence. The record showed that the state wished to introduce the mannequin during another officer's testimony, but the mannequin was within the jury's view before it was introduced and remained in the courtroom long after it was utilized. In addition to the mannequin, the state also offered evidence of 16 autopsy photos that displayed the officer's injuries. The Illinois Supreme Court noted that the use of physical evidence is guided by the principle that when "'spectacular exhibits having little probative value are offered for the principal purpose of arousing prejudicial emotions they should be promptly excluded.'" While Illinois courts are split on the question of admissibility of victim's clothing, the court held that a police officer's bloodied and brain splattered uniform is "uniquely 'charged with emotion'" and that the trial court erred in admitting the mannequin since the "nature and presentation of the uniform rendered the exhibit so disturbing that its prejudicial impact outweighed its probative value."

18. Trial Court May Allow Jury to View the Crime Scene Subject to an Abuse of Discretion Standard
People v. Durso, 40 Ill. 2d 242 (1968)

The trial court may allow a jury to view the crime scene subject to an abuse of discretion standard. Here, defendant argued that the trial court erred in not permitting the jury to go to the parking lot to view the vehicle in which the murder occurred. A witness testified that he saw the stabbing through an opening in the trunk that allowed him to view the inside of the car. To demonstrate the size of the opening, defense was allowed to use a cardboard model, and the state conducted an experiment to show what could potentially be seen through the opening. The Illinois Supreme Court held that it was not abuse of discretion for the trial court to deny the view since both the defense and prosecution had an opportunity to demonstrate through the use of various aids how large the opening was and how much could be seen through it. Thus, the court concluded, "no useful purpose would have been served by such a view."

19. Physical Evidence Is Admissible If There Is Proof to Connect It to the Defendant and the Crime

People v. Free, 94 Ill. 2d 378 (1983)

The Illinois Supreme Court has stated:

> The general rule is that physical evidence may be admitted provided there is proof to connect it with the defendant and the crime. See People v. Ashley, 18 Ill. 2d 272 (1960); People v. Miller, 40 Ill. 2d 154 (1968). It is only necessary that the object at least be suitable for the commission of the crime. *Miller*, 40 Ill. 2d 154 (1968), but it is not necessary that the object actually be used in committing the crime. People v. Magby, 37 Ill. 2d 197 (1967).

The Supreme Court held that the gun found in the defendant's home along with gun maintenance tools was relevant to show that defendant owned a gun and was familiar with guns in general.

Illinois Rules of Evidence Relevant to the Admissibility of Character Evidence

Rule 404. Character Evidence Not Admissible to Prove Conduct; Exceptions; Other Crimes

(a) Character Evidence Generally. Evidence of a person's character or a trait of character is not admissible for the purpose of proving action in conformity therewith on a particular occasion, except:

(1) **Character of Accused.** In a criminal case, evidence of a pertinent trait of character offered by an accused, or by the prosecution to rebut the same;

(2) **Character of Alleged Victim.** In a criminal case, and subject to the limitations imposed by section 115-7 of the Code of Criminal Procedure (725 ILCS 5/115-7), evidence of a pertinent trait of character of the alleged victim of the crime offered by an accused, or by the prosecution to rebut the same, or evidence of a character trait of peacefulness of the alleged victim offered by the prosecution in a homicide or battery case to rebut evidence that the alleged victim was the first aggressor;

(3) **Character of Witness.** Evidence of the character of a witness, as provided in Rules 607, 608, and 609.

(b) Other Crimes, Wrongs, or Acts. Evidence of other crimes, wrongs, or acts is not admissible to prove the character of a person in order to show action in conformity therewith except as provided by sections 115-7.3, 115-7.4, and 115-20 of the Code of Criminal Procedure (725 ILCS 5/115-7.3, 725 ILCS 5/115-7.4, and 725 ILCS 5/115-20). Such evidence may also be admissible for other purposes, such as proof of motive, opportunity, intent, preparation, plan, knowledge, identity, or absence of mistake or accident.

(c) In a criminal case in which the prosecution intends to offer evidence under subdivision (b), it must disclose the evidence, including statements of witnesses or a summary of the substance of any testimony, at a reasonable time in advance of trial, or during trial if the court excuses pretrial notice on good cause shown.

Adopted September 27, 2010, eff. January 1, 2011.

Official Comment

Evidence of character or a trait of character of a person for the purpose of proving that the person acted in conformity therewith on a particular occasion is not admissible, except in a criminal case to the extent provided for under Rule 404(a)(1) (regarding the character of the accused), and under Rule 404(a)(2) (regarding the character of the alleged victim). Rule 404(b) renders inadmissible evidence of other crimes, wrongs, or acts to prove the character of a person in order to show action in conformity therewith, but allows proof of other crimes, wrongs, or acts where they are relevant under statutes related to certain criminal offenses, as well as for other purposes, such as proof of motive, opportunity, intent, preparation, plan, knowledge, identity, or absence of mistake or accident.

AUTHOR'S COMMENTARY

Subject to well-defined limitations, evidence regarding the character of the accused or a victim is relevant and admissible as substantive evidence. Character evidence of witness, including that of the defendant or a victim, is not treated as substantive evidence; rather, it is viewed as evidence that affects the credibility of that individual as a witness.

Generally, character evidence is not admissible to prove that an individual acted in conformity with a character trait on a specific occasion. Pursuant to Illinois Rule of Evidence 404(a)(1), however, in a criminal case the accused may defend by introducing evidence of his or her pertinent trait of character. The prosecution has a limited right to rebut the evidence. The prosecution is not permitted to introduce character evidence of the accused in its case-in-chief, but is allowed to rebut with evidence related to the same character trait as that offered by the accused.

Pursuant to Illinois Rule of Evidence 404(a)(2), but subject to section 115-7 of the Code of Criminal Procedure (725 ILCS 5/115-7), the accused may introduce evidence of a pertinent character trait of the victim of the crime, and the prosecution may rebut such evidence. However, the victim's pertinent character trait may generally not be introduced through evidence of specific past acts, except as provided by Illinois Rule of Evidence 405(b). *See* MICHAEL H. GRAHAM, GRAHAM'S HANDBOOK OF ILLINOIS EVIDENCE § 404.1 (10th ed. 2010). Professor Graham has noted that the Illinois Supreme Court has "overlooked" this general prohibition in People v. Peeples, 155 Ill. 2d 422 (1993), where the court admitted evidence of victim's prior specific acts of attending church to show that the victim was a "trusting person" who would likely allow a stranger into her home. GRAHAM, GRAHAM'S HANDBOOK OF ILLINOIS EVIDENCE, at § 404.4.

In a homicide or a battery case, if the accused introduces evidence that the victim was the first aggressor, the prosecution may then rebut this evidence with evidence of the victim's character trait for peacefulness. Note that unlike the Federal Rule of Evidence 404(a)(2), the Illinois rule permits introduction of evidence of the victim's peaceful character not only in a homicide case but also in a battery case. Gino L. DiVito, *The Illinois Rules of Evidence: A Color-Coded Guide Containing the New Rules, the Committee's General and Specific Comments, a Comparison with the Federal Rules of Evidence, and Additional Commentary (Including the Federal Rules of Evidence as Amended Effective December 1, 2011)* (Jan. 1, 2012), at 32, http://www.tdrlawfirm.com/assets/downloads/Illinois_Rules_of_Evidence_Color-Coded_Guide.pdf [hereinafter DiVito, *Color-Coded Guide*].

Prior to the enactment of Illinois Rule of Evidence 404(b), the general Illinois common law rule was that evidence of other offenses committed by the defendant and which were not the subject of the prosecution was not relevant and therefore inadmissible against him or her. People v. Kliner, 185 Ill. 2d 81 (1998). Such evidence was viewed as too probative on the issue of guilt. Michelson v. United States, 335 U.S. 469 (1948). Illinois Rule of Evidence 404(b) has retained the common law rule prohibiting the admissibility of evidence of other crimes if its sole purpose is to establish the propensity of the accused to commit crimes. However, evidence that is relevant for a purpose other than to show propensity is admissible. The law draws no distinction between prior and subsequent crimes. Under this broad exception, evidence of other crimes is admissible if its purpose is to establish intent; knowledge; motive; absence of mistake or accident; identity; common scheme, plan, or design; or *modus operandi*. *See* People v. Wilson, 214 Ill. 2d 127 (2005); People v. Heard, 187 Ill. 2d 36 (1999); People v. Banks, 161 Ill. 2d 119 (1994); People v. Cruz, 162 Ill. 2d 314 (1994). Illinois Rule of Evidence 404(b) differs somewhat from the Federal Rule of Evidence 404(b) in effect prior to its stylistic amendment on December 1, 2011. DiVito, *Color-Coded Guide* at 33. Unlike Federal Rule of Evidence 404(b), Illinois Rule of Evidence 404(b) provides specific statutory exceptions that allow admissibility of propensity evidence. *Id.* The statutory exceptions allow admissibility of evidence of other specified offenses or convictions as propensity evidence in prosecutions for various sexual offenses, battery involving sexual penetration or sexual conduct, or criminal transmission of HIV (725 ILCS 5/115-7.3), offense of domestic violence (725 ILCS 5/115-7.4), and prior conviction for domestic battery against the same victim (725 ILCS 5/115-20).

RELEVANT STATUTORY AUTHORITY

The Illinois Rape Shield Law: Limiting Admissibility of Victim's Character Evidence 725 ILCS 5/115-7. Prior Sexual Activity or Reputation as Evidence

(a) In prosecutions for predatory criminal sexual assault of a child, aggravated criminal sexual assault, criminal sexual assault, aggravated criminal sexual abuse, criminal sexual abuse, or criminal transmission of HIV; and in prosecutions for battery and aggravated battery, when the commission of the offense involves sexual penetration or sexual conduct as defined in Section 11-0.1 of the Criminal Code of 1961; and with the trial or retrial of the offenses formerly known as rape, deviate sexual assault, indecent liberties with a child, and aggravated indecent liberties with a child, the prior sexual activity or the reputation of the alleged victim or corroborating witness under Section 115-7.3 of this Code is inadmissible except (1) as evidence concerning the past sexual conduct of the alleged victim or corroborating witness under Section 115-7.3 of this Code with the accused when this evidence is offered by the accused upon the issue of whether the alleged victim or corroborating witness under Section 115-7.3 of this Code consented to the sexual conduct with respect to which the offense is alleged; or (2) when constitutionally required to be admitted.

(b) No evidence admissible under this Section shall be introduced unless ruled admissible by the trial judge after an offer of proof has been made at a hearing to be held *in camera* in order to determine whether the defense has evidence to impeach the witness in the event that prior sexual activity with the defendant is denied. Such offer of proof shall include reasonably specific information as to the date, time and place of the past sexual conduct between the alleged victim or corroborating witness under Section 115-7.3 of this Code and the defendant. Unless the court finds that reasonably specific information as to date, time or place, or some combination thereof, has been offered as to prior sexual activity with the defendant, counsel for the defendant shall be ordered to refrain from inquiring into prior sexual activity between the alleged victim or corroborating witness under Section 115-7.3 of this Code and the defendant. The court shall not admit evidence under this Section unless it determines at the hearing that the evidence is relevant and the probative value of the evidence outweighs the danger of unfair prejudice. The evidence shall be admissible at trial to the extent an order made by the court specifies the evidence that may be admitted and areas with respect to which the alleged victim or corroborating witness under Section 115-7.3 of this Code may be examined or cross examined.

Effective July 1, 2011.

Evidence of Other Offenses, in Certain Cases, Is Also Admissible Under Section 115-7.3

725 ILCS 5/115-7.3. Evidence in Certain Cases

(a) This Section applies to criminal cases in which:

(1) the defendant is accused of predatory criminal sexual assault of a child, aggravated criminal sexual assault, criminal sexual assault, aggravated criminal sexual abuse, criminal sexual abuse, or criminal transmission of HIV;
(2) the defendant is accused of battery or aggravated battery when the commission of the offense involves sexual penetration or sexual conduct as defined in Section 12-12 of the Criminal Code of 1961;
(3) the defendant is tried or retried for any of the offenses formerly known as rape, deviate sexual assault, indecent liberties with a child, or aggravated indecent liberties with a child.

(b) If the defendant is accused of an offense set forth in paragraph (1) or (2) of subsection (a) or the defendant is tried or retried for any of the offenses set forth in paragraph (3) of subsection (a), evidence of the defendant's commission of another offense or offenses set forth in paragraph (1), (2), or (3) of subsection (a), or evidence to rebut that proof or an inference from that proof, may be admissible (if that evidence is otherwise admissible under the rules of evidence) and may be considered for its bearing on any matter to which it is relevant.

(c) In weighing the probative value of the evidence against undue prejudice to the defendant, the court may consider:

(1) the proximity in time to the charged or predicate offense;
(2) the degree of factual similarity to the charged or predicate offense; or
(3) other relevant facts and circumstances.

(d) In a criminal case in which the prosecution intends to offer evidence under this Section, it must disclose the evidence, including statements of witnesses or a summary of the substance of any testimony, at a reasonable time in advance of trial, or during trial if the court excuses pretrial notice on good cause shown.

(e) In a criminal case in which evidence is offered under this Section, proof may be made by specific instances of conduct, testimony as to reputation, or testimony in the form of an expert opinion, except that the prosecution may offer reputation testimony only after the opposing party has offered that testimony.

(f) In prosecutions for a violation of Section 10-2, 12-3.05, 12-4, 12-13, 12-14, 12-14.1, 12-15, 12-16, or 18-5 of the Criminal Code of 1961, involving the involuntary delivery of a controlled substance to a victim, no inference may be made about the fact that a victim did not consent to a test for the presence of controlled substances.

Effective July 1, 2011.

Evidence of Offenses of Domestic Violence Is Admissible Pursuant to Section 115-7.4

725 ILCS 5/115-7.4. Evidence in domestic violence cases

(a) In a criminal prosecution in which the defendant is accused of an offense of domestic violence as defined in paragraphs (1) and (3) of Section 103 of the Illinois Domestic Violence Act of 1986, evidence of the defendant's commission of another offense or offenses of domestic violence is admissible, and may be considered for its bearing on any matter to which it is relevant.

(b) In weighing the probative value of the evidence against undue prejudice to the defendant, the court may consider:

(1) the proximity in time to the charged or predicate offense;
(2) the degree of factual similarity to the charged or predicate offense; or
(3) other relevant facts and circumstances.

(c) In a criminal case in which the prosecution intends to offer evidence under this Section, it must disclose the evidence, including statements of witnesses or a summary of the substance of any testimony, at a reasonable time in advance of trial, or during trial if the court excuses pretrial notice on good cause shown.

(d) In a criminal case in which evidence is offered under this Section, proof may be made by specific instances of conduct, testimony as to reputation, or testimony in the form of an expert opinion, except that the prosecution may offer reputation testimony only after the opposing party has offered that testimony.

Effective August 23, 2007.

Evidence of a Prior Conviction Is Admissible Pursuant to Section 115-20

725 ILCS 5/115-20. Evidence of prior conviction.

(a) Evidence of a prior conviction of a defendant for domestic battery, aggravated battery committed against a family or household member as defined in Section 112A-3, stalking, aggravated stalking, or violation of an order of protection is admissible in a later criminal prosecution for any of these types of offenses when the victim is the same person who was the victim of the previous offense that resulted in conviction of the defendant.

(b) If the defendant is accused of an offense set forth in subsection (a) or the defendant is tried or retried for any of the offenses set forth in subsection (a), evidence of the defendant's conviction for another offense or offenses set forth in subsection (a) may be admissible (if that evidence is otherwise admissible under the rules of evidence) and may be considered for its bearing on any matter to which it is relevant if the victim is the same person who was the victim of the previous offense that resulted in conviction of the defendant.

(c) In weighing the probative value of the evidence against undue prejudice to the defendant, the court may consider:

(1) the proximity in time to the charged or predicate offense;
(2) the degree of factual similarity to the charged or predicate offense; or
(3) other relevant facts and circumstances.

(d) In a criminal case in which the prosecution intends to offer evidence under this Section, it must disclose the evidence, including statements of witnesses or a summary of the substance of any testimony, at a reasonable time in advance of trial, or during trial if the court excuses pretrial notice on good cause shown.

(e) In a criminal case in which evidence is offered under this Section, proof may be made by specific instances of conduct as evidenced by proof of conviction, testimony as to reputation, or testimony in the form of an expert opinion, except that the prosecution may offer reputation testimony only after the opposing party has offered that testimony.

Effective January 1, 1998.

PRIOR ILLINOIS CASE LAW

1. Sex Crime Victim's Reputation Was Traditionally Admissible

People v. Collins, 25 Ill. 2d 605 (1962)

Traditionally, Illinois courts allowed the introduction of general reputation evidence of a rape victim for unchastity and immorality when the defendant claimed that the victim consented to sexual intercourse. Specific acts of promiscuity were not admissible.

2. Limiting Admissibility of Character Evidence of Sex Crime Victim: The Illinois Rape Shield Law: 725 ILCS 5/115-7

People v. Summers, 353 Ill. App. 3d 367 (4th Dist. 2004)

Illinois has abrogated the common law rule that permitted admissibility of sex crime victim's reputation by statute (725 ILCS 5/115-7), but evidence of prior sexual activity with the defendant is admissible. The court summarized the evolution of the Illinois rape shield statute as follows:

> Illinois's rape-shield statute was enacted in 1978. The policy underlying the rape-shield statute is to prevent the defendant from harassing and humiliating the complaining witness with evidence of either her reputation for chastity or specific acts of sexual conduct with persons other than defendant, since such evidence has no bearing on whether she consented to sexual relations with the defendant. People v. Ellison, 123 Ill. App. 3d 615, 626 (1984). The supreme court expressed concern over the original statute's complete prohibition of evidence of the complainant's prior sexual activity with someone other than the defendant, noting that a defendant's constitutional rights may sometimes require the admission of such evidence. People v. Sandoval, 135 Ill. 2d 159, 174-75 (1990). Thereafter, the General Assembly in 1994 amended the rape-shield statute to expressly provide that the prior sexual activity of the complainant may be admitted "when constitutionally required." 725 ILCS 5/115-7(a) (West 1998).
>
> The constitution requires that a defendant "be permitted to offer certain evidence which was directly relevant to matters at issue in the case, notwithstanding that it concerned the victim's prior sexual activity." People v. Santos, 211 Ill. 2d 395, 405-06 (2004). Examples of direct relevance include evidence that complainant had sex a month before the alleged assault, which would explain physical evidence of a cleft hymen. People v. Anthony Roy W., 324 Ill. App. 3d 181, 186-87 (2001). Another example is evidence of a child victim's viewing of adult videotapes, which would explain her sexual knowledge, which had been submitted as evidence of abuse. People v. Mason, 219 Ill. App. 3d 76, 78-79 (1991).

Here, the defendant appealed his conviction of predatory criminal sexual assault of a child claiming that the trial court erred in excluding evidence of the victim's prior adjudication as a sex offender. The defendant argued that this evidence should have been admitted for impeachment purposes because it would show that the victim had sufficient sexual knowledge in order to make up this incident. The evidence was ultimately excluded by the trial judge who found that the prejudicial nature outweighed the probative value of the evidence and the alleged conduct was of a different nature than that occurring in the juvenile adjudication. The appellate court affirmed, stating that courts are "less concerned with prejudicial effect on a witness than prejudicial effect on a defendant," however, "[t]he rape-shield statute changes that dynamic." In order to prevent harassment and embarrassment of the victim, the court held it was not abuse of discretion to exclude this "minimally relevant" evidence.

3. Defendant Is Not Permitted to Inquire About Victim's Prior Sexual Conduct Not Involving Defendant

People v. Sandoval, 135 Ill. 2d 159 (1990)

The rape shield law bars the introduction of evidence from any party, including the prosecution. Here, the Illinois Supreme Court used a confrontation clause constitutional analysis for the first time to uphold the exclusion of evidence of prior sexual activity of a rape victim. The court also used the conventional statutory construction method to preclude such evidence. First, the Illinois Supreme Court found the rape shield law's language clear and unambiguous, precluding the introduction of reputation or specific act evidence from any party to the action, unless it relates to past sexual conduct between the victim and the accused. Further, the court disagreed with the appellate court's construction of the statute, namely, that the victim had relinquished her statutory protection when she testified during direct examination that she had never had anal sex with anyone other than the accused.

Second, the Illinois Supreme Court held that the confrontation clause of the sixth amendment is not violated where a defendant is not permitted to cross examine a rape victim on the subject of her direct examination testimony. The court reasoned that even if the complainant had engaged in anal sex with others, it was not relevant to the present sexual assault charge. The court explained that the rape shield statute was enacted to prevent the diversion of the jury's attention from the charged offense, namely that the victim was forced to have anal sex against her will on this particular occasion. The court added that the complainant's prior sexual activities were irrelevant and collateral to the sexual assault charged because these prior activities did not involve the victim with the accused. All that the confrontation clause requires is cross-examination as to relevant evidence.

Lastly, the court held that the victim did not open the door, or waive the statutory protection, when she testified on direct examination that she had never had anal sex with others, especially where the trial judge had instructed the jury to disregard such testimony and this testimony was in fact stricken. The Illinois Supreme Court distinguished this case from other cases where courts permit cross-examination of victims notwithstanding a statutory preclusion to impeach by prior inconsistent statements, evidence of other crimes, bias, prejudice, or motive.

4. Exceptions to the Illinois Rape Shield Statute

People v. Santos, 211 Ill. 2d 395 (2004)

The Illinois rape shield statute, 725 ILCS 5/115-7, "absolutely bars evidence of the alleged victim's prior sexual activity or reputation, subject to two exceptions: (1) evidence of past sexual activities with the accused, offered as evidence of consent; and (2) where the admission of such evidence is constitutionally required."

The Illinois Supreme Court reversed and remanded the appellate court's finding that the defendant could use two inconsistent out-of-court statements to impeach the victim's credibility in a rape trial. During the collection of "rape kit samples," the victim stated to hospital personnel that she had no other sexual activity in the preceding 72 hours of the alleged rape. However, upon discovery via DNA testing that the semen collected was not that of the defendant, the victim admitted that she had sexual intercourse with someone else on the day of the crime. The state argued that reference to a victim's past sexual activity was prohibited by the Illinois rape shield statute, and the Illinois Supreme Court agreed. The court held that the two inconsistent statements disclosed the victim's "prior sexual activity" and were protected from disclosure under the rape shield statute whether the statements were being used as impeachment evidence or character evidence.

5. Prior Accusation Evidence Not Admissible to Show Sex Victim's Interest, Bias, or Motive Against Defendant

People v. Cookson, 215 Ill. 2d 194 (2005)

Defendant was charged with predatory criminal sexual abuse and aggravated criminal sexual abuse. Prior to trial, the defendant sought to introduce evidence that the victim, a 7-year-old girl, had previously accused another individual of sexual assault, which DCFS concluded was unfounded, for purposes of impeaching the credibility of the victim. The defendant argued that the evidence was relevant to show her interest, bias, or motive to lie about the present accusation. The trial court refused to admit the evidence. On appeal, the defendant argued that the trial court abused its discretion in refusing to admit the evidence. The Illinois Supreme Court rejected the claim, finding that the proffered evidence was improper impeachment evidence because specific past instances of untruthfulness may not be used to impeach a witness' present truthfulness. Furthermore, it held that the evidence did not establish that the victim had an interest, bias, or motive to lie since the prior accusation involved a different individual. Therefore, the evidence was irrelevant.

For recent case law discussing the Illinois rape shield statute, see:

People v. Chromik, 408 Ill. App. 3d 1028 (3d Dist. 2011) (noting that defendant had no right to question victim regarding her past sexual activity pursuant to the rape shield law).

People v. Freeman, 404 Ill. App. 3d 978 (1st Dist. 2010) (finding that victim's statement that she had "never had sex before" the sexual assault was properly admitted as a statement to a treating physician to explain recent injuries to victim's hymen).

6. Voyeurism Does Not Fall Within the "Prior Sexual Activity with Defendant" Exception to the Rape Shield Statute

People v. Jones, 264 Ill. App. 3d 556 (1st Dist. 1993)

The court rejected the defendant's contention that voyeurism falls within the exception to the rape shield statute, 725 ILCS 5/115-7. It also rejected his argument that he was denied the right to confront his accusers and present a defense.

The first contention was an issue of first impression. The defendant argued that his observation of the alleged victim and co-defendant engaging in sex on a prior occasion constituted "past sexual conduct" between himself and the victim. Since no court had yet defined "past sexual conduct," the court started with a "clean slate." It first looked to the legislature's definition in section 12-12 as it applied to sections 12-13 through 12-18. It then looked to the intent of the legislature as the definition given in section 12-12 did not necessarily apply to section 115-7. The legislature, in promulgating the statute, sought to protect victims from irrelevant and embarrassing exposure of prior sex and promote effective law enforcement so that victims would be more forthcoming regarding sexual abuse. According to the court, the defendant's broad interpretation of "past sexual conduct" to include voyeurism would defeat the legislature's intent. The court held that the definition in section 12-12 was applicable to section 115-7. It concluded that the defendant's voyeurism did not fall within the exception because there was no "past sexual conduct" between the defendant and the victim.

As to the defendant's second allegation that the victim had motive to falsely accuse the defendant because she feared her mother would find out about a sexual encounter with the co-defendant, the court looked to People v. Gray, 209 Ill. App. 3d 407 (1991). In *Gray*, defendant was permitted to question the victim about her fear of being pregnant by another man because the evidence was relevant to show the victim may have falsely accused the defendant of the charged crime. Here, even though the victim may have had motive to falsely accuse the defendant, her prior sex with the co-defendant was not "legally or even logically relevant to the possible motive that the victim feared her mother's reaction." The past act shed no light on the issue at all. Although the court found some shared similarities between *Gray* and the case before it, it found that the only reason the testimony was admitted in *Gray* was because of the victim's fear of pregnancy. This made the prior sex with another person relevant. Only from this evidence could a jury reasonably infer that the victim made up the rape accusation. Here, nothing logically linked the victim's prior sex with the alleged motive to lie. Therefore, the defendant's right to confront his accuser was not violated.

7. Constitutionality of the Rape Shield Law
People v. Cornes, 80 Ill. App. 3d 166 (5th Dist. 1980)

In reviewing the constitutionality of the statute, the Illinois courts have overwhelmingly rejected numerous constitutional challenges to the statute. Here, the court stated:

> Defendant's right of confrontation necessarily includes the right to cross-examine witnesses, but that right does not extend to matters which are irrelevant and have little or no probative value. Complainant's past sexual conduct has no bearing on whether she has consented to sexual relations with defendant. The legislature recognized this fact and chose to exclude evidence of complainant's reputation for chastity as well as specific acts of sexual conduct with third persons in cases of rape and sexual deviate assault. The exclusion of this evidence does not prevent defendant from challenging or attacking complainant's credibility or veracity or otherwise utilizing cross-examination as an effective tool of impeachment. It merely denies defendant the opportunity to harass and humiliate the complainant at trial and divert the attention of the jury to issues not relevant to the controversy. At the same time, it provides an effective law enforcement tool by encouraging victims of rapes and other sexual assaults to report these crimes to the proper authorities without fear of having the intimate details of their past sexual activity brought before the public. The legislature was acting well within its powers in enacting reasonable legislation intended to eliminate the cruel and abusive treatment of the victim at trial by precluding the admission of prejudicial and irrelevant material and to promote the lawful administration of the criminal justice system.

8. Rape Shield Statute Barring Evidence of Past Sexual Conduct Between Defendant and Victim If Timely Notice Is Not Given Is Constitutional
Michigan v. Lucas, 500 U.S. 145 (1991)

The United States Supreme Court upheld the constitutionality of a rape shield statute which bars evidence of past consensual sexual relations between the accused and the victim if the defense fails to give notice to the prosecutor within 10 days of arraignment that it will seek to introduce such evidence. The Court stated that the notice and hearing requirement serves legitimate state interests: protecting rape victims against surprise, harassment, and unnecessary invasion of privacy. The requirement also protects the prosecution against surprise. These interests may justify the severe sanction of preclusion "in appropriate cases." The Court did not elaborate extensively upon the appropriate circumstances that may justify preclusion of such evidence. However, the Court discussed prior cases that had upheld the preclusion of probative evidence, demonstrating that such evidence may be excluded as a sanction to ensure compliance with valid discovery rules.

9. The Applicability of "Victim's Prior Sexual Knowledge" Exception in Illinois
People v. Warren, 162 Ill. App. 3d 430 (3d Dist. 1987)

The appellate court acknowledged that the rape shield statutes of various states have been construed to include a limited "victim's prior sexual knowledge" exception. Under this limitation, the defendant must first make a preliminary showing that the victim's knowledge or experience was similar to the sexual conduct charged against the defendant. Without deciding the legal question as to whether this exception should be recognized in the Illinois law, the court rejected its application on factual grounds. The court reasoned:

> In this case, defendant has not made a threshold showing that the minor victim was exposed to any prior sexual conduct whatsoever. The fact that he may have viewed the naked bodies of other children or, indeed, adults in his home is not sufficient to presume that he gained any more knowledge about sexual activity than he could have observed from bathing himself. We are not prepared to equate mere "nakedness" as "sexual experience." We find that the record before us falls far short of establishing even a reasonable suspicion or good-faith basis for subjecting the minor victim to inquiry into any prior sexual experience. On the basis of the record, it appears that what defendant proposes is no less than a trial after a trial of purely collateral matters. Under similar circumstances, courts have not hesitated to deny a defendant's request for further proceedings to determine whether an exception to the rape shield statute might apply.

10. Prior Sexual Conduct of a Child Victim Admissible to Show That Child's Knowledge of Sexual Activity Came from Someone Other Than Defendant
People v. Hill, 289 Ill. App. 3d 859 (5th Dist. 1997)

In an aggravated criminal sexual assault prosecution, the trial court barred evidence that the six-year-old victim had reported a prior fellatio incident with someone other than the defendant under the rape shield statute. Defendant sought to use this evidence to show that the victim's age-inappropriate knowledge came from someone other than him. The child was able to describe penile erection, ejaculate, ejaculation, and ejaculate's taste. The court noted that the rape shield statute would yield when needed to protect the defendant's constitutional rights to a full and fair defense. Each case was to be evaluated on its own to determine whether the prior sexual conduct was probative. The court held that "under proper circumstances, evidence of a child witness's prior sexual conduct is admissible to refute the inferences that flow from a display of unique sexual knowledge." However, the court cautioned, the exception is to be narrowly drawn and the trial judge must carefully examine the proof before admitting prior sexual conduct. In doing so:

> The prior sexual conduct must be sufficiently similar to defendant's alleged conduct to provide a relevant basis for its admission. It must engage the same sexual acts embodied in the child's testimony. Further, if the prior sexual conduct cannot fully rebut the knowledge displayed, if it fails to account for certain sexual details unique to the charged conduct, its admission should be precluded. Simply put, the prior sexual conduct must account for how the child could provide the testimony's sexual detail without having suffered defendant's alleged conduct.

In this case, defendant failed to meet the above requirements. The descriptions given by the victim of the two incidents were different and failed to show that defendant's proof could fully rebut the victim's unique sexual knowledge. There were too many sexual details that remained unaccounted for from the alleged prior incident. Accordingly, the trial court did not err in barring the evidence because the probative value was not sufficiently demonstrated. The necessary connection between the prior conduct and the victim's knowledge was lacking.

11. Evidence of Other Crimes as Propensity Evidence Not Admissible
Michelson v. United States, 335 U.S. 469 (1948)

The general rule is that evidence of defendant's offenses that are not the subject of the current prosecution is not relevant and therefore inadmissible against the defendant. Such evidence is viewed as too probative on the issue of guilt. The United States Supreme Court has prevented introduction of "defendant's prior trouble with the law, specific criminal acts, or ill name among his neighbors, even though such facts might logically be persuasive that he is by propensity a probable perpetrator of the crime. The inquiry is not rejected because character is irrelevant; on the contrary, it is said to weigh too much with the jury and to so overpersuade them as to prejudge one with a bad general record and deny him a fair opportunity to defend against a particular charge."

12. Other-Crimes Evidence Admissible Under 725 ILCS 5/115-7.3 As Long As Prejudicial Effect Does Not Substantially Outweigh Probative Value
People v. Donoho, 204 Ill. 2d 159 (2003)

Section 115-7.3 permits admissibility of evidence of defendant's prior offenses where defendant is on trial for specified sexual crimes. Defendant was charged with criminal sexual assault and aggravated criminal sexual abuse and had a 12- to 15-year-old offense of indecent liberties with a child, all qualifying offenses under Section 115-7.3. Defendant challenged the constitutionality of section 115-7.3, but the Illinois Supreme Court found that the statute did not violate equal protection or due process. Pursuant to the requirements of Section 115-7.3, the Illinois Supreme Court weighed the time lapse with the factual similarities of the offenses as well as other relevant circumstances and concluded that despite the long time lapse the prior offense was admissible. The court refused to give a "bright-line" rule regarding admissibility of convictions that might be too remote. It stressed the importance of conducting a balancing test to determine whether the evidence would be too prejudicial to be admitted. Despite the court's conclusion that the trial court did not abuse its discretion, it urged trial courts to be cautious in admitting prior sex crime convictions and urged them to engage in a meaningful assessment of the probative value versus the prejudicial effect.

For recent case law discussing this topic, see:

People v. Ross, 395 Ill. App. 3d 660 (1st Dist. 2009) (finding a 17-year-old sexual assault conviction relevant and admissible because of its factual similarity to the charged crime).

People v. Smith, 406 Ill. App. 3d 747 (3d Dist. 2010) (finding no abuse of discretion where trial court excluded defendant's alleged prior abuse of his sisters and daughters because the incidents were too remote in time as well as factually dissimilar to the charged crime).

13. Evidence of Defendant's Other Acts of Domestic Violence Admissible in Prosecution for Domestic Violence Pursuant to 725 ILCS 5/115-7.4
People v. Dabbs, 239 Ill. 2d 277 (2010)

Domestic violence defendant challenged the constitutionality of section 115-7.4(a) of the Illinois Code of Criminal Procedure, arguing that the section allowed admissibility of impermissible evidence of his prior domestic violence crimes. Section 115-7.4(a) states that "evidence of the defendant's commission of another offense or offenses of domestic violence is admissible" and such other-crimes evidence "may be considered for its bearing on any matter to which it is relevant." Defendant alleged that the statute was unconstitutional because it did not require a determination of relevance or a balancing of probative value against prejudicial effect and "mandate[d] the admission of propensity evidence, regardless of whether it [was] relevant." The Illinois Supreme Court disagreed, explaining that

> [t]he propensity rule is a negative rule, which prohibits use of evidence of a defendant's prior bad acts to show his propensity to commit crime. Exceptions to the rule allow the use of such evidence for a limited purpose, such as to show motive, identity, or lack of mistake. Even when allowed by an exception, other-crimes evidence may be excluded by the operation of another rule. Three examples come to mind.
>
> First, the evidence may be excluded because it is irrelevant. Relevance is a threshold requirement that must be met by every item of evidence. "All relevant evidence is admissible, except as otherwise provided by law. Evidence which is not relevant is not admissible." ILL. R. EVID. 402 (eff. Jan. 1, 2011). Although recently codified, this rule has always been a part of our common law rules of evidence.
>
> Second, the other-crimes evidence may be excluded because the risk of undue prejudice outweighs its probative value. "Although relevant, evidence may be excluded if its probative value is substantially outweighed by the danger of unfair prejudice, confusion of the issues, or misleading the jury, or by considerations of undue delay, waste of time, or needless presentation of cumulative evidence." ILL. R. EVID. 403 (eff. Jan. 1, 2011). Again, while this codified version of the rules is of recent origin, the need to balance probative value and the risk of unfair prejudice has long been a part of our common law.
>
> Third, the evidence may be excluded because it is offered in the form of a hearsay statement that does not meet a recognized exception to the hearsay rule. "Hearsay is not admissible except as provided by these rules, by other rules prescribed by the Supreme Court, or by statute as provided in Rule 101." ILL. R. EVID. 802 (eff. Jan. 1, 2011).
>
> Given the unified scheme of the rules of evidence, the threshold requirement of relevance would apply to the admission of evidence pursuant to section 115-7.4 even if the legislature had not specifically mentioned this requirement. However, the legislature was apparently aware of the relevance requirement when it enacted section 115-7.4 because it specifically provided that the other-crimes evidence "may be considered for its bearing on any matter to which it is relevant." 725 ILCS 5/115-7.4(a) (West 2008). Clearly, such evidence is not admissible under the statute if it is not relevant to an issue in the case.

The Supreme Court held that evidence of defendant's prior acts of domestic violence is admissible as long as there is a judicial determination at trial that the evidence is relevant and its probative value is not substantially outweighed by the risk of undue prejudice.

> *See also* People v. Peterson, 2011 IL App (3d) 100513 *appeal denied, judgment vacated* 2011 WL 6185448 (Ill. Nov. 30, 2011) (order directing appellate court to address appeal on the merits); (finding no abuse of discretion where trial court excluded as unduly prejudicial defendant's prior alleged acts of domestic violence because of their remoteness and factual dissimilarities to charged offense).

14. It Is an Abuse of Discretion to Refuse to Admit Evidence of Defendant's Acquittal to Rebut Other-Crimes Evidence
People v. Ward, 2011 IL 108690

Defendant's DNA recovered from one victim matched the DNA evidence obtained in an unsolved sexual assault from prior years. Defendant was acquitted at the first victim's trial. At the second victim's trial, the first victim testified pursuant to 725 ILCS 5/115-7.3 regarding defendant's alleged attack on her, but defendant was not allowed to present evidence that the jury acquitted him of the first assault charges. The appellate court upheld the trial court's decision, but the Illinois Supreme Court reversed. The Supreme Court found that the trial court abused its discretion in excluding the evidence of acquittal because the defendant did not have a chance to rebut the first victim's testimony and her testimony was highly prejudicial to him.

15. Evidence of Defendant's Acquittal of Prior Offenses May Be Admitted at Trial
Dowling v. United States, 493 U.S. 342 (1990)

Bank robbery defendant challenged admissibility of evidence of burglary, attempted burglary, and weapons offenses of which he was previously acquitted. Defendant argued that the prior acquittal of the robbery charges precluded the government from introducing the robbery victim's evidence in the present case. The United States Supreme Court disagreed. It found that the "prior acquittals did not determine an ultimate issue in the present case" because the government had to satisfy different burdens of proof with respect to defendant's prior alleged conduct and the conduct at issue. In the present case, government had to demonstrate that defendant was the perpetrator beyond a reasonable doubt, but introduction of other-crimes evidence pursuant to Federal Rule of Evidence 404(b) is permitted as long as "the jury can reasonably conclude that the act occurred and that the defendant was the actor." The court noted that "an acquittal in a criminal case does not preclude the Government from relitigating an issue when it is presented in a subsequent action governed by a lower standard of proof," and held that the government was not barred by the doctrine of collateral estoppel and could present the other-crimes evidence.

Defendant argued that his acquittals showed that he did not commit the prior crimes and that the trial court erred in admitting the other crimes evidence to establish identity. The Supreme Court, however, noted that to preclude introduction of the other-crimes evidence on the issue of identity in the present case, defendant was required to demonstrate that the issue of identity was actually previously decided. The Supreme Court found that the defendant failed to meet his burden of proof that he was not a participant in the prior crime because "he was not acquitted on the issue of identification." In the earlier trial defendant did not argue that he was not the perpetrator, but rather that he did not intend to commit burglary and entered the home with the intent to retrieve something that belonged to him. Thus, the Supreme Court found that the prior crimes evidence was properly admitted to show identity in the present case.

16. The Name and Nature of a Prior Felony Conviction Is Inadmissible Where Charged Offense Does Not Require Proof of Specific Felony Conviction
People v. Walker, 211 Ill. 2d 317 (2004)

The appellate court reversed and remanded jury verdicts finding the defendant guilty of unlawful sale of a firearm and unlawful possession of a weapon by a felon. In a motion *in limine*, the defense objected to the disclosure of a conviction for possession of a controlled substance and offered to stipulate to a felony conviction. The state refused the stipulation. The defense was concerned that the jury would use the evidence to view the defendant as a drug dealer. In the opening statement, the prosecutor stated, "Ladies and gentlemen, this case is about a drug deal gone bad and a man who is willing to take any step possible to make sure that he got paid for the drugs he sold. That man is the defendant." The trial judge allowed the prosecutor to publish a certificate of the defendant's conviction over objection. The appellate court held this to be reversible error.

The Illinois Supreme Court affirmed the appellate court and found that the unlawful possession of a weapon by a felon offense did not require proof of a specific felony conviction. The Supreme Court held that requiring the specific name and nature of the prior felony to be identified at trial was unnecessary and prejudicial. The court noted that while the United States Supreme Court decision in Old Chief v. United States, 519 U.S. 172 (1997), was not binding since it was based on a federal statute, its reasoning was nonetheless persuasive. The court thus held that the name and nature of the prior felony conviction was inadmissible where defendant offered to stipulate to his status as a felon because the diminished probative value of the record of the conviction is outweighed by the risk of unfair prejudice.

17. Evidence of Defendant's Prior Abuse of Victim Admissible to Show Motive, Intent and Lack of Accident

People v. Illgen, 145 Ill. 2d 353 (1991)

The Illinois Supreme Court held that in a first degree murder prosecution, evidence of defendant's prior abuse of the victim was admissible. The evidence was relevant to show motive, intent, and that the acts were not accidental. The evidence was probative, not too remote, sufficiently similar, and the probative value outweighed its prejudicial nature. The court found that the evidence tended to show defendant's criminal intent.

> Evidence which shows that an event was not caused by accident tends to show that it was caused intentionally. (2 D. LOUISELL & C. MUELLER, FEDERAL EVIDENCE § 140, at 224-25 (1985) (defining intent as "merely the absence of an accident").) Here, evidence of the defendant's prior unprovoked assaults on his wife tended to negate the likelihood that the shooting was an accident and thereby tended to prove his intent . . . . This evidence, taken with other evidence in the case, tends to make it more probable that the defendant acted with the criminal intent required for murder and less probable that his actions were inadvertent or the product of an innocent state of mind.
>
> ***
>
> [A] defendant's prior acts of violence against the victim may also provide evidence of motive, in this case, a hostility showing him likely to do further violence. (2 J. WIGMORE, EVIDENCE §§ 365(3), 397, at 364, 443 (Cahbourn rev. ed. 1979).) Here, the evidence that the defendant physically assaulted his wife throughout their marriage was relevant to show their antagonistic relationship and, thus, tended to establish the defendant's motive to kill her.
>
> Our holding is consistent with previous decisions which have held that evidence of a defendant's prior offense against the victim or persons in the same class with the victim is admissible to negate a claim that the victim's injury was accidental or inadvertent.

With regard to remoteness, the supreme court deferred to the trial court and its finding that the evidence was probative on the defendant's mental state and motive despite its remoteness, finding that "the admissibility of other crimes evidence should not, and indeed cannot, be controlled solely by the number of years that have elapsed between the prior offense and the crime charged." The prior offenses were also similar enough to the present crime to be admissible. The Supreme Court explained:

> It is well established that evidence of another offense may be used only when the other offense has some threshold similarity to the crime charged. "It is this similarity which increases the relevance of the evidence and ensures that it is not being used solely to establish the defendant's criminal propensities." People v. Bartall, 98 Ill. 2d 294, 310 (1983). Where evidence of prior bad acts is offered to prove *modus operandi* or that the crime charged was

> part of a common design or plan, there must be a high degree of identity between the facts of the crime charged and the other offense in which the defendant was involved.
>
> The same degree of identity between the two offenses is not necessary when evidence of the other crime if offered for some other purpose. People v. Kimbrough, 138 Ill. App. 3d 481, 487 (1985). Where, as in this case, evidence of the defendant's involvement in another offense is offered to prove the absence of an innocent frame of mind or the presence of criminal intent, mere general areas of similarity will suffice.

Finally, the probative value of the evidence outweighed the prejudicial effect of the prior offenses. The Supreme Court again deferred to the trial judge on this matter and found that especially since the trial judge gave limiting instructions on the use of this evidence, the prejudicial nature of the evidence was substantially limited and its prejudicial effect decreased.

18. Other-Crimes Evidence May Be Admissible to Establish Intent, Motive, or Identity
People v. Heard, 187 Ill. 2d 36 (1999)

The defendant was challenging the admissibility of three prior offenses as too prejudicial and irrelevant in the present case. The Illinois Supreme Court stated:

> Evidence of a crime for which a defendant is not on trial is not admissible if relevant merely to establish the defendant's propensity to commit crime. People v. Placek, 184 Ill. 2d 370, 385, (1998). Other-crimes evidence is admissible, however, when it is relevant for any purpose other than to show the defendant's propensity to commit a crime. People v. Illgen, 145 Ill. 2d 353, 365 (1991). For instance, other-crimes evidence is admissible to prove motive or intent. *Illgen*, 145 Ill. 2d at 364-65. Where other-crimes evidence is relevant for a permissible purpose, the trial court must still weigh the prejudicial effect of admitting the other-crimes evidence against its probative value. *Placek*, 184 Ill. 2d at 385. The admissibility of other-crimes evidence rests within the sound discretion of the trial court. *Placek*, 184 Ill. 2d at 385; People v. Robinson, 167 Ill. 2d 53, 63. As such, the trial court's decision will not be overturned absent a clear abuse of discretion. *Placek*, 184 Ill. 2d at 385; *Robinson*, 167 Ill. 2d at 63.

The court allowed evidence of three prior crimes committed by the defendant against the two victims to show intent and motive. The prior crimes showed that defendant was angry about the end of his relationship with one of the victims and upset that the two victims began a relationship together. The court found that the prior crimes showed that defendant had the motive and provided "further proof of defendant's identity as the shooter."

19. Similar Other-Crimes Evidence Admissible to Show Defendant's Intent and Lack of Mistake
People v. Wilson, 214 Ill. 2d 127 (2005)

The defendant was convicted of two counts of aggravated criminal sexual assault. The defendant contended that the trial court erred in admitting testimony of other similar crimes from two witnesses with respect to events similar to that with which he was charged. The defendant first claimed that such evidence was irrelevant because his intent was not at issue because he denied that he touched the students' breasts. The Supreme Court noted that the defendant had presented an innocent construction defense, namely that he did touch the girls but that his touching was not sexual, and therefore his intent was at issue. The Supreme Court reasoned that especially where the touching was subtle and may not have had a sexual purpose, other-crimes evidence is relevant and admissible to show intent and whether the touching was "incidental or accidental." The testimony of the other two girls was therefore relevant to show whether the defendant had sexual intent in touching the two girls in the current prosecution.

The defendant also argued that the four girls' testimony did not establish a pattern of behavior so distinctive as to establish a *modus operandi*. The Supreme Court disagreed, finding that the conduct was sufficiently similar since all four girls testified that the defendant touched their breasts. All incidents shared a common thread that the defendant engaged in similar innocuous conduct "that would afford defendant an opportunity to argue that the victims had 'misinterpreted' his actions if any complaints were made." The Supreme Court thus admitted the other-crimes evidence and concluded that its probative value outweighed any undue prejudice to the accused.

For additional cases discussing this topic, see:

People v. Burgess, 176 Ill. 2d 289 (1997) (Discussing admissibility of incidents of defendant's prior abuse of victim to show intent and absence of mistake).
People v. Whalen, 158 Ill. 2d 415 (1994) (Discussing admissibility of other-crimes evidence to establish intent and motive).
People v. Maxwell, 148 Ill. 2d 116 (1992) (Discussing admissibility of other-crimes evidence to show identity).
People v. Steidl, 142 Ill. 2d 204 (1991) (Discussing other-crimes evidence used to show defendant's motive in committing the crime).
People v. Bean, 137 Ill. 2d 65 (1990) (Discussing admissibility of other-crimes evidence to establish intent).
People v. Martin, 408 Ill. App. 3d 44 (1st Dist. 2011) (Discussing admissibility of other-crimes evidence to show identity).

20. Defendant's Prior Crime Against Victim Admissible to Show Motive and Intent If Limiting Instructions Are Given

People v. Lovejoy, 235 Ill. 2d 97 (2009)

During a homicide prosecution, state introduced evidence that defendant had previously sexually attacked the victim. It sought to show that defendant had motive and intent to kill the victim, as she was pursuing rape charges against him. Defendant argued that such evidence was prejudicial and should have been excluded. The Illinois Supreme Court found, however, that the trial court properly limited the evidence regarding the prior attack to avoid prejudice to the defendant. The trial court only allowed testimony that the victim had been assaulted, but did not allow evidence that the victim had named the perpetrator. Further, the trial court gave a limiting instruction to the jury to consider the other-crimes evidence only on the issue of motive and to decide whether defendant committed the prior offense and how to weigh that evidence.

See also People v. Moss, 205 Ill. 2d 139 (2001) (discussing trial court's proper limitation of other-crimes evidence admitted to show motive).

21. Evidence of Defendant's Solicitation to Commit Murder Against First Wife Not Admissible to Show Motive and Intent in Prosecution for Solicitation to Commit Murder Against Second Wife

People v. Thingvold, 145 Ill. 2d 441 (1991)

The Illinois Supreme Court in a solicitation to commit murder prosecution held that testimony by two witnesses whom defendant had solicited to kill his second wife was admissible to show that defendant intended for another person to kill her. However, testimony of a third witness, whom defendant had allegedly solicited 10 years earlier to kill his first wife, was inadmissible. With regard to the first two individuals, the court reasoned that:

> In terms of motive, both witnesses stated that the collection of insurance proceeds was the primary reason defendant wanted [his second wife] murdered. This was the common motive behind defendant's solicitation of these men. Consequently, the fact that defendant solicited two other men to kill [his second wife] for the purpose of obtaining insurance proceeds tends to prove that defendant solicited [another person] to kill [her] for the purpose of obtaining insurance proceeds . . . . Similarly, in terms of intent, the State had to prove that defendant intended for [the other person] to kill [his second wife] when he solicited him. The fact that defendant also solicited two other men to kill [his second wife] tends to prove that defendant actually intended for [the other person] to kill [her].

With regard to the third witness, the court found that:

> [T]he State was required to prove that defendant intended that [the other person] kill [his second wife] when he solicited him. The fact that defendant may have solicited [the third witness] nearly 10 years earlier to kill [his first wife] does not prove defendant intended to have [the other person] kill [his second wife]. Rather, [the third witness'] testimony is an example of evidence admitted to show defendant's propensity or disposition to commit crime. In terms of motive, it is difficult to understand the State's contention that because defendant discussed recovering insurance proceeds on [the first wife], defendant had a motive to seek [his second wife's] death.

State also sought to introduce evidence that defendant's second wife was later stabbed at work. There was some evidence showing that when defendant solicited individuals to kill his wife, he specifically indicated that she should be stabbed in the abdomen because a recent operation in that area would likely cause her to bleed to death. The trial court admitted the evidence of the stabbing. The Supreme Court found that the trial court erred because the state failed to connect defendant to the prior crime or show that defendant participated in it. While the state need not prove beyond a reasonable doubt that defendant participated in the other crime, "such proof must be more than a mere suspicion." Here, the state admitted that the attacker who stabbed defendant's wife was never identified or apprehended and the individuals solicited by defendant denied any participation in the stabbing. The court thus found that the other-crimes evidence must be excluded due to its "extremely prejudicial" nature.

22. Other-Crimes Evidence May Be Admissible to Establish Common Design If Crimes Are Sufficiently Similar

People v. Banks, 161 Ill. 2d 119 (1994)

The defendant was on trial for the murder of a 16-month-old victim. To establish evidence of a plan or design on the part of the defendant, the state introduced evidence that two other children suffered similar mistreatment by defendant. Defendant argued that the other crimes showing he abused two other children by leaving them in an unheated room with the windows open in the middle of December was prejudicial and its only purpose was to show his propensity to commit crimes. The Illinois Supreme Court stated:

> It is well established that evidence of collateral crimes is inadmissible if relevant only to establish the defendant's propensity to commit crimes. People v. Carlson, 92 Ill. 2d 440 (1982); People v. Lindgren, 79 Ill. 2d 129, 137 (1980); People v. Romero, 66 Ill. 2d 325, 330 (1977). However, evidence of other crimes committed by the accused may be admitted if it is probative of motive, intent, identity, absence of mistake or accident, the existence of a common

> design or plan, or *modus operandi*. People v. Jones, 156 Ill. 2d 225 (1993); People v. Lehman, 5 Ill. 2d 337, 342-43 (1955). "[I]t has been broadly held that evidence of other offenses is admissible if relevant for any purpose other than to show propensity to commit a crime." People v. McDonald, 62 Ill. 2d 448, 455 (1975).
>
> In order for evidence of another crime to be admissible to establish design or plan, the two offenses must be so similar that evidence of the other crime tends to prove the defendant guilty of the offense charged. People v. McKibbins, 96 Ill. 2d 176, 185 (1983).

The Supreme Court found that the other crimes were closely related to the charged crime, as the crimes against the two surviving children occurred at the same time as the crime against the victim and "distinct similarities existed" between the crimes. Indeed, the court found that it would have been difficult for the state to describe the circumstances leading to the victim's death without mentioning the abuse of the other two children. The court thus admitted the other-crimes evidence to establish plan or design on the part of the defendant.

23. Other-Crimes Evidence by Third Person Admissible to Show *Modus Operandi* or Common Plan Only If "High Degree of Identity" Exists Between Charged and Uncharged Offenses

People v. Cruz, 162 Ill. 2d 314 (1994)

Defendant argued that the trial court should have admitted other-crimes evidence concerning another individual who had confessed to the sexual assault and murder at issue and who committed similar crimes in the past. Defendant argued that evidence of the other-crimes committed by that person was relevant to corroborate this individual's confession to the crime, to establish *modus operandi*, and to show that defendant did not commit the charged crime. The court stated:

> Where other-crimes evidence is offered, it is admissible only where the other crime bears some threshold similarity to the crime charged. *See* People v. Illgen, 145 Ill. 2d 353, 372 (1991), quoting People v. Bartall, 98 Ill. 2d 294, 310 (1983). This threshold requirement serves to increase the relevancy of the evidence and ensures that the evidence is not being used solely to establish a defendant's criminal propensities. *See* People v. Bartall, 98 Ill. 2d at 310. In cases where evidence of other crimes is offered, however, to establish *modus operandi* or a common design or plan, a "high degree of identity" between the facts of the crime charged and the other offense has been required.

The Illinois Supreme Court determined that only one prior crime committed by the other person would be admissible under a *modus operandi* theory because it was the only crime sufficiently similar to the charged crime. In both crimes that person recklessly kidnapped a child, placed her in the car covered by a sheet, and sexually attacked the child while her hands were tied. The court found that the other crimes were admissible to corroborate that confession.

24. Other-Crimes Evidence Admissible to Show Continuing Narrative of the Charged Crime

People v. Adkins, 239 Ill. 2d 1 (2010)

Other-crimes evidence may be admitted as part of a continuing narrative where the facts "are all a part of the continuing narrative which concern the circumstances attending the entire transaction and they do not concern separate, distinct and disconnected crimes." On the other hand, "other-crimes evidence may not be admitted under the continuing-narrative exception, even when the crimes occur in close proximity, if the crimes are distinct and 'undertaken for different reasons at a different place at a separate time.' People v. Lindgren, 79 Ill. 2d 129 (1980)." The Illinois Supreme Court found that evidence of a burglary of victim's neighbor committed by the defendant immediately after the defendant robbed and murdered the victim was admissible to show a continuing narrative of the charged crime.

See also People v. Rutledge, 409 Ill. App. 3d 22 (1st Dist. 2011) (finding that account of incident recounted by a witness who rejected defendant's sexual advances and ran to the victim for help was admissible and relevant to show a continuing narrative).

25. Cumulative Other-Crimes Evidence Should Be Excluded If It Unduly Prejudices the Defendant

People v. Robinson, 167 Ill. 2d 53 (1995)

The trial court permitted the state to choose two out of eight prior crimes committed by the defendant so as to limit any prejudice against defendant stemming from the cumulative effect of such other-crimes evidence. Defendant argued that trial court abused its discretion in giving the state a choice, but the Illinois Supreme Court found that it was entirely within the trial court's discretion to give the state such a choice. Defendant further challenged the two crimes chosen by the state arguing that they were not sufficiently probative on the issue of identity because one crime occurred long time ago. The court rejected the claim and stated that

> [t]he admissibility of other-crimes evidence should not, and indeed cannot, be controlled solely by the number of years that have elapsed between the prior offense and the crime charged. The decision whether to admit or exclude such evidence must be made on a case-by-case basis by the trial judge responsible for evaluating the probative value of the evidence. People v. Illgen, 145 Ill. 2d 353, 370 (1991).

Defendant further argued that the crimes did not share distinctive features. State sought to establish *modus operandi* by showing that the prior crimes occurred in the same area, right outside the victims' garages during the early evening within seven days of each other. The court again found that the trial court did not abuse its discretion and properly admitted the evidence.

26. Evidence of Use of False Identification and Circumstances Surrounding Arrest Admissible to Show Identity and Explain Delay in Arrest

People v. Harris, 225 Ill. 2d 1 (2007)

Defendant appealed his jury conviction of two counts of first-degree murder, one count of attempted first-degree murder and two counts of aggravated battery for which he was sentenced to death, arguing that the trial court erred in admitting other-crimes evidence. The Illinois Supreme Court held that evidence of the defendant's capture in North Carolina was admissible to show the circumstances of his arrest and to explain the delay in his arrest. Evidence of his use of false identification was relevant to show his identity and consciousness of guilt. The court held that the trial court did not abuse its discretion in admitting evidence of drugs sold to a witness by the defendant because it was relevant to put the relationship between the defendant and the witness in context. The trial court conducted a balancing test to determine whether the probative value of the evidence substantially outweighed its prejudicial effect.

27. Error in State's Cryptic Referrals to Inadmissible Other-Crimes Evidence Harmless Due to Overwhelming Evidence of Defendant's Guilt

People v. Nieves, 193 Ill. 2d 513 (2000)

The Illinois Supreme Court held that in light of the overwhelming evidence against the defendant, the state's reference to "other incidents" committed by the defendant was not reversible error. The state introduced a portion of the defendant's out-of-court recorded statement, where he disclosed "other incidents" to the New York police department in addition to the present crime. Upon defense counsel's objection that the state was introducing this testimony only to show the defendant's propensity to commit crimes, the state responded that the evidence was relevant to explain the manner in which the defendant came to be in the custody of the Chicago police. While the court agreed with defense counsel that the mention of "other incidents" could not have been properly introduced under the state's theory, nonetheless, it was harmless error.

28. Admissibility of Other-Crimes Evidence Based on Whether the State Needs the Evidence to Establish Its Burden of Proof

People v. Cole, 29 Ill. 2d 501 (1963)

Trial court admitted evidence of two uncharged controlled substance sales in which defendant participated before the sale of narcotics at issue in this case. Defendant argued that introduction of the two prior sales was prejudicial. State offered the evidence to show why the present sale with the undercover police officer was carried out with such ease.

29. Other Crimes Evidence Inadmissible Where Trial Objectives Can Be Achieved by Less Prejudicial Means

People v. Lindgren, 79 Ill. 2d 129 (1980)

In a murder prosecution a state witness attempted to show that defendant was in the proximity of the murder scene shortly after the murder committing arson. The court held that it was prejudicial error to admit extensive testimony regarding defendant's alleged commission of arson where the witness could have testified about the time and place proximity without mentioning the alleged crime. The court stated that "[g]enerally, time and place proximity, without more, is an insufficient basis for permitting other-crimes evidence."

See also People v. Cortes, 181 Ill. 2d 249 (1998) (Finding harmless error where defendant's own witness volunteered other-crimes evidence during her testimony and trial court attempted to limit any prejudice to the defendant).

30. Other-Crimes Evidence May Be Used to Rebut Defense of Entrapment

People v. Placek, 184 Ill. 2d 370 (1998)

State introduced evidence that defendant had been dealing in "stolen" car parts at his controlled substance trial. Defendant argued that such evidence was irrelevant and highly prejudicial, as it did not relate to the charged offense. State argued that the evidence was critical to establishing that defendant had a prior relationship with an undercover officer. Defendant asserted a defense of entrapment, claiming that the officer induced him to deliver the cocaine. State sought to rebut this testimony through the prior crimes evidence. The court found that the other-crimes evidence was too prejudicial because it was entirely unrelated to the charged crime.

For additional cases discussing this topic, see:

People v. Gilliam, 172 Ill. 2d 484 (1996) (Other-crimes evidence found admissible to rebut claims of a coerced confession).

People v. Williams, 165 Ill. 2d 51 (1995) (Evidence of defendant's prior act showing his strength admissible to rebut defendant's claim that he was too weak to hurt the victim in the alleged manner).

31. Other-Crimes Evidence May Not Be Used to Bolster Witness Credibility
People v. Romero, 66 Ill. 2d 325 (1977)

Evidence of other crimes is not admissible if its purpose is to bolster the credibility of a state's witness. The state's witness overheard defendants discussing the burglary that they had committed and planning another one, and saw the defendants with the stolen property. The witness called the police and reported the crime as well as the defendants' plan to commit another crime. At trial, the witness testified as to the defendants' involvement in other crimes occurring subsequent to the charged crime. The trial court admitted the testimony to bolster the state's witness' credibility. The Illinois Supreme Court held that the admissibility of the evidence was error that required a new trial because the evidence was too prejudicial, considering that the defendants' convictions hinged on the state witness' testimony.

32. Prosecution May Not Use Other-Crimes Evidence Solely to Enhance Witness Credibility
People v. Thingvold, 145 Ill. 2d 441 (1991)

Defendant was charged with solicitation to commit murder of his wife. Approximately four months before defendant was charged with the present crime, defendant's wife was stabbed to death. The jury was not informed of the wife's death because there was no evidence connecting defendant to the crime. At trial, defendant testified that the individual that he solicited to kill his wife attempted to extort money from him. The individual allegedly threatened to tell the police that defendant gave him keys to his wife's car so that he could tamper with it.

After introduction of this evidence, state argued that defendant's testimony opened the door to evidence of the wife's homicide. State sought to call the individual whom defendant solicited to testify that he contacted defendant two weeks after his wife's murder and indicated to defendant that he did not kill defendant's wife "because defendant had found someone" else to do it. State planned to use the testimony about the wife's stabbing death to bolster the credibility of the individual solicited by defendant. The Supreme Court refused to admit the testimony, noting that other-crimes evidence is only admissible if "some showing is made that the other crime was actually committed and that the defendant took part in it." Here, prosecution failed to connect defendant to the prior crime.

State claimed that the other-crimes evidence should be admitted because defendant made the witness' credibility a "pivotal issue" at trial. State argued that other-crimes evidence is admissible "if it is relevant for any purpose other than to show the propensity to commit crime." The Supreme Court disagreed, noting that other-crimes evidence "is not admissible to bolster the credibility of a prosecution witness." The Supreme Court further found that "[a] more precise and accurate phrasing of this "well-established principle" is: '. . . that evidence of other crimes *committed by defendant* may be admitted if relevant to establish *any material question* other than the propensity of the defendant to commit a crime.'" The court reasoned that although the witness' credibility may have been "important to the State's ability to convict defendant," there was no evidence that the issue was "material." The Supreme Court reiterated that the state failed to connect defendant to the crime and concluded that the other-crimes evidence was inadmissible.

33. Use of Conversations Between Defendant and Informant Requires Reversal as Too Prejudicial
People v. Manning, 182 Ill. 2d 193 (1998)

Evidence was admitted that the defendant told an informant that if the informant gave him an alibi, the defendant would kill the primary witness against the informant. The court held such evidence inadmissible to show the defendant's ability to reason and communicate. The prejudicial effect of the evidence substantially outweighed its probative value.

34. Defense Counsel's Failure to Object to Other-Crimes Evidence May Constitute Ineffective Assistance of Counsel

People v. Evans, 209 Ill. 2d 194 (2004)

Defendant argued that his attorney was ineffective for failing to object to the admissibility of a police officer's testimony that defendant told him that he comes to the jail a lot and that he will be there "for a long time." The court found that counsel's failure to object could have been reasonable trial strategy and that defendant was not prejudiced by the use of this statement because of the substantial evidence of guilt against him.

Rule 405. Methods of Proving Character

(a) Reputation or Opinion. In all cases in which evidence of character or a trait of character of a person is admissible, proof may be made by testimony as to reputation, or by testimony in the form of an opinion.

(b) Specific Instances of Conduct.

(1) In cases in which character or a trait of character of a person is an essential element of a charge, claim, or defense, proof may also be made of specific instances of that person's conduct; and

(2) In criminal homicide or battery cases when the accused raises the theory of self-defense and there is conflicting evidence as to whether the alleged victim was the aggressor, proof may also be made of specific instances of the alleged victim's prior violent conduct.

Adopted September 27, 2010, eff. January 1, 2011.

Official Comment

Specific instances of a person's conduct as proof of a person's character or trait of character are not generally admissible as proof that the person acted in conformity therewith. Specific instances of a person's conduct are admissible, however, under Rule 405(b)(1), as proof of a person's character or a trait of character only in those limited cases (such as negligent entrustment, negligent hiring, and certain defamation actions), when a person's character or a trait of character is an essential element of a charge, claim, or defense. Specific instances of conduct are also admissible under Rule 405(b)(2) in criminal homicide or battery cases when the accused raises the theory of self-defense and there is conflicting evidence as to whether the alleged victim was the aggressor.

Committee Commentary

(4) Recommendations: The Committee recommended to the Illinois Supreme Court a limited number of changes to Illinois evidence law (1) where the particularized evidentiary principle was neither addressed by statute nor specifically addressed in a comprehensive manner within recent history by the Illinois Supreme Court, and (2) where prior Illinois law simply did not properly reflect evidentiary policy considerations or raised practical application problems when considered in light of modern developments and evidence rules adopted elsewhere with respect to the identical issue. The Committee identified, and the Illinois Supreme Court approved, recommendations [in the following area]:

(a) Opinion testimony is added to reputation testimony as a method of proof in Rule 405, when character evidence is admissible.
ILL. R. EVID. Committee Commentary § 4, pg. 4-5.

AUTHOR'S COMMENTARY

Illinois Rule of Evidence 405(a), while identical to the Federal Rule of Evidence 405(a), in effect prior to its stylistic amendment on December 1, 2011, represents a change to the Illinois common law. Gino L. DiVito, *The Illinois Rules of Evidence: A Color-Coded Guide Containing the New Rules, the Committee's General and Specific Comments, a Comparison with the Federal Rules of Evidence, and Additional Commentary* (*Including the Federal Rules of Evidence as Amended Effective December 1, 2011*) (Jan. 1, 2012), at 38, http://www.tdrlawfirm.com/assets/downloads/Illinois_Rules_of_Evidence_Color-Coded_Guide.pdf. Prior to the enactment of the Illinois Rules of Evidence, a party was permitted to prove character only through reputation testimony. People v. Lucas, 151 Ill. 2d 461 (1992). Illinois Rule of Evidence 405(a), however, now also allows proof of character through opinion evidence. ILL. R. EVID. Committee Commentary § 4, pg. 4-5.

Although the general rule is that evidence of specific instances of conduct is inadmissible, Illinois Rule of Evidence 405(b)(1) allows admissibility of such evidence in "limited cases (such as negligent entrustment, negligent hiring, and certain defamation actions), when a person's character or a trait of character is an essential element of a charge, claim, or defense." ILL. R. EVID. 405, Comment, pg. 16.

Consistent with the Illinois common law rule, Illinois Rule of Evidence 405(b)(2) permits admissibility of specific instances of the victim's prior violent behavior in battery or homicide cases where the accused asserts the defense of self-defense and it is unclear who the first aggressor was. ILL. R. EVID. 405, Comment, pg. 16; DiVito, *Color-Coded Guide* at 39.

Under the prior Illinois common law rule and now pursuant to Illinois Rule of Evidence 405, the victim's character for violence may be established by reputation or opinion or by specific evidence of the victim's prior acts of violence. *See* MICHAEL H. GRAHAM, GRAHAM'S HANDBOOK OF ILLINOIS EVIDENCE § 404.4 (10th ed. 2010); *see also* DiVito, *Color-Coded Guide* at 39. The defense may also introduce specific evidence of the victim's temper and disposition, including prior threats directed at the defendant. People v. Stombaugh, 52 Ill. 2d 130 (1972). Evidence of the victim's character for violence may be established by proof of prior convictions for violent or aggressive conduct. People v. Lynch, 104 Ill. 2d 194 (1984). For further discussion of prior Illinois common law rule pertaining to victim's character for violence, see RALPH RUEBNER, ILLINOIS CRIMINAL TRIAL EVIDENCE 59-60 (4th ed. 2001).

PRIOR ILLINOIS CASE LAW

1. Evidence of a Relevant Character Trait of the Accused May Be Used to Prove That the Accused Did Not Commit the Crime
People v. Lewis, 25 Ill. 2d 442 (1962)

The defense may introduce reputation evidence for a particular character trait of the accused as substantive proof that he or she did not commit the crime. Such evidence shows that the accused acted consistently with this character trait. Here, the court found that defendant's character trait for chastity was relevant in a rape prosecution.

2. Guidelines Regarding Admissibility of Character Evidence of the Accused by the Prosecution and Method of Proof
People v. Lucas, 151 Ill. 2d 461 (1992)

The Illinois Supreme Court has set out the following guidelines for the admissibility of character evidence:

> The prosecution may not present evidence of a defendant's bad character until the defendant puts his character in issue by presenting evidence of good character. People v. Lewis, 25 Ill. 2d 442 (1962); People v. Barrow, 133 Ill. 2d 226 (1989). Where it is admissible, evidence of character is confined to proof of general reputation at or prior to the alleged offense. It should also be confined to a time not very remote from the date of the alleged offense. [. . .] Reputation evidence may not be based upon specific acts of either bad conduct or good conduct.

3. Limiting Admissibility of Character Evidence of the Alleged Victim
People v. Davis, 29 Ill. 2d 127 (1963)

Generally, evidence of the victim's character is not relevant. However, in a homicide prosecution, the defendant may introduce evidence of the victim's character for violence and "prior threats or misconduct." Two conditions must be present to justify admissibility of character evidence:

a. The defendant relies on self-defense, and

b. Preliminary independent evidence establishes that the deceased was the initial aggressor.

Here, defendant was on trial for the stabbing death of his friend that occurred in the defendant's apartment. The evidence against defendant was entirely circumstantial. Defendant claimed self-defense and sought to introduce evidence of a disagreement he and the victim had two nights prior to the stabbing during which defendant called the police to remove the victim from his apartment. The trial court did not allow this evidence. The Illinois Supreme Court held that the trial court improperly excluded the evidence because the "refusal to admit [the] evidence prevented defendant from fully developing his defense of self-defense, and constituted prejudicial and reversible error."

4. Defense May Introduce Evidence of Deceased's Character Trait for Temper and Disposition
People v. Stombaugh, 52 Ill. 2d 130 (1972)

The defense may introduce specific evidence of the deceased's temper and disposition, including prior threats directed at the defendant "to show the circumstances confronting the defendant, the extent of his apparent danger, and the motive by which he was influenced. Such circumstances are relevant in that they tend to show the defendant's state of mind. In this area of proof, the defendant should be given substantial latitude."

See also People v. Salcedo, 2011 IL App (1st) 083148 (finding evidence of victim's prior aggression against empty parked car irrelevant because it did not make it more probable that victim would deliberately drive into defendant's occupied moving vehicle).

5. Defendant Must Have Been Aware of Deceased's Violent Tendencies Unless There Is Conflicting Evidence Surrounding the Homicide

People v. Lynch, 104 Ill. 2d 194 (1984)

Admissibility of evidence of the deceased's character trait for violence under a claim of self-defense is conditioned on the defendant's actual knowledge of the victim's violent tendencies. This knowledge

> necessarily affects his perceptions of and reactions to the victim's behavior. The same deadly force that would be unreasonable in an altercation with a presumably peaceful citizen may be reasonable in response to similar behavior by a man of known violent and aggressive tendencies. One can only consider facts one knows, however, and evidence of the victim's character is irrelevant to this theory of self-defense unless the defendant knew of the victim's violent nature.

However, if the evidence surrounding the homicide is conflicting as to what happened, evidence of specific prior violent behavior by the victim is admissible, regardless whether the defendant knew of its existence. The court stated:

> In this situation, whether the defendant knew of this evidence at the time of the event is irrelevant. If the jurors could see for themselves exactly what the defendant saw at the time, such circumstantial evidence would be unnecessary. However, the evidence of what happened here, as is often the case where self-defense is raised, is both incomplete and conflicting . . . . To decide what really occurred the jury needed all the available facts, including evidence of [the victim's] prior [three] convictions for battery.

Evidence of the victim's character for violence may be established by proof of prior convictions for violent or aggressive conduct. Battery "is *prima facie* probative enough of aggressive and violent tendencies to be admissible."

6. Prosecutor's Limited Right to Introduce Evidence of Victim's Reputation for Nonviolence

People v. Whiters, 146 Ill. 2d 437 (1992)

The prosecutor has a limited right to introduce evidence of the victim's reputation for nonviolence. It is admissible in his or her rebuttal case after the introduction by the defense of evidence of the victim's character trait for violence. The Illinois Supreme Court held that prosecution may also put on reputation evidence of the victim's peaceful character where defendant attacks the victim's character in his opening statement.

7. Evidence Suggestive of Other Criminal Conduct Inadmissible If Irrelevant and Prejudicial

People v. Arman, 131 Ill. 2d 115 (1989)

The Illinois Supreme Court found that the trial court erroneously admitted evidence that the defendant was under police surveillance and that his mug shots were on file with the police department. Detective testified that he obtained defendant's mug shot before meeting him. Court held testimony inadmissible as evidence of other crimes because it informed the jury that defendant had been previously arrested. The Supreme Court, however, noted:

> The erroneous admission at trial of mug shot evidence suggesting the defendant's involvement in unrelated offenses does not automatically warrant reversal. People v. Lewis, 103 Ill. 2d 111, 118-19 (1984); People v. Warmack, 83 Ill. 2d 112, 128-29 (1980). When the competent evidence in the record establishes the defendant's guilt beyond a reasonable doubt and it can be

> concluded that retrial without the erroneous admission of the challenged evidence would produce no different result, the conviction may be affirmed. *Warmack*, 83 Ill. 2d at 128-29; People v. Tranowski, 20 Ill. 2d 11 (1960).

The court held that even though it was erroneous to admit such evidence, in this case the error did not rise to reversible error because evidence of guilt was overwhelming.

8. Evidence of Attempt Bribery May Be Admitted as Circumstantial Evidence of Guilt
People v. Gambony, 402 Ill. 74 (1949)

Evidence that is otherwise suggestive of other criminal conduct may be admitted as circumstantial evidence of guilt. Such evidence evinces consciousness of guilt. For instance, courts have held flight, attempted escape or escape, tampering with or destroying evidence, intimidating a witness, use of an alias, or suicide threat admissible in the past. Here, the court stated that

> evidence introduced must be relevant to the guilt or innocence of the accused and such rule is not violated by the admission of evidence that plaintiff in error attempted to suppress evidence against himself. Any attempt by a party to a suit, either civil or criminal, to conceal or, by threats or otherwise, to suppress evidence or obstruct an investigation of an issue, is relevant upon the trial of such issue. In a criminal prosecution any attempted intimidation of a witness is properly attributable to a consciousness of guilt, and testimony relating thereto is relevant and admissible in evidence.

The defendant attempted to bribe prosecution witnesses so that they would not testify at his indecent liberties with a child trial. The court held that evidence of the bribery was relevant as it tended to show defendant's consciousness of guilt.

> *See also* People v. Abernathy, 402 Ill. App. 3d 736 (4th Dist. 2010) (admitting evidence that defendant started a fire to destroy proof of a domestic battery to show consciousness of guilt).

9. Defendant's Use of a False Alibi Is Probative of his Consciousness of Guilt and May Be Admitted
People v. Milka, 211 Ill. 2d 150 (2004)

Defendant on trial for murder could not provide a consistent alibi for the time of victim's murder. Defendant provided various alibi but subsequently recanted and changed his story. The court stated that "[a] false exculpatory statement is 'probative of a defendant's consciousness of guilt[,]" and "a false alibi can be a factor in establishing guilt beyond a reasonable doubt."

10. Evidence of Flight or Avoidance of Arrest May Be Considered as Tending to Prove Guilt
People v. Lewis, 165 Ill. 2d 305 (1995)

"The fact of flight, when considered in connection with all other evidence in a case, is a circumstance which may be considered by the jury as tending to prove guilt." Here, the defendant argued that state failed to show that he had knowledge of the offense and that he may be a suspect in the case. The court disagreed, reasoning that defendant need not have "actual knowledge of his possible arrest," and that "evidence from which such fact may be inferred" suffices. Defendant packed up a duffel bag full of clothes and left behind majority of his belongings which supported the inference of flight. Defendant argued that he was not fleeing Illinois but was rather going to California to surrender. The court held that while the defendant has the right to explain his conduct, the jury could weigh the evidence and make its own conclusions as to whether he was fleeing or merely leaving to surrender in another state.

11. Evidence of Defendant's DNA on File with the State Database Relevant and Admissible to Prove Defendant's Connection to the Crime
People v. Jackson, 232 Ill. 2d 246 (2009)

The Illinois Supreme Court reversed the appellate court's decision to remand the defendant's first degree murder conviction, a decision that was based on a finding that the trial court had inappropriately admitted a conversation between the state's attorney and a DNA expert that revealed that the defendant's DNA was on file with the CODIS database, thereby suggesting other-crimes evidence. According to the appellate court, the collection and storage of DNA is a relatively new process and the public perception is that such databases are specifically associated with criminal activity and evidence that the defendant's sample was stored in a DNA database was more prejudicial than probative. The Supreme Court disagreed, finding that an inference of past criminal wrongdoing from the testimony was merely speculative as there are many DNA databases that are kept for reasons unrelated to criminal activity, even among the CODIS indexes. Additionally the court found that although the term CODIS is popular in television crime dramas as a means to identify suspects using DNA, to conclude that jurors would assume that the defendant's DNA profile was stored solely for criminal identification is unwarranted. According to the court, the testimony was not unduly prejudicial because it was limited to the fact that the defendant's DNA profile matched DNA in the CODIS database and was necessary to show the steps of the investigation, to explain the state's case, and to connect the defendant to the crime.

12. Evidence of Defendant's Gang Affiliation May Be Admissible to Show Motive
People v. Smith, 141 Ill. 2d 40 (1990)

The court noted that evidence of gang affiliation is admissible if relevant and related to the crime charged, despite the fact "that, particularly in metropolitan areas, there may be strong prejudice against street gangs." The court further noted that "[i]t is generally held that evidence indicating the defendant was a member of a gang or was involved in gang-related activity is admissible to show common purpose or design, or to provide a motive for an otherwise inexplicable act."

The state's evidence here was flawed. The state sought to prove that defendant's membership in the King Cobras gang motivated the murder of the victim, but the court found that there was no evidence showing that defendant was a member of the gang or that he knew the victim had an altercation with the gang leader. The only evidence linking defendant to the gang leader who had a disagreement with the victim was that he was once seen in the presence of the gang leader. The court excluded the "inflammatory evidence of gang-related activity offered to support the 'motive' theory" because the evidence was "of little probative value and could do little more than 'excite a suspicion of guilt' in the minds of the jurors."

For other cases discussing this topic, see

People v. Lucas, 151 Ill. 2d 461 (1992) (finding that evidence of defendant's gang membership was relevant to show motive for murder of correctional officer where it indicated that defendant attended a gang meeting to plan retaliation against administration of the prison).

People v. Weston, 2011 IL App (1st) 092432 (finding evidence of defendant's gang membership to explain his conduct irrelevant and prejudicial where another explanation for defendant's actions was much more plausible).

13. Evidence of Defendant's Gang Membership Admissible to Strengthen Victim's Identification of Defendant as Perpetrator
People v. Gonzalez, 142 Ill. 2d 481 (1991)

In order for gang evidence to be admissible, the state must present sufficient proof that gang membership or activity is related to the crime charged. Once the state establishes that gang evidence is related to the crime, the evidence is admissible as long as it is relevant to an issue in dispute and its probative value is not substantially outweighed by its prejudicial effect. Here, the victim identified the defendant as the perpetrator. The reliability of the victim's description of the defendant was the primary issue in the case, and the gang-related evidence presented by victim was therefore relevant to explain the circumstances leading up to the defendant's identification. Police showed the victim a book filled with pictures of gang members, and the victim identified defendant as the perpetrator. Defendant argued that the relevance of the evidence of his gang membership was far outweighed by its prejudice, but the court noted that just because the evidence may be prejudicial, "[a]n accused may not insulate the trier of fact from his gang membership where it is relevant to the determination of the case." Thus, in this case, the court found that the evidence aided in the identification issue.

14. Admissibility of Evidence of Defendant's Gang Affiliation Not Unduly Prejudicial Where Defendant Admitted to Being a Gang Member and Referred to Rival Gangs
People v. Johnson, 208 Ill. 2d 53 (2003)

The defendant appealed his convictions for first degree murder and aggravated discharge of a firearm claiming evidence of his gang membership was improperly admitted. The Illinois Supreme Court held that the evidence was relevant because the defendant himself referred to the incident as involving rival gangs and admitted to being part of a gang. The evidence was minimally prejudicial, and it may have worked to the defendant's benefit by showing that the prosecution's witness (a rival gang member) would have a motive to lie about the defendant's participation in the shooting.

15. Defendant Should Not Be Unreasonably Restricted in Proving Motive or Bias of State's Witnesses Through Their Gang Affiliation
People v. Blue, 205 Ill. 2d 1 (2001)

At the start of trial for first-degree murder, the trial court provisionally granted the state's motion *in limine* to bar any reference to gang affiliation, but later granted the motion *in limine*, stating that the court's intent "was not to allow the cross-examination of the state's witnesses as to gang activity and gang membership." On appeal, the defendant contended that such evidence was relevant to expose the witnesses' bias against him. On review, the court noted that the discretion to impose limits on cross-examination may only be exercised "after the court has permitted sufficient cross-examination to satisfy the confrontation clause." The court instructed that a trial judge must afford the defense "the widest latitude to establish the witnesses' bias or hostile motivation." The court concluded that the state's motion *in limine* unreasonably restricted the defendant's cross-examination of the state's witnesses regarding any bias that may have motivated their testimony. In this case gang affiliation was relevant to assess witness credibility. The court found that the error in granting the motion *in limine* was not harmless. Although the state's evidence was strong, it was not overwhelming and the witnesses' testimony was not cumulative to that of other witnesses.

16. Certain Issues Regarding Gang Evidence Must Be Presented by an Expert
People v. Langford, 234 Ill. App. 3d 855 (1st Dist. 1992)

Certain issues in connection with gang evidence must be presented by expert testimony, generally by a police officer. Generally, an officer will testify to gang hierarchy, drug sales, gang life, rules, violations, and behavior. Such testimony is proper when the officer is qualified as an expert, the testimony is relevant, and the prejudicial effect of the testimony does not outweigh its probative value. Use of excessive detail about gang life may be reversible error.

Here, a police detective qualified as an expert on gangs testified that the shootings and killings occurred as a direct result of a gang dispute over drug territory. The court found that the officer's 10 years of experience with gang activity qualified him as an expert and that his testimony was relevant to establishing the motive for the shootings.

17. Jurors Must Be Questioned Regarding Gang Bias Where Gang Evidence Is Integral to Defendant's Trial
People v. Strain, 194 Ill. 2d 467 (2000)

Where evidence of gang membership and gang-related activity is to be an "integral" part of a trial, the defendant is entitled to have the potential jurors questioned during *voir dire* as to any gang bias they may have. However, the trial court has no *sua sponte* duty to do so. The trial court is only required to do so when an appropriate question is tendered prior to *voir dire* and the circumstances of the case require the court to probe the issue.

Here, defendant challenged the trial court's *voir dire* of jury members as insufficient to glean gang bias. The trial court only asked prospective jurors whether they or any family members have had involvement with street gangs. The Supreme Court stated that even though a jury member has never been involved with a gang, he or she may still "hold a negative opinion on the subject of gangs." The Supreme Court concluded that "[b]ecause of the trial court's refusal to probe for gang bias, defendant was denied an informed and intelligent basis on which to assert challenges for cause or to exercise peremptory challenges."

18. *Strain* Rule Does not Apply Retroactively on Collateral Review
People v. Sanders, 238 Ill. 2d 391 (2010)

The rule announced in *Strain*, 194 Ill. 2d 467 (2000), requiring inquiry into gang bias during *voir dire* does not apply retroactively to collateral proceedings.

19. Related Evidence Generally Inadmissible at a Capital Sentencing Hearing
Dawson v. Delaware, 503 U.S. 159 (1992)

The United States Supreme Court held that the first and fourteenth amendments bar the use of gang membership evidence during a capital sentencing hearing when such evidence is irrelevant to proving any aggravating circumstance. However, the court held that the erroneous use of such evidence is subject to a harmless error analysis.

20. Gang Affiliation Evidence Is Admissible in Limited Situations in Illinois During Capital Sentencing Hearing
People v. Brown, 172 Ill. 2d 1 (1996)

The Illinois Supreme Court held that pursuant to *Dawson*, "evidence of gang affiliation is admissible during a capital sentencing hearing to show a defendant's behavior, violations, and discipline while in prison," as well as "to rebut mitigating evidence offered by a defendant."

Other Types of Evidence

Rule 406. Habit; Routine Practice

Evidence of the habit of a person or of the routine practice of an organization, whether corroborated or not and regardless of the presence of eyewitnesses, is relevant to prove that the conduct of the person or organization on a particular occasion was in conformity with the habit or routine practice.

Adopted September 27, 2010, eff. January 1, 2011.

Committee Commentary

(3) Modernization: Where there was no conflict with statutes or recent Illinois Supreme Court or Illinois Appellate Court decisions, and where it was determined to be beneficial and uniformly or almost uniformly accepted elsewhere, the Committee incorporated into the Illinois Rules of Evidence uncontroversial developments with respect to the law of evidence as reflected in the Federal Rules of Evidence and the 44 surveyed jurisdictions. [One of t]he 14 instances of modernization of note [is] as follows:

(2) Rule 406. Habit; Routine Practice. Rule 406 confirms the clear direction of prior Illinois law that evidence of the habit of a person or of the routine practice of an organization, whether corroborated or not and regardless of the presence of eyewitnesses, is relevant to prove that the conduct of the person or organization on a particular occasion was in conformity with the habit or routine practice.

ILL. R. EVID. Committee Commentary § 3, pg. 2.

AUTHOR'S COMMENTARY

Illinois Rule of Evidence 406 has adopted the language of Federal Rule of Evidence 406, in effect prior to its stylistic amendment on December 1, 2011. Gino L. DiVito, *The Illinois Rules of Evidence: A Color-Coded Guide Containing the New Rules, the Committee's General and Specific Comments, a Comparison with the Federal Rules of Evidence, and Additional Commentary* (*Including the Federal Rules of Evidence as Amended Effective December 1, 2011*) (Jan. 1, 2012), at 41, http://www.tdrlawfirm.com/assets/downloads/Illinois_Rules_of_Evidence_Color-Coded_Guide.pdf. The commentary to Federal Rule of Evidence 406 explains the definition of habit evidence and distinguishes it from character evidence as follows:

> Character and habit are close akin. Character is a generalized description of one's disposition, or of one's disposition in respect to a general trait, such as honesty, temperance, or peacefulness. 'Habit,' in modern usage, both lay and psychological, is more specific. It describes one's regular response to a repeated specific situation. If we speak of character for care, we think of the person's tendency to act prudently in all the varying situations of life, in business, family life, in handling automobiles and in walking across the street. A habit, on the other hand, is the person's regular practice of meeting a particular kind of situation with a specific type of conduct, such as the habit of going down a particular stairway two stairs at a time, or of giving the hand-signal for a left turn, or of alighting from railway cars while they are moving. The doing of the habitual acts may become semi-automatic. [MCCORMICK, § 162, p. 340]. ***
>
> Agreement is general that habit evidence is highly persuasive as proof of conduct on a particular occasion. Again quoting MCCORMICK § 162, p. 341:
>
>> Character may be thought of as the sum of one's habits though doubtless it is more than this. But unquestionably the uniformity of one's response to habit is far greater than the

> consistency with which one's conduct conforms to character or disposition. Even though character comes in only exceptionally as evidence of an act, surely any sensible man in investigating whether X did a particular act would be greatly helped in his inquiry by evidence as to whether he was in the habit of doing it.

When disagreement has appeared, its focus has been upon the question what constitutes habit, and the reason for this is readily apparent. The extent to which instances must be multiplied and consistency of behavior maintained in order to rise to the status of habit inevitably gives rise to differences of opinion. Lewan, Rationale of Habit Evidence, 16 SYRACUSE L. REV. 39, 49 (1964). While adequacy of sampling and uniformity of response are key factors, precise standards for measuring their sufficiency for evidence purposes cannot be formulated.

The rule is consistent with prevailing views. Much evidence is excluded simply because of failure to achieve the status of habit. [. . .] In Levin v. United States, 119 U.S. App. D.C. 156, 338 F.2d 265 (1964), testimony as to the religious "habits" of the accused, offered as tending to prove that he was at home observing the Sabbath rather than out obtaining money through larceny by trick, was held properly excluded:

> It seems apparent to us that an individual's religious practices would not be the type of activities which would lend themselves to the characterization of 'invariable regularity.' [1 WIGMORE 520.] Certainly the very volitional basis of the activity raises serious questions as to its invariable nature, and hence its probative value." *Id.* at 272.

FED. R. EVID. 406, Advisory Committee Notes.

Traditionally in Illinois, evidence of a habit was generally only used in civil cases. *See e.g.*, Hardware State Bank v. Cotner, 55 Ill. 2d 240 (1973); Applehans v. Jurgenson, 336 Ill. 427 (1929). However, the new Illinois Rule of Evidence 406 should apply to criminal cases because it is neutral on its face and mirrors Federal Rule of Evidence 406, which has been applied in criminal cases. *See e.g.*, Levin v. United States, 338 F.2d 265 (D.C. Cir. 1964). Moreover, pursuant to Illinois Rule of Evidence 1101, the Illinois Rules of Evidence apply to "proceedings in the courts of Illinois" subject to stated exceptions. Illinois Rule of Evidence 406 states no exceptions, and therefore, it is applicable to civil and criminal proceedings alike.

Illinois Rule of Evidence 406 has confirmed "the clear direction of prior Illinois law" that habit evidence is admissible "whether corroborated or not and regardless of the presence of eyewitnesses."

ILL. R. EVID. Committee Commentary § 3, pg. 2.

PRIOR ILLINOIS CASE LAW

1. Evidence of Victim's Habit Admissible Subject to Judicial Discretion Where Proper Foundation Is Established

People v. Keller, 267 Ill. App. 3d 602 (1st Dist. 1994)

In a case of first impression in a criminal prosecution, the First District of the Illinois Appellate Court held that evidence of habit is admissible where a proper foundation is laid and subject to the trial judge's discretion. The court declined to decide whether habit evidence should be limited to a situation where no eyewitnesses exist. The court reasoned that the history of admitting habit evidence was uncertain and inconsistent. However, it found the better rule to admit such evidence. Here, the trial court did not abuse its discretion in admitting evidence that the decedent had a habit of carrying large sums of money on his person and every night left $50 in the register drawer.

See also People v. El, 83 Ill. App. 3d 31 (1st Dist. 1980) (noting but not applying a "rule followed in some jurisdictions that evidence of personal habits is admissible in all cases to prove that one acted in conformity with those habits at the time in question. (*See, e.g.*, FED. R. EVID. 406).").

Rule 407. Reserved [Subsequent Remedial Measures]

Committee Commentary

(1) Codification: . . . [T]he Committee incorporated into the Illinois Rules of Evidence the current law of evidence in Illinois whenever the Illinois Supreme Court or the Illinois Appellate Court had clearly spoken on a principle of evidentiary law within the last 50 or so years. Thus, . . . [t]he Committee reserved Rule 407, related to subsequent remedial measures, because Appellate Court opinions are sufficiently in conflict concerning a core issue that is now under review by the Supreme Court.

ILL. R. EVID. Committee Commentary § 1, pg. 1.

AUTHOR'S COMMENTARY

The Special Supreme Court Committee on Evidence has reserved Illinois Rule of Evidence 407 pertaining to subsequent remedial measures because there is currently no consensus among appellate court decisions with respect to admissibility of the evidence of remedial measures taken "after manufacture of a product but prior to an injury or harm allegedly caused by that product." Jablonski v. Ford Motor Co., 2011 IL 110096 (Illinois Supreme Court found that it "need not address" the issue); Gino L. DiVito, *The Illinois Rules of Evidence: A Color-Coded Guide Containing the New Rules, the Committee's General and Specific Comments, a Comparison with the Federal Rules of Evidence, and Additional Commentary (Including the Federal Rules of Evidence as Amended Effective December 1, 2011)* (Jan. 1, 2012), at 41, http://www.tdrlawfirm.com/assets/downloads/Illinois_Rules_of_Evidence_Color-Coded_Guide.pdf; ILL. R. EVID. Committee Commentary § 1, pg. 1. By its very nature the principle advanced in Federal Rule of Evidence 407 should not be applied in criminal prosecutions. At least one United States District Court has interpreted Federal Rule of Evidence 407 as inapplicable in criminal cases. United States v. Gallagher, CRIM. 89-00272-03, 1990 WL 52722 (E.D. Pa. Apr. 24, 1990) (finding "no legal authority or policy reasons supporting application of Rule 407 in a criminal action, and conclud[ing] that it is inapplicable" in a case where remedial measures were taken to "redress the wrong actually committed" rather than measures that would have made commission of the crime 'less likely to occur.').

Rule 408. Compromise and Offers to Compromise

(a) Prohibited Uses. Evidence of the following is not admissible on behalf of any party, when offered to prove liability for, invalidity of, or amount of a claim that was disputed as to validity or amount, or to impeach through a prior inconsistent statement or contradiction:

(1) furnishing or offering or promising to furnish—or accepting or offering or promising to accept—a valuable consideration in compromising or attempting to compromise the claim; and

(2) conduct or statements made in compromise negotiations regarding the claim.

(b) Permitted Uses. This rule does not require the exclusion of any evidence otherwise discoverable merely because it is presented in the course of settlement negotiations. This rule also does not require exclusion if the evidence is offered for purposes not prohibited by subdivision (a). Examples of permissible purposes include proving a witness' bias or prejudice; negating an assertion of undue delay; establishing bad faith; and proving an effort to obstruct a criminal investigation or prosecution.

Adopted September 27, 2010, eff. January 1, 2011.

Committee Commentary

(3) Modernization: Where there was no conflict with statutes or recent Illinois Supreme Court or Illinois Appellate Court decisions, and where it was determined to be beneficial and uniformly or almost uniformly accepted elsewhere, the Committee incorporated into the Illinois Rules of Evidence uncontroversial developments with respect to the law of evidence as reflected in the Federal Rules of Evidence and the 44 surveyed jurisdictions. [One of t]he 14 instances of modernization of note [is] as follows: ***

> **(3) Rule 408. Compromise and Offers to Compromise.** Prior Illinois law did not preclude admissibility of statements made in compromise negotiations unless stated hypothetically. Because they were considered a trap for the unwary, Rule 408 makes such statements inadmissible without requiring the presence of qualifying language.
> ILL. R. EVID. Committee Commentary § 3, pg. 2.

AUTHOR'S COMMENTARY

Illinois Rule of Evidence 408 alters the prior Illinois common law rule that excluded from evidence hypothetical statements made during compromise negotiations because the rule was a "trap for the unwary." ILL. R. EVID. Committee Commentary § 3, pg. 2. Illinois Rule of Evidence 408(a) now precludes admissibility of all statements made during compromise negotiations "when offered to prove liability for, invalidity of, or amount of a claim that was disputed as to validity or amount, or to impeach through a prior inconsistent statement or contradiction," regardless of how they were formulated.

Illinois Rule of Evidence 408 has adopted Federal Rule of Evidence 408(a)(1), in effect prior to its stylistic amendment on December 1, 2011. Gino L. DiVito, *The Illinois Rules of Evidence: A Color-Coded Guide Containing the New Rules, the Committee's General and Specific Comments, a Comparison with the Federal Rules of Evidence, and Additional Commentary* (*Including the Federal Rules of Evidence as Amended Effective December 1, 2011*) (Jan. 1, 2012), at 42, http://www.tdrlawfirm.com/assets/downloads/Illinois_Rules_of_Evidence_Color-Coded_Guide.pdf. Prior Illinois common law excluded only actual offers to compromise and compromises achieved during settlement negotiations, but the new Illinois Rule of Evidence 408(a)(2), after adopting a portion of Federal Rule of Evidence 408(a)(2), now excludes even "conduct or statements" made in connection with such negotiations. Edward Edinger Co. v. Willis, 260 Ill. App. 106 (3d Dist. 1931); Hook v. Bunch, 180 Ill. App. 39 (4th Dist. 1913).

Illinois Rule of Evidence 408(a)(2) did not adopt that portion of Federal Rule of Evidence 408(a)(2) which allows admissibility of "statements made in compromise negotiations regarding the claim [. . .] when offered in a criminal case and the negotiations related to a claim by a public office or agency in the exercise of regulatory, investigative, or enforcement authority." DiVito, *Color-Coded Guide* at 42. This portion was added to Federal Rule of Evidence 408(a)(2) in a 2006 amendment. FED. R. EVID. 408, Advisory Committee Notes (2006 Amendment). Pursuant to the amended language, Federal Rule of Evidence 408(a)(2)

> does not prohibit the introduction in a criminal case of statements or conduct during compromise negotiations regarding a civil dispute by a government regulatory, investigative, or enforcement agency. *See, e.g.*, United States v. Prewitt, 34 F.3d 436, 439 (7th Cir. 1994) (admissions of fault made in compromise of a civil securities enforcement action were

> admissible against the accused in a subsequent criminal action for mail fraud). Where an individual makes a statement in the presence of government agents, its subsequent admission in a criminal case should not be unexpected. The individual can seek to protect against subsequent disclosure through negotiation and agreement with the civil regulator or an attorney for the government.
>
> Statements made in compromise negotiations of a claim by a government agency may be excluded in criminal cases where the circumstances so warrant under Rule 403. For example, if an individual was unrepresented at the time the statement was made in a civil enforcement proceeding, its probative value in a subsequent criminal case may be minimal. But there is no absolute exclusion imposed by Rule 408.
>
> In contrast, statements made during compromise negotiations of other disputed claims are not admissible in subsequent criminal litigation, when offered to prove liability for, invalidity of, or amount of those claims.
>
> FED. R. EVID. 408, Advisory Committee Notes (2006 Amendment).

Prior to the 2006 amendment to Federal Rule of Evidence 408, "federal appellate courts were sharply divided over whether in criminal cases [Federal] Rule [of Evidence] 408 required the exclusion of statements made in compromise negotiations over civil claims." Robert A. Weninger, *Amended Federal Rule of Evidence 408: Trapping the Unwary*, 26 REV. LITIG. 401, 417 (2007). The United States Court of Appeals for the Seventh Circuit unequivocally found that the general exclusionary provision of Federal Rule of Evidence 408(a) did not apply to criminal cases, concluding that criminal defendant's statements to government authorities during settlement negotiations of a prior civil claim were admissible in a subsequent criminal prosecution. United States v. Prewitt, 34 F.3d 436, 439 (7th Cir. 1994). The adoption of the "partial exception for criminal cases" in Federal Rule of Evidence 408(a)(2), showed that the rule thereafter applied "to both civil and criminal litigation," United States v. Roti, 484 F.3d 934, 936 (7th Cir. 2007). Illinois, however, has not adopted the amended Federal Rule of Evidence 408(a)(2). *See* DiVito, *Color-Coded Guide* at 43. Illinois Rule of Evidence 408(a) therefore does not apply in criminal cases.

Illinois Rule of Evidence 408(b) differs from the Federal Rule of Evidence 408(b) in that it has added a statement that clarifies that evidence used during settlement negotiations that is "otherwise discoverable" is not shielded from disclosure simply because it was used during the negotiations. DiVito, *Color-Coded Guide* at 43. Federal Rule of Evidence 408 no longer contains this reference because it had been "deleted as superfluous." FED. R. EVID. 408, Advisory Committee Notes (2006 Amendment). The Advisory Committee Note states, however, that "even without the sentence, the Rule cannot be read to protect pre-existing information simply because it was presented to the adversary in compromise negotiations." FED. R. EVID. 408, Advisory Committee Notes (2006 Amendment).

Illinois Rule of Evidence 408(b), unlike Federal Rule of Evidence 408(b), allows the use of statements made during settlement negotiations to establish bad faith. DiVito, *Color-Coded Guide* at 43. Evidence of statements made in connection with settlement offers is also admissible under Illinois Rule of Evidence 408(b) when such evidence is offered to prove "witness' bias or prejudice," to negate "an assertion of undue delay," to establish bad faith, and to prove "an effort to obstruct a criminal investigation or prosecution." Federal Rule of Evidence 408(a)(2) likewise does not exclude statements made in an attempt to "'buy off' a complaining party" in federal criminal cases where "proving an effort to obstruct a criminal investigation or prosecution." FED. R. EVID. 408, Advisory Committee Notes (1972 Proposed Rule); United States v. Davis, 596 F.3d 852, 858 (D.C. Cir. 2010). The commentary to Federal Rule of Evidence 408 explains that

> [s]ince the rule excludes only when the purpose is proving the validity or invalidity of the claim or its amount, an offer for another purpose is not within the rule. [. . .] An effort to "buy off" the prosecution or a prosecuting witness in a criminal case is not within the policy of the rule of exclusion. McCORMICK § 251, p. 542.
>
> FED. R. EVID. 408, Advisory Committee Notes (1972 Proposed Rule).

Prior Illinois common law rule states that evidence of party's efforts "to conceal or, by threats or otherwise, to suppress evidence or obstruct an investigation of an issue, is relevant upon the trial of such issue." People v. Gambony, 402 Ill. 74 (1949) (admitting evidence of criminal defendant's attempt "to negotiate a settlement through bribery"); *but see* United States v. Davis, 596 F.3d 852, 858 (D.C. Cir. 2010) (interpreting amended Federal Rule of Evidence 408; finding that lower court abused its discretion in admitting evidence of a criminal defendant's offer to settle with a private party prior to the initiation of a criminal investigation because the offer was used to prove liability rather than to show an effort to obstruct a criminal investigation).

PRIOR ILLINOIS CASE LAW

1. Evidence That a Party Attempted to Obstruct an Investigation by Offering to Reach a Settlement Through Bribery Is Relevant and Admissible

People v. Gambony, 402 Ill. 74 (1949)

Defendant was charged with indecent liberties with a child and contributing to the delinquency of a minor. He contended on appeal that the trial court allowed inadmissible evidence pertaining to his alleged efforts to bribe certain state witnesses "to drop the case or testify in his favor." The Supreme Court disagreed, noting that the evidence showing that defendant attempted

> to negotiate a settlement through bribery [was admissible]. This evidence was proper and relevant as tending to show consciousness of guilt. This comes within the rule announced in the cases of People v. Bloom, 370 Ill. 144 (1938), People v. Borella, 362 Ill. 218 (1935), and People v. Tokoly, 313 Ill. 177 (1924), in which we held that all evidence introduced must be relevant to the guilt or innocence of the accused and such rule is not violated by the admission of evidence that plaintiff in error attempted to suppress evidence against himself. Any attempt by a party to a suit, either civil or criminal, to conceal or, by threats or otherwise, to suppress evidence or obstruct an investigation of an issue, is relevant upon the trial of such issue. In a criminal prosecution any attempted intimidation of a witness is properly attributable to a consciousness of guilt, and testimony relating thereto is relevant and admissible in evidence. *Bloom*, 370 Ill. 144; People v. Spaulding, 309 Ill. 292 (1923).

2. Evidence of Statements Made in Connection with Settlement Offers Is Admissible When Used to Prove Witness Bias or Prejudice

Batteast v. Wyeth Laboratories, Inc., 137 Ill. 2d 175 (1990)

A minor and his parents filed suit against a physician and a hospital for negligence and willful and wanton misconduct in their treatment of the minor patient who was injured by an overdose from a drug. The family also sued the manufacturer of the drug. The two lawsuits were consolidated. The family settled with the physician and the hospital. In the settlement agreement, the physician agreed that he would not "color, alter, or otherwise deviate from" his deposition testimony and that he would "vigorously continue to defend himself." The trial court entered an order *in limine* that prevented the manufacturer from cross-examining the physician about potential bias created by his settlement agreement with the plaintiffs. The manufacturer claimed on appeal that the physician "purchased a limitation on his own liability as long as he testified in accord with the agreement, and that it was error not to allow this bias to be brought to the attention of the jury." Plaintiffs argued that the agreement was neutral because either side could call the physician to testify and he would testify only consistently with his prior deposition. The Illinois Supreme Court disagreed with the plaintiffs' contention, explaining that

> [t]he Illinois position on this point is well established. If an extrajudicial agreement has the potential to bias a witness' testimony as to a relevant issue, disclosure is necessary to maintain the fairness and integrity of our judicial system. Tu Hou Lam v. Lynch Machinery Division of Lynch Corp., 178 Ill. App. 3d 229 (1988). *See* Gatto v. Walgreen Drug Co., 61 Ill. 2d 513 (1975); Pierce v. Commonwealth Edison Co., 101 Ill. App. 3d 272 (1981). We are not impressed with plaintiffs' contention that the agreement was neutral. [The physician] agreed to testify in a certain way, the same way he had testified in his deposition. Because plaintiffs imposed this term on the release, it was obviously the way they desired him to testify. A failure to comply with this undertaking would render him potentially liable to the plaintiffs for additional damages. Only the plaintiffs could enforce this agreement. The deposition itself had been taken before [the manufacturer] had been made a party, and, accordingly, [it] could not cross-examine the doctor at that time. This agreement clearly had a potential to affect and bias [the physician's] testimony, and the jury should have had the opportunity to take that fact into account in assessing his credibility. This error is of the utmost significance because the testimony of [the physician] is essential to the plaintiffs' position on proximate cause. This fact alone requires that the case be retried.

Rule 409. Payment of Medical and Similar Expenses

In addition to the provisions of section 8-1901 of the Code of Civil Procedure (735 ILCS 5/8-1901), evidence of furnishing or offering or promising to pay medical, hospital, or similar expenses occasioned by an injury is not admissible to prove liability for the injury.

Adopted September 27, 2010, eff. January 1, 2011.

(6) Referenced Statutes: Numerous existing statutes, the validity of which are not affected by promulgation of the Illinois Rules of Evidence, ILL. R. EVID. 101, relate in one form or another to the law of evidence. The Committee felt it was inappropriate, unnecessary and unwise to refer specifically to the abundance of statutory authority in an Appendix or otherwise. Reference is, however, made in the body of the text of the Illinois Rules of Evidence to certain statutes by citation or verbatim incorporation. Such references and the reasons therefor are as follows: ***

> **(3) Rule 409**: The parallel protection afforded by 735 ILCS 5/8-1901 with respect to payment of medical or similar expenses is specifically referenced in Rule 409 to preclude any possibility of conflict.
> ILL. R. EVID. Committee Commentary § 3, pg. 8.

AUTHOR'S COMMENTARY

Illinois legislature enacted 735 ILCS 5/8-1901 with the intent to prohibit the use of an offer to pay the medical bills of an injured person as an admission of liability for that injury. The statute evidences a public policy aimed at "encouraging assistance to an injured party." Sawicki v. Kim, 112 Ill. App. 3d 641 (2d Dist. 1983). Illinois Rule of Evidence 409 has incorporated section 8-1901. ILL. R. EVID. Committee Commentary § 3, pg. 8. Illinois Rule of Evidence 409 mirrors Federal Rule of Evidence 409, in effect prior to its stylistic amendment on December 1, 2011, except for the Illinois rule's reference to 735 ILCS 5/8-

1901. The Illinois statutory law was limited to civil cases. Illinois Rule of Evidence 409 does not apply to criminal cases, although there is some evidence that the language of Federal Rule of Evidence 409 may be "broad enough to cover proof of criminal liability," even though "common law decisions all involve the use of the evidence to establish civil liability." CHARLES ALAN WRIGHT & KENNETH W. GRAHAM, 23 FEDERAL PRACTICE & PROCEDURE, EVIDENCE § 5328 (1999) (Current through the 2011 Supplement).

RELEVANT STATUTORY AUTHORITY

Admission of Liability—Effect: 735 ILCS 5/8-1901

Sec. 8-1901. Admission of liability—Effect. The providing of, or payment for, medical, surgical, hospital, or rehabilitation services, facilities, or equipment by or on behalf of any person, or the offer to provide, or pay for, any one or more of the foregoing, shall not be construed as an admission of any liability by such person or persons. Testimony, writings, records, reports or information with respect to the foregoing shall not be admissible in evidence as an admission of any liability in any action of any kind in any court or before any commission, administrative agency, or other tribunal in this State, except at the instance of the person or persons so making any such provision, payment or offer.

> (Text of Section without the changes made by P.A. 94-677, which has been held unconstitutional in Lebron v. Gottlieb Memorial Hosp., 237 Ill. 2d 217 (2010), based on the act's inseverability provision. In *Lebron*, the Illinois Supreme Court does not discuss the principles embodied in section 5/8-1901. Changes proposed by 2011 Illinois House Bill No. 2887 (Feb. 22, 2011)).

Rule 410. Inadmissibility of Pleas, Plea Discussions, and Related Statements

Except as otherwise provided in this rule, evidence of the following is not admissible in any criminal proceeding against the defendant who made the plea or was a participant in the plea discussions:

(1) a plea of guilty which was later withdrawn;
(2) a plea of nolo contendere;
(3) any statement made in the course of any proceedings under Illinois Supreme Court Rule 402 regarding either of the foregoing pleas; or
(4) any statement made in the course of plea discussions which do not result in a plea of guilty or which result in a plea of guilty later withdrawn.

However, such a statement is admissible (i) in any proceeding wherein another statement made in the course of the same plea or plea discussions has been introduced and the statement ought in fairness be considered contemporaneously with it, or (ii) in a criminal proceeding for perjury or false statement if the statement was made by the defendant under oath, on the record and in the presence of counsel.

Adopted September 27, 2010, eff. January 1, 2011.

AUTHOR'S COMMENTARY

The new Illinois Rule of Evidence 410 supersedes prior Illinois Supreme Court Rule 402(f). The Illinois Supreme Court previously adopted Supreme Court Rule 402(f) to address the inadmissibility of plea discussions and agreements. The commentary to the new Illinois Rules of Evidence states that "[w]here redundancy exists between a rule contained in the Illinois Rules of Evidence and another Illinois Supreme Court rule, reference should be made solely to the appropriate Illinois rule of evidence." ILL. R. EVID. Committee Commentary § 7, pg. 9. It appears that rule 410 has incorporated rule 402(f), resulting in the

Supreme Court rule's redundancy. MICHAEL H. GRAHAM, GRAHAM'S HANDBOOK OF ILLINOIS EVIDENCE § 410.1, i (10th ed. 2010); Gino L. DiVito, *The Illinois Rules of Evidence: A Color-Coded Guide Containing the New Rules, the Committee's General and Specific Comments, a Comparison with the Federal Rules of Evidence, and Additional Commentary (Including the Federal Rules of Evidence as Amended Effective December 1, 2011)* (Jan. 1, 2012), at 45, http://www.tdrlawfirm.com/assets/downloads/Illinois_Rules_of_Evidence_Color-Coded_Guide.pdf. Reference should thus now be made solely to the Illinois Rule of Evidence 410.

RELEVANT ILLINOIS SUPREME COURT RULES

Illinois Supreme Court Rule 402(f)

Plea Discussions, Plea Agreements, Pleas of Guilty Inadmissible Under Certain Circumstances. If a plea discussion does not result in a plea of guilty, or if a plea of guilty is not accepted or is withdrawn, or if judgment on a plea of guilty is reversed on direct or collateral review, neither the plea discussion nor any resulting agreement, plea, or judgment shall be admissible against the defendant in any criminal proceeding.

> **Committee Comments.** Paragraph (f) adopts the prevailing view that once a guilty plea has been annulled by withdrawal or other means, it should not be subsequently admissible against the defendant in criminal proceedings. (*See* People v. Haycraft (1966), 76 Ill. App. 2d 149, 221 N.E.2d 317.) It follows that a plea discussion which has not resulted in a still-effective guilty plea should likewise be inadmissible, for otherwise defendants could engage in plea discussions only at their peril.
> Adopted June 26, 1970, effective July 1, 1997.

PRIOR ILLINOIS CASE LAW

1. Illinois Supreme Court Rule 402(f) Does Not Apply to Statements Made *After* Plea Agreement Has Been Accepted and Entered

People v. Connery, 296 Ill. App. 3d 384 (3d Dist. 1998)

Defendant confessed to his participation in a murder in a video-taped statement. Defendant then entered into a plea agreement requiring him to testify against his co-defendant in exchange for a 55-year sentence. During the plea bargain hearing, defendant affirmed that his confession was truthful and voluntary. Trial court accepted the agreement. Defendant did not testify at his co-defendant's trial and sought to withdraw his guilty plea, but the trial court denied his request. State argued that it was not required to uphold the plea bargain since defendant did not testify at his co-defendant's trial. The trial court then permitted defendant to withdraw his guilty plea. At trial, defendant repudiated his video-taped confession and state impeached him with his testimony from the plea bargain hearing. Defendant argued that it was error to admit the statements he made during the plea bargain hearing, but the court disagreed. It found that rule 402(f) does not extend to a defendant's statements at the plea hearing *after* the plea has been entered and accepted by the court because:

> the central policy behind Rule 402(f) is to prevent a jury from hearing of any statements made by a defendant during the process of attempting to reach a plea agreement, or the fact that a defendant had reached an agreement to plead guilty. Since the plea bargain process is completed when the plea is entered, statements made after an agreement has been reached and the plea has been entered are not covered by Rule 402(f). *See*, People v. Bennett, 222 Ill. App. 3d 188, 198 (1991).

2. Determination of Whether a Statement Is Plea-Related
People v. Friedman, 79 Ill. 2d 341 (1980)

The determination of whether a statement is plea-related and therefore protected by Supreme Court Rule 402(f), or merely an independent admission of the accused, which is not protected by the rule, is a factual one. In making that evaluation, Illinois courts apply a two-pronged subjective-objective test:

> [T]he boundaries of our rule must of necessity be delineated in relation to the reasonable expectations of the accused at the time the statement was made. In construing similar provisions of Rule 410 of the Federal Rules of Evidence and Rule 11(e)(6) of the Federal Rules of Criminal Procedure, the Federal courts have considered, first, whether the accused exhibited a subjective expectation to negotiate a plea, and, second, whether this expectation was reasonable under the totality of the objective circumstances, as relevant to the inquiry of whether a particular statement is plea related. [Citation omitted.] Because of the substantial similarity in the purpose of the Federal rules, we find this analysis equally applicable to the determination of when a statement is plea related under our rule. The characterization of a statement as plea related, and therefore inadmissible under Rule 402(f), must necessarily turn on the facts of each case.

Here, the accused asked an investigator from the Attorney General's office about "making a deal" and further stated general terms of a deal that he would be willing to accept. The court held that such statements were plea-related and therefore inadmissible because they were made during a "negotiation process." The court further noted that it

> [could not] agree that the parties must be seated at the negotiating table before our rule applies. A statement made as an offer to enter negotiation is indistinguishable from a statement made at an advanced stage of the negotiation process in terms of its impact upon a jury. Statements related to either stage of this process are equally devastating in the trial of the accused. In determining whether a statement is plea related, we do not require "a preamble explicitly demarcating the beginning of plea discussions." United States v. Herman, 544 F.2d 791, 797 (5th Cir. 1977). But where a preamble is delivered, such as defendant's inquiry related to "making a deal" in the present case, it cannot be ignored. See United States v. Brooks, 536 F.2d 1137 (6th Cir. 1976). This is a clear indication of defendant's intent to pursue plea negotiations. We find that defendant's unsolicited statement was a plea-related discussion and therefore inadmissible under Rule 402(f).

Rule 402(f) thus protects plea-related statements whether they are made during formal negotiations between counsel, or in an informal dialogue between the defendant and a representative of the state, such as an assistant state's attorney, assistant attorney general, investigator, or police officer. Whether the person to whom such a statement is made has actual authority to enter plea negotiations is but one factor a court must weigh in the equation. But the fact that this person does not have the actual authority to enter plea negotiations does not automatically render the statement admissible.

3. Defendant's Perception of the Agent's Negotiating Power Is Relevant to the Determination of the Existence of Plea Bargaining
People v. Hill, 78 Ill. 2d 465 (1980)

The Illinois Supreme Court emphasized that rule 402(f) ensures that "plea discussions may be conducted in an atmosphere of candor, free of the risk that statements made during negotiations will be used as evidence of guilt . . . ." Generally, it protects the defendant from the "devastating" effect of introducing the evidence of a withdrawn plea of guilty, a rejected plea of guilty, an offer to plead guilty, or a preliminary statement made as an offer to enter plea negotiations. Such evidence is not relevant as a matter of law, and it cannot be used substantively or for impeachment purposes.

Defendant was on trial for murder and conspiracy to commit murder after an individual solicited him to murder the victim. Defendant first murdered the wrong person but then finished the job by killing the intended victim as well. Defendant admitted to the crimes during discussion with the Assistant State's Attorney after asking to see "the head man" to "talk a deal." Assistant State's Attorney refused the defendant's offer. State introduced evidence concerning the defendant's admissions and defendant moved to exclude all testimony regarding the conversation as it involved his offer to plead guilty. State argued that the defendant's statements were admissible because the Assistant State's Attorney had no authority to conduct a plea bargaining negotiation. The court rejected the argument and noted that

> [t]he relevant factor is a defendant's perception of the government official's negotiating authority, not the official's actual authority. The twin goals of encouraging unrestrained plea negotiations and assuring fairness to defendants dictate that any statements made by a defendant as part of an effort to reach a plea agreement must be excluded; it makes no difference that the defendant's efforts are misguided because the official cannot or will not accept the offer. (quoting United States v. Herman, 544 F.2d 791 (5th Cir. 1977)).

4. Illinois Supreme Court Rule 402(f) Does Not Bar "Mere Offers to Cooperate"
People v. Hart, 214 Ill. 2d 490 (2005)

Detective testified that he advised defendant of his rights during an interview and stated that he knew that the defendant had participated in an armed robbery. Defendant responded by asking what the detective could do for him if he cooperated. During closing argument, the prosecutor told the jury that the defendant was seeking some leniency via cooperation and that "only guilty men want to know what they get if they cooperate." Defense counsel did not object to either statement, and the defendant was convicted of armed robbery and aggravated fleeing or attempting to elude a police officer. On appeal, the Supreme Court of Illinois stated that Supreme Court Rule 402(f) was not intended to bar "mere offers to cooperate with the police." Instead, offers to cooperate must be accompanied by "rudiments of the negotiation process" to constitute negotiations. Here, the defendant did not ask for the detective to make contact with the state's attorney, did not say how he would cooperate, nor did he discuss pleading guilty. Therefore, the testimony of the detective and the prosecutor's closing argument did not violate Rule 402(f).

See also People v. Rivera, 409 Ill. App. 3d 122 (1st Dist. 2011), *appeal allowed*, 955 N.E.2d 478 (Ill. 2011) (finding that more than "mere offer to cooperate" occurred where defendant discussed a possible deal with assistant state's attorney and offered to confess in exchange for a specific sentence).

5. Circumstances May Indicate That It Is Not Objectively Reasonable for Defendant to Believe He or She Is Engaged in Plea Negotiations
People v. Jones, 219 Ill. 2d 1 (2006)

A jury convicted the defendant of first degree murder. While the defendant was in custody, he made several statements to law enforcement officials. On August 15, 1994, the defendant gave and signed a written statement to detectives outlining the terms he would be willing to accept if he were allowed to plead guilty. The detectives directed the defendant to do so and informed him that the statement was for the state's attorney. The defendant also made recorded statements to law enforcement officers on July 27 and August 16. The trial court admitted each of the statements in evidence. The defendant appealed, and the appellate court remanded the case for a new trial because the August 15 statement contained the "rudiments of the negotiation process," and therefore, it was inadmissible as a plea related statement. A jury in the second trial convicted the defendant. At the second trial, the court admitted the defendant's other two statements from July 27 and August 16. Once again the defendant appealed, and this time the appellate court affirmed.

On appeal to the Illinois Supreme Court, the defendant argued that the trial court had erred in admitting the statements from July 27 and August 16 because they were plea related. The court discussed its earlier cases which had held that the rudiments of negotiation must be present in order for a statement to be plea related. Also, it must be objectively reasonable for the accused to believe that he or she was engaged in plea related negotiations. The court determined that the totality of circumstances here indicated that it was not objectively reasonable for the defendant to believe that he was engaged in plea negotiations. During the two statements in question, the defendant did not give information to strike a deal; he did not confess to the murder; his statements were not prompted by a desire to seek leniency. Instead the defendant made exculpatory statements seeking to exonerate himself from the murder. In the two statements the defendant did not indicate a desire to plead guilty, nor did the detectives lead the defendant to believe that they could make a plea deal for him. The court concluded that nothing in the record showed that the statements of July 27 and August 16 were plea related, therefore, the court held that the statements were admissible.

6. Defendant's Knowing and Voluntary Waiver of Exclusionary Provisions of Plea-Statement Rules Is Enforceable; Statements May Be Used as Impeachment Evidence
United States v. Mezzanatto, 513 U.S. 196 (1995)

The United States Supreme Court held that defendant's statements made during plea discussions on federal drug charges could be used against him for impeachment purposes at his subsequent trial for those charges where bargaining failed and defendant knowingly and voluntarily waived their use. Plea discussions are generally inadmissible under Federal Rule of Evidence 410 and Federal Rule of Civil Procedure 11(e)(6). The Supreme Court reasoned that inadmissibility could be waived. First, the Court has consistently held that a broad array of constitutional and statutory provisions, although containing no express waiver clause, are presumed to be waivable. Second, the Court has consistently found that the Federal Rules of Civil Procedure are presumptively waivable. Third, evidentiary rules have specifically been held waivable. In sum, the Court held "[b]ecause the plea-statement Rules were enacted against a background presumption that legal rights generally, and evidentiary provisions specifically, are subject to waiver by voluntary agreement of the parties, we will not interpret Congress' silence as an implicit rejection of waivability."

The Court rejected all three challenges to waivability. First, defendant argued that the Rules provide a "guarantee [to] fair trial procedure" that is not waivable. In rejecting this argument, the Court found that waiver would "enhance[] the truth-seeking function of trials and will result in more accurate verdicts." Thus, instead of undermining the fact-finding process, it will improve it. The Court further found that the Rules were "a privilege of the defendant" which could be waived or varied at the parties' request. This is evidenced by the fact that the Rules allow the accused to offer such statements for his or her own benefit. "Thus the plea-statement Rules expressly contemplate a degree of party control that is consonant with the background presumption of waivability."

Next, defendant argued that waiver was inconsistent with the purpose of the Rules which was to encourage voluntary statements. Although the Ninth Circuit below viewed the claim from the perspective of accused persons and that they would lose out, the Supreme Court looked to the prosecutors' side finding they too may be discouraged from entering negotiations if waiver were not allowed. Thus, this would defeat the Rules. "If prosecutors were precluded from securing such agreements, they might well decline to enter into cooperation discussions in the first place and might never take this potential first step toward a plea bargain." Additionally:

> A sounder way to encourage settlement is to permit the interested parties to enter into knowing and voluntary negotiations without any arbitrary limits on their bargaining chips. To use the Ninth Circuit's metaphor, if the prosecutor is interested in 'buying' the reliability assurance that accompanies a waiver agreement, then precluding waiver can only stifle the market for plea bargains. A defendant can 'maximize' what he has to 'sell' only if he is permitted to offer what the prosecutor is most interested in buying. And while it is certainly true that prosecutors often need help from the small fish in the conspiracy in order to catch the big ones, that is no reason to preclude waiver altogether. If prosecutors decide that certain crucial information will be gained only by preserving the inadmissibility of plea statements, they will agree to leave intact the exclusionary provisions of the plea-statement Rules.

Finally, defendant argued that waiver would invite prosecutorial overreaching and abuse. The Court stated: "[t]he mere potential for abuse of prosecutorial bargaining power is an insufficient basis for foreclosing negotiation altogether." Moreover, the Court believed that a majority of prosecutors would act in good faith and not abuse their power.

In conclusion, the Court stated that the appropriate response to defendant's concern for abuse "is to permit case-by-case inquiries into whether waiver agreements are the product of fraud or coercion. We hold that absent some affirmative indication that the agreement was entered into unknowingly or involuntarily, an agreement to waive the exclusionary provisions of the plea-statements Rules is valid and enforceable."

7. Use of Defendant's Prior Guilty Plea in a Subsequent Prosecution for Victim's Death Permissible

People v. Williams, 188 Ill. 2d 365 (1999)

The court upheld the use of defendant's prior guilty plea for attempted murder in a subsequent murder prosecution following the victim's death some years later. The court concluded that a "direct consequence" of the guilty plea was not its subsequent use in evidence at a murder trial. Direct consequences were limited to the "penal consequence[s] of that plea." The subsequent use in a murder prosecution had nothing to do with defendant's sentence following his guilty plea for attempted murder. The Supreme Court noted that both the trial court and the appellate court overlooked the "narrow definition of a direct consequence of a guilty plea as relating to the sentence imposed on the plea."

Rule 411. Liability Insurance

Evidence that a person was or was not insured against liability is not admissible upon the issue whether the person acted negligently or otherwise wrongfully. This rule does not require the exclusion of evidence of insurance against liability when offered for another purpose, such as proof of agency, ownership, or control, or bias or prejudice of a witness.

Adopted September 27, 2010, eff. January 1, 2011.

AUTHOR'S COMMENTARY

Prior Illinois common law excluded evidence in civil cases pertaining to a person's coverage or lack of coverage by liability insurance as irrelevant on the issue of his or her negligence or wrongful conduct. Kavanaugh v. Parret, 379 Ill. 273 (1942). Illinois Rule of

Evidence 411 has retained this common law exclusion and has adopted the language of the Federal Rule of Evidence 411 which was in effect until its stylistic amendment on December 1, 2011. Gino L. DiVito, *The Illinois Rules of Evidence: A Color-Coded Guide Containing the New Rules, the Committee's General and Specific Comments, a Comparison with the Federal Rules of Evidence, and Additional Commentary* (*Including the Federal Rules of Evidence as Amended Effective December 1, 2011*) (Jan. 1, 2012), at 46, http://www.tdrlawfirm.com/assets/downloads/Illinois_Rules_of_Evidence_Color-Coded_Guide.pdf.

Illinois Rule of Evidence 411 is generally not applicable in criminal cases. One author has raised the issue of the applicability of Federal Rule of Evidence 411 in criminal prosecutions involving arson for liability insurance proceeds. STEPHEN A. SALTZBURG ET AL., 1 FEDERAL RULES OF EVIDENCE MANUAL § 411, pg. 651 (7th ed. 1998). Professor Saltzburg has concluded that the policy behind Federal Rule of Evidence 411 does not require courts to bar evidence of liability insurance because the evidence is not used "to prove that a person acted 'wrongfully,'" but rather to show that its existence "tended to make a particular individual take a specific action in an effort to take advantage of that insurance policy." *Id.*

PRIOR ILLINOIS CASE LAW

Evidence of Liability Insurance Is Generally Irrelevant and Inadmissible

Kavanaugh v. Parret, 379 Ill. 273 (1942)

Plaintiff in a personal injury case arising out of a collision of an automobile with a bicycle filed an affidavit out of the presence of the jury that showed that defendant had liability insurance. The plaintiff, with the trial court's permission, questioned jurors whether any of them were insured by that insurance company. The Illinois Supreme Court found that the question posed to the jurors was improper in that its

> only effect [. . .] was to advise the jury that the insurance company was making the defense and was liable for the payment of any judgment rendered.
>
> ***
>
> As announced in Mithen v. Jeffery, 259 Ill. 372 (1913), Smithers v. Henriquez, 368 Ill. 588 (1938), and Edwards v. Hill-Thomas Lime & Cement Co., 378 Ill. 180 (1941), it is improper to inform the jury, either directly or indirectly, that the defendant is insured against liability on a judgment that may be entered against him in the trial of the case. [. . .]
>
> ***
>
> In this case it is clear from the record that the question put not only was not necessary to plaintiff's right to a fair trial but could serve only to prejudice the defendant. It is a matter of common knowledge that ofttimes casualty insurance policies cover only a portion of the liability arising on a judgment entered against the insured. Whether the defendant has someone to help him pay a judgment, if one is rendered against him, has nothing to do with the case on trial, and to bring it into the lawsuit is to import an influence having nothing to do with the merits of the case and designed only to aid the plaintiff at the expense of the defendant. It would be no more unfair to show that plaintiff is insured, either by contract with his attorney, or otherwise, against the payment of any costs or attorney's fees, in case he loses. Neither makes for a fair and just trial of the lawsuit and neither should be permitted.

Chapter 3

Article V – Privileges

Rule 501. General Rule

Principles as Interpreted by the Illinois Courts

Attorney-Client Privilege: Common Law Rule in Illinois

Marital Privilege: 725 ILCS 5/115-16

Physician-Patient Privilege: 735 ILCS 5/8-802

Therapist-Patient Privilege: 740 ILCS 110/10

Rape Crisis Counselor Privilege: 735 ILCS 5/8-802.1

Domestic Violence Counselor or Advocate Privilege: 750 ILCS 60/227 & 750 ILCS 60/227.1

Privilege for Statements Made by Victims of Violent Crimes to Counselors of Such Victims: 735 ILCS 5/8-802.2

Licensed Clinical Social Workers' Privilege: 225 ILCS 20/16

Genetic Counselor's Privilege: 225 ILCS 135/90

Clergy Privilege: 735 ILCS 5/8-803

Accountant's Privilege: 225 ILCS 450/27

Reporter's Privilege: 735 ILCS 5/8-901

Parent-Child Privilege

Governmental Privileges

Secret Surveillance Location Privilege

Informant's Privilege: 735 ILCS 5/8-802.3

Interpreter's Privilege: 735 ILCS 5/8-911

Interpreter for the Deaf and Hard of Hearing Privilege: 735 ILCS 5/8-912

Chapter 3

Article V – Privileges

Rule 501. General Rule

Except as otherwise required by the Constitution of the United States, the Constitution of Illinois, or provided by applicable statute or rule prescribed by the Supreme Court, the privilege of a witness, person, government, state, or political subdivision thereof shall be governed by the principles of the common law as they may be interpreted by Illinois courts in the light of reason and experience.

Adopted September 27, 2010, eff. January 1, 2011.

Principles as Interpreted by the Illinois Courts

AUTHOR'S COMMENTARY

Illinois recognizes that certain social and professional relationships must be protected by the law. Confidential communications between certain persons must be shielded from disclosure to accomplish a societal goal that seeks to enhance the quality of the relationship through the free flow of communication. Therefore, otherwise relevant and reliable evidence will be excluded at trial.

The Attorney-Client Privilege: Common Law Rule in Illinois

AUTHOR'S COMMENTARY

The attorney-client privilege is a common law rule in Illinois. The essential elements of the attorney-client privilege are:

a. Person seeks legal advice;
b. from a professional legal advisor in his or her capacity as such;
c. the communication relates to that purpose;
d. the communication is made in confidence;
e. the communication is made by the client;
f. the communication is permanently protected;
g. from disclosure by the attorney;
h. except where the protection is waived by the client; and
i. the privilege survives the death of the client.

RELEVANT ILLINOIS SUPREME COURT RULES

1. The Illinois Rules of Professional Conduct as Implemented by Order of the Illinois Supreme Court

Rule 1.6: Confidentiality of Information

(a) A lawyer shall not reveal information relating to the representation of a client unless the client gives informed consent, the disclosure is impliedly authorized in order to carry out the representation, or the disclosure is permitted by paragraph (b) or required by paragraph (c).

(b) A lawyer may reveal information relating to the representation of a client to the extent the lawyer reasonably believes necessary:

(1) to prevent the client from committing a crime in circumstances other than those specified in paragraph (c);
(2) to prevent the client from committing fraud that is reasonably certain to result in substantial injury to the financial interests or property of another and in furtherance of which the client has used or is using the lawyer's services;
(3) to prevent, mitigate or rectify substantial injury to the financial interests or property of another that is reasonably certain to result or has resulted from the client's commission of a crime or fraud in furtherance of which the client has used the lawyer's services;
(4) to secure legal advice about the lawyer's compliance with these Rules;
(5) to establish a claim or defense on behalf of the lawyer in a controversy between the lawyer and the client, to establish a defense to a criminal charge or civil claim against the lawyer based upon conduct in which the client was involved, or to respond to allegations in any proceeding concerning the lawyer's representation of the client; or
(6) to comply with other law or a court order.

(c) A lawyer shall reveal information relating to the representation of a client to the extent the lawyer reasonably believes necessary to prevent reasonably certain death or substantial bodily harm.

(d) Information received by a lawyer participating in a meeting or proceeding with a trained intervener or panel of trained interveners of an approved lawyers' assistance program, or in an intermediary program approved by a circuit court in which nondisciplinary complaints against judges or lawyers can be referred, shall be considered information relating to the representation of a client for purposes of these Rules.

Adopted July 1, 2009, effective January 1, 2010.

Comment

[1] This Rule governs the disclosure by a lawyer of information relating to the representation of a client during the lawyer's representation of the client. See Rule 1.18 for the lawyer's duties with respect to information provided to the lawyer by a prospective client, Rule 1.9(c)(2) for the lawyer's duty not to reveal information relating to the lawyer's prior representation of a former client and Rules 1.8(b) and 1.9(c)(1) for the lawyer's duties with respect to the use of such information to the disadvantage of clients and former clients.

[2] A fundamental principle in the client-lawyer relationship is that, in the absence of the client's informed consent, the lawyer must not reveal information relating to the representation. See Rule 1.0(e) for the definition of informed consent. This contributes to the trust that is the hallmark of the client-lawyer relationship. The client is thereby encouraged to seek legal assistance and to communicate fully and frankly with the lawyer even as to embarrassing or legally damaging subject matter. The lawyer needs this information to represent the client effectively and, if necessary, to advise the client to refrain from wrongful conduct. Almost without exception, clients come to lawyers in order to determine their rights and what is, in the complex of laws and regulations, deemed to be legal and correct. Based upon experience, lawyers know that almost all clients follow the advice given, and the law is upheld.

[3] The principle of client-lawyer confidentiality is given effect by related bodies of law: the attorney-client privilege, the work product doctrine and the rule of confidentiality

established in professional ethics. The attorney-client privilege and work product doctrine apply in judicial and other proceedings in which a lawyer may be called as a witness or otherwise required to produce evidence concerning a client. The rule of client-lawyer confidentiality applies in situations other than those where evidence is sought from the lawyer through compulsion of law. The confidentiality rule, for example, applies not only to matters communicated in confidence by the client but also to all information relating to the representation, whatever its source. A lawyer may not disclose such information except as authorized or required by the Rules of Professional Conduct or other law. *See also* Scope.

[4] Paragraph (a) prohibits a lawyer from revealing information relating to the representation of a client. This prohibition also applies to disclosures by a lawyer that do not in themselves reveal protected information but could reasonably lead to the discovery of such information by a third person. A lawyer's use of a hypothetical to discuss issues relating to the representation is permissible so long as there is no reasonable likelihood that the listener will be able to ascertain the identity of the client or the situation involved.

Authorized Disclosure

[5] Except to the extent that the client's instructions or special circumstances limit that authority, a lawyer is impliedly authorized to make disclosures about a client when appropriate in carrying out the representation. In some situations, for example, a lawyer may be impliedly authorized to admit a fact that cannot properly be disputed or to make a disclosure that facilitates a satisfactory conclusion to a matter. Lawyers in a firm may, in the course of the firm's practice, disclose to each other information relating to a client of the firm, unless the client has instructed that particular information be confined to specified lawyers.

Disclosure Adverse to Client

[6] Although the public interest is usually best served by a strict rule requiring lawyers to preserve the confidentiality of information relating to the representation of their clients, the confidentiality rule is subject to limited exceptions. Paragraph (c) recognizes the overriding value of life and physical integrity and requires disclosure reasonably necessary to prevent reasonably certain death or substantial bodily harm. Such harm is reasonably certain to occur if it will be suffered imminently or if there is a present and substantial threat that a person will suffer such harm at a later date if the lawyer fails to take action necessary to eliminate the threat. Thus, a lawyer who knows from information relating to a representation that a client or other person has accidentally discharged toxic waste into a town's water must reveal this information to the authorities if there is a present and substantial risk that a person who drinks the water will contract a life-threatening or debilitating disease and the lawyer's disclosure is necessary to eliminate the threat or reduce the number of victims.

[6A] Paragraph (b)(1) preserves the policy of the 1980 Illinois Code of Professional Responsibility and the 1990 Illinois Rules of Professional Conduct that permitted a lawyer to reveal the intention of a client to commit a crime. This general provision would permit disclosure where the client's intended conduct is a crime, including a financial crime, and the situation is not covered by paragraph (c).

[7] Paragraph (b)(2) is a limited exception to the rule of confidentiality that permits the lawyer to reveal information to the extent necessary to enable affected persons or

appropriate authorities to prevent the client from committing fraud, as defined in Rule 1.0(d), that is reasonably certain to result in substantial injury to the financial or property interests of another and in furtherance of which the client has used or is using the lawyer's services. Such a serious abuse of the client-lawyer relationship by the client forfeits the protection of this Rule. The client can, of course, prevent such disclosure by refraining from the wrongful conduct. Like paragraph (b)(1), paragraph (b)(2) does not require the lawyer to reveal the client's misconduct, but the lawyer may not counsel or assist the client in conduct the lawyer knows is criminal or fraudulent. See Rule 1.2(d). *See also* Rule 1.16 with respect to the lawyer's obligation or right to withdraw from the representation of the client in such circumstances, and Rule 1.13(c), which permits the lawyer, where the client is an organization, to reveal information relating to the representation in limited circumstances.

[8] Paragraph (b)(3) addresses the situation in which the lawyer does not learn of the client's crime or fraud until after it has been consummated. Although the client no longer has the option of preventing disclosure by refraining from the wrongful conduct, there will be situations in which the loss suffered by the affected person can be prevented, rectified or mitigated. In such situations, the lawyer may disclose information relating to the representation to the extent necessary to enable the affected persons to prevent or mitigate reasonably certain losses or to attempt to recoup their losses. Paragraph (b)(3) does not apply when a person who has committed a crime or fraud thereafter employs a lawyer for representation concerning that offense.

[9] A lawyer's confidentiality obligations do not preclude a lawyer from securing confidential legal advice about the lawyer's personal responsibility to comply with these Rules. In most situations, disclosing information to secure such advice will be impliedly authorized for the lawyer to carry out the representation. Even when the disclosure is not impliedly authorized, paragraph (b)(4) permits such disclosure because of the importance of a lawyer's compliance with the Rules of Professional Conduct.

[10] Where a legal claim or disciplinary charge alleges complicity of the lawyer in a client's conduct or other misconduct of the lawyer involving representation of the client, the lawyer may respond to the extent the lawyer reasonably believes necessary to establish a defense. The same is true with respect to a claim involving the conduct or representation of a former client. Such a charge can arise in a civil, criminal, disciplinary or other proceeding and can be based on a wrong allegedly committed by the lawyer against the client or on a wrong alleged by a third person, for example, a person claiming to have been defrauded by the lawyer and client acting together. The lawyer's right to respond arises when an assertion of such complicity has been made. Paragraph (b)(5) does not require the lawyer to await the commencement of an action or proceeding that charges such complicity, so that the defense may be established by responding directly to a third party who has made such an assertion. The right to defend also applies, of course, where a proceeding has been commenced.

[11] A lawyer entitled to a fee is permitted by paragraph (b)(5) to prove the services rendered in an action to collect it. This aspect of the Rule expresses the principle that the beneficiary of a fiduciary relationship may not exploit it to the detriment of the fiduciary.

[12] Other law may require that a lawyer disclose information about a client. Whether such a law supersedes Rule 1.6 is a question of law beyond the scope of these Rules.

When disclosure of information relating to the representation appears to be required by other law, the lawyer must discuss the matter with the client to the extent required by Rule 1.4. If, however, the other law supersedes this Rule and requires disclosure, paragraph (b)(6) permits the lawyer to make such disclosures as are necessary to comply with the law.

[13] A lawyer may be ordered to reveal information relating to the representation of a client by a court or by another tribunal or governmental entity claiming authority pursuant to other law to compel the disclosure. Absent informed consent of the client to do otherwise, the lawyer should assert on behalf of the client all nonfrivolous claims that the order is not authorized by other law or that the information sought is protected against disclosure by the attorney-client privilege or other applicable law. In the event of an adverse ruling, the lawyer must consult with the client about the possibility of appeal to the extent required by Rule 1.4. Unless review is sought, however, paragraph (b)(6) permits the lawyer to comply with the court's order.

[14] Paragraph (b) permits disclosure only to the extent the lawyer reasonably believes the disclosure is necessary to accomplish one of the purposes specified. Where practicable, the lawyer should first seek to persuade the client to take suitable action to obviate the need for disclosure. In any case, a disclosure adverse to the client's interest should be no greater than the lawyer reasonably believes necessary to accomplish the purpose. If the disclosure will be made in connection with a judicial proceeding, the disclosure should be made in a manner that limits access to the information to the tribunal or other persons having a need to know it and appropriate protective orders or other arrangements should be sought by the lawyer to the fullest extent practicable.

[15] Paragraph (b) permits but does not require the disclosure of information relating to a client's representation to accomplish the purposes specified in paragraphs (b)(1) through (b)(6). In exercising the discretion conferred by this Rule, the lawyer may consider such factors as the nature of the lawyer's relationship with the client and with those who might be injured by the client, the lawyer's own involvement in the transaction and factors that may extenuate the conduct in question. A lawyer's decision not to disclose as permitted by paragraph (b) does not violate this Rule. Disclosure may be required, however, by other Rules. Some Rules require disclosure only if such disclosure would be permitted by paragraph (b). See Rules 1.2(d), 4.1(b), and 8.1. Rules 3.3 and 8.3, on the other hand, require disclosure in some circumstances regardless of whether such disclosure is permitted by this Rule.

Withdrawal

[15A] If the lawyer's services will be used by a client in materially furthering a course of criminal or fraudulent conduct, the lawyer must withdraw, as stated in Rule 1.16(a)(1). The lawyer may give notice of the fact of withdrawal regardless of whether the lawyer decides to disclose information relating to a client's representation as permitted by paragraph (b). The lawyer may also withdraw or disaffirm any opinion or other document that had been prepared for the client or others. Where the client is an organization, the lawyer must also consider the provisions of Rule 1.13.

Acting Competently to Preserve Confidentiality

[16] A lawyer must act competently to safeguard information relating to the representation of a client against inadvertent or unauthorized disclosure by the lawyer or other persons

who are participating in the representation of the client or who are subject to the lawyer's supervision. See Rules 1.1, 5.1 and 5.3.

[17] When transmitting a communication that includes information relating to the representation of a client, the lawyer must take reasonable precautions to prevent the information from coming into the hands of unintended recipients. This duty, however, does not require that the lawyer use special security measures if the method of communication affords a reasonable expectation of privacy. Special circumstances, however, may warrant special precautions. Factors to be considered in determining the reasonableness of the lawyer's expectation of confidentiality include the sensitivity of the information and the extent to which the privacy of the communication is protected by law or by a confidentiality agreement. A client may require the lawyer to implement special security measures not required by this Rule or may give informed consent to the use of a means of communication that would otherwise be prohibited by this Rule.

Former Client
[18] The duty of confidentiality continues after the client-lawyer relationship has terminated.

See Rule 1.9(c)(2). See Rule 1.9(c)(1) for the prohibition against using such information to the disadvantage of the former client.

Lawyers' Assistance and Court Intermediary Programs
[19] Information about the fitness or conduct of a law student, lawyer or judge may be received by a lawyer while participating in an approved lawyers' assistance program. Protecting the confidentiality of such information encourages law students, lawyers and judges to seek assistance through such programs. Without such protection, law students, lawyers and judges may hesitate to seek assistance, to the detriment of clients and the public. Similarly, lawyers participating in an approved intermediary program established by a circuit court to resolve nondisciplinary issues among lawyers and judges may receive information about the fitness or conduct of a lawyer or judge. Paragraph (d) therefore provides that any information received by a lawyer participating in an approved lawyers' assistance program or an approved circuit court intermediary program will be protected as confidential client information for purposes of the Rules. *See also* Comment [5] to Rule 8.3.

Rule 1.8: Conflict of Interest; Current Clients; Specific Rules
*** (b) A lawyer shall not use information relating to representation of a client to the disadvantage of the client unless the client gives informed consent, except as permitted or required by these Rules. ***

Adopted July 1, 2009, effective January 1, 2010.

Comment
*** Use of Information Related to Representation
[5] Use of information relating to the representation to the disadvantage of the client violates the lawyer's duty of loyalty. Paragraph (b) applies when the information is used to benefit either the lawyer or a third person, such as another client or business associate of the lawyer. For example, if a lawyer learns that a client intends to purchase and develop several parcels of land, the lawyer may not use that information to purchase one of the parcels in competition with the client or to recommend that another client make such a purchase. The Rule does not prohibit uses that do not disadvantage the client. For example, a lawyer who learns a government agency's interpretation of trade legislation

during the representation of one client may properly use that information to benefit other clients. Paragraph (b) prohibits disadvantageous use of client information unless the client gives informed consent, except as permitted or required by these Rules. See Rules 1.2(d), 1.6, 1.9(c), 3.3, 4.1(b), 8.1 and 8.3. ***

Rule 1.9: Duties to Former Clients

(a) A lawyer who has formerly represented a client in a matter shall not thereafter represent another person in the same or a substantially related matter in which that person's interests are materially adverse to the interests of the former client unless the former client gives informed consent.

(b) A lawyer shall not knowingly represent a person in the same or a substantially related matter in which a firm with which the lawyer formerly was associated had previously represented a client

(1) whose interests are materially adverse to that person; and
(2) about whom the lawyer had acquired information protected by Rules 1.6 and 1.9(c) that is material to the matter; unless the former client gives informed consent.

(c) A lawyer who has formerly represented a client in a matter or whose present or former firm has formerly represented a client in a matter shall not thereafter:

(1) use information relating to the representation to the disadvantage of the former client except as these Rules would permit or require with respect to a client, or when the information has become generally known; or
(2) reveal information relating to the representation except as these Rules would permit or require with respect to a client.

Adopted July 1, 2009, effective January 1, 2010.

Comment

[1] After termination of a client-lawyer relationship, a lawyer has certain continuing duties with respect to confidentiality and conflicts of interest and thus may not represent another client except in conformity with this Rule. Under this Rule, for example, a lawyer could not properly seek to rescind on behalf of a new client a contract drafted on behalf of the former client. So also a lawyer who has prosecuted an accused person could not properly represent the accused in a subsequent civil action against the government concerning the same transaction. Nor could a lawyer who has represented multiple clients in a matter represent one of the clients against the others in the same or a substantially related matter after a dispute arose among the clients in that matter, unless all affected clients give informed consent. See Comment [9]. Current and former government lawyers must comply with this Rule to the extent required by Rule 1.11.

[2] The scope of a "matter" for purposes of this Rule depends on the facts of a particular situation or transaction. The lawyer's involvement in a matter can also be a question of degree. When a lawyer has been directly involved in a specific transaction, subsequent representation of other clients with materially adverse interests in that transaction clearly is prohibited. On the other hand, a lawyer who recurrently handled a type of problem for a former client is not precluded from later representing another client in a factually distinct problem of that type even though the subsequent representation involves a position adverse to the prior client. Similar considerations can apply to the reassignment of military lawyers between defense and prosecution functions within the same military jurisdictions.

The underlying question is whether the lawyer was so involved in the matter that the subsequent representation can be justly regarded as a changing of sides in the matter in question.

[3] Matters are "substantially related" for purposes of this Rule if they involve the same transaction or legal dispute or if there otherwise is a substantial risk that confidential factual information as would normally have been obtained in the prior representation would materially advance the client's position in the subsequent matter. For example, a lawyer who has represented a businessperson and learned extensive private financial information about that person may not then represent that person's spouse in seeking a divorce. Similarly, a lawyer who has previously represented a client in securing environmental permits to build a shopping center would be precluded from representing neighbors seeking to oppose rezoning of the property on the basis of environmental considerations; however, the lawyer would not be precluded, on the grounds of substantial relationship, from defending a tenant of the completed shopping center in resisting eviction for nonpayment of rent. Information that has been disclosed to the public or to other parties adverse to the former client ordinarily will not be disqualifying. Information acquired in a prior representation may have been rendered obsolete by the passage of time, a circumstance that may be relevant in determining whether two representations are substantially related. In the case of an organizational client, general knowledge of the client's policies and practices ordinarily will not preclude a subsequent representation; on the other hand, knowledge of specific facts gained in a prior representation that are relevant to the matter in question ordinarily will preclude such a representation. A former client is not required to reveal the confidential information learned by the lawyer in order to establish a substantial risk that the lawyer has confidential information to use in the subsequent matter. A conclusion about the possession of such information may be based on the nature of the services the lawyer provided the former client and information that would in ordinary practice be learned by a lawyer providing such services.

Lawyers Moving Between Firms

[4] When lawyers have been associated within a firm but then end their association, the question of whether a lawyer should undertake representation is more complicated. There are several competing considerations. First, the client previously represented by the former firm must be reasonably assured that the principle of loyalty to the client is not compromised. Second, the rule should not be so broadly cast as to preclude other persons from having reasonable choice of legal counsel. Third, the rule should not unreasonably hamper lawyers from forming new associations and taking on new clients after having left a previous association. In this connection, it should be recognized that today many lawyers practice in firms, that many lawyers to some degree limit their practice to one field or another, and that many move from one association to another several times in their careers. If the concept of imputation were applied with unqualified rigor, the result would be radical curtailment of the opportunity of lawyers to move from one practice setting to another and of the opportunity of clients to change counsel.

[5] Paragraph (b) operates to disqualify the lawyer only when the lawyer involved has actual knowledge of information protected by Rules 1.6 and 1.9(c). Thus, if a lawyer while with one firm acquired no knowledge or information relating to a particular client of the firm, and that lawyer later joined another firm, neither the lawyer individually nor the second firm is disqualified from representing another client in the same or a related matter

even though the interests of the two clients conflict. See Rule 1.10(b) for the restrictions on a firm once a lawyer has terminated association with the firm.

[6] Application of paragraph (b) depends on a situation's particular facts, aided by inferences, deductions or working presumptions that reasonably may be made about the way in which lawyers work together. A lawyer may have general access to files of all clients of a law firm and may regularly participate in discussions of their affairs; it should be inferred that such a lawyer in fact is privy to all information about all the firm's clients. In contrast, another lawyer may have access to the files of only a limited number of clients and participate in discussions of the affairs of no other clients; in the absence of information to the contrary, it should be inferred that such a lawyer in fact is privy to information about the clients actually served but not those of other clients.

[7] Independent of the question of disqualification of a firm, a lawyer changing professional association has a continuing duty to preserve confidentiality of information about a client formerly represented. See Rules 1.6 and 1.9(c).

[8] Paragraph (c) provides that information acquired by the lawyer in the course of representing a client may not subsequently be used or revealed by the lawyer to the disadvantage of the client. However, the fact that a lawyer has once served a client does not preclude the lawyer from using generally known information about that client when later representing another client.

[9] The provisions of this Rule are for the protection of former clients and can be waived if the client gives informed consent. With regard to the effectiveness of an advance waiver, see Comment [22] to Rule 1.7. With regard to disqualification of a firm with which a lawyer is or was formerly associated, see Rule 1.10.
Adopted July 1, 2009, effective January 1, 2010.

2. Illinois Supreme Court Rule 412(j)(i)
Illinois Supreme Court Rule 412(j)(i): Matters Not Subject to Disclosure.
(i) *Work Product.* Disclosure under this rule and Rule 413 shall not be required of legal research or of records, correspondence, reports or memoranda to the extent that they contain the opinions, theories or conclusions of the State or members of its legal or investigative staffs, or of defense counsel or his staff.

Effective October 1, 1971; amended October 1, 1976, effective November 15, 1976; amended June 15, 1982, effective July 1, 1982; amended March 1, 2001, effective immediately, except when in the opinion of the trial, Appellate, or Supreme Court the application of the amended provisions in a particular case pending at the time the amendment becomes effective would not be feasible or would work an injustice, in which case former procedures would apply.

PRIOR ILLINOIS CASE LAW

1. The Attorney-Client Privilege Protects Confidential Communications Between Client and Counsel Where Client Seeks Legal Advice
People v. Adam, 51 Ill. 2d 46 (1972)

Illinois gives full recognition to the common law privilege that protects from disclosure certain confidential communications made between a client and his or her attorney. The purpose of this privilege is to promote the free flow of communication between the two so "that one who is, or seeks to become a client, may consult freely with counsel without fear of compelled disclosure of information communicated by him to the attorney . . . ."

2. Communications Must Be Made by Client to Attorney or Attorney's Assistants and Agents in a Confidential Manner
People v. Knippenberg, 66 Ill. 2d 276 (1977)

The communication must be made by the client to the attorney in a confidential manner. However, that confidentiality is not destroyed where the client communicates with the attorney's investigator, secretary, stenographer, or clerk. Here, defendant's counsel hired an investigator to assist him in the case. The investigator interviewed the defendant about the crime and later wrote a summary of the interview. The prosecution gained access to the investigator's summary and used it to impeach defendant's testimony at trial. Defendant initially did not object to the use of the summary, but later raised an objection that was overruled. The appellate court found that although the communication was privileged, the improper reference to it was merely harmless error. On appeal to the Illinois Supreme Court, defendant maintained that the communication was privileged and that its introduction was seriously prejudicial to him. The Illinois Supreme Court considered the defendant's argument and adopted Wigmore's view:

> Professor Wigmore considered it clear that the communication did not have to be directly with the attorney. He observed:
>
> > It has never been questioned that the privilege protects communications to the attorney's clerks, and his other agents (including stenographers) for rendering his services. The assistance of these agents being indispensable to his work and the communications of the client being often necessarily committed to them by the attorney or by the client himself, the privilege must include all the persons who act as the attorney's agents. 8 WIGMORE, EVIDENCE sec. 2301, at 583 (McNaughton Rev. Ed. 1961).
>
> The People's contention that the privilege should not apply here because, it is claimed, the investigator was not necessary or essential to communication between the defendant and his attorney is unimpressive. As the use of law clerks, secretaries and stenographers is common and necessary for an attorney as a practical matter, realities of practice often require an attorney's use of investigators. "The attorney's obligation to investigate fully and without delay is of course basic. It is the duty of the [defense] lawyer to conduct a prompt investigation of the circumstances of the case." ABA Standards, The Defense Function sec. 4.1 (1971).

The Illinois Supreme Court determined that the improper references to the contents of defendant's communications with the investigator were a "clear and indefensible" violation of the attorney-client privilege requiring a new trial.

3. Rule 711 Licensed Law Student Is Considered a Professional Legal Advisor for Purposes of the Attorney-Client Privilege
People v. Williams, 97 Ill. 2d 252 (1983)

The defendant argued that his communications made to his representative, a law student with a Rule 711 license, were privileged. The court stated:

> Although the attorney-client privilege does not usually extend to communications with a law student (8 WIGMORE, EVIDENCE sec. 2300 (McNaughton rev. ed. 1961)), [the law student here] was a person authorized under our Rule 711 to appear in court for limited purposes. As such, we will consider for purposes of this argument that he was acting as [defendant's] legal

> representative in the place of a licensed attorney and assume that the privilege extended to secrets or confidential communications between [the law student] and the defendant.

4. Probation Officer Is Not Considered a Professional Legal Advisor for Purposes of the Attorney-Client Privilege

People v. Williams, 97 Ill. 2d 252 (1983)

Defendant asserted that his communication with a probation officer was confidential and privileged. The court, however, found that communications between defendant and the probation officer were not privileged because

> [t]he situation does not present the same concerns that support the attorney-client or physician-client privilege, *viz*, that the defendant will not be candid and will not make disclosures to the professional out of fear that the information will later be used against him. . . . [A] defendant awaiting sentencing has no obligation to speak to a probation officer or to aid in the preparation of a presentence report.

5. The Attorney-Client Privilege Protects Only Communications Between Client and Counsel Necessary for Procurement of Legal Advice or Representation

People v. Simms, 192 Ill. 2d 348 (2000)

An imprisoned defendant physically assaulted his wife and forced her to perform a sexual act during visiting hours while another prisoner and his attorney were present. The attorney who observed the incident testified for the state at defendant's second stage death sentencing hearing. Defendant argued that the court erred in allowing the attorney to testify because the information she possessed was confidential. Defendant also contended that his trial counsel was ineffective in failing to object to the attorney's testimony and that his appellate counsel was ineffective for failing to argue trial counsel's ineffectiveness. The court disagreed, reasoning that the incident was not confidential as it occurred in the presence of other individuals in a room that was under video surveillance. The court noted that "defendant's voluntary disclosure of information, or other matters subject to being testified to, in the presence of opposing counsel or any other third person who is not the agent of the defendant or his attorney is not privileged."

Defendant further argued that the attorney who observed his conduct in the prison visiting room was his counsel, and that an attorney-client relationship existed. One year after the incident in the visiting room, the attorney was again visiting a client at the prison and defendant asked to speak with her. Defendant told the attorney to ask the prosecutor if a deal could be worked out in his case. The defendant's wife and the attorney also discussed possible fees if defendant retained the attorney. The defendant could not pay the attorney's fees, however, and the attorney turned down the possibility of representing defendant. Defendant did not seek to have the attorney appointed as his counsel by the court. The court noted:

> The attorney-client relationship is a voluntary, contractual relationship that requires the consent of both the attorney and client. *In re* Chicago Flood Litigation, 289 Ill. App. 3d 937, 941 (1st Dist. 1997). As explained in Corti v. Fleisher, 93 Ill. App. 3d 517, 521 (1st Dist. 1981), the relationship "is only created by a retainer or an offer to retain or a fee paid. De Wolf v. Strader, 26 Ill. 225 (1961). It cannot be created by the attorney alone or by an attorney and a third party who has no authority to act." [. . .] Being a consensual relationship, "[t]he client must manifest [his] authorization that the attorney act on [his] behalf, and the attorney must indicate [her] acceptance of the power to act on the client's behalf." Simon v. Wilson, 291 Ill. App. 3d 495, 509 (1st Dist. 1997).

The court concluded that no attorney-client relationship existed here between the attorney and defendant because there was no "consultation by a layperson with an attorney for the purpose of securing that attorney's legal advice on a particular matter."

See also People v. Marcofsky, 219 Ill. App. 230 (1st Dist. 1920) (finding that wife's statement to attorney who represented her in a divorce proceeding that she would prosecute her husband for pandering unless he returned her jewelry was not protected by the attorney-client privilege because it was not made for purposes of securing attorney's legal advice).

6. Factual Information That Does Not Contain Defense Opinions, Theories, or Conclusions Is Not Protected by the Attorney-Client Privilege
People v. Sutherland, 223 Ill. 2d 187 (2006)

Here, the defendant argued that the trial court had erred in denying his motion to bar the testimony of a defense investigator, because her information was protected by the work product rule and by the attorney-client privilege. The witness was called by the state in the retrial to rebut the alibi testimony presented by the defendant's mother. Illinois Supreme Court Rule 412(j)(i) states that research, records and correspondence are not subject to discovery if they contain the "opinions, theories or conclusions" of counsel or those employed by counsel. The Illinois Supreme Court held that the trial court did not abuse its discretion in allowing the testimony because the investigator was able to testify without revealing anything more than a factual account of alibi evidence. The substance of the investigator's testimony did not contain her impressions or reactions and thus is not protected from discovery by the work product doctrine or the attorney client privilege.

7. The Attorney-Client Privilege Does Not Protect a Client Seeking Legal Assistance to Achieve Illegal Goals; The Crime-Fraud Exception to the Attorney-Client Privilege
United States v. Zolin, 491 U.S. 554 (1989)

The IRS as part of its investigation of tax returns of an individual requested certain documents and tapes. The District Court ruled that some of the requested documents should be disclosed but that the tapes were protected from disclosure by the attorney-client privilege. The IRS requested the trial court to conduct an *in camera* review of the tapes, but the court rejected that request. The Court of Appeals affirmed. The United States Supreme Court noted that the "crime-fraud" exception to the attorney-client privilege applies where communications are "in furtherance of a future crime or fraud." Here, the Supreme Court considered what proof is necessary to establish the crime-fraud exception. The court held that rather than requiring independent evidence to show that the exception applied, the trial court should conduct an *in camera* evaluation of the materials sought to be exempted from the attorney-client privilege. The burden of establishing that the communication is within the crime-fraud exception falls upon the party challenging the application of the privilege. To establish this exception, the United States Supreme Court has held that:

> *[I]n camera* review may be used to determine whether allegedly privileged attorney client communications fall within the crime fraud exception . . . . [H]owever . . . before a district court may engage in *in camera* review at the request of the party opposing the privilege, that party must present evidence sufficient to support a reasonable belief that *in camera* review may yield evidence that establishes the exception's applicability. Finally . . . the threshold showing to obtain *in camera* review may be met by using any relevant evidence, lawfully obtained, that has not been adjudicated to be privileged.

8. Court May Conduct an *in Camera* Hearing If There Is Evidence to Support Good Faith Belief by a Reasonable Person That the Crime-Fraud Exception May Apply

United States v. Boender, 649 F.3d 650 (7th Cir. 2011)

Defendant on trial for bribery of a local official, violations of campaign contribution limits and endeavoring to obstruct justice challenged his convictions. Defendant argued that his convictions were based on inadmissible attorney-client privileged communications. The district court, over defendant's objection, conducted an *in camera* hearing to determine whether the crime-fraud exception to the attorney-client privilege applied. The district court found that the crime-fraud exception applied and held that the communications were not privileged. Defendant appealed. The Seventh Circuit upheld the district court's holding, noting that

> [t]o establish the crime-fraud exception, and thus defeat the [attorney-client] privilege, the government must "present *prima facie* evidence that gives color to the charge by showing some foundation in fact." United States v. BDO Seidman, 492 F.3d 806, 818 (7th Cir. 2007). Such evidence then allows the district court to require the defendant "to come forward with an explanation for the evidence offered against [the privilege]." *Id.* The district court then exercises its discretion in accepting or rejecting the proffered explanation. The court may, if necessary, examine the privileged communications themselves to determine whether they further a crime or fraud, so long as there is a "showing of a factual basis adequate to support a good faith belief by a reasonable person that *in camera* review of the materials may reveal evidence to establish the claim that the crime-fraud exception applies." United States v. Zolin, 491 U.S. 554, 572 (1989).

Defendant alleged that there was insufficient evidence to conduct an *in camera* hearing and that the government should not have been allowed to attend the hearing and to cross-examine defendant's attorneys. The Seventh Circuit, however, found that the district court had sufficient basis on which to conduct an *in camera* review as it had reason to believe that such a hearing would disclose whether the crime-fraud exception would apply.

With respect to the defendant's argument that the government should not have been permitted to attend the *in camera* hearing, the Seventh Circuit noted that the guidelines set forth by the United States Supreme Court in *Zolin* permitted "greater flexibility for district courts to balance the need to safeguard the privilege with the need to prevent abuse." The Seventh Circuit reasoned that where documentary evidence is at issue, an *in camera* examination by the judge will usually suffice, but where live testimony is involved, the courts have a choice between an *ex parte* hearing or an adversarial proceeding. The Seventh Circuit noted that "[a]lthough district courts may conduct crime-fraud exception hearings *ex parte* where the circumstances demand it, such proceedings are contrary to the adversarial nature of our judicial system. So a presumption against using *ex parte* proceedings should be a factor weighing in favor of adversarial proceedings when they occur." Even though there might be a risk of the government discovering privileged information during the *in camera* hearing, the Seventh Circuit concluded that such risk was minimal in this case as the district court ordered the transcript of the hearing to be sealed and forbid the government from using any information that was privileged.

9. Illinois Guidelines Regarding the Crime-Fraud Exception to the Attorney-Client Privilege

In re Marriage of Decker, 153 Ill. 2d 298 (1992)

The Illinois Supreme Court adopted United States v. Zolin, 491 U.S. 554 (1989). It also provided additional guidance for Illinois trial courts in evaluating such situations. First, the court found it advisable for another trial judge to conduct the *in camera* review once the proponent satisfies the initial inquiry. Such review would ensure that the assigned judge would not be privy to privileged information in the event he or she must later rule on an issue affected by it. The Supreme Court explained that while

> the approach espoused in *Zolin* [is] a sensible solution to the problem of establishing the crime-fraud exception to the attorney-client privilege, . . . we caution and instruct the trial courts of this State in a few areas. Because of the inherent problem involved in a trial court's viewing information that may in fact be privileged, and then later ruling on an issue which the privileged information may affect, it would be prudent, where possible, to have another trial judge conduct the *in camera* inspection once the initial threshold has been met and the court has determined that an *in camera* inspection is proper.

Second, the *in camera* questioning should "be as limited as possible to initially keep the actual information itself confidential." Therefore, the judge should begin the questioning with narrow questions such as "Did your client ask your advice on how to commit this [specific illegal] act, knowing it to be unlawful?" Finally, the trial court should stay any contempt order pending appellate review when the attorney refuses to disclose the information in good faith.

10. The Attorney-Client Privilege Does Not Protect Client Identity Unless Client Would Be Substantially Prejudiced by Disclosure
People v. Williams, 97 Ill. 2d 252 (1983)

Here, defendant pleaded guilty to kidnapping, rape and murder. Defendant argued that his legal representative should not have been allowed to testify regarding his demeanor and actions during their meeting at a courthouse. Defendant argued that their communications were protected by the attorney-client privilege.

While meeting with his representative and attending court, defendant held a kidnapping victim locked in the trunk of his car. The representative later testified at defendant's trial for the kidnapping, robbery, rape and murder of the victim who had been locked in the trunk. The representative testified that he had never met the defendant before their meeting at the courthouse and that the defendant responded to his name. The representative noted that the defendant appeared "articulate, well-dressed, calm and quite normal." Defendant contended that the representative should not have been permitted to testify, but the court disagreed. The Illinois Supreme Court explained that the representative's testimony did not pertain to confidential communication with his client, but rather constituted a general observation of defendant's appearance that was not privileged.

Defendant further argued that his representative improperly testified as to his identity at trial. The Supreme Court noted that the identity of a client is not privileged "unless he would be prejudiced in some substantial way." The court reasoned that there was no prejudice in the representative's disclosure of this information because defendant had pleaded guilty and his identity was thus not at issue. The court concluded that disclosure of defendant's identity did not substantially prejudice him.

11. The Attorney-Client Privilege Protects Confidential Communications Between Client and Counsel That Have Not Been Waived by the Client
People v. Adam, 51 Ill. 2d 46 (1972)

The attorney-client privilege does not apply if the client waives the privilege through disclosure of the confidential information. Here, the court found that client's disclosure at a grand jury hearing of when and how she obtained the attorney's services and about conversations she had with the attorney effectively waived the attorney-client privilege. The client was called to testify before a grand jury investigating obstruction of justice in a murder investigation. Client's attorney was also called to testify before the grand jury, but refused to answer questions aimed at discovering (1) when he first became the client's lawyer, (2) the circumstances of his employment, and (3) certain conversations with the client. The trial court held the attorney in contempt of court. The attorney appealed, arguing that he refused to answer the court's questions because the matters at issue were protected by the attorney-client privilege. State noted, however, that the matters were not privileged as the client had already waived the privilege by testifying about them. The attorney contended that the client did not waive the privilege because she had been granted immunity and her testimony was thus "compelled and involuntary."

The Illinois Supreme Court found that the client's grant of immunity and subsequent testimony under compulsion were not dispositive of the issues presented. The Supreme Court noted that "[u]nder modern procedures process is available, with rare exception, to compel attendance of witnesses either in court or for deposition and in that sense, most testimony is given under compulsion." The determinative factor in this case, the court explained, is whether the client timely asserted the privilege. The Supreme Court determined that the client waived her privilege as to the first and third questions asked by the trial court because the client testified about them after consulting with her attorney during the grand jury hearing. With respect to the second question, regarding the circumstances of the attorney's employment for the client, the Supreme Court reasoned that it could "not be determined from the record and briefs whether there were in fact privileged matters communicated to the defendant, and if so, in whose presence, and for what purpose, nor can it be determined whether [the client] testified to any such communications." The Supreme Court concluded that it could not be said that defendant was in contempt for his refusal to answer the second question, and remanded for further proceedings.

12. Where a Client Reveals Portions of Conversation with Attorney, Those Revelations Amount to a Waiver of the Attorney-Client Privilege as to the Remainder of the Conversation or Communication About the Same Subject Matter

In re Grand Jury, Jan. 246, 272 Ill. App. 3d 991 (1st Dist. 1995)

Two attorneys refused to disclose the content of a conversation they had with a former client before a grand jury and were found in contempt of court. The former client revealed in a deposition that she discussed with her attorneys the receipt of "financial benefits" from a congressman whom she had accused of sexual misconduct. The appellate court found that the client waived the attorney-client privilege with respect to these conversations because she had disclosed them in her deposition. The court explained that

> [t]he attorney-client privilege is an "evidentiary privilege [which] provides limited protection to communications from the client by prohibiting their unauthorized disclosure in judicial proceedings." *In re* Marriage of Decker, 153 Ill. 2d 298, 312 (1992). The definition and application of the attorney-client privilege has been explained as follows: (1) where legal advice of any kind is sought; (2) from a professional legal adviser in his capacity as such; (3) the communications relating to that purpose; (4) made in confidence; (5) by the client; (6) are at his instance permanently protected; (7) from disclosure by himself or by the legal adviser; (8) except the protection be waived. People v. Adam, 51 Ill. 2d 46, 48 (1972).
>
> The purpose of the attorney-client privilege "is to enable a person to consult freely and openly with an attorney without any fear of compelled disclosure of the information communicated." *Decker*, 153 Ill. 2d at 312-13. However, the client may waive this privilege when he or she

> voluntarily discloses the privileged information. ***Decker***, 153 Ill. 2d at 313; Estate of Hoover, 226 Ill. App. 3d 422, 431 (1992); Rapps v. Keldermans, 257 Ill. App. 3d 205 (1993); Fidelity & Casualty Co. v. Mobay Chemical Corp., 252 Ill. App. 3d 992 (1992); Newton v. Meissner, 76 Ill. App. 3d 479 (1979). By [the client] giving the deposition and then making it public, it was not confidential.
>
> Although voluntary disclosure of confidential information does not effectively waive an attorney-client privilege as to all other non-disclosed communications that may have taken place (Estate of Hoover, 226 Ill. App. 3d 422, 431 (1992)), where a client reveals portions of her conversation with her attorney, those revelations amount to a waiver of the attorney-client privilege as to the remainder of the conversation or communication about the same subject matter. People v. O'Banner, 215 Ill. App. 3d 778, 793 (1991).

The appellate court observed that the client's statements in her deposition pertaining to "financial benefits" were "so broad that they encompassed all discussions she had with [her attorneys] involving any financial benefits, either legal or illegal, that she received from [the congressman]." The court concluded that the client waived the attorney-client privilege as to the subject matter of "financial benefits" received and that her attorneys could not use the attorney-client privilege to refuse to answer questions about such benefits before the grand jury.

13. Illinois Courts Apply One of Three Standards in Determining the Existence of Waiver of the Attorney-Client Privilege

Dalen v. Ozite Corp., 230 Ill. App. 3d 18 (2d Dist. 1992)

The Illinois appellate court has noted that there are

> three general approaches courts have used to analyze [. . .] questions of waiver of the attorney-client privilege: a subjective analysis, an objective analysis, and a balancing test. Golden Valley Microwave Foods, Inc. v. Weaver Popcorn Co., Inc., 132 F.R.D. 204, 208 (N.D. Ind. 1990). Under a subjective analysis, inadvertent disclosure can never result in a true waiver because "there was no intention to waive the privilege, and one cannot waive the privilege without intending to do so." Golden Valley, 132 F.R.D. at 208, citing Connecticut Mutual Life Insurance Co. v. Shields, 18 F.R.D. 448, 451 (S.D.N.Y. 1955). Under an objective analysis, the court need only confirm that the document was made available to opposing counsel; "the 'confidentiality' of the document has been 'breached' by the disclosure, thereby destroying the basis for the continued existence of the privilege." *Golden Valley*, 132 F.R.D. at 208, citing Underwater Storage, Inc. v. United States Rubber Co., 314 F. Supp. 546, 548-49 (D.D.C. 1970). And lastly, under the balancing test, a court considers five factors to determine if a party waived the attorney-client privilege: "(1) the reasonableness of the precautions taken to prevent the disclosure; (2) the time taken to rectify the error; (3) the scope of the discovery; (4) the extent of the disclosure; and (5) the overriding issue of fairness." *Golden Valley*, 132 F.R.D. at 209, citing Bud Antle, Inc. v. Grow Tech Inc., 131 F.R.D. 179, 193 (N.D. Cal. 1990).

See also People v. Murry, 305 Ill. App. 3d 311 (2d Dist. 1999) (applying the subjective analysis test where co-defendant inadvertently testified at defendant's trial about privileged information she disclosed to an attorney who at the time represented her and the defendant).

14. Communications Are Not Privileged If Client Directs Attorney to Disclose Communications to a Non-Agent Third Party
People v. Werhollick, 45 Ill. 2d 459 (1970)

Communications that the client intends his or her attorney to disclose to a person who is not an agent of the attorney or of the client are not privileged. Here, the defendant's attorney attempted to impeach a witness' credibility by showing that he was a former narcotics user and a current informant who was promised leniency by the police if he testified in the present case. The witness specifically denied that he had received promises of leniency or immunity in return for his assistance in convicting the defendant. The court found that it was proper to call the attorney who had represented the witness at the preliminary hearings on the witness' three burglary indictments to testify concerning the circumstances under which he was released from jail. The Illinois Supreme Court stated:

> Matters which the client intends his attorney to disclose to a third person (who is not the agent of either the client or the attorney) are not privileged. Dickerson v. Dickerson, 322 Ill. 492; Spencer v. Burns, 413 Ill. 240. Thus, any offer or acceptance of an offer made by [the informant] through his attorney to the State's Attorney to become a prosecution witness in return for a promise of leniency or immunity is not privileged.

15. The Attorney-Client Privilege Applies to Communications Between Defendant and a Non-Testifying Mental Health Expert
People v. Knuckles, 165 Ill. 2d 125 (1995)

The attorney-client privilege protects communications between defendant and a psychiatric expert, as long as the expert does not testify at trial. Defendant does not waive the attorney-client privilege by asserting an insanity defense. Thus, the attorney-client privilege "protects communications between a defendant who raises an insanity defense and a psychiatrist employed by defense counsel to aid in the preparation of the defense, if the psychiatrist will not testify and the psychiatrist's notes and opinions will not be used in the formulation of the other defense experts' trial testimony." Here, the court rejected the state's contention that the privilege is waived when the defense presents an insanity defense. The privilege is not waived as long as the medical provider does not testify at trial and his or her notes and opinions will not be used by another expert for trial testimony. The court noted that public policy reasons favor such a decision. Finally, the court declined to adopt a generalized public interest exception to its ruling which would allow the state to overcome the privilege.

16. Defendant Waives the Attorney-Client Privilege If Experts Testify at Trial
People v. Wagener, 196 Ill. 2d 269 (2001)

Homicide defendant argued that a conversation he had with his attorney regarding possible penalties for a capital crime was privileged. Defendant, however, had disclosed a police report containing a record of the conversation to his testifying expert witnesses. The court found that defendant waived the attorney-client privilege with respect to those conversations.

17. Attorney's Mere Testimony That Client Waived Confidentiality Is Insufficient to Constitute Waiver
People v. Ortega, 209 Ill. 2d 354 (2004)

Two defendants were charged in connection with the sale of a controlled substance to an undercover police officer. The sale was arranged by an informant who worked for the undercover officer. One attorney represented both defendants at trial. The attorney's brother, who was his law partner, represented the informant in connection with criminal charges stemming from the controlled substance sale. The informant claimed that the undercover officer promised him that charges against him would be dropped if he arranged for the sale. The charges against the informant, however, were not dropped, and the attorney's brother represented the informant in an attempt to enforce the officer's promise to the informant. The trial judge found that the officer made no promises to the informant. The informant then pleaded guilty and was sentenced to probation. Based on this information, the prosecution in the defendants' joint case sought to disqualify their attorney based on a conflict of interest. The informant's attorney subsequently told the defendants' attorney information he obtained from the informant because he thought the informant "would" waive the attorney-client privilege. The trial court granted the state's motion to disqualify the defendants' attorney, finding a *per se* conflict of interest. Defendants appealed and the appellate court reversed, finding that the defendants had waived their right to conflict-free counsel. The Illinois Supreme Court reversed and held that an attorney's testimony to a trial court judge that his client waived confidentiality and conflict was inadequate to prove the waiver. The court reasoned that the mere fact that the informant "would" waive confidentiality of his communications with the attorney does not mean that he "did" waive it, or that the informant understood what it meant to waive confidentiality. The court held that the attorney's testimony was a "legal conclusion that may or may not be supported by the facts" and that the "alleged waiver" was not in the record.

18. The Attorney-Client Privilege Survives the Client's Death
Swidler & Berlin v. United States, 524 U.S. 399 (1998)

The United States Supreme Court held that the federal common law attorney-client privilege survives the client's death. The majority of the justices reasoned that the fear of posthumous disclosure could dissuade clients from speaking frankly to their attorneys because of concerns over possible civil liability, harm to the clients' reputations, or harm to family or friends. Three justices dissented in an opinion written by Justice O'Connor who argued that the attorney-client privilege should be qualified after the client's death in the context of criminal trials. The client's posthumous interest in confidentiality should be balanced against the criminal defendant's right to exculpatory evidence or a compelling law enforcement need for information.

The Marital Privilege

Author's Commentary

At common law, a husband and wife were generally not competent to testify for or against each other. "The disqualification was rested in part upon their interest, in part upon the common-law notion of unity of husband and wife, and in part upon a desire to promote domestic tranquility." People v. Palumbo, 5 Ill. 2d 409, 413 (1955). The common law also recognized a marital privilege "which protected confidential communications made between husband and wife during coverture." *Id.* By statute, Illinois has removed the disqualification of a spouse as a witness but has preserved the testimonial privilege subject to certain exceptions:

> In criminal cases, husband and wife may testify for or against each other. Neither, however, may testify as to any communication or admission made by either of them to the other or as to any conversation between them during marriage, except in cases in which either is charged with an offense against the person or property of the other, in case of spouse abandonment, when the interests of their child or children or of any child or children in either spouse's care, custody, or control are directly involved, when either is charged with or under investigation for

> an offense under Section 11-1.20, 11-1.30, 11-1.40, 11-1.50, 11-1.60, 12-13, 12-14, 12-14.1, 12-15, or 12-16 of the Criminal Code of 1961 and the victim is a minor under 18 years of age in either spouse's care, custody, or control at the time of the offense, or as to matters in which either has acted as agent of the other. 725 ILCS 5/115-16

See People v. Hall, 194 Ill. 2d 305 (2000). Pursuant to the statute and under prior Illinois common law, if one spouse is charged with criminal conduct against the other spouse or his or her property, communications relevant to the charge are not privileged. 725 ILCS 5/115-16; *see e.g.*, People v. Mullinax, 67 Ill. App. 3d 936, 939 (4th Dist. 1979) (noting that "[t]he defendant, having been charged with the assault and attempted murder of his wife and the arson of her automobile, cannot seriously contend that this threatening communication, which [was] relevant to those charges, [was] privileged."); *see also* Bassett v. United States, 137 U.S. 496, 503 (1890) (noting that neither spouse may be "examined as to any communication made by one to the other during the marriage; but this exception does not apply [. . .] to a criminal action or proceeding for a crime committed by one against the other."). Where interests of children are "directly involved," the privilege is also not available. *See* People v. Eveans, 277 Ill. App. 3d 36 (4th Dist. 1996) (holding that defendant's former husband could testify against her in her prosecution for murdering two of her children); People v. Burton, 102 Ill. App. 3d 148, 152 (4th Dist. 1981) (noting that wife's testimony about admissions made to her by defendant husband concerning acts of aggravated incest committed against his eight- and nine-year-old stepdaughters was not barred by privilege).

Although not expressly stated in the statute, the marital privilege extends only to confidential communications. People v. Orange, 121 Ill. 2d 364 (1988). The communicating spouse is the holder of the privilege. Therefore, the non-communicating spouse cannot waive the privilege. *Hall*, 194 Ill. 2d at 334. The marital privilege is not available if a third person learns of the oral communication by eavesdropping. People v. Simpson, 68 Ill. 2d 276 (1977). "Similarly, one may testify who learns the contents of a written communication from one spouse to another by interception, or through loss or misdelivery by the custodian." *Id.* at 280. But if the eavesdropping or disclosure of a written communication is brought about by the "betrayal or connivance" of the non-communicating spouse, the privilege will protect the communication from disclosure. *Id.* at 280.

Generally, the marital privilege only protects confidential communications, but conduct or an act that is expressive in nature and is clearly intended to be a substitute for the spoken or written word is also protected by the privilege. People v. Derr, 316 Ill. App. 3d 272 (5th Dist. 2000); People v. Krankel, 105 Ill. App. 3d 988 (3d Dist. 1982). However, non-communicative conduct is not privileged. *Krankel*, 105 Ill. App. 3d at 992. The privilege also does not protect matters in which a spouse acted as the other spouse's agent. People v. Hommerson, 399 Ill. App. 3d 405 (2d Dist. 2010). The marital privilege may yield to the accused's right to confront witnesses against him or her. People v. Foskey, 136 Ill. 2d 66 (1990).

Relevant Statutory Authority

The Marital Privilege: 725 ILCS 5/115-16

§ 115-16. Witness disqualification.

***

In criminal cases, husband and wife may testify for or against each other. Neither, however, may testify as to any communication or admission made by either of them to the other or as to any conversation between them during marriage, except in cases in which either is charged with an offense against the person or property of the other, in case of spouse abandonment, when the interests of their child or children or of any child or children in either spouse's care, custody, or control are directly involved, when either is charged with or under investigation for an offense under Section 11-1.20, 11-1.30, 11-1.40, 11-1.50, 11-1.60, 12-13, 12-14, 12-14.1, 12-15, or 12-16 of the Criminal Code of 1961 and the victim is a minor under 18 years of age in either spouse's care, custody, or control at the time of the offense, or as to matters in which either has acted as agent of the other.

Effective July 1, 2011.

PRIOR ILLINOIS CASE LAW

1. At Common Law, Husband and Wife Were Not Competent to Testify For or Against Each Other and Marital Privilege Protected Their Confidential Communications

People v. Palumbo, 5 Ill. 2d 409 (1955)

At common law, both husband and wife were incompetent to testify for or against each other. "The disqualification was rested in part upon their interest, in part upon the common law notion of unity of husband and wife, and in part upon a desire to promote domestic tranquility." The common law recognized a marital privilege "which protected confidential communications made between husband and wife during coverture."

2. Illinois Has Removed the Disqualification of Spouses Through Statute (725 ILCS 5/115-16) but Retains the Marital Privilege

People v. Hall, 194 Ill. 2d 305 (2000)

By statute, Illinois has removed the disqualification of a spouse as a witness but has preserved the testimonial privilege subject to certain exceptions. Husband and wife, in criminal cases, may not testify as to "any communication or admission made by either of them to the other or as to any conversation between them during marriage." The holder of the privilege may waive the privilege. Here, the husband was on trial for first-degree murder and argued that his conversations with his wife regarding his instructions for her to send him a gun through FedEx and to secure a storage unit he rented were privileged. Defendant, however, did not invoke the marital privilege during his wife's testimony, and therefore waived the privilege. The court further found, under a plain error analysis, that even if defendant had objected to his wife's testimony, the wife could testify regarding her own conduct in purchasing the gun and sending it to defendant. Considering the strong evidence against defendant, the court also found that evidence was not closely balanced and that admissibility of wife's testimony regarding the storage locker did not constitute plain error.

3. Marital Privilege Protects Only Confidential Communications Between Spouses

People v. Orange, 121 Ill. 2d 364 (1988)

Defendant argued that a conversation he had with his wife in jail was confidential and protected by the marital privilege. The court found, however, that it was unclear whether the conversation was confidential, as there was some evidence suggesting that a third person, a potential alibi witness, was present. Further, the court noted, defendant waived the marital privilege when he failed to object to his wife's testimony at trial. Defendant alleged that his counsel was ineffective for failing to object to the wife's testimony, but the court concluded that even if the counsel's conduct was deficient, the defendant was not denied effective assistance of counsel as the evidence of his guilt was overwhelming.

4. Marital Privilege Does Not Protect Non-Communicative Conduct
People v. Derr, 316 Ill. App. 3d 272 (5th Dist. 2000)

The court was required to determine if a description by one spouse of the other spouse's nonverbal conduct was a protected "communication" under the marital privilege. The court stated:

> Implicit in the term "communication" is speech. *See* People v. Krankel, 105 Ill. App. 3d 988, 991 (3d Dist. 1982). Certain acts, however, may also constitute communication, such as a nod of the head. See People v. Murphy, 241 Ill. App. 3d 918, 924 (1st Dist. 1992); *Krankel*, 105 Ill. App. 3d at 991. In order to fall within the privilege, though, the nonverbal conduct must clearly be a substitute for oral communications. The mere description by one spouse of general, noncommunicative conduct is not protected by the marital privilege. See *Krankel*, 105 Ill. App. 3d at 991.

Murder defendant's ex-wife, who was married to defendant at the time of the crime, testified that defendant showed her the victim's body, she saw defendant put the body in the trunk of his car, and she followed defendant to a levee where he threw some of victim's jewelry in the water. The Fifth District of the Illinois Appellate Court determined that the decision of the trial court to admit the testimony of the ex-wife's description of her then-spouse's non-verbal conduct was not communication, and therefore it would not be protected by the marital privilege.

5. Illinois Rejects a "Joint Criminal Enterprise" Exception to the Marital Privilege
People v. Krankel, 105 Ill. App. 3d 988 (3d Dist. 1982)

Defendant's ex-wife testified at his burglary and theft trial. The ex-wife was married to the defendant during the time of the commission of the crime. She testified that she and defendant discussed stealing her grandmother's silverware and drove to her grandmother's house. Once at the house, defendant broke in and they both entered. Defendant found the silverware and asked his ex-wife how he should pack it up. She suggested that he wrap it in a towel. Defendant then packed up the silverware and carried it out of the house. The defendant and his ex-wife then drove to a pawn shop and sold the silverware. At trial, defendant denied taking part in the robbery and claimed that he had only agreed to help his ex-wife sell some silverware she claimed was a gift from her grandmother. Defendant argued that his ex-wife should not have been allowed to testify about their conversations and his conduct during their marriage. The trial court rejected defendant's arguments, finding that the ex-wife was allowed to testify because she committed the crime in concert with defendant while engaged in a joint criminal enterprise. The Third District of the Illinois Appellate Court reversed and remanded the case, noting that Illinois does not recognize a "joint criminal enterprise" exception to the marital privilege. The Third District held that confidential communications between the defendant and his ex-wife during their marriage were protected, and that the trial court erred in permitting those into evidence. The ex-wife, however, was properly permitted to describe non-communicative conduct of the defendant.

6. Marital Privilege Does Not Protect Matters in Which Spouse Acted as Other Spouse's Agent
People v. Hommerson, 399 Ill. App. 3d 405 (2d Dist. 2010)

After committing murder, defendant told his wife to lie to the police about his whereabouts during the time the murder occurred. After being interviewed by the police, the defendant instructed his wife to register under a fictitious name at a motel and to borrow a car. Wife then drove the defendant to the Mexican border. The Second District of the Illinois Appellate

Court found that the wife was acting solely for the defendant's benefit when she followed his directions by lying about his activities on the day of the murder, borrowing a car, and driving him to the Mexican border. The Second District concluded that defendant's wife acted as his agent and that therefore their communications were not privileged.

7. Generally Marital Privilege Is Not Available If Third Person Overhears the Communication by Interception or Eavesdropping
People v. Simpson, 68 Ill. 2d 276 (1977)

The marital privilege is not available if a third person learns of the oral communication by eavesdropping. "[O]ne may testify who learns the contents of a written communication from one spouse to another by interception, or through loss or misdelivery by the custodian." But if the eavesdropping or disclosure of a written communication is brought about by the betrayal or connivance of the noncommunicating spouse, the privilege will protect the communication from disclosure. This exception only applies if a communication is revealed "through no conscious act of the protesting spouse, to a third party."

Here, the court found that the exception did not apply because the defendant, as holder of the privilege, revealed and confirmed the content of a prior privileged communication. Defendant's wife came into an interrogation room occupied by defendant and police officers, and stated that defendant told her he had shot and killed a woman. In response to the wife's allegations, defendant stated "Yes, but I told you later I was lying." The court held that the officers could testify as to defendant's public statement.

8. Presence of Third Persons Who Are Capable of Understanding the Communication Destroys the Marital Privilege
People v. Sanders, 99 Ill. 2d 262 (1983)

The court found that the "presence of children of the spouses destroys confidentiality unless they are too young to understand what is being said." Defendant argued that his conversations with his wife in front of his children, ages 13, 10 and 8, were privileged. The court rejected the claim because the oldest child was present when the conversations occurred, and nothing indicated that the child "was not old enough or sufficiently bright to understand."

9. Child Interest Exception to the Spousal Privilege
People v. Eveans, 277 Ill. App. 3d 36 (4th Dist. 1996)

The court held that defendant's former husband was not barred from testifying against her as his testimony fell within the interests of the child exception in her prosecution for murdering two of her children. The court rejected defendant's contention that no interest of the children was involved since they were dead, demonstrating the absurdity of the results if her contention prevailed. It stated that under defendant's argument:

> A spouse could testify when the other spouse admitted to attempting to murder their child, because the child would presumably still be in the care, custody, or control of the innocent spouse. However, the innocent spouse could not testify when the other spouse admitted to succeeding in murdering their child, under the theory a dead child is no longer in anyone's care, custody, or control.

The court then noted that the exception covers the interest of any children in the parents' care, custody, or control at the time of the trial and at the time of the offense. Moreover,

> [w]hen a child is murdered by a parent the State stands in its place to serve several continuing interests directly involved in a criminal prosecution of that parent for murder: the interest in seeing the murderer brought to justice, the interest in protecting other children from violent

acts of physical abuse committed by the same defendant, and the interest in deterring similar behavior in other potentially abusive parents.

The court further reasoned that the purpose behind the rule—to preserve marital harmony—was not served in such situations. Where one spouse admits killing a child to another spouse, "there is no marital harmony left to preserve."

10. Marital Privilege Does Not Defeat Defendant's Right to Confrontation of Witnesses
People v. Foskey, 136 Ill. 2d 66 (1990)

In addition to the statutory exceptions, the marital privilege may not defeat a defendant's constitutional right to confront and cross-examine witnesses. Here, the Illinois Supreme Court held that the defendant's Sixth Amendment right to confront witnesses superseded his wife's marital privilege during cross-examination of her as a prosecution witness. The court stated that the marital privilege may yield to constitutional rights where the challenged evidence is critical and the purposes underlying the privilege would not be served. Here, the public policy for the privilege—marital harmony—had already been defeated by the wife's cooperation with the police and her testimony against the husband at trial. In this prosecution for possession of heroin with the intent to deliver, the wife was an important witness whose credibility was extremely relevant and important. Consequently, the court held that the accused may use evidence of letters and conversations in which she allegedly admitted that she had fabricated a story of conspiracy to murder police officers to cross-examine his wife, notwithstanding the fact he was allowed to cross examine his wife as to bias and drug use.

The Physician-Patient Privilege

Author's Commentary

Illinois did not recognize a physician-patient privilege at common law. People *ex rel.* Department of Professional Regulation v. Manos, 202 Ill. 2d 563 (2002). The legislature, however, has created a statutory physician-patient privilege pursuant to 735 ILCS 5/8-802. The statutory privilege protects confidential information a physician acquires that is "necessary to enable" the physician to professionally serve the patient. 735 ILCS 5/8-802. The statutory privilege is subject to several exceptions that allow a physician to disclose privileged matters. *See* 735 ILCS 5/8-802.

Relevant Statutory Authority

The Physician-Patient Privilege: 735 ILCS 5/8-802

§ 8-802. Physician and patient. No physician or surgeon shall be permitted to disclose any information he or she may have acquired in attending any patient in a professional character, necessary to enable him or her professionally to serve the patient, except only (1) in trials for homicide when the disclosure relates directly to the fact or immediate circumstances of the homicide, (2) in actions, civil or criminal, against the physician for malpractice, (3) with the expressed consent of the patient, or in case of his or her death or disability, of his or her personal representative or other person authorized to sue for personal injury or of the beneficiary of an insurance policy on his or her life, health, or physical condition, (4) in all actions brought by or against the patient, his or her personal representative, a beneficiary under a policy of insurance, or the executor or administrator of his or her estate wherein the patient's physical or mental condition is an issue, (5) upon an issue as to the validity of a document as a will of the patient, (6) in any criminal action where the charge is either first degree murder by abortion, attempted abortion or abortion, (7) in actions, civil or criminal, arising from the filing of a report in compliance with the Abused and Neglected Child

Reporting Act, (8) to any department, agency, institution or facility which has custody of the patient pursuant to State statute or any court order of commitment, (9) in prosecutions where written results of blood alcohol tests are admissible pursuant to Section 11-501.4 of the Illinois Vehicle Code, (10) in prosecutions where written results of blood alcohol tests are admissible under Section 5-11a of the Boat Registration and Safety Act, (11) in criminal actions arising from the filing of a report of suspected terrorist offense in compliance with Section 29D-10(p)(7) of the Criminal Code of 1961, or (12) upon the issuance of a subpoena pursuant to Section 38 of the Medical Practice Act of 1987; the issuance of a subpoena pursuant to Section 25.1 of the Illinois Dental Practice Act; the issuance of a subpoena pursuant to Section 22 of the Nursing Home Administrators Licensing and Disciplinary Act; or the issuance of a subpoena pursuant to Section 25.5 of the Workers' Compensation Act.

In the event of a conflict between the application of this Section and the Mental Health and Developmental Disabilities Confidentiality Act (740 ILCS 110/1 *et seq.*) to a specific situation, the provisions of the Mental Health and Developmental Disabilities Confidentiality Act shall control.

Effective June 28, 2011.

Abused and Neglected Child Reporting Act: 325 ILCS 5/4

§ 4. Persons required to report; privileged communications; transmitting false report. Any physician, resident, intern, hospital, hospital administrator and personnel engaged in examination, care and treatment of persons, surgeon, dentist, dentist hygienist, osteopath, chiropractor, podiatrist, physician assistant, substance abuse treatment personnel, funeral home director or employee, coroner, medical examiner, emergency medical technician, acupuncturist, crisis line or hotline personnel, school personnel (including administrators and both certified and non-certified school employees), educational advocate assigned to a child pursuant to the School Code, member of a school board or the Chicago Board of Education or the governing body of a private school (but only to the extent required in accordance with other provisions of this Section expressly concerning the duty of school board members to report suspected child abuse), truant officers, social worker, social services administrator, domestic violence program personnel, registered nurse, licensed practical nurse, genetic counselor, respiratory care practitioner, advanced practice nurse, home health aide, director or staff assistant of a nursery school or a child day care center, recreational program or facility personnel, law enforcement officer, licensed professional counselor, licensed clinical professional counselor, registered psychologist and assistants working under the direct supervision of a psychologist, psychiatrist, or field personnel of the Department of Healthcare and Family Services, Juvenile Justice, Public Health, Human Services (acting as successor to the Department of Mental Health and Developmental Disabilities, Rehabilitation Services, or Public Aid), Corrections, Human Rights, or Children and Family Services, supervisor and administrator of general assistance under the Illinois Public Aid Code, probation officer, animal control officer or Illinois Department of Agriculture Bureau of Animal Health and Welfare field investigator, or any other foster parent, homemaker or child care worker having reasonable cause to believe a child known to them in their professional or official capacity may be an abused child or a neglected child shall immediately report or cause a report to be made to the Department.

Any member of the clergy having reasonable cause to believe that a child known to that member of the clergy in his or her professional capacity may be an abused child as defined in item (c) of the definition of "abused child" in Section 3 of this Act shall immediately report or cause a report to be made to the Department.

Any physician, physician's assistant, registered nurse, licensed practical nurse, medical technician, certified nursing assistant, social worker, or licensed professional counselor of any office, clinic, or any other physical location that provides abortions, abortion referrals, or contraceptives having reasonable cause to believe a child known to him or her in his or her professional or official capacity may be an abused child or a neglected child shall immediately report or cause a report to be made to the Department.

(Italicized text has been inserted by P.A. 97-0254, effective January 1, 2012).

If an allegation is raised to a school board member during the course of an open or closed school board meeting that a child who is enrolled in the school district of which he or she is a board member is an abused child as defined in Section 3 of this Act, the member shall direct or cause the school board to direct the superintendent of the school district or other equivalent school administrator to comply with the requirements of this Act concerning the reporting of child abuse. For purposes of this paragraph, a school board member is granted the authority in his or her individual capacity to direct the superintendent of the school district or other equivalent school administrator to comply with the requirements of this Act concerning the reporting of child abuse.

***

Whenever such person is required to report under this Act in his capacity as a member of the staff of a medical or other public or private institution, school, facility or agency, or as a member of the clergy, he shall make report immediately to the Department in accordance with the provisions of this Act and may also notify the person in charge of such institution, school, facility or agency, or church, synagogue, temple, mosque, or other religious institution, or his designated agent that such report has been made. Under no circumstances shall any person in charge of such institution, school, facility or agency, or church, synagogue, temple, mosque, or other religious institution, or his designated agent to whom such notification has been made, exercise any control, restraint, modification or other change in the report or the forwarding of such report to the Department.

The privileged quality of communication between any professional person required to report and his patient or client shall not apply to situations involving abused or neglected children and shall not constitute grounds for failure to report as required by this Act or constitute grounds for failure to share information or documents with the Department during the course of a child abuse or neglect investigation. If requested by the professional, the Department shall confirm in writing that the information or documents disclosed by the professional were gathered in the course of a child abuse or neglect investigation.

A member of the clergy may claim the privilege under Section 8-803 of the Code of Civil Procedure.

Any office, clinic, or any other physical location that provides abortions, abortion referrals, or contraceptives shall provide to all office personnel copies of written information and training materials about abuse and neglect and the requirements of this Act that are provided to employees of the office, clinic, or physical location who are required to make reports to the Department under this Act, and instruct such office personnel to bring to the attention of an employee of the office, clinic, or physical location who is required to make reports to the Department under this Act any reasonable suspicion that a child known to him or her in his or her professional or official capacity may be an abused child or a neglected child. In addition to the above persons required to report suspected cases of abused or neglected children, any other person may make a report if such person has reasonable cause to believe a child may be an abused child or a neglected child.

(Italicized text has been inserted by P.A. 97-0254, effective January 1, 2012).

Any person who enters into employment on and after July 1, 1986 and is mandated by virtue of that employment to report under this Act, shall sign a statement on a form prescribed by the Department, to the effect that the employee has knowledge and understanding of the reporting requirements of this Act. The statement shall be signed prior to commencement of the employment. The signed statement shall be retained by the employer. The cost of printing, distribution, and filing of the statement shall be borne by the employer.

The Department shall provide copies of this Act, upon request, to all employers employing persons who shall be required under the provisions of this Section to report under this Act.

Any person who knowingly transmits a false report to the Department commits the offense of disorderly conduct under subsection (a)(7) of Section 26-1 of the "Criminal Code of 1961." Any person who violates this provision a second or subsequent time shall be guilty of a Class 3 felony.

Any person who knowingly and willfully violates any provision of this Section other than a second or subsequent violation of transmitting a false report as described in the preceding paragraph, is guilty of a Class A misdemeanor for a first violation and a Class 4 felony for a second or subsequent violation; except that if the person acted as part of a plan or scheme having as its object the prevention of discovery of an abused or neglected child by lawful authorities for the purpose of protecting or insulating any person or entity from arrest or prosecution, the person is guilty of a Class 4 felony for a first offense and a Class 3 felony for a second or subsequent offense (regardless of whether the second or subsequent offense involves any of the same facts or persons as the first or other prior offense).

A child whose parent, guardian or custodian in good faith selects and depends upon spiritual means through prayer alone for the treatment or cure of disease or remedial care may be considered neglected or abused, but not for the sole reason that his parent, guardian or custodian accepts and practices such beliefs.

A child shall not be considered neglected or abused solely because the child is not attending school in accordance with the requirements of Article 26 of the School Code, as amended.

Nothing in this Act prohibits a mandated reporter who reasonably believes that an animal is being abused or neglected in violation of the Humane Care for Animals Act from reporting animal abuse or neglect to the Department of Agriculture's Bureau of Animal Health and Welfare.

A home rule unit may not regulate the reporting of child abuse or neglect in a manner inconsistent with the provisions of this Section. This Section is a limitation under subsection (i) of Section 6 of Article VII of the Illinois Constitution on the concurrent exercise by home rule units of powers and functions exercised by the State.

For purposes of this Section "child abuse or neglect" includes abuse or neglect of an adult resident as defined in this Act.

Effective August 15, 2011.

Reporting of Blood or Urine Test Results: 625 ILCS 5/11-501.4-1

§ 11-501.4-1. Reporting of test results of blood or urine conducted in the regular course of providing emergency medical treatment.

(a) Notwithstanding any other provision of law, the results of blood or urine tests performed for the purpose of determining the content of alcohol, other drug or drugs, or intoxicating compound or compounds, or any combination thereof, in an individual's blood or urine conducted upon persons receiving medical treatment in a hospital emergency room for injuries resulting from a motor vehicle accident shall be disclosed to the Department of State Police or local law enforcement agencies of jurisdiction, upon request. Such blood or urine tests are admissible in evidence as a business record exception to the hearsay rule only in prosecutions for any violation of Section 11-501 of this Code or a similar provision of a local ordinance, or in prosecutions for reckless homicide brought under the Criminal Code of 1961.

(b) The confidentiality provisions of law pertaining to medical records and medical treatment shall not be applicable with regard to tests performed upon an individual's blood or urine under the provisions of subsection (a) of this Section. No person shall be liable for civil damages or professional discipline as a result of the disclosure or reporting of the tests or the evidentiary use of an individual's blood or urine test results under this Section or Section 11-501.4 or as a result of that person's testimony made available under this Section or Section 11-501.4, except for willful or wanton misconduct.

Effective January 1, 2000.

Boat Registration and Safety Act: 625 ILCS 45/5-11a (renumbered as 625 ILCS 45/5-16a by P.A. 88-670, eff. Dec. 2, 1994)

§ 5-16a. Admissibility of chemical tests of blood or urine conducted in the regular course of providing emergency medical treatment.

(a) Notwithstanding any other provision of law, the written results of blood or urine alcohol tests conducted upon persons receiving medical treatment in a hospital emergency room are admissible in evidence as a business record exception to the hearsay rule only in prosecutions for any violation of Section 5-16 of this Act or a similar provision of a local ordinance or in prosecutions for reckless homicide brought under the Criminal Code of 1961, when:

(1) the chemical tests performed upon an individual's blood or urine were ordered in the regular course of providing emergency treatment and not at the request of law enforcement authorities; and

(2) the chemical tests performed upon an individual's blood or urine were performed by the laboratory routinely used by the hospital.

Results of chemical tests performed upon an individual's blood or urine are admissible into evidence regardless of the time that the records were prepared.

(b) The confidentiality provisions of law pertaining to medical records and medical treatment shall not be applicable with regard to chemical tests performed upon an individual's blood or urine under the provisions of this Section in prosecutions as specified in subsection (a) of this Section. No person shall be liable for civil damages as a result of the evidentiary use of the results of chemical testing of an individual's blood or urine under this Section or as a result of that person's testimony made available under this Section.

Effective Aug. 11, 2009.

Offenses Affecting Public Health, Safety, and Decency—Terrorism: 720 ILCS 5/29D-10

§ 29D-10. Definitions. As used in this Article, where not otherwise distinctly expressed or manifestly incompatible with the intent of this Article:

*** (p) "Render criminal assistance" means to do any of the following with the intent to prevent, hinder, or delay the discovery or apprehension of, or the lodging of a criminal charge against, a person who he or she knows or believes has committed an offense under this Article or is being sought by law enforcement officials for the commission of an offense under this Article, or with the intent to assist a person in profiting or benefiting from the commission of an offense under this Article:

***

(7) provide expert services or expert assistance to the person. Providing expert services or expert assistance shall not be construed to apply to: (1) a licensed attorney who discusses with a client the legal consequences of a proposed course of conduct or advises a client of legal or constitutional rights and (2) a licensed medical doctor who provides emergency medical treatment to a person whom he or she believes has committed an offense under this Article if, as soon as reasonably practicable either before or after providing such treatment, he or she notifies a law enforcement agency.

Effective Jan. 1, 2011.

Medical Practice Act of 1987: 225 ILCS 60/38

§ 38. The Disciplinary Board or Department has power to subpoena and bring before it any person in this State and to take testimony either orally or by deposition, or both, with the same fees and mileage and in the same manner as is prescribed by law for judicial procedure in civil cases.

The Disciplinary Board, upon a determination that probable cause exists that a violation of one or more of the grounds for discipline listed in Section 22 has occurred or is occurring, may subpoena the medical and hospital records of individual patients of physicians licensed under this Act, provided, that prior to the submission of such records to the Disciplinary Board, all information indicating the identity of the patient shall be removed and deleted. Notwithstanding the foregoing, the Disciplinary Board and Department shall possess the power to subpoena copies of hospital or medical records in mandatory report cases under Section 23 alleging death or permanent bodily injury when consent to obtain records is not provided by a patient or legal representative. Prior to submission of the records to the Disciplinary Board, all information indicating the identity of the patient shall be removed and deleted. All medical records and other information received pursuant to subpoena shall be confidential and shall be afforded the same status as is proved information concerning medical studies in Part 21 of Article VIII of the Code of Civil Procedure. The use of such records shall be restricted to members of the Disciplinary Board, the medical coordinators, and appropriate staff of the Department designated by the Disciplinary Board for the purpose of determining the existence of one or more grounds for discipline of the physician as provided for by Section 22 of this Act. Any such review of individual patients' records shall be conducted by the Disciplinary Board in strict confidentiality, provided that such patient records shall be admissible in a disciplinary hearing, before the Disciplinary Board, when necessary to substantiate the grounds for discipline alleged against the physician licensed under this Act, and provided further, that nothing herein shall be deemed to supersede the provisions of Part 21 of Article VIII of the "Code of Civil Procedure", as now or hereafter amended, to the extent applicable. ***

Effective November 23, 2011.

Illinois Dental Practice Act: 225 ILCS 25/25.1

Sec. 25.1. Subpoena powers.

(a) The Department, upon a determination by the chairperson of the Board that reasonable cause exists that a violation of one or more of the grounds for discipline set forth in Section 23 or Section 24 of this Act has occurred or is occurring, may subpoena the dental records of individual patients of dentists and dental hygienists licensed under this Act.

(b) Notwithstanding subsection (a) of this Section, the Board and the Department may subpoena copies of hospital, medical, or dental records in mandatory report cases alleging death or permanent bodily injury when consent to obtain the records has not been provided by a patient or a patient's legal representative. All records and other information received pursuant to a subpoena shall be confidential and shall be afforded the same status as information concerning medical studies under Part 21 of Article VIII of the Code of Civil Procedure. The use of these records shall be restricted to members of the Board, the dental coordinator, and appropriate Department staff designated by the Secretary for the purpose of determining the existence of one or more grounds for discipline of the dentist or dental hygienist as provided for in Section 23 or Section 24 of this Act.

(c) Any review of an individual patient's records shall be conducted by the Department in strict confidentiality, provided that the patient records shall be admissible in a disciplinary hearing before the Secretary, the Board, or a hearing officer designated by the Department when necessary to substantiate the grounds for discipline alleged against the dentist or dental hygienist licensed under this Act.

(d) The Department may provide reimbursement for fees and mileage associated with its subpoena power in the same manner prescribed by law for judicial procedure in a civil case.

(e) Nothing in this Section shall be deemed to supersede the provisions of Part 21 of Article VIII of the Code of Civil Procedure, now or hereafter amended, to the extent applicable.

(f) All information gathered by the Department during any investigation, including information subpoenaed under this Act and the investigative file, shall be kept for the confidential use of the Secretary, the dental coordinator, the Board's attorneys, the dental investigative staff, authorized clerical staff, and persons employed by contract to advise the dental coordinator or the Department as provided in this Act, except that the Department may disclose information and documents to (i) a federal, State, or local law enforcement agency pursuant to a subpoena in an ongoing criminal investigation or (ii) a dental licensing authority of another state or jurisdiction pursuant to an official request made by that authority. Any information or documents disclosed by the Department to a federal, State, or local law enforcement agency may only be used by that agency for the investigation and prosecution of a criminal offense. Any information or documents disclosed by the Department to a dental licensing authority of another state or jurisdiction may only be used by that authority for investigations and disciplinary proceedings with regards to a license.

This subsection (f) applies only to causes of action accruing on or after the effective date of this amendatory Act of the 96th General Assembly.

> Effective July 23, 2010. Section scheduled to be repealed on January 1, 2016. Section 4.26 of the Regulatory Sunset Act (5 ILCS 80/4.26) provides for the repeal of the Illinois Dental Practice Act effective January 1, 2016, unless, under 5 ILCS 80/4, the General Assembly enacts legislation providing for its continuation.

Nursing Home Administrators Licensing and Disciplinary Act: 225 ILCS 70/22

Sec. 22. Subpoena power.

The Board or Department has power to subpoena and bring before it any person in this State and to take testimony either orally or by deposition, or both, with the same fees and mileage and in the same manner as is prescribed by law for judicial proceedings in civil cases.

The Department, upon a determination that probable cause exists that a violation of one or more of the grounds for discipline listed in Section 17 has occurred or is occurring, may subpoena the records of an individual licensed under this Act provided that prior to the submission of such records to the Board, all information indicating the identity of any resident shall be removed and deleted. The use of such records shall be restricted to members of the Board and appropriate staff of the Department for the purpose of determining the existence of one or more grounds for discipline of the nursing home administrator as provided for by Section 17 of this Act. Any such review of individual residents' records shall be conducted by the Board in strict confidentiality, provided that such resident records shall be admissible in a disciplinary hearing, before the Department, when necessary to substantiate the grounds for discipline alleged against the administrator licensed under this Act, and provided further that nothing herein shall be deemed to supersede the provisions of Part 21 of Article VIII of the Code of Civil Procedure, as now or hereafter amended, to the extent applicable.

The Secretary, the designated hearing officer, and any member of the Board have the power to administer oaths at any hearing that the Department is authorized to conduct and any other oaths authorized in an Act administered by the Department.

> Effective December 31, 2007. Section scheduled to be repealed on January 1, 2018. Section 4.28 of the Regulatory Sunset Act (5 ILCS 80/4.28) provides for the repeal of the Nurse Practice Act effective January 1, 2018, unless, under 5 ILCS 80/4, the General Assembly enacts legislation providing for its continuation.

Workers' Compensation Act: 820 ILCS 305/25.5

Sec. 25.5. Unlawful acts; penalties.

*** (c) The Department of Insurance shall establish a fraud and insurance non-compliance unit responsible for investigating incidences of fraud and insurance non-compliance pursuant to this Section. The size of the staff of the unit shall be subject to appropriation by the General Assembly. It shall be the duty of the fraud and insurance non-compliance unit to determine the identity of insurance carriers, employers, employees, or other persons or entities who have violated the fraud and insurance non-compliance provisions of this Section. The fraud and insurance non-compliance unit shall report violations of the fraud and insurance non-compliance provisions of this Section to the Special Prosecutions Bureau of the Criminal Division of the Office of the Attorney General or to the State's Attorney of the county in which the offense allegedly occurred, either of whom has the authority to prosecute violations under this Section.

With respect to the subject of any investigation being conducted, the fraud and insurance noncompliance unit shall have the general power of subpoena of the Department of Insurance, including the authority to issue a subpoena to a medical provider, pursuant to Section 8-802 of the Code of Civil Procedure. ***

> Effective June 28, 2011.

PRIOR ILLINOIS CASE LAW

1. Illinois Did Not Recognize a Physician-Patient Privilege at Common Law

People *ex rel.* Department of Professional Regulation v. Manos, 202 Ill. 2d 563 (2002)

The Illinois Supreme Court has noted that "[a]t common law, communications between a doctor and a patient were not privileged."

2. There Is No Physician-Patient Privilege Recognized by Federal Common Law

Patterson v. Caterpillar, Inc., 70 F.3d 503 (7th Cir. 1995)

Petitioner was diagnosed with multiple sclerosis and went on disability leave of absence from work. Individuals on such leave were qualified to receive their full salary as long as they met the employer's requirements for being "totally disabled." Petitioner was treated by various doctors and remained on disability leave of absence for five years. The employer conducted a review of individuals on disability and investigated the petitioner. The investigation disclosed that the petitioner was not totally disabled and the employer terminated his benefits. Petitioner sued the employer. At trial, the employer called one of petitioner's treating doctors to testify. Petitioner objected to such testimony and asserted that his medical records were confidential and protected by the physician-patient privilege. The Seventh Circuit rejected petitioner's claim relying on Federal Rule of Evidence 501 and found that federal common law does not recognize the physician-patient privilege.

3. The Statutory Physician-Patient Privilege Protects Confidential Information Physician Acquires That Is Necessary to Enable the Physician to Professionally Serve the Patient
People *ex rel.* Department of Professional Regulation v. Manos, 202 Ill. 2d 563 (2002)

The legislature enacted a physician-patient privilege that protects "certain information obtained by a physician or surgeon in his professional relationship with a patient." 735 ILCS 5/8-802. The Illinois Supreme Court held, as a matter of first impression, that dentists are "surgeons" within the meaning of the physician-patient privilege. The court recognized that while the Department of Professional Regulation has broad investigatory powers, these powers, however, do not override the interests of the physician-patient privilege. Therefore, providing patient records, even with names and other identifying information deleted, would violate the physician-patient privilege. The Supreme Court noted:

> The primary purpose of the physician-patient privilege is to encourage free disclosure between a doctor and a patient and to protect the patient from embarrassment and invasion of privacy that disclosure would entail. See LoCoco v. XL Disposal Corp., 307 Ill. App. 3d 684, 689 (3d Dist. 1999), citing People v. Herbert, 108 Ill. App. 3d 143, 149 (1st Dist. 1982). The physician-patient privilege is one of trust and confidence in which the patient knowingly seeks the doctor's assistance and the doctor knowingly accepts the person as a patient. See *XL Disposal Corp.*, 307 Ill. App. 3d at 689, quoting Reynolds v. Decatur Memorial Hospital, 277 Ill. App. 3d 80, 85 (4th Dist. 1996). The legislature has recognized the patient's interest in maintaining confidentiality in his or her dealings with a physician or surgeon by enacting the physician-patient privilege in section 8-802. People v. Bickham, 89 Ill. 2d 1, 6 (1982). As with other statutory privileges, the physician-patient privilege is a legislative balancing between relationships that society feels should be fostered through the shield of confidentiality and the interests served by disclosure of the information. See Parkson v. Central DuPage Hospital, 105 Ill. App. 3d 850, 854 (1st Dist. 1982). Lastly, the physician-patient privilege is for the benefit of the patient and is not to be used as a shield by doctors. *Bickham*, 89 Ill. 2d at 6.

The defendants, two dentists, refused to produce two patient records and appointment schedules in response to a subpoena *duces tecum* issued by the plaintiff. The circuit court granted plaintiff's motion for summary judgment and ordered the defendants to produce the documents, redacting any patient identifying information. The appellate court affirmed in part, holding that the defendants must produce the patient appointment schedules containing names and addresses of patients treated, but ordered that the Department could not compel the dentists to produce the dental records because they were privileged.

On appeal, the Illinois Supreme Court affirmed and rejected the Department's argument that the Civil Administrative Code empowers the Department to compel production of any documentation the agency deems relevant to its investigation. The Supreme Court held that the Department's investigatory powers do not supersede the privilege. The Supreme Court concluded that the physician-patient privilege applies to dentists, reasoning that while dentists are not physicians, they are surgeons because they perform operations. Therefore, because dentists are surgeons, any "information acquired by dentists in attending any patient in a professional character, necessary to enable dentists to professionally serve the patient, are confidential for purposes of the physician-patient privilege." The Department argued that redaction of patients' names would sufficiently safeguard their privacy. The Illinois Supreme Court disagreed, explaining that even deletion of the patients' names from their medical records would not safeguard the patients' privacy. The Supreme Court explained that the Department already knew the names of the two patients whose records it requested, and that it would not be a difficult task to match the names of the patients to their records, thus easily discovering information protected by the physician-patient privilege.

4. Patients' Medical Records Including Patients' Identities Are Protected If Disclosure Would Also Reveal Information Used by Physician to Professionally Serve the Patient
Defilippis v. Gardner, 368 Ill. App. 3d 1092 (2d Dist. 2006)

Plaintiff filed a malpractice claim against doctor and hospital for damages resulting from negligent medical treatment. Plaintiff requested and the trial court ordered disclosure of the names and addresses of 20 of defendants' patients who had undergone the same procedure as plaintiff. Defendants refused to disclose the identities of their patients and asserted the physician-patient privilege. The plaintiff argued that House v. Swedish American Hospital, 206 Ill. App. 3d 437 (1990), was determinative of the issue. The court in *House* found that a patient's identity could be disclosed where a patient attacked the plaintiff in a hospital and plaintiff was suing the hospital for negligence. The Second District of the Illinois Appellate Court distinguished *House*, noting that while disclosure of patient's name in *House* did not reveal any confidential communications, the disclosure of patients' names here would necessarily expose their diagnosis and the type of treatment they received. The Second District concluded that such disclosure would violate the physician-patient privilege as it would show information "necessary to enable [the physician to] professionally . . . serve the patient" 735 ILCS 5/8-802.

See also Coy v. Washington County Hosp. Dist., 372 Ill. App. 3d 1077 (2007) (finding non-party patients' identity protected by physician-patient privilege).

But see People v. Florendo, 95 Ill. 2d 155 (1983) (holding that a grand jury issuing a subpoena *duces tecum* requesting the disclosure of patients' identities is entitled to the information despite the fact that it reveals the treatment patients received).

5. Patient's Medical Records Requested by Grand Jury Subpoena *Duces Tecum* Are Protected by the Physician-Patient Privilege Unless the Patient Consents
People v. Bickham, 89 Ill. 2d 1 (1982)

A grand jury investigation of a physician's criminal conduct relating to malpractice or abortion may outweigh the patient's right of privacy because courts recognize "the desirability in maintaining the breadth of the grand jury's power to conduct investigations regarding criminal violations." The legislature created the privilege for the patient's benefit, but it was not the legislative intent that a physician would use it as a shield against criminal investigation. In all other grand jury investigations, the privilege protects the information from disclosure, unless the patient consents to the disclosure of confidential information.

Here, defendant physician received a grand jury subpoena for the medical records of 63 patients, but the purpose of the grand jury investigation was not revealed. Defendant argued that he was not allowed to disclose medical records of the women whose identities were known. 62 of the women refused to consent to the disclosure of their medical records to the grand jury, and one woman was deceased. The representative of the deceased woman's estate signed the consent form. The court held that defendant would not have to disclose the records of the 62 women because state failed to show that defendant was the subject of a criminal action for malpractice or abortion, but that defendant would be compelled to disclose the record of the deceased woman as a valid consent had been signed for her records.

6. Patients' Identities Requested by a Grand Jury Subpoena *Duces Tecum* Not Protected by the Physician-Patient Privilege

People v. Florendo, 95 Ill. 2d 155 (1983)

Defendant, a president of a medical group providing abortion services, refused to turn over documents pursuant to a grand jury subpoena *duces tecum* that would identify his public-aid-recipient patients. Defendant argued that the physician-patient privilege protected the patients' identity because disclosure of the information would expose the type of treatment the patients received where clinic only provided abortion-related services. The Illinois Supreme Court disagreed, finding that while it is important to maintain confidentiality of patients' records, it is also important to ensure that a grand jury can conduct its investigations in a meaningful manner. Pursuant to People v. Bickham, 89 Ill. 2d 1 (1982), the grand jury may access patients' medical records only with the patients' consent. Without disclosure of the patients' names, the Supreme Court reasoned, the state would not be able to obtain consent from the patients for the disclosure of their records. The Supreme Court concluded that the defendant would be required to disclose patients' identities because the subpoena did not request confidential medical information, and because of the "public's interest in the [grand jury's] investigation of criminal activities." The Supreme Court explained that to hold otherwise would allow physicians to shield themselves from prosecution for their own misconduct.

But see People *ex rel.* Department of Professional Regulation v. Manos, 202 Ill. 2d 563 (2002) (noting that removal of patients' identifying information from medical records during investigations by governmental body regulating physicians is insufficient to safeguard the patients' privacy and violates the physician-patient privilege; but also finding that disclosure of appointment schedules containing names and addresses of patients was proper and did not violate the physician-patient privilege).

7. Homicide and Physical/Mental Condition at Issue Exceptions to the Physician-Patient Privilege

People v. Botsis, 388 Ill. App. 3d 422 (1st Dist. 2009)

In an aggravated reckless driving and reckless homicide prosecution, the defendant's medical history of fainting incidents was admissible under two exceptions to the physician-patient privilege rule. As to the homicide exception set forth in 735 ILCS 5/8-802.1, the court found that the medical disclosures directly related to the circumstances of the homicide and were probative of the defendant's recklessness because he was unconscious at the scene. As to the exception for actions brought against a patient in which the patient's physical condition is at issue 735 ILCS 5/8-802.4, the court held that the defendant's physical and mental condition were in issue because his state of consciousness was relevant to determining the issue of recklessness.

8. Medical Records Are Not Privileged per Section 5/11-501.4-1 of the Motor Vehicle Code and Disclosure Is Constitutional

People v. Jung, 192 Ill. 2d 1 (2000)

The defendant was involved in a one car accident and the sergeant administering first aid to defendant smelled alcohol on his breath. Defendant admitted to the sergeant that he had been drinking and driving. Defendant was taken to the emergency room and his blood was drawn. The blood test results were immediately disclosed to the police pursuant to 625 ILCS 5/11-501.4-1. Section 5/11-501.4-1 permits disclosure of "the results of blood or urine tests performed for the purpose of determining the content of alcohol, other drugs, or both, in an individual's blood or urine . . . [during] medical treatment in a hospital emergency room for injuries resulting from a motor vehicle accident." These medical records are not protected by the physician-patient privilege. Defendant argued that section 5/11-501.4-1 is unconstitutional. The Illinois Supreme Court disagreed, noting that

> Under the instant statute, the medical information which may be disclosed to police is strictly confined to the results of physician-ordered blood or urine tests. Given that life, limb and property are seriously threatened by drunken driving and given the all too common reality that a driver involved in a motor vehicle accident may be intoxicated, waiver of a driver's privacy interest in his blood or urine test results in this situation is reasonable and does not violate his constitutional right to privacy.

For other cases also discussing this topic, see:

People v. Ogle, 313 Ill. App. 3d 813 (1st Dist. 2000) (finding that blood-alcohol test results were not subject to the physician-patient privilege).

People v. Ernst, 311 Ill. App. 3d 672 (2d Dist. 2000) (finding that section 11-501.4-1 specifically authorizes medical providers to report blood-alcohol test results to the police without prior judicial authorization).

The Therapist-Patient Privilege

AUTHOR'S COMMENTARY

One Illinois trial court recognized at common law a special need for protection of communications between a psychotherapist and a patient. Binder v. Ruvell, Civil Docket 52C2535 (Ill. Cir. 1952). Some have noted, however, that the trial court's decision in *Binder* was "generally considered without justification in law." Ralph Slovenko, *Psychiatry and a Second Look at the Medical Privilege*, 6 WAYNE L. REV. 175, 196 (1959-1960). It appears that the privilege was not recognized in common law and this trial court decision is the only case in which an Illinois court explicitly protected the therapist-patient relationship before the statute was enacted. *See* MICHAEL H. GRAHAM, GRAHAM'S HANDBOOK OF ILLINOIS EVIDENCE § 503.1 (10th ed. 2010). The therapist-patient privilege is now recognized in all 50 states by statute or common law and in Illinois by 740 ILCS 110/10. Norskog v. Pfiel, 197 Ill. 2d 60, 72 (2001).

RELEVANT STATUTORY AUTHORITY

The Therapist-Patient Privilege: 740 ILCS 110/10 (The Mental Health and Developmental Disabilities Confidentiality Act)

The Mental Health and Developmental Disabilities Confidentiality Act § 10. (a) Except as provided herein, in any civil, criminal, administrative, or legislative proceeding, or in any proceeding preliminary thereto, a recipient, and a therapist on behalf and in the interest of a recipient, has the privilege to refuse to disclose and to prevent the disclosure of the recipient's record or communications.

(1) Records and communications may be disclosed in a civil, criminal or administrative proceeding in which the recipient introduces his mental condition or any aspect of his services received for such condition as an element of his claim or defense, if and only to the extent the court in which the proceedings have been brought, or, in the case of an administrative proceeding, the court to which an appeal or other action for review of an administrative determination may be taken, finds, after *in camera* examination of testimony or other evidence, that it is

relevant, probative, not unduly prejudicial or inflammatory, and otherwise clearly admissible; that other satisfactory evidence is demonstrably unsatisfactory as evidence of the facts sought to be established by such evidence; and that disclosure is more important to the interests of substantial justice than protection from injury to the therapist-recipient relationship or to the recipient or other whom disclosure is likely to harm. Except in a criminal proceeding in which the recipient, who is accused in that proceeding, raises the defense of insanity, no record or communication between a therapist and a recipient shall be deemed relevant for purposes of this subsection, except the fact of treatment, the cost of services and the ultimate diagnosis unless the party seeking disclosure of the communication clearly establishes in the trial court a compelling need for its production. However, for purposes of this Act, in any action brought or defended under the Illinois Marriage and Dissolution of Marriage Act, or in any action in which pain and suffering is an element of the claim, mental condition shall not be deemed to be introduced merely by making such claim and shall be deemed to be introduced only if the recipient or a witness on his behalf first testifies concerning the record or communication.

***

(3) In the event of a claim made or an action filed by a recipient, or, following the recipient's death, by any party claiming as a beneficiary of the recipient for injury caused in the course of providing services to such recipient, the therapist and other persons whose actions are alleged to have been the cause of injury may disclose pertinent records and communications to an attorney or attorneys engaged to render advice about and to provide representation in connection with such matter and to persons working under the supervision of such attorney or attorneys, and may testify as to such records or communication in any administrative, judicial or discovery proceeding for the purpose of preparing and presenting a defense against such claim or action.

(4) Records and communications made to or by a therapist in the course of examination ordered by a court for good cause shown may, if otherwise relevant and admissible, be disclosed in a civil, criminal, or administrative proceeding in which the recipient is a party or in appropriate pretrial proceedings, provided such court has found that the recipient has been as adequately and as effectively as possible informed before submitting to such examination that such records and communications would not be considered confidential or privileged. Such records and communications shall be admissible only as to issues involving the recipient's physical or mental condition and only to the extent that these are germane to such proceedings.

***

(6) *Records and communications may be disclosed to a court-appointed therapist, psychologist, or psychiatrist for use in determining a person's fitness to stand trial if the records were made within the 180-day period immediately preceding the date of the therapist's, psychologist's or psychiatrist's court appointment. These records and communications shall be admissible only as to the issue of the person's fitness to stand trial.* Records and communications may be disclosed when such are made during treatment which the recipient is ordered to undergo to render him fit to stand trial on a criminal charge, provided that the disclosure is made only with respect to the issue of fitness to stand trial.

[Italicized text added by P.A. 97-566, effective January 1, 2012].

***

(8) Records or communications may be disclosed when such are relevant to a matter in issue in any action brought under this Act and proceedings preliminary thereto, provided that any information so disclosed shall not be utilized for any other purpose nor be redisclosed except in connection with such action or preliminary proceedings.

(9) Records and communications of the recipient may be disclosed in investigations of and trials for homicide when the disclosure relates directly to the fact or immediate circumstances of the homicide.

(10) Records and communications of a deceased recipient may be disclosed to a coroner conducting a preliminary investigation into the recipient's death under Section 3-3013 of the Counties Code. However, records and communications of the deceased recipient disclosed in an investigation shall be limited solely to the deceased recipient's records and communications relating to the factual circumstances of the incident being investigated in a mental health facility.

(11) Records and communications of a recipient shall be disclosed in a proceeding where a petition or motion is filed under the Juvenile Court Act of 1987 and the recipient is named as a parent, guardian, or legal custodian of a minor who is the subject of a petition for wardship as described in Section 2-3 of that Act or a minor who is the subject of a petition for wardship as described in Section 2-4 of that Act alleging the minor is abused, neglected, or dependent or the recipient is named as a parent of a child who is the subject of a petition, supplemental petition, or motion to appoint a guardian with the power to consent to adoption under Section 2-29 of the Juvenile Court Act of 1987.

***

(b) Before a disclosure is made under subsection (a), any party to the proceeding or any other interested person may request an *in camera* review of the record or communications to be disclosed. The court or agency conducting the proceeding may hold an *in camera* review on its own motion. When, contrary to the express wish of the recipient, the therapist asserts a privilege on behalf and in the interest of a recipient, the court may require that the therapist, in an *in camera* hearing, establish that disclosure is not in the best interest of the recipient. The court or agency may prevent disclosure or limit disclosure to the extent that other admissible evidence is sufficient to establish the facts in issue. The court or agency may enter such orders as may be necessary in order to protect the confidentiality, privacy, and safety of the recipient or of other persons. Any order to disclose or to not disclose shall be considered a final order for purposes of appeal and shall be subject to interlocutory appeal.

***

(d) No party to any proceeding described under paragraphs (1), (2), (3), (4), (7), or (8) of subsection (a) of this Section, nor his or her attorney, shall serve a subpoena seeking to obtain access to records or communications under this Act unless the subpoena is accompanied by a written order issued by a judge, authorizing the disclosure of the records or the issuance of the subpoena. No such written order shall be issued without written notice of the motion to the recipient and the treatment provider. Prior to issuance of the order, each party or other person entitled to notice shall be permitted an opportunity to be heard pursuant to subsection (b) of this Section. No person shall comply with a subpoena for records or communications under this Act, unless the subpoena is accompanied by a written order authorizing the issuance of the subpoena or the disclosure of the records. Each subpoena duces tecum issued by a court or administrative agency or served on any person pursuant to this subsection (d) shall include the following language: "No person shall comply with a subpoena for mental health records or communications pursuant to Section 10 of the Mental Health and Developmental Disabilities Confidentiality Act, 740 ILCS 110/10, unless the subpoena is accompanied by a written order that authorizes the issuance of the subpoena and the disclosure of records or communications."

(e) When a person has been transported by a peace officer to a mental health facility, then upon the request of a peace officer, if the person is allowed to leave the mental health facility within 48 hours of arrival, excluding Saturdays, Sundays, and holidays, the facility director shall notify the local law enforcement authority prior to the release of the person. The local law enforcement authority may re-disclose the information as necessary to alert the appropriate enforcement or prosecuting authority.

(f) A recipient's records and communications shall be disclosed to the Inspector General of the Department of Human Services within 10 business days of a request by the Inspector General (i) in the course of an investigation authorized by the Department of Human Services Act and applicable rule or (ii) during the course of an assessment authorized by the Abuse of Adults with Disabilities Intervention Act and applicable rule. The request shall be in writing and signed by the Inspector General or his or her designee. The request shall state the purpose for which disclosure is sought. Any person who knowingly and willfully refuses to comply with such a request is guilty of a Class A misdemeanor. A recipient's records and communications shall also be disclosed pursuant to subsection (g-5) of Section 1-17 of the Department of Human Services Act in testimony at health care worker registry hearings or preliminary proceedings when such are relevant to the matter in issue, provided that any information so disclosed shall not be utilized for any other purpose nor be redisclosed except in connection with such action or preliminary proceedings.

Effective January 1, 2012.

(Note that statutory text related to civil proceedings only has been omitted.)

Definitions: 740 ILCS 110/2

§ 2. The terms used in this Act, unless the context requires otherwise, have the meanings ascribed to them in this Section. ***

"Confidential communication" or "communication" means any communication made by a recipient or other person to a therapist or to or in the presence of other persons during or in connection with providing mental health or developmental disability services to a recipient. Communication includes information which indicates that a person is a recipient.

Effective December 1, 1997.

PRIOR ILLINOIS CASE LAW

1. One Illinois Trial Court Recognized the Special Need for Protection of Communications Between a Psychotherapist and a Patient at Common Law

Binder v. Ruvell, Civil Docket 52C2535 (Ill. Cir. 1952)

Psychiatrist treating a patient refused to testify about his treatment of the patient relying on the physician-patient privilege. The trial court noted that at the time, "no immunity [arose] from any professional relationship other than that of lawyer and client" in Illinois and that there was no statutory privilege protecting communications between the therapist and patient. The trial court, however, considered the public policy of Illinois with respect to the issue. The court observed that although "the physician and patient relationship does not enjoy immunity," the therapist-patient relationship may be protected because of the "vital difference[s]" between the two. The court explained that a psychiatrist would not succeed in his or her treatment "unless there is complete confidence in the mind of the patient . . . in the secrecy of the things transpiring in the doctor's chambers." The physician-patient relationship does not require such secrecy because a physician does not delve deeply into the subconscious mind of the patient but only treats specific physical illnesses. The court concluded that the confidential communications between the psychiatrist and patient were privileged.

2. Federal Common Law Protects Confidential Communications Made in the Course of a Psychotherapist-Patient Relationship

Jaffee v. Redmond, 518 U.S. 1 (1996)

The United States Supreme Court recognized a psychotherapist-patient privilege under Federal Rule of Evidence 501 and that confidential communications made in the course of diagnosis or treatment are protected from compelled disclosure. The Court also rejected a balancing component which would make confidentiality contingent upon the trial court's later determination of relative importance of the patient's private interests and the evidentiary need for the disclosure.

In recognizing the privilege, the Court first pointed out that Federal Rule of Evidence 501 authorizes federal courts to define new privileges based on reason and experience. The Court further found that the privilege served both private and public interests. As to private interests, the privilege protects confidential communications which are necessary for development of trust and confidence in treatment.

> Effective psychotherapy . . . depends upon an atmosphere of confidence and trust in which the patient is willing to make a frank and complete disclosure of facts, emotions, memories, and fears. Because of the sensitive nature of the problems for which individuals consult psychotherapists, disclosure of confidential communications made during counseling sessions may cause embarrassment or disgrace. For this reason, the mere possibility of disclosure may impede development of the confidential relationship necessary for successful treatment.

The privilege also serves the public function, since it serves to facilitate treatment for individuals who suffer from mental and emotional problems. The Court stated that the mental health of our citizens is just as important as their physical health.

As further support, the Court stated that all 50 states and the District of Columbia have adopted a psychotherapist-patient privilege. In light of this, "any State's promise of confidentiality would have little value if the patient were aware that the privilege would not be honored in a federal court. Denial of the federal privilege therefore would frustrate the purposes of the state legislation that was enacted to foster these confidential communications."

Because the therapist in this case was a social worker, the Court was required to address whether the privilege applies to such individuals. In finding that the privilege does apply, it looked to the fact that social workers provide a significant amount of mental care treatment and that a vast majority of the states extend their privilege to social workers. As an example of this trend, the Supreme Court noted in a footnote that Illinois extends the protections of the privilege by broadly defining the term "therapists" to include "social workers" (740 ILCS 110/2 and 740 ILCS 110/10). As a final note, the Court stated it was not "necessary nor feasible to delineate [the] full contours [of the privilege] in a way that would 'govern all conceivable future questions in this area.'"

3. The Therapist-Patient Privilege Is Recognized in All 50 States by Statute or Common Law and in Illinois by 740 ILCS 110/10

Norskog v. Pfiel, 197 Ill. 2d 60 (2001)

The Illinois Supreme Court noted that:

> All 50 states, the District of Columbia and the federal courts recognize a psychiatrist-patient privilege, either by statute or common law. Jaffee v. Redmond, 518 U.S. 1, 12 (1996). Clearly, this reflects an understanding that people will increasingly avail themselves of needed treatment if they are confident that their privacy will be protected. It is in the public interest, then, that we zealously guard against erosion of the confidentiality privilege.

Plaintiffs, parents of a murdered victim, brought wrongful death and survival claims against patient who committed the murder and action for negligent supervision against his parents. Plaintiffs alleged at trial that the patient had received mental health services and defendants objected to the admissibility of such evidence based on the Mental Health and Developmental Disabilities Confidentiality Act ("Act"). Defendants claimed that the mental health information requested by plaintiffs was privileged. Plaintiffs argued that defendant had waived the privilege because (1) the patient asserted the insanity defense at his criminal trial, and (2) the patient's mental health information was revealed at his fitness examination and (3) the information was also disclosed to school officials and a probation officer.

With respect to the plaintiffs' first argument, the Supreme Court explained that the patient had not waived the privilege pursuant to section 10(a)(1) of the Act at his criminal trial by asserting the insanity defense because he did not go to trial but rather pleaded guilty. Thus, he never had the chance to assert the affirmative defense of insanity. In considering the plaintiffs' second argument, the Supreme Court found that patient did not waive the privilege pursuant to section 10(a)(4) of the Act by participating in a court-ordered fitness examination in his criminal case because the examiner did not inform the patient about possible disclosure of the information in a subsequent civil proceeding. Finally, the Supreme Court rejected the plaintiffs' third argument by noting that the mere fact that the patient and his parents shared his mental health records with school officials and a probation officer did not indicate that the patient intended to waive confidentiality.

Plaintiffs further asserted that the information should not be protected by the privilege because considerations of fundamental fairness require its disclosure. The Supreme Court rejected the plaintiffs' argument and concluded that the patient and his parents were not using the therapist-patient privilege as a sword "to exploit or subvert the legal process," but rather to shield certain confidential information. The Supreme Court observed that the parents were actually at a disadvantage by not disclosing the information because the mental health records could have helped them defend against allegations "that they failed to take action to control [their son's] behavior." The Supreme Court concluded that fundamental fairness did not require disclosure.

4. The Therapist-Patient Privilege, unlike the Physician-Patient Privilege, Protects the Patient's Identity

People v. Doe, 211 Ill. App. 3d 962 (1st Dist. 1991)

The therapist patient privilege under the Mental Health and Developmental Disabilities Confidentiality Act, unlike the physician-patient privilege (735 ILCS 5/8-802), is not qualified by the condition that the communications be "necessary to enable him [or her] to professionally serve" the patient. Instead, any communication made to the therapist during or "in connection with providing mental health or developmental disability services" is privileged, including "information which indicates that a person is *a recipient*" (740 ILCS 110/2) (emphasis added).

Here, a grand jury issued a subpoena *duces tecum* to a therapist at a mental health facility, requiring her to disclose "any and all information on all male tenants" of the facility to the grand jury in a "John Doe investigation" for homicide. The First District of the Illinois

Appellate Court held that information identifying male residents of the mental health facility was privileged, distinguishing People v. Florendo, 95 Ill. 2d 155 (1983). In *Florendo*, the Illinois Supreme Court relied on 735 ILCS 5/8-802 to find that the physician-patient privilege did not protect disclosure of a patient's identity at a grand jury proceeding because that information was not necessary to enable the physician to treat the patient. The First District, however, held that identities of mental health patients were protected by the therapist-patient privilege because disclosure of such facts would necessarily reveal information indicating that they were treatment *recipients*.

The First District further refused to apply the homicide exception in this case because state failed to show that disclosure of the patients' identities related "directly" to the "immediate circumstances" of a homicide. The court concluded that the state was merely embarking on a "fishing expedition" as it conceded that there were no leads in the case.

5. The Therapist-Patient Privilege Only Protects Communications Between Patients and Therapists Where Patients Are Seeking Treatment
Johnston v. Weil, 241 Ill. 2d 169 (2011)

Plaintiffs, an ex-wife and her parents, filed a complaint against ex-wife's former husbands, children's counselors and ex-husbands' attorneys for violations of the Mental Health and Developmental Disabilities Confidentiality Act as a result of dissemination of certain information during divorce proceedings. Plaintiffs argued that a psychiatrist appointed pursuant to 750 ILCS 5/604(b) to evaluate them for a child custody matter was a mental health provider within the meaning of the therapist-patient privilege statute and thus the conversations between plaintiffs and psychiatrist were confidential and privileged. The Illinois Supreme Court disagreed, finding that the therapist-patient statute "only applies to situations in which the patient is seeking treatment for a mental health condition." Here, the plaintiffs were not "recipients" within the meaning of the statute and the psychiatrist was not retained to treat plaintiffs, but rather to evaluate them in a domestic relations proceeding.

6. Statements Related to the Immediate Circumstances of a Homicide Are Admissible Under the Therapist-Patient Privilege
People v. Wilson, 164 Ill. 2d 436 (1994)

Defendant made oral statements to the prison therapist regarding his accomplice in armed robbery and murder. The therapist recounted defendant's statements at trial. Defendant argued that the statements were inadmissible and subject to the therapist-patient privilege, but the court disagreed. The court found that the statements were directly related to the facts and immediate circumstances of the homicide with which defendant was charged, and therefore the statements were admissible.

7. Court May Order *in Camera* Review of Patient's Medical Records If Patient Places His or Her Condition in Issue
Goldberg v. Davis, 151 Ill. 2d 267 (1992)

The accused, a psychiatrist subject to disciplinary proceedings stemming from his sexual misconduct with a patient, sued the patient's former psychiatrist seeking access to the patient's medical records. The circuit court ordered the former psychiatrist to disclose the records for *in camera* review. The former psychiatrist refused to reveal the patient's records claiming a therapist-patient privilege. Illinois Supreme Court found that the patient's records were not privileged because the patient's mental condition was an element of the sexual misconduct claim. Further, the accused and the former psychiatrist differed regarding the precise diagnosis of the patient, and the court determined that a "diagnosis [was] significant to the issue of whether any sexual misconduct occurred." Specifically, the accused claimed that the patient's allegations were not based in reality. The former psychiatrist, however, argued that patient's belief that the accused was engaged in a sexual relationship with her was real. The Supreme Court concluded that an *in camera* examination of the patient's records could help settle the issue of whether the patient's belief that improper conduct occurred was based on reality or fiction.

8. The Therapist-Patient Privilege May Protect Even Communications Made Outside of the Formal Treatment Process

People v. Gemeny, 313 Ill. App. 3d 902 (2d Dist. 2000)

The state sought to introduce threatening voice recordings that the defendant had left on his court-appointed therapist's voice mail. The defendant objected, claiming that the recordings were privileged communications and should be protected from disclosure under the Mental Health and Developmental Disabilities Confidentiality Act. The appellate court agreed. Although the state asserted that voice mail was not meant to be "protected communication" within the context of the Confidentiality Act, the court disagreed on two grounds. First, the court reasoned that "giving the words used to define 'communication' their plain and ordinary meanings, [the] messages, whatever their precise content, were made 'in connection with providing mental health . . . services.'" Secondly, the court held that long-standing policy to "encourage complete candor between patient and therapist" would best be preserved by not limiting the definition of "communication" in the context of the Confidentiality Act to just those communications that occur in formal treatment sessions.

9. The Therapist-Patient Privilege Applies to Records Created Pursuant to Treatment That Occurred Prior to the Effective Date of the Statute

Wisniewski v. Kownacki, 221 Ill. 2d 453 (2006)

The plaintiff filed suit against the defendants alleging that a Catholic priest had sexually abused him between 1973 and 1978. The plaintiff also alleged fraud and conspiracy against the Diocese, claiming that the Diocese knew that the priest had molested another child in the past before transferring him to the site of the abuse in question. The plaintiff also alleged that the priest had received mental health treatment and alcohol counseling prior to the transfer. During discovery, the plaintiff sought disclosure of the priest's mental health and alcohol counseling records. The defendants alleged that the records were privileged under the Mental Health and Developmental Disabilities Confidentiality Act (Confidentiality Act) (740 ILCS 110/1 *et seq.* (West 2002)) and the Alcoholism and Other Drug Abuse and Dependency Act (Dependency Act) (20 ILCS 301/30-5 *et seq.* (West 2002)). The trial court disagreed and ruled that they must disclose the records because they were made prior to the enactment of the legislation. The defendants refused to turn over the records, and as a result the trial court held them in contempt, fined them and awarded the plaintiff's attorney fees. The appellate court affirmed the order of production but vacated the order holding the defendants in contempt.

On further appeal, the Illinois Supreme Court ruled that the applicability of the Confidentiality Act and the Dependency Act did not depend on retroactive/prospective analysis because the disclosure of records only "takes place in the present or the future." The court reasoned that "applying the nondisclosure provisions of the Confidentiality Act and the Dependency Act to pre-enactment treatment records and communications would not impair anyone's rights with respect to past transactions." The protection from disclosure contemplated by the statutes covered mental health records and alcohol treatment records created prior to the enactment of the statutes. However, the court did not rule on whether the priest may invoke the privileges under the statutes in the present case. The court noted that there are several exceptions that permit disclosure under the statutes and remanded the case to the trial court to determine if any statutory exceptions are applicable to the instant matter.

10. Defendant May Waive the Therapist-Patient Privilege Through Assertion of Insanity or Intoxication Defense
People v. Kashney, 111 Ill. 2d 454 (1986)

Two defendants' appeals were consolidated at the Illinois Supreme Court due to a common question arising under 725 ILCS 5/104-14(a). Section 104-14(a) states:

> § 104-14. Use of Statements Made During Examination or Treatment. (a) Statements made by the defendant and information gathered in the course of any examination or treatment ordered under Section 104-13, 104-17 or 104-20 shall not be admissible against the defendant unless he raises the defense of insanity or the defense of drugged or intoxicated condition, in which case they shall be admissible only on the issue of whether he was insane, drugged, or intoxicated. The refusal of the defendant to cooperate in such examinations shall not preclude the raising of the aforesaid defenses but shall preclude the defendant from offering expert evidence or testimony tending to support such defenses if the expert evidence or testimony is based upon the expert's examination of the defendant.

Murder defendant argued on appeal that his statements made to court-appointed psychiatrists were inadmissible at his trial because they were protected by the therapist-patient privilege and he did not present a defense of insanity. Defendant did not explicitly present the defense of insanity, but did suggest that he was insane at the time he confessed to the crime, believing that he was coerced into confessing by a demon that overtook one of the investigating officers. The appellate court held that state could use defendant's statements for purposes of impeachment. The Illinois Supreme Court agreed, noting that under 725 ILCS 5/104-14(a), defendant waived statutory protection by introducing substance of statements made during court ordered fitness examination through testimony of examining psychiatrist to support claim that confession was coerced by demonic possession.

Second defendant was charged with rape and asserted that he suffered from post-traumatic stress syndrome and that the sexual encounter with the victim was consensual. Defendant met with a court-ordered psychologist who then testified at trial regarding statements made to her by the defendant. The court noted that section 104-14(a) only allows for use of defendant's statements if he raised the defense of insanity, but that the defendant did not assert the affirmative defense during trial. Defendant denied he committed the crime and called his own psychiatrist to explain why he may have verbally abused the victim during a consensual sexual encounter. The court concluded that the introduction of post-traumatic stress syndrome evidence did not raise affirmative defense of insanity, and therefore confidentiality was protected.

11. Patient's Waiver of the Therapist-Patient Privilege Bars Reliance on the Privilege at a Future Trial
Novak v. Rathnam, 106 Ill. 2d 478 (1985)

The therapist-patient privilege may be asserted by a patient, a physician, or a hospital acting on behalf of the patient. Only the patient, who is the holder of the privilege, may waive it. A psychiatrist testified at his patient's murder trial and disclosed privileged information for the purpose of establishing the patient's insanity at the time of the crime. The father of the victim subsequently sued the psychiatrist for wrongful death and sought to depose the psychiatrist regarding his treatment of the patient. The psychiatrist asserted the therapist-patient privilege and refused to submit to a deposition. The court noted that

> [i]f there is a disclosure of confidential information by the individual for whose benefit the privilege exists, or if he permits such a disclosure, the privilege is waived and cannot be reasserted. Wigmore states:
>
> > A waiver at a *former trial* should bar a claim of the [therapist-patient] privilege at a later trial, for the original disclosure takes away once and for all the confidentiality sought to be protected by the privilege. To enforce it thereafter is to seek to preserve a privacy which exists in legal fiction only." (Emphasis in original.) 8 WIGMORE, EVIDENCE sec. 2389(4), at 860-61 (McNaughton rev. ed. 1961).

Here, the patient had previously waived the therapist-patient privilege at the criminal trial, and a "waiver of the privilege involved in a prior proceeding will be regarded as a waiver of the privilege in a subsequent proceeding."

12. Privilege Against Self-Incrimination Bars Introduction of Defendant's Statements to Court-Ordered Psychiatrist Absent Consent or Warnings and Intelligent Waiver
Estelle v. Smith, 451 U.S. 454 (1981)

The United States Supreme Court held that the Fifth Amendment privilege against self-incrimination bars the use at a capital sentencing hearing of compelled statements made by a defendant during a court-ordered psychiatric examination absent consent or adequate warnings and intelligent waiver of constitutional rights. The Court also held that an examination held after attachment of the Sixth Amendment right to counsel is a "critical stage," and therefore the defendant is entitled to the assistance of counsel.

13. Defendant's Sixth Amendment Right of Confrontation Not Denied by Refusal to Grant Access to Prosecution Witness' Privileged Mental Health Records
People v. Bean, 137 Ill. 2d 65 (1990)

Defendant's sixth amendment right of confrontation was not violated where witness' mental health records remained privileged but defense counsel was allowed to explore witness' mental health on cross-examination to expose potential bias. The court noted:

> This public interest [in maintaining the confidentiality of mental health records], and the individual recipient's interest, in maintaining the secrecy of this personal information in order to assist the individual's recovery justifies its protection from the unlimited scrutiny of a criminal defendant or defense counsel wielding the sixth amendment as a weapon before which all other interests must fall. . . . [J]ust as a trial judge can limit cross-examination to prevent inquiries that are irrelevant, repetitive, or too time-consuming, that harass the witness, or that threaten to distract the jury from the actual issues by unduly emphasizing details of the witness' life, a defendant's access to statutorily privileged information can be limited by the same considerations. Thus, when the patient or a therapist asserts the privilege, a trial judge can review *in camera*, without disclosure to any attorneys, a witness' mental health records and disclose only those portions that are relevant when that relevance is not outweighed by other factors.

Defendant argued that the trial court unfairly limited the disclosure of prosecution witness' mental health records, but the court disagreed. The court found that the only mental health information that was not disclosed to the defendant was information that was irrelevant to defendant's case. The Supreme Court noted that the trial court properly disclosed all information relevant to defendant's case, such as the witness' past alcohol and drug abuse, and properly allowed defendant to explore these issues on cross-examination.

Rape Crisis Counselor Privilege: 735 ILCS 5/8-802.1

AUTHOR'S COMMENTARY

Illinois has statutorily created a privilege for records and communications made between a rape crisis counselor and an alleged victim of a sex crime. 735 ILCS 5/8-802.1. Communications made in the course of providing information, counseling, or advocacy are privileged. A rape crisis counselor includes a psychologist, social worker, or volunteer who works for a rape crisis organization. Absent the victim's consent, a rape crisis counselor cannot disclose any confidential communications nor be examined in a criminal proceeding regarding these communications. People v. Foggy, 121 Ill. 2d 337 (1988).

RELEVANT STATUTORY AUTHORITY

Privilege for Statements Made by a Victim of a Sexual Offense to Rape Crisis Personnel: 735 ILCS 5/8-802.1

§ 8-802.1. Confidentiality of Statements Made to Rape Crisis Personnel

(a) Purpose. This Section is intended to protect victims of rape from public disclosure of statements they make in confidence to counselors of organizations established to help them. On or after July 1, 1984, "rape" means an act of forced sexual penetration or sexual conduct, as defined in Section 11-0.1 of the Criminal Code of 1961, as amended, including acts prohibited under Sections 11-1.20 through 11-1.60 or 12-13 through 12-16 of the Criminal Code of 1961, as amended. Because of the fear and stigma that often results from those crimes, many victims hesitate to seek help even where it is available at no cost to them. As a result they not only fail to receive needed medical care and emergency counseling, but may lack the psychological support necessary to report the crime and aid police in preventing future crimes.

(b) Definitions. As used in this Act:

(1) "Rape crisis organization" means any organization or association the major purpose of which is providing information, counseling, and psychological support to victims of any or all of the crimes of aggravated criminal sexual assault, predatory criminal sexual assault of a child, criminal sexual assault, sexual relations between siblings, criminal sexual abuse and aggravated criminal sexual abuse.

(2) "Rape crisis counselor" means a person who is a psychologist, social worker, employee, or volunteer in any organization or association defined as a rape crisis organization under this Section, who has undergone 40 hours of training and is under the control of a direct services supervisor of a rape crisis organization.

(3) "Victim" means a person who is the subject of, or who seeks information, counseling, or advocacy services as a result of an aggravated criminal sexual assault, predatory criminal sexual assault of a child, criminal sexual assault, sexual relations within families, criminal sexual abuse, aggravated criminal sexual abuse, sexual exploitation of a child, indecent solicitation of a child, public indecency, exploitation of a child, promoting juvenile prostitution as described in subdivision (a)(4) of Section 11-14.4, or an attempt to commit any of these offenses.

(4) "Confidential communication" means any communication between a victim and a rape crisis counselor in the course of providing information, counseling, and advocacy. The term includes all records kept by the counselor or by the

organization in the course of providing services to an alleged victim concerning the alleged victim and the services provided.

(c) Waiver of privilege.

(1) The confidential nature of the communication is not waived by: the presence of a third person who further expresses the interests of the victim at the time of the communication; group counseling; or disclosure to a third person with the consent of the victim when reasonably necessary to accomplish the purpose for which the counselor is consulted.

(2) The confidential nature of counseling records is not waived when: the victim inspects the records; or in the case of a minor child less than 12 years of age, a parent or guardian whose interests are not adverse to the minor inspects the records; or in the case of a minor victim 12 years or older, a parent or guardian whose interests are not adverse to the minor inspects the records with the victim's consent, or in the case of an adult who has a guardian of his or her person, the guardian inspects the records with the victim's consent.

(3) When a victim is deceased, the executor or administrator of the victim's estate may waive the privilege established by this Section, unless the executor or administrator has an interest adverse to the victim.

(4) A minor victim 12 years of age or older may knowingly waive the privilege established in this Section. When a minor is, in the opinion of the Court, incapable of knowingly waiving the privilege, the parent or guardian of the minor may waive the privilege on behalf of the minor, unless the parent or guardian has been charged with a violent crime against the victim or otherwise has any interest adverse to that of the minor with respect to the waiver of the privilege.

(5) An adult victim who has a guardian of his or her person may knowingly waive the privilege established in this Section. When the victim is, in the opinion of the court, incapable of knowingly waiving the privilege, the guardian of the adult victim may waive the privilege on behalf of the victim, unless the guardian has been charged with a violent crime against the victim or otherwise has any interest adverse to the victim with respect to the privilege.

(d) Confidentiality. Except as provided in this Act, no rape crisis counselor shall disclose any confidential communication or be examined as a witness in any civil or criminal proceeding as to any confidential communication without the written consent of the victim or a representative of the victim as provided in subparagraph (c).

(e) A rape crisis counselor may disclose a confidential communication without the consent of the victim if failure to disclose is likely to result in a clear, imminent risk of serious physical injury or death of the victim or another person. Any rape crisis counselor or rape crisis organization participating in good faith in the disclosing of records and communications under this Act shall have immunity from any liability, civil, criminal, or otherwise that might result from the action. In any proceeding, civil or criminal, arising out of a disclosure under this Section, the good faith of any rape crisis counselor or rape crisis organization who disclosed the confidential communication shall be presumed.

(f) Any rape crisis counselor who knowingly discloses any confidential communication in violation of this Act commits a Class C misdemeanor.

Effective July 1, 2011.

Prior Illinois Case Law

1. Absent Rape Victim's Consent, Confidential Rape Crisis Counselor Communications Are Privileged

People v. Foggy, 121 Ill. 2d 337 (1988)

Defendant argued that the court's refusal to disclose communications between rape victim and a rape crisis counselor violated his due process and confrontation rights and impaired his right to present a defense. Defendant requested an *in camera* inspection of communications pertaining to the commission of the alleged crime. The trial court quashed defendant's subpoena seeking disclosure, finding that the communications were privileged and that defendant's confrontation rights would not be violated as the victim would be subject to cross-examination when she testified in court. The Illinois Supreme Court relied on Davis v. Alaska, 415 U.S. 308 (1974), where the United States Supreme Court held that defendant's confrontation rights were violated when he was prevented from fully conducting impeachment of a state's witness with his juvenile record. The Supreme Court in *Davis* noted that "[t]he State's policy interest in protecting the confidentiality of a juvenile offender's record cannot require yielding of so vital a constitutional right as the effective cross-examination for bias of a defense witness." Here, the trial court found that the defendant's request for information "did not represent critical or irreplaceable information," was only general and did not show how disclosure of the materials would be helpful to his defense.

The Supreme Court further examined the legislative intent behind 735 ILCS 5/8-802.1 and determined that legislature reinforced the policy of confidentiality when it removed a provision that permitted *in camera* review of records, broadened the confidentiality statement and added a penalty for disclosure of confidential information. The Supreme Court noted that this strong legislative intent of strengthening confidentiality and the absence of information or reason to believe that victim's communications with rape therapist would provide basis for impeachment required that the information remain confidential. The Supreme Court therefore concluded:

> In sum, section 8-802.1 of the Code of Civil Procedure evinces a strong public policy in favor of the confidentiality of communications between sexual assault victims and counselors. Unlike the defendant in *Davis* who knew of specific information that could show bias or motive to fabricate on the part of the prosecution witness, and who had no other means of achieving that end, the defendant here has offered no reason to believe that the victim's counseling records would provide a source of impeaching material unavailable from other sources. We conclude that the defendant was not denied due process, nor was his confrontation right violated, by the trial judge's refusal in this case to conduct an *in camera* inspection of the victim's counseling records.

Domestic Violence Counselor or Advocate Privilege: 750 ILCS 60/227 & 750 ILCS 60/227.1

Relevant Statutory Authority

Privileged Communications Between Domestic Violence Counselors and Victims: 750 ILCS 60/227

§ 227. Privileged communications between domestic violence counselors and victims.

(a) As used in this Section:

(1) "Domestic violence program" means any unit of local government, organization, or association whose major purpose is to provide one or more of the following:

information, crisis intervention, emergency shelter, referral, counseling, advocacy, or emotional support to victims of domestic violence.

(2) "Domestic violence advocate or counselor" means any person (A) who has undergone a minimum of forty hours of training in domestic violence advocacy, crisis intervention, and related areas, and (B) who provides services to victims through a domestic violence program either on an employed or volunteer basis.

(3) "Confidential communication" means any communication between an alleged victim of domestic violence and a domestic violence advocate or counselor in the course of providing information, counseling, or advocacy. The term includes all records kept by the advocate or counselor or by the domestic violence program in the course of providing services to an alleged victim concerning the alleged victim and the services provided. The confidential nature of the communication is not waived by the presence at the time of the communication of any additional persons, including but not limited to an interpreter, to further express the interests of the domestic violence victim or by the advocate's or counselor's disclosure to such an additional person with the consent of the victim when reasonably necessary to accomplish the purpose for which the advocate or counselor is consulted.

(4) "Domestic violence victim" means any person who consults a domestic violence counselor for the purpose of securing advice, counseling or assistance related to one or more alleged incidents of domestic violence.

(5) "Domestic violence" means abuse as defined in the Illinois Domestic Violence Act.

(b) No domestic violence advocate or counselor shall disclose any confidential communication or be examined as a witness in any civil or criminal case or proceeding or in any legislative or administrative proceeding without the written consent of the domestic violence victim except (1) in accordance with the provisions of the Abused and Neglected Child Reporting Act or (2) in cases where failure to disclose is likely to result in an imminent risk of serious bodily harm or death of the victim or another person.

(c) A domestic violence advocate or counselor who knowingly discloses any confidential communication in violation of this Act commits a Class A misdemeanor.

(d) When a domestic violence victim is deceased or has been adjudged incompetent by a court of competent jurisdiction, the guardian of the domestic violence victim or the executor or administrator of the estate of the domestic violence victim may waive the privilege established by this Section, except where the guardian, executor or administrator of the estate has been charged with a violent crime against the domestic violence victim or has had an Order of Protection entered against him or her at the request of or on behalf of the domestic violence victim or otherwise has an interest adverse to that of the domestic violence victim with respect to the waiver of the privilege. In that case, the court shall appoint an attorney for the estate of the domestic violence victim.

(e) A minor may knowingly waive the privilege established by this Section. Where a minor is, in the opinion of the court, incapable of knowingly waiving the privilege, the parent or guardian of the minor may waive the privilege on behalf of the minor, except where such parent or guardian has been charged with a violent crime against the minor or has had an Order of Protection entered against him or her on request of or on behalf of the minor or otherwise has any interest adverse to that of the minor with respect to the waiver of the privilege. In that case, the court shall appoint an attorney for the minor child who shall be compensated in accordance with Section 506 of the Illinois Marriage and Dissolution of Marriage Act.

(f) Nothing in this Section shall be construed to limit in any way any privilege that might otherwise exist under statute or common law.

(g) The assertion of any privilege under this Section shall not result in an inference unfavorable to the State's cause or to the cause of the domestic violence victim.

Effective January 1, 1993.

Other Privileged Information: 750 ILCS 60/227.1

Except as otherwise provided in this Section, no court or administrative or legislative body shall compel any person or domestic violence program to disclose the location of any domestic violence program or the identity of any domestic violence advocate or counselor in any civil or criminal case or proceeding or in any administrative or legislative proceeding. A court may compel disclosure of the location of a domestic violence program or the identity of a domestic violence advocate or counselor if the court finds, following a hearing, that there is clear and convincing evidence that failure to disclose would be likely to result in an imminent risk of serious bodily harm or death to a domestic violence victim or another person. If the court makes such a finding, then disclosure shall take place *in camera*, under a restrictive protective order that does not frustrate the purposes of compelling the disclosure, and the information disclosed shall not be made a part of the written record of the case. Effective January 1, 1993.

Prior Illinois Case Law

See generally, People v. Griffith, 249 Ill. App. 3d 1046 (1st Dist. 1993).

Privilege for Statements Made by Victims of Violent Crimes to Counselors of Such Victims: 735 ILCS 5/8-802.2

Relevant Statutory Authority

Confidentiality of Statements Made to Personnel Counseling Victims of Violent Crimes: 735 ILCS 5/8-802.2

§ 8-802.2. Confidentiality of statements made to personnel counseling victims of violent crimes.

(a) Purpose. This Section is intended to protect victims of violent crimes from public disclosure of statements they make in confidence to counselors of organizations established to help them. Because of the fear and trauma that often result from violent crimes, many victims hesitate to seek help even where it is available and may therefore lack the psychological support necessary to report the crime and aid police in preventing future crimes.

(b) Definitions. As used in this Act, "violent crimes" include, but are not limited to, any felony in which force or threat of force was used against the victim or any misdemeanor which results in death or great bodily harm to the victim.

(c) Confidentiality. Where any victim of a violent crime makes a statement relating to the crime or its circumstances during the course of therapy or consultation to any counselor, employee or volunteer of a victim aid organization, the statement or contents thereof shall not be disclosed by the organization or any of its personnel unless the maker of the statement consents in writing or unless otherwise directed pursuant to this Section.

If in any judicial proceeding, a party alleges that such statements are necessary to the determination of any issue before the court and written consent to disclosure has not been given, the party may ask the court to consider the relevance and admissibility of the statements. In such a case, the court shall hold a hearing *in camera* on the relevance of the statements. If the court finds them relevant and admissible to the issue, the court shall order the statements to be disclosed.

Effective January 1, 1990.

Prior Illinois Case Law

There has been no case law discussing this privilege.

Licensed Clinical Social Worker-Patient Privilege: 225 ILCS 20/16 *et seq.*

Author's Commentary

Illinois legislature has created a statutory licensed clinical social worker-patient privilege pursuant to 225 ILCS 20/16 *et seq*. The social worker-patient privilege does not apply to information obtained while investigating child abuse or neglect. People v. McKean, 94 Ill. App. 3d 502 (2d Dist. 1981).

Relevant Statutory Authority

Privileged Communications and Exceptions: 225 ILCS 20/16 *et seq.*

§ 16. Privileged Communications and Exceptions.

1. No licensed clinical social worker or licensed social worker shall disclose any information acquired from persons consulting the social worker in a professional capacity, except that which may be voluntarily disclosed under the following circumstances:

(a) In the course of formally reporting, conferring or consulting with administrative superiors, colleagues or consultants who share professional responsibility, including a professional responsibility to maintain confidentiality, in which instance all recipients of such information are similarly bound to regard the communication as privileged;

(b) With the written consent of the person who provided the information;

(c) In case of death or disability, with the written consent of a personal representative, other person authorized to sue, or the beneficiary of an insurance policy on the person's life, health or physical condition;

(d) When a communication reveals the intended commission of a crime or harmful act and such disclosure is judged necessary by the licensed clinical social worker or licensed social worker to protect any person from a clear, imminent risk of serious mental or physical harm or injury, or to forestall a serious threat to the public safety;

(e) When the person waives the privilege by bringing any public charges against the licensee; or

(f) When the information is acquired during the course of investigating a report or working on a case of elder abuse, neglect, or financial exploitation by a designated Elder Abuse Provider Agency and disclosure of the information is in accordance with the provisions of Section 8 of the Elder Abuse and Neglect Act.

2. When the person is a minor under the laws of the State of Illinois and the information acquired by the licensed clinical social worker or licensed social worker indicates the minor was the victim or subject of a crime, the licensed clinical social worker or licensed social

worker may be required to testify in any judicial proceedings in which the commission of that crime is the subject of inquiry and when, after *in camera* review of the information that the licensed clinical social worker or licensed social worker acquired, the court determines that the interests of the minor in having the information held privileged are outweighed by the requirements of justice, the need to protect the public safety or the need to protect the minor, except as provided under the Abused and Neglected Child Reporting Act.

3. Any person having access to records or any one who participates in providing social work services or who, in providing any human services, is supervised by a licensed clinical social worker or licensed social worker, is similarly bound to regard all information and communications as privileged in accord with this Section.

4. Nothing shall be construed to prohibit a licensed clinical social worker or licensed social worker from voluntarily testifying in court hearings concerning matters of adoption, child abuse, child neglect or other matters pertaining to children, except as provided under the Abused and Neglected Child Reporting Act.

5. The Mental Health and Developmental Disabilities Confidentiality Act, as now or hereafter amended, is incorporated herein as if all of its provisions were included in this Act.

> Effective July 23, 2009. Section 4.28 of the Regulatory Sunset Act (5 ILCS 80/4.28) provides for the repeal of the Clinical Social Work and Social Work Practice Act effective January 1, 2018, unless, under 5 ILCS 80/4, the General Assembly enacts legislation providing for its continuation.

Prior Illinois Case Law

Social Worker-Patient Privilege Does Not Apply to Information Obtained while Investigating Child Abuse or Neglect

People v. McKean, 94 Ill. App. 3d 502 (2d Dist. 1981)

The Second District of the Illinois Appellate Court found that the social worker-patient privilege does not apply where "abused or neglected children are involved." The defendant was charged with aggravated incest after he sought mental health counseling and told a social worker that he had abused his six and ten-year-old stepdaughters. The social worker reported the defendant's statements to the police and prosecuting authorities pursuant to the Abused and Neglected Child Reporting Act. The court rejected defendant's privilege claim, reasoning that not only was the information not privileged but also that the social worker had an affirmative duty to report child abuse.

See also People v. Morton, 188 Ill. App. 3d 95 (4th Dist. 1989) (permitting hospital counselor to testify about statements defendant made to her in an aggravated criminal sexual assault of a child prosecution).

Genetic Counselor Privilege: 225 ILCS 135/90

Relevant Statutory Authority

Privileged Communications and Exceptions: 225 ILCS 135/90

§ 90. Privileged communications and exceptions.

(a) With the exception of disclosure to the physician performing or supervising a genetic test and to the referring physician licensed to practice medicine in all its branches, advanced practice nurse, or physician assistant, no licensed genetic counselor shall disclose any information acquired from persons consulting the counselor in a professional capacity, except that which may be voluntarily disclosed under any of the following circumstances:

(1) In the course of formally reporting, conferring, or consulting with administrative superiors, colleagues, or consultants who share professional responsibility, in which instance all recipients of the information are similarly bound to regard the communication as privileged.

(2) With the written consent of the person who provided the information and about whom the information concerns.

(3) In the case of death or disability, with the written consent of a personal representative.

(4) When a communication reveals the intended commission of a crime or harmful act and such disclosure is judged necessary in the professional judgment of the licensed genetic counselor to protect any person from a clear risk of serious mental or physical harm or injury or to forestall a serious threat to the public safety.

(5) When the person waives the privilege by bringing any public charges or filing a lawsuit against the licensee.

(b) Any person having access to records or anyone who participates in providing genetic counseling services, or in providing any human services, or is supervised by a licensed genetic counselor is similarly bound to regard all information and communications as privileged in accord with this Section.

(c) The Mental Health and Developmental Disabilities Confidentiality Act is incorporated herein as if all of its provisions were included in this Act. In the event of a conflict between the application of this Section and the Mental Health and Developmental Disabilities Confidentiality Act to a specific situation, the provisions of the Mental Health and Developmental Disabilities Confidentiality Act shall control.

Effective July 27, 2010. Section 4.25 of the Regulatory Sunset Act (5 ILCS 80/4.25) provides for the repeal of the Genetic Counselor Licensing Act effective January 1, 2015, unless, under 5 ILCS 80/4, the General Assembly enacts legislation providing for its continuation.

PRIOR ILLINOIS CASE LAW

There has been no case law discussing this privilege.

Clergy Privilege

AUTHOR'S COMMENTARY

Illinois did not recognize a common law clergy-penitent privilege. Binder v. Ruvell, Civil Docket 52C2535 (Ill. Cir. 1952). In 1954, at a symposium held after the American Bar Association had recommended the adoption of a set of "Uniform Rules of Evidence," it was noted that "Illinois, in accordance with the common law, does not expressly recognize the priest-penitent privilege . . . [and that] the privilege exists *sub silentio*." Comments, *A Symposium on the Uniform Rules of Evidence and Illinois Evidence Law, Confidential Privileges*, 49 N.W. L. REV. 481, 538-541 (1954) (citing WIGMORE, EVIDENCE § 2394 (3d ed. 1940). Moreover, it was explained that since there was no case law or legislation "on this subject in Illinois, it would seem that the common law of this state is still to the effect that communications between a priest and penitent are not privileged." *Id.* A survey of Illinois case law between the years 1952 until 1961 when the clergy privilege was first codified revealed no other court decisions discussing the privilege, suggesting that the state courts recognized no common law clergy-penitent privilege. *See also* MICHAEL H. GRAHAM, GRAHAM'S HANDBOOK OF ILLINOIS EVIDENCE § 503.2 (10th ed. 2010).

The Illinois legislature has enacted a statutory clergy privilege under 735 ILCS 5/8-803. The privilege protects only a communication with a clergy person who is acting in his or her capacity as a spiritual advisor when the information is obtained. People v. McNeal, 175 Ill. 2d 335 (1997).

RELEVANT STATUTORY AUTHORITY

Clergy: 735 ILCS 5/8-803

§ 8-803. Clergy.

A clergyman or practitioner of any religious denomination accredited by the religious body to which he or she belongs, shall not be compelled to disclose in any court, or to any administrative board or agency, or to any public officer, a confession or admission made to him or her in his or her professional character or as a spiritual advisor in the course of the discipline enjoined by the rules or practices of such religious body or of the religion which he or she professes, nor be compelled to divulge any information which has been obtained by him or her in such professional character or as such spiritual advisor.

Effective July 1, 1982.

PRIOR ILLINOIS CASE LAW

1. Illinois Recognized No Common Law Clergy-Penitent Privilege

Binder v. Ruvell, Civil Docket 52C2535 (Ill. Cir. 1952)

The trial court in *dictum* made one of the earliest references in the Illinois courts to the fact that the "priest and penitent relationship does not enjoy immunity." The court's statement came nine years before the enactment of the first Illinois statute codifying a clergy-penitent privilege in 1961.

2. The Federal Clergy-Communicant Privilege Is Based on Common Law

United States v. Dube, 820 F.2d 886 (7th Cir. 1987)

The Seventh Circuit recognized the clergy-penitent privilege and noted that the privilege

> is limited to private communications rooted in confidence and trust. The privilege 'recognizes the human need to disclose to a spiritual counselor, in total and absolute confidence, what are believed to be flawed acts or thoughts and to receive priestly consolation and guidance in return.' Trammel v. United States, 445 U.S. 40, 45 (1980). If, however, one seeks out the clergy only for income tax avoidance, we see no more need for a protective privilege than if the taxpayer had consulted his butcher or barber. The taxpayer is not a penitent seeking spiritual relief from his sins, only a citizen seeking relief from his obligation to pay taxes.

Here, defendant consulted a pastor to determine how he could avoid paying income taxes. The Seventh Circuit found that defendant was not consulting the pastor in confidence about spiritual matters and therefore their communications were not protected by the clergy-penitent privilege.

See also Trammel v. United States, 445 U.S. 40 (1980) (recognizing a "priest-penitent" privilege in *dicta*).

3. Illinois Has Enacted a Statutory Clergy Privilege Under 735 ILCS 5/8-803 Protecting Only Communication Where Clergy Person Is Acting in Capacity of a Spiritual Advisor When Information Is Obtained
People v. McNeal, 175 Ill. 2d 335 (1997)

Pursuant to 735 ILCS 5/8-803, the party asserting the clergy privilege must prove all of the elements of the privilege before the privilege may be recognized. It must be shown that the statements were made in confidence, that they were made to a clergy person who was acting as a spiritual advisor, and that their disclosure would be against the tenets of that religion. Either the clergy person or the communicant may assert the privilege, and each may object to the testimonial disclosure of confidential communications. If the clergy person does not object to the divulging of confidential communications, the communicant has the burden to show that disclosure would be in violation of that religion.

A murder defendant confessed to the crimes to his brother who had been ordained a minister of the Church of the Second Coming. Defendant argued that communications with his brother were confidential and protected by the clergy privilege. The Illinois Supreme Court found that while defendant's brother could be considered a clergy person despite the fact that his church had no presence in the United States, there was no evidence that he was acting in his professional character or as a spiritual advisor when defendant confessed his crimes. Moreover, defendant's brother disclosed most of these communications at the grand jury proceeding without raising the clergy privilege or stating that it is against his religion to divulge such information. The Illinois Supreme Court concluded that it was proper for the trial court to deny defendant's motion *in limine* to exclude his brother's statements, as the defendant failed to prove that the clergy person privilege applied here.

4. Breach of the Clergy Privilege May Be Cured by Exclusion of Evidence
People v. Burnidge, 178 Ill. 2d 429 (1997)

Defendant was a counselor to a church youth group and was charged with aggravated criminal sexual assault. A minister found out about defendant's conduct and referred him to another minister for counseling. The minister was also a psychologist. He reported the incident to DCFS, and DCFS advised him that he was not required to report the incident as a clergy person but that he was required to report it as a psychologist. The minister then submitted a written report to DCFS in which he described the incident as related by the defendant but he did not name the defendant. The defendant contended on appeal that the entire prosecution had to be "quashed" because his arrest and charges were the "fruits of the poisonous tree," claiming that the police would never have learned of the incident had the minister not submitted a report. In this regard, he claimed that the conversations between himself and the minister were privileged.

The Illinois Supreme Court held that even if the conversations were privileged, the incidents were not secret because the victim testified about them and the defendant had previously acknowledged to victim's family that he had committed the acts charged. Although the victim's father told the ministers at the church that he wanted to solve the incident within the church, he testified at trial that he kept the possibility of filing criminal charges in mind throughout the process. The court found that the independent source doctrine applied as there was no evidence that the victim or her family had intended to keep the matter secret or at the least within the church only. Moreover, the trial court granted defendant appropriate relief by barring use of the minister's report and not allowing the minister to reveal what defendant had told him. Dismissal of the case was too drastic a remedy for the breach of confidentiality.

Chief Justice Freeman specially concurred, with Justice Bilandic joining. He stated that the Fourth Amendment exclusionary rule was not applicable to privilege cases and that the majority should not even have suggested that it may be.

Accountant's Privilege

AUTHOR'S COMMENTARY

Illinois did not recognize a common law accountant's privilege. Dorfman v. Rombs, 218 F. Supp. 905 (N.D. Ill. 1963). Illinois has enacted a statutory accountant's privilege under 225 ILCS 450/27. The privilege protects from disclosure information obtained by an accountant in his or her confidential capacity. *In re* October 1985 Grand Jury No. 746, 124 Ill. 2d 466 (1988).

RELEVANT STATUTORY AUTHORITY

Accountant's Privilege: 225 ILCS 450/27

§ 27. Accountant as Witness. A licensed or registered certified public accountant shall not be required by any court to divulge information or evidence which has been obtained by him in his confidential capacity as a licensed or registered certified public accountant. This Section shall not apply to any investigation or hearing undertaken pursuant to this Act.

Effective May 19, 2006.

Section 4.24 of the Regulatory Sunset Act (5 ILCS 80/4.24) provides for the repeal of the Illinois Public Accounting Act effective January 1, 2014, unless, under 5 ILCS 80/4, the General Assembly enacts legislation providing for its continuation.

PRIOR ILLINOIS CASE LAW

1. Illinois Recognized No Common Law Accountant's Privilege
Dorfman v. Rombs, 218 F. Supp. 905 (N.D. Ill. 1963)

The United States District Court for the Northern District of Illinois, in examining the Illinois statutory accountant's privilege noted that there existed "no accountant client or accountant privilege at common law." Here, the accountant received a subpoena to disclose information pertaining to one of his clients sought by the Internal Revenue Service. The client to whom the information pertained filed an injunction to prevent the accountant from disclosing the requested materials. The court refused to restrain disclosure, noting that the Illinois accountant privilege could not be raised by the client on the accountant's behalf, and rather could only be asserted by the accountant.

2. Federal Common Law Recognized No Accountant's Privilege
Couch v. United States, 409 U.S. 322 (1973)

The United States Supreme Court noted that "no confidential accountant-client privilege exists under federal law, and no state created privilege has been recognized in federal cases." Defendant urged the court to recognize the confidential relationship between an accountant and a client by invoking the Fourth and Fifth Amendments' protections, but the court refused. The Supreme Court emphasized that creation of such privilege would not be justified in the context of a criminal tax investigation. The Supreme Court concluded:

> We hold today that no Fourth or Fifth Amendment claim can prevail where, as in this case, there exists no legitimate expectation of privacy and no semblance of governmental compulsion against the person of the accused. It is important, in applying constitutional

> principles, to interpret them in light of the fundamental interests of personal liberty they were meant to serve. Respect for these principles is eroded when they leap their proper bounds to interfere with the legitimate interest of society in enforcement of its laws and collection of the revenues.

3. Illinois Has Enacted a Statutory Accountant's Privilege Under 225 ILCS 450/27 Protecting from Disclosure Information Obtained by Accountant in His or Her Confidential Capacity

In re October 1985 Grand Jury No. 746, 124 Ill. 2d 466 (1988)

A public accountant cannot be compelled to reveal information or evidence obtained in his or her confidential capacity as a public accountant; however information which a client gives to his or her accountant for tax preparation is not privileged. Here, a grand jury issued a subpoena *duces tecum* directed to a public accountant to disclose copies of state and federal income tax returns prepared by the accountant for the defendant, as well as any material provided by the accountant to the defendant, and any of accountant's "worksheets or workpapers" used in preparation of the tax returns. The public accountant asserted that the accountant's privilege protected from disclosure the information requested and that he was therefore not required to divulge such documents.

The appellate court held that the privilege did not apply to the information requested because it "did not originate in confidence that it would not be disclosed." The Illinois Supreme Court agreed and further noted that "[t]here can be little expectation of privacy where records are handed to an accountant, knowing that mandatory disclosure of much of the information therein is required in an income tax return." (quoting Couch v. United States, 409 U.S. 322 (1973)). The Supreme Court concluded that "information given an accountant to prepare a client's tax returns and the accountant's workpapers in preparing the returns thus are not confidential."

Reporter's Privilege

Author's Commentary

The Illinois reporter's privilege evolved from the constitutional guarantee of a free press. *In re* Special Grand Jury, 104 Ill. 2d 419 (1984). Illinois has enacted a qualified reporter's privilege under 735 ILCS 5/8-901 *et seq.*, which protects against compelled disclosure of a reporter's information source. *Id.* The public interest in the functioning of a grand jury is essential however, and may justify the divestiture of the reporter's privilege. People v. Pawlaczyk, 189 Ill. 2d 177 (2000).

Relevant Statutory Authority

Reporter's Privilege: 735 ILCS 5/8-901 *et seq.*

§ 8-901. Source of information.

No court may compel any person to disclose the source of any information obtained by a reporter except as provided in Part 9 of Article VIII of this Act.

Effective September 16, 1985.

§ 8-903. Application to court.

(a) In any case, except a libel or slander case, where a person claims the privilege conferred by Part 9 of Article VIII of this Act, the person or party, body or officer seeking the information so privileged may apply in writing to the circuit court serving the county where the hearing, action or proceeding in which the information is sought for an order divesting the person named therein of such privilege and ordering him or her to disclose his or her source of the information.

Effective September 16, 1985.

§ 8-906. Consideration by Court.
In granting or denying divestiture of the privilege provided in Part 9 of Article VIII of this Act the court shall have due regard to the nature of the proceedings, the merits of the claim or defense, the adequacy of the remedy otherwise available, if any, the relevancy of the source, and the possibility of establishing by other means that which it is alleged the source requested will tend to prove.

Effective September 23, 1983.

§ 8-907. Court's findings.
An order granting divestiture of the privilege provided in Part 9 of Article VIII of this Act shall be granted only if the court, after hearing the parties, finds:

(1) that the information sought does not concern matters, or details in any proceeding, required to be kept secret under the laws of this State or of the Federal government; and
(2) that all other available sources of information have been exhausted and, either, disclosure of the information sought is essential to the protection of the public interest involved or, in libel or slander cases, the plaintiff's need for disclosure of the information sought outweighs the public interest in protecting the confidentiality of sources of information used by a reporter as part of the news gathering process under the particular facts and circumstances of each particular case.

If the court enters an order divesting the person of the privilege granted in Part 9 of Article VIII of this Act it shall also order the person to disclose the information it has determined should be disclosed, subject to any protective conditions as the court may deem necessary or appropriate.

Effective September 16, 1985.

§ 8-909. Contempt.
A person refusing to testify or otherwise comply with the order to disclose the source of the information as specified in such order, after such order becomes final, may be adjudged in contempt of court and punished accordingly.

Effective July 1, 1982.

PRIOR ILLINOIS CASE LAW

1. Illinois Reporter's Privilege Evolved from a Common Law Recognition of Constitutional Guarantees of Free Press

In re Special Grand Jury, 104 Ill. 2d 419 (1984)

The Illinois Supreme Court has noted that "[t]he reporter's privilege has evolved from a common law recognition that the compelled disclosure of a reporter's sources could compromise the news media's first amendment right to freely gather and disseminate information."

2. No Federal Constitutional Right Based on the First Amendment to Protect Reporters from Disclosing Criminal Conduct of Confidential News Sources Before Criminal Grand Jury

Branzburg v. Hayes, 408 U.S. 665 (1972)

Grand jury issued a subpoena *duces tecum* directed to reporters who, through work-related research, observed various individuals participating in criminal activities. The reporters refused to disclose the names of the individuals asserting a qualified reporter's privilege, arguing that they

> should not be forced either to appear or to testify before a grand jury or at trial until and unless sufficient grounds are shown for believing that [they] possess[] information relevant to a crime the grand jury is investigating, that the information . . . is unavailable from other sources, and that the need for the information is sufficiently compelling to override the claimed invasion of First Amendment interests occasioned by the disclosure.

The United States Supreme Court considered that reporters are free to use confidential sources in their work and that the grand jury subpoena is not an attempt to require them to disclose all of their sources "indiscriminately." The Supreme Court noted that the reporters, like other ordinary citizens, are obligated to answer the grand jury's questions when it is investigating the commission of a crime. The reporters argued, however, that the burden of requiring them to disclose their confidential sources would result in later difficulties in providing informative news stories. The Supreme Court, however, reasoned that "[a]t common law, courts consistently refused to recognize the existence of any privilege authorizing a newsman to refuse to reveal confidential information to a grand jury." The Supreme Court noted that

> courts have applied the presumption against the existence of an asserted testimonial privilege, United States v. Bryan, 339 U.S. 323, 331 (1950), and have concluded that the First Amendment interest asserted by the newsman was outweighed by the general obligation of a citizen to appear before a grand jury or at trial, pursuant to a subpoena, and give what information he possesses. . . .[A]lthough a few recent cases, such as Caldwell v. United States, 434 F.2d 1081 (9th Cir. 1970), have recognized and given effect to some form of constitutional newsman's privilege. See State v. Knops, 49 Wis. 2d 647, 183 N.W.2d 93 (1971) (dictum); Alioto v. Cowles Communications, Inc., C.A. No. 52150 (ND Cal. 1969); *In re* Grand Jury Witnesses, 322 F. Supp. 573 (ND Cal. 1970); People v. Dohrn, Crim. No. 69-3808 (Cook County, Ill., Cir. Ct. 1970).

The Supreme Court determined that reporters generally have no privilege protecting them from testifying before state or federal criminal grand juries and refused to provide a First Amendment reporter's privilege for this purpose.

Justice Powell, in a concurring opinion, emphasized the "limited nature of the Court's holding" noting that

> The Court does not hold that newsmen, subpoenaed to testify before a grand jury, are without constitutional rights with respect to the gathering of news or in safeguarding their sources. . . . As indicated in the concluding portion of the opinion, the Court states that no harassment of newsmen will be tolerated. If a newsman believes that the grand jury investigation is not being conducted in good faith he is not without remedy. Indeed, if the newsman is called upon to give information bearing only a remote and tenuous relationship to the subject of the investigation, or if he has some other reason to believe that his testimony implicates confidential source relationship without a legitimate need of law enforcement, he will have

> access to the court on a motion to quash and an appropriate protective order may be entered. The asserted claim to privilege should be judged on its facts by the striking of a proper balance between freedom of the press and the obligation of all citizens to give relevant testimony with respect to criminal conduct. The balance of these vital constitutional and societal interests on a case-by-case basis accords with the tried and traditional way of adjudicating such questions. In short, the courts will be available to newsmen under circumstances where legitimate First Amendment interests require protection.

3. Illinois Has Enacted a Qualified Reporter's Privilege Under 735 ILCS 5/8-901 *et seq. That* Protects Against Compelled Disclosure of a Reporter's Information Source
In re Special Grand Jury, 104 Ill. 2d 419 (1984)

Illinois provides qualified statutory protection against compelled disclosure of a reporter's information source pursuant to 735 ILCS 5/8-901 *et seq*. Section 8-906 guides the court's determination of granting or denying disclosure. Pursuant to section 8-906, the court "shall have due regard to the nature of the proceedings, the merits of the claim or defense, the adequacy of the remedy otherwise available, if any, the relevancy of the source, and the possibility of establishing by other means that which it is alleged the source requested will tend to prove." Section 8-907 prevents the granting of an order of divestiture if the information sought is a government secret, and if all available sources of information have not been exhausted. The Illinois Supreme Court has recognized that section 8-906, "when read with section 8-907, reflect[s] a clear legislative intent to create a standard which balances the reporter's first amendment rights against the public interest in the information sought and the practical difficulties in obtaining the information elsewhere."

As to what constitutes a showing "that all other available sources of information have been exhausted," the Illinois Supreme Court stated that there is no "precise formula or definition" and that the determination will be made on the specific facts of each case. This case by case determination is consistent with the "tried and traditional way" of adjudicating these questions. In Illinois, the court is to weigh the freedom of the press against the factors enumerated in sections 8-906 and 8-907 and strike a proper balance.

Here, a complaint was filed with the Judicial Inquiry Board against a circuit court judge for his use of inappropriate language during two juvenile court hearings. The Board conducted an investigation and obtained transcripts of those hearings. Information from those transcripts was leaked to the newspapers. A special grand jury was constituted to investigate the disclosure of the confidential information from the juvenile hearing proceedings. The Illinois Supreme Court determined that the trial court erred in finding that all available sources of information had been exhausted. The Supreme Court explained that there were at least three persons who had access to the confidential information and who could have provided sworn testimony of relevant information to the grand jury. The court concluded that "the proof of exhaustion of alternative sources here was insufficient to justify divestiture of the reporter's privilege."

4. Public Interest in the Functioning of a Grand Jury Is Essential and May Justify Divestiture of the Reporter's Privilege
People v. Pawlaczyk, 189 Ill. 2d 177 (2000)

A former chief of the police was accused in the local newspaper and by a television station of being a prime suspect in a rape investigation. The former chief was later cleared. He brought suit for libel, slander, and the tort of false light against the television and newspaper reporters. The plaintiff deposed various individuals, including two reporters, the local mayor and the city commissioner. The mayor and commissioner both claimed that they did not speak to the media regarding the case. The two reporters asserted their statutory privilege and did not divulge their sources until the court divested them of their privilege. The first reporter implicated the mayor and did not appeal her divestiture. The second reporter would not divulge his sources and appealed the divestiture. The plaintiff subsequently withdrew his motion to divest the second reporter of his privileges as it was no longer necessary in light of first reporter's divestiture.

The State's Attorney initiated a grand jury investigation to charge the mayor and commissioner with perjury. At the grand jury hearing, the two reporters asserted their statutory privileges and refused to reveal whether the mayor and commissioner were their sources for the news story. The special prosecutor moved to divest the news reporters of their privilege and the circuit court granted his request, noting that the first reporter was collaterally estopped from raising the privilege since she had already divulged the information in the civil suit and she never appealed the divestiture order in that case. The reporters appealed. The first reporter argued that she was not collaterally estopped from challenging the divestiture because the issues were not identical. The Illinois Supreme Court agreed:

> . . . the test for divestiture under the Act varies slightly when the divestiture proceedings arise in the course of a lawsuit for libel or slander, as opposed to when the divestiture request arises in other actions. The chief difference lies in the proof the movant must adduce concerning any "public interest" at stake in the proceedings. A court granting divestiture in a libel/slander action must be convinced that the public's "need for disclosure of the information sought outweighs the public interest in protecting the confidentiality of sources of information used by a reporter." 735 ILCS 5/8-907(2) (West 1998). In all other cases, the movant must demonstrate that "disclosure of the information sought is essential to the protection of the public interest involved." 735 ILCS 8-907(2).

The Supreme Court concluded that the first news reporter was not collaterally estopped because no "identical question" was resolved in the prior civil proceeding. The Supreme Court then proceeded to consider whether the reporters were properly divested of their privileges. The reporters argued that the circuit court improperly divested them of their privileges, alleging that the privileged information was not relevant to the grand jury investigation in determining whether the mayor and commissioner committed perjury, and that disclosure was not essential to the public interest. The Supreme Court disagreed, finding that the information regarding defendants' sources was relevant because the "privileged information will make any one of the elements of perjury more or less probable." In other words, the reporters' information will determine whether the mayor or the commissioner, or both, were their sources, and if so, that will show that one or both committed perjury.

Reporters further argued that the special prosecutor failed to show that disclosure was essential to the public interest. The court found, however, that disclosure was vital to the grand jury's investigative function and that thus the reporters were properly divested of the privilege.

Parent-Child Privilege

Author's Commentary

Currently, Illinois does not recognize a parent-child privilege. People v. Sanders, 99 Ill. 2d 262 (1983). The Illinois courts, however, may act pursuant to Illinois Rule of Evidence 501 to recognize a constitutionally based parent-child privilege that would protect the "private realm of family life which the state cannot enter." Griswold v. Connecticut, 381 U.S. 479 (1965); *see e.g.*, Matter of A. & M., 61 A.D.2d 426 (N.Y. A.D. 1978) (recognizing a parent-child privilege based on the constitutional right to privacy).

PRIOR ILLINOIS CASE LAW

1. The Right to Privacy Protects the Familial Relationship
Griswold v. Connecticut, 381 U.S. 479 (1965)

The United States Supreme Court indicated a willingness to protect the familial relationship when it struck down a state statute that criminalized the provision of contraceptives to married couples by medical providers. The Supreme Court noted that the First Amendment protects the right of association and the right to privacy and stressed that the Fourth and Fifth Amendments protect "against all governmental invasions 'of the sanctity of a man's home and the privacies of life.'" Thus, the Supreme Court emphasized that there is a "private realm of family life which the state cannot enter."

2. No Federal Common Law Privilege Exists Protecting Communications Between Parent and Child
United States v. Davies, 768 F.2d 893 (7th Cir. 1985)

Defendant on trial for conspiring to transport stolen merchandise and concealing stolen merchandise argued that certain evidence acquired by federal agents from his daughter should be suppressed as a violation of the parent-child privilege. The agents approached defendant's daughter on a sidewalk and asked her whether she knew how her father could be reached. She hesitantly provided the agents with a telephone number. Pursuant to the information gained from defendant's daughter, the agents began surveillance of the apartment where defendant and his accomplice hid the stolen merchandise. Defendant argued that he gave the phone number to his daughter "in confidence and for emergency use," and that any evidence obtained as a result of the disclosure of that number should be suppressed.

The Seventh Circuit disagreed, noting that an examination of common law pursuant to the Federal Rule of Evidence 501 revealed that a majority of the circuits have rejected the parent-child privilege. The Seventh Circuit explicitly rejected the reasoning of the Nevada District Court in *In re* Agosto, 553 F. Supp. 1298 (D. Nev. 1983), that found a parent-child privilege existed pursuant to the "constitutional protections for the family's rights to privacy" of the First Amendment. The Seventh Circuit cautioned that although the United States Constitution "protects the sanctity of the family," such "generalized claims . . . must give way to the overriding needs of the truth-seeking process." Moreover, the court reasoned, even if a parent-child privilege existed the defendant would not be able to avail himself of it here. The Seventh Circuit explained that the privilege only applies to testimony and that defendant failed to show that his daughter would be called as a witness at his trial. The Seventh Circuit therefore refused to suppress the evidence against defendant and declined to recognize a parent-child privilege.

3. New York Has Explicitly Recognized a Parent-Child Privilege Based on Constitutional Grounds
Matter of A. & M., 61 A.D.2d 426 (N.Y. A.D. 1978)

The prosecution sought to introduce a minor child's incriminating statements to his parents about an alleged arson. One New York court has recognized that a parent-child privilege existed protecting the minor's statements based on the constitutional right to privacy. The court based its decision on the importance of preserving the family relationship, noting:

> [T]he [Supreme] [C]ourt [in Griswold v. Connecticut, 381 U.S. 479 (1965)] articulated for the first time a fundamental right of privacy of constitutional dimension and signaled the willingness of the court to prevent encroachment by the State into certain enclaves of private life.

***

> The role of the family, particularly that of the mother and father, in establishing a child's emotional stability, character and self-image is universally recognized. The erosion of this influence would have a profound effect on the individual child and on society as a whole. Child psychologists and behavioral scientists generally agree that it is essential to the parent-child relationship that the lines of communication remain open and that the child be encouraged to "talk out" his problems.
>
> ***
>
> Surely the thought of the State forcing a mother and father to reveal their child's alleged misdeeds, as confessed to them in private, to provide the basis for criminal charges is shocking to our sense of decency, fairness and propriety.

The court then discussed the importance of privacy within the family unit and reviewed constitutional precedent:

> The course of constitutional law is filled with instances wherein the interests of the State in achieving a legitimate goal have been balanced against the rights of individual privacy guaranteed by the Constitution. *See, e.g.*, cases cited in Roe v Wade, 410 U.S. 113 (1973). The State has a legitimate interest in the process of fact-finding necessary to discover, try and punish criminal behavior. Branzburg v Hayes, 408 U.S. 665 (1972). Nevertheless, if it is determined that the information sought here was divulged by the boy in the context of the familial setting for the purpose of obtaining support, advice or guidance, we believe that the interest of society in protecting and nurturing the parent-child relationship is of such overwhelming significance that the State's interest in fact-findings must give way.

The court concluded that "the communications made by a minor child to his parents within the context of the family relationship may, under some circumstances, lie within the "private realm of family life which the state cannot enter." Prince v. Massachusetts, 321 U.S. 158 (1944). For instance, the court noted that requiring parents to appear when called to testify at a grand jury proceeding investigating their children is proper and would not infringe upon family privacy because parents could request to quash the subpoena or assert the parent-child privilege once they appear before the grand jury.

4. Illinois Does Not Recognize a Parent-Child Privilege
People v. Sanders, 99 Ill. 2d 262 (1983)

The defendant urged the Illinois Supreme Court to recognize a new testimonial privilege to protect communications between parents and their children. The court stated that the source of all privileges in Illinois, with the exception of the long standing common law attorney-client privilege, is statutory. Declining to judicially introduce an additional privilege, the court was constrained by the legislature's lack of interest in extending the interspousal communications privilege to communications between parent and child. The court noted that broadening the existing privilege may result in exclusion of relevant evidence and could work against the truth seeking function of legal proceedings. Another factor in the court's decision was that the proposed privilege would require not only judicial initiation but also that the court extend the privilege to include children of only one spouse. Here, the child was the son of the wife but not of the defendant. The Supreme Court reasoned that "to recognize such a privilege under our judicial authority, it would be impossible to contain it logically from spreading to conversations with other relatives in whom a person might normally confide, or even to close friends." Further, the Supreme Court explained that since privileges exclude relevant evidence and "work against the truthseeking function of legal proceedings," they should be strictly construed.

The parent child privilege has been recognized by courts in some jurisdictions on the basis that certain communications are intimately associated with the family and, when confidential in nature, fall within that category of constitutionally protected communications. The Illinois Supreme Court, however, distinguished those cases on the ground that they raised questions about whether a parent or child could be compelled against his or her will to testify against the other. Here, the testimony was given by the defendant's wife of her own free will. The Illinois Supreme Court found this to be a significant difference. The proposed constitutional privilege relies on conjecture that a family member faced with the choice would either aid in the conviction of a loved one, commit perjury on the stand, or risk a contempt of court citation for refusing to testify. The harshness of this choice, the court believed, would have the effect of "sundering the family relationship."

5. Child Requesting Parent's Presence May Constitute Invocation of Fifth Amendment Right to Counsel

United States *ex rel.* Riley v. Franzen, 653 F.2d 1153 (7th Cir. 1981)

Defendant on trial for murder argued that a request to see his father shortly after he was arrested and imprisoned constituted an invocation of his Fifth Amendment right to counsel. The Seventh Circuit examined Fare v. Michael C., 442 U.S. 707 (1979), which held that a juvenile defendant's request to see his probation officer did not constitute an invocation of the Fifth Amendment right to counsel. The Seventh Circuit considered that in *Fare* the communications between the juvenile and probation officer were unprivileged, and consequently raised the issue whether defendant's communications with his father were privileged under Illinois law. The court found that Illinois does not recognize the parent-child privilege, but did note that "unlike the probation officer in *Fare*, [defendant's] father is not a state employee duty bound to report his son's wrongdoing." Moreover, the court noted that

> the parent-child relationship is appreciably different from that between a juvenile and his probation officer. A parent may significantly aid a juvenile in asserting his Fifth Amendment privilege. The parent may be, or be able to provide, an attorney for the child. Even a lay parent, unlike a probation officer, may not encourage the suspect to talk with the police or feel bound to report any confession which the child may make in confidence. Indeed, because of these and other considerations, many states require parental consultation in order for a juvenile's confession to be admissible. (Citations omitted). While we believe that such a rule exceeds the requirements of the Constitution, it illustrates the important role that a parent may play during a custodial interrogation of a child and militates in favor of the case-by-case approach which we adopt with respect to requests for a parent.

The Seventh Circuit then considered the circumstances of the case to determine whether defendant's request constituted invocation of his Fifth Amendment right to counsel. The court determined that the proper evaluation of the circumstances involves an examination of the defendant's and the parent's abilities. The court noted that while defendant was technically a juvenile, he lived independently of his parents and had dropped out of school. Moreover, defendant had previous interactions with the police although none involved *Miranda* warnings, interrogation or help of an attorney. Defendant also testified that he understood the *Miranda* warnings. Defendant's father, on the other hand, had no legal training and thus could not have been of assistance in protecting defendant's Fifth Amendment rights. The Seventh Circuit explained that

> because of the special problems associated with uncounseled confessions by juveniles, *In re* Gault, 387 U.S. 1, 55 (1967), it probably is desirable as a matter of policy for police to consent to a juvenile suspect's request for his parents or guardian during an interrogation . . . . [S]ome

> states either by statute or through case law, prohibit the admission into evidence of the confession of a juvenile whose parent, guardian or attorney was not present when the child was advised of his rights, when the waiver decision was made, or both, even if no request for a parent was made.

The Seventh Circuit concluded that based on the circumstances here, however, defendant had not invoked the right to counsel or to silence by requesting to see his father.

Governmental Privileges

AUTHOR'S COMMENTARY

Currently, Illinois does not recognize a "deliberative process privilege." People *ex rel.* Birkett v. City of Chicago, 184 Ill. 2d 521 (1998). Some courts and academics have attributed the origins of the "deliberative process privilege" to Kaiser Aluminum & Chem. Corp. v. United States, 157 F. Supp. 939 (Ct. Cl., 1958), an early United States Court of Claims decision. *See e.g.*, Marriott Int'l Resorts, L.P. v. United States, 437 F.3d 1302, 1304 (Fed. Cir. 2006); Michael N. Kennedy, *Escaping The Fishbowl: A Proposal To Fortify The Deliberative Process*, 99 NW. U. L. REV. 1769, 1779 (2005). The public policy favoring the adoption of this privilege is the support of "open, frank discussion" in "confidential intra-agency advisory opinions." *Kaiser Aluminum*, 157 F. Supp. 945-46.

PRIOR ILLINOIS CASE LAW

1. Governmental "Deliberative Process Privilege" Is Historically Based in the Common Law

Kaiser Aluminum & Chem. Corp. v. United States, 157 F. Supp. 939 (Ct. Cl., 1958)

The Court of Claims permitted the government to claim a privilege with respect to an advisory opinion on an intra-office policy with respect to the sale of three aluminum manufacturing plants. The plaintiff claimed breach by government on a contract for the sale of the aluminum plants. The plaintiff sought disclosure of various documents and the government disclosed all documents except for one. The document was written by the Special Assistant to the War Assets Liquidator and contained "recommendations and advice on program policy." Government argued that disclosure of the document was "contrary to the national interest." The court noted that a privilege for these types of documents has never been recognized before by the U.S. courts, but indicated that in England a similar privilege existed. The court reasoned that the public policy favoring adoption of this privilege is support of "open, frank discussion between subordinate and chief concerning administrative action." The court concluded that confidential intra-agency advisory opinions

> belong to that class of governmental documents that are privileged from inspection as against public interest but not absolutely. It is necessary therefore to consider the circumstances around the demand for this document in order to determine whether or not its production is injurious to the consultative functions of government that the privilege of non-disclosure protects.

The court determined that the document was privileged as it would be against the public interest for the United States government to be forced to disclose an advisory opinion. The court, however, refused the plaintiff's request for an *in camera* examination of the intra-departmental memorandum because

> the encouragement of open expression of opinion as to governmental policy [would be] somewhat impaired by a requirement to submit the evidence even unilaterally. When the head

> of an agency claims privilege from discovery on the ground of public interest, which is recognized as a basis for the claim, it seems to us a judicial examination of the sought-for evidence itself should not be required without a much more definite showing of necessity than appears here. We have adverted to the fact that all the contracts are available to the plaintiff, and also the factual situation of the plants. No fraud is charged, no duality of interest, only a breach of the terms of open contracts. We do not think this record shows the need for examination of the privileged document. To require it here would mean the creation of an absolute right for judicial examination and determination of all evidence whose discovery the executive deemed contrary to the public interest.

The court concluded that an *in camera* inspection can only be granted with a prior "definite showing by plaintiff of facts indicating reasonable cause" for such examination.

2. Illinois Does Not Recognize a "Deliberative Process" Privilege
People *ex rel.* Birkett v. City of Chicago, 184 Ill. 2d 521 (1998)

The Illinois Supreme Court refused to adopt a "deliberative process privilege." The privilege would protect from disclosure "certain classes of intra-agency communications offered in the course of governmental decisionmaking." The City of Chicago sought to bar all plans and discussions of future proposed alterations, modifications, and construction at O'Hare on the basis of privilege. The Supreme Court rejected this argument, concluding that the adoption of such privilege would have adverse effects. Alternatively, if such a privilege were to be adopted, it is best left to the legislature.

The Supreme Court noted that a similar privilege was widely recognized in the federal courts, that the primary purpose of the privilege was to ensure the frank exchange of advice and opinions in the course of a governmental body's decision and policy making, and that the privilege was allowed because the courts believed a "chilling effect" would occur if governmental communications were not protected. However, privileges are strongly disfavored as they work against the truth seeking process. Furthermore, if privileges are not applied uniformly, public trust in government integrity may be undermined. Therefore, to adopt a privilege, the court must find that a sufficiently important interest outweighs the need for probative evidence.

The Supreme Court also rejected the City's argument that because the Illinois Freedom of Information Act (FOIA) contains such a privilege, a general policy is in effect that bars disclosure of pre-decisional matters. While this is evidence of a policy favoring confidentiality, it did not necessarily mean that the legislature sought to create an evidentiary privilege. The concerns of FOIA revolve around providing citizens with information regarding the affairs of the government. These concerns are not the same concerns at issue when an individual is involved in litigation and requires governmental information to establish his or her case. The Supreme Court reasoned that it would be unfair to permit the government to withhold relevant evidence on the one hand while requiring an individual to disclose everything. The Supreme Court further found that where such a privilege has been recognized by the federal court, it was in cases where high-level government officials were involved or matters of national security were at issue. Finally, the Supreme Court stated that although courts can adopt evidentiary privileges, a four-prong test must be met which was not satisfied in this case.

Secret Surveillance Location Privilege

AUTHOR'S COMMENTARY

The secret surveillance location privilege is based on the common law "informant's privilege." People v. Price, 404 Ill. App. 3d 324, 330 (1st Dist. 2010). The purpose of the secret surveillance privilege is "to protect sources from retaliation and to encourage their continuing cooperation with law enforcement." *Id.* Illinois recognizes a qualified privilege against disclosure of secret surveillance locations. People v. Criss, 294 Ill. App. 3d 276, 281 (4th Dist. 1998). To determine whether the privilege applies in a given case, the courts balance the public interest in confidentiality of law enforcement sources against the defendant's interest in presenting a defense. People v. Stokes, 392 Ill. App. 3d 335 (1st Dist. 2009).

PRIOR ILLINOIS CASE LAW

1. Secret Surveillance Location Privilege Is Based on Common Law
People v. Price, 404 Ill. App. 3d 324 (1st Dist. 2010)

The First District of the Illinois Appellate Court discussed the surveillance privilege as follows: The surveillance privilege is a common-law privilege that is based on and evolved from the related "informant's privilege," which is widely recognized in federal and state courts and has been codified in Illinois. *See* 735 ILCS 5/8-802.3 (West 2008).

***

> The purpose of the informant's privilege, and consequently of the surveillance privilege, is twofold: to protect sources from retaliation and to encourage their continuing cooperation with law enforcement. (internal citations omitted) However, these public interests must be balanced against a defendant's constitutional right to a fair trial, making the informant's privilege a qualified privilege, not an absolute privilege.

2. Illinois Recognizes a Qualified Privilege Against Disclosure of Secret Surveillance Locations
People v. Criss, 294 Ill. App. 3d 276 (4th Dist. 1998)

The Fourth District of the Illinois Appellate Court held that the state has a qualified privilege to protect against the disclosure of secret surveillance locations during pretrial hearings. The court noted that other jurisdictions, including Massachusetts, Pennsylvania, and the District of Columbia, recognize such a privilege. The court reasoned that the policy justifications for a surveillance location privilege are analogous to the informant's privilege. Recognizing the privilege would protect police officers as well as building owners who allow their property to be used for criminal surveillance. The court also held that the standard for determining whether a secret surveillance location should be disclosed at trial should be the same standard which is used to determine whether an informant's identity should be disclosed. The trial court should balance the public interest in confidentiality against the defendant's interest in presenting a defense and in testing the credibility of identification witnesses. The court noted that "even if [the] defendant cannot overcome the surveillance location privilege, defense counsel should be permitted to cross-examine the police officers' observations with respect to distance, weather, and any possible obstructions."

3. State Has the Burden to Prove That the Surveillance Privilege Applies
People v. Price, 404 Ill. App. 3d 324 (1st Dist. 2010)

Defendant, on trial for possession of a controlled substance with intent to deliver, argued that the trial court violated his sixth amendment right by improperly limiting his questioning of state witness regarding his surveillance location. The trial court repeatedly prevented defense counsel from cross-examining the witness about his surveillance location. The First District found that state "bears the initial burden of proof and must demonstrate that the surveillance privilege" applies because "[l]ike the informant's privilege on which it is based, surveillance privilege only applies where its underlying purposes are served." The court further noted:

> The State therefore carries its burden of proof by presenting evidence to the court that the surveillance location was either (1) on private property with the permission of the owner, or (2) in a location that is useful and whose utility would be compromised by disclosure. *See* People v. Criss, 294 Ill. App. 3d 276, 280-81 (4th Dist. 1998). Once the State has carried its burden of proof, the defense bears the burden of persuasion and can overcome the privilege by showing that the surveillance location "is relevant and helpful to the defense" or is "essential to the fair determination of a cause." Roviaro v. United States, 353 U.S. 53, 60-61 (1957). The trial court must balance the public interests underlying the surveillance privilege against the need of the defendant for disclosure in order to defend himself at trial, based on the specific facts of each individual case. Factors include but are not limited to "the crime charged, the possible defenses, the possible significance of the [witness's] testimony, and other relevant factors." *Roviaro*, 353 U.S. at 62. To aid in making this determination, the trial court may require the surveillance officer to disclose the surveillance location *in camera* outside of the presence of both the State and the defense.
>
> ***
>
> A trial court has more discretion in declining to order the disclosure of an informant's identity during a preliminary hearing than it does at trial. See McCray v. Illinois, 386 U.S. 300, 310 (1967); People v. Vauzanges, 158 Ill. 2d 509, 520 (1994); People v. Williams, 38 Ill. 2d 150, 153 (1967).
>
> ***
>
> At a pretrial hearing, therefore, the defendant must make a "strong showing that the disclosure of the location is material or necessary to his defense and that his need for the information outweighs the public's interest in keeping the location secret" in order to compel disclosure. *Criss*, 294 Ill. App. 3d at 281. In contrast, due process requires that at trial the defendant need only show that the location is "relevant and helpful to the defense of an accused, or is essential to the fair determination of a cause" in order to overcome the privilege. *Roviaro*, 353 U.S. at 60-61.

The court found that in this case the trial court did not properly apply the surveillance location privilege because it failed to determine whether state had met its initial burden of establishing the existence of the privilege and to then examine whether defense had overcome the state's claim. The First District explained that during defense questioning of an officer about his surveillance location, the trial court sustained state's objection without first establishing that state had met its burden of establishing that the privilege applied. The trial court thus erroneously recognized the application of the privilege without requiring the state to carry its burden of proof. Furthermore, instead of investigating whether defendant then overcame the state's proof, the trial court merely accepted the application of the privilege by stating that it does not "require police officers to give up their surveillance spots." The First District concluded that the trial court abused its discretion by failing to balance the interests of the state and the defendant.

4. Defendant Can Overcome the Surveillance Privilege Through Proof That Location Is so Materially Necessary to Defense as to Outweigh the Public Interest
People v. Stokes, 392 Ill. App. 3d 335 (1st Dist. 2009)

The court held that defendant can overcome the surveillance privilege by showing that disclosure of the secret location is materially necessary for his defense, and that his need in obtaining the location outweighs the public interest of keeping the location confidential. The court reiterated the rule set forth in People v. Knight, 323 Ill. App. 3d 1117 (2001), that the court should conduct an *in camera* hearing to determine whether the privilege applies. Where the case against the defendant "turns exclusively on an officer's testimony, disclosure must almost always be ordered." In this case, the error in failing to conduct an *in camera* hearing was harmless because several officers testified about their role in the investigation and arrest of the defendant.

5. It May Be Proper to Limit the Scope of Defendant's Cross-examination of Testifying Officer to Protect the Public Interest in Keeping Surveillance Location Secret
People v. Quinn, 332 Ill. App. 3d 40 (1st Dist. 2002)

The defendant appealed a conviction of possession of a controlled substance with intent to deliver within 1000 feet of a church. Prior to his arrest, defendant was under surveillance by Chicago police officers at a distance of 75 to 100 feet away with the aid of binoculars. The officers observed him selling narcotics 613 feet away from a church. On appeal, defendant contended that his rights to confront witnesses against him were violated when he was precluded from questioning the testifying officer on cross-examination about the exact surveillance location. On review, the court noted that a defendant's right to confront a witness against him is not absolute and that the scope of the cross-examination may be limited by the trial court. Moreover, the state enjoys a qualified privilege regarding the disclosure of surveillance locations to "protect the public interest in keeping the exact surveillance location secret." Here, the trial judge allowed the defendant to extensively cross-examine the testifying officer about the surveillance, lighting conditions, and possible obstructions. Under these circumstances, the court held that the trial court did not abuse its discretion when it limited the scope of the defendant's cross-examination of the officer.

Informant's Privilege

AUTHOR'S COMMENTARY

The Illinois Supreme Court Rule 412(j)(ii) addresses the matter of informants and states that "[d]isclosure of an informant's identity shall not be required where his identity is a prosecution secret and a failure to disclose will not infringe the constitutional rights of the accused. Disclosure shall not be denied hereunder of the identity of witnesses to be produced at a hearing or trial." In 2006, the legislature codified the informant's privilege in 735 ILCS 5/8-802.3. Rule 101 of the new Illinois Rules of Evidence states that "[a] statutory rule of evidence is effective unless in conflict with a rule or a decision of the Illinois Supreme Court." The informant's privilege statute appears to be consistent with Supreme Court Rule 412(j)(ii) and prior Illinois case law. *See* MICHAEL H. GRAHAM, GRAHAM'S HANDBOOK OF ILLINOIS EVIDENCE § 505.9 (10th ed. 2010).

RELEVANT ILLINOIS SUPREME COURT RULES

Illinois Supreme Court Rule 412(j)(ii) Addressing the Matter of Informants: Matters Not Subject to Disclosure.

(ii) *Informants*. Disclosure of an informant's identity shall not be required where his identity is a prosecution secret and a failure to disclose will not infringe the constitutional rights of the accused. Disclosure shall not be denied hereunder of the identity of witnesses to be produced at a hearing or trial.

Effective October 1, 1971; amended October 1, 1976, effective November 15, 1976; amended June 15, 1982, effective July 1, 1982; amended March 1, 2001, effective immediately, except when in the opinion of the trial, Appellate, or Supreme Court the application of the amended provisions in a particular case pending at the time the amendment becomes effective would not be feasible or would work an injustice, in which case former procedures would apply.

Committee Comments

The value of informants to effective law enforcement is so highly regarded that encouragement of their use, through protection of their identity, has resulted in the development of one of the few privileges accorded to the State. The public interest in protecting the sources of information concerning the commission of crimes is served by providing for the nondisclosure of the identity of informants except when compelling circumstances require it. Disclosure should only be required when constitutional problems are raised or when the informant's identity is to be disclosed at trial (although a protective order under Rule 414(d) might still be in order). The cases which have established this privilege include McCray v. Illinois, 386 U.S. 300 (1967), Roviaro v. United States, 353 U.S. 53 (1957), People v. White, 16 N.Y.2d 270, 266 N.Y.S.2d 100, 213 N.E.2d 438 (1965), and Commonwealth v. Carter 208 Pa. Super. 245, 222 A.2d 475 (1966), aff'd mem., 209 Pa. Super. 732, 226 A.2d 215 (1967).

RELEVANT STATUTORY AUTHORITY

Informant's Privilege: 735 ILCS 5/8-802.3

§ 8-802.3. Informant's privilege.

(a) Except as provided in subsection (b), if an individual (i) submits information concerning a criminal act to a law enforcement agency or to a community organization that acts as an intermediary in reporting to law enforcement and (ii) requests anonymity, then the identity of that individual is privileged and confidential and is not subject to discovery or admissible in evidence in a proceeding.

(b) There is no privilege under subsection (a) if a court, after a hearing *in camera*, finds that the party seeking discovery or the proponent of the evidence has shown that:

(1) the identity of an individual who submits information concerning a criminal act is sought or offered in a court proceeding involving a felony or misdemeanor;
(2) the evidence is not otherwise available; and
(3) nondisclosure infringes upon a constitutional right of an accused, or there is a need for the evidence that substantially outweighs the interest in protecting confidentiality.

(c) The court may impose such sanctions as are necessary to enforce its order.

Effective January 1, 2006.

PRIOR ILLINOIS CASE LAW

1. Informant's Privilege and the Defendant's Constitutional Right to Present a Defense
Roviaro v. United States, 353 U.S. 53 (1957)

The United States Supreme Court recognized the informant's privilege and noted that its purpose "is the furtherance and protection of the public interest in effective law enforcement." Defendant was charged with the sale and transportation of a controlled substance under a federal statute. A government informant permitted a narcotics agent to hide in the trunk of his car while he conducted a drug sale. The informant drove to meet with defendant and two law enforcement vehicles trailed behind. Defendant got into the informant's car and directed him to an address. The narcotics agent could hear the conversation between the defendant and the informant from the trunk. After the car reached the address, the defendant got out and picked up a small package from a nearby tree.

Defendant gave the package to the informant and left in his own vehicle. The package contained heroin. The police later arrested defendant. At the police station, the defendant was confronted with the informant. Informant, however, denied ever meeting defendant or knowing who he was. At trial, police officers and the narcotics agent testified. The defendant repeatedly sought disclosure of informant's identity, but the trial court refused based on application of the informant's privilege.

The Supreme Court found that the trial court committed prejudicial error and that the informant's privilege did not apply here. The Supreme Court explained that the informant was "an active participant in the crime," and that nondisclosure of the informant's identity would be manifestly unfair to the defendant. The Supreme Court reasoned that the informant's identity was highly relevant in this case because the informant was a material witness. The mere cross-examination of the police officers would not "substitute for an opportunity to examine the man who had been nearest to [the defendant] and took part in the transaction." The Supreme Court noted that the informant participated in the transaction and could provide valuable testimony at defendant's trial that may reveal entrapment. The informant was also the only person who could corroborate or contradict the police officers' testimony. The Supreme Court concluded that where "disclosure of an informer's identity is relevant and helpful to the defense of an accused, or is essential to a fair determination of a cause, the privilege must give way."

2. Informant's Privilege Prevails at a Suppression Hearing and Refusal to Divulge Informant's Identity at Such a Hearing Does Not Violate Defendant's Due Process or Confrontation Rights
McCray v. Illinois, 386 U.S. 300 (1967)

Police officers received a tip from a reliable informant that defendant was selling drugs. The officers stopped defendant while he was walking down the street, searched him and recovered heroin. Before trial, defendant filed a motion to suppress the drugs as evidence based on an alleged violation of his Fourth amendment rights. The trial court conducted a hearing but denied defendant's motion to suppress. Defendant appealed, arguing that the hearing was "constitutionally deficient." At the hearing, defense counsel inquired about informant's identity on cross-examination of the arresting officers, but the state objected and asserted the informant's privilege. The trial court sustained the objection. Defendant argued that the trial court violated his due process and confrontation rights when it prevented the disclosure of the informant's identity. The United States Supreme Court disagreed, relying on the "well-settled Illinois law" and upholding the informant's privilege:

> When the issue is not guilt or innocence, but, as here, the question of probable cause for an arrest or search, the Illinois Supreme Court has held that police officers need not invariably be required to disclose an informant's identity if the trial judge is convinced, by evidence submitted in open court and subject to cross-examination, that the officers did rely in good faith upon credible information supplied by a reliable informant.

Here, the defendant requested that the Supreme Court require disclosure of an informant's identity at any preliminary hearing where officers relied on information supplied by an informer. The Supreme Court declined to adopt such a rule, noting that neither the due process clause nor the Sixth Amendment right to confrontation required such result. The Supreme Court explained that the officers here were subject to thorough cross-examination that disclosed in great detail the information they learned from the informant. The Supreme Court noted that the trial court found the officers' testimony credible and rejected the notion that the due process clause would require a judge to assume that the officers were lying. Moreover, the Supreme Court found that defendant's right to confront witnesses against him was not violated when the officers refused to disclose the informant's identity on cross-examination. The Supreme Court reasoned that finding of such a violation would prevent every witness on cross-examination from asserting a testimonial privilege.

3. Informant's Privilege Gives Way Where Informant's Identity Is Relevant to the Defense or Is Essential to a Fair Determination of a Cause
People v. Williams, 45 Ill. 2d 319 (1970)

Defendant argued that the trial court wrongfully protected the identity of an informant who signed the complaint for a search warrant of defendant's apartment. The search yielded drugs. At trial, defendant sought to call the informant to the stand and claimed that the nondisclosure of informant's identity denied her due process. To resolve the issue, the Illinois Supreme Court examined and distinguished Roviaro v. United States, 353 U.S. 53 (1957), noting that here, unlike in *Roviaro*,

> there was no participation [by the informant] in the crime, the police evidence was clear and the circumstances surrounding the raid supported the conviction for knowingly possessing narcotics. We believe the requirements of fundamental fairness have been met in this case and we believe that the testimony of the informer would have been of little help to the defense in view of the independent evidence by which the crime . . . was proved.

Also see the following cases for further discussion on this topic:

People v. Vauzanges, 158 Ill. 2d 509 (1994) (remanding to determine whether trial court conducted *in camera* review of informant's files).

People v. Scott, 34 Ill. 2d 41 (1966) (finding proper non-disclosure where defendant failed to show informant's identity crucial to presentation of defense).

People v. Connie, 34 Ill. 2d 353 (1966) (finding non-disclosure proper where informant did not participate in serving warrant or in defendant's arrest).

People v. Beattie, 31 Ill. 2d 257 (1964) (holding that trial court improperly struck officer testimony regarding informant; in the absence of the information there was no probable cause for arrest).

People v. Durr, 28 Ill. 2d 308 (1963) (finding proper non-disclosure where informant did not participate in the crime).

People v. Mack, 12 Ill. 2d 151 (1957) (finding refusal to disclose identity of informant who signed search warrant proper where informant's identity not helpful to defense or necessary for determination of cause).

4. Prosecution Is Not Required to Disclose Identity of an Informant Who Is Not a Material Witness on the Issue of Guilt or Innocence of Defendant
People v. Smith, 40 Ill. 2d 501(1968)

Defendant, convicted of illegal possession of narcotics, argued on appeal that prosecution should have been required to produce the informant at a preliminary hearing. The informant was an affiant on a search warrant application contending that he bought narcotics from defendant. Defendant argued that he should have had an opportunity to cross-examine the informant. Defendant reasoned that "if he did in fact sell narcotics to the affiant-informer his identity must be known to him, thereby vitiating the traditional reasons favoring an informer's privilege, i.e., to protect him from possible retribution and to maintain his usefulness as a purveyor of information." The Illinois Supreme Court disagreed, noting that prosecution is generally "not required to disclose the identity of an informer who is not a material witness on the issue of the guilt or innocence of the defendant at trial." The Supreme Court further stated that the prosecution need not disclose an informant's identity simply because he "communicated his information to the police through the medium of a search warrant." The Supreme Court concluded that it was not clear that defendant knew who the informant was, and therefore the prosecution had a legitimate interest in refusing to disclose the informant's identity.

See also People v. Williams, 38 Ill. 2d 150 (1967) (finding non-disclosure of informant's identity proper where informant's testimony was not "of significant value" on issue of guilt or innocence).

5. Defendant May Be Entitled to Disclosure of Informant's Identity to Assert Entrapment Defense
People v. Woods, 139 Ill. 2d 369 (1990)

Controlled substances and armed violence defendant argued that the trial court erred in refusing to disclose the identity and address of an informant. Defendant sought to show that the informant introduced defendant to an undercover police officer, urged defendant to sell drugs to the officer and provided defendant with the drugs that defendant admitted to selling. The appellate court found that the informant's testimony would be essential to the establishment of defendant's entrapment defense. The Illinois Supreme Court affirmed the appellate court's holding, reasoning that although the informant was not an active participant in the crime, he may have "facilitated and perhaps induced" the crime. The Supreme Court further found that the state's introduction of evidence regarding the informant at trial must have indicated the informant's identity to the defendant. The undercover police officer testified that he was introduced to the defendant by one specific individual-the informant. Moreover, defendant testified at trial that he was introduced to the officer by that same individual. Thus, the court noted that since defendant already knew who the informant was,

> disclosure of the informant's identity on the record was not actually intended for defendant's enlightenment but in order that, as a matter of law, defendant might be aided in procuring [the informant's] attendance at trial or in overcoming [his] unwillingness to testify. Nevertheless, any such defense motive would not in itself defeat any right of defendant to disclosure of the informant's identity. On the contrary, under both [Illinois Supreme Court] Rule 412(j)(ii) and Roviaro v. United States, 353 U.S. 53 (1957), such failure of the informant's identity to constitute a prosecution secret would tend to defeat the State's privilege of nondisclosure. In that event, preexisting knowledge by defendant of the informant's identity might affect the question whether nondisclosure prejudiced defendant but would not govern whether disclosure

> should have been made. [. . .] In other words, considerations of fundamental fairness may overcome the State's privilege against disclosing an informant's identity.

The Supreme Court found that disclosure of informant's identity in this case was necessary as "any public interest in shielding it failed to outweigh defendant's need for it." The trial court's failure to disclose the informant's identity, the Supreme Court concluded, was not harmless error.

For other cases discussing this topic, see:

People v. Chaney, 63 Ill. 2d 216 (1976) (finding prejudicial error for the state not to inform court or defendant of informer's identity when state became aware that informer was to be called as defense witness).

People v. Lewis, 57 Ill. 2d 232 (1974) (finding defendant entitled to disclosure of informant's name and address unless state could establish danger to informant).

Interpreter's Privilege

RELEVANT STATUTORY AUTHORITY

Interpreter's Privilege: 735 ILCS 5/8-911

§ 8-911. Language interpreter's privilege.

(a) A "language interpreter" is a person who aids a communication when at least one party to the communication has a language difficulty.

(b) If a communication is otherwise privileged, that underlying privilege is not waived because of the presence of the language interpreter.

(c) The language interpreter shall not disclose the communication without the express consent of the person who has the right to claim the underlying privilege.

Effective September 12, 2007.

PRIOR ILLINOIS CASE LAW

There has been no case law discussing this privilege.

Interpreter for the Deaf and Hard of Hearing Privilege

RELEVANT STATUTORY AUTHORITY

Interpreter for the Deaf and Hard of Hearing Privilege: 735 ILCS 5/8-912

§ 8-912. Interpreter for the deaf and hard of hearing's privilege.

(a) An "interpreter for the deaf and hard of hearing" is a person who aids communication when at least one party to the communication has a hearing loss.

(b) An interpreter for the deaf and hard of hearing who interprets a conversation between a hearing person and a deaf person is deemed a conduit for the conversation and may not disclose or be compelled to disclose by subpoena the contents of the conversation that he or she facilitated without the written consent of all persons involved who received his or her professional services.

(c) All communications that are recognized by law as privileged shall remain privileged even in cases where an interpreter for the deaf and hard of hearing is utilized to facilitate such communications.

(d) Communications may be voluntarily disclosed under the following circumstances:

(1) the formal reporting, conferring, or consulting with administrative superiors, colleagues, or consultants who share similar professional responsibility, in which instance all recipients of such information are similarly bound to regard the communication as privileged;
(2) a person waives the privilege by bringing any public charges against an interpreter for the deaf and hard of hearing, including a person licensed under the Interpreter for the Deaf Licensure Act of 2007; and
(3) a communication reveals the intended commission of a crime or harmful act and such disclosure is judged necessary by the interpreter for the deaf and hard of hearing to protect any person from a clear, imminent risk of serious mental or physical harm or injury or to forestall a serious threat to public safety.

(e) (Blank).

January 1, 2010.

PRIOR ILLINOIS CASE LAW

There has been no case law discussing this privilege.

Chapter 4

Chapter 4

Article VI – Witnesses

Competency

Rule 601. General Rule of Competency

Every person is competent to be a witness, except as otherwise provided by these rules, by other rules prescribed by the Supreme Court, or by statute.

Adopted September 27, 2010, eff. January 1, 2011.

AUTHOR'S COMMENTARY

Illinois Rule of Evidence 601 codifies existing Illinois common law and recognizes the role of the legislative process in this area of the law. People v. Smith, 152 Ill. 2d 229 (1992).

RELEVANT STATUTORY AUTHORITY

Witness Competency: 725 ILCS 5/115-14

§ 115-14. Witness Competency. (a) Every person, irrespective of age, is qualified to be a witness and no person is disqualified to testify to any matter, except as provided in subsection (b). ***

(b) A person is disqualified to be a witness if he or she is:

(1) Incapable of expressing himself or herself concerning the matter so as to be understood, either directly or through interpretation by one who can understand him or her; or

(2) Incapable of understanding the duty of a witness to tell the truth.

(c) A party may move the court prior to a witness' testimony being received in evidence, requesting that the court make a determination if a witness is competent to testify. The hearing shall be conducted outside the presence of the jury and the burden of proof shall be on the moving party.

Effective January 1, 1989.

Court May Not Order Mental Examination of Sex Victim: 725 ILCS 5/115-7.1

§ 115-7.1. Court may not order mental examination of sex victim. Except where explicitly authorized by this Code or by the Rules of the Supreme Court of Illinois, no court may require or order a witness who is the victim of an alleged sex offense to submit to or undergo either a psychiatric or psychological examination.

Effective January 1, 1984.

Witness Disqualification: 725 ILCS 5/115-16

§ 115-16. Witness disqualification. No person shall be disqualified as a witness in a criminal case or proceeding by reason of his or her interest in the event of the case or proceeding, as a party or otherwise, or by reason of his or her having been convicted of a crime; but the interest or conviction may be shown for the purpose of affecting the credibility of the witness. A defendant in a criminal case or proceeding shall only at his or her own request be deemed a competent witness, and the person's neglect to testify shall not create a presumption against the person, nor shall the court permit a reference or comment to be made to or upon that neglect. [. . .]

Effective July 1, 2011.

Abuse or Neglect Proceedings: 705 ILCS 405/2-18(4)(d)

(4)(d) There shall be a rebuttable presumption that a minor is competent to testify in abuse or neglect proceedings. The court shall determine how much weight to give to the minor's testimony, and may allow the minor to testify in chambers with only the court, the court reporter and attorneys for the parties present.

Effective August 20, 2010.

Interested Witness: 735 ILCS 5/8-101

§ 8-101. Interested witness. No person shall be disqualified as a witness in any action or proceeding, except as hereinafter stated, by reason of his or her interest in the event thereof, as a party or otherwise, or by reason of his or her conviction of any crime; but such interest or conviction may be shown for the purpose of affecting the credibility of such witness; and the fact of such conviction may be proven like any fact not of record, either by the witness himself or herself (who shall be compelled to testify thereto) or by any other witness cognizant of such conviction, as impeaching testimony, or by any other competent evidence.

Effective July 1, 1982.

Prior Illinois Case Law

1. A Witness Is Competent to Testify Unless Party Challenging Competency Shows Otherwise

People v. Smith, 152 Ill. 2d 229 (1992)

Defendant on trial for murder and aggravated criminal sexual assault argued that a four-year-old witness' hearsay statements should not have been allowed into evidence. Immediately following the murder of her babysitter, police asked the minor witness about what happened. Although the minor did not testify at trial, the police officer who interviewed her testified about statements she made immediately following the murder. The trial court admitted the officer's testimony under the excited utterance hearsay exception. Defendant first challenged the admissibility of the statements under the excited utterance hearsay exception but the Illinois Supreme Court found that the trial court properly admitted them under this exception. Defendant then contended that it was unfair to admit the hearsay statements because the trial court never determined that the minor witness was competent to testify. The Supreme Court rejected this argument, noting "that absent a showing by *defendant*, [the witness] was qualified to testify in spite of her young age" (citing 725 ILCS 5/115-14). The Supreme Court further emphasized that "declarant's competency is not relevant to the admission of excited utterances."

2. 725 ILCS 5/115-14 Removed the Common Law Requirement of Automatic Witness Competency Hearing for Witnesses Under 14 Years of Age

People v. Trail, 197 Ill. App. 3d 742 (4th Dist. 1990)

The court held that the trial court's refusal to allow a 12-year-old witness to testify was error, although it was not reversible. The court recognized that 725 ILCS 5/115-14 discarded the former rigid common law rule that had mandated competency hearings for all witnesses under 14 years of age. In this case, the trial court erred in excluding the witness because of his age and "eagerness to testify." The appellate court concluded that the trial judge's exclusion order was motivated improperly by a finding that the testimony lacked credibility. It stated that "[i]t is not the trial court's role to evaluate witnesses and to permit the testimony of only those witnesses the court finds credible."

For other decisions discussing this issue, see:

People v. Jones, 123 Ill. 2d 387 (1988) (finding an unresponsive witness with a legal guardian competent to testify).

People v. Titone, 115 Ill. 2d 413 (1986) (finding use of drugs by witness relevant in assessing her credibility).

People v. Nash, 36 Ill. 2d 275 (1966) (noting that a psychopath has the ability to observe, recollect, and communicate and is therefore a competent witness).

Harrison v. Thackaberry, 248 Ill. 512 (1911) (finding that a witness' inability to hear does not violate defendant's right to cross-examine as long as witness meets test of competency).

3. If a Party Objects to a Child's Competency to Testify, Court Should Hold a Preliminary Competency Hearing

People v. Garcia, 97 Ill. 2d 58 (1983)

When a party objects to a child's competency to testify, a judge should hold a preliminary hearing. This is usually accomplished outside of the jury's presence, but in the court's discretion the examination may be held in the presence of the jury. It is the degree of intelligence, the ability to understand the meaning of a witness' oath, and a moral duty to tell the truth, not the child's age, that determine competency. In determining the minor's degree of intelligence, the judge should consider whether the minor is sufficiently mature to:

(1) "receive correct impressions by her senses"
(2) recollect these impressions;
(3) understand questions and narrate answers intelligently; and
(4) "appreciate the moral duty to tell the truth."

This is not a rigid formula, and the judge's determination will be sustained on appeal absent an abuse of discretion.

Here, the Illinois Supreme Court found that the trial court properly conducted a competency hearing to determine that an 11-year-old witness was competent to testify. The trial court inquired as to the witness' age, school information and whether she understood the difference between telling the truth and telling a lie.

4. Witnesses Are Competent to Testify As Long As They Possess the Requisite Capacities to Observe, Recollect, and Communicate

People v. Williams, 147 Ill. 2d 173 (1991)

A person is not disqualified from testifying merely because he or she has a mental illness, physical disability, drug dependency, or an intellectual disability. Here, the defendant challenged the trial court's determination that an accomplice witness once treated with acute schizophrenic reaction was competent to testify. The Illinois Supreme Court held that the trial court did not abuse its discretion in finding the witness competent. The Supreme Court found that since there was no evidence that the witness exhibited at the time of the crime or continued to exhibit symptoms of the disability, she was competent to testify. The Supreme Court noted:

> A witness is competent to testify if he has the capacity to observe, recollect, and communicate, and his mental deficiency is considered only insofar as it affects credibility. People v. Jones, 123 Ill. 2d 387, 405 (1988); *see* People v. Dixon, 22 Ill. 2d 513, 515-16 (1961). Thus, sanity is not the test of competency. People v. Seel, 68 Ill. App. 3d 996, 1006 (1st Dist. 1979). Likewise, an individual [with an intellectual disability] is legally competent to testify so long as he possesses the requisite capacities, and the burden to show otherwise is upon the party questioning competency. People v. Spencer, 119 Ill. App. 3d 971, 977 (1st Dist. 1983). The

> determination of whether a witness is competent to testify is within the sound discretion of the trial court and may be arrived at either through preliminary inquiry or by observing the witness' demeanor and ability to testify during trial. *See Spencer*, 119 Ill. App. 3d at 976; People v. Ford, 139 Ill. App. 3d 894, 901 (5th Dist. 1985).

5. Accomplice Is Competent to Testify For or Against the Defendant
People v. Williams, 147 Ill. 2d 173 (1991)

Defendant was convicted of murder, aggravated kidnapping and rape. An accomplice testified against him at trial. Defendant argued that the testimony of the accomplice was insufficient to prove him guilty of the crime beyond a reasonable doubt because it "lacked 'an absolute conviction of truth' and was not meaningfully corroborated." The Illinois Supreme Court noted that an accomplice, or one who admits his or her participation in the commission of a crime with the defendant, is competent to testify for or against the defendant, and his or her testimony is admissible regardless of whether it is corroborated by other evidence or testimony. Such testimony should be rejected by the fact finder, however, if it is shown that the accomplice has hopes of reward from the prosecution, unless his or her testimony "carries with it absolute conviction of its truth."

The Supreme Court acknowledged that the witness presented several inconsistent statements, forgot information and denied knowledge of the crimes, but noted that the jury had found her credible despite all of these deficiencies. The Supreme Court pointed out that "the testimony of an accomplice witness, whether corroborated or uncorroborated, is sufficient to sustain a criminal conviction 'if it convinces the jury of the defendant's guilt beyond a reasonable doubt.'" The Supreme Court concluded that the evidence was sufficient to sustain defendant's conviction.

6. Court May Not Order a Psychological Examination of a Sex Crime Victim but Defendant May Request to Have Own Expert Evaluate Victim for Evidence of Rape Trauma Syndrome If Victim Consents
People v. Wheeler, 151 Ill. 2d 298 (1992)

Defendant was charged with aggravated criminal sexual assault. State sought to introduce evidence that the victim suffered from rape trauma syndrome. Defendant requested that the trial court order the victim to submit to a psychological examination by defendant's expert. The trial court denied his motion and defendant argued on appeal that the trial court violated his fair trial rights. The Illinois Supreme Court explained that

> [a] defendant's right to due process is the right to a fundamentally fair trial, including the right to present witnesses in his own behalf. Chambers v. Mississippi, 410 U.S. 284, 294 (1973). "Few rights are more fundamental than that of an accused to present witnesses in his own defense." *Chambers*, 410 U.S. at 302. In this case the trial court did not preclude defendant from presenting his own expert witness. Rather, because defendant's expert was prevented from personally examining the victim the basis on which the expert could form an opinion was limited.

The Supreme Court noted that historically the Illinois courts had the "discretionary power to order a sex-offense victim to submit to a psychological examination if the defendant presented a compelling reason for the exam." The practice thus opened victim's competency and credibility "to attack based merely on the nature of the offense" and resulted in intimidation of "sex-offense victims through psychological examinations."

Two statutes were later enacted, 725 ILCS 5/115-7.1 and 725 ILCS 5/115-7.2, to protect a victim of a sexual crime from embarrassment and harassment resulting from the practice of submitting such victims to psychological evaluations. 725 ILCS 5/115-7.1 forbids a mental examination of a sex crime victim and 725 ILCS 5/115-7.2 allows an expert to testify as to any evidence that a sex crime victim has suffered from post-traumatic stress syndrome. The Supreme Court explained that 725 ILCS 5/115-7.2 does not deal with the issue of victim's competency or credibility as a witness, but rather permits expert testimony about rape trauma syndrome as substantive evidence to determine whether a sexual assault happened or not.

Here, the Supreme Court observed that the defendant was not attacking the credibility of the victim but was merely seeking to rebut the state's evidence that the assault happened pursuant to section 5/115-7.2. The Supreme Court sought to balance the victim's right to be free from intrusions of privacy against the defendant's right to a fair trial and concluded that with the victim's consent the defendant should be allowed to have an expert examine her to determine whether she suffered from rape trauma syndrome. If, however, the victim does not consent to such an examination, the state may only introduce syndrome evidence from a non-examining expert.

7. Court May Not Order a Physical Examination of a Sex Crime Victim
People v. Lopez, 207 Ill. 2d 449 (2003)

Defendant charged with aggravated criminal sexual abuse sought to have the three-year-old victim undergo a gynecological examination. The Supreme Court recognized that in People v. Glover, 49 Ill. 2d 78 (1971), the court stated that if defendant provides a "compelling reason," a court may order a psychiatric examination of a sex crime victim. The Supreme Court here overruled *Glover*, reasoning that pursuant to 725 ILCS 5/115-7.1, a court has no authority to order a mental examination of a sexual assault victim. The Supreme Court extended this prohibition to court ordered physical examinations, explaining that

> the legislature's decision to prohibit trial courts from ordering the mental examination of complaining witnesses provides further support for our decision to likewise proscribe trial courts from ordering physical examinations.

The Supreme Court then examined its decision in People v. Wheeler, 151 Ill. 2d 298 (1992), where it held that the state was precluded from presenting evidence with respect to rape trauma syndrome from an examining expert where the victim refused to undergo an examination at defendant's request. The state, however, could still introduce this type of evidence from a non-examining expert. The rationale for this rule was based on the victim's right to be free from intrusions of privacy balanced against a defendant's right to a fair trial. The Supreme Court noted that the same considerations and rights were at issue when a defendant seeks a physical examination of a sex crime victim. The Supreme Court explained:

> Victims of sexual assault should no more be subjected to physical examinations by experts proffered by the defense than they should be required to submit to psychological evaluations. The effects of both types of examinations can be intolerably harassing and intimidating and can cause further harm to the victim. . . . . We believe that this court struck the proper balance between a victim's right to be free of intrusion and a defendant's right to a fair trial, and that the *Wheeler* holding should be applicable in cases where defendants seek either psychological or physical examinations of victims in sexual offense cases.

Thus, the Supreme Court held that "a trial court cannot order the physical examination of a complaining witness in a sex offense case." Additionally, the Supreme Court warned that

> [t]o ensure a defendant's constitutional rights to a fair trial is not compromised by the inability to obtain an independent physical examination, trial courts should exercise vigilance when rendering decisions on what evidence the State is allowed to produce.

Specifically:

> [W]hen a trial court rules on the admission of evidence in a sex offense case where a defendant has requested the physical examination of a complaining witness and the witness refuses to submit to the examination, the court must balance the due process rights of the defendant against the privacy rights of the alleged victim, by decision what medical evidence, if any, the State is allowed to introduce.

8. Court Should Not Order Psychiatric Evaluation of Witness for Impeachment Purposes Because Defendant May Impeach the Witness with Evidence of General Reputation for Truth and Veracity
People v. Nash, 36 Ill. 2d 275 (1966)

Defendant was convicted of murder. On appeal he argued that the trial court should have ordered a psychiatric evaluation to impeach the credibility of the state's key witness who was with the defendant during the commission of the crime. The defendant claimed that the witness was a psychopath and should not be believed. He sought to show that "a psychopath tends to be more untruthful than other persons," but the Illinois Supreme Court disagreed, noting that "psychiatrists are not in agreement" on this point. The Illinois Supreme Court found that the trial court did not err in denying defendant's request for a psychiatric evaluation of the witness because such evidence is "unnecessary to raise the issue of whether a witness is a psychopath, from which a jury could infer that he possesses the characteristic of untruthfulness, when direct evidence of a witness's reputation for truthfulness is admissible."

9. Witness' Hypnotically Induced or Refreshed Testimony May Be Admitted Subject to Strict Limitations
People v. Cohoon, 104 Ill. 2d 295 (1984)

The Illinois Supreme Court skirted the question of whether hypnotically induced or refreshed testimony of a witness is *per se* inadmissible, stating:

> We need not and do not decide whether hypnosis induced testimony is sufficiently suspect *per se* to hold it inadmissible. [The special agent who hypnotized the victim] testified that an individual under hypnosis might 'confabulate' or 'make up and fill in things that they can't remember.' He acknowledged that it was not possible for the hypnotist to determine what was truth and what was confabulation. This is consistent with the findings contained in the recognized treatises on the subject of hypnosis, and illustrative is the statement contained in Orne, The Use and Misuse of Hypnosis in Court, 27 Int'l J. Clinical & Experimental Hypnosis 311 (1979). Dr. Orne, discussing the difficulties which may be encountered through the forensic use of hypnosis, said:
>
> > The hypnotic suggestion to relive a past event, particularly when accompanied by questions about specific details, puts pressure on the subject to provide information for which few, if any, actual memories are available. This situation may jog the subject's memory and produce some increased recall, but it will also cause him to fill in details that are plausible but consist of memories or fantasies from other times. It is extremely difficult to know which aspects of hypnotically aided recall are historically accurate and which aspects have been confabulated. [Citation omitted].
> >
> > Though it is possible that accurate information is recovered, the important effects that motivation can exert on memory—hypnotically enhanced or otherwise—must be taken into account in assessing the "memories" that are obtained. [Citation omitted].

Here, the Supreme Court determined that the pretrial photographic identification of the defendant by the rape victim who, *inter alia*, had been hypnotized shortly before the identification procedure was impermissibly suggestive. The appellate court opinion (120 Ill. App. 3d 62 (5th Dist. 1983)), however, addressed the question directly. The court examined several factors, stating:

> Although the officer in the case at bar did not have extended or elaborate training in hypnosis, the transcript of the hypnotic session shows that his 30 hours of training were sufficient to prevent him from attempting to influence the witness. Moreover, as the victim testified at trial, her hypnotic session brought out only one descriptive detail not previously offered, that the rapist had big ears. Given that the hypnotist in the case at bar had formal training in hypnosis, we hold he was sufficiently competent to satisfy the requirements of People v. Smrekar, 68 Ill. App. 3d 379 (4th Dist. 1979). In addition to showing the hypnotist to be competent, there is no indication from the record that the procedure was fraught with suggestive influences since the victim altered the description under hypnosis in only one minor way. Other corroborative evidence did exist and the witness described how she had ample opportunity to view the rapist during the crime. Given the circumstances of this case, we find that the hypnotically enhanced testimony was helpful to the trier of fact in arriving at the truth and was properly admitted pursuant to People v. Smrekar.

Thus, hypnotically induced or refreshed testimony could be admissible subject to strict limitations, and ultimately the question is one of weight and credibility.

10. Categorical Exclusion of All Post-Hypnotic Testimony of Defendant Violates Defendant's Right to Testify on His or Her Behalf
Rock v. Arkansas, 483 U.S. 44 (1987)

Defendant was charged with manslaughter for the shooting death of her husband. She could not remember many details of the incident and submitted to pretrial hypnosis twice in hopes of refreshing her memory. During the hypnosis sessions the defendant could not remember any additional details than she had already provided to the police. After the hypnosis ended, however, she was able to recall that while fighting with her husband on the night of the shooting she was holding the gun but did not have her finger on the trigger and that the gun fired after her husband grabbed her arm. A gun expert evaluated the gun and determined that the gun was defective and could fire even without someone pulling the trigger. State subsequently filed a motion to exclude all hypnotically-induced testimony at trial and the trial court granted the motion pursuant to a state rule of evidence. The United States Supreme Court noted that

> logically included in the accused's right to call witnesses whose testimony is "material and favorable to his defense," United States v. Valenzuela-Bernal, 458 U.S. 858, 867 (1982), is a right to testify himself, should he decide it is in his favor to do so. In fact, the most important witness for the defense in many criminal cases is the defendant himself. There is no justification today for a rule that denies an accused the opportunity to offer his own testimony. Like the truthfulness of other witnesses, the defendant's veracity . . . can be tested adequately by cross-examination.

The Supreme Court concluded that the *per se* state rule prohibiting defendant's hypnotically refreshed testimony serves to "arbitrarily" exclude material portions of defendant's testimony and was not a justified limitation on defendant's constitutional right to testify.

11. Hypnotically Induced Testimony Is Generally Inadmissible in Illinois
People v. Zayas, 131 Ill. 2d 284 (1989)

Here, the appellate court concluded that hypnotically enhanced testimony should not be permitted. The court reached this conclusion after examining judicial trends and the scientific community's view that such evidence is inherently unreliable:

> [T]he overwhelming majority of jurisdictions which have considered this issue bar from the courtroom any hypnotically enhanced testimony. [Citations omitted].
>
> This growing body of authority rejecting the courtroom use of hypnotically enhanced testimony is also reflected in the legal and scientific literature . . . .
>
> A more recent survey of the scientific community's view of this issue also clearly supports exclusion of such evidence. [Citation omitted]. The author notes that after what he describes as an exhaustive review of the scientific research on hypnosis and memory, the Council on Scientific Affairs of the American Medical Association concluded that hypnosis should not be used to prepare witnesses for trial. He also cites research showing that: hypnotized subjects respond incorrectly to leading questions twice as often as nonhypnotized subjects; false memories from hypnotic recall may actually replace the original memory; hypnosis does not improve facial identification and may facilitate false positive identifications; hypnosis does not improve the accuracy of recall but does significantly increase the subject's confidence in the recollection.

On further appeal, the Illinois Supreme Court agreed that hypnotically induced testimony is unreliable and therefore inadmissible. The Supreme Court carved out two exceptions:

> (a) a previously hypnotized witness may testify on condition that the proponent of the witness can establish that the testimony is based solely on independent pre-hypnotic recall, and
>
> (b) consistent with *Rock v. Arkansas*, a criminal defendant has a constitutional right to testify even if he or she was previously hypnotized.

12. Witness' Prior Conviction Does Not Disqualify Witness from Testifying
People v. Naylor, 229 Ill. 2d 584 (2008)

The Illinois Supreme Court noted:

> At common law, any person convicted of an infamous crime was deemed incompetent to be a witness and was not permitted to testify in any civil or criminal trial. This disqualification was based on the belief that conviction of such a crime rendered the prospective witness inherently unworthy of trust. People v. Spates, 77 Ill. 2d 193, 201-02 (1979); *see generally* 2 J. WIGMORE, EVIDENCE §§ 519 through 521 (Chadbourn rev. ed. 1979). In Illinois, this harsh rule is abrogated [. . .] in criminal cases by section 115-16 of the Code of Criminal Procedure of 1963 (725 ILCS 5/115-16 (West 2006) (originally enacted at ILL. REV. STAT. 1874, ch. 38, par. 426)). Th[is] statute[] provide[s] that no person shall be disqualified to testify based on a prior conviction, but such conviction may be admitted to affect the credibility of the witness. 725 ILCS 5/115-16 (West 2006); *Spates*, 77 Ill. 2d at 202.

Rule 602. Lack of Personal Knowledge

A witness may not testify to a matter unless evidence is introduced sufficient to support a finding that the witness has personal knowledge of the matter. Evidence to prove personal knowledge may, but need not, consist of the witness' own testimony. This rule is subject to the provisions of Rule 703, relating to opinion testimony by expert witnesses.

Adopted September 27, 2010, eff. January 1, 2011.

AUTHOR'S COMMENTARY

Illinois Rule of Evidence 602 codifies existing common law principles and is identical to Federal Rule of Evidence 602 in effect until its stylistic amendment on December 1, 2011. *See* People v. Rosenbaum, 299 Ill. 93 (1921); Gino L. DiVito, *The Illinois Rules of Evidence: A Color-Coded Guide Containing the New Rules, the Committee's General and Specific Comments, a Comparison with the Federal Rules of Evidence, and Additional Commentary* (*Including the Federal Rules of Evidence as Amended Effective December 1, 2011*) (Jan. 1, 2012), at 64, http://www.tdrlawfirm.com/assets/downloads/Illinois_Rules_of_Evidence_Color-Coded_Guide.pdf.

PRIOR ILLINOIS CASE LAW

1. Witness May Only Testify as to Facts Within His or Her Personal Knowledge
People v. Rosenbaum, 299 Ill. 93 (1921)

Defendant on trial for forgery argued that the trial court erred when it refused to allow opinion testimony by a lay witness that the defendant did not forge the signature on the instrument. The Supreme Court found that the trial court did not err because the witness knew nothing about the facts and it was "not competent for the witness to state his mere conclusion or opinion that plaintiff in error did not write the forged signature, or pass the forged instrument, in the absence of personal knowledge of those facts."

Rule 603. Oath or Affirmation

Before testifying, every witness shall be required to declare that the witness will testify truthfully, by oath or affirmation, administered in a form calculated to awaken the witness' conscience and impress the witness' mind with the duty to do so.

Adopted September 27, 2010, eff. January 1, 2011.

AUTHOR'S COMMENTARY

Illinois Rule of Evidence 603 codifies existing Illinois common law and statutory principles and is identical to Federal Rule of Evidence 603 in effect prior to its stylistic amendment on December 1, 2011. *See* 5 ILCS 255/3; 5 ILCS 255/4; Diaz v. Kelley, 275 Ill. App. 3d 1058 (1st Dist. 1995); Gino L. DiVito, *The Illinois Rules of Evidence: A Color-Coded Guide Containing the New Rules, the Committee's General and Specific Comments, a Comparison with the Federal Rules of Evidence, and Additional Commentary* (*Including the Federal Rules of Evidence as Amended Effective December 1, 2011*) (Jan. 1, 2012), at 64, http://www.tdrlawfirm.com/assets/downloads/Illinois_Rules_of_Evidence_Color-Coded_Guide.pdf.

RELEVANT STATUTORY AUTHORITY

Form of Oath: 5 ILCS 255/3

§ 3. Whenever any person shall be required to take an oath before he enters upon the discharge of any office, place or business, or on any other lawful occasion, it shall be lawful for any person empowered to administer the oath to administer it in the following form, to-wit: The person swearing shall, with his hand uplifted, swear by the ever-living God, and shall not be compelled to lay the hand on or kiss the gospels.

Effective July 1, 1874.

Affirmation: 5 ILCS 255/4

§ 4. Whenever any person required to take or subscribe an oath, as aforesaid, and in all cases where an oath is upon any lawful occasion to be administered, and such person shall have conscientious scruples against taking an oath, he shall be admitted, instead of taking an oath, to make his solemn affirmation or declaration in the following form to-wit: You do solemnly, sincerely and truly declare and affirm. Which solemn affirmation or declaration shall be equally valid as if such person had taken an oath in the usual form; and every person guilty of falsely and corruptly declaring, as aforesaid, shall incur and suffer the like pains and penalties as are or shall be inflicted on persons convicted of willful and corrupt perjury.

Effective July 1, 1874.

PRIOR ILLINOIS CASE LAW

1. Witness May Affirm Rather Than Take an Oath and Inquiry into Reasons for Affirmation Generally Not Permitted Because It May Unnecessarily Bring Issue of Religion Before Trier of Fact

Diaz v. Kelley, 275 Ill. App. 3d 1058 (1st Dist. 1995)

Defendant sought to impeach a witness with his failure to take an oath before testifying, intending to show that the witness took an oath during his deposition. The witness testified that he has never taken an oath. The First District of the Illinois Appellate Court affirmed the trial court's limitation of the impeachment because "such impeachment would unnecessarily bring the issue of religion before the jury."

Rule 604. Interpreters

An interpreter is subject to the provisions of these rules relating to qualification as an expert and the administration of an oath or affirmation to make a true translation.

Adopted September 27, 2010, eff. January 1, 2011.

AUTHOR'S COMMENTARY

Illinois Rule of Evidence 604 codifies existing Illinois common law and statutory principles and is identical to Federal Rule of Evidence 604 in effect prior to its stylistic amendment on December 1, 2011. *See* 725 ILCS 140/1; 725 ILCS 120/4.5; 725 ILCS 120/5; People v. Murphy, 21 Ill. 2d 149 (1961); Gino L. DiVito, *The Illinois Rules of Evidence: A Color-Coded Guide Containing the New Rules, the Committee's General and Specific Comments, a Comparison with the Federal Rules of Evidence, and Additional Commentary (Including the Federal Rules of Evidence as Amended Effective December 1, 2011)* (Jan. 1, 2012), at 65, http://www.tdrlawfirm.com/assets/downloads/Illinois_Rules_of_Evidence_Color-Coded_Guide.pdf.

RELEVANT STATUTORY AUTHORITY

Criminal Proceeding Interpreter Act: 725 ILCS 140/0.01 *et seq.*

Appointment of Interpreter: 725 ILCS 140/1

§ 1. Whenever any person accused of committing a felony or misdemeanor is to be tried in any court of this State, the court shall upon its own motion or that of defense or prosecution determine whether the accused is capable of understanding the English language and is capable of expressing himself in the English language so as to be understood directly by counsel, court or jury. If the court finds the accused incapable of so understanding or so expressing himself, the court shall appoint an interpreter for the accused whom he can understand and who can understand him. In compliance with the federal Americans with Disabilities Act of 1990, the right to communications access through a sign language interpreter or other means shall extend to a person with a disability who is accused of a violation of any penal statute of this State.

Effective August 5, 1993.

Procedures to Implement the Rights of Crime Victims: 725 ILCS 120/4.5

§ 4.5. Procedures to implement the rights of crime victims. To afford crime victims their rights, law enforcement, prosecutors, judges and corrections will provide information, as appropriate of the following procedures:

***

(b) The office of the State's Attorney:

***

(7) shall provide notice to the crime victim of the right to have a translator present at all court proceedings and, in compliance with the federal Americans with Disabilities Act of 1990, the right to communications access through a sign language interpreter or by other means.
Effective January 1, 2012.

Rights of Witnesses: 725 ILCS 120/5

§ 5. Rights of Witnesses.

(a) Witnesses as defined in subsection (b) of Section 3 of this Act shall have the following rights:

***

(4) to be provided with notice by the Office of the State's Attorney, where necessary, of the right to have a translator present whenever the witness' presence is required and, in compliance with the federal Americans with Disabilities Act of 1990, to be provided with notice of the right to communications access through a sign language interpreter or by other means.
Effective January 1, 2009.

Prior Illinois Case Law

1. Appointment of Interpreter Is Within the Discretion of the Trial Court and Abuse of Discretion Occurs Only Where Refusal to Appoint Results in Deprivation of a Basic Right

People v. Murphy, 21 Ill. 2d 149 (1961)

At a controlled substance trial defendant argued that he was deprived of a fair trial where court failed to appoint an interpreter to translate an informant witness' testimony. The Illinois Supreme Court noted that appointment of an interpreter is within the discretion of the trial court and that nothing here indicated that either of the parties, the jury or the judge could not understand the witness. The Supreme Court concluded that although the witness' speech was "broken and ungrammatical," no deprivation of any of defendant's basic rights occurred.

Rule 605. Competency of Judge as Witness

The judge presiding at the trial may not testify in that trial as a witness. No objection need be made in order to preserve the point.

Adopted September 27, 2010, eff. January 1, 2011.

Author's Commentary

Illinois Rule of Evidence 605 codifies Illinois common law principles and is identical to Federal Rule of Evidence 605 in effect prior to its stylistic amendment on December 1, 2011. *See* Ill. S. Ct. R. 62; Ill. S. Ct. R. 63; 725 ILCS 5/114-5; People v. Ernest, 141 Ill. 2d 412 (1990); Gino L. DiVito, *The Illinois Rules of Evidence: A Color-Coded Guide Containing the New Rules, the Committee's General and Specific Comments, a Comparison with the Federal Rules of Evidence, and Additional Commentary (Including the Federal*

Rules of Evidence as Amended Effective December 1, 2011) (Jan. 1, 2012), at 65, http://www.tdrlawfirm.com/assets/downloads/Illinois_Rules_of_Evidence_Color-Coded_Guide.pdf.

RELEVANT ILLINOIS SUPREME COURT RULES

Illinois Supreme Court Rule 62

Canon 2: A Judge Should Avoid Impropriety and the Appearance of Impropriety in All of the Judge's Activities

A. A judge should respect and comply with the law and should conduct himself or herself at all times in a manner that promotes public confidence in the integrity and impartiality of the judiciary.

B. A judge should not allow the judge's family, social, or other relationships to influence the judge's judicial conduct or judgment. A judge should not lend the prestige of judicial office to advance the private interests of others; nor should a judge convey or permit others to convey the impression that they are in a special position to influence the judge. *A judge should not testify voluntarily as a character witness*. (emphasis added)

> Adopted December 2, 1986, effective January 1, 1987; amended October 15, 1993, effective immediately.
>
> **Committee Commentary**
>
> This canon is substantially identical to ABA Canon 2. Public confidence in the judiciary is eroded by irresponsible or improper conduct by judges. A judge must avoid all impropriety and appearance of impropriety. A judge must expect to be the subject of constant public scrutiny. A judge must therefore accept restrictions on his or her conduct that might be viewed as burdensome by the ordinary citizen and should do so freely and willingly.
>
> The testimony of a judge as a character witness injects the prestige of judicial office into the proceeding in which the judge testifies and may be misunderstood to be an official testimonial. This canon, however, does not afford a judge a privilege against testifying in response to an official summons.

Illinois Supreme Court Rule 63

Canon 3: A Judge Should Perform the Duties of Judicial Office Impartially and Diligently

The judicial duties of a judge take precedence over all the judge's other activities. The judge's judicial duties include all the duties of the judge's office prescribed by law. In the performance of these duties, the following standards apply:

A. Adjudicative Responsibilities.

***

(8) A judge shall perform judicial duties without bias or prejudice. A judge shall not, in the performance of judicial duties, by words or conduct manifest bias or prejudice, including but not limited to bias or prejudice based upon race, sex, religion, national origin, disability, age, sexual orientation or socioeconomic status, and shall not permit staff, court officials and others subject to the judge's direction and control to do so.

C. Disqualification.

(1) *A judge shall disqualify himself or herself in a proceeding in which the judge's impartiality might reasonably be questioned, including but not limited to*

instances where: *** (e) *the judge* or the judge's spouse, or a person within the third degree of relationship to either of them, or the spouse of such a person:

***

(iv) *is* to the judge's knowledge *likely to be a material witness in the proceeding.* (emphasis added)

Adopted December 2, 1986, effective January 1, 1987; amended June 12, 1987, effective August 1, 1987; amended November 25, 1987, effective November 25, 1987; amended August 6, 1993, effective immediately; amended October 15, 1993, effective immediately; amended March 26, 2001, effective immediately; amended April 1, 2003, effective immediately; amended December 5, 2003, effective immediately; amended April 16, 2007, effective immediately.

Committee Commentary

***

A judge must perform judicial duties impartially and fairly. A judge who manifests bias on any basis in a proceeding impairs the fairness of the proceeding and brings the judiciary into disrepute. A judge must be alert to avoid behavior that may be perceived as prejudicial.

RELEVANT STATUTORY AUTHORITY

Substitution of Judge in a Criminal Case: 725 ILCS 5/114-5

§ 114-5. Substitution of judge.

(a) Within 10 days after a cause involving only one defendant has been placed on the trial call of a judge the defendant may move the court in writing for a substitution of that judge on the ground that such judge is so prejudiced against him that he cannot receive a fair trial. Upon the filing of such a motion the court shall proceed no further in the cause but shall transfer it to another judge not named in the motion. The defendant may name only one judge as prejudiced, pursuant to this subsection; provided, however, that in a case in which the offense charged is a Class X felony or may be punished by death or life imprisonment, the defendant may name two judges as prejudiced.

(b) Within 24 hours after a motion is made for substitution of judge in a cause with multiple defendants each defendant shall have the right to move in accordance with subsection (a) of this Section for a substitution of one judge. The total number of judges named as prejudiced by all defendants shall not exceed the total number of defendants. The first motion for substitution of judge in a cause with multiple defendants shall be made within 10 days after the cause has been placed on the trial call of a judge.

(c) Within 10 days after a cause has been placed on the trial call of a judge the State may move the court in writing for a substitution of that judge on the ground that such judge is prejudiced against the State. Upon the filing of such a motion the court shall proceed no further in the cause but shall transfer it to another judge not named in the motion. The State may name only one judge as prejudiced, pursuant to this subsection.

(d) In addition to the provisions of subsections (a), (b) and (c) of this Section the State or any defendant may move at any time for substitution of judge for cause, supported by affidavit. Upon the filing of such motion a hearing shall be conducted as soon as possible after its filing by a judge not named in the motion; provided, however, that the judge named in the motion need not testify, but may submit an affidavit if the judge wishes. If the motion is allowed, the case shall be assigned to a judge not named in the motion. If the motion is denied the case shall be assigned back to the judge named in the motion.

Effective July 1, 1987.

PRIOR ILLINOIS CASE LAW

1. Judge May Not Be a Material Witness in a Proceeding Over Which He or She Is Presiding

People v. Ernest, 141 Ill. 2d 412 (1990)

Defendant filed a motion for substitution of judge in a civil proceeding. The presiding judge denied the motion and defendant then requested the issuance of a discovery subpoena to the presiding judge without asking leave to do so. Defendant was found in contempt. The appellate court affirmed, reasoning that a presiding judge could not be a witness in a proceeding before him. One dissenting judge noted, however, that the presiding judge was only requested to appear at a deposition and not to testify at trial. The Illinois Supreme Court affirmed, noting that pursuant to Illinois Supreme Court Rule 63, a judge should excuse himself if he is "likely to be a material witness in the proceeding." The Supreme Court further noted that even if the presiding judge's order refusing substitution was erroneous, defendant was required to follow the order until it was modified or reversed. The Supreme Court found defendant in contempt of court for the violation of the trial order.

2. Party Must Establish Actual Prejudice in Petition for Substitution of Judge for Cause

People v. Jones, 219 Ill. 2d 1 (2006)

Defendant convicted of first degree murder contended on appeal that the trial court improperly ruled on his petition for substitution of a judge for cause pursuant to 725 ILCS 5/114-5(d). Defendant contended that the trial judge was biased against him because he did not force the state to comply with discovery orders and when defendant raised allegations of prosecutorial misconduct, the trial judge stated that he was "outraged" by such accusations. The Illinois Supreme Court explained that

> [i]n order to prevail, defendant must demonstrate that there are facts and circumstances which indicate that the trial judge was prejudiced. People *ex rel.* Baricevic v. Wharton, 136 Ill. 2d 423, 439 (1990); *see also* People v. Mercado, 244 Ill. App. 3d 1040, 1045-46 (1st Dist. 1993). Prejudice is defined as 'animosity, hostility, ill will, or distrust towards this defendant.' People v. Patterson, 192 Ill. 2d 93, 131 (2000), quoting People v. Vance, 76 Ill. 2d 171, 181 (1979); *see also Mercado*, 244 Ill. App. 3d at 1047, quoting *Vance*, 76 Ill. 2d at 181. A movant bears the burden of establishing actual prejudice, not just the possibility of prejudice. *Patterson*, 192 Ill. 2d at 131; *see Mercado*, 244 Ill. App. 3d at 1045. A reviewing court will not disturb a trial court's determination absent a finding against the manifest weight of the evidence. *See Mercado*, 244 Ill. App. 3d at 1047.

The Supreme Court observed that the trial court properly found that defendant failed to show actual prejudice. Although the trial judge's comments may have been "intemperate," there was no evidence that the judge "harbored animus" toward the defendant. Moreover, the judge properly held hearings on state's compliance with various discovery orders and thus the trial court's order denying defendant's petition was not against the manifest weight of the evidence.

Cf. In re Marriage of O'Brien, 2011 IL 109039 (resolving inconsistencies among the lower courts and holding that in civil cases pursuant to 735 ILCS 5/2-1001, substitution for cause "may be granted only where the party can establish actual prejudice").

Rule 606. Competency of Juror as Witness

(a) At the Trial. A member of the jury may not testify as a witness before that jury in the trial of the case in which the juror is sitting. If the juror is called so to testify, the opposing party shall be afforded an opportunity to object out of the presence of the jury.

(b) Inquiry Into Validity of Verdict or Indictment. Upon an inquiry into the validity of a verdict or indictment, a juror may not testify as to any matter or statement occurring during the course of the jury's deliberations or to the effect of anything upon that or any other juror's mind or emotions as influencing the juror to assent to or dissent from the verdict or indictment or concerning the juror's mental processes in connection therewith. But a juror may testify (1) whether any extraneous prejudicial information was improperly brought to the jury's attention, (2) whether any outside influence was improperly brought to bear upon any juror, or (3) whether there was a mistake in entering the verdict onto the verdict form. A juror's affidavit or evidence of any statement by the juror may not be received concerning a matter about which the juror would be precluded from testifying.

Adopted September 27, 2010, eff. January 1, 2011.

AUTHOR'S COMMENTARY

Illinois Rule of Evidence 606(a) codifies Illinois common law principles and is the same as Federal Rule of Evidence 606(a) in effect prior to its stylistic amendment on December 1, 2011. *See* Gino L. DiVito, *The Illinois Rules of Evidence: A Color-Coded Guide Containing the New Rules, the Committee's General and Specific Comments, a Comparison with the Federal Rules of Evidence, and Additional Commentary (Including the Federal Rules of Evidence as Amended Effective December 1, 2011)* (Jan. 1, 2012), at 65, http://www.tdrlaw firm.com/assets/downloads/Illinois_Rules_of_Evidence_Color-Coded_Guide.pdf. The Illinois Supreme Court previously adopted Federal Rule of Evidence 606(b) in People v. Holmes, 69 Ill. 2d 507 (1978).

PRIOR ILLINOIS CASE LAW

1. Juror Testimony Is Generally Inadmissible to Impeach a Jury Verdict but a Verdict May Be Set Aside as a Result of Outside Influences That Prejudice Defendant
People v. Hobley, 182 Ill. 2d 404 (1998)

The Illinois Supreme Court stated that a jury verdict may not generally be impeached by juror testimony. The Supreme Court explained that there are "sound public policy considerations underlying this rule." The rule seeks to preserve the finality of verdicts and to protect jurors from harassment by a defeated party seeking a reason to overturn the judgment. The rule also protects the jurors' undertaking a frank discussion during their deliberations. The Supreme Court noted, however, that "[t]he rule against admitting juror testimony to impeach a verdict does not . . . preclude juror testimony or affidavits which are offered as proof of improper extraneous influences on the jury." A verdict will only be set aside if such improper outside influences on the jury prejudiced the defendant. To show prejudice, the Supreme Court indicated that

> jurors may testify as to the nature of outside influences or communications, but evidence relating to the effect of such influences on the mental processes of the jurors is inadmissible. People v. Holmes, 69 Ill. 2d 507, 514 (1978). Accordingly, because the actual effect of the conduct on the minds of the jurors cannot be proved, the standard to be applied is whether the

> conduct involved 'such a probability that prejudice will result that it is [to be] deemed inherently lacking in due process.' *Holmes*, 69 Ill. 2d at 514.

Here, the defendant alleged that he was deprived of due process because some jurors were intimidated by non-jurors during sequestration. The jurors were dining in the hotel where they were sequestered and some of the other diners yelled at them in a coercive manner and told them to "hang" the defendant because he was guilty and deserved the death penalty. The jurors testified that they were intimidated and feared for their well-being. The Supreme Court found that the defendant made "a substantial showing that he was deprived of due process" and granted an evidentiary hearing on the claim. The Supreme Court explained that "private communications with a juror during trial about the matter pending before the jury are considered presumptively prejudicial."

2. Allegations of Juror Exposure to Improper Outside Influence Only Raise a Presumption of Prejudice and Shift the Burden to the State to Establish That Such Contacts Were Harmless

People v. Williams, 209 Ill. 2d 227 (2004)

Murder defendant argued in his post-conviction petition that juror misconduct deprived him of a fair trial. One juror provided an affidavit stating that another juror "had a conversation" with her husband about the case. A letter from the jury commission requesting jurors to call defendant's attorney was sent but no jurors responded. Defendant argued that the trial court erred in failing to hold an evidentiary hearing, noting that the juror affidavit established the possibility of improper outside influence on the jury.

The Supreme Court described the situations in which the testimony or affidavit of a juror is offered in an attempt to impeach a jury verdict that have been divided into two broad categories. When the juror's testimony or affidavit has been offered to prove the motive, method, or process by which the jury reached its verdict, the courts, almost without exception, have held the testimony or affidavit inadmissible. In contrast, when the testimony or affidavit has been offered as proof of conditions or events brought to the attention of the jury, without any attempt to show its effect on the deliberations or mental processes, most jurisdictions hold such proof admissible.

The Supreme Court considered that in People v. Hobley, 182 Ill. 2d 404 (1998), where jurors were yelled at and intimidated, an evidentiary hearing was warranted as the incident involved "prejudicial outside influences" on the jury. The Supreme Court further noted that there is a difference between permissible juror testimony or affidavit about extraneous interference and impermissible inquiry into jurors' "mental processes." Evidence of juror's mental process and the effect the extraneous matters had on their decision-making is inadmissible. Allegations of juror exposure to improper outside influence are only enough to "raise a presumption of prejudice and to shift the burden to the State to establish that such contacts were harmless." The affidavit in this case, however, failed to show the nature of the allegedly improper conversation the juror had with her husband and was as such insufficient to show that the conversation was prejudicial. The Supreme Court concluded that defendant was not entitled to an evidentiary hearing and that the trial court properly dismissed the claim of juror misconduct.

3. Evidence Revealing the Jury's Mental Processes Is Inadmissible

People v. Holmes, 69 Ill. 2d 507 (1978)

The Illinois Supreme Court, in drawing a distinction between the exclusion of juror testimony or affidavits to show the motive, method or process of the jury and the admissibility of such testimony or affidavit for the purposes of showing external factors that may have affected the jury, quoted Justice William J. Brennan, Jr. from an opinion he had authored while serving on the New Jersey Supreme Court. Justice Brennan stated:

> The better reasoned decisions support the exclusion of jurors' testimony as to their mental processes, not upon the discredited basis of the policies against self stultification and avoidance of jury tampering, perjury or other fraudulent practices, but upon the sounder ground that, being personal to each juror, the working of the mind of any of them cannot be subjected to the test of other testimony, and therefore that such testimony should not be received to overthrow the verdict to which all assented . . . .
>
> Where, however, jurors' testimony goes, not to the motives or methods or processes by which they reached the verdict, but merely to the existence of conditions or the occurrence of events bearing on the verdict, that basis of policy does not exist, and this is whether the condition happens or the event occurs in or outside of the jury room. Evidence of the actual effect of the extraneous matter upon jurors' minds can and should be excluded, as such evidence implicates their mental processes, but receiving their evidence as to the existence of the condition or the happening of the event, particularly when the consequences are governed according to whether capacity for adverse prejudice inheres in the condition or event itself supplies evidence which can be put to the test of other testimony (and thus sound policy is satisfied) and at the same time the evidence can serve to avert, as here, a grave miscarriage of justice, which it is certainly the first duty of a court of conscience to prevent if at all possible.

The Illinois Supreme Court reviewed the defendant's allegation that the jury had improperly conducted its own investigation concerning the evidence. The Supreme Court adopted Federal Rule of Evidence 606(b), noting that

> a juror should be permitted to testify "whether extraneous prejudicial information was improperly brought to the jury's attention or whether any outside influence was improperly brought to bear upon any juror." We hold, therefore that the circuit court erred in holding that it could not consider the allegations made in defendant's motion for new trial and the affidavit filed in support thereof.

4. Allegations That Jurors Improperly Considered Defendant's Prior Conviction for the Same Crime and His Failure to Testify in This Trial During Deliberations Are Not Admissible

People v. Nitz, 219 Ill. 2d 400 (2006)

Defendant was on trial for first degree murder. He was previously convicted of this murder, but the Illinois Supreme Court reversed the trial court's dismissal of defendant's post-conviction petition and remanded the case for a new trial. Defendant was again convicted of the same murder and appealed. Defendant alleged that improper outside influences on the jury prejudiced him. A juror submitted an affidavit post-trial that contended that jurors lied during *voir dire* when they answered that they could presume defendant's innocence until proven guilty. The juror alleged that during their deliberations the other jurors considered defendant's prior conviction for the crime at issue which was later reversed, and his failure to testify in the present trial. The trial court ruled that the juror affidavit was inadmissible "because it addressed the nature and process of jury deliberations." The Supreme Court agreed and found that the allegations in the affidavit were "not subject to extraneous proof" and were thus inadmissible. The Supreme Court explained that the allegations in the juror affidavit "cannot be verified by evidence other than the jury's own motive, method, or process." The Supreme Court concluded that although the jurors may have lied during *voir dire*, the trial court did not abuse its discretion in excluding the juror affidavit.

Impeachment

Rule 607. Who May Impeach

The credibility of a witness may be attacked by any party, including the party calling the witness, except that the credibility of a witness may be attacked by the party calling the witness by means of a prior inconsistent statement only upon a showing of affirmative damage. The foregoing exception does not apply to statements admitted pursuant to Rules 801(d)(1)(A), 801(d)(1)(B), 801(d)(2), or 803.

Adopted September 27, 2010, eff. January 1, 2011.

Committee Commentary

(7) Redundancy: Where redundancy exists between a rule contained in the Illinois Rules of Evidence and another Illinois Supreme Court rule, reference should be made solely to the appropriate Illinois rule of evidence.

ILL. R. EVID. Committee Commentary § 7, pg. 9.

AUTHOR'S COMMENTARY

Illinois common law "voucher rule" traditionally prohibited a party from impeaching its own witness. People v. Wesley, 18 Ill. 2d 138 (1959). Under the "voucher rule," a party could not impeach its witness in any manner. *Id.* Illinois courts subsequently began to carve various exceptions to the rules, such as the "hostile witness" rule and the "court's witness rule," resulting in the "erosion" of the "voucher rule." *Id.* at 150. A hostile witness is one who, when called to the stand, begins to testify and appears unwilling, evasive, and unfriendly. A party was permitted to show that its witness had unexpectedly given "surprise testimony" against it that was contradictory to his or her prior statements. *Id.* at 151. This was limited to refreshing recollection or "awakening his conscience." *Id.* Moreover, where neither party would want to "vouch" for a witness, the witness was called as the "court's witness" and was subject to cross-examination by both parties. People v. Weaver, 92 Ill. 2d 545 (1982). Next, the Illinois Supreme Court addressed the issue in Illinois Supreme Court Rule 238. Rule 238 initially required the showing of surprise before a party could impeach its own witness. ILL. REV. STAT. 1967, chap. 110A, par. 238. Rule 238 was subsequently amended. For a thorough historical account of the development of Illinois Supreme Court Rule 238, see RALPH RUEBNER, ILLINOIS CRIMINAL TRIAL EVIDENCE 147-49 (4th ed. 2001).

The amended Illinois Supreme Court Rule 238 "liberalized" trial practice to allow a party to impeach its own witness. People v. Tate, 87 Ill. 2d 134 (1981). Courts interpreting the amended Rule 238(a) required that affirmative damage be shown before a party calling the witness could impeach its own witness with a prior inconsistent statement. People v. Cruz, 162 Ill. 2d 314 (1994). The amended Rule 238 also removed the "voucher rule" and the "court's witness rule," but retained a modified "hostile witness" rule in section (b). Under the amended rule, there was no meaningful distinction between a hostile witness and any other witness, because a hostile witness could be examined by cross-examination. Therefore, a hostile witness could be subjected to impeachment like any other witness.

The new Illinois Rule of Evidence 607, in conjunction with Illinois Rule of Evidence 611(c), has effectively superseded Illinois Supreme Court Rule 238. Rule 607 has retained the language of Supreme Court Rule 238(a), but has removed any reference to hostile witness contained in Supreme Court Rule 238(b). The Committee Commentary to the Illinois Rules of Evidence notes, "Where redundancy exists between a rule contained in the Illinois Rules of Evidence and another Illinois Supreme Court rule, reference should be made solely to the appropriate Illinois rule of evidence." ILL. R. EVID. Committee Commentary § 7, pg. 9. Professor Graham has indicated that after the enactment of Rule of

Evidence 607, Supreme Court Rule 238(a) has "become redundant and thus subject to repeal." MICHAEL H. GRAHAM, GRAHAM'S HANDBOOK OF ILLINOIS EVIDENCE xxi-xxii (10th ed. 2010). Professor Graham has likewise concluded that Supreme Court Rule 238(b) has effectively been repealed by the enactment of Illinois Rule of Evidence 611(c). *Id.* Illinois Rule of Evidence 611(c) states, "When a party calls a hostile or an unwilling witness or an adverse party or an agent of an adverse party as defined by section 2-1102 of the Code of Civil Procedure (735 ILCS 5/2-1102), interrogation may be by leading questions."

The consequence of the enactment of Rule 607 is that any party may attack the credibility of a witness. Professor Graham has further noted that a party impeaching "a witness it has called to testify by means of a prior inconsistent statement that is not admissible as substantive evidence" must show affirmative damage, although "surprise need not be shown." GRAHAM at § 607.4. The affirmative damage requirement has been "added to codify Illinois common law." Gino L. DiVito, *The Illinois Rules of Evidence: A Color-Coded Guide Containing the New Rules, the Committee's General and Specific Comments, a Comparison with the Federal Rules of Evidence, and Additional Commentary (Including the Federal Rules of Evidence as Amended Effective December 1, 2011)* (Jan. 1, 2012), at 67, http://www.tdrlawfirm.com/assets/downloads/Illinois_Rules_of_Evidence_Color-Coded_Guide.pdf. Pursuant to Illinois Rules of Evidence 801(d)(1)(A), 801(d)(1)(B), 801(d)(2), or 803, no showing of affirmative damage is necessary where a prior inconsistent statement is used as substantive evidence. ILL. R. EVID. 607. Moreover, the Illinois Rape Shield Statute, 725 ILCS 5/115-7, prevents a defendant from impeaching a sex crime victim with evidence excluded by the statute.

RELEVANT ILLINOIS SUPREME COURT RULES

Illinois Supreme Court Rule 433

Rule 433. Impeachment of Witnesses; Hostile Witnesses

The impeachment of witnesses and the examination of hostile witnesses in criminal cases is governed by Rule 238.

> Adopted September 29, 1978, effective November 1, 1978; amended February 19, 1982, effective April 1, 1982.

Illinois Supreme Court Rule 238

Rule 238. Impeachment of Witnesses; Hostile Witnesses

(a) The credibility of a witness may be attacked by any party, including the party calling the witness.

(b) If the court determines that a witness is hostile or unwilling, the witness may be examined by the party calling the witness as if under cross-examination.

> Amended February 19, 1982, effective April 1, 1982; amended April 11, 2001, effective immediately.

RELEVANT STATUTORY AUTHORITY

The Rape Shield Statute: 725 ILCS 5/115-7

§ 115-7. a. In prosecutions for predatory criminal sexual assault of a child, aggravated criminal sexual assault, criminal sexual assault, aggravated criminal sexual abuse, criminal sexual abuse, or criminal transmission of HIV; and in prosecutions for battery and aggravated battery, when the commission of the offense involves sexual penetration or sexual conduct as defined in Section 11-0.1 of the Criminal Code of 1961; and with the trial or retrial of the offenses formerly known as rape, deviate sexual assault, indecent liberties with a child, and aggravated indecent liberties with a child, the prior sexual activity or the reputation of the alleged victim or corroborating witness under Section 115-7.3 of this Code is inadmissible except (1) as evidence concerning the past sexual conduct of the alleged victim or corroborating witness under Section 115-7.3 of this Code with the accused when this evidence is offered by the accused upon the issue of whether the alleged victim or corroborating witness under Section 115-7.3 of this Code consented to the sexual conduct with respect to which the offense is alleged; or (2) when constitutionally required to be admitted.

b. No evidence admissible under this Section shall be introduced unless ruled admissible by the trial judge after an offer of proof has been made at a hearing to be held *in camera* in order to determine whether the defense has evidence to impeach the witness in the event that prior sexual activity with the defendant is denied. Such offer of proof shall include reasonably specific information as to the date, time and place of the past sexual conduct between the alleged victim or corroborating witness under Section 115-7.3 of this Code and the defendant. Unless the court finds that reasonably specific information as to date, time or place, or some combination thereof, has been offered as to prior sexual activity with the defendant, counsel for the defendant shall be ordered to refrain from inquiring into prior sexual activity between the alleged victim or corroborating witness under Section 115-7.3 of this Code and the defendant. The court shall not admit evidence under this Section unless it determines at the hearing that the evidence is relevant and the probative value of the evidence outweighs the danger of unfair prejudice. The evidence shall be admissible at trial to the extent an order made by the court specifies the evidence that may be admitted and areas with respect to which the alleged victim or corroborating witness under Section 115-7.3 of this Code may be examined or cross examined.

Effective July 1, 2011.

Rights of Defendant: 725 ILCS 185/11

§ 11. No person shall be interviewed by a pretrial services agency unless he or she has first been apprised of the identity and purpose of the interviewer, the scope of the interview, the right to secure legal advice, and the right to refuse cooperation. Inquiry of the defendant shall carefully exclude questions concerning the details of the current charge. Statements made by the defendant during the interview, or evidence derived therefrom, are admissible in evidence only when the court is considering the imposition of pretrial or post-trial conditions to bail or recognizance, or when considering the modification of a prior release order.

Effective July 1, 1987.

PRIOR ILLINOIS CASE LAW

1. Traditionally a Party Could Not Impeach Its Own Witness

People v. Wesley, 18 Ill. 2d 138 (1959)

Illinois used to follow the common law “voucher rule” that prohibited a party from discrediting its own witness. Under the voucher rule, a party could not impeach its witness in any manner. Thus, a witness could not be impeached by a showing of bias, interest, corruption, or conviction or by the use of a prior inconsistent statement. A party was permitted to show, however, that its witness had unexpectedly given testimony against it that was contradictory to his or her prior statements. This was limited to refreshing recollection or “awakening his conscience.” The Illinois Supreme Court explained that

> [i]t is a general rule that a party who calls a witness to testify cannot directly impeach his testimony, but certain exceptions indicate that the rule may be in the process of erosion. Thus, where the witness unexpectedly gives testimony against the party calling him, such party has the right of examination to show that the witness gave surprise testimony and to specifically call his attention to former inconsistent statements made by him for the purpose of refreshing his memory or awakening his conscience to the end that he may relent and speak the truth if he is lying.

2. Historically Court Had the Ability to Call Witness Where Neither Party Would Vouch for the Credibility of Witness
People v. Weaver, 92 Ill. 2d 545 (1982)

The court's witness doctrine was developed in response to situations where neither the state nor the defendant could or would vouch for the credibility of a witness. At the discretion of the trial court a witness would be called as a court's witness and subjected to cross-examination by both parties. Examination on collateral matters was prohibited. The testimony had to be crucial, related to direct issues in the case, and necessary to prevent a miscarriage of justice. A court's witness could be impeached by a prior inconsistent statement, if his or her testimony had affirmatively damaged, rather than failed to support, the position of the impeaching party. The Illinois Supreme Court explained that

> [t]he designation of a hostile witness as a court's witness is meant to allow a party to call an important witness whose truthfulness is in doubt without fear that if the witness says something that hurts the party's case, he won't be able to impeach him. Thus a court's witness can be impeached if he says something that damages the party's case and he can then be examined with leading questions.

3. Party May Impeach Any Witness by a Prior Inconsistent Statement as Long as Affirmative Damage Is Established
People v. Cruz, 162 Ill. 2d 314 (1994)

Illinois Supreme Court Rule 238 removed the limitations of the "voucher rule." A party may impeach any witness by a prior inconsistent statement as long as it can show that the witness' testimony has damaged the impeaching party's position. The Illinois Supreme Court defined the meaning of damage. It stated:

> 'Damage' . . . does not occur where a party interrogates a witness about a fact which would be favorable to the examiner if true, but then receives a reply which is merely negative in its effect on the examiner's case . . . . Such testimony is merely disappointing and not damaging since the examiner's case is no worse off than if the witness had not testified. 'Affirmative damage results only from testimony that gives positive aid to an adversary's case.'

The purpose of rule 238 is to destroy the credibility of the witness and not to establish the truth of the impeaching material. To foster the purpose of the rule, courts must vigorously enforce the damage requirement.

For additional case law pertaining to impeachment of a witness by means of a prior inconsistent statement, see analysis of Rule 613: Prior Statements of Witnesses.

4. Witness May Not Be Impeached on a Collateral Matter
People v. Collins, 106 Ill. 2d 237 (1985)

Two defendants were charged with armed robbery, kidnapping and murder. Defendants were found guilty and sentenced to death. One of the defendants argued that it was error to allow state to impeach his alibi witness concerning her activities three days before the murders took place because such evidence was collateral to the issues at trial. The alibi witness testified that she and the defendant went to see a kung-fu movie at a movie theater three days before the crime. The state called the manager of the movie theater to testify that on that day there was not a kung-fu movie playing at the theater. The Illinois Supreme Court noted:

> The latitude to be allowed on cross-examination and rebuttal is a matter within the sound discretion of the trial court, and a reviewing court should not interfere unless there has been a clear abuse of discretion resulting in manifest prejudice to the defendant. People v. Peter, 55 Ill. 2d 443, 451-52 (1973); People v. Columbo, 118 Ill. App. 3d 882, 966 (1st Dist. 1983). Generally, any permissible kind of impeaching matter may be developed on cross-examination, since one of the purposes of cross-examination is to test the credibility of the witnesses. *Columbo*, 118 Ill. App. 3d at 966; People v. Mannen, 46 Ill. App. 3d 61, 64 (3d Dist. 1977). However, the cross-examiner may not impeach a witness on a collateral matter; he must accept the witness' answer. *Columbo*, 118 Ill. App. 3d at 966; McCormick, Evidence sec. 47, at 98 (2d ed. 1972). The test to be applied in determining if a matter is collateral is whether the matter could be introduced for any purpose other than to contradict. People v. Moore, 105 Ill. App. 3d 264, 272 (1st Dist. 1981); People v. Byer, 75 Ill. App. 3d 658, 669 (1st Dist. 1979). The application of the "collateral" test, like the latitude allowed in cross-examination and rebuttal, is best left "largely in the control of the trial court." 3A WIGMORE, EVIDENCE sec. 1003, at 964 (Chadbourn rev. 1970).

The Supreme Court found that the state's cross-examination of the alibi witness was proper. The Supreme Court considered that the witness testified more than eight months after the murders occurred and concluded that her testimony about the defendant's activities three days before the murder was relevant to her ability to recall the events that occurred on the day of the murder.

5. State May Impeach the Defendant with Statements Obtained in Violation of His or Her Sixth Amendment Right to Counsel

Michigan v. Harvey, 494 U.S. 344 (1990)

The United States Supreme Court found that a voluntary statement obtained during police initiated interrogation once a criminal defendant has invoked his sixth amendment right to counsel may not be admitted as substantive evidence at trial, but may be used as impeachment evidence. The Supreme Court found that such statement may be used to impeach the defendant because

> use of statements so obtained for impeachment purposes is a different matter. If a defendant exercises his right to testify on his own behalf, he assumes a reciprocal 'obligation to speak truthfully and accurately,' Harris v. New York, 401 U.S. 222, 225 (1971), and we have consistently rejected arguments that would allow a defendant to 'turn the illegal method by which evidence in the Government's possession was obtained to his own advantage, and provide himself with a shield against contradiction of his untruths.'

6. State May Impeach Defendant with an Otherwise Voluntary Statement Obtained in Violation of *Miranda*

Harris v. New York, 401 U.S. 222 (1971)

Defendant testified at his sale of a controlled substance trial. He admitted to making the sale but contended that he used baking powder to defraud the buyer. On cross-examination the prosecutor asked defendant whether he could remember statements he had made immediately after he was arrested. These statements partially contradicted his statements elicited on direct examination. Defendant claimed that he could not remember most of those statements. The prosecutor placed the document containing defendant's prior statements on the record for possible use on appeal, but the jury did not view it. The impeaching statements were otherwise inadmissible because defendant had not been given *Miranda* warnings prior to making them. The United States Supreme Court noted that "[i]t does not follow from *Miranda* that evidence inadmissible against an accused in the prosecution's case in chief is barred for all purposes, provided of course that the trustworthiness of the evidence satisfies legal standards." The Supreme Court concluded that:

> Every criminal defendant is privileged to testify in his own defense, or to refuse to do so. But that privilege cannot be construed to include the right to commit perjury. *See* United States v. Knox, 396 U.S. 77 (1969); *cf.* Dennis v. United States, 384 U.S. 855 (1966). Having voluntarily taken the stand, petitioner was under an obligation to speak truthfully and accurately, and the prosecution here did no more than utilize the traditional truth-testing devices of the adversary process. [. . .] The shield provided by *Miranda* cannot be perverted into a license to use perjury by way of a defense, free from the risk of confrontation with prior inconsistent utterances. We hold, therefore, that petitioner's credibility was appropriately impeached by use of his earlier conflicting statements.

7. Defendant May Not Be Impeached with Post-Arrest Silence Following *Miranda* Warnings

Doyle v. Ohio, 426 U.S. 610 (1976)

Two defendants were arrested for the sale of 10 pounds of marijuana. At their respective trials, the defendants contended that the individual with whom they completed the sale framed them. The individual was working with the police and promised the police to buy 10 pounds of marijuana from the defendants. Each defendant testified, however, that the individual brought the 10 pounds of marijuana to sell to them. When he realized that the defendants only wanted about two pounds of the illegal substance, he allegedly threw the money supplied by the police officers into their car and ran off with the marijuana. To impeach this testimony, the prosecution cross-examined each defendant about his failure to tell the police the "frameup" story after he was arrested. Defense objections to this line of questioning were overruled. The United States Supreme Court held that impeachment by defendant's post-arrest silence following *Miranda* warnings violated the due process clause of the fourteenth amendment. The Supreme Court explained:

> The warnings mandated by [*Miranda*], as a prophylactic means of safeguarding Fifth Amendment rights, (citation omitted), require that a person taken into custody be advised immediately that he has the right to remain silent, that anything he says may be used against him, and that he has a right to retained or appointed counsel before submitting to interrogation. Silence in the wake of these warnings may be nothing more than the arrestee's exercise of these *Miranda* rights. Thus, every post-arrest silence is insolubly ambiguous because of what the State is required to advise the person arrested. *See* United States v. Hale, supra, 422 U.S. 171, 177 (1975). Moreover, while it is true that the *Miranda* warnings contain no express assurance that silence will carry no penalty, such assurance is implicit to any person who receives the warnings. In such circumstances, it would be fundamentally unfair and a deprivation of due process to allow the arrested person's silence to be used to impeach an explanation subsequently offered at trial.

8. Defendant May Be Impeached with Pre-Arrest Silence

Jenkins v. Anderson, 447 U.S. 231 (1980)

The United States Supreme Court refused to apply Doyle v. Ohio, 426 U.S. 610 (1976), to bar impeachment of defendant by pre-arrest silence. Defendant was charged with murder and claimed self-defense. During cross-examination, the prosecution elicited from the defendant information that after the stabbing death of the victim the defendant did not turn himself into police custody for two weeks. In his closing argument, the prosecutor again noted defendant's pre-arrest silence, suggesting that had the defendant acted in self-defense, he would have spoken out about it earlier. Defendant argued that prosecution's references to his pre-arrest silence violated the fifth amendment's right to silence as applied to the states through the fourteenth amendment as well as the fundamental fairness guaranteed by the fourteenth amendment. The United States Supreme Court disagreed, explaining that

> [i]n this case, no governmental action induced petitioner to remain silent before arrest. The failure to speak occurred before the petitioner was taken into custody and given *Miranda* warnings. Consequently, the fundamental unfairness present in *Doyle*, is not present in this case. We hold that impeachment by use of prearrest silence does not violate the Fourteenth Amendment.

The Supreme Court further clarified that its holding

> does not force any state court to allow impeachment through the use of prearrest silence. Each jurisdiction remains free to formulate evidentiary rules defining the situations in which silence is viewed as more probative then prejudicial. We merely conclude that the use of prearrest silence to impeach a defendant's credibility does not violate the Constitution.

9. Author's Commentary: Impeachment of Defendant by Post-Arrest/Pre-*Miranda* Silence in Illinois

In 1979, the Illinois Supreme Court held in People v. Beller, 74 Ill. 2d 514 (1979), that defendant may not be impeached by his post-arrest, pre-*Miranda* silence. The Illinois Supreme Court had extended the rule articulated by the United States Supreme Court in Doyle v. Ohio, 426 U.S. 610 (1976), to prohibit impeachment of the defendant even where no *Miranda* warnings had been given. In 1982, however, the United States Supreme Court held in Fletcher v. Weir, 455 U.S. 603 (1982), that there is no constitutional violation when the defendant is impeached by his silence that occurs after his arrest but before he is informed of any *Miranda* warnings. The Supreme Court permitted the states to decide on their own the extent to which a testifying defendant may be impeached by his or her post-arrest/pre-*Miranda* silence in such cases.

Post-*Fletcher*, Illinois courts continue to find the use of defendant's post-arrest pre-*Miranda* silence impermissible although admissibility of such evidence is not deemed a constitutional violation. There is disagreement about the effect of *Fletcher* on *Beller*. Some courts, such as the Second District of the Illinois Appellate Court in People v. McMullin, 138 Ill. App. 3d 872 (2d Dist. 1985), have found that the rule prohibiting impeachment by post-arrest silence whether or not *Miranda* warnings had been given was "rooted in Illinois evidentiary law" and was left "unaltered" by *Fletcher*. Others hold that *Beller* is no longer good law in light of *Fletcher*, but nevertheless continue to find impeachment of defendant by post-arrest, pre-*Miranda* silence impermissible. *See* People v. Homes, 274 Ill. App. 3d 612 (1st Dist. 1995). Ultimately, the current rule in Illinois as interpreted by the Illinois Appellate Court remains consistent with the holding in *Beller* that a defendant may not be impeached by his post-arrest, pre-*Miranda* silence. The courts have, however, carved out exceptions to this rule. *See* People v. Quinonez, 2011 IL App (1st) 092333. Defendant may be impeached with his or her post-arrest silence when the accused testifies that he or she made an exculpatory statement to the police at the time of the arrest, and when the accused makes a post-arrest statement that is inconsistent with the exculpatory trial testimony. *Id.*; People v. Simmons,

293 Ill. App. 3d 806 (2d Dist. 1998); People v. McMullin, 138 Ill. App. 3d 872 (2d Dist. 1985). The Illinois Supreme Court recently found in People v. Adams, 2012 IL 111168, that where defendant testifies that he or she made exculpatory statements at the time of the arrest, the prosecutor does not improperly attack defendant's post-arrest silence by commenting on the fact that defendant had an opportunity to perfect his or her account of the arrest.

10. Illinois Law Before *Fletcher v. Weir*: Defendant May Not Be Impeached by Post-Arrest Silence When No *Miranda* Warnings Have Been Given
People v. Beller, 74 Ill. 2d 514 (1979)

Defendant was convicted of burglary and felony theft. After defendant was arrested, but before he received any *Miranda* warnings, he asked the police whether they had arrested a particular individual in connection with the burglary. The defendant never asked about any other person's arrest. At trial, defendant testified that he innocently purchased the stolen items from a thief. In closing argument, state referred to defendant's failure to raise the "innocent purchase" defense at the time of his arrest. The state sought to show that defendant's "innocent purchase" defense was a fabrication. In support, the state claimed that although defendant asked about one person's arrest, he failed to ask about the thief's arrest. State argued that defendant's failure to inquire about the thief showed that defendant was the thief's accomplice. Defendant contended that the state's closing argument violated his right to a fair trial. The Illinois Supreme Court agreed, observing that

> [a] threshold question in this case is whether the [. . .] rule [in Doyle v. Ohio, 426 U.S. 610 (1976),] is applicable when there is no evidence that defendant was previously given the *Miranda* warnings. We hold that the rule is applicable. The *Miranda* warnings do not confer rights on a defendant; they merely advise a defendant, who may be ignorant or intimidated, that he possesses such rights. Since every arrested person has the right to remain silent and may be aware of this right even in the absence of *Miranda* warnings, post-arrest silence remains "insolubly ambiguous."

The Supreme Court explained that in this case the defendant's failure to ask about the thief's arrest did not unambiguously contradict his later testimony that he innocently bought the stolen goods from the thief. The Supreme Court explained that only where

> defendant's earlier and later statements are manifestly inconsistent, the prosecutor may properly impeach the defendant by means of the earlier statement, and he derives no added and prejudicial advantage from establishing that when the defendant made the first statement he failed to make the contradictory second statement.

Although the Supreme Court concluded that the prosecutor's comments on defendant's silence were erroneous, it found the error harmless beyond a reasonable doubt due to substantial evidence of guilt.

11. Impeachment of Defendant by His or Her Post-Arrest Silence Before *Miranda* Warnings Have Been Given Is Not a Constitutional Violation
Fletcher v. Weir, 455 U.S. 603 (1982)

Defendant was involved in a fight with the victim during which the victim was stabbed. The victim died from his injuries. Defendant left the scene without reporting the incident to the police. After defendant's arrest but before he received any *Miranda* warnings, the defendant offered no exculpatory statements in his defense. At his trial, defendant testified that he had acted in self-defense. On cross-examination, the state asked defendant why he had not claimed self-defense when he was arrested. Defendant contended that such line of questioning was improper pursuant to Doyle v. Ohio, 426 U.S. 610 (1976), but the United States Supreme Court disagreed. The Supreme Court explained that the situation present here was different from *Doyle* because prosecution here sought to impeach defendant with his post-arrest silence *before* any *Miranda* warnings had been given. The Supreme Court observed that

> [i]n the absence of the sort of affirmative assurances embodied in the *Miranda* warnings, we do not believe that it violates due process of law for a State to permit cross-examination as to postarrest silence when a defendant chooses to take the stand. A State is entitled, in such situations, to leave to the judge and jury under its own rules of evidence the resolution of the extent to which postarrest silence may be deemed to impeach a criminal defendant's own testimony.

The United States Supreme Court noted that it would be fundamentally unfair to penalize a defendant for exercising silence by impeaching him or her with silence. The Supreme Court, however, made it clear this prohibition applied only to silence that follows *Miranda* warnings. The Supreme Court held that a defendant may be impeached by his post-arrest silence before *Miranda* warnings had been given. On the question of the admissibility of post-arrest, pre-*Miranda* silence, the United States Supreme Court left it to the states to develop their own rules of evidence.

12. Illinois Law after *Fletcher: Beller* Is No Longer Valid Law
People v. Homes, 274 Ill. App. 3d 612 (1st Dist. 1995)

Defendant was convicted of first degree murder, aggravated battery with a firearm, armed violence and aggravated battery. State impeached defendant with a defense witness' post-arrest pre-*Miranda* silence. Defendant argued that the state committed a *Doyle* violation. The First District of the Illinois Appellate Court disagreed, explaining that defendant could not assert violation of another person's constitutional rights because these rights were personal. Moreover, the First District noted that

> [d]efendant improperly relies on People v. Beller, 74 Ill. 2d 514, 521-22 (1979), which extended the *Doyle* rule to situations where there is no evidence that the defendant had been given *Miranda* warnings. Three years after *Beller* was decided, the U.S. Supreme Court held in Fletcher, 455 U.S. at 607, that there is no due process violation when a defendant is cross-examined regarding his post-arrest silence if *Miranda* warnings had not been given. We must conclude, therefore, that *Beller* is no longer the law.

13. Although Introduction of Defendant's Post-Arrest Pre-*Miranda* Silence Is Not a Constitutional Violation, It Is Prohibited in Illinois
People v. Sanchez, 392 Ill. App. 3d 1084 (3d Dist. 2009)

Defendant did not testify at his trial and it was not clear whether he had been given *Miranda* warnings after he was arrested. State introduced evidence of defendant's post-arrest silence. The Third District of the Illinois Appellate Court found that

> "[u]nder Illinois evidentiary law, it is impermissible to impeach a defendant with his or her post-arrest silence, regardless of whether the silence occurred before or after the defendant was given *Miranda* warnings." People v. Clark, 335 Ill. App. 3d 758, 763 (3d Dist. 2002). Evidence of the defendant's post-arrest silence is considered neither material [n]or relevant to proving or disproving the charged offense. *Clark*, 335 Ill. App. 3d 758.

14. Defendant Improperly Impeached with Post-Arrest Silence May Be Entitled to a New Trial

People v. Quinonez, 2011 IL App (1st) 092333

Defendant was charged with possession of a controlled substance. Arresting police officers testified that they observed defendant arguing with another man on a street corner and stopped to investigate. As they approached the men, defendant allegedly dropped a clear plastic bag containing what appeared to be cocaine. The officer immediately seized the bag and placed defendant under arrest. A further search of the defendant revealed another clear bag. The substance in the bags was later confirmed to be cocaine.

Defendant testified at trial that from the moment the police officers stepped out of their vehicle to the time they arrested him it took only a few seconds. He denied at trial that he had dropped a plastic bag of cocaine or that he had any such bag in his pockets. He testified, however, that the man with him may have been attempting to put something in his hands and pockets and may have planted the drugs on him before he was arrested. On cross-examination, state asked defendant if, between the time the police approached him on the street and the time the officers arrested him, he told them about the man's conduct. Defense counsel objected to this line of questioning because it concerned post-arrest silence, but the trial court overruled the objection. Defendant's landlady testified at trial that she observed defendant's arrest and confirmed that she did not see defendant drop anything. State again reiterated in closing argument that defendant said nothing to the police officers during the encounter about the man planting drugs on him, suggesting that because defendant said nothing, no drugs were planted.

Defendant argued on appeal that his conviction should be reversed due to the state's improper impeachment with his post-arrest silence. The First District of the Illinois Appellate Court agreed, explaining that

> the Illinois evidentiary rule generally prohibits impeachment of a criminal defendant with his post-arrest silence, regardless of whether it occurred before or after he was given *Miranda* warnings, because under those circumstances, that silence is not considered relevant or material. People v. Clark, 335 Ill. App. 3d 758, 763 (3d Dist. 2002). However, courts have held that there are two exceptions to the general rule, where that post-arrest silence will be considered relevant. McMullin, 138 Ill. App. 3d 872, 877 (2d Dist. 1985). Pursuant to those exceptions, a defendant's post-arrest silence may be used to impeach his trial testimony: (1) when defendant testifies at trial that he made an exculpatory statement to the police at the time of his arrest; and (2) when he makes a post-arrest statement that is inconsistent with his exculpatory trial testimony. People v. Simmons, 293 Ill. App. 3d 806, 811 (2d Dist. 1998); *see also McMullin*, 138 Ill. App. 3d at 877. However, in contrast to a defendant's post-arrest silence, his silence prior to arrest may properly be used by the State to impeach his trial testimony under Illinois law. People v. Graves, 142 Ill. App. 3d 885, 889-90 (1st Dist. 1986).

The First District determined that because the police officers almost immediately arrested defendant upon approaching him, the state improperly referred to his post-arrest silence in cross-examining him at trial and in closing arguments. The First District further found that neither of the exceptions applied because defendant made no statements that could be deemed inconsistent with his testimony at trial. The First District concluded that the error was not harmless because state's questioning and closing comments undermined his credibility in a trial where the result hinged on the jury believing either the defendant or the police officers.

15. Defendant May Be Impeached with Post-Arrest Silence When Defendant Testifies That He or She Made an Exculpatory Statement to the Police at the Time of Arrest

People v. Simmons, 293 Ill. App. 3d 806 (2d Dist. 1998)

Defendant was convicted of unlawful use of a weapon by a felon and possession of a firearm without a firearm owner's identification card. He was a back seat passenger during a traffic stop, and police arrested him after he exited the vehicle and they saw a handgun in the middle of the back seat where he had been sitting. Defendant said nothing to the officers after he was arrested. At trial, defendant testified that he got into his friend's car but that he did not know the driver of the car. He further stated that after he got into the back seat, he observed that it was cluttered with a "lot of stuff." He also argued that he did not have a gun and did not know anything about the gun found in the car. The state referred to defendant's post-arrest silence and his failure to argue that the gun was not his. The Second District explained that

> [a] defendant's postarrest silence may be used for impeachment purposes when the defendant testifies at trial that he gave an exculpatory statement to the police when arrested or if the defendant made a prior inconsistent statement to the police after his arrest.

The Second District concluded that the state's remarks were improper and

> did not fall within either exception to the rule against using a defendant's postarrest silence against him. The State was not attempting to elicit impeachment. The defendant did not testify that he told the police that he did not know anything about the gun and did not know it was in the car. Further, the defendant's exculpatory testimony was not inconsistent with anything the defendant said to the police.

16. Defendant May Be Impeached with Post-Arrest Silence When His or Her Post-Arrest Statement Is Inconsistent with His or Her Trial Testimony
People v. McMullin, 138 Ill. App. 3d 872 (2d Dist. 1985)

Defendant was charged with burglary after he and two of his friends stopped at a house and loaded two ladders and a snow blower onto their pick-up truck. Defendant argued that he was unaware that his friends were stealing the ladders and the snow blower. Defendant explained that one of his friends asked him to use the truck to help get some of his things from his landlord's house. When defendant received the complaint charging him with the crime, he allegedly told the officer that he should have been charged with "possession of stolen property instead of burglary." On cross-examination of defendant, state asked why defendant did not simply say "you should not charge me with burglary because I don't know anything." Defense objection to this line of questioning was overruled by the trial court. In its closing argument state again referred to defendant's post-arrest failure to give the police an exculpatory statement. Defendant argued that the state's remarks were improper.

The Second District of the Illinois Appellate Court stated that "evidence of a defendant's post-arrest silence is inadmissible because such evidence is neither material nor relevant, having no tendency to prove or disprove the charge against a defendant." The Second District noted that this rule was "rooted in Illinois evidentiary law" and was left "unaltered" by Fletcher v. Weir, 455 U.S. 603 (1982). The Second District held that although "Illinois evidentiary rule permits the use of a defendant's post-arrest failure to tell the police his exculpatory story when the statements made by a defendant after arrest are definitely and manifestly inconsistent with his exculpatory trial testimony," the exception did not apply here. The Second District found that the defendant's statement when he received the complaint was not "manifestly inconsistent" with his trial testimony—in both statements defendant claimed that he did not steal. The court concluded that the error was not harmless beyond a reasonable doubt.

17. Where Defendant Testifies That He or She Made Exculpatory Statements at the Time of the Arrest, Prosecutor Does Not Attack Defendant's Post-Arrest Silence by Commenting on the Fact That Defendant Had an Opportunity to Perfect His or Her Account of the Arrest

People v. Adams, 2012 IL 111168

Defendant was charged with possession of a controlled substance. At trial, the arresting officers testified that they found the drugs in one of defendant's pockets, but did not mention that defendant made any exculpatory statements during the encounter. Defendant, however, testified that the drugs were found on the ground near him and that he told the police at the time of the arrest that he had not dropped any drugs. In its closing argument, the state argued that defendant had two and a half years to come up with this story. Defendant contended that the state impermissibly impeached him with his post-arrest silence. The Third District of the Illinois Appellate Court disagreed, explaining that under the "unique facts of this case," although the prosecutor's statements did pertain to defendant's silence, the statements were permissible because they "challenge[d] defendant's testimony as to his behavior after the arrest." The appellate court observed that such impeachment is permissible where defendant testifies at trial to an exculpatory version of events and claims that he gave the police the same account when he was arrested. The Illinois Supreme Court also disagreed with defendant's contention that the prosecutor "'implicitly' attack[ed] defendant's post-arrest silence, in violation of Doyle v. Ohio, 426 U.S. 610 (1976)," explaining that

> [i]n *Doyle*, the United States Supreme Court held that, after a defendant has received his *Miranda* warnings, it is a due process violation for a prosecutor to comment on a defendant's postarrest silence at trial for the purpose of impeaching the defendant's testimony. That did not occur here. In this case, when the prosecutor made the comment about how defendant "had time to think about and plan [his] testimony, he was merely assailing [defendant's] credibility." State v. Mendoza, 262 P.3d 266, 270 (Idaho 2011). As one court has explained:
>
> > The prosecutor did not use petitioner's earlier silence to suggest that his exculpatory testimony was untrue; instead, he commented on petitioner's credibility as a witness by alluding to petitioner's opportunity to perfect his account. As the Supreme Court noted in Portuondo v. Agard, 529 U.S. 61, 68 (2000):
> >
> > > Allowing comment upon the fact that a defendant's presence in the courtroom provides him a unique opportunity to tailor his testimony is appropriate . . . to the central function of the trial, which is to discover the truth.
> >
> > The prosecutor's comment in this case was more like that in *Portuondo* than in *Doyle*; there was no error." Melendez v. Scribner, No. CIV S-03-1593, 2006 WL 2520301, at *12 (E.D. Cal. Aug. 30, 2006).
> >
> > We agree with this reasoning and hold that the prosecutor did not err when he stated that defendant "had two and a half years to come up" with his story. See also, e.g., Tri Dung Nguyen v. Felker, No. C 07-2479, 2009 WL 1246693 (N.D. Cal. May 5, 2009).

18. Impeachment Exception to the Exclusionary Rule Allowing State to Introduce Illegally Obtained Evidence to Impeach Defendant's Testimony Cannot Be Used to Impeach Testimony of All Defense Witnesses

James v. Illinois, 493 U.S. 307 (1990)

In People v. James, 123 Ill. 2d 523 (1988), the Illinois Supreme Court, in a case of first impression, held that the prosecution may use the defendant's custodial statements that were previously suppressed under the Fourth Amendment to rebut the testimony of a defense witness who "testifies on direct examination in a manner squarely at odds with evidence which has been suppressed . . . ." The court limited the impeachment, stating that "only statements made on direct examination may be impeached and there must be a direct, material relationship between the trial testimony and the impeaching evidence."

The United States Supreme Court reversed and held that the impeachment exception to the exclusionary rule should not be expanded to the testimony of all defense witnesses. The Court reasoned that the truth seeking rationale supporting the impeachment of the defendant witness does not apply with equal force to his or her witnesses. Furthermore, the threat of a prosecution for perjury is more likely to deter a defense witness from lying than to deter a defendant. Also, expanding the impeachment exception would deter the defendant from calling witnesses who would otherwise provide probative evidence. Lastly, such expansion would weaken the deterrence of police misconduct, which is the underlying rationale of the exclusionary rule.

19. State May Not Impeach Defendant with a Pretrial Services Report
People v. Bennett, 257 Ill. App. 3d 299 (1st Dist. 1993)

In a case of first impression, the First District of the Illinois Appellate Court held that a pretrial services report obtained pursuant to the Pretrial Services Act, 725 ILCS 185/11, cannot be used to impeach the defendant. In this case, statements the defendant made to a probation officer during his interview were used to impeach him. The First District found that the trial court erred when it allowed the state to do so. First, the language of the act itself clearly and unambiguously prohibits use of any statements given during the interview process for impeachment purposes. The act states that

> [s]tatements made by the defendant during the [pretrial] interview, or evidence derived therefrom, are admissible in evidence only when the court is considering the imposition of pretrial or posttrial conditions to bail or recognizance, or when considering the modification of a prior release order.

Moreover, if the court allows impeachment use, it would have a "chilling" effect on the purpose of the act so that defendants would be reluctant to cooperate or provide accurate information. Although the First District found that the trial court erred, it found this error harmless because, under the totality of the circumstances, the trial result would not have been different absent the error.

20. State May Not Impeach Defendant with Results of a Preliminary Breath Test
People v. Bass, 351 Ill. App. 3d 1064 (4th Dist. 2004)

The Fourth District of the Illinois Appellate Court held that results of a preliminary breath screening test (PBT) could not be used by the state in rebuttal to impeach the defendant's testimony that he was not intoxicated at the time of arrest. The defendant was pulled over, and when questioned by the arresting officer, admitted that he had two beers before driving. The arresting officer administered a field sobriety test and PBT which resulted in a reading of 0.120. At trial, the defendant testified that he did not have any alcoholic beverages on the night of his arrest. The Fourth District found that the relevant statute, 625 ILCS 5/11-501.5, authorizes the defendant to use results of the PBT in his defense and permits state to use the test results to show existence of probable cause at the time of arrest. The Fourth District concluded however that pursuant to the plain meaning of the statute, the legislature did not intend to allow use of such test results to impeach the testimony of the accused.

21. Sixth Amendment of the United States Constitution Protects the Accused's Right to Confront Witness by Cross-Examination About Any Bias, Interest, or Motive to Testify Falsely
Davis v. Alaska, 415 U.S. 308 (1974)

At defendant's trial for burglary and grand larceny of a safe, a prosecution witness testified that he saw the defendant prying open a safe with a crowbar. The witness was 16 years old at the time he witnessed defendant's actions and had turned 17 years old by the time of trial. Prosecution sought to bar evidence of the witness' juvenile record. At the time of trial the witness was on probation for the commission of two burglaries. Defendant sought to use the witness' juvenile adjudication to show his bias (but not to impeach his general character), arguing that the witness may have incorrectly identified the defendant in his haste to avoid any appearance of wrongdoing. The defendant intended to show that the witness was afraid that his probation would be revoked if the police thought he had been involved in the burglary. The trial court granted the prosecution's motion to preclude introduction of witness' juvenile record pursuant to a state law. During cross-examination defense counsel asked the witness whether he was apprehensive about the police possibly believing that he had committed the crime and the witness responded in the negative. Defense counsel was attempting to show that the witness may have had motive to lie to the police about defendant's involvement in the burglary due to his prior juvenile adjudications for burglary. The United States Supreme Court noted that the witness' answer to defense questioning was "self-serving" and may not have been entirely truthful considering that while the witness was reporting a burglary he had prior juvenile adjudications for two burglaries. The Supreme Court explained that one

> particular attack on the witness' credibility is effected by means of cross-examination directed toward revealing possible biases, prejudices, or ulterior motives of the witness as they may relate directly to issues or personalities in the case at hand. The partiality of a witness is subject to exploration at trial, and is 'always relevant as discrediting the witness and affecting the weight of his testimony.' 3A J. WIGMORE, EVIDENCE § 940, p. 775 (Chadbourn rev. 1970). We have recognized that the exposure of a witness' motivation in testifying is a proper and important function of the constitutionally protected right of cross-examination. Greene v. McElroy, 360 U.S. 474, 496 (1959).

The Supreme Court observed that although it was not clear that the jury would have believed the defendant's argument that the witness was biased, the jury was entitled to consider such evidence. The "accuracy and truthfulness of [the witness'] testimony were key elements in the State's case against [the defendant]" and the Supreme Court reasoned that the defendant should have been able to expose other facts from which the jury could have evaluated the witness' credibility. The Supreme Court concluded that the defendant was denied the right to effective confrontation of witnesses against him, explaining that defendant

> sought to introduce evidence of [the witness'] probation for the purpose of suggesting that [he] was biased and, therefore, that his testimony was either not to be believed in his identification of [the defendant] or at least very carefully considered in that light. Serious damage to the strength of the State's case would have been a real possibility had [defendant] been allowed to pursue this line of inquiry. In this setting we conclude that the right of confrontation is paramount to the State's policy of protecting a juvenile offender. Whatever temporary embarrassment might result to [the witness] or his family by disclosure of his juvenile record—if the prosecution insisted on using him to make its case—is outweighed by [defendant's] right to probe into the influence of possible bias in the testimony of a crucial identification witness.

See also Olden v. Kentucky, 488 U.S. 227 (1988) (finding that black defendant accused of raping a white woman should have been allowed to impeach the woman's testimony that she lived with her mother with evidence of her cohabitation with another black man, who was the only corroborating state witness, to show that defendant and woman engaged in consensual sexual relations and that she lied to protect her relationship with her boyfriend when she accused defendant of raping her).

22. Article I Section 8 of the Illinois Constitution Protects Defendant's Right to Cross-Examine a Witness as to Bias, Prejudice, or Motive
People v. Gonzalez, 104 Ill. 2d 332 (1984)

The trial court prevented all references to gang affiliation of a testifying witness. The Illinois Supreme Court found that such limitation violated defendant's constitutional right to confront witnesses against him pursuant to the sixth and fourteenth amendments of the United States Constitution and Article 1, section 8 of the Illinois Constitution. The Supreme Court held that defendant was entitled to cross-examine witnesses about gang affiliation to elicit evidence of any possible bias, prejudice or motive.

23. Impeachment by Showing Bias, Interest, or Motive Must Give Rise to an Inference That Witness Has Something to Gain or Lose by Testifying
People v. Triplett, 108 Ill. 2d 463 (1985)

Defendant on trial for murder argued that the trial court erred in limiting his cross-examination of a juvenile witness about his juvenile record to elicit evidence of possible bias. The juvenile witness allegedly saw defendant commit the crime but initially refused to speak to the police about what he saw. It was not until the police threatened to put the witness in jail that he told them what he observed. The witness testified that he saw defendant enter a gas station while holding a gun and putting the gun to the gas station attendant's back. The witness then stated that he heard one shot being fired. At the time of trial the witness was on probation resulting from a delinquency adjudication, had 10 prior delinquency petitions filed against him, and had other prior "contacts" with the police. The Illinois Supreme Court noted that impeachment by showing bias, interest or motive on the part of the witness requires that "'the evidence used must give rise to the inference that the witness has something to gain or lose by his testimony' and, therefore, the evidence used must not be remote or uncertain." Defendant here sought to show that the witness' prior "contacts" with the police gave him an incentive to cooperate with the police especially after police officers threatened him that if he did not tell them all he knew they would imprison him. The Illinois Supreme Court concluded that this evidence was too remote to be admissible because the "contacts" did not show that the witness had something to gain or lose by testifying.

24. Evidence That Witness Was Arrested or Charged with a Crime Used to Show That Witness Is Biased Need Only Give Rise to the Inference That Witness Has Something to Gain or Lose by Testifying
People v. Davis, 185 Ill. 2d 317 (1998)

Defendant on trial for aggravated criminal sexual assault, aggravated kidnapping, robbery and concealment of a homicidal death argued that he was deprived of his right to cross-examine a prosecution witness about a pending criminal charge. The witness was charged with rape of a child. State argued that since the witness was not convicted of the crime, impeachment with such evidence was improper. Moreover, the state contended that there was no evidence that the witness had been promised leniency regarding the charge. The trial court precluded a specific mention of the pending charge except a reference that it was a felony, and permitted defense to cross-examine the witness about possible promises of leniency. The Illinois

Supreme Court noted that

> [a] defendant need not show that a promise of leniency has in fact been made to the witness, or that an expectation of special favor exists in the mind of the witness; rather, the evidence used need only give rise to the inference that the witness has something to gain or lose by testifying.

The Supreme Court explained that although defendant may have been limited in his cross-examination of the prosecution witness, the evidence against him was overwhelming and any error that may have occurred was harmless.

25. Evidence of Bias, Motive, or Interest Must Not Be Remote or Speculative
People v. Lucas, 151 Ill. 2d 461 (1992)

If the evidence of bias, interest, or motive is remote or speculative, the trial court may prohibit or limit the cross-examination because the jury must be able to infer from proper evidence that the witness has something to gain or lose by his or her testimony. Here, defendant argued that the trial court violated his sixth amendment right to confront witnesses against him by preventing him from impeaching the credibility of a prosecution witness with a prior bad act to show that the witness was biased. The defendant sought to show that the witness had a motive to testify against defendant because he was seeking leniency from the prosecution in exchange for testimony. The witness had previously attacked prison guards and was hoping to gain favor from the adjustment committee by testifying for the prosecution. The Illinois Supreme Court disagreed, explaining that the committee did not consider the witness' testimony for the prosecution as a factor in evaluating his eligibility for parole. The Supreme Court noted that the evidence of bias, interest or motive offered by the defendant was too speculative to be admitted because there was no evidence that the witness received leniency for testifying. The Supreme Court concluded that defendant was not denied his right to confront witnesses against him.

26. Evidence of an Unrelated Pending Civil Suit Against Witness Generally Not Admissible to Impeach as Too Remote or Speculative
People v. Nelson, 235 Ill. 2d 386 (2009)

Defendant was charged with multiple murders and confessed to the crimes. On appeal, defendant claimed that his confession was coerced. He sought to introduce evidence of an unrelated civil suit pending against the interrogating officers. The civil suit was brought by an individual who had been interrogated by the same officers as defendant and who falsely confessed to the murder of his daughter. He was ultimately exonerated via DNA evidence and all charges against him were dropped. The Illinois Supreme Court refused to admit evidence of the other suit to show that the officers used similar interrogation techniques on the defendant and forced him to confess because the evidence was too remote and speculative.

27. Evidence of Arrest or Charge of Crime May Be Used to Show That Witness May Have Interest, Bias, or Motive to Testify Falsely
People v. Galloway, 59 Ill. 2d 158 (1974)

The state's key witness testified that she sold defendant the heroin he was charged with obtaining. The witness was a police informant who was a drug addict and had been a prostitute. Defendant sought the witness' arrest record for impeachment purposes. The state asked the witness and a police officer for whom she was an informant about any pending charges against her, but both denied that she had been arrested in the period between the defendant's arrest and the trial. Defendant later discovered that the witness was arrested on a charge of armed robbery shortly before his trial commenced. Her police record showed that she had over 80 arrests and that a few of them were stricken on motion by the state. The Illinois Supreme Court noted that

> [w]hile neither evidence of an arrest nor indictment may ordinarily be admissible to impeach credibility generally, an arrest or charge of a crime may be shown, or inquired into, where it reasonably could tend to show that the witness's testimony might be influenced by interest, bias, or motive to testify falsely.

The Supreme Court found that defendant was entitled to examine the witness' record to show her bias. The Supreme Court explained that the witness and the police officer were both aware that she had a recent arrest and that the false representation of the arrest record was "so lacking in fundamental fairness as to deprive an accused of due process of law."

Rule 608. Evidence of Character Witness

The credibility of a witness may be attacked or supported by evidence in the form of opinion or reputation, but subject to these limitations: (1) the evidence may refer only to character for truthfulness or untruthfulness, and (2) evidence of truthful character is admissible only after the character of the witness for truthfulness has been attacked by opinion or reputation evidence or otherwise.

Adopted September 27, 2010, eff. January 1, 2011.

Committee Commentary

(4) Recommendations. The Committee recommended to the Illinois Supreme Court a limited number of changes to Illinois evidence law (1) where the particularized evidentiary principle was neither addressed by statute nor specifically addressed in a comprehensive manner within recent history by the Illinois Supreme Court, and (2) where prior Illinois law simply did not properly reflect evidentiary policy considerations or raised practical application problems when considered in light of modern developments and evidence rules adopted elsewhere with respect to the identical issue. The Committee identified, and the Illinois Supreme Court approved, recommendations in only two areas. [One of those areas is as follows]:

> (a) Opinion testimony is added to reputation testimony as a method of proof in Rule 405, when character evidence is admissible, and in Rule 608 with respect to character for truthfulness.

ILL. R. EVID. Committee Commentary § 4, pg. 4.

AUTHOR'S COMMENTARY

Prior to the enactment of the Illinois Rules of Evidence, testimony pertaining to a witness' character for truthfulness or untruthfulness could only be introduced by reputation evidence. People v. Nash, 36 Ill. 2d 275 (1966). The new Illinois Rule of Evidence 608, however, has adopted the language of the Federal Rule of Evidence 608(a), in effect prior to its stylistic amendment on December 1, 2011, and has changed Illinois law to now allow both reputation testimony and opinion testimony concerning a witness' character for truthfulness or untruthfulness. *See* Gino L. DiVito, *The Illinois Rules of Evidence: A Color-Coded Guide Containing the New Rules, the Committee's General and Specific Comments, a Comparison with the Federal Rules of Evidence, and Additional Commentary* (*Including the Federal Rules of Evidence as Amended Effective December 1, 2011*) (Jan. 1, 2012), at 68-69, http://www.tdrlawfirm.com/assets/downloads/Illinois_Rules_of_Evidence_Color-Coded_Guide.pdf [hereinafter DiVito, *Color-Coded Guide*]. The rule provides that once a witness' character for truthfulness has been attacked, reputation or opinion evidence of the truthful character of the witness may be introduced.

Illinois has not adopted Federal Rule of Evidence 608(b) but instead retains Illinois common law principles. Federal Rule of Evidence 608(b) states in the relevant part that

> [e]xcept for a criminal conviction under Rule 609, extrinsic evidence is not admissible to prove specific instances of a witness's conduct in order to attack or support the witness's character for truthfulness. But the court may, on cross-examination, allow them to be inquired into if they are probative of the character for truthfulness or untruthfulness of:
>
> (1) the witness; or
> (2) another witness whose character the witness being cross-examined has testified about.
> FED. R. EVID. 608(b) (effective Dec. 1, 2011).

Unlike Federal Rule of Evidence 608(b), Illinois Rule of Evidence 608 has retained the common law rule and does not allow inquiry into a witness' prior specific instances of untruthfulness or bad acts. DiVito, *Color-Coded Guide* at 69. Generally, a party may not impeach a witness by showing that on a prior occasion the witness had committed a "bad act" or engaged in immoral conduct, because such evidence is not probative of testimonial veracity. *See* People v. Butler, 58 Ill. 2d 45 (1974) (finding inquiry into defendant's co-habitation with various women improper but harmless beyond a reasonable doubt). As an exception to this rule, a party may impeach a witness, through cross-examination, by showing that the witness is or was engaged in an "unlawful and disreputable occupation and activity." *See* People v. Crump, 5 Ill. 2d 251 (1955) (finding that defendant should have been permitted to inquire into accomplice witness' drug addiction). But even when this exception is utilized, the proponent of the evidence must still demonstrate the relevancy of the evidence.

Illinois common law also differs from Federal Rule of Evidence 608(b) in that in Illinois "it is generally improper to ask one witness to comment directly on the credibility of another witness . . . as '[q]uestions of credibility are to be resolved by the trier of fact.'" People v. Becker, 239 Ill. 2d 215, 236 (2010); *see* Chapter 1; DiVito, *Color-Coded Guide* at 69.

PRIOR ILLINOIS CASE LAW

1. Witnesses May Be Impeached by Evidence of General Reputation for Truth and Veracity

People v. Nash, 36 Ill. 2d 275 (1966)

Any witness, including a defendant who testifies, may be impeached by evidence showing his or her general reputation for truth and veracity. The Illinois Supreme Court explained that "[i]t has always been permissible to show that a witness, including the accused in a criminal case, if he takes the stand, has a bad reputation for truth and veracity." Evidence attacking the witness' reputation for truth and veracity is inadmissible until he or she takes the stand and testifies.

Here, defendant argued that the trial court should have ordered a psychiatric evaluation of the state's key witness who was with the defendant during the commission of the crime to impeach the witness. The defendant claimed that the witness was a psychopath and should not be believed. The Illinois Supreme Court found that the trial court did not err in denying defendant's request for a psychiatric evaluation of the witness because such evidence is "unnecessary to raise the issue of whether a witness is a psychopath, from which a jury could infer that he possesses the characteristic of untruthfulness, when direct evidence of a witness's reputation for truthfulness is admissible."

2. Where Defendant Voluntarily Testifies, State May Impeach with His or Her Reputation for Truth and Veracity
People v. Bakutis, 377 Ill. 386 (1941)

The rule that precludes the state from offering substantive evidence of the defendant's bad character unless the defendant first offers evidence of good character has no application to the impeachment process of the defendant witness. Defendant argued that it was improper to allow state to rebut with testimony of witnesses testifying about defendant's character since defendant introduced no character evidence. The court noted:

> The rule with reference to attacking the character of the defendant before evidence of good character is offered on his part, has no application to testimony concerning reputation for truth and veracity of a witness. The rule has always been that where a defendant voluntarily takes the stand, his testimony is to be subjected to the same test and treated the same as was the testimony of any other witness. It has always been permissible, in cases where the defendant has voluntarily testified, to offer proof that his reputation for truth and veracity is bad.

3. Evidence of Reputation for Truth and Veracity Is Admissible Only After Witness' Credibility Is Placed in Issue
Tedens v. Schumers, 112 Ill. 263 (1884)

Employee of a general store was alleged to have taken $4,000 worth of goods from his employers, the owners of the store. The employers owed the employee $2,100 and had given him a check for this amount before they found out about his theft of the goods. The employee contended at trial that the employers took the $2,100 check back from him, but it was unclear whether the employers took the money back in satisfaction of the employee's debt or whether they were holding on to it until they could more precisely ascertain the amount taken by the employee. At trial, the employee called several witnesses to testify as to his character for truth and veracity. The employee argued that he properly called character witnesses because other witnesses contradicted their testimony. The Illinois Supreme Court disagreed, noting that "a witness can not call witnesses to support his general character for truth and veracity until it is assailed. Mere contradictions, or different versions by witnesses, do not justify the application of the rule that he may call witnesses to support his character for truth."

4. Reputation Witness Must Have Adequate Knowledge About Subject of the Testimony
People v. Ulrich, 30 Ill. 2d 94 (1963)

Before a witness may be impeached by evidence of a bad reputation for truth and veracity, a proper foundation must be laid and a question in proper form must be asked of the reputation witness. A proper foundation is established by showing that the reputation witness has sufficient knowledge of the witness being impeached and that the evidence of general reputation is based on the reputation witness' contact with neighbors and associates of the witness, rather than the reputation witness' own observations or personal opinion. Here, defendant argued that a reputation witness testifying against him had insufficient knowledge about his reputation for truth and veracity because the basis for the witness' testimony was formed 12 years before trial. The Illinois Supreme Court disagreed, noting that the fact that the witness did not see or speak to defendant for several years

> has no bearing on [witness'] conversations with members of the community in which defendant resided regarding defendant's reputation for truth and veracity for any other period

> of time. . . . [R]eputation witnesses must have adequate knowledge about the subject of their testimony but the claim of that knowledge is *prima facie* sufficient. Here the defendant did not establish by cross-examination that the reputation witness had knowledge that related only to a period 12 years prior to the trial.

5. Testimony of the Reputation Witness Must Not Relate to Specific Instances of Untruthfulness

People v. Cookson, 215 Ill. 2d 194 (2005)

Defendant was convicted of predatory criminal sexual assault and aggravated criminal sexual abuse. Defendant sought to impeach the child victim with evidence that she had previously accused a third person of sexual assault. Defendant intended to use the evidence to show that the victim confused the defendant with the third person. The Illinois Supreme Court acknowledged that the victim's credibility was unquestionably at issue because there was no testimony from independent eyewitnesses supporting her allegations and no physical evidence linking the defendant to the alleged abuse. Generally, the Supreme Court observed, the use of reputation evidence is the proper way to impeach a witness' trait for truthfulness. Here, however, the defendant sought to introduce evidence of specific past instances of untruthfulness on the part of the child victim for purposes of impeaching her credibility. The Supreme Court explained that evidence of specific past instances of untruthfulness may not be used to impeach the truthfulness of a witness. The Supreme Court emphasized that

> the proper procedure for impeaching a witness' reputation for truthfulness is through the use of reputation evidence and not through [. . .] evidence of specific past instances of untruthfulness. People v. Kliner, 185 Ill. 2d 81, 173 (1998); People v. West, 158 Ill. 2d 155, 162 (1994) (rejecting the argument evidence of specific acts of untruthfulness should be admitted to impeach a child witness because the child was too young to have developed a reputation in the community). This rule applies with equal force to all witnesses, regardless of age. People v. Williams, 139 Ill. 2d 1, 21 (1990). This case has not presented us with any compelling basis for altering this rule in cases involving sexual abuse allegations, and we take this opportunity to reaffirm that principle.

See also People v. West, 158 Ill. 2d 155 (1994) (rejecting defendant's argument that child was too young to have a reputation for truth and finding impeachment of a child witness with specific instances of untruthfulness improper).

6. Reputation Witness May Be Asked Whether He or She Would Believe the Person Under Oath

People v. Lehner, 326 Ill. 216 (1927)

If the reputation witness testifies that a witness has a bad reputation for truth and veracity, the party calling him or her may also ask whether, based on the witness' general reputation for truth and veracity, he or she would believe such person under oath. The reputation witness' answer must rest on his or her knowledge of the witness' general reputation for truth and veracity in the community.

See also People v. West, 246 Ill. App. 3d 1070 (1st Dist. 1993) (finding it proper to inquire whether reputation witness actually heard the reputation discussed in the community).

Rule 609. Impeachment by Evidence of Conviction of Crime

(a) General Rule. For the purpose of attacking the credibility of a witness, evidence that the witness has been convicted of a crime, except on a plea of nolo contendere, is admissible but only if the crime, (1) was punishable by death or imprisonment in excess of one year under the law under which the witness was convicted, or (2) involved dishonesty or false statement regardless of the punishment unless (3), in either case, the court determines that the probative value of the evidence of the crime is substantially outweighed by the danger of unfair prejudice.

(b) Time Limit. Evidence of a conviction under this rule is not admissible if a period of more than 10 years has elapsed since the date of conviction or of the release of the witness from confinement, whichever is the later date.

(c) Effect of Pardon, Annulment, or Certificate of Rehabilitation. Evidence of a conviction is not admissible under this rule if (1) the conviction has been the subject of a pardon, annulment, certificate of rehabilitation, or other equivalent procedure, and (2) the procedure under which the same was granted or issued required a substantial showing of rehabilitation or was based on innocence.

(d) Juvenile Adjudications. Evidence of juvenile adjudications is generally not admissible under this rule. The court may, however, allow evidence of a juvenile adjudication of a witness other than the accused if conviction of the offense would be admissible to attack the credibility of an adult and the court is satisfied that admission in evidence is necessary for a fair determination of the issue of guilt or innocence.

(e) Pendency of Appeal. The pendency of an appeal therefrom does not render evidence of a conviction inadmissible. Evidence of the pendency of an appeal is admissible.

Adopted September 27, 2010, eff. January 1, 2011.

Official Comment

Rule 609 represents a codification of a draft of FED. R. EVID. 609, as adopted by the Illinois Supreme Court in People v. Montgomery, 48 Ill. 2d 510, 268 N.E.2d 695 (1971). Rule 609(d) is a codification of the *Montgomery* holding related to the admissibility of juvenile adjudications for impeachment purposes. Rule 609(d) may conflict with section 5-150(1)(c) of the Juvenile Court Act (705 ILCS 405/5-150(1)(c)), which arguably makes such adjudications admissible for impeachment purposes. Concerning that issue, it should be noted that in People v. Harris, 231 Ill. 2d 582 (2008), the Supreme Court held that juvenile adjudications are admissible for impeachment purposes when a defendant opens the door to such evidence (in that case, by testifying that "I don't commit crimes"). Because of its holding, which was based on the defendant's own testimony, the court declined to consider whether section 5-150(1)(c) overrides the common law prohibition against such use. The codification of *Montgomery* in Rule 609(d) is not intended to resolve this issue.

Committee Commentary

(2) Statute Validity: The Committee believes it avoided affecting the validity of existing statutes promulgated by the Illinois legislature. There is a possible conflict between Rule 609(d) and section 5-150(1)(c) of the Juvenile Court Act (705 ILCS 405/5-150(1)(c)) with respect to the use of juvenile adjudications for impeachment purposes. That possible conflict, however, is not the result of promulgation of Rule 609(d) because that rule simply codifies the Illinois Supreme Court's adoption of the 1971 draft of Fed. R. Evid. 609 in People v. Montgomery, 47 Ill. 2d 510 (1971). As noted in the Comment to Rule 609(d), the present codification is not intended to resolve the issue concerning the effect of the statute. Moreover, the Illinois Rules of Evidence permit the Illinois legislature to act in the future with respect to the law of evidence as long as the particular legislative enactment is not in conflict with an Illinois Supreme Court rule or an Illinois Supreme Court decision. *See* ILL. R. EVID. 101. ILL. R. EVID. Committee Commentary § 2, pg. 2.

AUTHOR'S COMMENTARY

The Illinois Supreme Court had previously adopted the 1971 draft of Federal Rule of Evidence 609 in what came to be known as the *Montgomery* Rule. People v. Montgomery, 47 Ill. 2d 510 (1971). The new Illinois Rule of Evidence 609 has adopted the *Montgomery* standard. ILL. R. EVID. Committee Commentary § 2, pg. 2. The new Illinois rule differs from the 1971 Federal Rule of Evidence 609 in that it changed the words "court" and "witness" for "judge" and "he." *See* MICHAEL H. GRAHAM, GRAHAM'S HANDBOOK OF ILLINOIS EVIDENCE § 609.1 (10th ed. 2010).

Illinois Rule of Evidence 101 provides that "a statutory rule of evidence is effective unless in conflict with a rule or a decision of the Illinois Supreme Court." The Comment to Rule 101 notes that a possible conflict may exist with "the statute discussed in the commentary to Rule 609(d)." The statute, 705 ILCS 405/5-150(1)(c), states that

> [e]vidence and adjudications in proceedings under [the Juvenile Court Act of 1987] shall be admissible [. . .] in proceedings under this Act or in criminal proceedings in which anyone who has been adjudicated delinquent under Section 5-105 is to be a witness *including the minor or defendant if he or she testifies*, and *then only for purposes of impeachment and pursuant to the rules of evidence for criminal trials*. (emphasis added).

The Illinois Supreme Court initially did not reach the issue of whether section 5-150(1)(c) of the Juvenile Court Act changed the common law *Montgomery* rule and allowed admissibility of a testifying defendant's prior juvenile adjudication in People v. Harris, 231 Ill. 2d 582 (2008). Instead, the Supreme Court in *Harris* found that a testifying accused may be impeached on cross-examination by a prior juvenile conviction if he or she opens the door to such evidence by providing testimony that may be misleading to the trier of fact. The Illinois Supreme Court recently resolved the issue left unanswered in *Harris* in People v. Villa, 2011 IL 110777. The Supreme Court in *Villa* held that section 5-150(1)(c) did not change the *Montgomery* rule and reaffirmed that evidence of a juvenile adjudication is generally inadmissible against a testifying defendant unless it is "in accordance with *Montgomery* and its progeny."

ILLINOIS CASE LAW UNDER THE NEW ILLINOIS RULES OF EVIDENCE

1. Evidence of a Juvenile Adjudication Is Generally Inadmissible Against a Testifying Accused

People v. Villa, 2011 IL 110777

Defendant was charged with aggravated battery with a firearm and aggravated discharge of a firearm. He gave signed inculpatory statements to interrogating police officers after he was arrested. Defendant subsequently recanted his statements. He filed a motion *in limine* prior to trial to bar state from using his juvenile adjudication for burglary as impeachment evidence. The trial court denied defendant's motion and permitted the prosecution to use the prior juvenile adjudication for impeachment purposes.

Defendant testified at trial that he did not commit the crime. He was asked why he gave a statement to the police admitting that he participated in it. Defendant responded that he had "never been in a situation like this before," that he had never been in prison and that he was scared. Defendant explained that he had never been arrested, interrogated, or charged as an adult. State challenged defendant's testimony and defendant further clarified that he had been interviewed by the same police officers before, but that he was a juvenile at that time.

Defendant distinguished the two police encounters and noted that he was previously interviewed as a juvenile and had never before been charged as an adult. The state offered a certified copy of defendant's juvenile adjudication and repeatedly argued during trial and in closing argument that this adjudication indicated that "defendant's trial testimony was not truthful." Defendant appealed and the appellate court affirmed, relying on the reasoning in People v. Harris, 231 Ill. 2d 582 (2008). The appellate court held that defendant was properly impeached with evidence of his prior juvenile adjudication after he opened the door to such evidence.

The Illinois Supreme Court reversed, finding that the trial court and the appellate court both erred in allowing state to impeach defendant with his prior juvenile adjudication. The Supreme Court noted the conflict in the appellate court. It observed that some districts reconciled section 5-150(1)(c) of the Juvenile Court Act with *Montgomery* and held that juvenile adjudications were generally inadmissible against a testifying defendant, while others, like the appellate court here, found that the statutory provision "trumps *Montgomery*" and allowed impeachment of a testifying defendant with a prior juvenile adjudication. The Supreme Court observed that

> the holding of *Montgomery* relating to juvenile adjudications has now been codified as Rule 609(d) of the Illinois Rules of Evidence (ILL. R. EVID. 609(d) (eff. Jan. 1, 2011)). We need not consider the effect, if any, of this codification because it postdates defendant's trial by over two years. Moreover, the comment to Rule 609 expressly states that the codification of the *Montgomery* holding was not intended to resolve any conflict between *Montgomery* and section 5-150(1)(c) of the Act. ILL. R. EVID. 609, cmt. (eff. Jan. 1, 2011); *see also* ILL. R. EVID. Committee Commentary (eff. Jan. 1, 2011) (recognizing a possible conflict between Rule 609(d) and section 5-150(1)(c) of the Act and stating that codification "is not intended to resolve the issue concerning the effect of the statute").

The state argued that defendant's prior juvenile adjudication was admissible because the statutory provision removed any prohibition against such impeachment contained in *Montgomery*. The Supreme Court disagreed, holding that "section 5-150(1)(c) of the Act allows the admission of juvenile adjudications against a testifying defendant for impeachment only in accordance with *Montgomery* and its progeny. We therefore overrule the appellate decision under review to the extent it holds that section 5-150(1)(c) changed the rule adopted in *Montgomery*."

After resolving this primary issue, the Illinois Supreme Court noted that its holding did "not absolutely resolve whether defendant's juvenile adjudication should have been admitted." The Supreme Court therefore considered this issue, observing that

> [i]n ruling that defendant had opened the door to admission of his juvenile adjudication, the appellate court relied on this court's opinion in People v. Harris, 231 Ill. 2d 582 (2008). In *Harris*, the defendant, when asked on direct examination whether he had committed the crimes in question, testified:
>
>> 'No sir. There is no possible way that I could have committed this crime. I mean people who commit robberies, things like that, have a motive, have a reason for doing things like that. But I am a professional man. I work. I go to college. I went to Robert Morris, ICC, Midstate. I mean, it's no reason—I mean I live a productive life. I live just like any of the 12 jurors, like you live. *I don't commit crimes*.' (Emphasis added.) *Harris*, 231 Ill. 2d at 584-85.
>
> The trial court allowed the State to impeach defendant with evidence of his two most recent juvenile adjudications. In judging whether the trial court had abused its discretion, we

> determined that the "pivotal question" on review was whether the defendant was attempting to mislead the jury about his criminal background when he testified, "I don't commit crimes." *Id.* at 590. "If he was, then he 'opened the door' and the trial court was well within its discretion to allow the admission of defendant's prior adjudications for purposes of impeachment. If he was not, then defendant's testimony was not a proper basis for the admission of that evidence." *Id.*
>
> The defendant in *Harris* maintained that his answer was merely a present tense statement of how he conducts his life and was not meant to misstate or falsify his juvenile record. We concluded that even if true, "it is just as reasonable to construe defendant's answer as a comprehensive denial of ever having engaged in criminal activity, which amounts to an outright lie." (Emphasis in original.) *Id.* at 591. Thus, we found the trial court did not abuse its discretion when it permitted the State to impeach the defendant with two prior juvenile adjudications. *Id.*

Here, the Supreme Court distinguished *Harris*, explaining that defendant had not opened the door to admissibility of his prior juvenile adjudication by stating that he had never been arrested or charged as an adult before and had never been in prison. The Supreme Court noted that the state conceded that defendant had never been imprisoned. The Supreme Court explained that defendant also had not preemptively introduced his prior adjudication to lessen its prejudicial impact on the trier of fact. The Supreme Court also noted that defendant was not attempting to mislead the jury. Although the state was permitted to cross-examine defendant about prior police questioning, the Supreme Court found that the state was prohibited from disclosing his prior criminal history. The court observed that there was very little evidence of defendant's guilt and his credibility was crucial to a determination of his guilt. The court concluded that the evidentiary error in admitting his prior juvenile adjudication was therefore not harmless beyond a reasonable doubt.

PRIOR ILLINOIS CASE LAW

1. Impeachment of a Witness by Evidence of Prior Conviction: The *Montgomery* Rule

People v. Montgomery, 47 Ill. 2d 510 (1971)

The rule of impeachment in Illinois, commonly known as the *Montgomery* rule, is entirely discretionary. Here, the Illinois Supreme Court adopted the 1971 draft of the Federal Rule of Evidence 609. The Supreme Court found that defendant's 21-year-old prior conviction was erroneously admitted in evidence as it was too remote and not relevant to defendant's present credibility. The Supreme Court observed that pursuant to the Federal Rule of Evidence 609, a party seeking to introduce a prior conviction of a witness must show that the conviction qualifies under the rule. A conviction qualifies when the prior crime

> (1) was punishable by death or imprisonment in excess of one year under the law under which he was convicted, or (2) involved dishonesty or false statement regardless of the punishment . . . [and (3) less] than 10 years has elapsed since the date of conviction or of the release of the witness from confinement, whichever is the later date.

Once the party has established a qualifying conviction, the burden will be on the party opposing admissibility of the conviction to show that the probative value is substantially outweighed by its prejudicial effect. The Illinois Supreme Court explained that in exercising its discretion to allow the impeachment or to exclude the evidence, the trial court should look to a number of relevant factors, including

> the nature of the prior crimes, . . . the length of the criminal record, the age and circumstances of the defendant, and, above all, the extent to which it is more important to the search for truth in a particular case for the jury to hear the defendant's story than to know of a prior conviction.

In determining whether the probative value of a prior crime is substantially outweighed by unfair prejudice to the defendant, a court should consider "the nature of the crime, nearness or remoteness, subsequent career of the person, and whether the crime was similar to the one charged." The Supreme Court noted that the accused, as distinguishable from any other witness, enjoys the constitutional right to testify in his or her own defense, yet impeachment may chill that right. If the defendant does testify, there is a real danger that a jury may confuse the impeachment value of prior conviction evidence, even with a limiting instruction, with substantive use of such evidence and conclude that the defendant has a propensity to commit crime. In this case, the Supreme Court determined that the prior conviction did not have a rational relationship to defendant's present credibility.

2. Only Prior Convictions Relevant to Defendant's Credibility as a Witness Are Admissible
People v. Williams, 161 Ill. 2d 1 (1994)

The Illinois Supreme Court held that *Montgomery* does not authorize the admissibility of any and all prior convictions, but only those that pertain to defendant's "testimonial credibility." Although the Supreme Court did not set forth a *per se* rule that voluntary manslaughter convictions would never be admissible against a defendant in a murder prosecution, in the case before it, the *Montgomery* requirements were not met and the defendant's prior conviction for voluntary manslaughter was not admissible. There was no evidence that the conviction had any relationship to the defendant's truthfulness as a witness. The conviction was admitted for the impermissible purpose of showing defendant's guilt in the instant case.

3. People v. Williams, 161 Ill. 2d 1 (1994), Did Not Alter the Three-Prong *Montgomery* Rule but Rather Emphasized the Importance of Applying the Balancing Test
People v. Williams, 173 Ill. 2d 48 (1996)

Subsequent to People v. Williams, 161 Ill. 2d 1 (1994), the Illinois Appellate Court inconsistently interpreted the holding of that case. Some cases held that *Williams* modified or changed the rule in *Montgomery*, e.g., felony convictions are no longer admissible, but only those convictions reflecting on defendant's veracity are; other cases held to the contrary, finding all felony convictions, even if they do not impact on credibility are admissible. The Illinois Supreme Court re-addressed the issue here. The court held that "*Williams* does not alter the three-prong rule set forth in *Montgomery*. Rather, this court in *Williams* was expressing concern about the indiscriminate admission of all prior felony convictions for impeachment purposes absent application of the critical balancing test mandated by *Montgomery*."

4. Party Seeking to Impeach Has the Burden of Presenting Proper Evidence of an Impeaching Conviction
People v. Yost, 78 Ill. 2d 292 (1980)

Defendant was charged with the murder of his wife. State sought to introduce his prior conviction for felonious assault that occurred 10 years and 10 months before his trial. Defendant was sentenced to two to four years although the record did not show his date of release or whether he had been imprisoned at all. Defendant argued that this prior conviction was more than 10 years old and thus should not be admitted. State urged the court to presume that he had served at least the minimum of two years imprisonment, causing the conviction to be within the 10-year limitation. The Illinois Supreme Court refused to so presume, noting that "[t]he party seeking to impeach testimony has the responsibility of presenting proper evidence of an impeaching conviction."

5. Trial Court Should Rule on Defendant's Motion to Bar Prior Convictions Before Defendant Testifies Unless There Is Compelling Reason to Delay Ruling

People v. Patrick, 233 Ill. 2d 62 (2009)

The Illinois Supreme Court settled the issue of the proper time for ruling on a motion to bar prior convictions for impeachment of the defendant. Here, the Supreme Court considered a consolidated appeal by two defendants. The first defendant was on trial for first degree murder. During trial the defendant filed a motion *in limine* seeking to bar the state from presenting evidence of his prior convictions. Defendant had three prior convictions for possession of a controlled substance. The judge refused to rule on the motion prior to defendant's testimony. Defendant testified and the state impeached him with his prior convictions for possession of a controlled substance. Defendant raised a theory of self-defense and was convicted of second degree murder. The defendant argued on appeal that the trial court erred by refusing to rule on his motion until after the he testified.

The Supreme Court recognized that a defendant's decision to testify is generally made only after the strength of the state's evidence is fully and properly evaluated. The court also noted that the defendant benefits from an early ruling on the admissibility of prior convictions evidence by being able to make strategic decisions about his defense. Here, the defendant argued self-defense and the Supreme Court emphasized that it was important for him to know whether his prior convictions could be used for impeachment before he took the stand. Moreover, state repeatedly argued that the jury should not believe "a three-time convicted felon." The Supreme Court held that, unless some compelling reason to delay the ruling exists, the trial court should rule on a defendant's motion to bar prior convictions before the defendant testifies. The Supreme Court further explained that situations requiring the defendant to testify prior to the court making its decision would be exceedingly rare. The court found that the trial judge did not articulate any justification for delaying the ruling, and its decision was "arbitrary and without reason." The Supreme Court held that the trial court's failure to rule on the defendant's motion *in limine* on the admissibility of prior convictions, when it had sufficient information to make the ruling, constituted an abuse of discretion. The Supreme Court remanded for a new trial.

The second defendant was charged with attempted first degree murder, armed violence and aggravated battery. He sought to bar use of his four prior convictions, three of which were for armed violence, aggravated battery, and a controlled substance offense as impeachment during trial. The trial judge granted the defendant's motion *in limine* in part by excluding one of his four convictions but reserved ruling on the other three convictions that included armed violence, aggravated battery, and a controlled substance offense until defendant testified. Defendant chose not to testify at trial. The Supreme Court concluded that the defendant failed to preserve the issue of trial court's failure to consider his motion *in limine* because he did not testify at trial.

6. Defendant's Claim of Improper Impeachment with a Prior Conviction Is Reviewable Only If Defendant Testifies

Luce v. United States, 469 U.S. 38 (1984)

Defendant was charged with conspiracy and possession of cocaine with intent to distribute. Defendant filed a motion to preclude the government from using a prior conviction for possession of a controlled substance to impeach him. Defendant did not testify at trial and was convicted. The United States Court of Appeals for the Sixth Circuit held that because defendant did not testify, the District Court's ruling on his motion was not reviewable. The United States Supreme Court affirmed, observing that when defendant does not testify it is impossible for the reviewing court to determine whether the probative value of the prior conviction would have been outweighed by its prejudicial effect on the defendant in light of his or her testimony. Moreover, there is no way to determine whether prosecution would have even used the prior conviction to impeach the defendant's testimony. The Supreme Court concluded that a defendant's claim of improper impeachment with a prior conviction is preserved for review only if defendant testifies.

7. Trial Court's Withholding of Ruling on Defendant's Motion *in Limine* Does Not Require Reversal If Defendant Does Not Testify at Trial

People v. Averett, 237 Ill. 2d 1 (2010)

The Illinois Supreme Court considered a consolidated appeal to determine whether defendants were entitled to relief. Defendants moved *in limine* to preclude the use of their prior convictions for impeachment purposes. The trial court deferred ruling on the motions *in limine*. Neither defendant testified at trial. On appeal, defendants argued that the trial court's blanket policy to defer rulings on motions *in limine* violated their right to testify. The Illinois Supreme Court reiterated its decision in People v. Patrick, 233 Ill. 2d 62 (2009), that a trial court abuses its discretion when it exercises a blanket policy of withholding its rulings on motions *in limine* regarding prior convictions until the defendant testifies. The Supreme Court considered whether defendants were entitled to relief even though they did not testify because the trial court had a "blanket policy" of deferring rulings on motions *in limine* before defendants testified.

Defendants first argued that the trial court's policy constituted structural error. The Supreme Court noted that a structural error occurs only in a few select cases and is so serious as to render a criminal trial "fundamentally unfair or unreliable in determining guilt or innocence." The Supreme Court refused to recognize structural error in this case because the error here did not necessarily render the trial fundamentally unfair or unreliable because it did "not affect the framework of the trial process. Rather, it [was] simply an error within the trial proceedings."

Defendants further argued that the ruling was constitutional error as it violated their right to testify at trial. The Supreme Court reasoned that defendants were not prevented from testifying at trial by the trial court's policy, and noted that defendants may be "required to weigh the possibility of being impeached with their prior convictions along with other factors in determining whether to testify. The defendants' constitutional right to testify was not violated by any deterrent effect on their testimony due to the risk of being impeached with their prior convictions."

Defendants then contended that the trial court's blanket policy to defer ruling on their motions *in limine* was plain error because it deprived them of fair trial. The Supreme Court dismissed this argument as well, reasoning that courts cannot speculate on the possible testimony the defendants could have offered had they testified at trial. The Supreme Court refused to apply the plain-error analysis here and concluded that none of defendants' arguments were persuasive and that the defendants' decision not to testify rendered this issue unreviewable.

8. Defendant's Refusal to Testify Because Prosecution Seeks to Impeach with a Prior Conviction Will Not Alone Demonstrate Prejudice
People v. Leonard, 83 Ill. 2d 411 (1980)

Defendant was convicted of murder. Trial court permitted impeachment use of defendant's prior convictions for forgery and delivery of a controlled substance. Defendant informed the trial court that if the impeachment evidence were allowed, he would not testify at trial. Defendant argued on appeal that the introduction of his prior convictions denied his constitutional right to present a defense. The Illinois Supreme Court reasoned that where the prosecution seeks to impeach the defendant with a prior conviction, the defendant's refusal to testify, standing alone, will not provide a sufficient basis to conclude that he or she was prejudiced. The Supreme Court explained that defendant's choice not to testify was a matter of trial strategy and that he failed to show any other prejudice or how such prejudice substantially outweighed the probative value of the evidence.

9. Error in Withholding Ruling on Defendant's Motion to Bar Prior Convictions When Defendant Testifies Is Subject to Harmless Error Analysis
People v. Mullins, 242 Ill. 2d 1 (2011)

Defendant was charged with possession of a controlled substance with intent to deliver. Before trial he filed a motion *in limine* to bar use of his three prior felony narcotics convictions as impeachment. The trial court reserved its decision on the motion until after defendant testified. After defendant testified, the parties presented arguments weighing the probative value and prejudicial effect of prior convictions during a sidebar conference. The trial court admitted defendant's 2001 controlled substance conviction but excluded two earlier convictions. The parties stipulated to the 2001 conviction. The appellate court held that the trial court erred in deferring its ruling on defendant's motion *in limine* until defendant testified and remanded the case for a new trial. On further appeal, the Illinois Supreme Court considered whether the trial court erroneously admitted defendant's 2001 conviction, and whether the ruling to defer was harmless.

Defendant contended that the trial court failed to properly conduct the balancing analysis per *Montgomery*, and erroneously permitted state to impeach his credibility with a prior conviction for the same offense with which he was charged. The Supreme Court recognized that use of a prior conviction that is "similar to a crime for which the defendant is on trial is not automatically barred." Moreover, the Supreme Court explained that it was not necessary for the trial court to state on the record that it was conducting the balancing test or to make explicit that it was doing so pursuant to *Montgomery*. The trial court clearly weighed the probative value of the impeachment evidence against its prejudicial effect when it excluded earlier convictions and provided limiting instructions to the jury to clarify the narrow use for which the evidence was admissible.

The Supreme Court then considered whether the trial court committed harmless error in deferring its ruling on defendant's motion *in limine* using the following factors: (1) the defendant's need to testify, (2) whether parties mentioned defendant's prior conviction in argument, and (3) the strength of evidence against the defendant. The Supreme Court first noted that the defendant's need to testify in this case was great because the prosecution presented strong evidence and without his testimony there were "significant gaps" in his theory of the case. Moreover, defendant's alibi witness failed to actually provide an alibi and placed defendant at the scene of crime. The Supreme Court then evaluated whether the state mentioned defendant's prior convictions during trial but found no evidence that any improper references were made to defendant's propensity to commit the current crime. Finally, the Supreme Court noted that the prosecution presented a strong case via the unimpeached testimony of three police officers who observed defendant participating in the sale of a controlled substance. The Supreme Court concluded that "any error in delaying the ruling was harmless beyond a reasonable doubt. If the court's error were removed, we are convinced that a retrial would end with the same result."

Defendant also argued that trial court's error was not harmless because jurors considered the prior 2001 conviction during their deliberations pointing to the fact that the jury requested a copy of the stipulation while it was deliberating. The Supreme Court determined that the mere fact that the jury requested the stipulation was not "dispositive of whether the trial court's error in delaying its ruling on defendant's motion to bar that evidence is harmless, because any conclusion based on the jury's question is necessarily speculative." Although the stipulation may have played "some role" in defendant's conviction, the Supreme Court refused to speculate about the extent to which the jury considered it and why it may have requested it.

10. Defendant Who Preemptively Introduces Evidence of a Prior Conviction on Direct Examination May Not Challenge Admissibility of That Evidence

Ohler v. United States, 529 U.S. 753 (2000)

The defendant preemptively introduced evidence of her prior conviction on direct examination and then claimed on appeal that the trial court erred in its *in limine* ruling allowing the government to use the evidence of her prior conviction for impeachment purposes. Noting the 1990 amendment to FRE 609 that allows a defendant-witness to introduce evidence of her prior conviction on direct examination, the United States Supreme Court held that a "defendant who preemptively introduces evidence of a prior conviction on direct examination may not on appeal claim that the admission of such evidence was error."

11. Trial Court May Not Allow the "Mere Fact" of a Prior Conviction Without Disclosing the Nature of the Conviction for Impeachment

People v. Atkinson, 186 Ill. 2d 450 (1999)

Defendant was charged with burglary and testified at trial. Trial court permitted state to introduce defendant's two prior convictions for burglary for impeachment purposes. On appeal, defendant argued that the trial court should have only informed the jury that defendant had two prior felony convictions without naming the specific crimes. The appellate court agreed, holding that the trial court should have used the "mere fact" method of impeachment and that the jury should have only been informed of the "mere fact" that defendant had been convicted twice before of two unidentified felonies. The Illinois Supreme Court reversed, explaining that pursuant to the third factor of the *Montgomery* test, the trial court must conduct a balancing test. In conducting this test, "the trial judge should consider, *inter alia*, the nature of the prior conviction, its recency and similarity to the present charge, other circumstances surrounding the prior conviction, and the length of the witness' criminal record." The Supreme Court reasoned that

> it is the nature of a past conviction, not merely the fact of it, that aids the jury in assessing a witness' credibility. . . . The mere-fact approach undermines the *Montgomery* rule and inhibits the jury's evaluation of a witness' credibility by eliminating the jury's consideration of the nature of the past crime.

The Supreme Court further observed that non-disclosure of the nature of the specific prior crime would be prejudicial to the defendant because it could result in jury speculating that the conviction was for a more serious crime. Conversely, under *Montgomery*, there is no room for speculation. The Supreme Court concluded that

> [t]he *Montgomery* rule, which balances the jury's role in evaluating the witness' credibility with the unfair prejudice to the defendant, shall continue to be undisturbed as the method governing admission of evidence of a prior conviction to impeach the credibility of a witness. Thus, trial courts should not consider the mere-fact method of impeachment.

Note that pursuant to People v. Cox, 195 Ill. 2d 378 (2001), the Supreme Court's ruling in *Atkinson* applies retroactively to all cases pending when the opinion was announced.

12. Use of Mere-Fact Method of Impeachment Does Not Constitute Plain Error
People v. Harvey, 211 Ill. 2d 368 (2004)

The Illinois Supreme Court considered three consolidated cases dealing with the use of the "mere fact" method of impeachment by prior conviction.

The first defendant was charged with murder and kidnapping. After the close of the evidence, state presented a jury instruction in reference to defendant's prior convictions. Defense counsel objected, arguing that the state had not presented evidence of the convictions during trial. The trial court overruled the objection reasoning that the trial court permitted state to reopen its case. The trial court allowed the state only to refer to the prior conviction as a felony offense and the parties stipulated that the defendant had been convicted of two felony convictions. Defendant appealed, arguing that he did not agree to the use of "mere fact" impeachment.

The second defendant was charged with unlawful possession of stolen vehicles and aggravated possession of stolen vehicles. In an oral motion *in limine* the defendant requested that his prior felony conviction for burglary of a motor vehicle be barred or, in the alternative, that the "mere fact" method of impeachment be used. The state consented to the use of "mere fact" method of impeachment. Defendant was convicted and contended that the trial court erred in using the "mere fact" method of impeachment.

The third defendant was charged with vehicular invasion, aggravated battery, intimidation and unlawful restraint. Defense counsel sought to exclude evidence of defendant's prior burglary, theft and two aggravated battery convictions. Counsel agreed to the use of "mere fact" impeachment. Defendant appealed, arguing that the trial court erred in permitting use of the "mere fact" method of impeachment.

The Supreme Court observed that "[t]here is no question the trial court in each of these three consolidated cases committed error by employing mere-fact impeachment." The Supreme Court found, however, that none of the defendants preserved the issue for review. The Supreme Court concluded that if defendant agrees to the use of or requests improper mere fact impeachment, he or she cannot later complain of its use on appeal. Use of mere fact impeachment by the court, while improper, does not constitute plain error.

13. Non-testifying Declarant of Excited Utterance May Not Be Impeached by Prior Conviction
People v. Johnson, 271 Ill. App. 3d 962 (4th Dist. 1995)

In this case of first impression, the Fourth District of the Illinois Appellate Court held that a non-testifying declarant of an excited utterance cannot be impeached by a prior conviction. It reasoned that the reliability of an excited utterance is derived from the excited state of the declarant who lacks the opportunity to fabricate a lie. Such statements are the product of sense and not of thoughtful or self-interested reflection. Admissibility rests upon the circumstances surrounding the making of the statement and not on the reliability of the declarant. The court concluded that since the "declarant's credibility is immaterial to the veracity of the excited utterance, the declarant's prior criminal convictions are also irrelevant to the veracity of an excited utterance."

14. Evidence of a Prior Conviction Is Not Admissible If More Than 10 Years Have Elapsed Since the Date of Conviction or the Release of the Witness from Confinement, Whichever Is the More Recent Date

People v. Warmack, 83 Ill. 2d 112 (1980)

Defendant was charged with murder and armed robbery. State sought to prohibit the impeachment of one of its witnesses with an 11-year-old felony conviction of attempted robbery. The Supreme Court found that impeachment of the witness by her attempted robbery conviction was improper because the conviction occurred 11 years before the current trial and the witness was not imprisoned. The witness was put on probation and although her probationary period may have extended to within nine years of this trial, the Supreme Court noted that "the expiration date of a witness' probationary period is not a consideration in determining when the time requirements for admissibility are met."

15. Date of Trial Is the End Point of the *Montgomery* 10-Year Time Limit of Impeachment by Prior Conviction

People v. Naylor, 229 Ill. 2d 584 (2008)

The trial court held that the end date for *Montgomery*'s 10-year rule was the date the defendant allegedly committed the charged offense, rather than the date of trial. In doing so, the trial court admitted the defendant's conviction of aggravated battery in a case involving his alleged sale of heroin. The defendant was tried 13 years and 8 months after his battery conviction. However, the date on which he was charged with the drug-related offense was only 9 years and 3 months after the conviction.

Here, the state failed to present evidence as to the date of the defendant's release from confinement on the battery conviction so the appellate court used the date of conviction until the date of the new trial as the relevant time period and found that the battery conviction fell outside of the 10-year limit. The Illinois Supreme Court held that setting *Montgomery*'s end date as the date the defendant allegedly committed the charged offense improperly presumes the defendant's guilt. The Supreme Court also found that *Montgomery* constitutes a *per se* rule which stands for the proposition that after 10 years, a conviction is no longer relevant for issues of credibility, therefore, the trial court's discretion cannot be expanded at the expense of the rationale for the 10-year rule. The Supreme Court added that in a majority of trials, witnesses have not been charged with any offenses, so for purposes of impeachment of witnesses, setting the *Montgomery* end date as the date the defendant committed the charged offense "would not make sense."

16. Any Misdemeanor Which Has as Its Basis Lying, Cheating, Deceiving, or Stealing Is a Crime Involving Dishonesty for Impeachment Purposes

People v. Spates, 77 Ill. 2d 193 (1979)

Defendant was convicted of armed robbery and argued on appeal that the trial court erroneously permitted state to impeach him with his prior misdemeanor theft conviction. Before trial, defendant filed a motion *in limine* to bar the prior theft conviction but the trial court rejected the motion. The Illinois Supreme Court "propose[d] as a guideline that any misdemeanor, which has as its basis lying, cheating, deceiving or *stealing*, bears a reasonable relation to testimonial deceit and should be admissible for impeachment purposes" (emphasis added). The Supreme Court concluded that a misdemeanor theft conviction is a crime involving dishonesty and was properly used as impeachment evidence against defendant.

See also People v. Malone, 78 Ill. 2d 34 (1979) (finding prior misdemeanor theft convictions admissible to impeach armed robbery defendant).

17. Trial Court Did Not Abuse Its Discretion in Admitting All of Defendant's Numerous Prior Misdemeanor Theft Convictions at Defendant's Robbery-Murder Trial to Demonstrate a "Consistent Pattern of Dishonesty"
People v. McKibbins, 96 Ill. 2d 176 (1983)

Defendant was found guilty of murder, armed robbery, and armed violence. He made a motion *in limine* to bar use of his previous convictions for impeachment purposes. State sought to introduce defendant's prior 20 convictions for theft, most of which were misdemeanors within the 10 years prior to trial. The trial court permitted introduction of these prior convictions. Defendant contended that trial court erred because it did not balance the probative value against the prejudicial effect of prior convictions when it failed to limit their number. He further claimed that the mere fact that the trial court would admit these prior convictions prevented him from testifying because he was afraid of the prejudicial impact of the evidence.

The Illinois Supreme Court, however, found that trial courts have discretionary authority to determine whether prior convictions will be admitted for impeachment and that the trial court here properly recognized and applied the balancing test. The trial court need not articulate reasons for allowing the prior conviction as impeachment evidence, but the record must reflect that the trial judge did in fact apply the balancing test.

The Supreme Court then considered the nature of the crimes, their remoteness, defendant's career subsequent to the crimes as well as their similarity to the charged offense. The Supreme Court explained that the prior convictions were correctly admitted despite their number because the crimes here, mostly theft misdemeanors were not

> crimes of violence from which the jury might infer that the defendant had a propensity for committing such crimes and thus probably committed the murder with which he was charged. The career of the defendant subsequent to these convictions does not demonstrate a change of character but rather a continuation of deceitful conduct. The prior convictions covered the entire 10-year-period limit of *Montgomery*. Therefore, although some may have been remote, defendant's conduct demonstrated a consistent pattern of dishonesty. The probative value of such evidence as it relates to the defendant's credibility was extremely convincing and far outweighed any prejudicial impact that the evidence would have on the question of the defendant's guilt of the violent crime of murder.

The Supreme Court concluded that the trial court did not abuse its discretion by admitting all of these prior crimes. The Supreme Court indicated that to cut down on the number of these crimes would be a complex exercise and might result in shielding the jury from the reality that the defendant had an extensive record of dishonesty. Moreover, the fact that defendant may have been prevented from testifying here was merely a "consequence of his own wrongdoing."

18. Proof of Arrests, Indictments, Charges, and Evidence of Commission of a Crime or Jury Verdicts Are Not "Convictions" for Impeachment Purposes
People v. Mason, 28 Ill. 2d 396 (1963)

The Illinois Supreme Court explained that to conduct impeachment by a prior conviction,

> only conviction may be proved, and proof of arrests, indictments, charges or actual commission of crime are not admissible. People v. Hoffman, 399 Ill. 57 (1948); People v. Newman, 261 Ill. 11 (1913). The rule prevailing in most jurisdictions and supported by the great weight of authority is that it is not permissible to show that a witness has been arrested,

charged with a criminal offense, or confined in prison, or to inquire as to such fact upon cross-examination, where no conviction is shown, for the purpose of impairing his credibility.

19. Conviction of Misdemeanor Not Involving Dishonesty or False Statement or a Charge Resulting in Supervision Are Not Qualifying Convictions for Impeachment Under *Montgomery*
People v. Schuning, 106 Ill. 2d 41 (1985)

Defendant was charged with rape. State impeached his credibility with two prior convictions, one for criminal trespass and the other for retail theft. The retail theft conviction was discharged after defendant successfully completed a period of supervision. The Illinois Supreme Court found that the impeachment with the prior convictions was improper. First, the Supreme Court reasoned, criminal trespass is a misdemeanor that does not involve dishonesty or false statement and therefore is not an impeachable offense under *Montgomery*. Second, the Supreme Court considered the retail theft charge and noted that use of it for impeachment was also inappropriate because it resulted in supervision rather than a conviction. The Supreme Court explained that "the successful completion of a period of supervision does not result in a conviction" and is not a proper basis for impeachment under *Montgomery*.

See also People v. Stover, 89 Ill. 2d 189 (1982) (finding resisting or obstructing a peace officer a misdemeanor which does not involve dishonesty or a false statement)

20. Criminal Trespass to a Vehicle Is Not a Crime Involving Dishonesty or False Statement
Knowles v. Panopoulos, 66 Ill. 2d 585 (1977)

Father brought a wrongful death action after his son, a passenger on a motorcycle driven by his step-brother, died in a collision with the defendant's car. The step-brother testified on plaintiff's behalf at trial. The defendant introduced and the trial court admitted the step-brother's prior misdemeanor conviction for criminal trespass to a vehicle for impeachment purposes. Plaintiff argued that the conviction was inadmissible to impeach a non-party witness in a civil case. Although the Illinois Supreme Court found that *Montgomery* applied to civil cases, it found and that the misdemeanor conviction here was inadmissible because the conviction was neither for a crime of dishonesty nor punishable by more than one year in prison. The Supreme Court concluded that the conviction was unfairly prejudicial to the plaintiff and was erroneously admitted at trial.

21. Admissibility of a Prior Conviction for Impeachment Is Unaffected by a Pending Appeal and Impeached Witness May Introduce Evidence of the Appeal
People v. Bey, 42 Ill. 2d 139 (1969)

Defendant testified at his trial for burglary that he had previously been convicted of a felony. On cross-examination state asked defendant if he had been convicted of any other felonies in the past. Defense objected to the question but the trial court overruled the objection and ordered defendant to answer. Defendant conceded that he had previously been convicted of burglary. An appeal was pending in the earlier burglary conviction and defendant argued that it was improperly admitted for impeachment because of the pendency of the appeal. The Illinois Supreme Court disagreed, noting that a trial court's judgment "is still a determination of guilt which stands until it is reversed." The Supreme Court concluded that although a prior conviction is not rendered inadmissible merely because an appeal is pending, the impeached witness may explain the pendency of an appeal.

22. Impeachment of Defendant by Prior Conviction Reversed Because of Constitutional Violation of Defendant's Right to Counsel Is Reversible Error
People v. Martin-Trigona, 111 Ill. 2d 295 (1986)

Defendant was convicted of theft and forgery. State impeached the defendant with a prior federal conviction for mail fraud. After defendant's state conviction for theft and forgery, the United States Court of Appeals for the Seventh Circuit reversed defendant's federal mail fraud conviction finding a violation of defendant's right to the assistance of counsel at trial. Defendant subsequently appealed his theft and forgery convictions arguing that they were tainted by the use of the reversed federal conviction. State contended that the introduction of defendant's federal conviction was harmless error because there was overwhelming evidence of defendant's guilt. The Illinois Supreme Court disagreed, noting that it may be reversible error to admit a prior conviction that was reversed due to a constitutional error. The Supreme Court concluded that defendant was entitled to a new trial because the trier of fact improperly relied upon his prior conviction to determine guilt or innocence in the present case and that the error could not be determined to be harmless beyond a reasonable doubt.

23. Defendant May Be Impeached on Cross-Examination by Prior Juvenile Convictions If He or She Opens the Door to Such Evidence
People v. Harris, 231 Ill. 2d 582 (2008)

Defendant was charged with armed robbery. He was 19 years old at the time he committed the crime and 20 years old by the time the case went to trial. The case went to trial three times because the jury could not reach a unanimous verdict twice. Defendant testified at the third trial and stated that he didn't commit the crime in question and that in general he did not commit crimes. State sought to introduce defendant's prior convictions as impeachment evidence to rebut defendant's false contention that he did not commit crimes. The trial court permitted state to introduce certified copies of defendant's two most recent juvenile convictions for aggravated battery and aggravated discharge of a firearm.

Defendant argued on appeal that his prior juvenile convictions were improperly admitted because he did not open the door to such evidence. In the alternative, even if he had opened the door to the evidence, defendant argued that the trial court should have instructed state to confront him with the prior convictions on cross-examination and allowed defendant an opportunity to rehabilitate his credibility. The Illinois Supreme Court disagreed. The Supreme Court noted that a defendant may open the door to otherwise inadmissible evidence. The Supreme Court explained that the trial court had the best opportunity to assess the meaning of defendant's testimony and held that the trial court did not abuse its discretion in determining that defendant was attempting to mislead the jury when he testified that he did not commit crimes. With respect to defendant's second argument, the Supreme Court reasoned that

> as a general rule, "it is improper to cross-examine a defendant about a prior conviction even where the conviction has been properly introduced into evidence." People v. Coleman, 158 Ill. 2d 319, 337 (1994). And while this rule is not always enforced when a defendant opens the door to such cross-examination (*see, e.g.*, People v. Bey, 42 Ill. 2d 139, 147 (1969); *Coleman*, 158 Ill. 2d at 337), admission of a certified copy of the prior conviction remains the preferred form of impeachment even under those circumstances.

State further argued for the first time that even if the trial court erred in admitting the juvenile records because defendant opened the door to such evidence, the prior convictions were admissible pursuant to section 5-150(1)(c) of the Juvenile Court Act. The Supreme Court declined to consider this issue as it already decided that the trial court correctly decided the issue.

24. Proper Method of Impeaching Defendant with a Prior Conviction Is to Offer in Evidence the Record of Conviction or an Authenticated Copy in Rebuttal
People v. Flynn, 8 Ill. 2d 116 (1956)

The Illinois Supreme Court explained that the proper method of impeaching defendant is to offer into evidence the record of conviction or an authenticated copy in rebuttal. The defendant may not be cross-examined about a prior conviction. The Illinois Supreme Court explained this prohibition:

> This court has repeatedly held that it is improper to cross examine a defendant as to his conviction of a crime. [Citations omitted]. In People v. Kosearas, 408 Ill. 179, 181 (1951), the court stated: 'To repeat what was said in People v. Decker, 310 Ill. 234 (1923), there is no question more damaging to a defendant with a jury than one which suggests or intimates that he is a criminal or has been charged with criminal offenses. Such damage is magnified twofold when it is elicited from a defendant on cross examination and he is compelled to testify against himself.' Defendant's conviction of a prior felony may be shown to affect his credibility by offering the record of his conviction, or an authenticated copy thereof, in evidence, [citation omitted], and not otherwise.

25. Cross-Examination of a Witness Other Than the Defendant About Prior Convictions Is Proper Impeachment
People v. Halkens, 386 Ill. 167 (1944)

Proof of the prior conviction of a witness other than the defendant may be established by cross-examination of the witness. The record of conviction or a certified copy is not necessary. The Illinois Supreme Court explained the need to apply a different rule to a witness other than the defendant testifying at trial:

> A witness, not a defendant, however, is in a different position. In the first place it cannot affect anything except his credibility, because, not being on trial, neither the jury nor the court can use it in administering punishment. Also, it will not subject him to the same hazards to which a defendant is subject in being before the court as a criminal. And finally, the State in many cases, being unaware of whom the defendant may call as witnesses, may be left at a disadvantage in being unable to ascertain whether the credibility of the witness is liable to be impeached by a previous conviction.

26. Impeachment of a Witness other Than Defendant Who Denies Existence of a Prior Conviction Requires Formal Proof of Evidence of Prior Conviction
People v. Wallenberg, 24 Ill. 2d 350 (1962)

If a witness other than the defendant is cross-examined about a prior conviction but the witness denies the prior conviction, the party seeking to impeach the witness must introduce evidence of the prior conviction. Here, prosecution asked a defense witness whether he had previously been convicted of robbery, but the witness denied the prior conviction. Prosecution then failed to show that the prior conviction existed. The Supreme Court concluded that the trial court was required to strike the prosecution's inquiry from the record.

27. Listing of Name in a Certified Copy of Conviction Raises a Rebuttable Presumption of Identity of the Person
People v. Davis, 95 Ill. 2d 1 (1983)

The listing of a name in a certified copy of conviction gives rise to a rebuttable presumption of the identity of the person. Here, the prosecution introduced certified copies of defendant's two prior convictions for murder and attempted murder. Defendant argued that introduction of the prior convictions was improper because the prosecution failed to establish that he was the same person who committed the prior crimes. The defendant's name and the name on the prior convictions were identical. The Illinois Supreme Court noted that "identity of name gives rise to a rebuttable presumption of identity of person." The Supreme Court explained that since defendant did not deny that he committed the prior crimes, he was not prejudiced by state's proof of the prior convictions via certified copies.

28. If Prior Conviction Is in a Name Other Than That of Defendant Who Is Being Impeached and Defendant Refuses to Stipulate, Prosecution Must Prove Identity

People v. Malone, 78 Ill. 2d 34 (1979)

Where the conviction is in a name other than that of the defendant who is being impeached and the defendant refuses to stipulate that he or she is the same person, the party seeking to impeach must prove that the defendant is the same person previously convicted. Here, the state read certified copies of two prior misdemeanor theft convictions into the record to impeach defendant's credibility. The prior convictions, however, contained a name different from that of the defendant and defendant refused to stipulate that those were his prior convictions. A technician testified that the fingerprints taken in the prior convictions matched each other and that these fingerprints also matched those of the defendant in the current trial. Defendant contended that introduction of such testimony prejudiced him because it called too much attention to the prior convictions. The Illinois Supreme Court disagreed, noting that

> [a]lthough proof of prior convictions for impeachment purposes need not be made beyond a reasonable doubt (People v. Stewart, 23 Ill. 2d 161, 164 (1961); People v. Buford, 396 Ill. 158, 161 (1947)), such proof includes identification of the defendant as the same person convicted in the previous case. People v. Davis, 65 Ill. 2d 157 (1976). Inasmuch as, here, the names were different on the prior convictions and defendant refused to stipulate that he was the same person, the State was required to prove that defendant was, in fact, the same person as was convicted earlier.
>
> ***
>
> While it may have been preferable, as defendant suggests, for the judge to take this evidence *[i]n camera*, we find no reversible error here, where the singularity of identities was clearly established and where the State was permitted to elicit only such testimony as was necessary to establish identity. Moreover, the jury was instructed that evidence of defendant's previous convictions was to be considered only insofar as it may have affected his credibility, and not as evidence of guilt of the crime charged. Defendant's challenge to the reading of the two conviction statements is not well taken [because] this is the proper method by which a defendant's credibility may be impeached with a prior conviction.

29. Defendant May Preemptively Disclose Prior Conviction to Lessen the Impact of the Evidence

People v. Spates, 77 Ill. 2d 193 (1979)

Defendant charged with armed robbery moved *in limine* to bar admissibility of his prior convictions at trial. The trial court rejected the motion. Defendant then preemptively introduced his prior conviction in evidence to lessen its impact, and argued on appeal that forcing him to introduce his prior conviction denied him a fair trial. Defendant sought review of the issue concerning the admissibility of his former conviction. The Illinois Supreme Court noted that while a party waives the right to raise as error action taken by the court at the instance of that party; it is quite another matter when, after an exclusionary motion is denied, the party himself raises a matter so as to lessen its impact, when the party knows that if he does not raise it, the opponent will. The difference is that, in the first instance, the request and the subsequent assertion of error are inconsistent with one another. In the second instance the aim is consistent: once the motion to exclude the matter is denied, the party must try to limit the effect the matter will have on the trier of fact. He has not waived the issue by raising it; he has merely tried to ensure that it does the least damage to his witness' credibility. Under the precise facts presented herein, that is what the defendant has done. Therefore the defendant has properly preserved this issue for review. Compare People v. Price, 41 Ill. App. 3d 1059 (1976), with People v. Rudolph, 50 Ill. App. 3d 559 (1977).

Rule 610. Religious Beliefs or Opinions

Evidence of the beliefs or opinions of a witness on matters of religion is not admissible for the purpose of showing that by reason of their nature the witness' credibility is impaired or enhanced.

Adopted September 27, 2010, eff. January 1, 2011.

AUTHOR'S COMMENTARY

Illinois Rule of Evidence 610 codifies Illinois common law principles and is "identical" to Federal Rule of Evidence 610 in effect prior to its stylistic amendment on December 1, 2011. *See* People v. Nevitt, 135 Ill. 2d 423 (1990); Gino L. DiVito, *The Illinois Rules of Evidence: A Color-Coded Guide Containing the New Rules, the Committee's General and Specific Comments, a Comparison with the Federal Rules of Evidence, and Additional Commentary* (*Including the Federal Rules of Evidence as Amended Effective December 1, 2011*) (Jan. 1, 2012), at 78, http://www.tdrlawfirm.com/assets/downloads/Illinois_Rules_of_Evidence_Color-Coded_Guide.pdf.

PRIOR ILLINOIS CASE LAW

Witness' Religious Beliefs or Opinions Are Not Admissible to Impair or Enhance Credibility but May Be Admissible to Show Bias

People v. Nevitt, 135 Ill. 2d 423 (1990)

Defendant on trial for aggravated criminal sexual assault argued that the trial court erred in permitting prosecution to question a witness about her religious beliefs. The witness was a director of a day care center where defendant was employed and where he allegedly sexually assaulted a three-year-old boy. The prosecution questioned the witness about holding weekly theological lectures at the day care center. The defendant argued that such questioning was improper. The Illinois Supreme Court noted that "[a]lthough a witness' religious convictions are not admissible for the purposes of impairing or enhancing credibility," the inquiry into the witness' beliefs here was not improper. The Supreme Court explained that the prosecution was merely attempting to reveal the witness' bias in protecting the day care center's reputation in the community, and that the trial court properly limited the questioning by sustaining objections "when the prosecution's questions strayed too far."

See also People v. Ballinger, 36 Ill. 2d 620 (1967) (finding a nine-year-old witness who was an "infrequent church-goer" competent to testify because a witness' religious beliefs are not a factor in determining competency).

Mode and Scope of Examination of Witnesses

Rule 611. Mode and Order of Interrogation and Presentation

(a) Control by Court. The court shall exercise reasonable control over the mode and order of interrogating witnesses and presenting evidence so as to (1) make the interrogation and presentation effective for the ascertainment of the truth, (2) avoid needless consumption of time, and (3) protect witnesses from harassment or undue embarrassment.

(b) Scope of Cross-Examination. Cross-examination should be limited to the subject matter of the direct examination and matters affecting the credibility of the witness. The court may, in the exercise of discretion, permit inquiry into additional matters as if on direct examination.

(c) Leading Questions. Leading questions should not be used on the direct examination of a witness except as may be necessary to develop the witness' testimony. Ordinarily leading questions should be permitted on cross-examination. When a party calls a hostile or an unwilling witness or an adverse party or an agent of an adverse party as defined by section 2-1102 of the Code of Civil Procedure (735 ILCS 5/2-1102), interrogation may be by leading questions.

Adopted September 27, 2010, eff. January 1, 2011.

Committee Commentary

(6) Referenced Statutes: Numerous existing statutes, the validity of which are not affected by promulgation of the Illinois Rules of Evidence ILL. R. EVID. 101, relate in one form or another to the law of evidence. The Committee felt it was inappropriate, unnecessary and unwise to refer specifically to the abundance of statutory authority in an Appendix or otherwise. Reference is, however, made in the body of the text of the Illinois Rules of Evidence to certain statutes by citation or verbatim incorporation. Such references and the reasons therefor are as follows:

(4) Rule 611(c): 735 ILCS 5/2-1102 provides a definition of adverse party or agent with respect to hostile witnesses as to whom interrogation may be by leading questions. ILL. R. EVID. Committee Commentary § 6, pg. 8.

AUTHOR'S COMMENTARY

The new Illinois Rule of Evidence 611 specifies the mode and order of interrogation of witnesses and presentation of evidence at trial. Rule 611(c) indicates that leading questions are generally reserved for cross-examination of witnesses but may be proper in certain situations on direct examination. Rule 611(c), according to Professor Graham, has "effectively replaced" Illinois Supreme Court Rule 238(b) and 433. MICHAEL H. GRAHAM, GRAHAM'S HANDBOOK OF ILLINOIS EVIDENCE xxi-xxii (10th ed. 2010). Illinois Rule of Evidence 611(c) "is almost identical" to Federal Rule of Evidence 611(c), in effect prior to its stylistic amendment on December 1, 2011,

> except that FRE 611(c)'s "a witness identified with an adverse party" has been deleted because its inclusion would represent an expansion of Illinois law [and] would have altered the provisions of Supreme Court Rule 238(b), which allows questions as if under cross-examination of a "hostile or unwilling" witness, without any reference to "a witness identified with an adverse party."

Gino L. DiVito, *The Illinois Rules of Evidence: A Color-Coded Guide Containing the New Rules, the Committee's General and Specific Comments, a Comparison with the Federal Rules of Evidence, and Additional Commentary (Including the Federal Rules of Evidence as*

Amended Effective December 1, 2011) (Jan. 1, 2012), at 79, http://www.tdrlawfirm.com/assets/downloads/Illinois_Rules_of_Evidence_Color-Coded_Guide.pdf. Supreme Court Rule 238(b), which governs impeachment of witnesses in civil as well as criminal cases pursuant to Supreme Court Rule 433, states that a party may cross-examine a hostile or unwilling witness.

Relevant Illinois Supreme Court Rules

Illinois Supreme Court Rule 432

Rule 432. Opening Statements

Opening statements in criminal cases are governed by Rule 235. Renumbered October 1, 1971.

Illinois Supreme Court Rule 235

Rule 235. Opening Statements

As soon as the jury is impaneled the attorney for the plaintiff may make an opening statement. The attorney for the defendant may immediately follow with an opening statement. An opening statement may not be made at any other time, except in the discretion of the trial court.

Committee Comments

This is a revision of Rule 6.4 of the Uniform Rules for the Circuit Courts of Illinois.

Illinois Supreme Court Rule 433

Rule 433. Impeachment of Witnesses; Hostile Witnesses

The impeachment of witnesses and the examination of hostile witnesses in criminal cases is governed by Rule 238.

Adopted September 29, 1978, effective November 1, 1978; amended February 19, 1982, effective April 1, 1982.

Illinois Supreme Court Rule 238

Rule 238. Impeachment of Witnesses; Hostile Witnesses

(a) The credibility of a witness may be attacked by any party, including the party calling the witness.

(b) If the court determines that a witness is hostile or unwilling, the witness may be examined by the party calling the witness as if under cross-examination.

Amended February 19, 1982, effective April 1, 1982; amended April 11, 2001, effective immediately.

Prior Illinois Case Law

1. Opening Statement Should Outline Only Matters and Inferences Party Intends to Prove at Trial

People v. Smith, 141 Ill. 2d 40 (1990)

Defendant on trial for murder of a prison warden argued that the prosecutor in his opening statement improperly alleged that the defendant was in a gang and that the evidence would prove it. The evidence introduced against defendant, however, did not show that he was a gang member. The Illinois Supreme Court noted:

> An opening statement may include a discussion of the evidence and matters which may reasonably be inferred from the evidence. People v. Warmack, 83 Ill. 2d 112, 126 (1980). "Counsel may summarily outline what he expects the evidence admissible at trial will show

> [citations], but no statement may be made in opening which counsel does not intend to prove or cannot prove." Gillson v. Gulf, Mobile & Ohio R.R. Co. (1969), 42 Ill. 2d 193, 197 (1969); People v. Robinson, 163 Ill. App. 3d 754, 776 (1987). It is not, however, necessarily grounds for reversal that an opening statement refers to evidence which later proves to be inadmissible. Reversible error only occurs where the remarks are attributable to deliberate misconduct of the prosecutor and result in substantial prejudice to the defendant. Miller v. John, 208 Ill. 173, 177 (1904); People v. Robinson, 163 Ill. App. 3d 754, 776-77 (1987); People v. Trass, 136 Ill. App. 3d 455, 465 (1985).

The Supreme Court found that the opening statement remarks were not indicative of prosecutorial misconduct because the trial court excluded the evidence from consideration by the jury. The Supreme Court concluded, however, that the remarks taken together with other improper references to gang-related motive for the murder during closing argument warranted remand for a new trial.

2. It Is the Trial Court's Duty to Control the Proceedings to Safeguard Defendant's Right to a Fair Trial

People v. Bernette, 30 Ill. 2d 359 (1964)

The Illinois Supreme court noted that "[i]t is always the duty of a trial court to control proceedings to insure that an accused receives a fair and impartial trial." Here, the court found that highly prejudicial and irrelevant evidence admitted at trial should have been rejected on trial court's own motion. Prosecution, on direct examination of the victim's widow, elicited the fact that the deceased victim left behind young children. In closing argument the prosecutor again reiterated this fact. Defendant argued that the prosecution's argument was "irrelevant and highly prejudicial and served only to infuriate and inflame the jury against him." The Illinois Supreme Court agreed, noting that the evidence was irrelevant and so prejudicial that the trial court should have "refused it on its own motion."

3. Order of Proof Is Subject to the Broad Discretion of the Trial Court

People v. Waller, 67 Ill. 2d 381 (1977)

Defendant stabbed her husband to death and testified at her trial. She claimed that the stabbing was an accident. Prosecution called the husband's sister to testify on rebuttal about defendant's and her husband's prior argument to show that the killing was not accidental. The sister testified that during the prior argument she witnessed the defendant wielding a knife and threatening her husband with it. Defendant argued that the sister's testimony was improperly admitted in rebuttal and should have been introduced as part of the state's case-in-chief. The Illinois Supreme Court disagreed, noting that

> the order of proof in a criminal case is subject to the broad discretion of the trial court. The court may admit rebuttal evidence which would tend to 'explain, repel, contradict or disprove the evidence of the defendant,' even if such evidence also would have been admissible as part of the State's case in chief before the State closed. People v. Daugherty, 43 Ill. 2d 251, 255 (1969).

4. Scope of Cross-Examination Is Limited by Subject of Direct Examination and May Address Matters Affecting Witness Credibility

People v. Blue, 205 Ill. 2d 1 (2001)

The Illinois Supreme Court has noted that

> a criminal defendant's constitutional right to confrontation includes the right to cross-examine. Douglas v. Alabama, 380 U.S. 415 (1965). *** The scope of a defendant's cross-examination

> is limited to the subject of direct examination and '[a]ny permissible matter which affects the witness's credibility.' People v. Kliner, 185 Ill. 2d 81 (1998); *see* 1 J. Strong, McCormick on Evidence § 22, at 97 (5th ed. 1999). We have noted repeatedly that the court enjoys discretion to impose reasonable limits on such cross-examination to assuage concerns about harassment, prejudice, jury confusion, witness safety, or repetitive and irrelevant questioning (*see, e.g.*, People v. Frieberg, 147 Ill. 2d 326, 357 (1992)), but this discretionary authority arises only after the court has permitted sufficient cross-examination to satisfy the confrontation clause.

The Supreme Court further indicated that although denial of defendant's the right to effectively cross-examine a witness is very serious, the error may be deemed harmless after consideration of the following factors:

> the importance of the witness' testimony in the prosecution's case, whether the testimony was cumulative, the presence or absence of evidence corroborating or contradicting the testimony of the witness on material points, the extent of cross-examination otherwise permitted, and, of course, the overall strength of the prosecution's case." Delaware v. Van Arsdall, 475 U.S. 673, 684 (1986). Accord People v. Davis, 185 Ill. 2d 317, 338 (1998); People v. Young, 128 Ill. 2d 1, 43-44 (1989); *see also*, People v. Wilkerson, 87 Ill. 2d 151, 157 (1981) (confrontation clause case enumerating three approaches for measuring harmless error).

Here, defendant argued that the trial court erroneously prevented him from cross-examining three witnesses against him about their gang affiliation. Defendant sought to show that the witnesses belonged to the same rival gang as the murder victim and were testifying to retaliate for his death. The Illinois Supreme Court agreed, noting that the trial court's error was not harmless beyond a reasonable doubt because the witnesses' "gang affiliation was relevant to their credibility." The Supreme Court observed that the witnesses' testimony was not cumulative and was contradicted on some points by other witnesses. Moreover, although cross-examination of the witnesses elicited the fact that they were friends with the victim, it did not reveal the fact that they were all members of the same gang. Defendant was thus not able to clearly show the witnesses' bias. The Supreme Court concluded that even though the state's case was strong, the evidence against defendant was not overwhelming and that the defendant should have been allowed to cross-examine the witnesses to elicit evidence of bias.

> *See also* People v. Kitchen, 159 Ill. 2d 1 (1994) (finding that state properly showed defense witness' bias on cross-examination about the fact that the house where the witness lived was owned by the drug dealer who employed the defendant).

5. Cross-Examiner May Question Witness About Anything That Explains, Modifies, or Discredits Testimony Elicited on Direct Examination

People v. Barr, 51 Ill. 2d 50 (1972)

The cross-examiner may question the witness about any matter that explains, modifies, or discredits what he or she said on direct examination. Here, defendant was charged with armed robbery and rape after a group of youths pulled a woman out of her car, raped her and robbed her husband at gun point. A state witness testified on direct examination that he was acquainted with defendant and had seen him with a gun during the commission of the crime. During cross-examination, the witness conceded that he had been inside of the victim's car after the crime and that he had not spoken to the police about the crime. Defendant sought to show that the witness received leniency for testifying against him, but the state successfully objected to such testimony as being beyond the scope of direct examination. Defendant argued that he should have been able to cross-examine the witness to show his possible motive to testify falsely. The Illinois Supreme Court agreed, explaining that the witness

> had corroborated the identification testimony of the complainants, and inquiry into his possession of the victims' car and possible criminal charges arising therefrom was, in our judgment, permissible for purposes of impeachment. We accordingly hold that trial court's restriction on this inquiry was an abuse of discretion and prejudicial error.

6. Defendant Alleging on Direct Examination That Confession to an Uncharged Crime Was Coerced Opens Door to Inquiry into Uncharged Crime on Cross-Examination

People v. Kokoraleis, 132 Ill. 2d 235 (1989)

Defendant on trial for murder testified on direct examination that his confession to various murders was coerced. He explained that the police described other murders to him, beat him, threatened him, and that afterwards he gave oral and written statements confessing to the present murder and to several other murders. The state presented evidence of defendant's participation in two other similar murders. The trial court barred evidence of other murders. During cross-examination the state asked defendant whether the assistant state's attorney present during his confession informed him of various facts of a murder that was originally excluded by the trial court. The state presented gruesome details regarding this murder. Defendant argued that he had been prejudiced by the introduction of this evidence. The Supreme Court observed that defendant first spoke about the murder on direct examination when he explained how the police coerced his confession to various murders, including the one excluded by the trial court. The Supreme Court found that the defendant had opened the door to the introduction of the evidence about the uncharged and originally excluded murder.

7. Trial Court Has Discretion to Limit the Extent of Cross-Examination

People v. Klepper, 234 Ill. 2d 337 (2009)

Defendant was charged with disorderly conduct for falsely telling a police officer that his neighbor had attempted to hit him with his car. A witness disagreed with defendant's story and testified that she was watching from her kitchen window and that she saw defendant calling the police after his neighbor passed him by in his car without incident. The neighbor also denied that he had tried to run over the defendant in his vehicle. Trial court permitted brief testimony showing that defendant and his neighbor had an ongoing "feud," but did not allow defense counsel to extensively explore the topic on cross-examination. Defendant contended that he was deprived of his right to confront witnesses against him when the trial court limited his cross-examination of state witnesses about possible bias. He alleged that the witness who testified to seeing the incident from her kitchen window also had past disagreements with the defendant. Defendant contended that he should have had more opportunity to explore this bias. The Illinois Supreme Court disagreed and explained:

> The confrontation clause of the sixth amendment of the United States Constitution (U.S. Const., amend. VI) guarantees a defendant the right to cross-examine a witness against him for the purpose of showing the witness' bias, interest or motive to testify falsely. Davis v. Alaska, 415 U.S. 308 (1974); People v. Kirchner, 194 Ill. 2d 502, 536 (2000); People v. Harris, 123 Ill. 2d 113, 144 (1988). The exposure of a witness' motivation is an important function of the constitutionally protected right of cross-examination. Greene v. McElroy, 360 U.S. 474 (1959); *Harris*, 123 Ill. 2d at 144. However, a trial judge may impose limits on a defense counsel's inquiry into the potential bias of a prosecution witness without offending defendant's sixth amendment right. Delaware v. Van Arsdall, 475 U.S. 673, 679 (1986); *Harris*, 123 Ill. 2d at 144. A trial judge retains wide latitude to impose reasonable limits based on concerns about harassment, prejudice, confusion of the issues, the witness' safety, or interrogation that is repetitive or of little relevance. *Delaware v. Van Arsdall*, 475 U.S. at 679; *Harris*, 123 Ill. 2d at 144. As the United States Supreme Court observed in Delaware v. Fensterer, 474 U.S. 15, 20

> (1985), 'the Confrontation Clause guarantees an opportunity for effective cross-examination, not cross-examination that is effective in whatever way, and to whatever extent, the defense might wish.' *Harris*, 123 Ill. 2d at 144, quoting *Fensterer*, 474 U.S. at 20. *** [T]he question in each case must finally be whether defendant's inability to make the inquiry created a substantial danger of prejudice by depriving him of the ability to test the truth of the witness's direct testimony. *** Thus, if a review of the entire record reveals that the fact-finder has been made aware of adequate factors concerning relevant areas of impeachment of a witness, no constitutional question arises merely because the defendant has been prohibited on cross-examination from pursuing other areas of inquiry. *Harris*, 123 Ill. 2d at 145.

The Supreme Court found that in this case the record showed that the fact finder was well-informed about any witness bias and that any potential bias was sufficiently revealed on cross-examination and during defendant's own testimony. Additionally, a police officer who had previously responded to incidents between defendant and his neighbor testified about his observations. The Supreme Court concluded that any bias was well-explored and that the trial court "acted within its wide latitude in limiting cross-examination."

8. Defendant's Right to Cross-Examination Is Not Violated by Admitting Witness' Out-of-Court Statement As Long As Witness Testifies and Is Subject to Cross-Examination
People v. Flores, 128 Ill. 2d 66 (1989)

Defendant was charged with armed robbery and murder. A witness for the prosecution testified at trial under a grant of immunity. On direct examination the witness testified that he could not remember speaking with the defendant about the murder. Moreover, while the witness remembered testifying before a grand jury, he could not recall what he testified about. Prosecution gave the witness a transcript of the grand jury proceedings to refresh his memory. Defendant argued that the witness' loss of memory deprived the defendant from cross-examining him about his grand jury testimony and violated his right to confrontation. The Supreme Court disagreed, explaining that

> [t]he confrontation clause is not violated by admitting a declarant's out-of-court statements, as long as the declarant is testifying as a witness and subject to full and effective cross-examination. Delaware v. Fensterer, 474 U.S. 15, 20 (1985); California v. Green, 399 U.S. 149, 158 (1970). Contrary to the defendant's assertions, a gap in the witness' recollection concerning the content of a prior statement does not necessarily preclude an opportunity for effective cross-examination.

Accordingly, the Supreme Court reasoned that a witness' inability to recall prior out-of-court statements does not violate the defendant's right to confrontation so long as the witness is physically in court, available for cross-examination, and answers the questions asked. The Supreme Court referred to United States v. Owens, 484 U.S. 554 (1988), where the court noted that the opportunity to effectively cross-examine a witness:

> is not denied when a witness testifies as to his current belief but is unable to recollect the reason for that belief. It is sufficient that the defendant has the opportunity to bring out such matters as the witness's bias, his lack of care and attentiveness, his poor eyesight, and even (what is often a prime objective of cross-examination, *see* 3A J. WIGMORE, EVIDENCE § 995, pp. 931-932 (J. Chadbourn rev. 1970)) the very fact that he has a bad memory.

See also People v. Kirchner, 194 Ill. 2d 502 (2000) (finding no violation of defendant's sixth amendment right to confrontation where trial court refused to order a state witness to undergo a psychological and psychiatric evaluation because defendant had sufficient opportunity to impeach witness with relevant mental health records).

9. Defendant Should Be Allowed Widest Latitude in Cross-Examination of a Witness to Establish Bias

People v. Mason, 28 Ill. 2d 396 (1963)

Defendant was charged with the sale of a controlled substance. At trial, two police officers who arrested him pursuant to an informant's tip testified. The informant did not testify. On cross-examination of one of the officers, defense counsel asked him whether he had recently been suspended from acting as a police officer and whether he was a defendant in an ongoing criminal case. State objected and court sustained the objection. Defendant argued that the trial court improperly limited his cross-examination of the officer. The Illinois Supreme Court agreed, noting that the indictment of the officer who arrested the defendant and was one of two witnesses testifying against him was relevant to show his bias or prejudice against defendant. Although cross-examination is usually limited to matters introduced by direct examination, the cross-examiner may go beyond the scope of direct examination to impeach the witness. The Supreme Court explained:

> The scope of cross-examination is generally within the trial court's discretion. However, the widest latitude should generally be allowed the defendant in cross-examination for the purpose of establishing bias. People v. Naujokas, 25 Ill. 2d 32 (1962). In the present case the trial court cut off all inquiry on subjects with respect to which the defense was entitled to a reasonable cross-examination. This was an abuse of discretion and prejudicial error.

For additional case law governing an accused's right to confrontation of witnesses, see Chapter 7.

10. Prosecution's Unsupported Persistent Insinuations of Defendant's Misconduct on Cross-Examination of Defense Witnesses and Defendant Deny Accused a Fair Trial

People v. Nuccio, 43 Ill. 2d 375 (1969)

Defendant, a former police officer, was on trial for the murder of a young victim who ran away from the officer after a restaurant owner called the police about a disturbance at his restaurant. Two state witnesses testified that the defendant often came to the restaurant and intimidated the youths who gathered there. On cross-examination of defendant and various defense witnesses the state insinuated that defendant engaged in a pattern of misconduct, including beating the youths and threatening the life of the victim as well as allegations of sexual misconduct with the victim's girlfriend. All defense witnesses including the defendant denied such allegations. State subsequently failed to call rebuttal witnesses, although many of them were in the courtroom and were available. The Illinois Supreme Court noted that the improper questioning by the state showed "intent on the part of the prosecution to prejudice defendant in the eyes of the court." While leading questions are proper, a cross-examiner should not inject unsupported insinuations into the questioning process. The cross-examiner should not ask questions unless he or she is able and ready to produce evidence to contradict a denial from the witness. The Supreme Court further observed that the evidence of guilt in this case was not overwhelming and depended largely on witness credibility and testimony. In addition,

> there appear in the record substantial numbers of unsupported insinuations which, if considered, could have seriously impeached the credibility of the defendant and his witnesses, and there is no indication of the court's awareness of this impropriety even though it is brought to his attention, it is our opinion that justice and fundamental fairness demand that the defendant be afforded a new trial free from such prejudicial misconduct.

But see People v. Del Vecchio, 105 Ill. 2d 414 (1985) (finding no reversible error for prosecutor's improper remarks where evidence of defendant's guilt was overwhelming).

11. Unresponsive Answer on Cross-Examination Should Generally Be Stricken
People v. Burris, 49 Ill. 2d 98 (1971)

Defendant was on trial for murder. During cross-examination of the victim's son, defense counsel asked him to limit his answer to "what he had heard," and not to "what he had seen." The witness responded that the counsel was attempting to "twist the questions around" and that counsel should instead ask him directly about anything he wanted to know. Defense counsel subsequently requested the court to instruct the jury that the witness' remarks were "unfair, harmful, prejudicial and detrimental" to the defendant. The trial court declined to so instruct the jury. The Illinois Supreme Court upheld the trial court's decision and noted that:

> Generally, if a witness on cross-examination gives an answer not responsive to a question on motion the unresponsive portion will be stricken. (6 CALLAGHAN'S ILLINOIS EVIDENCE, sec. 17.08.) However, this outburst was not an answer to a question, nor a statement concerning anything involved in the trial. It can best be described as an argument between the witness and counsel.

12. Leading Questions Are Generally Improper on Direct Examination of a Witness
People v. Schladweiler, 315 Ill. 553 (1925)

The Illinois Supreme Court considered whether the state improperly asked minor witnesses leading questions. The Supreme Court noted that

> [t]he test of a leading question is whether it suggests the answer thereto by putting into the mind of the witness the words or thought of such answer. Leading questions, to be incompetent, must refer to material matters, and occur where no necessity for them appears. Whether or not such necessity exists is a matter resting largely in the discretion of the trial court, an abuse of which discretion will amount to prejudicial error. Questions merely directing the attention of the witness to the subject-matter of the inquiry are not suggestive or leading in any proper sense. People v. Elliott, 272 Ill. 592 (1916).

The Supreme Court observed that although some of the questions may have been leading, during the material portions of the testimony the minor witnesses "testified from their recollection" about what happened and not by reason of the questioning by the state.

13. Trial Court May in Its Discretion Permit Leading Questions During Direct Examination of an Unresponsive Witness
People v. Merritt, 367 Ill. 521 (1937)

Defendant argued that the trial court improperly allowed the state to ask leading questions of its witness. The witness was reluctant and unresponsive. The Illinois Supreme Court noted that

> [t]he propriety of permitting leading questions is a matter within the sound discretion of the court, and is not a ground for reversal unless there has been an abuse of the discretion, resulting in substantial injury. Maguire v. People, 219 Ill. 16 (1905); People v. Brown, 273 Ill. 169 (1916).

Here, the Supreme Court found that the trial court did not abuse its discretion by allowing leading questions because the topics stated in unresponsive manner were later elicited on cross-examination of other witnesses.

14. Scope of Redirect Examination Is Within Trial Court's Discretion and Is Designed to Remove Unfavorable Inferences Raised by Cross-Examination

People v. Harris, 123 Ill. 2d 113 (1988)

The scope of redirect examination is limited to matters raised on cross-examination. It is not to be used as a review of the witness' direct examination. A party may examine its witness to remove unfavorable impressions or inferences created by the cross-examination.

Here, imprisoned defendants were charged with the murder and conspiracy to commit murder of a fellow inmate who was a member of a rival gang. Defendants argued that the trial court erred in admitting the entire record of a witness' grand jury testimony during the state's redirect examination of the witness. The witness testified on direct examination that he saw one of the defendants strike the victim with a baseball bat. On cross-examination defense counsel impeached the witness with two prior inconsistent statements concerning whether the defendant was wearing gloves and where he disposed of the bat. The state introduced the witness' entire grand jury testimony on redirect examination to rehabilitate his credibility.

Defendants argued that admissibility of the grand jury testimony as a prior consistent statement was erroneous. Defendants claimed that because the witness' good-time credits were revoked before the victim was murdered, the witness sought to restore his good-time credits by testifying against defendants. Defendants thus contended that because the witness' motive to fabricate already existed at the time he gave the grand jury testimony, the testimony could not be admitted as a prior consistent statement. The Illinois Supreme Court disagreed, observing that the witness consistently denied that he had made a deal with the prosecution for the restoration of his good-time credit in exchange for his testimony. Moreover, defendants failed to show through independent evidence that such a deal existed. The Supreme Court concluded that admissibility of the grand jury testimony on redirect examination was proper under the circumstances.

Defendants further argued that admissibility of the entire grand jury testimony on redirect was improper to rehabilitate the witness on only two matters. The Supreme Court agreed, explaining that admissibility of the entire record "improperly bolstered [the witness'] trial testimony." The Supreme Court nevertheless concluded that under the totality of circumstances the error was harmless, noting that

> in light of defense counsel's extensive cross-examination and impeachment of [the witness'] credibility in several important areas, we find it unlikely that the introduction of the entire testimony could have affected the jury's verdict. The scope of redirect examination lies within the sound discretion of the trial court, and we will not reverse the trial court's decision unless it is a clear abuse of discretion resulting in manifest prejudice to the defendant. People v. Cowper, 145 Ill. App. 3d 1074, 1083-84 (2d Dist. 1986). We cannot say that the trial court's decision allowing the State to read the entire transcript resulted in reversible error.

For other decisions discussing this topic, see:

People v. Chambers, 179 Ill. App. 3d 565 (2d Dist. 1989) (concluding that state improperly elicited evidence on redirect examination of alleged threats made by defendant to state witness as this testimony was irrelevant and unfairly prejudicial to defendant).

People v. Davis, 92 Ill. App. 3d 426 (3d Dist. 1981) (finding state's redirect examination eliciting evidence of threats against state witness made by co-defendant proper after defendant testified and suggested that witness who testified about threats had improper motives or fabricated evidence).

15. Questioning on Re-Cross-Examination Is Limited to the Scope of the Redirect Examination
People v. Franklin, 135 Ill. 2d 78 (1990)

Defendant was charged with murder. At trial, the victim's grandfather testified that on the day of the murder he saw his grandson enter a vehicle driven by the defendant. The grandfather noted that he had seen the defendant in his neighborhood on several occasions prior to the murder. On cross-examination the grandfather conceded that on the day of the murder he saw the front of defendant's face, but that he saw it for "[n]o more than a second." At a preliminary hearing, however, the grandfather had testified that he saw the back of defendant's head and then a side of his face. Defendant argued that the trial court erred in not permitting him to impeach the grandfather on recross-examination with his previous failure to inform the police that he had encountered defendant on other occasions prior to the murder.

The Illinois Supreme Court disagreed, noting that defendant had every opportunity to question the witness on cross-examination and had sufficiently made the jury aware of any inconsistencies in his testimony. Moreover, defense counsel's question regarding the grandfather's omission was "outside the scope of redirect examination." The Supreme Court explained:

> As a general rule cross-examination is limited to the scope of the direct examination. People v. Matthews, 18 Ill. 2d 164, 173 (1959). Circumstances, however, may be developed on cross-examination that lie 'within the knowledge of the witness which explain, qualify, discredit or destroy his direct testimony,' even though that material may not have been raised on direct examination. People v. Williams, 66 Ill. 2d 478, 486, (1977), quoting S. GARD, ILLINOIS EVIDENCE MANUAL R. 471 (1963). Recross-examination, in contrast, is limited to responding to the testimony brought out on redirect examination. People v. Kline, 92 Ill. 2d 490, 503 (1982). *See also* R. RUEBNER, ILLINOIS CRIMINAL TRIAL EVIDENCE ch. 4, at 97 (1986); M. GRAHAM, CLEARY & GRAHAM'S HANDBOOK OF ILLINOIS EVIDENCE § 611.12, at 395-97 (4th ed. 1984).

See also People v. Kline, 92 Ill. 2d 490 (1982) (finding state objection to defense counsel's question about victim's ownership of a camera on re-cross-examination proper and not an attempt to conceal the fact that no camera was missing because the question exceeded the scope of redirect examination).

16. State May Argue Only Facts and Legitimate Inferences Drawn from the Evidence in Its Closing Argument
People v. Smith, 141 Ill. 2d 40 (1990)

State, in its closing argument at a trial for the murder of a prison warden, contended that the defendant was a gang member who killed the warden because he was strongly opposed to gang activity in the prison. State only introduced general evidence of gang activity in the prisons and failed to directly tie the defendant to such activity. The Illinois Supreme Court observed that the state failed to show evidence at trial that would support the allegation that defendant was a member of a gang. The Supreme Court noted:

> State is permitted wide latitude in closing argument and may argue to the jury facts and legitimate inferences drawn from the evidence. People v. Turner, 128 Ill. 2d 540, 560 (1989); People v. Cisewski, 118 Ill. 2d 163, 175 (1987); People v. Williams, 40 Ill. 2d 522, 530 (1968). It is, however, improper for the prosecutor to argue assumptions or facts not based upon evidence in the case or to present to the jury what amounts to his own testimony. People v. Beier, 29 Ill. 2d 511, 517 (1963); People v. Rothe, 358 Ill. 52, 56 (1934). Furthermore, it is

> improper for the prosecutor to do or say anything in argument the only effect of which will be to inflame the passion or arouse the prejudice of the jury against the defendant, without throwing any light on the question for decision. People v. Dukes, 12 Ill. 2d 334, 342-43 (1957). Improper remarks will not merit reversal unless they result in substantial prejudice to the defendant, considering the context of the language used, its relationship to the evidence, and its effect on the defendant's rights to a fair and impartial trial. People v. Thompkins, 121 Ill. 2d 401, 445 (1988); People v. Pittman, 93 Ill. 2d 169, 176 (1982); People v. Bryant, 94 Ill. 2d 514 (1983).

The Supreme Court concluded that the state's remarks during the closing argument, together with similarly improper remarks made during the opening statements and at trial, warranted a new trial.

17. Prosecutor May Not Argue in Closing Argument That Police Officer's Testimony Should Be Believed Because he Would Not Jeopardize His Job by Lying Where No Evidence Supporting the Inference Was Introduced at Trial

People v. Adams, 2012 IL 111168

Defendant was charged with possession of a controlled substance. At trial, the arresting officers testified that they found the drugs in one of defendant's pockets. Defendant, however, testified that the drugs were found on the ground near him and that he told the police at the time of the arrest that he had not dropped any drugs. In its closing argument, the state argued that if the jury believed the defendant, then it also had "to believe that [the arresting officer was] risking his credibility, his job, and his freedom over 0.8 grams of cocaine." The Illinois Supreme Court explained that

> it is improper for a prosecutor to argue assumptions or facts not based upon evidence in the case (see, e.g., People v. Smith, 141 Ill. 2d 40, 60 (1990)). [. . .]
>
> ***
>
> Whether a prosecutor may properly make the statements at issue here has divided our appellate court. Compare, e.g., People v. Fields, 258 Ill. App. 3d 912, 920-21 (1994) (improper), with People v. Bennett, 304 Ill. App. 3d 69, 71-72 (1999) (proper). However, the weight of authority in other jurisdictions, particularly in the federal courts, holds that such comments are improper. See, e.g., United States v. Pungitore, 910 F.2d 1084, 1125 (3d Cir. 1990); United States v. Gallardo-Trapero, 185 F.3d 307, 319 (5th Cir. 1999); United States v. Martinez, 981 F.2d 867, 871 (6th Cir. 1992); United States v. Swiatek, 819 F.2d 721, 731 (7th Cir. 1987); United States v. McMath, 559 F.3d 657, 668 (7th Cir. 2009); United States v. Weatherspoon, 410 F.3d 1142, 1146 (9th Cir. 2005); United States v. Boyd, 54 F.3d 868, 870 (D.C. Cir. 1995); *see also, e.g.*, State v. Mussey, 893 A.2d 701, 705 (N.H. 2006); Spain v. State, 872 A.2d 25, 31 (Md. 2005); City of Williston v. Hegstad, 562 N.W.2d 91, 94-95 (N.D. 1997).
>
> ***
>
> We agree with the majority view. The prosecutor's comments in this case were impermissible speculation, as no evidence was introduced at trial from which it could be inferred that the testifying officers would risk their careers if they testified falsely. See, e.g., *Gallardo-Trapero*, 185 F.3d at 320 (prosecutor's argument that agents would not lie because it would place their careers at risk was improper because it referred to evidence not in the record); *Martinez*, 981 F.2d at 871 (same); *Pungitore*, 910 F.2d at 1125 (holding argument improper where there was "no evidence backing the prosecutor's comments that the U .S. Attorneys and law enforcement officers could not have behaved as unscrupulously as defense counsel alleged they did without violating their oaths of office and jeopardizing their careers"). Further, "[b]y invoking unspecified, but assumed, punitive consequences or sanctions that might result if a police

> officer testifies falsely, a prosecutor's arguments imply that a police officer has a greater reason to testify truthfully than any other witness with a different type of job" (*Spain*, 872 A.2d at 32), thus violating the principle that "a prosecutor may not argue that a witness is more credible because of his status as a police officer" (People v. Clark, 186 Ill. App. 3d 109, 115-16 (1989). *See also, e.g.*, *Weatherspoon*, 410 F.3d at 1146 (comments such as those at issue here constituted improper vouching because they "clearly urged that the existence of legal and professional repercussions served to ensure the credibility of the officers' testimony"). For these reasons, we hold [that] the prosecutor's remarks were improper.

Rule 612. Writing Used to Refresh Memory

If a witness uses a writing to refresh memory for the purpose of testifying, either—

(1) while testifying, or

(2) before testifying, an adverse party is entitled to have the writing produced at the hearing, to inspect it, to cross-examine the witness thereon, and to introduce in evidence for the purpose of impeachment those portions which relate to the testimony of the witness. If it is claimed that the writing contains matters not related to the subject matter of the testimony the court shall examine the writing *in camera*, excise any portions not so related, and order delivery of the remainder to the party entitled thereto. Any portion withheld over objections shall be preserved and made available to the appellate court in the event of an appeal. If a writing is not produced or delivered pursuant to order under this rule, the court shall make any order justice requires, except that in criminal cases when the prosecution elects not to comply, the order shall be one striking the testimony or, if the court in its discretion determines that the interests of justice so require, declaring a mistrial.

Adopted September 27, 2010, eff. January 1, 2011.

Author's Commentary

Illinois Rule of Evidence 612 is similar to Federal Rule of Evidence 612, in effect prior to its stylistic amendment on December 1, 2011, but makes it clear that in Illinois a writing used to refresh a witness' memory may be introduced only for the limited purpose of impeachment. *See* Gino L. DiVito, *The Illinois Rules of Evidence: A Color-Coded Guide Containing the New Rules, the Committee's General and Specific Comments, a Comparison with the Federal Rules of Evidence, and Additional Commentary* (*Including the Federal Rules of Evidence as Amended Effective December 1, 2011*) (Jan. 1, 2012), at 80-81, http://www.tdrlawfirm.com/assets/downloads/Illinois_Rules_of_Evidence_Color-Coded_Guide.pdf. Illinois Rule of Evidence 612, unlike the Federal Rule of Evidence 612, does not require a court to make a preliminary determination that "justice requires the party" to have the option of using a writing to refresh memory before testifying. *Id.* at 80-81.

Prior Illinois Case Law

1. Party May Refresh a Witness' Recollection by Showing the Witness a Document Before or During Testimony

People v. Griswold, 405 Ill. 533 (1950)

Defendant was on trial for killing his wife. After he was arrested, a police officer questioned the defendant and dictated a memorandum of what defendant had said to a court reporter. The officer later testified as a rebuttal witness at defendant's trial. Before testifying, the officer read over the memorandum to refresh his memory. The Illinois Supreme Court upheld this practice, explaining that

> [t]he rule in this State permits a witness to testify only to facts within his knowledge and recollection. He is allowed to refresh and assist his memory by the use of a written instrument, memorandum, or entry in a book. The writing need not be made by the witness himself, and it need not be an original writing; he need only inspect what is recorded, so he can speak to the facts from his own recollection.

2. Party Using a Writing to Refresh a Witness' Memory Must Lay Proper Foundation by Showing That Witness Has No Recollection

People v. Shatner, 174 Ill. 2d 133 (1996)

Defendant was convicted of first degree murder, armed robbery and arson. A witness at trial testified that she could not remember making a particular statement to a detective investigating the crime. Defense counsel sought to refresh her memory by showing her a detective's report about her statements pertaining to that evening that would show she had made a prior inconsistent statement. State objected and the trial court sustained the objection. Defendant contended that the trial court violated his right to confront witnesses against him. The Illinois Supreme Court disagreed, noting that the defendant, rather than refreshing the witness' recollection with the report, was attempting to impeach her with the report. The Supreme Court observed that defendant could only impeach the witness via the detective's testimony at trial. Moreover, even if defendant was only attempting to refresh the witness' recollection with the report, he failed to lay proper foundation. The Supreme Court stated that although

> a police report may be used to refresh recollection[, . . .] it is fundamental that a witness' memory can be refreshed only after it has been established that the witness has no memory concerning the facts in question. [citation omitted] If a witness has testified that his memory is exhausted, a written memorandum may be used to refresh and assist his memory, but the manner and mode of refreshing a witness' memory rests within the discretion of the trial court.

Here, the witness only testified that she could not remember making one statement to the detective. The Supreme Court found that defendant failed to show that witness could remember nothing about the events that took place the night before the murder and was thus not entitled to refresh the witness' recollection with the report.

Rule 613. Prior Statements of Witnesses

(a) Examining Witness Concerning Prior Statement. In examining a witness concerning a prior statement made by the witness, whether written or not, the statement need not be shown nor its contents disclosed to the witness at that time, but on request the same shall be shown or disclosed to opposing counsel.

(b) Extrinsic Evidence of Prior Inconsistent Statement of Witness. Extrinsic evidence of a prior inconsistent statement by a witness is not admissible unless the witness is first afforded an opportunity to explain or deny the same and the opposing party is afforded an opportunity to interrogate the witness thereon, or the interests of justice otherwise require. This provision does not apply to admissions of a party-opponent as defined in Rule 801(d)(2).

Adopted September 27, 2010, eff. January 1, 2011.

Committee Commentary

(3) Modernization: Where there was no conflict with statutes or recent Illinois Supreme Court or Illinois Appellate Court decisions, and where it was determined to be beneficial and uniformly or almost uniformly accepted elsewhere, the Committee incorporated into the Illinois Rules of Evidence uncontroversial developments with respect to the law of evidence as reflected in the Federal Rules of Evidence and the 44 surveyed jurisdictions. [One of t]he 14 instances of modernization of note [is] as follows: ***

> **(4) Rule 613(a).** Examining Witness Concerning Prior Statement. Rule 613(a) provides that a prior inconsistent statement need not be shown to a witness prior to cross-examination thereon. Illinois Central Railroad v. Wade, 206 Ill. 523, 69 N.E. 565 (1903), was to the contrary.
>
> ILL. R. EVID. Committee Commentary § 3, pg. 2.

AUTHOR'S COMMENTARY

Illinois Rule of Evidence 613 has changed the Illinois common law with respect to confronting a witness with a prior inconsistent statement. *See* MICHAEL H. GRAHAM, GRAHAM'S HANDBOOK OF ILLINOIS EVIDENCE § 613.1 (10th ed. 2010). The requirement that a party examining a witness disclose evidence of the witness' prior inconsistent statement before questioning the witness about its substance "has not been followed by trial courts in actual practice" and has been "formally discarded in favor of surprise" by Rule 613(a). GRAHAM at § 613.1. Justice DiVito opines that the new rule

> arguably represents a change in Illinois law (but not necessarily in practice), because in Illinois Central Railroad Co. v. Wade, 206 Ill. 523 (1903), the supreme court required that written statements be shown to the cross-examined witness. [. . .] Contrary to the contention that the added language represents a change in Illinois law, however, note that IRE 613(a) addresses merely the method of questioning a witness about a prior statement, while IRE 613(b) addresses the prerequisites for admitting the extrinsic evidence in order to complete the impeachment of the witness, which includes affording the witness an opportunity to explain or deny the prior statement, and affording the opposing party an opportunity to question the witness about it.

Gino L. DiVito, *The Illinois Rules of Evidence: A Color-Coded Guide Containing the New Rules, the Committee's General and Specific Comments, a Comparison with the Federal Rules of Evidence, and Additional Commentary* (*Including the Federal Rules of Evidence as Amended Effective December 1, 2011*) (Jan. 1, 2012), at 81-82, http://www.tdrlawfirm.com/assets/downloads/Illinois_Rules_of_Evidence_Color-Coded_Guide.pdf. The examining party must, however, disclose the statement to the opposing counsel if requested to do so pursuant to Rule 613(a).

PRIOR ILLINOIS CASE LAW

1. Historically a Party Seeking to Impeach Witness with a Prior Inconsistent Statement Was Required to Disclose Its Contents to the Witness

Illinois Cent. R. Co. v. Wade, 206 Ill. 523 (1903)

An employee of a bridge-building company was injured on the job. He brought suit alleging lack of due care exercised by his employer. A witness testifying for defense stated that the employer was at fault. To impeach the witness, defendant's counsel showed the witness previous statement made and signed by him concluding that plaintiff could have avoided the accident. The witness admitted that he had signed the statement but denied that it was correct in its entirety. Defendant sought to enter the document containing the statement into evidence. The trial court refused, explaining that the witness did not deny making the prior statement and no further proof was necessary. The Illinois Supreme Court disagreed with the trial court's ruling, noting that the trial court confused "the rule as to the foundation to be laid to authorize the admission of oral impeaching statements of a witness with the foundation necessary to justify the offer to introduce contradictory statements made in writing and signed by the witness." The Supreme Court explained that prior contradictory out-of-court statements of a witness, whether made orally or in writing, are admissible for purposes of impeachment and not as substantive evidence. Specifically, the Supreme Court further clarified that:

> When it is desired to impeach a witness by proof of oral statements made by him out of court contradictory upon a material point of his testimony given from the witness stand, it is requisite that a foundation for the introduction of such oral statements be made by asking the witness if he did not, at a given time and place, in the presence of specified persons, make the supposed contradictory statements. But where the supposed contradictory statements were reduced to writing by the witness, or signed by him, a sufficient foundation for the introduction of the writing is laid by showing the paper to the witness, allowing him to inspect it and to read it if he desires, and proving by him or others that the signature thereto is his genuine signature. Having laid the foundation for the introduction of the writings as impeaching testimony, the proper practice (as was the course pursued by counsel for the appellate company in the present case) was to offer the writings in evidence with the other testimony in the same behalf.

2. Party May Impeach a Witness by Prior Inconsistent Statements and Material Omissions after Substantial Compliance with Foundation Requirements
People v. Henry, 47 Ill. 2d 312 (1970)

When a witness' testimony is inconsistent with a prior out-of-court statement, or if in a witness' trial testimony there is a material omission of matters contained in the witness' prior out-of-court statement, evidence of the prior statement and the fact of such omission are admissible to impeach the credibility of the witness. The Illinois Supreme Court explained:

> Where, as here, it is claimed there has been a material omission of matters contained in a prior statement from later testimony it is logical that the fact of such omission should be admissible. Wigmore says: 'A failure to assert a fact, when it would have been natural to assert it, amounts in effect to an assertion of the nonexistence of the fact.' [Citations omitted].

Impeachment by omission is only permitted where the omission is of such a character that its inclusion would be expected and its omission unexpected. Impeachment via prior inconsistent statement does not require literal inconsistency between the witness' testimony and his or her prior statement. Before a prior inconsistent statement can be used to impeach a witness, a proper foundation must be laid during the cross-examination of the witness. The foundation is established if the witness is informed of the time, place, and circumstances of the statement, the persons present, and the substance of the prior statement. The purpose of the foundation requirement is to avoid surprise and to provide the witness an opportunity to explain the prior statement. The Illinois Supreme Court found that substantial compliance with the rule is sufficient, and rigidity in establishing a proper foundation for a prior inconsistent statement is not demanded. Here, the defendant failed to meet the conventional requirements to establish foundation for impeachment through evidence of prior inconsistent statements. The Supreme Court found, however, that the reasons behind establishing foundation were satisfied and the court concluded that defendant should have been allowed to impeach the credibility of a key witness.

For other decisions discussing this topic, see:

People v. Cobb, 97 Ill. 2d 465 (1983) (finding that where state witness testified she never told anyone that she expected a reward for testifying for the prosecution, defense should have been able to question impeaching witness about a contrary statement made to her by the state witness).

People v. Smith, 78 Ill. 2d 298 (1980) (concluding that a witness may not be impeached by a prior inconsistent statement if the foundation laid is too general in nature).

3. Proper Foundation Must Be Laid to Impeach Identification Witness with Sketch of a Suspect

People v. Yates, 98 Ill. 2d 502 (1983)

The Illinois Supreme Court found that proper foundation was laid to impeach an identification witness with a composite sketch of a suspect. The police artist unequivocally testified that the sketch was prepared at the direction of the witness and that after viewing the completed sketch, the witness adopted it as an accurate portrayal of the suspect, despite a later denial by the identifying witness that he had agreed to its accuracy.

See also People v. Nance, 54 Ill. App. 3d 109 (5th Dist. 1977) (laying adequate foundation of written prior inconsistent statement when witness admits signing the writing and does not repudiate its accuracy; if witness repudiates accuracy or denies knowledge, testimony from a person who was present when the statement was made is necessary).

4. Generally, a Prior Inconsistent Statement of a Witness May Be Used for Impeachment but Not as Substantive Evidence

People v. Collins, 49 Ill. 2d 179 (1971)

Except in instances where a prior inconsistent statement meets certain requirements, a prior inconsistent statement of a witness may only be used for impeachment and may not be used as substantive evidence. Here, the Illinois Supreme Court stated:

> It has been the rule in this State, as it has been the rule generally in this country, that only the testimony given by the witness upon oath in court, subject to cross examination, is to be considered as substantive evidence, and that a prior contradictory statement of a witness is received in evidence only for the purpose of impeaching the credibility of the witness.

5. Prior Statements Need Not Completely Contradict the Witness' Testimony for Impeachment Purposes but Must Relate to a Material Issue

People v. Henry, 47 Ill. 2d 312 (1970)

Two defendants were convicted of murder in the beating death of a victim because they suspected he was an FBI agent. Defendants sought to impeach the testimony of a key state witness. The witness testified on cross-examination that the police made no promises to her in exchange for her testimony. Defendants intended to introduce two witnesses who had a prior conversation with the state witness during which the state witness told them that she only testified because police told her that they would "hold her" in custody if she did not give them a statement. Moreover, the witnesses would testify as to other statements of the state witness where she admitted that police promised her that is she "played ball with them, they would play ball with her." The Illinois Supreme Court found that although "no prior inconsistent statement in the usual sense was involved, [. . .] inconsistency in the literal sense is not always required for impeachment." The Supreme Court observed that it would have been natural for the state witness to mention the alleged coercion and that because her credibility was "highly important, even pivotal question," the defendants should have had an opportunity to impeach her with the prior inconsistent statement.

6. Defendant May Not Impeach a Sex Crime Victim with Evidence Excluded by the Rape Shield Statute

People v. Santos, 211 Ill. 2d 395 (2004)

A defendant in a criminal sexual assault prosecution may not impeach the victim by using evidence which is otherwise excluded by the rape shield statute in 725 ILCS 5/115-7. Here, the Illinois Supreme Court reversed and remanded the appellate court's finding that the defendant could use two inconsistent out-of-court statements to impeach the victim's credibility in a rape trial. The defendant sought to admit these two conflicting statements, made when the victim reported the crime, to show that the victim had lied, thereby casting doubt on everything she had stated pertaining to the events between her and the defendant. During the collection of "rape kit samples," the victim stated to hospital personnel that she had not engaged in other sexual activity in the preceding 72 hours of the alleged rape. However, upon discovery via DNA testing that the semen collected was not that of the defendant, the victim admitted that she had sexual intercourse with someone else on the day of the crime. The state argued that reference to a victim's past sexual activity was prohibited by the Illinois rape shield law, and the Illinois Supreme Court agreed. The court held that the two inconsistent statements disclosed the victim's "prior sexual activity" and were protected from disclosure under the rape shield statute regardless whether the statements were being used as impeachment evidence rather than character evidence. Since neither exception to the rape shield statute applied here, the court reversed the appellate court on this point and remanded for a new trial. Chief Justice McMorrow entered a strong dissent from the majority's reasoning, stating that:

> under the specific facts presented, the majority errs in mechanically applying the provisions of the rape shield statute, thereby excluding evidence which is relevant and necessary to defendant's ability to defend against the charges brought against him . . . . [T]he majority too broadly construes the provisions of the rape shield statute at the expense of too narrowly construing the constitutional rights of the defendant.

7. Even Though Witness Admits to Making Prior Inconsistent Statement, His or Her Prior Statement May Be Introduced into Evidence

People v. Bradford, 106 Ill. 2d 492 (1985)

Defendant on trial for indecent liberties with a child argued that the state improperly used the victim's prior inconsistent statements as substantive evidence of his guilt. The victim testified that defendant did not have intercourse with her but admitted making contradictory statement to department of criminal investigations agents that she had intercourse with him. The Illinois Supreme Court noted that "[t]he prosecution was not precluded here from introducing the prior inconsistent statements even though [the victim] had admitted making the statements. The State may choose to have the impeaching statements introduced into evidence." citing People v. Williams, 22 Ill. 2d 498 (1961).

8. If Witness Denies or Cannot Recall Making of the Prior Inconsistent Statement, Cross-Examiner Must Prove That the Statement Was Made

People v. Moore, 54 Ill. 2d 33 (1973)

Murder defendant gave testimony on direct examination that was inconsistent with his prior oral statements to the police. State inquired whether defendant had made the prior statements and defendant denied making such statements. State next introduced defendant's prior inconsistent statements through the testimony of a police officer. Defendant argued that introduction of the statements violated his rights as they constituted "vicious insinuations of criminal misconduct." The Illinois Supreme Court found, however, that

> [a] familiar mode of impeaching a witness is by showing that he has at some time prior to the trial made a statement inconsistent with his testimony. It is proper on cross-examination to ask him if he had made such a prior inconsistent statement. If he denies having done so, it is incumbent upon the cross-examiner to offer evidence that such a statement was, in fact, made. People v. Burbank, 53 Ill. 2d 261, 269 (1972).

9. State Impeaching Defendant with a Prior Inconsistent Statement Must Prove Statement Via Extrinsic Evidence If Defendant Denies Making the Statement
People v. Williams, 204 Ill. 2d 191 (2003)

The defendant appealed convictions of two counts of first-degree murder and two counts of contributing to the criminal delinquency of a juvenile. The defendant was allegedly involved in a shooting that took place in 1997. On appeal, he argued that the trial court abused its discretion when it allowed the state to impeach him with facts not in evidence. During its cross-examination of defendant, the state asked him questions about conversations he had with a cell block acquaintance. The defense originally intended to call the acquaintance as a witness, but he flipped and wanted to testify for the state in exchange for a deal. The acquaintance claimed that defendant had tried to bribe him to testify that he knew a third party not involved in the case had committed the murder. The state asked defendant questions that implied he had in fact tried to bribe the acquaintance, all of which he denied. The defense never called the acquaintance as a witness, and the state did not call him as a rebuttal witness.

The Supreme Court stated the general rule that "the State may not impeach a witness on cross-examination with a prior inconsistent statement unless the State can prove the statement with extrinsic evidence if the witness denies making it." The Supreme Court went on to say that "[t]he inherent danger posed by such cross-examination questions is that the jury will ignore the witness' denial, make a presumption that the insinuation created by the question is accurate, and substitute the presumption for proof." The Supreme Court held that "[c]learly, the State's failure to call [the acquaintance] in rebuttal was error." Although the Supreme Court found that defendant had forfeited his right to review the claim when he did not object to the state's failure to perfect the impeachment at trial and to include the issue in a post-trial motion, it agreed with him that the issue warranted review under the plain error doctrine. Here, the Supreme Court reversed, noting that

> the State's error in failing to call [the acquaintance] as a rebuttal witness deprived the defendant of a fair trial . . . . The State's questions created the insinuation that the defendant, conscious of his guilt, tried to bribe [the acquaintance] with money and drugs to finger [a third person] in an attempt to secure an acquittal. This insinuation became unanswerable when the state did not call [the acquaintance] in rebuttal. Particularly where, as here, the state presented strong, but not overwhelming evidence of the defendant's guilt, the damaging and prejudicial effect of such a strategy is obvious.

10. Witness Impeached by Prior Inconsistent Statement Must Have an Opportunity to Explain the Statement and Show Circumstances Under Which It Was Made
People v. Hicks, 28 Ill. 2d 457 (1963)

Defendant was charged with rape. The victim testified that her attacker wore a small-brimmed hat and dark tweed coat and used a knife during the crime. When defendant failed to pay rent, his landlord locked him out and moved a box of his possessions to a locked room. Defendant's hat, coat, and knife were found by the police in the locked room. The victim identified the items as those the perpetrator wore and used during the attack on September 28.

Defendant told a police officer that he lived in his apartment until September 30, two days after the crime occurred, and that he had the coat hanging in his apartment until that date. Defendant's landlord, however, testified that he locked defendant out of his apartment on September 27, the day before the crime took place, and that defendant did not have access to his possessions after that date. At trial, contrary to defendant's prior statements, defendant testified that he only lived in the apartment until September 27 and spent the rest of September at his friend's house. On cross-examination the state asked defendant whether he had been in his apartment on September 30, and defendant responded that he had been locked out on the 27th. Defense counsel then attempted to rehabilitate defendant's credibility by asking him about the date he was locked out of his apartment. The state objected and trial court sustained the objections. Defendant argued that the trial court improperly limited defense counsel's attempts at rehabilitation after defendant had been impeached by proof of his prior inconsistent statement.

The Illinois Supreme Court noted that where a witness has been impeached by a prior inconsistent statement, the witness must be given an opportunity on redirect examination to explain the statement and to show the circumstances under which it was made. Other portions of the prior statement that qualify or explain the inconsistency may be brought out on redirect examination. Questions on redirect examination designed to elicit testimony from the witness that the prior statement is false and that the witness' testimony at trial is true, without any explanation of the inconsistency, are improper. The Supreme Court remanded for a new trial.

11. State May Only Use Defendant's Voluntary Statement, Confession, or Admission to Impeach

People v. Peterson, 74 Ill. 2d 478 (1978)

The trial court found defendant's confession to have been "the result of 'psychological coercion' and of failure to warn of the right to discontinue questioning." The court further noted that the involuntary confession could not be used to impeach the defendant's testimony as any statement that is used to impeach must be a voluntary statement, confession or admission. A mere technical *Miranda* violation, however, does not preclude use of such a statement for impeachment purposes.

12. State May Impeach Defendant with Documents Submitted by Defendant in Connection with Motion to Suppress Evidence If Defendant Testifies at Trial

People v. Sturgis, 58 Ill. 2d 211 (1974)

Defendant denied possessing a controlled substance when he was arrested but filed a motion to suppress the evidence of the controlled substance retrieved by the police during his arrest. Defendant argued that it was improper to allow impeachment with statements contained in his motion to suppress because of a "tension" created by such impeachment—"if an accused elects to proceed with the motion, he may later be impeached at trial by matters raised at the suppression hearing if he denies implication in the offense." The Illinois Supreme Court disagreed, noting that prior testimony of the defendant at a hearing to suppress evidence or statements contained in documents that the defendant voluntarily attested to in conjunction with a motion to suppress evidence may be used to impeach his or her contradictory testimony at trial.

13. Witness May Not Be Impeached with Specific Collateral Instances of Untruthfulness

People v. Cookson, 215 Ill. 2d 194 (2005)

Defendant was convicted of predatory criminal sexual assault and aggravated criminal sexual abuse. The Illinois Supreme Court rejected the defendant's argument that evidence of previous sexual assault accusations made by the victim against a third person was admissible to impeach her credibility and to demonstrate her confusing the defendant with the third person. The Supreme Court acknowledged that the victim's credibility was unquestionably at issue because there was no testimony from independent eyewitnesses supporting her allegations and no physical evidence linking the defendant to the alleged abuse. Generally, the Supreme Court observed that the use of reputation evidence is the proper way to impeach a witness' trait for truthfulness. A party may also impeach a witness through a showing of bias, interest, or motive to testify falsely, but such evidence should not be remote or uncertain. Here, however, the defendant sought to introduce evidence of specific past instances of untruthfulness on the part of the child victim for purposes of impeaching her credibility.

The Supreme Court concluded that evidence of abuse allegedly committed against the victim by a third person did not establish her bias against the accused. The evidence of the "false" allegation also failed to show that the victim had an improper interest or motive to lie about being abused by the defendant. The Supreme Court also explained that evidence of specific past instances of untruthfulness may not be used to impeach the truthfulness of a witness. The Supreme Court emphasized that

> the proper procedure for impeaching a witness' reputation for truthfulness is through the use of reputation evidence and not through [. . .] evidence of specific past instances of untruthfulness. People v. Kliner, 185 Ill. 2d 81, 173, 235 Ill. Dec. 667, 705 N.E.2d 850 (1998); People v. West, 158 Ill. 2d 155, 162, 198 Ill. Dec. 393, 632 N.E.2d 1004 (1994) (rejecting the argument evidence of specific acts of untruthfulness should be admitted to impeach a child witness because the child was too young to have developed a reputation in the community). This rule applies with equal force to all witnesses, regardless of age. People v. Williams, 139 Ill. 2d 1, 21, 150 Ill. Dec. 544, 563 N.E.2d 431 (1990). This case has not presented us with any compelling basis for altering this rule in cases involving sexual abuse allegations, and we take this opportunity to reaffirm that principle.

Moreover, the Supreme Court held that the only inference the jury could draw from such evidence is that the victim had lied about being abused by the defendant, since the evidence suggested that she had lied about being abused by a third person.

Finally, the finding of the Department of Children and Family Services (DCFS) that the victim's allegation of abuse against the third person was unfounded was also properly excluded. The Supreme Court observed that evidence of this type failed to establish that a victim had any interest, bias, or motive to lie about the particular defendant at issue.

14. An Expert Witness May Not Be Impeached with Prior Disciplinary Record That Is Collateral to the Ultimate Issue

People v. Sims, 192 Ill. 2d 592 (2000)

The Illinois Supreme Court affirmed the trial court's decision to grant the state's motion *in limine*, which effectively barred defense counsel from impeaching an expert witness on cross-examination with questions relating to his disciplinary record. The misconduct evident in the disciplinary record was determined to be collateral to the ultimate issues in the case. Authorities agree that "[c]ross-examination is proper whenever the prosecution has sufficient 'leverage' over the witness justifying the defendant's claim that the witness has an interest or bias, or that there is corruption or coercion that would tend to make the witness testify falsely." Here, the Supreme Court, in the absence of any evidence other than the mere existence of the disciplinary agreement, could not conclude that the state's expert was under any "leverage" by the state to falsify his testimony.

15. Matter Is Not Collateral to the Ultimate Issue If It Is Relevant and Introduced for Purpose Other Than to Contradict
People v. Collins, 106 Ill. 2d 237 (1985)

State sought to impeach defendant's alibi witness who claimed that she and defendant went to see a kung-fu movie three days before the armed robbery, aggravated kidnapping and murder with which defendant was charged. On rebuttal the state called a manager for the movie theater who testified that there was not a kung-fu movie playing on the day alleged by the witness. The defendant contended that state's impeachment concerned a collateral matter and was impermissible. The Supreme Court found, however, that the state was permitted to impeach the witness because the issue was not collateral. The Supreme Court explained that "[t]he test to be applied in determining if a matter is collateral is whether the matter could be introduced for any purpose other than to contradict." Here, the Supreme Court concluded that the trial court did not abuse its discretion in allowing the state to impeach the witness' testimony because her testimony was relevant to her "ability to recall" her and defendant's activities prior to the day the crimes were committed.

Rule 614. Calling and Interrogation of Witnesses by Court

(a) Calling by Court. The court may, on its own motion or at the suggestion of a party, call witnesses, and all parties are entitled to cross-examine witnesses thus called.

(b) Interrogation by Court. The court may interrogate witnesses, whether called by itself or by a party.

(c) Objections. Objections to the calling of witnesses by the court or to interrogation by it may be made at the time or at the next available opportunity when the jury is not present.

Adopted September 27, 2010, eff. January 1, 2011.

AUTHOR'S COMMENTARY

Illinois Rule of Evidence 614 codifies Illinois common law principles and is identical to Federal Rule of Evidence 614, in effect prior to its stylistic amendment on December 1, 2011. Gino L. DiVito, *The Illinois Rules of Evidence: A Color-Coded Guide Containing the New Rules, the Committee's General and Specific Comments, a Comparison with the Federal Rules of Evidence, and Additional Commentary* (*Including the Federal Rules of Evidence as Amended Effective December 1, 2011*) (Jan. 1, 2012), at 67, http://www.tdrlawfirm.com/assets/downloads/Illinois_Rules_of_Evidence_Color-Coded_Guide.pdf; *see* People v. Givens, 237 Ill. 2d 311 (2010); People v. Nevitt, 135 Ill. 2d 423 (1990).

PRIOR ILLINOIS CASE LAW

1. Trial Court's Questioning of Witnesses Must Be Fair and Impartial
People v. Nevitt, 135 Ill. 2d 423 (1990)

The questioning by a trial judge must be fair and impartial. It must not show the court's bias against any party. The judge must not reveal an opinion—by word or conduct—on the facts in evidence, the veracity of witnesses, or the guilt or innocence of the defendant. Here, the defendant was on trial for aggravated criminal sexual assault. Defendant contended on appeal that the trial court "displayed bias in favor of the prosecution and engaged in abusive conduct toward defense counsel and a defense witness." Defendant argued that during a pretrial hearing on his motion to suppress certain statements the trial court asked witnesses about "defendant's sobriety, whether the assistant State's Attorney properly identified herself, the circumstances surrounding defendant's presence at the police station, the use of any force against defendant and whether any promises were made to defendant before he confessed." The Illinois Supreme Court noted that

> [g]enerally, a trial judge has discretion to question witnesses in order to elicit truth or clarify issues which seem obscure. People v. Wesley, 18 Ill. 2d 138, 155 (1959). The propriety of each examination depends on the circumstances of the case. People v. Hopkins, 29 Ill. 2d 260, 265 (1963), and rests largely within the discretion of the trial judge. People v. Palmer (1963), 27 Ill. 2d 311, 314 (1963). However, this discretion is not unlimited. A judge must be fair and impartial, even when outside the hearing of the jury. People v. Giacomino, 347 Ill. 523, 529 (1932).

The Supreme Court concluded that the trial court did not abuse its discretion in this case because defendant raised the various allegations and the trial court was required to consider each before ruling on defendant's motion to suppress.

For other decisions discussing this topic, see:

People v. Falaster, 173 Ill. 2d 220 (1996) (finding that trial court did not abuse discretion in asking expert witness to clarify whether she would expect a 13-year-old sex abuse victim to be more inaccurate in her initial description of the attack and more accurate in her later recollection of the event).

People v. Tyner, 30 Ill. 2d 101 (1964) (finding abuse of discretion where trial judge accused state witness of lying and concealing facts beneficial to state).

People v. Jackson, 409 Ill. App. 3d 631 (1st Dist. 2011) (finding abuse of discretion where trial judge "adopted a prosecutorial role" in questioning an expert witness and relying on prior personal knowledge).

2. Judge May Not Assume the Role of Advocate
People v. Givens, 237 Ill. 2d 311 (2010)

The Illinois Supreme Court found that the appellate court exceeded role as neutral arbiter by reversing defendant's conviction based on theory not raised by defendant at trial. Defendant was convicted of possession of a controlled substance. The appellate court held that trial counsel was ineffective in not challenging the police search on basis of lack of consent and reversed the case for a hearing on the issue. The Illinois Supreme Court vacated the appellate court's decision and observed that

> Illinois law is well settled that other than for assessing subject matter jurisdiction, 'a reviewing court should not normally search the record for unargued and unbriefed reasons to reverse a trial court judgment.' [citation omitted].
>
> ***
>
> [W]e conclude that the appellate court stepped over the line from neutral jurist to that of an advocate for defendant to raise and rule on issues that were neither controlled by clear precedent nor dictated by an interest in a just result.

Exclusion of Witnesses

Rule 615. Exclusion of Witnesses

At the request of a party the court shall order witnesses excluded so that they cannot hear the testimony of other witnesses, and it may make the order of its own motion. This rule does not authorize exclusion of (1) a party who is a natural person, or (2) an officer or employee of a party which is not a natural person designated as its representative by its attorney, or (3) a person whose presence is shown by a party to be essential to the presentation of the party's cause, or (4) a person authorized by law to be present.

Adopted September 27, 2010, eff. January 1, 2011.

AUTHOR'S COMMENTARY

Illinois Rule of Evidence 615 codifies Illinois common law principles and is almost identical to the Federal Rule of Evidence 615, in effect prior to its amendment on December 1, 2011, except that it has substituted the word "law" for "statute." Gino L. DiVito, *The Illinois Rules of Evidence: A Color-Coded Guide Containing the New Rules, The Committee's General and Specific Comments, A Comparison with the Federal Rules of Evidence, and Additional Commentary (Including the Federal Rules of Evidence as Amended Effective December 1, 2011)* (Jan. 1, 2012), at 67, http://www.tdrlawfirm.com /assets/downloads/Illinois_Rules_of_Evidence_Color-Coded_Guide.pdf; *see* People v. Mack, 25 Ill. 2d 416 (1962).

RELEVANT STATUTORY AUTHORITY

Prosecution for Sex Offenses; Victims Under 18 Years; Persons Excluded from Proceedings: 725 ILCS 5/115-11

§ 115-11. In a prosecution for a criminal offense defined in Article 11 or in Section 11-1.20, 11-1.30, 11-1.40, 11-1.50, 11-1.60, 12-13, 12-14, 12-14.1, 12-15 or 12-16 of the "Criminal Code of 1961", where the alleged victim of the offense is a minor under 18 years of age, the court may exclude from the proceedings while the victim is testifying, all persons, who, in the opinion of the court, do not have a direct interest in the case, except the media.

Effective July 1, 2011.

PRIOR ILLINOIS CASE LAW

1. Exclusion of Witnesses Is Within the Trial Court's Discretion
People v. Mack, 25 Ill. 2d 416 (1962)

Witnesses may be excluded during the taking of testimony on the motion of the defense, the state's attorney, or the court. The motion is generally allowed, but the power to exclude witnesses is exercised within the discretion of the trial court. Defendant "has no absolute right to have witnesses excluded." Defendant here argued that the trial court erred in not excluding the arresting officer. The Supreme Court noted that "[i]t is a common practice for a trial court, in granting a motion to exclude witnesses, to except, at the request of the State's Attorney, one witness for the People, frequently, but not always, one of the arresting officers." A material witness for the prosecution, usually a police officer, may remain in the courtroom to assist the prosecutor. If the court denies the motion to exclude, the ruling must be rational and not arbitrary. The Supreme Court here found that the lower court did not abuse its discretion in excluding all witnesses except one of the arresting officers.

2. Court May Exclude the Public from Young Sex Victim's Trial Proceedings
People v. Holveck, 141 Ill. 2d 84 (1990)

The trial judge has discretion to exclude the public from the trial proceedings during the testimony of young sex victims. The trial judge here excluded the general public from the courtroom, but permitted the victims' family members, a psychologist and the media to remain. The court considered the victims' age and interests of the victims and their families as well as the defendant's rights. The Illinois Supreme Court upheld the trial judge's decision to clear the courtroom of "persons without an interest" to protect the young victims.

3. Exclusion Order Is Valid If It Meets the Statutory Requirements of 725 ILCS 5/115-11
People v. Falaster, 173 Ill. 2d 220 (1996)

At an aggravated criminal sexual assault trial, the trial judge excluded defendant's nephews and the nephew's grandfather from the courtroom during 14-year-old victim's testimony. Defendant argued that the trial court improperly excluded these spectators and that the partial closure of the proceedings violated his federal and state constitutional rights to a fair trial. The defendant contended that exclusion of spectators must satisfy the stringent limitations for closure of judicial proceedings to the media and the public. The Illinois Supreme Court disagreed, however, reasoning that those stringent limitations are inapplicable here and that trial court's order for closure is valid if it satisfies the statutory requirements of 725 ILCS 5/115-11.

4. Party Seeking to Introduce Testimony of a Special Witness Must Disclose the Contents of the Evidence, Show That It Is Necessary and That Efforts Have Been Made to Secure It Via Other Means
People v. Rodriguez, 402 Ill. App. 3d 932 (1st Dist. 2010)

The special witness doctrine applies when a party plans on calling a prosecutor, judge or news reporter to testify.

> Pursuant to the special witness doctrine, when a party in a criminal case requests the testimony of a special witness, including a judge, that party must (1) specify the testimony to be elicited from the witness; (2) state why the testimony is necessary and relevant to the party's case; and (3) state what efforts have been made to secure the same evidence through other means.

If the proponent fails to establish each prong of the test, the special witness must be excluded. Defendant argued that the trial court abused its discretion in allowing a judge to testify because the judge's testimony was duplicative and not necessary to the State's case. The First District of the Illinois Appellate Court agreed but found the error harmless.

Chapter 5

Chapter 5

Article VII – Opinions and Expert Testimony

Opinion Evidence by Lay Witnesses

Rule 701. Opinion Testimony by Lay Witnesses

If the witness is not testifying as an expert, the witness' testimony in the form of opinions or inferences is limited to those opinions or inferences which are (a) rationally based on the perception of the witness, and (b) helpful to a clear understanding of the witness' testimony or the determination of a fact in issue, and (c) not based on scientific, technical, or other specialized knowledge within the scope of Rule 702.

Adopted September 27, 2010, eff. January 1, 2011.

AUTHOR'S COMMENTARY

Before the enactment of the Illinois Rules of Evidence, the Illinois Supreme Court relied on the Federal Rules of Evidence with respect to lay witness testimony. Specifically, in 1985 the Illinois Supreme Court by case law adopted Federal Rule of Evidence 701(a) and (b), which is identical to Illinois Rule of Evidence 701(a) and (b) currently in effect. *See* Freeding-Skokie Roll-Off Serv. v. Hamilton, 108 Ill. 2d 217 (1985); Gino L. DiVito, *The Illinois Rules of Evidence: A Color-Coded Guide Containing the New Rules, the Committee's General and Specific Comments, a Comparison with the Federal Rules of Evidence, and Additional Commentary (Including the Federal Rules of Evidence as Amended Effective December 1, 2011)* (Jan. 1, 2012), at 85, http://www.tdrlawfirm.com/assets/downloads/Illinois_Rules_of_Evidence_Color-Coded_Guide.pdf.

The Illinois Rules of Evidence have adopted Federal Rule of Evidence 701, in effect prior to its stylistic amendment on December 1, 2011, in its entirety, including section (c) which was added in 2000. The Federal Advisory Committee Note to Federal Rule of Evidence 701 explains that section (c) was added to Federal Rule 701

> to eliminate the risk that the reliability requirements set forth in [Federal] Rule 702 will be evaded through the simple expedient of proffering an expert in lay witness clothing. Under the amendment, a witness' testimony must be scrutinized under the rules regulating expert opinion to the extent that the witness is providing testimony based on scientific, technical, or other specialized knowledge within the scope of Rule 702. [. . .] The amendment makes clear that any part of a witness' testimony that is based upon scientific, technical, or other specialized knowledge within the scope of Rule 702 is governed by the standards of Rule 702.
>
> FED. R. EVID. 701 (Federal Advisory Committee Notes, 2000 Amendments)

PRIOR ILLINOIS CASE LAW

1. Lay Witness Opinion Testimony Must Be Based on Witness' Own Perceptions

People v. Novak, 163 Ill. 2d 93 (1994) *abrogated by* People v. Kolton, 219 Ill. 2d 353 (2006) on a separate issue

Defendant, a boys' baseball coach, was convicted of aggravated criminal sexual assault. In his defense, defendant claimed that he did not assault the victim but only performed a "set of muscle strength and flexibility exercises." A personal trainer and a college athletics director were called by the state and testified as lay witnesses that they would have never performed such exercises on 10- to 13-year-old boys. Defendant argued that their testimony should not have been permitted because they were not experts on the topic of athletic training. The Illinois Supreme Court found that the witnesses' testimony was not admissible as lay opinion testimony, explaining that

> [l]ay witness opinion testimony is admissible where the facts could not otherwise be adequately presented or described to the fact finder in such a way as to enable the fact finder to form an opinion or reach an intelligent conclusion. Lay witnesses may relate their opinions or conclusions on what they observed because it is sometimes difficult to describe a person's mental or physical condition, character or reputation, or the emotions manifest by his or her acts; or things that occur and can be observed, including speed, appearance, odor, flavor, and temperature. United States v. Skeet, 665 F.2d 983, 985 (9th Cir. 1982); accord People v. Burton, 6 Ill. App. 3d 879, 886 (1st Dist. 1972); 1 S. GARD, ILLINOIS EVIDENCE MANUAL § 7:03 (2d ed. 1979).
>
> The limitation that lay witness opinion testimony be rationally based on the witness' perception reflects the general requirement that a witness must have personal knowledge of the matter to testify to it. Joy Manufacturing Co. v. Sola Basic Industries, Inc., 697 F.2d 104, 111 (3d Cir. 1982); accord FED. R. EVID. 602; M. GRAHAM, CLEARY & GRAHAM'S HANDBOOK OF ILLINOIS EVIDENCE § 701.1, at 482 (5th ed. 1990).) The testimony must be based on concrete facts perceived from the witness' own senses. Randolph v. Collectramatic, Inc., 590 F.2d 844, 847-48 (10th Cir. 1979); 1 J. STRONG, MCCORMICK ON EVIDENCE § 11, at 46 n. 22 (4th ed. 1992); 1 S. GARD, ILLINOIS EVIDENCE MANUAL § 7:02 (2d ed. 1979). Personal knowledge of a fact cannot be based on the statement of another. United States v. Owens, 789 F.2d 750, 754 (9th Cir. 1986). The limitation essentially requires that the fact finder receive the best evidence available—first-hand knowledge rather than second-hand knowledge. United States v. Hoffner, 777 F.2d 1423, 1425 (10th Cir. 1985); *Joy Manufacturing Co.*, 697 F.2d at 111.

The Supreme Court concluded that the witnesses did not observe defendant performing the exercises and therefore could not have had first-hand knowledge about his technique and their propriety. Although the Supreme Court found that the witnesses could not give lay opinion testimony, it held that the witnesses properly testified as experts.

2. Witness May Only Testify as to Facts Within His or Her Personal Knowledge
People v. Rosenbaum, 299 Ill. 93 (1921)

Defendant on trial for forgery argued that the trial court erred when it refused to allow opinion testimony by a witness claiming that the witness did not think the defendant forged the signature on the instrument. The Illinois Supreme Court found that the trial court did not err because the witness knew nothing about the facts and it was "not competent for the witness to state his mere conclusion or opinion that plaintiff in error did not write the forged signature, or pass the forged instrument, in the absence of personal knowledge of those facts."

3. Lay Witness May Express Opinion on Facts Within His or Her Personal Knowledge That Are Helpful to the Trier of Fact
Freeding-Skokie Roll-Off Serv. v. Hamilton, 108 Ill. 2d 217 (1985)

Defendant was involved in a car accident with the plaintiff. Plaintiff and another witness testified at trial that the accident "could not have been avoided." Defendant contended that the testimony was improper because only the jury could have decided the issue and argued that a lay witness may not testify to an ultimate issue in the case.

The Illinois Supreme Court noted that generally a lay witness may not express an opinion or draw inferences from facts but may only testify about facts that he or she personally knows and recalls. The Supreme Court, relying on Federal Rule of Evidence 704, explained that "lay opinion testimony is admissible even on the ultimate issue to be decided by the trier of fact." Moreover, the Supreme Court adopted Federal Rule of Evidence 701. The Supreme Court, quoting United States v. Jackson, 688 F.2d 1121 (7th Cir. 1982), explained that under Federal Rule 701 opinion testimony of a lay witness is admissible

> whenever the witness cannot adequately communicate to the jury the facts upon which his or her opinion is based. United States v. Skeet, 665 F.2d 983, 985 (9th Cir. 1982). The theory behind Rule 701 'is that wherever inference and conclusions can be drawn by the jury as well as by the witness, the witness is superfluous; . . . a lay opinion is received because and whenever his facts cannot be so told as to make the jury as able as he to draw the inference.' 7 Wigmore on Evidence (Chadbourn rev. 1978) sec. 1917.8 at 10 (emphasis in original). Thus, in order to conclude that such testimony is admissible, the court must find that the witness' testimony is based upon his or her personal observation and recollection of concrete facts [citation omitted], and that those facts cannot be described in sufficient detail to adequately convey to the jury the substance of the testimony. The Advisory Committee Notes to Rule 701 indicate that direct and cross-examination of the lay witness testifying as to his or her opinion is relied upon to verify the accuracy of the testimony." *Jackson*, 688 F.2d 1121, 1124.

Here, the Illinois Supreme Court concluded that the witnesses' testimony explaining that the accident could not have been avoided was not helpful to the trier of fact. The Supreme Court observed that the witnesses' explanation of the facts upon which their testimony was based was sufficient to give the jury a thorough understanding upon which to draw their conclusions. Therefore, the witnesses' conclusions were "superfluous" and their admissibility constituted error.

4. Lay Witness May Express Opinion on Matters Difficult to Reproduce If the Opinion Is One That Others Could Make and Understand
People v. Armstrong, 183 Ill. 2d 130 (1998)

Defendant was convicted of murder, armed robbery, and residential burglary. At the sentencing hearing, the custodian of records at the Illinois Department of Corrections testified that he had worked at the department for 16 years and had never seen a worse disciplinary record than that of the defendant. Defendant contended that the trial court abused its discretion by admitting the testimony. The Illinois Supreme Court disagreed, noting that witness was a custodian of records who had testified about issues relevant to trial that were in his personal knowledge. The Supreme Court explained that a lay witness may

> express opinion based on his observations where it is difficult or impossible for [the witness] to reproduce for the jury the totality of the conditions perceived and where the opinion given is one that men in general are accustomed to, and capable of, making, comprehending, and understanding. People v. Sprinkle, 74 Ill. App. 3d 456, 464-65 (1979).

For other decisions discussing this topic, see:

People v. Hanson, 238 Ill. 2d 74 (2010) (permitting defendant's sister's testimony as lay witness opinion that after the murders she told a police officer that she thought her brother committed the crime).

People v. Claussen, 367 Ill. 430 (1937) (allowing police officer who observed defendant and described him during his testimony to testify as to his opinion of defendant's age).

Opinion Evidence by Expert Witnesses

Rule 702. Testimony by Experts

If scientific, technical, or other specialized knowledge will assist the trier of fact to understand the evidence or to determine a fact in issue, a witness qualified as an expert by knowledge, skill, experience, training, or education, may testify thereto in the form of an opinion or otherwise. Where an expert witness testifies to an opinion based on a new or novel scientific methodology or principle, the proponent of the opinion has the burden of showing the methodology or scientific principle on which the opinion is based is sufficiently established to have gained general acceptance in the particular field in which it belongs.

Adopted September 27, 2010, eff. January 1, 2011.

Comment

Rule 702 confirms that Illinois is a *Frye* state. The second sentence of the rule enunciates the core principles of the *Frye* test for admissibility of scientific evidence as set forth in Donaldson v. Central Illinois Public Service Co., 199 Ill. 2d 63, 767 N.E.2d 314 (2002).

Committee Commentary

(1) Codification: With the exception of the two areas discussed below under "Recommendations," the Committee incorporated into the Illinois Rules of Evidence the current law of evidence in Illinois whenever the Illinois Supreme Court or the Illinois Appellate Court had clearly spoken on a principle of evidentiary law within the last 50 or so years. Thus, Rule 702 retains the *Frye* standard for expert opinion evidence pursuant to the holding in Donaldson v. Central Illinois Public Service Co., 199 Ill. 2d 63, 767 N.E.2d 314 (2002). The Committee reserved Rule 407, related to subsequent remedial measures, because Appellate Court opinions are sufficiently in conflict concerning a core issue that is now under review by the Supreme Court.

ILL. R. EVID. Committee Commentary § 1, pg. 1.

AUTHOR'S COMMENTARY

Illinois courts, unlike federal courts, retain the *Frye* standard for determining admissibility of expert evidence. Comment to ILL. R. EVID. 702; ILL. R. EVID. Committee Commentary § 1, pg. 1; *see also* Gino L. DiVito, *The Illinois Rules of Evidence: A Color-Coded Guide Containing the New Rules, the Committee's General and Specific Comments, a Comparison with the Federal Rules of Evidence, and Additional Commentary* (*Including the Federal Rules of Evidence as Amended Effective December 1, 2011*) (Jan. 1, 2012), at 86, http://www.tdrlawfirm.com/assets/downloads/Illinois_Rules_of_Evidence_Color-Coded_Guide.pdf. The *Frye* test requires a showing that a particular theory or method relied upon by an expert is "generally accepted" in the relevant scientific field. Donaldson v. Central Illinois Public Service Co., 199 Ill. 2d 63 (2002).

The federal courts have, however, abandoned the *Frye* standard and have adopted a standard of relevancy based in Daubert v. Merrell Dow Pharmaceuticals, Inc., 509 U.S. 579 (1993), for admissibility of expert evidence. The *Daubert* test requires reliable and relevant expert testimony to be based on scientific knowledge, and to be helpful to the trier of fact in determining the issues at hand. General acceptance of the scientific method or theory is not a pre-condition but may be a helpful factor.

The difference between the two standards appears unclear, but it has been argued that the *Daubert* standard places more discretion in the judiciary to decide whether expert testimony is relevant and admissible by empowering courts to more closely inspect the evidence, whereas the *Frye* standard is much more deferential to the scientific community's evaluation and ultimate acceptance or rejection of expert evidence. *See* Edward K. Cheng & Albert H. Yoon, *Does Frye or Daubert Matter? A Study of Scientific Admissibility Standards*, 91 VA. L. REV. 471, 472 (2005); *see also* MICHAEL H. GRAHAM, GRAHAM'S HANDBOOK OF ILLINOIS EVIDENCE § 702.10 (10th ed. 2010) (noting the "narrower gatekeeping role" of the trial court under *Frye*); *and see* General Electric Co. v. Joiner, 522 U.S. 136 (1997) (explaining that federal courts admit a "broader range of scientific testimony"). Some, however, argue that whether courts apply *Daubert* or *Frye*, "the practical results are essentially the same." Cheng & Yoon, *Does* Frye *or* Daubert *Matter?* 91 VA. L. REV. at 472. For a detailed discussion of the developments of the *Frye* and *Daubert* tests, see RALPH RUEBNER, ILLINOIS CRIMINAL TRIAL EVIDENCE 195-203 (4th ed. 2001).

Illinois courts permit admissibility of a range of scientific evidence presented by qualified experts at trial. For instance, Illinois courts approve the admissibility of statistical evidence through the testimony of expert witnesses. Whenever such evidence is used, the trial judge must be on guard to ensure that the jury is not confused or misled by the evidence. It may be said that statistical evidence is not relevant if it tends to confuse or mislead. Such evidence may be viewed as being too probative in that it dilutes the prosecutor's burden of proof.

Illinois also recognizes the admissibility of syndrome evidence. Its foundation is a model of universal signs and symptoms that usually occur together and are characteristic of a certain abnormality. This model is relevant in establishing an element of a crime or of a defense to the charge in a particular case and should be admitted in evidence. *See* People v. Oaks, 169 Ill. 2d 409 (1996), *abrogated on other grounds by In re* G.O., 191 Ill. 2d 37 (2000). It may also be used to rebut a defense. *Id.*

Scientific evidence has also been helpful in exonerating wrongly convicted persons. Consequently, the legislature has provided convicted individuals with the ability to seek and present fingerprint, ballistic, and DNA evidence long after their convictions in an effort to demonstrate that they are actually innocent. Statutory law allows such individual to present a motion in the trial court for fingerprint or forensic testing that was not available to him or her at trial pursuant to 725 ILCS 5/116-3. *Id.* There is no time limit on defendant's ability to file this motion. *See* 725 ILCS 5/116-3; *see also* 90th Ill. Gen. Assemb., House Proceedings, April 15, 1997, at 13 (explaining that "[w]hen it's a wrong person behind bars, there shouldn't be a time limit").

RELEVANT STATUTORY AUTHORITY

Prosecution for Illegal Sexual Act Perpetrated upon a Victim; Admissibility of Evidence; Post-traumatic Stress Syndrome: 725 ILCS 5/115-7.2

§ 115-7.2. In a prosecution for an illegal sexual act perpetrated upon a victim, including but not limited to prosecutions for violations of Sections 11-1.20 through 11-1.60 or 12-13 through 12-16 of the Criminal Code of 1961, or ritualized abuse of a child under Section 12-33 of the Criminal Code of 1961, testimony by an expert, qualified by the court relating to any recognized and accepted form of post-traumatic stress syndrome shall be admissible as evidence.

Effective July 1, 2011.

Motion for Fingerprint, Integrated Ballistic Identification System, or Forensic Testing Not Available at Trial Regarding Actual Innocence: 725 ILCS 5/116-3

§ 116-3. Motion for fingerprint, Integrated Ballistic Identification System, or forensic testing not available at trial regarding actual innocence.

(a) A defendant may make a motion before the trial court that entered the judgment of conviction in his or her case for the performance of fingerprint, Integrated Ballistic Identification System, or forensic DNA testing, including comparison analysis of genetic marker groupings of the evidence collected by criminal justice agencies pursuant to the alleged offense, to those of the defendant, to those of other forensic evidence, and to those maintained under subsection (f) of Section 5-4-3 of the Unified Code of Corrections, on evidence that was secured in relation to the trial which resulted in his or her conviction, and:

(1) was not subject to the testing which is now requested at the time of trial; or
(2) although previously subjected to testing, can be subjected to additional testing utilizing a method that was not scientifically available at the time of trial that provides a reasonable likelihood of more probative results. Reasonable notice of the motion shall be served upon the State.

(b) The defendant must present a *prima facie* case that:

(1) identity was the issue in the trial which resulted in his or her conviction; and
(2) the evidence to be tested has been subject to a chain of custody sufficient to establish that it has not been substituted, tampered with, replaced, or altered in any material aspect.

(c) The trial court shall allow the testing under reasonable conditions designed to protect the State's interests in the integrity of the evidence and the testing process upon a determination that:

(1) the result of the testing has the scientific potential to produce new, noncumulative evidence materially relevant to the defendant's assertion of actual innocence even though the results may not completely exonerate the defendant;
(2) the testing requested employs a scientific method generally accepted within the relevant scientific community.

(d) If evidence previously tested pursuant to this Section reveals an unknown fingerprint from the crime scene that does not match the defendant or the victim, the order of the Court shall direct the prosecuting authority to request the Illinois State Police Bureau of Forensic Science to submit the unknown fingerprint evidence into the FBI's Integrated Automated Fingerprint Identification System (AIFIS) for identification.

Effective October 23, 2007.

PRIOR ILLINOIS CASE LAW

1. Expert Opinion Evidence Is Admissible as an Aid to the Trier of Fact in Reaching Its Conclusion

People v. Jordan, 103 Ill. 2d 192 (1984)

The Illinois Supreme Court restated the general rule of admissibility of an expert's testimony this way:

> It is well established that an individual will be permitted to testify as an expert if his experience and qualifications afford him knowledge which is not common to lay persons and where such testimony will aid the trier of fact in reaching its conclusion. [Citation omitted]. The burden of establishing the qualifications of an expert witness is on the proponent of his testimony, and it is within the discretion of the trial court to determine whether the witness has been qualified. [Citation omitted]. Further, in rendering an opinion, the expert must rely upon scientific theories which have gained general acceptance in his field. [Citations omitted].

Here, defendant was charged with murder and armed robbery. Police investigators recovered the victim's skull and bones and an autopsy showed that the victim's teeth were pink. The Supreme Court found no abuse of discretion in allowing the state's forensic odontologists' testimony about the cause of "pink tooth phenomenon," including the fact that strangulation is a cause of pink tooth and a possible cause of death. The court based its finding on the following factors: the witnesses were questioned at length about their education and experience in the field; the study of pink tooth phenomenon was included in their field of expertise; their theory was not rejected by defense witnesses; the theory was outside the realm of knowledge of lay persons; and the experts' testimony aided the fact finder in understanding the theory and its significance.

2. Expert Testimony Is Admissible Only If Relevant to the Issues in the Case
People v. Nelson, 235 Ill. 2d 386 (2009)

Defendant was charged with multiple murders and confessed to the crimes. He later argued that his confession was coerced. A clinical psychologist examined defendant and administered the Gudjonsson Suggestibility Scale (GSS) which is used to evaluate an individual's "susceptibility to giving a false confession," and helps "gauge[] the extent to which a person may be persuaded to change his answers to questions." The psychologist concluded that defendant was "very shy, submissive, deferential, accommodating, and introverted," and that he was very likely to accept information that might not be entirely true. The trial court found that although GSS appeared to be generally accepted in the psychological community, it was not a "reliable test to determine a person's suggestibility to admit to a crime." The trial court concluded that the test did not meet the *Frye* requirements and evidence related to it was inadmissible. The Illinois Supreme Court found that the trial court erroneously applied the "*Frye*-plus-reliability test," but concluded that any error was harmless because defendant failed to show evidence that the officers used a method of interrogation that would have induced him to change his story. The Supreme Court concluded that expert testimony about GSS evidence was irrelevant in this case.

3. Testifying Expert Must Be Properly Qualified
People v. Park, 72 Ill. 2d 203 (1978)

The burden of establishing the qualifications of an expert witness belongs to the proponent of his or her testimony. That burden is not diluted or eliminated altogether merely because the opponent of the testimony has an opportunity to cross-examine the expert witness about his or her qualifications. The Illinois Supreme Court held that a deputy sheriff who had not been trained to identify marijuana and who relied on his belief that he had seen marijuana on 40 prior occasions was not qualified to testify as an expert witness. His opinion that the substance was in fact marijuana should not have been admitted. The Illinois Supreme Court observed that:

> [W]hile the value of pregnant sows and stolen auto parts might be readily assimilated with only limited experience, the ability to draw fine distinctions between fingerprints and ballistic markings requires more thorough and systematic study. The positive identification of cannabis without the aid of chemical and microscopic analysis falls in the latter category, because it simply is far too likely that a nonexpert would err in his conclusions on this matter, and taint the entire fact finding process. Cross examination often is a clumsy, counterproductive and therefore ineffective means of purging that taint.

The Supreme Court further noted that the burden of establishing an expert's qualifications is not uniform in every case. Instead, it is measured in accordance with the following rule:

> [T]he degree and manner of knowledge and experience required of an alleged expert is directly related to the complexity of the subject matter and the corresponding likelihood or error by one insufficiently familiar therewith.

4. Expert May Be Qualified by Knowledge, Skill, Practical Experience, Training, or Education, but a Professional License or Formal Training Is Not Required

Thompson v. Gordon, 221 Ill. 2d 414 (2006)

Defendant was driving and had to swerve to avoid another car. Her car crossed the median and collided with another vehicle. Two individuals in the other vehicle died as a result of the accident. An administrator of the decedents' estates brought suit against defendant and the designers of the intersection where the accident occurred, claiming that their design fell below the normal standard of care, and that the designers had failed to provide an adequate barrier between traffic traveling in the opposite direction. The plaintiff retained the services of a civil engineer as her expert. The engineer was not licensed as an engineer in Illinois but was licensed as a professional engineer in the District of Columbia. The defendants filed a motion for summary judgment, arguing that the facts did not give rise to any duty of care owed by the defendants to the plaintiff. In opposition to the motion, the plaintiff submitted an affidavit by the engineer opining that under an ordinary standard of care the defendants should have installed a Jersey median in the intersection to prevent a vehicle from crossing over into on-coming traffic. The defendants filed a motion to strike the engineer's affidavit on the basis that he was not qualified to be an expert, since he did not have an Illinois license to render engineering services. The trial court agreed with the defendants and struck the affidavit.

The Illinois Supreme Court disagreed, explaining that the trial court only took into consideration that the engineer was not licensed in the State of Illinois in striking his affidavit. The Supreme Court found that a license is one factor in determining whether an individual is qualified as an expert, but that the trial court should have also considered whether his knowledge, skill, experience, training, or education afforded him a basis beyond that of an average lay person in assessing whether he was competent to testify as an expert. The Supreme Court explained that

> '[t]here is no predetermined formula for how an expert acquires specialized knowledge or experience and the expert can gain such through practical experience, scientific study, education, training or research.' People v. Miller, 173 Ill. 2d 167, 186 (1996). Thus, '[f]ormal academic training or specific degrees are not required to qualify a person as an expert; practical experience in a field may serve just as well to qualify him.' Lee v. Chicago Transit Authority, 152 Ill. 2d 432, 459 (1992). An expert need only have knowledge and experience beyond that of an average citizen. *Miller*, 173 Ill. 2d at 186. Expert testimony, then, is admissible 'if the proffered expert is qualified by knowledge, skill, experience, training, or education, and the testimony will assist the trier of fact in understanding the evidence.' Snelson v. Kamm, 204 Ill. 2d 1, 24 (2003).

The Supreme Court reasoned that licensure in Illinois is not a mandatory prerequisite to admissibility of an expert opinion. Additionally, an important inquiry is whether the engineer's testimony would aid the trier of fact in reaching its conclusions. The Illinois Supreme Court did not rule that the trial court must accept the testimony of the expert; rather, it held that the trial court had abused its discretion by looking "solely" to the fact that the engineer did not have an Illinois license to practice engineering.

Ultimately whether a witness is or is not qualified as an expert is a question that the trial judge must resolve in the exercise of his or her discretion.

5. The Subject Matter of the Expert Testimony Must Be Beyond the Realm of Common Knowledge or Experience of Lay Persons
People v. Becker, 239 Ill. 2d 215 (2010)

Defendant was charged with predatory criminal sexual assault of his three-year-old daughter. State introduced out-of-court statements of the victim in evidence pursuant to 725 ILCS 5/115-10, which provides for admissibility of evidence of a child victim's statement if it is found to be sufficiently reliable. Defendant sought to have an expert testify about the reliability of the child witness' statements. The expert had reviewed the child's out-of-court statements as they were recorded in interview notes, transcripts and videos. The expert concluded that the child could not give a reliable statement on the stand. After a section 115-10 hearing, the trial court refused to allow the expert to testify, noting that the jury should be entitled to determine whether the child's statements were reliable or a result of suggestive interview techniques. The Illinois Supreme Court noted that

> [e]xpert testimony is only necessary when the subject is both particularly within the witness's experience and qualifications and beyond that of the average juror's, and when it will aid the jury in reaching its conclusion. People v. Cloutier, 156 Ill. 2d 483, 501 (1993); People v. Enis, 139 Ill. 2d 264, 288 (1990). Expert testimony is not admissible on matters of common knowledge unless the subject is difficult to understand and explain. People v. Gilliam, 172 Ill. 2d 484, 513 (1996). A trial court does not err in barring expert testimony where the matter at issue is not beyond the ken of the average juror. Watkins v. Schmitt, 172 Ill. 2d 193, 206-07 (1996).

Here, the Supreme Court concluded that the expert's testimony seeking to show that a child could have been influenced by suggestive interrogation was not beyond the understanding and capability of an average juror.

See also People v. Mertz, 218 Ill. 2d 1 (2005) (finding harmless error in admissibility of profiler testimony that was cumulative and within the realm of jurors' common knowledge).

6. Only Scientific Principle or Theory "Generally Accepted" in the Relevant Field Can Serve as Basis for Expert Testimony at Trial
Frye v. United States, 293 F. 1013 (D.C. Cir. 1923)

An expert witness may give an opinion based on scientific principle or theory. As a foundational requirement, the proponent of the witness must establish that the opinion rests on a scientific principle or theory that has gained "general acceptance" in his or her particular field. This may be difficult in some cases. Here, defendant on trial for murder was given a systolic blood pressure deception test that measured changes in his blood pressure to determine whether he was being truthful. Defendant sought to have the results of the test admitted at trial. The government objected. The United States Court of Appeals for the District of Columbia sided with the government, observing that

> [j]ust when a scientific principle or discovery crosses the line between the experimental and demonstrable stages is difficult to define. Somewhere in this twilight zone the evidential force of the principle must be recognized, and while courts will go a long way in admitting expert testimony deduced from a well-recognized scientific principle or discovery, the thing from which the deduction is made must be sufficiently established to have gained general acceptance in the particular field in which it belongs.

> We think the systolic blood pressure deception test has not yet gained such standing and scientific recognition among physiological and psychological authorities as would justify the courts in admitting expert testimony deduced from the discovery, development, and experiments thus far made.

7. Federal Courts Have Rejected the *Frye* Standard and Adhere to the *Daubert* Standard for Admissibility of Expert Scientific Testimony

Daubert v. Merrell Dow Pharmaceuticals, Inc., 509 U.S. 579 (1993)

The United States Supreme Court rejected the *Frye* standard for admissibility of expert scientific testimony and instead held that the Federal Rules of Evidence, in particular Federal Rule of Evidence 702, is the appropriate standard in trials in federal courts.

Here, the parents of children born with serious birth defects sued the company marketing an anti-nausea drug ingested by the children's mothers during pregnancy. Defendant presented expert testimony that concluded that there was no link between the anti-nausea drug and birth defects based on numerous published studies. Plaintiffs countered with their own experts who testified that there was a causal link based on other studies and an unpublished "reanalysis" of the previously published studies relied on by the defendant. The District Court applied the "general acceptance" standard and granted the defendant's motion for summary judgment. The District Court reasoned that the plaintiffs' evidence did not meet the standard because the studies relied on by the plaintiffs were not published or subject to peer review. United States Court of Appeals for the Ninth Circuit affirmed, relying on Frye v. United States, 293 F. 1013 (D.C. Cir. 1923). The United States Supreme Court, however, determined that reliance on *Frye* was erroneous because the Federal Rules of Evidence superseded it. Federal Rule of Evidence 702 provided:

> If scientific, technical, or other specialized knowledge will assist the trier of fact to understand the evidence or to determine a fact in issue, a witness qualified as an expert by knowledge, skill, experience, training, or education, may testify thereto in the form of an opinion or otherwise.

The Supreme Court reasoned that Rule 702 did not incorporate the *Frye* standard of "general acceptance" and that the drafters of the Federal Rules of Evidence sought to relax the traditional limits on the admissibility of opinion evidence. The Supreme Court explained that under the new standard, court should first determine whether expert's testimony is based on scientific knowledge, and then consider whether the testimony would be helpful to the trier of fact. The Supreme Court emphasized that the courts must still ensure that expert testimony admitted is relevant and reliable. Specifically, to be considered scientific, the expert's opinion should "have a reliable basis in the knowledge and experience of his discipline." The courts should thus assess "whether the reasoning or methodology underlying the testimony is scientifically valid and of whether that reasoning or methodology properly can be applied to the facts in issue." The Supreme Court enumerated various factors to consider in determining whether the scientific technique will assist the trier of fact such as whether the theory has been tested, subjected to peer review, and its rate of error. The Supreme Court observed that although existence of widespread or "general acceptance" in the relevant community may be "an important factor in ruling particular evidence admissible," it is not "a necessary precondition to the admissibility of scientific evidence under the Federal Rules of Evidence." The Supreme Court remanded for further proceedings consistent with its opinion.

On remand, the Ninth Circuit held that the testimony of plaintiffs' experts was inadmissible because the experts failed to show the existence of any methodology used to achieve their conclusions, or that their findings were subject to peer review or any external source that would validate their theory.

8. The *Daubert* Standard Applies to All Expert Testimony in the Federal Courts
Kumho Tire Co. v. Carmichael, 526 U.S. 137 (1999)

The United States Supreme Court extended the holding of *Daubert* to all expert testimony. The United States Supreme Court reasoned that Federal Rule of Evidence 702 does not distinguish between "scientific" and other specialized knowledge and that in practice it is often difficult, if not impossible, to draw a distinction between scientific matters and other specialized areas.

9. The Federal Appellate Review Standard on Decisions to Admit or Exclude Scientific Evidence Is Abuse of Discretion
General Electric Co. v. Joiner, 522 U.S. 136 (1997)

The United States Supreme Court held that the standard of review applicable to a trial judge's decision to admit or bar expert testimony under Daubert v. Merrell Dow Pharmaceuticals, Inc., 509 U.S. 579 (1993), is an abuse of discretion. The Supreme Court found that the Court of Appeals erred in reviewing the district court judge's decision to deny expert testimony because it applied an overly "stringent" standard of review and failed to give the trial judge's decision the deference it was due. According to the Court, "while the Federal Rules of Evidence allow district courts to admit a somewhat broader range of scientific testimony than would have been admissible under *Frye*, they leave in place the 'gatekeeper' role of the trial judge in screening such evidence."

The Court further rejected defendant's contention that the focus of *Daubert* was on the "principles and methodology" rather than on the "conclusions" generated from them, and, therefore, the district court erred because it only disagreed with the expert's conclusion. The Court stated that:

> [C]onclusions and methodology are not entirely distinct from one another. Trained experts commonly extrapolate from existing data. But nothing in either *Daubert* or the Federal Rules of Evidence requires a district court to admit opinion evidence which is connected to existing data only by the ipse dixit of the expert. A court may conclude that there is simply too great an analytical gap between the data and the opinion proffered.

10. Illinois Adheres to the *Frye* Standard for Admissibility of Expert Testimony
Donaldson v. Central Illinois Public Service Co., 199 Ill. 2d 63 (2002), *abrogated by In re* Commitment of Simons, 213 Ill. 2d 523 (2004) with respect to standard of review

The parents of four children diagnosed with neuroblastoma, a rare form of cancer, sued the owner of a former gas manufacturing plant. The manufacture of gas produced as byproduct coal tar. The plant owner buried 50,000 gallons of the byproduct below ground on site and later sold the land without disclosing its presence to the new owner or to state and federal environmental agencies. The site was surrounded by a park, residential buildings and a forest. The new owner of the site discovered the tar while doing excavation work. Unaware that it was a biohazard, the new owner transported the tar to a rural farm. After the tar was uncovered, some members of the community began smelling strange odors, and experiencing headaches and nausea. During the two years following the excavation on the site, four children were diagnosed with neuroblastoma. The parents of the children sued the owner of the plant and the jury awarded them damages. Two weeks before trial defendant filed a motion for a *Frye* hearing to determine whether the testimony of plaintiffs' experts was admissible. The trial court denied the motion due to time concerns, but conducted an informal

Frye hearing nonetheless. On appeal, defendant contended that the trial court committed reversible error by denying its motion, but the Illinois Supreme Court found that any error was harmless in light of the trial court's informal hearing and familiarity with the experts' methodologies.

Defendant also contended that the trial court erroneously permitted "unfounded expert opinion testimony." The defendant argued that the Supreme Court should adopt a "*Frye*-plus-reliability" standard that requires a court to determine whether the opinion is reliable even after it has concluded that the methodology is generally accepted under *Frye*. The Supreme Court refused to adopt such a standard noting that "the exclusive test for the admission of expert testimony is governed by the standard first expressed in Frye v. United States, 293 F. 1013 (D.C. Cir. 1923)." The Supreme Court further explained that

> [t]he *Frye* standard, commonly called the "general acceptance" test, dictates that scientific evidence is only admissible at trial if the methodology or scientific principle upon which the opinion is based is "sufficiently established to have gained general acceptance in the particular field in which it belongs." *Frye*, 293 F. at 1014. First, "general acceptance" does not concern the ultimate conclusion. Rather, the proper focus of the general acceptance test is on the underlying methodology used to generate the conclusion. If the underlying method used to generate an expert's opinion are reasonably relied upon by the experts in the field, the fact finder may consider the opinion—despite the novelty of the conclusion rendered by the expert. *** [G]eneral acceptance does not require that the methodology be accepted by unanimity, consensus, or even a majority of experts. A technique, however, is not "generally accepted" if it is experimental or of dubious validity. Thus, the *Frye* rule is meant to exclude methods new to science that undeservedly create a perception of certainty when the basis for the evidence or opinion is actually invalid.
>
> ***
>
> Only novelty requires that the trial court conduct a *Frye* evidentiary hearing to consider general acceptance. We recognize that a "new" or "novel" scientific technique is not always easy to identify, especially in light of constant scientific advances in our modern era. Generally, however, a scientific technique is "new" or "novel" if it is "original or striking" or does "not resembl[e] something formerly known or used." Webster's Third New International Dictionary 1546 (1993).
>
> Once a principle, technique, or test has gained general acceptance in the particular scientific community, its general acceptance is presumed in subsequent litigation; the principle, technique, or test is established as a matter of law.

Plaintiffs' experts testified by the "extrapolation method" that the release of the coal tar into the air surrounding the residential community was likely the cause of the children's neuroblastoma. Defendant contended that the experts' testimony and conclusions were novel and thus inadmissible pursuant to *Frye*. The Supreme Court concluded that the method of extrapolation was generally accepted in the experts' respective fields and was thus admissible under *Frye*. The Supreme Court explained that although the experts could not conclusively determine that the tar was the cause of the cancer because of the lack of scientific study on the subject of the causes of neuroblastoma, the experts extrapolated from other scientific studies to draw the conclusion that a cause-and-effect relationship existed. The Supreme Court held that the trial court did not err in admitting the experts' testimony because extrapolation was generally accepted in the scientific community at issue.

11. Dual Standard of Review Applies to Admissibility of Expert Scientific Testimony Under *Frye*

In re Commitment of Simons, 213 Ill. 2d 523 (2004)

The trial court, in a bench trial, found the defendant to be a sexually violent person under the Sexually Violent Persons Commitment Act (725 ILCS 207/1 *et seq.* (West 2002)) and committed him to the custody of the Department of Health and Human Services. Prior to trial, the defendant filed a motion *in limine* to exclude the testimony of the state's two expert witnesses. The defendant argued that the opinions were based on novel scientific actuarial instruments, such as the MnSOST-R and the Static-99, that had not yet been accepted in the relevant field; and that therefore the trial court should have excluded the evidence under *Frye*. The trial court disagreed with the defendant and held that the actuarial instruments were not novel, and therefore, not within the strictures of *Frye*. It further reasoned that even if the actuarial instruments are novel, they have gained general acceptance in the relevant field and therefore pass the admissibility standard of *Frye*. At trial, both state's experts testified that based on their evaluation of the defendant using actuarial assessment methods their opinion was that the defendant posed a significant risk of committing another sexually violent crime. On appeal, the defendant argued that the trial court had erred in admitting the testimony of the experts without conducting a *Frye* hearing. The appellate court agreed and reversed the trial court's judgment in an unpublished opinion pursuant to Illinois Supreme Court Rule 23.

On further appeal, the Illinois Supreme Court adopted a dual standard of review for the admissibility of expert scientific testimony. First, the qualifications of an expert scientific witness to testify in a particular subject area and the relevancy of the testimony are within the trial court's discretion and will be reviewed by an abuse of discretion standard. Secondly, a trial court's *Frye* analysis will be subject to a *de novo* review. Under a *de novo* review, a reviewing court may use materials outside the trial court record to determine if a *Frye* hearing is needed, and if so, it must determine whether the technique is generally accepted in the scientific community. The Illinois Supreme reversed the appellate court's ruling, holding that the use of actuarial risk assessment is generally accepted by psychological and psychiatric professionals who evaluate sex offenders' recidivism. The court noted that several jurisdictions that have determined the admissibility of actuarial risk assessment tests have determined that such tests are generally accepted by the relevant scientific community. Also, some jurisdictions mandate the use of actuarial risk assessment tests in their civil commitment hearings. The court did not hold that actuarial risk assessment is subject to the *Frye* standard, but even if it is, tests such as the MnSOST-R and the Static-99 are admissible under *Frye*. Therefore, the trial court did not err in admitting the testimony of the state's expert witnesses.

See also People v. Nelson, 235 Ill. 2d 386 (2009) (reaffirming that a dual standard of review applies to admissibility of expert testimony under *Frye*).

12. Admissibility of Scientific Testimony Pursuant to *Frye* Requires Proper Foundation and Balancing of Probative Value Against Unfair Prejudice

People v. McKown, 236 Ill. 2d 278 (2010)

Defendant contended that a Horizontal Gaze Nystagmus (HGN) test does not meet the *Frye* standards. An HGN test may preliminarily determine alcohol impairment and is often used by police officers in conducting sobriety checkpoints. The Illinois Supreme Court held that HGN testing met the *Frye* standard. The Supreme Court determined that HGN testing was generally accepted in the scientific field to show alcohol consumption and possible impairment. For an HGN test to be admissible into evidence, however, the state must lay the proper foundation: the HGN test was administered according to NHTSA protocol by a properly trained officer.

Finally, the ultimate determination of admissibility of evidence requires the trial court to balance the probative value against unfair prejudice.

See also People v. Basler, 193 Ill. 2d 545 (2000) (finding that defendant did not preserve for review the issue of whether HGN tests are ever admissible in DUI prosecutions).

For additional examples of Illinois courts' treatment of scientific evidence pursuant to *Frye*, see:

In re Commitment of Sandry, 367 Ill. App. 3d 949 (2d Dist. 2006) (holding that penile plethysmograph is generally accepted and admissible to indicate future dangerousness of sex offenders).

People v. Cumbee, 366 Ill. App. 3d 476 (2d Dist. 2006) (finding expert evidence regarding luminol testing admissible pursuant to *Frye*).

People v. Evans, 369 Ill. App. 3d 366 (4th Dist. 2006) (noting that bloodstain-pattern analysis is generally accepted in the law enforcement and scientific community and admissible pursuant to *Frye*).

People v. Wilke, 367 Ill. App. 3d 130 (3d Dist. 2006) (noting that mathematical yield evidence is not a novel scientific method and does not require a *Frye* hearing).

People v. Davis, 304 Ill. App. 3d 427 (2d Dist. 1999) (finding that lip print evidence is generally accepted within the forensic science community and admissible under *Frye*).

People v. DiGiacomo, 71 Ill. App. 3d 56 (2d Dist. 1979) (concluding that mathematical odds evidence indicating probability that physical evidence incriminated defendant is admissible).

13. Electrophoretic Testing of Dried Blood and Using Super Glue to Develop Latent Fingerprints Admissible Under the *Frye* Standard

People v. Eyler, 133 Ill. 2d 173 (1989)

In a case of first impression, the Illinois Supreme Court held that electrophoretic testing of dried blood is a reliable method of detecting genetic markers in blood and is generally accepted in the scientific community. Consequently, expert testimony on electrophoretic testing of dried bloodstains is admissible, even when the forensic scientist who testifies is a member of the police department. The Supreme Court also held that expert testimony regarding the super gluing technique or process which develops and compares latent fingerprints is generally accepted by the relevant scientific community under the *Frye* standard. Consequently, fingerprints which had been developed with the super gluing process were properly admitted in evidence.

14. Neutron-Activation Analysis Is Generally Accepted and Admissible

People v. Johnson, 114 Ill. 2d 170 (1986)

Defendant was convicted of murder, attempted murder, aggravated kidnapping, and deviate sexual assault. An FBI special agent testified at trial about neutron-activation analysis of bullets and cartridges recovered at defendant's home and crime scene. The agent indicated that the bullets recovered from the crime scene were likely once packaged in the cartridge recovered from defendant's home. Defendant argued that the agent's testimony was irrelevant and inconclusive. The Illinois Supreme Court described

> neutron-activation analysis [as] a two-phase method of instrumental chemical analysis, which detects, in parts per million, trace elements in a sample of material for the purpose of identifying the source of the material.
>
> ***

> [The Supreme Court concluded that] neutron-activation analysis has come to be accepted as a consistently reliable forensic-science technique, with a majority of jurisdictions holding that the results of such tests are admissible in criminal proceedings. E.g., Chatom v. State, 348 So. 2d 838 (Ala. 1977); Keith v. State, 612 P.2d 977 (Alaska 1980); Mills v. State, 476 So. 2d 172 (Fla. 1985); State v. Warden, 100 Idaho 21, 592 P.2d 836 (1979); State v. Ulrich, 187 Mont. 347, 609 P.2d 1218 (1980); State v. Journey, 201 Neb. 607, 271 N.W.2d 320 (1978); Commonwealth v. Sangricco, 475 Pa. 179, 379 A.2d 1342 (1977). We are persuaded by the reasoning of those courts in so doing and likewise believe that any lack of certitude in a qualified expert's testimony, or inconclusiveness in the results of an otherwise reliable neutron-activation analysis, goes to the weight and not the admissibility of such evidence.

15. Expert Shoeprint Identification Is Admissible as Circumstantial Evidence
People v. Campbell, 146 Ill. 2d 363 (1992)

Defendant was charged with residential burglary. Owners of the home defendant burglarized found muddy shoeprints on the linoleum floors of the living room and dining room areas. Police investigators also recovered a fingerprint from a videotape container. A shoeprint identification expert testified at trial that the shoeprints found in the home were consistent with the shoes recovered from the defendant. The Illinois Supreme Court held that shoeprint identification evidence was admissible as circumstantial evidence. Here, the shoeprint identification evidence along with evidence of opportunity and flight were sufficient to sustain defendant's guilt beyond a reasonable doubt. The court stated about shoeprint evidence:

> [If] there are significant general and individual characteristics, such as would provide a basis for a positive identification, shoeprint evidence may be as reliable and as trustworthy as any other evidence.

The court further explained that:

> [W]hen shoes are worn, even for a limited period of time, the soles begin to show peculiar signs of wear, nail marks, cuts, and other accidental markings. Consequently, shoeprints may offer sufficient individual, unique markings and characteristics upon which to base a positive identification.

In testing the weight to be given to shoeprint evidence, the court, relying on State v. Palmer, 230 N.C. 205 (1949), noted the following:

> [E]vidence of shoeprints has no legitimate or logical tendency to identify an accused as the perpetrator of a crime unless the attendant circumstances support this triple inference: (1) That the shoeprints were found at or near the place of the crime; (2) that the shoeprints were made at the time of the crime; and (3) that the shoeprints correspond to shoes worn by the accused at the time of the crime. [Citation omitted].

The Supreme Court decided the case without reference to *Frye*.

16. RFLP Method of DNA Profiling and the Product Rule Are Generally Accepted in the Scientific Community and Admissible
People v. Hickey, 178 Ill. 2d 256 (1997)

The Illinois Supreme Court held that the fragment length polymorphis (RFLP) method of DNA profiling and use of the product rule were admissible in defendant's aggravated criminal sexual assault prosecution. The product rule is generally used to determine the frequency with which a DNA profile occurs in a population. The Supreme Court noted that both the method and the product rule have been generally accepted in the relevant scientific community.

17. Canine-Based Evidence Is Generally Inadmissible in Illinois Because It Is Too Unreliable and Prejudicial
People v. Cruz, 162 Ill. 2d 314 (1994)

Defendant contended that the trial court erroneously admitted canine-based evidence at his trial. A police officer testified that his two bloodhounds could track human scent and "possessed a success rate of '85 percent' based on the number of their 'finds.'" On cross-examination the officer conceded that the dog's effectiveness in tracking may be affected by weather conditions. Prosecutor used the canine-based evidence to argue that defendant was lying about his conduct on the day of the kidnapping, rape, and murder of the victim. The Illinois Supreme Court found that the trial court erred in admitting the bloodhound evidence and noted that

> bloodhound evidence is inadmissible to establish any factual proposition in a criminal proceeding in Illinois. Having reviewed those cases admitting such evidence, we remain unpersuaded that this class of evidence is reliable. Moreover, we recognize that the real danger posed by admitting bloodhound evidence lies not simply in its fallibility, but in its potential to prejudice. 'It is well known that the exercise of a mysterious power not possessed by human beings begets in the minds of many people a superstitious awe ***. The very name by which the animal is called has a direct tendency to enhance the impressiveness of the performance ***,' quoting People v. Pfanschmidt, 262 Ill. 411, 458 (1914).

The Supreme Court decided the case without mention of *Frye*.

See also People v. Acri, 277 Ill. App. 3d 1030 (3d Dist. 1996) (finding that uncorroborated canine-based evidence is generally inadmissible in Illinois because it is not generally accepted under *Frye*).

But see People v. Reeves, 314 Ill. App. 3d 482 (1st Dist. 2000) (finding evidence that police dogs sniffed victim's home and alerted to presence of narcotics admissible because not used to support element of offense but to corroborate testimony that defendant and victims engaged in drug transactions).

18. Expert Testimony on Actuarial Risk Assessment Is Generally Accepted and Admissible on the Subject of Sex Offender's Risk of Recidivism
In re Commitment of Simons, 213 Ill. 2d 523 (2004)

Defendant was found to be a sexually violent person under the Sexually Violent Persons Commitment Act (725 ILCS 207/1 *et seq.*). Defendant contended that the trial court erroneously admitted scientific testimony regarding actuarial risk assessment to determine that if he were allowed back into the general population he would likely reoffend.

The Illinois Supreme Court held that actuarial risk assessment of sexually violent offenders is generally accepted and admissible, as shown by the acceptance after extensive litigation of the subject in 19 other states. Other courts either found that the scientific testimony is generally accepted or that the *Frye* test was inapplicable. The Illinois Supreme Court concluded that

> [a]fter careful consideration, [. . .] there is no question that [actuarial risk assessment] is generally accepted by professionals who assess sexually violent offenders and therefore is perfectly admissible in a court of law. As of this writing, experts in at least 19 other states rely upon actuarial risk assessment in forming their opinions on sex offenders' risks of recidivism. [. . .] As importantly, we were unable to identify any state outside of Illinois in which expert testimony based upon actuarial risk assessment was deemed inadmissible on the question of sex offender recidivism.

***

> Finally, we note that the academic literature contains many articles confirming the general acceptance of actuarial risk assessment by professionals who assess sexually violent offenders for risk of recidivism. In one article, the authors maintain that actuarial risk assessment 'is a state-of-the-art technique, and courts should insist that it be employed as a major instrument of risk assessment.' (citation omitted).

19. Battered Child Syndrome Evidence May Be Admitted to Prove Intent Although It Does Not Provide Identity of Perpetrator
Estelle v. McGuire, 502 U.S. 62 (1991)

Defendant was convicted of the second-degree murder of his six-month-old daughter. The child exhibited bruising on her chest and an autopsy revealed that she had suffered extensive damage to her internal organs and there was evidence of "prior rectal tearing and fractured ribs." Two physicians testified on the basis of the prior injuries that the victim was a battered child. The California Court of Appeals explained that the "syndrome exists when a child has sustained repeated and/or serious injuries by nonaccidental means," and held that evidence of the syndrome was properly admitted at trial. Defendant then filed a petition for habeas corpus relief and the United States Court of Appeals for the Ninth Circuit granted it. The Ninth Circuit found that the syndrome evidence was improperly admitted at trial because there was no evidence linking defendant to the prior injuries and defendant did not claim at trial that the injuries were result of an accident.

The United States Supreme Court reversed, noting that "[w]hen offered to show that certain injuries are a product of child abuse, rather than accident, evidence of prior injuries is relevant even though it does not purport to prove the identity of the person who might have inflicted those injuries." The Supreme Court observed that since the state charged defendant with intentional killing, it had a burden to prove that the child's death was not accidental, and battered child syndrome evidence purports to do just that. The Supreme Court concluded that the evidence was admissible on the issue of intent.

20. Trier of Fact's Determination That Victim Died of Shaken Baby Syndrome Based on Conflicting Expert Testimony Will Be Upheld as Long as After Viewing the Evidence in the Light Most Favorable to the Prosecution, Any Rational Trier of Fact Could Have Found the Essential Elements of the Crime Beyond a Reasonable Doubt
Cavazos v. Smith, 132 S. Ct. 2 (2011)

The defendant, the victim's grandmother, was charged with assault of a child resulting in death. She claimed that the victim was sleeping but seemed unresponsive. After she picked the child up, she tried to shake it or twist it to wake it up. The child then "went limp" and she called the police. Doctors initially thought that the victim died from sudden infant death syndrome, but the coroner determined that he died from shaken baby syndrome after conducting an autopsy. Several experts testified about the cause of death at trial over the course of seven days, providing conflicting testimony about the cause of death. The cause of death was difficult to determine because the child died so quickly. The jury convicted defendant.

The appellate court affirmed and the California Supreme Court refused to grant further appeal. In subsequent habeas corpus proceedings, the United States District Court for the Central District of California found that the evidence was sufficient to support the conviction. The United States Court of Appeals for the Ninth Circuit reversed, finding that there was "no evidence to permit an expert conclusion one way or the other" on the cause of death because there was "no physical evidence of . . . tearing or shearing, and no other evidence supporting death by violent shaking." It found that the state's experts "reached [their] conclusion because there was no evidence in the brain itself of the cause of death." The United States Supreme Court strongly disagreed, noting that

> evidence is sufficient to support a conviction so long as "after viewing the evidence in the light most favorable to the prosecution, any rational trier of fact could have found the essential elements of the crime beyond a reasonable doubt. [. . .] The jury was presented with competing views of how [the victim] died. It was made aware of the various experts' qualifications and their familiarity with both the subject of [shaken baby syndrome] and the physical condition of [the victim's] body. It observed the attorneys for each party cross-examine the experts and elicit concessions from them. The State's experts, whom the jury was entitled to believe, opined that the physical evidence was consistent with, and best explained by, death from sudden tearing of the brainstem caused by shaking. The Ninth Circuit's assertion that these experts "reached [their] conclusion because there was no evidence in the brain itself of the cause of death" is simply false. There was "evidence in the brain itself." The autopsy revealed indications of recent trauma to [the victim's] brain, such as subdural and subarachnoid hemorrhaging, hemorrhaging around the optic nerves, and the presence of a blood clot between the brain's hemispheres. The autopsy also revealed a bruise and abrasion on the lower back of [the victim's] head. These affirmative indications of trauma formed the basis of the experts' opinion that [the victim] died from shaking so severe that his brainstem tore. Defense counsel made certain that the jury understood that the prosecution's experts were unable to identify the precise point of tearing itself. [T]he experts explained why the location of the tear was undetectable: "[The victim's] death happened so quickly that the effects of the trauma did not have time to develop." [citation omitted]. According to the prosecutions' experts, there was simply no opportunity for swelling to occur around the brainstem before [the victim] died. In light of the evidence presented at trial, the Ninth Circuit plainly erred in concluding that the jury's verdict was irrational.

21. Battered Child Syndrome Evidence Is Admissible to Show That Parent's Explanation of Child's Injuries Is Improbable

People v. Oaks, 169 Ill. 2d 409 (1996), *abrogated on other grounds by In re* G.O., 191 Ill. 2d 37 (2000)

Defendant was charged with first degree murder and aggravated battery of a child. In the guilt phase of the trial, the state introduced the testimony of various medical experts to show that the injuries suffered by the victim were not the result of an accident. The emergency room physician testified that the child's mother provided contradicting accounts explaining the child's injuries and that he observed bruises in various stages of healing on the victim's body. A CAT scan showed bleeding in the victim's brain and an X ray showed a fracture of his clavicle. The physician diagnosed the victim with battered child syndrome. Another state expert, a pediatrician, testified that after a review of the victim's medical records he concluded that the child died due to the "shaken/impact syndrome" and the battered child syndrome. Defendant contended that he did not have the intent to kill or cause great bodily harm to the child and that the injuries were a result of the child's accidental fall earlier that day. The state introduced a prior incident in which the victim had suffered similar injuries. Defendant argued that such evidence was not admissible. The Illinois Supreme Court disagreed, noting that the prior injuries were consistent with those in the present case and that expert testimony regarding battered child syndrome indicated that all injuries were consistent with battered child syndrome. The Supreme Court concluded that evidence of prior injuries was sufficiently similar to the fatal injuries and was therefore admissible.

See also People v. Platter, 89 Ill. App. 3d 803 (2d Dist. 1980) (finding that battered child syndrome evidence was properly admitted to help determine the factual issues in the case which included whether the child's injuries were the result of an accident or defendant's physical abuse).

22. Defendant Seeking to Assert Battered Child Syndrome as an Affirmative Defense Should Have an Opportunity to Conduct *Voir Dire* of Expert
People v. Shanahan, 323 Ill. App. 3d 835 (1st Dist. 2001)

Defendant wished to assert the battered child syndrome as an affirmative defense to the charge against him of killing his father. The trial court refused to allow evidence in the form of expert testimony regarding the scientific validity of the battered child syndrome defense. Moreover, the trial court did not conduct *voir dire* of the expert to determine the nature of his testimony. On appeal, defendant argued that the trial court denied his right to present a defense by barring the admissibility of the proposed expert testimony and by refusing to hold a hearing concerning the evidence. Defendant contended that the battered child syndrome was not a novel scientific theory and was not subject to the *Frye* test.

The First District of the Illinois Appellate Court recognized that "[n]o other Illinois case has addressed the question of admissibility of battered child syndrome" as evidence of self-defense. The First District found that it was reversible error to deny *voir dire* of the expert. The First District remanded the case for the trial court to ascertain whether the expert's testimony related to syndromes not yet recognized in Illinois cases and to conduct a *Frye* hearing to determine whether that syndrome had gained general acceptance in the psychological community.

23. Battered Wife Syndrome Evidence Is Admissible to Support Theory That Defendant Killed Husband in Self-Defense
People v. Minnis, 118 Ill. App. 3d 345 (4th Dist. 1983)

Defendant was convicted of murder of her husband. Defendant's husband died after a struggle following sexual and physical abuse. To dispose of evidence, defendant dismembered his body. Defendant sought to introduce evidence that she suffered from the battered wife syndrome to explain why she dismembered her husband's body. The trial court excluded this evidence, noting that this was a traditional self-defense case and that the syndrome evidence would not add anything to her defense. The Fourth District of the Illinois Appellate Court reversed, observing that refusal to admit the syndrome evidence may have violated the defendant's right to present a defense. The Fourth District explained that

> [t]he prosecutor used the dismemberment as substantive evidence to prove defendant's consciousness of guilt. A defendant clearly has the right to introduce evidence to rebut the State's evidence of consciousness of guilt. People v. Manion, 67 Ill. 2d 564 (1977). The State's use of the dismemberment evidence rendered any explanation of it which would be consistent with innocence vital to the defendant's case. By ruling that expert evidence on the syndrome was irrelevant and by denying defense counsel his right to make an offer of proof, the trial court took much too narrow a view of the matter.

Battered wife syndrome evidence is relevant and admissible to explain within the context of a self-defense theory why the defendant murdered her husband. A number of jurisdictions allow expert evidence on the syndrome to explain why the abuse suffered by the spouse over a period of time caused her on a particular day to reasonably believe that her life was in danger and forcing her to use deadly force against her battering husband.

24. If Victim Refuses to Submit to an Examination by Defendant's Expert to Determine Evidence of Rape Trauma Syndrome, State May Not Introduce Evidence of an Examining Expert on the Matter

People v. Wheeler, 151 Ill. 2d 298 (1992)

Defendant was charged with aggravated criminal sexual assault. Pursuant to 725 ILCS 5/115-7.2, the state sought to introduce evidence that the victim suffered from rape trauma syndrome, which consists of a "cluster of psychological symptoms common to victims of sexual assault." In response, defendant requested the court to allow defendant's expert to examine the victim, or to exclude state's proposed syndrome evidence. The trial court denied defendant's request. Defendant contended that the trial court's denial of his motion constituted a violation of due process. Defendant claimed that section 115-7.2, in conjunction with section 115-7.1, which prevents the court from ordering a mental examination of a sex victim, deprived him of a fair trial.

The Illinois Supreme Court found that the trial court's order violated defendant's right to due process. The Illinois Supreme Court observed that subjecting a victim of a sexual crime to a psychological examination to determine the victim's competency and credibility is impermissible because such an examination could prove to be harassing, but that

> [u]nlike psychological evidence regarding the victim's competency and credibility as a witness, evidence of rape trauma syndrome is substantive evidence that a sexual assault occurred. By showing that a complainant suffers from psychological symptoms common to most victims of sexual assault, this evidence tends to support the proposition that the complainant was also the victim of a sexual assault.

The Supreme Court explained that because the state used evidence of rape trauma syndrome to show that the victim was abused, defendant should have had an opportunity to examine the victim as well to prove that the victim was not suffering from the syndrome. The state contended that the defendant had an opportunity to review the state's expert's reports and was not, therefore, completely deprived of presenting evidence on the subject. The Supreme Court, however, observed that there are "inherent qualitative differences between testimony from an examining expert and a nonexamining expert," and that an "expert who has personally examined a victim is in a better position to render an opinion than is an expert who has not done so." The Supreme Court held that the defendant had a due process right to have the victim examined by a defense expert to rebut the state's evidence of rape trauma syndrome. Further, the Supreme Court noted that the state may not introduce an examining expert's testimony unless the victim consents to an examination by a defense expert. If the victim refuses, the state can only present non-examining expert testimony. On the other hand, if the victim consents to an examination by the defense, then "[s]uch an examination . . . shall be conducted by an expert qualified by the court [citation omitted] and shall be strictly limited to whether the victim has symptoms consistent with 'any recognized and accepted form of post-traumatic stress syndrome.'" Furthermore, "[a]ny report generated by the defense expert's examination of the victim is discoverable by the prosecution."

25. Child Sexual Abuse Accommodation Syndrome Is Generally Accepted in the Psychological Community

People v. Atherton, 406 Ill. App. 3d 598 (2d Dist. 2010)

Defendant was charged with predatory criminal sexual assault of a child. State introduced the testimony of an expert about the child-sexual-abuse-accommodation syndrome. Defendant contended on appeal that the trial court erred when it refused to conduct a *Frye* hearing on the admissibility of syndrome evidence because it took judicial notice of prior Illinois decisions that did not rely on a *Frye* hearing in admitting such evidence. The Second District of the Illinois Appellate Court found that the trial court properly relied on prior Illinois decisions that comprehensively discussed the syndrome and accepted it into evidence by conducting an analysis similar to that undertaken during a *Frye* hearing.

The Second District of the Illinois Appellate Court explained that the child-sexual-abuser-accommodation syndrome

> is actually a pattern of five behavioral characteristics often observed in children who have been sexually abused. The characteristics are secrecy, helplessness, entrapment or accommodation, delayed or unconvincing disclosure, and retraction. [The child welfare supervisor who had worked with sexually abused children] stated that secrecy means the child keeps the abuse a secret and that it can be the result of an explicit or implied threat. Helplessness refers to an imbalance of power between the child and the authority figure who is abusing. Entrapment or accommodation means the child feels trapped by the abuse and learns ways to deal with it. Disclosure is usually delayed and given only in increments. The eventual disclosure may conflict with what actually happened due to the child's inability to recall detail. Retraction often happens after a child discloses and feels guilt, fear, or shame. [The child welfare supervisor] acknowledged that some studies had called the syndrome into question; however, she believed it was generally accepted.

Defendant also argued that the expert testifying about the syndrome was not properly qualified because she was not a psychologist and did not have any training pertaining to the syndrome. Moreover, the expert never interviewed the victim and therefore lacked the "in-depth knowledge" necessary to diagnose her. The Second District disagreed, finding that the expert gained her knowledge through experience and that because her testimony was only a general opinion on how offenders and child victims act after abuse, she was qualified to testify as an expert.

Defendant further argued that evidence of the syndrome was irrelevant and should have been excluded because the victim did not exhibit many of the symptoms of the syndrome but the Second District concluded that the evidence was relevant to explain to the trier of fact "the dynamics of a sexually abusive relationship," and the evidence was admissible pursuant to 725 ILCS 5/115-7.2.

26. Expert Evidence on Child Sexual Abuse Accommodation Syndrome Indicating That Victim Received Psychiatric Treatment after Assault Irrelevant and Inadmissible

People v. Hodor, 341 Ill. App. 3d 853 (2d Dist. 2003)

The defendant appealed a jury conviction of criminal sexual assault after he was charged with molesting his teenage stepdaughter. Prior to trial, the trial court granted defendant's motion *in limine*, barring any statements the stepdaughter had made to counselors during psychological examinations. When asked by state why the stepdaughter began counseling, her therapist responded that she "had reported that she had been sexually abused." The Second District of the Illinois Appellate Court allowed the statement over defense counsel's objection, but prohibited the state from inquiring about the details. The therapist further testified that the victim "presented with some very serious trauma reaction symptoms primarily." Over defendant's objection, a counseling supervisor testified that her "treatment goal for [the victim] was to minimize the effects of sexual trauma." The state also presented expert testimony about "child sex abuse accommodation syndrome."

On appeal, defendant asserted that he was denied his right to a fair trial when the state was permitted to introduce testimony of the therapist and counseling supervisor. The Second District of the Illinois Appellate Court agreed with the defendant, and discussed a prior case in which the court had held that testimony that a victim had undergone psychiatric treatment was irrelevant to the issue of the defendant's guilt or innocence, and use of such evidence was reversible error. The court stated that the testimony from the therapist and counseling supervisor was vague and did not discuss "behavioral patterns typically manifested by victims of sexual abuse or whether [the victim's] behavior was consistent with known syndromes" and therefore not within the purview of section 115-7.2 as the state argued. The Second District found, however, that the testimony of a clinical counselor who described "the characteristics of child sexual abuse accommodation syndrome" was admissible because it explained "the behavioral patterns typically manifested by victims of sexual abuse."

27. Defendant Is Entitled to DNA Testing Not Available at Trial Pursuant to 725 ILCS 5/116-3 If He or She Establishes Identity as a Central Issue in the Case and a Sufficient Chain of Custody of the Evidence to Be Tested

People v. Shum, 207 Ill. 2d 47 (2003)

Defendant was convicted of murder, feticide, attempted murder, and rape. The trial court dismissed defendant's post-conviction petition and refused to order DNA testing requested by defendant pursuant to 725 ILCS 5/116-3. The DNA testing was not available at the time of defendant's trial. Defendant consistently denied his involvement in the crime and contended that identity of the assailant was at issue. Defendant claimed actual innocence arguing that DNA testing of a rape kit recovered from the victim could show that defendant did not commit the crime. The Illinois Supreme Court explained that

> [u]nder section 116-3, the trial court evaluates whether DNA testing has the potential to produce new evidence "materially relevant" to defendant's actual-innocence claim. This phrase has been interpreted to include evidence that will "significantly advance" defendant's claim; the evidence need not exonerate defendant by itself.

The Illinois Supreme Court concluded that defendant had established a *prima facie* case for DNA testing because "he established that identity was a central issue and that the evidence was subject to a secure chain of custody." Moreover, the DNA evidence could "significantly advance" defendant's claim of actual innocence because it could show that defendant's DNA is not a match. The Supreme Court found that the trial court erred in denying DNA testing in this case.

See also People v. Johnson, 205 Ill. 2d 381 (2002) (finding sufficient chain of custody to allow DNA testing pursuant to 725 ILCS 5/116-3 where rape kit would have remained in the custody of the circuit court clerk after defendant's conviction).

28. Defendant Who Pleaded Guilty Is Not Entitled to DNA Testing Pursuant to 725 ILCS 5/116-3

People v. O'Connell, 227 Ill. 2d 31 (2007)

Defendant pleaded guilty to first degree murder, aggravated criminal sexual assault and armed robbery. Defendant filed a motion for DNA testing after his appeal and post-conviction proceedings. The trial court denied his motion. The Illinois Supreme Court held, as a matter of first impression, that defendant was not entitled to DNA testing pursuant to 725 ILCS 5/116-3 because

> [t]he plain and unambiguous language of section 116-3 permits a motion for DNA testing only when a defendant has been *convicted following a trial* contesting identity. Accordingly, as a matter of law, defendants who plead guilty may not avail themselves of section 116-3. Those defendants are a separate group who have not contested identity at trial. [emphasis in original].

Rule 703. Bases of Opinion Testimony by Experts

The facts or data in the particular case upon which an expert bases an opinion or inference may be those perceived by or made known to the expert at or before the hearing. If of a type reasonably relied upon by experts in the particular field in forming opinions or inferences upon the subject, the facts or data need not be admissible in evidence.

Adopted September 27, 2010, eff. January 1, 2011.

AUTHOR'S COMMENTARY

The Illinois Supreme Court adopted the original version of Federal Rule of Evidence 703 in Wilson v. Clark, 84 Ill. 2d 186 (1981). Adoption of the Federal Rule of Evidence 703 represented a major change in Illinois evidence law in that it allowed an expert witness to express an opinion based on facts that were not in evidence. The rule applied to all forms of expert opinion before the rule's adoption, such as "expert opinions based on firsthand observation, hypothetical questions, or presentation of data outside the court." Wilson v. Clark, 84 Ill. 2d 186, 193 (1981). Prior Illinois common law rule required that in propounding a hypothetical question to an expert, the elements of the hypothetical needed an evidentiary basis in the record and the hypothetical had to contain all material facts to form the basis of the opinion. *Id.* Now, a hypothetical question may contain facts not in evidence as long as the data or facts relied upon by the expert are reliable. *Id.*

Federal Rule of Evidence 703 was amended subsequent to the Supreme Court's adoption in *Wilson v. Clark*. Federal Advisory Committee's Note, 56 F.R.D. 183, 283. The version of the Federal Rule of Evidence 703 existing at the time of the Supreme Court's adoption in *Wilson v. Clark* is almost identical to the new Illinois Rule of Evidence 703, except that the new rule substituted a gender neutral term "expert" for "him" in the first sentence. The amended version of Federal Rule 703 was not adopted in Illinois. *See* Gino L. DiVito, *The Illinois Rules of Evidence: A Color-Coded Guide Containing the New Rules, the Committee's General and Specific Comments, a Comparison with the Federal Rules of Evidence, and Additional Commentary (Including the Federal Rules of Evidence as Amended Effective December 1, 2011)* (Jan. 1, 2012), at 88-89, http://www.tdrlawfirm.com/assets/downloads/Illinois_Rules_of_Evidence_Color-Coded_Guide.pdf.

The most recently amended Federal Rule of Evidence 703 states that "if the facts or data [relied upon by an expert in forming an opinion] would otherwise be inadmissible, the proponent of the opinion may disclose them to the jury only if their probative value in helping the jury evaluate the opinion substantially outweighs their prejudicial effect." FED. R. EVID. 703 (eff. Dec. 1, 2011). Illinois Rule of Evidence 703 contains no such balancing requirement and permits experts to base their opinion on inadmissible facts or data if they are "of a type reasonably relied upon by experts in the particular field." ILL. R. EVID. 703. Justice DiVito therefore explains that Illinois courts should rely on Illinois Rule of Evidence 403, which mirrors Federal Rule of Evidence 403, "in determining whether to allow or exclude the disclosure of inadmissible facts or data that the expert reasonably relied upon." DiVito, *Color-Coded Guide* at 88. Illinois courts therefore "must determine whether or not the probative value of the disclosure is substantially outweighed by the danger of unfair prejudice." DiVito, *Color-Coded Guide* at 88. Moreover, pursuant to Illinois Rules of Evidence 602 and 703, an expert witness, unlike a lay witness, may express an opinion even though the witness is relying on facts not in his or her personal knowledge. *See* MICHAEL H. GRAHAM, GRAHAM'S HANDBOOK OF ILLINOIS EVIDENCE at § 602.1 (10th ed. 2010).

PRIOR ILLINOIS CASE LAW

1. Expert Witness May Express an Opinion Based on Facts That Are Not in Evidence
Wilson v. Clark, 84 Ill. 2d 186 (1981)

Patient brought suit against a physician for alleged negligent medical treatment. Plaintiff claimed that the trial court improperly admitted his hospital records in evidence without establishing a proper foundation, and erroneously allowed an expert to respond to a hypothetical question based on these records. The medical records contained charts, reports, physician orders and nurses' notes. Defense counsel then asked the expert whether, based on these records and other assumed facts the defendant conformed to the degree of care required of him. The Illinois Supreme Court noted that although the medical records were admitted without proper foundation, an expert may rely on such records. The Illinois Supreme Court then discussed and adopted rules 703 and 705 of the Federal Rules of Evidence as they existed at the time the case was decided. Under the then-existing Federal Rule of Evidence 703 an expert may give an opinion based on facts or data derived from any one of three separate sources:

a. firsthand observation of the witness;
b. presentation of data at the trial; or
c. presentation of data to the witness outside of the courtroom and other than by his or her own perception.

The Supreme Court reasoned that "due to the high degree of reliability of hospital records, an expert may give his response to a hypothetical question based on facts contained in those records, even if the hospital records themselves are not in evidence." The Supreme Court departed from the Illinois practice of requiring that a hypothetical question contain only proved facts, and followed the modern state and federal trend of liberalizing various trial procedures. The Supreme Court concluded that the "key element in applying Federal Rule 703 is whether the information upon which the expert bases his opinion is of a type that is reliable."

2. An Expert May Give an Opinion Based Upon Facts Not in Evidence If They Are of Type Reasonably Relied on by Experts in the Particular Field
People v. Nieves, 193 Ill. 2d 513 (2000)

The Illinois Supreme Court held that an expert may give an opinion based upon facts that are not in evidence if those facts are of a type reasonably relied on by experts in the particular field. The state's expert forensic pathologist formulated his expert opinion regarding the victim's death based on the autopsy file prepared by a then retired medical examiner who had performed the autopsy. The Supreme Court found that since the medical expert had formulated his opinion from the autopsy file that "included autopsy photographs, a postmortem examination report, a toxicologic analysis report, an evidence receipt, diagrams made by the medical examiner while he conducted the autopsy, an investigator's report, and other administrative documents," his opinion was based on the "type of evidence reasonably relied upon by experts in the field of forensic pathology to form their opinions as to the cause and manner of death."

3. Analysts Certifying That a Substance Seized from Defendant Is a Controlled Substance Must Testify at Trial to Comport with the Defendant's Sixth Amendment Right to Confrontation
Melendez-Diaz v. Massachusetts, 129 S. Ct. 2527 (2009)

The United States Supreme Court held that defendant was entitled to be confronted with analysts who generated reports introduced at trial attesting that a recovered substance was cocaine. The United States Supreme Court noted that the analysts' reports contained testimonial statements for purposes of defendant's sixth amendment right to be confronted with witnesses against him. If analysts were unavailable, the reports would be admissible only if defendant had a prior opportunity to cross-examine the analysts.

See also Bullcoming v. New Mexico, 131 S. Ct. 2705 (2011) (holding that analyst who certified blood-alcohol analysis report must testify as to the truth of the statements in the report unless it is shown that analyst is unavailable and accused had prior opportunity to cross-examine).

4. Expert Testimony That Relies on Inadmissible Hearsay Is Nonetheless Proper to Explain Basis of Opinion
People v. Lovejoy, 235 Ill. 2d 97 (2009)

The Illinois Supreme Court held that a medical examiner's testimony as to toxicology testing performed by someone else did not violate Crawford v. Washington, 541 U.S. 36 (2004). The United States Supreme Court in *Crawford* held that testimonial out-of-court statements by a witness are barred unless the witness is unavailable and defendant had a prior opportunity to cross-examine her. The Illinois Supreme Court reasoned that the evidence was not admitted to prove the truth of the matter asserted and thus did not implicate defendant's right to confrontation. The medical examiner interpreted the results of the testing and the Supreme Court found that the expert was only explaining the steps he took in rendering his expert opinion. The Supreme Court observed that

> [t]his court has long held that prohibitions against the admission of hearsay do not apply when an expert testifies to underlying facts and data, not admitted into evidence, for the purpose of explaining the basis of his opinion. People v. Nieves, 193 Ill. 2d 513, 528 (2000); People v. Sutherland, 223 Ill. 2d 187 (2006).

For additional cases pertaining to the bases of expert opinion, see:

Williams v. Illinois, 132 S. Ct. 2221 (2012) (finding that expert may testify about non-testifying third party's findings to form opinions).

People v. Leach, 405 Ill. App. 3d 297 (1st Dist. 2010) *appeal allowed*, 239 Ill. 2d 572 (2011) (finding testimony of medical examiner who had not conducted the victim's autopsy was not hearsay and was admissible).

5. Expert Witness May Draw Conclusions About mtDNA Sequencing Evidence Obtained by a Third Party
People v. Sutherland, 223 Ill. 2d 187 (2006)

The defendant claimed that the trial court erred in denying his motion to take the deposition of an expert who testified at trial about mtDNA sequencing and the results that her laboratory reached. The Illinois Supreme Court held that the trial court did not abuse its discretion in denying the motion to depose because the state made significant disclosures to the defendant about mtDNA evidence and the expert had already testified at length during a *Frye* hearing. The defendant also argued that portions of her testimony were not admissible because she drew conclusions based on results that were obtained by lab technicians rather than from her own work and the technicians were not called as witnesses. The court disagreed, reasoning that since the witness was qualified as an expert she could give opinion testimony based on facts not in evidence as long as they were of the type reasonably relied on by experts in her particular field.

6. Expert May Testify as to Probability or Possibility Based on Certain Assumed Facts

People v. Ceja, 204 Ill. 2d 332 (2005)

The defendant appealed a conviction of first-degree murder. Defendant and another person who was tried separately were accused of the murder of two rival gang members. Testimony showed that defendant and the other person stole a Chevy Tahoe from a dealership in Westmont, Illinois. Two days later, eyewitnesses saw a Tahoe, which was later determined to be the Tahoe stolen from the dealership, approach alongside a Lincoln and fire several shots into the vehicle. The two passengers in the Lincoln were killed. After a long police chase, the Tahoe was cornered in an alley. Three men ran from the vehicle. Soon thereafter, defendant and the other person were found by police dogs hiding in a bush two blocks from where the Tahoe had stopped. Defendant told the police where one of the weapons had been discarded. In a jury trial, defendant was convicted and sentenced to death. Former Governor George Ryan commuted his sentence to natural life without the possibility of parole.

On appeal, defendant argued that he was deprived of a fair trial because, *inter alia*, the state's use of glass evidence retrieved from his shoe and compared to the glass from the Tahoe lacked a reasonable scientific basis and therefore the expert witness testimony should have been excluded. The state's expert had testified that there was a "good probability" that the glass fragment from defendant's shoe came from the broken window of the Tahoe. Because the sample taken from the shoe was so small—the size of a pinhead—the state's expert had to measure the glass' refractive index. A comparison of the two glass samples showed that they had an "association," and the expert determined from that association that there was a "good probability of common origin." Defendant presented his own expert who opined that the state's witness' reference to a refractive index and database to determine a frequency of occurrence was not scientific. Nonetheless, since the defendant failed to object to the testimony of the state's expert at trial and did not include the issue in his post-trial motion, the Illinois Supreme Court regarded the matter as waived. The Supreme Court rejected defendant's request to consider the issue under the plain error doctrine since the evidence was not so closely balanced that the case hinged on the glass fragment evidence, and the alleged error was not so substantial so as to deprive defendant of a fair trial. The Supreme Court noted that an "expert may not state a judgment or opinion based on conjecture. However, 'an expert opinion couched in terms of probabilities or possibilities based upon certain assumed facts is not improper or inadmissible.'"

7. An Expert Witness May Rely on Defendant's Statements in Forming a Diagnosis

People v. Anderson, 113 Ill. 2d 1 (1986)

The Illinois Supreme Court held that a psychiatric expert who reasonably relies on what a criminal defendant tells him or her may relate these statements if they figure in his or her diagnosis. Here, defendant committed a murder and raised the defense of insanity. He presented the testimony of a psychiatrist who reviewed defendant's psychiatric and criminal records and concluded that defendant likely could not have conformed his conduct to the requirements of the law and was unable to appreciate the criminality of his actions. State objected to the testimony because it relied on defendant's "self-serving" statements, but the Supreme Court found that "an expert must be allowed to repeat those statements if relevant to explaining the opinion to the jury," and that any possibility that defendant lied may be revealed on cross-examination of the expert.

See also People v. Gacy, 125 Ill. 2d 117 (1988) (finding that although the trial judge impermissibly precluded the experts from "quot[ing] the defendant directly, they were often permitted to convey the substance of his statements through paraphrases, answers to hypothetical questions, and narrative recitation of information provided by the defendant in their conversations with him").

8. An Expert Witness May Not Rely Only on Defendant's Self-Serving Statements in Forming Opinion on Defendant's Insanity
People v. Britz, 123 Ill. 2d 446 (1988)

Defendant was charged with murder, kidnapping, robbery, and rape of a victim. Defendant sought to introduce experts who would testify that he was insane during the commission of the crime due to chronic voluntary intoxication from drugs and alcohol. The reports submitted by the experts were based solely on defendant's claims of how much he drank prior to and on the day of the murder. The trial court held that the experts could only testify about their conclusions on defendant's insanity based on objective tests, but after a hearing it was determined that none of the experts could testify. The Illinois Supreme Court found that trial court properly limited expert witnesses from testifying about defendant's alleged mental illness resulting from voluntary abuse of drugs and alcohol where supporting evidence was mostly based on defendant's self-serving statements. The Supreme Court relied on Wilson v. Clark, 84 Ill. 2d 186 (1981) and distinguished People v. Anderson, 113 Ill. 2d 1 (1986), explaining that in this case the experts did not

> rely on any other reports in assessing defendant's alleged substance abuse disorder. They did not refer, either before or after their examination of defendant, to reports made by the officers, the statements of witnesses, or the reports from the rehabilitative center or centers in which defendant allegedly received treatment. They did not speak to friends or members of his family. The bases of their opinions rely substantially on the statements of defendant. This court does not believe that *Wilson v. Clark* in combination with *People v. Anderson* allows for such an extension of the rule. To allow an expert to rely solely on self-serving statements made by the defendant to determine his sanity defense permits this court to circumvent and abrogate the intent and meaning of the Federal Rules of Evidence and the rules announced in *Wilson* and *Anderson*. If this court were to allow such testimony, it would open the door for a defendant to tell his side of the story without the possibility of being cross-examined.

9. Opposing Party May Cross-Examine Expert Witness About Bias or Interest If Evidence Is Not Too Speculative or Remote
People v. Bull, 185 Ill. 2d 179 (1998)

The Illinois Supreme Court held that the trial court properly barred defendant from cross-examining the state's DNA expert regarding his disciplinary record. The Supreme Court found that the evidence was too remote and speculative to show the witness had something to gain or lose by the testimony. The Supreme Court explained that particularly where the discipline occurred two years after the witness had completed the DNA testing in defendant's case, such evidence was too remote and speculative.

See also Sears v. Rutishauser, 102 Ill. 2d 402 (1984) (holding that trial court abused its discretion in preventing defense from cross-examining plaintiff's medical expert about extent of patient referrals from plaintiff's attorney).

Rule 704. Opinion on Ultimate Issue

Testimony in the form of an opinion or inference otherwise admissible is not objectionable because it embraces an ultimate issue to be decided by the trier of fact.

Adopted September 27, 2010, eff. January 1, 2011.

AUTHOR'S COMMENTARY

Illinois Rule of Evidence 704, in accordance with Illinois common law, permits lay and expert witnesses to express an opinion on the ultimate issue of fact if it will aid the trier of fact. *See* People v. Harris, 132 Ill. 2d 366 (1989). In 1985, Illinois adopted Federal Rule of Evidence 704(a) by case law, stating that "[t]estimony in the form of an opinion or inference otherwise admissible is not objectionable because it embraces an ultimate issue to be decided by the trier of fact." Freeding-Skokie Roll-Off Serv. v. Hamilton, 108 Ill. 2d 217 (1985). In accordance with common law, the Illinois Rules of Evidence also adopted section (a) of Federal Rule of Evidence 704, in effect prior to its stylistic amendment on December 1, 2011, but had not adopted Federal Rule of Evidence 704(b). *See* Gino L. DiVito, *The Illinois Rules of Evidence: A Color-Coded Guide Containing the New Rules, the Committee's General and Specific Comments, a Comparison with the Federal Rules of Evidence, and Additional Commentary (Including the Federal Rules of Evidence as Amended Effective December 1, 2011)* (Jan. 1, 2012), at 90, http://www.tdrlawfirm.com /assets/downloads/Illinois_Rules_of_Evidence_Color-Coded_Guide.pdf. Illinois Rule of Evidence 704 did not adopt section (b) of the Federal Rule because Illinois common law, unlike Federal Rule of Evidence 704(b), allows experts to testify in the form of opinion testimony about defendant's mental state or condition at the time the crime was committed. *See* People v. Ward, 61 Ill. 2d 559 (1975).

PRIOR ILLINOIS CASE LAW

1. Witness May Testify on an Ultimate Issue in the Case

People v. Harris, 132 Ill. 2d 366 (1989)

A witness may express an opinion on the ultimate issue of fact as an aid to the trier of fact. The defendant was convicted of murder, aggravated criminal sexual assault, and aggravated kidnapping. The victim's body was found partially clothed near an oil processing plant. Defendant argued on appeal that testimony of a physician who supervised the victim's autopsy was improper because it concerned an ultimate issue in the case and was based on matters "within the common ken of jurors." The physician testified that based on how the victim's body was found and the various injuries to her, he concluded that she had been sexually assaulted. The Illinois Supreme Court found that the expert properly testified and

> was competent to render an opinion on the question whether the victim had been sexually assaulted. We believe that the basis for his opinion could properly include not only the medical evidence concerning the nature and extent of the victim's injuries, but also the other circumstances referred to, including the evidence pertaining to her disappearance and eventual discovery. His expertise and training qualified him as an expert on the matters at issue here. The jury remained free to accept or reject this testimony.

2. Witness May Express Opinion on Ultimate Issue in the Case If Such Testimony Is Helpful to the Trier of Fact

Freeding-Skokie Roll-Off Serv. v. Hamilton, 108 Ill. 2d 217 (1985)

Plaintiff and defendant were involved in a car accident. Plaintiff and another witness testified at trial that the accident "could not have been avoided." Defendant contended that the testimony was improper because only the jury could have decided the issue and argued that a lay witness may not testify to an ultimate issue in the case. The Illinois Supreme Court noted that generally a lay witness may not express an opinion or draw inferences from facts but may only testify about facts that he or she personally knows and recalls. The Supreme Court, relying on Federal Rule of Evidence 704, noted that

> lay opinion testimony is admissible even on the ultimate issue to be decided by the trier of fact. Federal Rule 704 provides:
>
> > "Testimony in the form of an opinion or inference otherwise admissible is not objectionable because it embraces an ultimate issue to be decided by the trier of fact." FED. R. EVID. 704.
>
> Relaxation of the proscription of opinions on the ultimate issue has not, however, affected the requirement that to be admissible opinion testimony must be of assistance to the trier of fact.

The Supreme Court concluded that the witnesses' testimony here was not helpful to the trier of fact because the witnesses' explanation of the facts upon which their testimony was based was sufficient to give the jury a thorough understanding upon which to draw their own conclusions.

3. Expert or Lay Witness May Provide Opinion on Ultimate Issue Because Trier of Fact Is Not Required to Accept the Conclusion
People v. Terrell, 185 Ill. 2d 467 (1998)

The Illinois Supreme Court held that when a witness testifies to an ultimate issue in the case, "the trier of fact is not required to accept the witness' conclusion and, therefore, such testimony cannot be said to usurp the province of the jury." Defendant was charged with murder and aggravated criminal sexual assault of a 15-month-old victim. A police detective testified at trial that "he had never before seen injuries like those suffered by the victim." Defendant argued that the officer's testimony was erroneously admitted as expert testimony and that he improperly testified as to an ultimate issue of fact in the case, specifically as to the exceptionally brutal or heinous nature of the crime.

The Supreme Court disagreed, explaining that regardless of whether the officer was an expert, he could have testified as to an ultimate issue in a case. Moreover, the officer's testimony was properly admissible as lay opinion: the officer had previously worked on cases involving sexual crimes against children, he investigated the current case and he personally observed the condition of the victim after the attack. The Supreme Court concluded that the officer's testimony was helpful to the trier of fact and was properly admitted.

4. Lay Witness May Give Opinion on a Person's Mental Condition Based on Personal Observation
People v. Fair, 159 Ill. 2d 51 (1994)

Defendant was charged with two murders and the jury found him guilty. Defendant argued that it was improper for the trial court to limit the testimony of his common law wife about whether she believed defendant was addicted to cocaine at the time he committed the murders. The Illinois Supreme Court disagreed, observing that the evidence presented at trial showed that defendant had not used cocaine for a couple of months before the murders and that defendant had not previously claimed he was under the influence of cocaine during the murders. The Supreme Court noted that "a lay witness may give his opinion regarding the mental condition of an individual based on personally observed facts, which must be stated in detail." The Supreme Court explained that defendant's wife was able to testify about defendant's prior cocaine use and that her testimony apprised the jury that defendant may have been a heavy user of cocaine. The Supreme Court concluded that although limitation of her testimony may have been erroneous, the error was harmless.

For other decisions discussing this topic, see:

People v. Sprinkle, 74 Ill. App. 3d 456 (1979) (explaining that lay witness may offer opinion testimony on issue of intoxication if knowledge is based on personal observation and experience)

People v. Williams, 38 Ill. 2d 115 (1967) (noting that although lay witness may give opinion testimony about a person's sanity based on personal observation, in this case the evidence was properly excluded due to its lack of probative value).

People v. Hauke, 335 Ill. 217 (1929) (noting that lay witness properly testified that defendant appeared "nervous and upset" on the morning of the shooting).

5. Lay Testimony May Suffice to Establish Psychological Injury Resulting from the Crime

People v. Hudson, 228 Ill. 2d 181 (2008)

Whether or not expert testimony is needed depends on the particular facts of the case. Here, the defendant appealed his home invasion conviction arguing that the trial court erred in relying solely on lay testimony to conclude that the victim was psychologically injured. Although the court noted that expert testimony was needed to show psychological injury in some cases, lay testimony of the victim and her mother was sufficient to demonstrate injury in this case. The undisputed facts of the case indicated that a 16-year-old girl had been grabbed in the middle of the night in her own home by a strange man who was wearing no pants. In this case, the court found that jurors could reasonably find that the circumstances of the offense may cause psychological injury to the victim.

6. Lay Witness May Testify as to Opinion of Defendant's Sanity or Insanity If Based Upon Personally Observed Facts

People v. Wright, 111 Ill. 2d 128 (1985)

Defendant was charged with murder, attempted murder, home invasion, residential burglary, attempted rape, and armed robbery. Defendant entered an apartment where a mother and her daughter lived. He murdered the mother and attempted to murder the daughter, but she survived. At trial, defendant testified that he was not able to control his actions on the night of the crime. Defense counsel attempted to cross-examine the daughter about her opinion regarding defendant's sanity on the night he attacked her. State objected to the line of questioning and trial court sustained the objection. Defendant contended on appeal that the trial court improperly limited the cross-examination on the "crucial" issue of his sanity. The Illinois Supreme Court found that

> [i]t is well established that a lay witness may give his opinion regarding the mental condition of an individual based on personally observed facts, which must be stated in detail. People v. Smothers, 55 Ill. 2d 172, 174 (1973); People v. Williams, 38 Ill. 2d 115, 123 (1967); CLEARY & GRAHAM, ILLINOIS EVIDENCE sec. 704.3 (3d ed. 1979); 4 CALLAGHAN'S ILLINOIS EVIDENCE sec. 7.27 (1964). Nevertheless, "the scope of cross-examination rests largely in the discretion of the trial court, and we will overturn its ruling only where an abuse of that discretion results in manifest prejudice to the defendant." People v. Owens, 102 Ill. 2d 88, 103 (1984).

The Supreme Court concluded that the trial judge did not abuse its discretion in limiting the cross-examination of the daughter because it appeared from the record that she was unable to give an opinion as to defendant's sanity or insanity at the time of the attack. The Supreme Court observed that the daughter could only conclude that defendant's actions were "vicious" but not abnormal, and that her description of defendant's actions "fully apprised" the jury of defendant's actions.

7. Expert May Testify in the Form of Opinion Testimony Based on Personal Observations and Data Reasonably Relied Upon by Experts in the Particular Field About Whether Defendant Was Sane or Insane at the Time of the Crime
People v. Ward, 61 Ill. 2d 559 (1975)

An expert witness may express an opinion on the ultimate issue of fact as an aid to the trier of fact. Here, the Illinois Supreme Court found that a psychiatrist could give an opinion on the ultimate issue of the defendant's sanity or insanity. Defendant was convicted of murder and argued on appeal that the state did not prove his sanity beyond a reasonable doubt. Defendant called a clinical psychologist who evaluated him to testify. The psychologist concluded that defendant was schizophrenic and had a very low IQ.

The state's expert in rebuttal was a psychiatrist who also examined defendant and supervised another psychiatrist's evaluation of him. The testifying psychiatrist relied on various reports that were initially not in evidence. Defense counsel, however, requested that these reports be admitted in evidence. The reports included defendant's medical records and a letter written by the other examining psychiatrist. The letter detailed the other psychiatrist's conclusion that defendant was "legally sane" at the time of the commission of the crime.

On appeal, defendant objected to the admissibility of the psychiatrist's testimony regarding the letter, contending that the testimony constituted inadmissible hearsay offered to prove that defendant was sane at the time he committed the crime. The Illinois Supreme Court disagreed, noting that the letter was drafted "under the direction and supervision" of the testifying psychiatrist and that he was available for cross-examination. Moreover, the Supreme Court emphasized that the psychiatrist did not merely recite the non-testifying psychiatrist's opinion as to defendant's sanity, but rather expressed his own opinion about defendant's sanity and general mental health based on the letter, his review of defendant's medical records and on a personal observation of defendant. The Supreme Court found that the psychiatrist could give an opinion on the ultimate issue of the defendant's sanity or insanity because an expert witness may express an opinion on the ultimate issue of fact as an aid to the trier of fact.

The Illinois Supreme Court also rejected defendant's challenge to the admissibility of the letter. The Supreme Court observed that the letter was part of medical records that the defendant requested to be admitted during trial. The Supreme Court noted that the records and the letter would not have been in evidence without defendant's request that they be admitted. The Supreme Court explained that as long as "such reports are of a type customarily utilized by the medical profession, then these reports may be used as factors by an expert in the determination of his opinion as to an accused's sanity even though the reports are not admitted into evidence."

Rule 705. Disclosure of Facts or Data Underlying Expert Opinion

The expert may testify in terms of opinion or inference and give reasons therefor without first testifying to the underlying facts or data, unless the court requires otherwise. The expert may in any event be required to disclose the underlying facts or data on cross-examination.

Adopted September 27, 2010, eff. January 1, 2011.

Author's Commentary

The Illinois Supreme Court adopted the Federal Rule of Evidence 705 in Wilson v. Clark, 84 Ill. 2d 186 (1981), and "drastically" altered the common law with respect to the issue of disclosure of facts or data underlying an expert opinion. Michael H. Graham, Graham's

HANDBOOK OF ILLINOIS EVIDENCE § 705.1 (10th ed. 2010). Before the adoption of Federal Rule 705 by Illinois courts, an expert was required to disclose the basis for his or her opinion "as a safeguard of reliability." GRAHAM at § 705.1. The new Illinois Rule of Evidence 705 has adopted Federal Rule of Evidence 705 relied on in *Wilson v. Clark*, except that it made the language gender neutral by deleting a reference to expert's reasons as "his." The language of Illinois Rule 705 is now identical to the language of Federal Rule of Evidence 705 in effect prior to its stylistic amendment on December 1, 2011. Gino L. DiVito, *The Illinois Rules of Evidence: A Color-Coded Guide Containing the New Rules, the Committee's General and Specific Comments, a Comparison with the Federal Rules of Evidence, and Additional Commentary* (*Including the Federal Rules of Evidence as Amended Effective December 1, 2011*) (Jan. 1, 2012), at 91, http://www.tdrlawfirm.com/assets/downloads/Illinois_Rules_of_Evidence_Color-Coded_Guide.pdf. In accordance with Illinois common law, Illinois Rule 705 now permits an expert to testify without disclosing underlying facts supporting his or her opinion except where required on cross-examination. People v. Wagener, 196 Ill. 2d 269 (2001).

PRIOR ILLINOIS CASE LAW

1. An Expert Witness May Give an Opinion Without Disclosing Underlying Facts Supporting That Opinion

Wilson v. Clark, 84 Ill. 2d 186 (1981)

The Illinois Supreme Court adopted the Federal Rules of Evidence 703 and 705, noting that pursuant to Rule 705,

> an expert may give an opinion without disclosing the facts underlying that opinion. [. . .] Under [Federal] Rule 705 the burden is placed upon the adverse party during cross-examination to elicit the facts underlying the expert opinion. Bryan v. John Bean Division of FMC Corp., 566 F.2d 541, 545 (5th Cir. 1978). The advisory committee's note to Rule 705 allows an expert opinion without disclosure of underlying facts whether the opinion is based on firsthand or secondhand information. In light of Illinois' extensive pretrial discovery procedures, this does not place an undue burden on the cross-examining party.

The Supreme Court further explained that adoption of the Federal Rules of Evidence 703 and 705 "comports with the modern trend of liberalizing certain trial procedures" and "eliminates the time-consuming process of posing long hypothetical questions that afford an opportunity to sum up or reiterate the evidence in the middle of a case."

2. Expert Witness May Be Cross-Examined to Elicit Facts Underlying Expert Opinion

People v. Wagener, 196 Ill. 2d 269 (2001)

Defendant was charged with murder and concealment of a homicidal death. He claimed insanity at trial and had various mental health experts testify on his behalf. Defendant disclosed a police report, containing some of his statements, to his testifying expert witnesses to help them determine whether he was sane at the time of the crime. The Supreme Court found that defendant had waived any privilege with respect to those statements because he disclosed them to testifying experts, and that the state properly cross-examined his experts with respect to the contents of the report. The Illinois Supreme Court explained that

> the general rule [is] that experts may be cross-examined for the purpose of discrediting their testimony, as well as to ascertain which factors were taken into account and which were disregarded in arriving at these conclusions. People v. Williams, 181 Ill. 2d 297, 329 (1998). Opposing counsel is allowed to cross-examine an expert with respect to material which he has

reviewed but upon which he did not rely. People v. Page, 156 Ill. 2d 258, 275 (1993), quoting People v. Pasch, 152 Ill. 2d 133, 179 (1992). Indeed, counsel may venture beyond the facts supported by the record in inquiring as to what changes of conditions would affect his opinion. *Williams*, 181 Ill. 2d at 329; *Page*, 156 Ill. 2d at 275; *Pasch*, 152 Ill. 2d at 179. Thus the general rule would allow the State to cross-examine the experts with the content of a report included among the materials which they considered in forming their opinions.

3. Expert Witness May Be Impeached with Reports and Conclusions of Other Experts

People v. Pasch, 152 Ill. 2d 133 (1992)

The Illinois Supreme Court determined to what extent an expert may be questioned regarding reports and conclusions of other experts he or she did not rely on in coming to his or her conclusion. In this case, the court allowed the state to impeach the defendant's expert witness with reports and documents the expert did not review in forming his opinion. By allowing such questioning, the court felt that the examiner could test the knowledge and fairness of the expert by inquiring into what changes of conditions would affect his opinion. Moreover, this line of questioning allowed the jury to see what factors the expert took into account in forming an opinion and, more importantly, what factors the expert did not consider. This would allow the jury to properly evaluate the expert's opinion.

Chapter 6

Chapter 6

Article VIII – Hearsay

Definitions

Rule 801. Definitions
The following definitions apply under this article:

(a) Statement. A "statement" is (1) an oral or written assertion or (2) nonverbal conduct of a person, if it is intended by the person as an assertion.

(b) Declarant. A "declarant" is a person who makes a statement.

(c) Hearsay. "Hearsay" is a statement, other than one made by the declarant while testifying at the trial or hearing, offered in evidence to prove the truth of the matter asserted.

(d) Statements Which Are Not Hearsay. A statement is not hearsay if

(1) Prior Statement by Witness. In a criminal case, the declarant testifies at the trial or hearing and is subject to cross-examination concerning the statement, and the statement is

(A) inconsistent with the declarant's testimony at the trial or hearing, and—

(1) was made under oath at a trial, hearing, or other proceeding, or in a deposition, or

(2) narrates, describes, or explains an event or condition of which the declarant had personal knowledge, and

(a) the statement is proved to have been written or signed by the declarant, or

(b) the declarant acknowledged under oath the making of the statement either in the declarant's testimony at the hearing or trial in which the admission into evidence of the prior statement is being sought or at a trial, hearing, or other proceeding, or in a deposition, or

(c) the statement is proved to have been accurately recorded by a tape recorder, videotape recording, or any other similar electronic means of sound recording; or

(B) one of identification of a person made after perceiving the person.

(2) Admission by Party-Opponent. The statement is offered against a party and is (A) the party's own statement, in either an individual or a representative capacity, or (B) a statement of which the party has manifested an adoption or belief in its truth, or (C) a statement by a person authorized by the party to make a statement concerning the subject, or (D) a statement by the party's agent or servant concerning a matter within the scope of the agency or employment, made during the existence of the relationship, or (E) a statement by a coconspirator of a party during the course and in furtherance of the conspiracy, or (F) a statement by a person, or a person on behalf of an entity, in privity with the party or jointly interested with the party.
Adopted September 27, 2010, eff. January 1, 2011.

Committee Commentary

(3) Modernization: Where there was no conflict with statutes or recent Illinois Supreme Court or Illinois Appellate Court decisions, and where it was determined to be beneficial and uniformly or almost uniformly accepted elsewhere, the Committee incorporated into the Illinois Rules of Evidence uncontroversial developments with respect to the law of evidence as reflected in the Federal Rules of Evidence and the 44 surveyed jurisdictions. [Some of t]he 14 instances of modernization of note are as follows: ***

(5) Rule 801(d). Statements Which Are Not Hearsay.
Rule 801(d)(1)(A) codifies an Illinois statute (725 ILCS 5/115-10.1) that applies only in criminal cases. It makes admissible as "not hearsay" (rather than as a hearsay exception) a prior inconsistent statement of a declarant who testifies at a trial or a hearing and is subject to cross-examination, when the prior inconsistent statement was given under oath at a trial, hearing, or other proceeding, or in a deposition, or under other specified circumstances. The rule does not apply in civil cases. Rule 801(d)(1)(B) also codifies an Illinois statute (725 ILCS 5/115-12). It makes admissible as "not hearsay" a declarant's prior statement of identification of a person made after perceiving that person, when the declarant testifies at a trial or hearing in a criminal case and is subject to cross-examination concerning the statement. Rule 801(d)(2) provides substantive admissibility, as "not hearsay," for admissions of a party-opponent.

(6) Rule 801(d)(2)(D). Statement by a Party's Agent or Servant.
Rule 801(d)(2)(D) confirms the clear direction of prior Illinois law that a statement by a party's agent or servant concerning a matter within the scope of the agency or employment, made during the existence of the relationship, constitutes an admission of a party-opponent.
ILL. R. EVID. Committee Commentary § 3, pg. 2-3.

(6) Referenced Statutes: Numerous existing statutes, the validity of which are not affected by promulgation of the Illinois Rules of Evidence, Ill. R. Evid. 101, relate in one form or another to the law of evidence. The Committee felt it was inappropriate, unnecessary and unwise to refer specifically to the abundance of statutory authority in an Appendix or otherwise. Reference is, however, made in the body of the text of the Illinois Rules of Evidence to certain statutes by citation or verbatim incorporation. Such references and the reasons therefor are as follows:

(5) Rule 801(d)(1): The provisions of 725 ILCS 5/115-10.1, dealing with prior inconsistent statements in a criminal case, are incorporated nearly verbatim in Rule 801(d)(1)(A) in the interests of completeness and convenience. Similar treatment is given to prior statements of identification, 725 ILCS 5/115-12, in Rule 801(d)(1)(B).
ILL. R. EVID. Committee Commentary § 6, pg. 8-9.

AUTHOR'S COMMENTARY

Illinois Rule of Evidence 801(a)-(c)

Illinois Rule of Evidence 801(a)-(c) provides definitions for "statement," "declarant," and "hearsay." Pursuant to the definition of a "statement" contained in Illinois Rule of Evidence 801(a), the out-of-court declaration may be an oral or written statement or assertive nonverbal conduct that is intended by the declarant to be a communication. Sections (a) through (c) of the Illinois Rule of Evidence 801 are identical to the Federal Rule of Evidence 801(a)-(c) effective December 1, 1997. *See* Gino L. DiVito, *The Illinois Rules of Evidence: A Color-Coded Guide Containing the New Rules, the Committee's General and*

Specific Comments, a Comparison with the Federal Rules of Evidence, and Additional Commentary (Including the Federal Rules of Evidence as Amended Effective December 1, 2011) (Jan. 1, 2012), at 95, http://www.tdrlawfirm.com/assets/downloads/Illinois_Rules_of_Evidence_Color-Coded_Guide.pdf.

Illinois Rule of Evidence 801(d)(1)(A): Statements That Are Not Hearsay—Prior Inconsistent Statement of Declarant Witness

The long-standing Illinois common law rule classified a prior inconsistent statement of a witness as hearsay. Such statement could be used solely as impeachment evidence of a declarant witness whose trial testimony conflicted with his or her out-of-court statement. People v. Gant, 58 Ill. 2d 178 (1974). The Illinois legislature subsequently enacted 725 ILCS 5/115-10.1, which allows admissibility of some prior inconsistent statements as substantive evidence in criminal trials. Section 5/115-10.1 has in turn been codified by the new Illinois Rule of Evidence 801(d)(1)(A). *See* ILL. R. EVID. Committee Commentary § 3, pg. 2-3.

Illinois Rule of Evidence 801(d)(1)(A)(1) addresses prior inconsistent statements of a witness made under oath at a trial, hearing, other proceeding, or in a deposition, but mirrors only a portion of Federal Rule of Evidence 801(d)(1)(A), in effect prior to its stylistic amendment on December 1, 2011. *See* Gino L. DiVito, *The Illinois Rules of Evidence: A Color-Coded Guide Containing the New Rules, the Committee's General and Specific Comments, a Comparison with the Federal Rules of Evidence, and Additional Commentary (Including the Federal Rules of Evidence as Amended Effective December 1, 2011)* (Jan. 1, 2012), at 96, http://www.tdrlawfirm.com/assets/downloads/Illinois_Rules_of_Evidence_Color-Coded_Guide.pdf. Illinois Rule of Evidence 801(d)(1)(A)(2), in adopting 725 ILCS 5/115-10.1, goes far beyond the narrow scope of Federal Rule of Evidence 801(d)(1)(A) ("statement given under oath subject to the penalty of perjury at a trial, hearing, or other proceeding, or in a deposition"). Under section 115-10.1, and now Illinois Rule of Evidence 801(d)(1)(A)(2), the setting for the out-of-court statement is not limited to a trial, hearing, or other proceeding, or a deposition. This expansion invites the admissibility of untrustworthy evidence where even minimal indicia of reliability, an oath, for example, are missing.

A police interrogation may yield an unreliable statement, perhaps the product of mistake, fabrication, or duress. Yet under section 5/115-10.1 and now under Illinois Rule of Evidence 801(d)(1)(A)(2), if the statement is written or signed by the declarant or is accurately recorded by the police, it will be admitted substantively in a criminal trial. For example, the statement of a crime witness who honestly misperceived the events of a crime or the defendant's conduct, given shortly after the event and videotaped by the police, would be admitted as substantive evidence, even though the declarant, who is now a witness, having had an opportunity to reflect on the events, expresses grave doubts about the accuracy of his or her prior statement. The same result could occur if the declarant had deliberately fabricated a story for the police but at trial exposed the statement as a lie. Perhaps the most troubling situation is where the police coerce the declarant into giving a statement that is false or that does not accurately reflect the truth. The fact that the statement had been written or signed by the declarant who has personal knowledge, or was accurately recorded by the police, should provide no cure for the involuntariness of that statement.

Unlike Illinois Rule of Evidence 607, which requires a showing of affirmative damage where a prior inconsistent statement is used to impeach a party's own witness, Illinois Rules of Evidence 801(d)(1)(A), 801(d)(1)(B), 801(d)(2), and 803, require no showing of affirmative damage when an out-of-court statement is admitted substantively.

Prior Consistent Statements

Illinois Rule of Evidence 801 has not adopted Federal Rule of Evidence 801(d)(1)(B), effective December 1, 2011, (permitting substantive admissibility of a statement if the "declarant testifies and is subject to cross-examination about a prior statement, and the statement [. . .] is consistent with the declarant's testimony and is offered to rebut an express or implied charge that the declarant recently fabricated it or acted from a recent improper influence or motive in so testifying"), and has retained the Illinois common law rule that prior consistent statements are admissible solely to rehabilitate an impeached witness but cannot be used as substantive evidence. People v. Walker, 211 Ill. 2d 317 (2004). But see Justice DiVito who asserts that "Illinois allows [prior consistent] statements to be admitted [. . .] for their corroborative value." Gino L. DiVito, *The Illinois Rules of Evidence: A Color-Coded Guide Containing the New Rules, the Committee's General and Specific Comments, a Comparison with the Federal Rules of Evidence, and Additional Commentary* (*Including the Federal Rules of Evidence as Amended Effective December 1, 2011*) (Jan. 1, 2012), at 98, http://www.tdrlawfirm.com/assets/downloads/Illinois_Rules_of_Evidence_Color-Coded_Guide.pdf. Illinois courts, however, have followed the "general rule that a witness may not testify as to statements he made out-of-court for the purpose of corroborating his testimony given at the trial relative to the same subject." People v. Clark, 52 Ill. 2d 374, 389 (1972); *see also* People v. Lambert, 288 Ill. App. 3d 450 (2d Dist. 1997) (reasoning that "corroboration by repetition 'preys on the human failing of placing belief in that which is most often repeated.'"). A prior consistent statement is admissible as rehabilitation evidence to rebut a charge or an inference that the witness has a motive to testify falsely or that the witness has recently fabricated his or her testimony.

Illinois Rule of Evidence 801(d)(1)(B): Statements That Are Not Hearsay—Prior Identification by Declarant Witness Subject to Cross-Examination

Trial testimony that on a prior occasion the victim had identified the defendant as his or her assailant is highly probative. It may be presented by the testimony of the out-of-court declarant or by a witness to the out-of-court identification procedure. The testimony may establish that the victim had made an identification and explain how the victim had accomplished the identification of the defendant by such means as a line-up, showup, photograph, sketch, or Identi-kit composites.

Before the enactment of the Illinois Rules of Evidence, Illinois common law followed a rule that allowed a victim to testify at trial about his or her out-of-court identification of the defendant. Because the out-of-court declarant was available for cross-examination, the evidence was allowed. However, the admissibility of the evidence was limited: it could only corroborate the victim's in-court identification of the defendant but could not be used as substantive evidence of the defendant's guilt. The Illinois legislature subsequently modified the common law rule and designated such statement as non-hearsay pursuant to 725 ILCS 5/115-12. ILL. R. EVID. Committee Commentary § 3, pg. 2-3. Since the corroboration limitation has been eliminated by the statute, and the new Illinois Rule of Evidence 801(d)(1)(B) has codified section 5/115-12, an out-of-court identification is now admissible as substantive evidence of the defendant's guilt. ILL. R. EVID. Committee Commentary § 3, pg. 2-3.

Illinois Rule of Evidence 801(d)(2): Admission by Party-Opponent

Before the enactment of the Illinois Rules of Evidence, a party's out-of-court admission was considered hearsay but admissible substantively as an exception to the hearsay rule. *In re* Estate of Rennick, 181 Ill. 2d 395 (1998). Pursuant to Rule 801(d)(2), such admissions are now considered "not hearsay." ILL. R. EVID. Committee Commentary § 3, pg. 2-3.

The silence of the accused may be treated as an admission. The Illinois common law treated this out-of-court statement as a tacit or implied admission of guilt if the accused remained silent in the face of an accusation of criminal conduct. Such evidence was received with caution and only when it affirmatively appeared that the accused was addressed or questioned about the crime for which he or she was subsequently prosecuted. People v. McCain, 29 Ill. 2d 132, 135 (1963) (noting that a "natural reaction of an innocent person would be to deny the accusation, and that silence is an admission of guilt, proof of defendant's silence is essential to the admission of the declaration"). An evasive or unresponsive reply to an accusation would also constitute a tacit admission from which guilt could be implied. *See* People v. Wright, 65 Ill. App. 2d 23 (1st Dist. 1965).Where the silence followed advice from the accused's attorney or was deemed as the exercise of the privilege against self-incrimination, silence could not be admitted as an admission. People v. Redd, 135 Ill. 2d 252 (1990). The foregoing treatment of silence remains unaffected by the adoption of the Illinois Rules of Evidence.

The defendant may not introduce his or her own out-of-court exculpatory statements. Such statements are hearsay. Such self-serving statements are not reliable because the accused may have a motive to fabricate favorable evidence relating to his or her innocence. *See* People v. Jones, 26 Ill. 2d 300 (1962). A defendant's exculpatory out-of-court statement that denies his or her criminal responsibility but is false is admissible as circumstantial evidence of guilt. *See* People v. Gutierrez, 105 Ill. App. 3d 1059 (2d Dist. 1982).

Illinois Rule of Evidence 801(d)(2)(D) has adopted Federal Rule of Evidence 801(d)(2)(D), effective December 1, 1997, and has "confirm[ed] the clear direction of prior Illinois law that a statement by a party's agent or servant concerning a matter within the scope of the agency or employment, made during the existence of the relationship, constitutes an admission of a party-opponent." ILL. R. EVID. Committee Commentary § 3, pg. 2-3. The Committee Commentary to the Federal Rule of Evidence 801(d)(2)(D) explained that

> [t]he tradition has been to test the admissibility of statements by agents, as admissions, by applying the usual test of agency. Was the admission made by the agent acting in the scope of his employment? Since few principals employ agents for the purpose of making damaging statements, the usual result was exclusion of the statement. Dissatisfaction with this loss of valuable and helpful evidence has been increasing. A substantial trend favors admitting statements related to a matter within the scope of the agency or employment.
> FED. R. EVID. 801, Advisory Committee Notes (1972 Proposed Rules).

Prior to the adoption of this standard, Illinois common law followed "[t]raditional agency principles" in determining whether the statement of an agent was treated as an admission of the principal. People v. Cruz, 162 Ill. 2d 314 (1994). The traditional common law approach required an agent to be authorized to speak on behalf of the principal. Jenkins v. Dominick's Finer Foods, Inc., 288 Ill. App. 3d 827 (1st Dist. 1997). Some Illinois appellate court decisions subsequently began to recognize the federal standard as the "modern trend." Pietruszynski v. McClier Corp., Architects & Engineers, Inc., 338 Ill. App. 3d 58 (1st Dist. 2003); Pavlik v. Wal-Mart Stores, Inc., 323 Ill. App. 3d 1060 (1st Dist. 2001); Vojas v. Kmart Corp., 312 Ill. App. 3d 544 (5th Dist. 2000). The federal standard does not require that the agent have the authority to speak on behalf of the principal. *See* Gino L. DiVito, *The Illinois Rules of Evidence: A Color-Coded Guide Containing the New Rules, the Committee's General and Specific Comments, a Comparison with the Federal Rules of Evidence, and Additional Commentary (Including the Federal Rules of Evidence as Amended Effective December 1, 2011)* (Jan. 1, 2012), at 97-98, http://www.tdrlawfirm.com/assets/downloads/Illinois_Rules_of_Evidence_Color-Coded_Guide.pdf [hereinafter DiVito, *Color-Coded Guide*]. Illinois Rule of Evidence 801(d)(2)(D) has therefore abandoned the common law approach in favor of the federal standard, and now requires only that the statement is one made "within the scope of the agency or employment [and] during the existence of the relationship."

Pursuant to Illinois Rule of Evidence 801(d)(2)(E), the statement of a co-conspirator is no longer admitted as an exception to the hearsay rule but is now treated as "not hearsay" and is admissible against the defendant and all other conspirators. However, Illinois has rejected the Federal Rules of Evidence model that permits the contents of the out-of-court statement as partial proof of the existence of the conspiracy and of the participation in it by the declarant and the defendant. Illinois has retained the common law principle that requires proof of a conspiracy by independent evidence. People v. Goodman, 81 Ill. 2d 278 (1980). Illinois Rule of Evidence 801(d)(2) has not incorporated the last paragraph of Federal Rule of Evidence 801(d)(2), effective December 1, 2011, which states that "[t]he statement must be considered but does not by itself establish [. . .] the existence of the conspiracy or participation in it under (E)." *See* Bourjaily v. United States, 483 U.S. 171 (1987) (providing the federal standard). Pursuant to Illinois Rule of Evidence 801(d)(2), statements admitted pursuant to subdivisions (C), (D), (E) and (F) must "be based on the relationships specified independently of the contents of the statement." DiVito, *Color-Coded Guide* at 99.

Illinois Rule of Evidence 801(d)(2) also differs from Federal Rule of Evidence 801(d)(2), in effect prior to its stylistic amendment on December 1, 2011, in that it has an additional section (F) which allows for the admissibility of a statement against a party if that statement is "by a person, or a person on behalf of an entity, in privity with the party or jointly interested with the party." Section (F) codifies Illinois common law principles. DiVito, *Color-Coded Guide* at 99.

Relevant Statutory Authority

Admissibility of Prior Inconsistent Statements: 725 ILCS 5/115-10.1

§ 115-10.1. Admissibility of Prior Inconsistent Statements. In all criminal cases, evidence of a statement made by a witness is not made inadmissible by the hearsay rule if
(a) the statement is inconsistent with his testimony at the hearing or trial, and (b) the witness is subject to cross-examination concerning the statement, and (c) the statement—

(1) was made under oath at a trial, hearing, or other proceeding, or
(2) narrates, describes, or explains an event or condition of which the witness had personal knowledge, and

(A) the statement is proved to have been written or signed by the witness, or
(B) the witness acknowledged under oath the making of the statement either in his testimony at the hearing or trial in which the admission into evidence of the prior statement is being sought, or at a trial, hearing, or other proceeding, or
(C) the statement is proved to have been accurately recorded by a tape recorder, videotape recording, or any other similar electronic means of sound recording.

Nothing in this Section shall render a prior inconsistent statement inadmissible for purposes of impeachment because such statement was not recorded or otherwise fails to meet the criteria set forth herein.

Effective July 1, 1984.

Substantive Admissibility of Prior Identification. 725 ILCS 5/115-12

§ 115-12. Substantive Admissibility of Prior Identification.

A statement is not rendered inadmissible by the hearsay rule if (a) the declarant testifies at the trial or hearing, and (b) the declarant is subject to cross-examination concerning the statement, and (c) the statement is one of identification of a person made after perceiving him.

Effective January 1, 1984.

Illinois Case Law Under the New Illinois Rules of Evidence

1. Prior Consistent Statements Are Inadmissible Substantively

People v. Walker, 211 Ill. 2d 317 (2004)

Defendant was charged with unlawful possession of a weapon by a felon and unlawful sale of firearms. Defendant and two teenage girls were together on the evening the crime took place. Both girls testified against defendant under a grant of immunity that he placed a gun into one girl's pocket immediately before the three were confronted by the police. The girls initially gave the police statements that "didn't match" because they were scared. They later gave written statements that were consistent with their testimony at trial. The state moved to have one girl's written statement consistent with her trial testimony introduced at trial. Defendant contended on appeal that the statement was improperly admitted as substantive evidence. The Illinois Supreme Court agreed, observing that the prosecutor explicitly argued that the statement was admissible substantively in his argument and in closing remarks, indicating that it "tells the truth." The Supreme Court agreed with the appellate court which noted that

> in Illinois, prior consistent statements may be admitted to rebut a charge or inference that the witness is motivated to testify falsely or to rebut the inference that the witness' testimony is of recent fabrication, but may not be admitted substantively to corroborate the witness' testimony. People v. Williams, 147 Ill. 2d 173 (1991).
>
> ***
>
> In its appeal to this court, the State challenges the appellate court's holding on this matter. The State does not take exception to the appellate court's statement of the law and concedes that prior consistent statements are generally inadmissible, but may be admitted *for the limited purpose* of rebutting inferences that the witness is motivated to testify falsely or that the testimony is of recent fabrication. People v. Emerson, 97 Ill. 2d 487, 500-01 (1983). Rather, the State disputes the appellate court's finding that, in the case at bar, [the girl's] prior consistent statement was admitted substantively, arguing that the record shows that the evidence was admitted under the exception, that is, for the limited purpose of rebutting the inference that [the girl] was motivated to lie. The State also argues that the appellate court should not have addressed the error because defendant waived it. The State also makes a harmless error argument.
>
> ***
>
> We find the State's arguments unavailing. We agree with the appellate court that the record suggests that [the girl's] prior consistent statement was admitted substantively. The prosecutor's arguments at trial reveal confusion over the extent to which a prior consistent statement may be admitted. When arguing for admission of [the girl's] written statement into evidence, the prosecutor asked that it be admitted "*as substantive evidence* under the hearsay

> rule." (Emphasis added.) Later, when seeking the admission of the State's exhibits, the prosecutor, with regard to [her] second written statement, argued: "[I]n that context, to counter that inference, [you can] admit *as substantive evidence* a prior consistent statement, and I think that that's exactly what we're trying to do and it's proper for that reason." (Emphasis added.) Later, in closing argument, the prosecutor used [her] prior consistent statement substantively, arguing that it "tells the truth." Also, when arguing in favor of sending the statement back to the jury, the prosecutor argued: "Both are admissible *as substantive evidence*. And with respect to the hearsay exception for rebutting the inference of fabrication, I think they're [the jury] entitled to consider it, especially in light of their request to see them." (Emphasis added.)

The Supreme Court found that the trial court failed to provide limiting instructions with respect to the statement and allowed the statement to be used for substantive purposes. The Supreme Court concluded that although the statement was admitted substantively, it need not decide whether the error warranted reversal because it had already decided to reverse defendant's conviction on another basis.

2. Prior Consistent Statement Is Admissible Solely for Rehabilitative Purposes
People v. Lambert, 288 Ill. App. 3d 450 (2d Dist. 1997)

Defendant was convicted of first degree murder. Defendant's half-brother and nephew were the only eyewitnesses linking defendant to the murder, and they both provided written statements to the police. The prosecutor read the written statements at trial and defense objected. The trial court overruled the objection and admitted the statement. The Second District of the Illinois Appellate Court reversed and noted that

> Illinois follows the common-law rule [. . .] that, where admission is allowed, a prior consistent statement is permitted solely for rehabilitative purposes and not as substantive evidence. People v. Weinger, 101 Ill. App. 3d 857, 874 (1981); People v. Hudson, 86 Ill. App. 3d 335, 340 (1980); People v. Hahn, 39 Ill. App. 3d 969 (1976); R. STEIGMANN, ILLINOIS EVIDENCE MANUAL § 23:37, at 310 (3d ed. 1995). The rationale for this common-law rule is that corroboration by repetition 'preys on the human failing of placing belief in that which is most often repeated.' [citations omitted]. In other words, 'mere repetition does not imply veracity.' Coltrane v. United States, 418 F.2d 1131, 1140 (D.C. 1969); *see also* 4 J. WIGMORE, EVIDENCE § 1126 (Chadbourn rev. ed. 1972). Credibility should not depend upon the number of times a witness has repeated the same story, as opposed to the inherent trustworthiness of the story. [citation omitted]. Where the common law applies and a prior consistent statement is admitted into evidence, an instruction from the court instructing the jury of its limited rehabilitative purpose is proper.

3. Prior Consistent Statement Is Admissible to Rebut a Charge or an Inference That Witness Is Motivated to Testify Falsely or That Witness' Testimony Is of Recent Fabrication
People v. Williams, 147 Ill. 2d 173 (1991)

Defendant was convicted of murder, aggravated kidnapping and rape after a gas station attendant and his girlfriend went missing and were found murdered in and near an abandoned warehouse. A woman who witnessed the murder testified at defendant's grand jury proceeding. State introduced her testimony as a prior consistent statement at defendant's trial. Defendant contended for the first time on appeal that her testimony was erroneously admitted as a prior consistent statement because the witness had the same motive to fabricate her testimony when she gave it as at trial. The Illinois Supreme Court disagreed, noting that the trial court properly found that the witness' statement qualified as a prior consistent statement because defense "raised an inference that [her] trial testimony was motivated by expectations of leniency and was of recent fabrication." The Supreme Court explained that

> [a] witness may not be corroborated on direct examination by proof of prior statements consistent with his testimony. People v. Powell, 53 Ill. 2d 465, 472 (1973). Moreover, when a witness is impeached by means of a prior inconsistent statement, if a consistent statement does not disprove or explain the making of the inconsistent statement, it is not admissible. M. GRAHAM, CLEARY & GRAHAM'S HANDBOOK OF ILLINOIS EVIDENCE § 611.14 (5th ed. 1990).) However, prior consistent statements are admissible to rebut a charge or an inference that the witness is motivated to testify falsely or that his testimony is of recent fabrication, and such evidence is admissible to show that he told the same story before the motive came into existence or before the time of the alleged fabrication. People v. Clark, 52 Ill. 2d 374, 389 (1972); People v. Titone, 115 Ill. 2d 413, 423 (1986); *see also* People v. Harris, 123 Ill. 2d 113, 139 (1988); M. GRAHAM, CLEARY & GRAHAM'S HANDBOOK OF ILLINOIS EVIDENCE § 611.14 (5th ed. 1990).

PRIOR ILLINOIS CASE LAW

1. Hearsay Evidence Is an Out-of-Court Statement Offered to Prove the Truth of the Matter Asserted

People v. Olinger, 176 Ill. 2d 326 (1997)

Defendant was charged with multiple murders. On appeal he contended that his trial counsel was ineffective for failing to call his co-defendant to testify about a statement he previously had made to the police. The co-defendant previously told the police that a third person who had a drug dispute with the victims had told him he was planning to hurt the victims on the day the murders occurred. The Illinois Supreme Court noted that this statement was inadmissible hearsay. The court explained that "[h]earsay evidence is an out-of-court statement offered to prove the truth of the matter asserted, and it is generally inadmissible due to its lack of reliability unless it falls within an exception to the hearsay rule." The Supreme Court concluded that no hearsay exception applied in this case and the statement was, therefore, not admissible.

2. The Presence or Absence in Court of the Declarant of an Out-of-Court Statement Is Irrelevant to a Determination of Whether the Statement Is Hearsay

People v. Lawler, 142 Ill. 2d 548 (1991)

Defendant was convicted of aggravated criminal sexual assault. The incident occurred one evening while the victim was driving home. Defendant pulled his car up next to the victim's and told her that her car tire was loose and might fall off. The victim pulled her car over and defendant wielded a weapon and threatened her. The victim asked the defendant if she could call her family because they would be worried about her if she did not check in with them. The victim called her father who became concerned for her safety. Her father asked her several questions to which she answered "yes" or "no." From the victim's answers her father understood that she was with a man who was armed and that she could not leave. Her father told her to try to get to a specific restaurant where he would have the police waiting. The evidence of this telephone conversation was admitted at trial through the victim's and her father's testimony. The appellate court reversed defendant's conviction, finding that the conversation was erroneously admitted because it was inadmissible hearsay. The Illinois Supreme Court agreed and explained that

> [h]earsay evidence is an out-of-court statement offered to prove the truth of the matter asserted, and is generally inadmissible unless it falls within an exception. People v. Carpenter, 28 Ill. 2d

> 116, 121 (1963). The State argues that a statement from a witness as to his own prior out-of-court statement cannot violate the hearsay rule, because the witness will testify at trial with the safeguards of an oath and cross-examination, reducing the risk of perjured testimony. Adoption of the State's rationale would essentially obliterate a good portion of the hearsay rule. As has been noted, "[t]he presence or absence in court of the declarant of the out-of-court statement is *** irrelevant to a determination as to whether the out-of-court statement is hearsay." M. GRAHAM, CLEARY & GRAHAM'S HANDBOOK OF ILLINOIS EVIDENCE § 801.1, at 564-65 (5th ed. 1990).

The Supreme Court found that the conversation was offered to prove truth of the matter asserted and was inadmissible hearsay. The Supreme Court also concluded that no exception to the hearsay rule applied.

3. Out-of-Court Statement Is Not Hearsay and Is Admissible If Offered for Some Purpose Other Than to Establish the Truth of the Matter Asserted
People v. Hanson, 238 Ill. 2d 74 (2010)

Detective was allowed to testify at trial regarding a conversation he had with defendant's sister in which she told the detective that she thought defendant was involved in the murder of his parents, sister and brother-in-law. Defendant argued that the testimony was inadmissible hearsay. The Supreme Court disagreed, noting that

> [a]n out-of-court statement is admissible if it is offered for some purpose other than to establish the truth of the matter asserted and does not constitute hearsay. People v. Banks, 237 Ill. 2d 154 (2010). In this case, the State did not seek to admit [the sister's] statements to prove that defendant was guilty or even to prove that [she] thought defendant was guilty. Instead, Detective['s] testimony provided context for his investigation and for testimony pertaining to defendant's state of mind based on defendant's response to [his] questioning.

4. Evidence Is Not Hearsay If Offered for Independent Purpose Other Than Establishing the Truth of Matter Asserted Such as to Explain the Nature of Police Investigation
People v. Banks, 237 Ill. 2d 154 (2010)

If the evidence is offered for an independent purpose other than establishing the truth of the matter asserted, it is not hearsay. Here, defendant was charged with first degree murder, attempt, armed robbery, aggravated vehicular hijacking, aggravated kidnapping, aggravated discharge of a firearm, possession of a stolen motor vehicle, and aggravated unlawful restraint. A police officer testified at trial that he received a series of "flash" messages that informed him that a vehicle was taken in a carjacking, and was then involved in a hit and run accident. Police chased the vehicle, saw defendant exit and run away from the vehicle, and ultimately arrested him. Defendant argued that the evidence pertaining to the series of "flash" messages was inadmissible hearsay because it served to identify him as the perpetrator. The Illinois Supreme Court disagreed, noting that

> [t]he admission of an out-of-court statement that is not offered to prove the truth of the matter asserted but rather to explain the investigatory procedure followed in a case is proper (see, e.g., People v. Jones, 153 Ill. 2d 155, 160-61 (1992)) and to show that the police officers had probable cause to arrest on the basis of the communication (see People v. Louisville, 241 Ill. App. 3d 772, 781 (1st Dist. 1992)). Because [the officer] was not part of the initial investigation, the admission of the flash messages explained the course of the investigation, the subsequent actions of the police officers, which included a high-speed chase, a car crash into a CTA elevated-train pillar, a foot chase, and the basis for placing defendant under arrest.

For other decisions discussing this topic, see:

People v. Simms, 143 Ill. 2d 154 (1991) (finding officer's testimony that defendant's brother stated that defendant admitted to committing the murder was not hearsay because it was offered to show why police continued interrogating defendant).

People v. Williams, 181 Ill. 2d 297 (1998) (admitting 911 tape to help explain officers' conduct).

People v. Pulliam, 176 Ill. 2d 261 (1997) (admitting bystanders' statements to help explain investigative steps taken by police).

People v. Ransom, 65 Ill. 2d 339 (1976) (finding that physician's testimony that the body on which he performed an autopsy had a tag bearing a certain name was not hearsay because it was offered to establish chain of custody of the body rather than identity).

Williams v. Illinois, 132 S. Ct. 2221 (2012) (finding that expert's testimony about non-testifying third party's findings is not hearsay).

5. An Out-of-Court Statement Used to Impeach a Witness Is Not Hearsay
People v. Silagy, 101 Ill. 2d 147 (1984)

An out-of-court statement that is used as impeachment evidence is not hearsay. Defendant on trial for the murder of his girlfriend and her sister raised an insanity defense. A psychiatrist testified that based on defendant's history and his review of reports of other psychiatrists who treated defendant, it was his opinion that defendant was sexually and physically dangerous. On cross-examination, the psychiatrist admitted that another psychiatrist on whose report he partially relied in forming his opinion concluded that defendant was not sexually dangerous. Defendant argued that the trial court erred in admitting this testimony claiming it was hearsay. The Illinois Supreme Court disagreed, explaining that the statement was not hearsay since it was offered to impeach the psychiatrist witness. The Supreme Court noted that

> '[h]earsay evidence is testimony in court or written evidence, of a statement made out-of-court, such statement being offered as an assertion to show the truth of matters asserted therein, and thus resting for its value upon the credibility of the out-of-court asserter.' People v. Carpenter, 28 Ill. 2d 116, 121 (1963); People v. Rogers, 81 Ill. 2d 571 (1980); MCCORMICK, EVIDENCE sec. 246, at 584 (2d ed. 1972). The admission concerning [the other psychiatrist's] diagnosis at what was a substantially earlier time [. . .] was elicited, not "to show the truth of matters asserted therein," but for the purpose of impeaching [the testifying psychiatrist]. [. . .] That the defendant had previously been diagnosed as not sexually dangerous was offered to show and did show that the previous medical reports on which [the testifying psychiatrist] in part formed his opinion were not clear, unequivocal and undisputed.

6. Not Every Out-of-Court Statement of a Declarant Witness Is Necessarily Hearsay
People v. Clark, 52 Ill. 2d 374 (1972)

An out-of-court statement of a declarant witness is not excludable on the basis of hearsay if the opponent has an opportunity to cross-examine the declarant at trial about his or her statement. Here, a witness testified that defendant was at her house at the time of the crime. She also sought to testify that she told police officers who searched her home that defendant was at her house at this time. She made these statements to the officers weeks after the crime occurred and after the defendant had been identified by several witnesses in a lineup. The trial court prevented the witness from testifying as to what she said to the police officers. Defendant argued on appeal that the trial court erred in excluding this evidence, and state argued that the testimony was properly excluded as hearsay. The Illinois Supreme Court found that the witness' testimony was not hearsay because she

> was not offering to testify as to a statement made by a third person, but as to a statement she, herself, had made on a previous occasion. Therefore, the fundamental basis for excluding the hearsay evidence-lack of opportunity for cross-examination-[wa]s absent. (citations omitted) Although not within the purview of the hearsay rule, the exclusion of the statement the witness made to the police officer is supported by the general rule that a witness may not testify as to statements he made out-of-court for the purpose of corroborating his testimony given at the trial relative to the same subject. People v. Wesley, 18 Ill. 2d 138 (1959); People v. Fox, 269 Ill. 300 (1915). However, to rebut a charge or an inference that the witness is motivated to testify falsely or that his testimony is of recent fabrication, evidence is admissible that he told the same story before the motive came into existence or before the time of the alleged fabrication. Lyon v. Oliver, 316 Ill. 292 (1925); CLEARY, HANDBOOK OF ILLINOIS EVIDENCE (2d ed. 1963), sec. 9.12.

The Supreme Court concluded that although the statement was not hearsay, it was properly excluded because it

> was made several weeks after the killing and after the defendant had been identified in a lineup by witnesses to the killing. Every motive for fabricating a false statement existed [when the witness made her statement to the police officers] that existed at the time of the trial. The trial court properly excluded the testimony concerning her prior statement.

7. Prior Inconsistent Statement of a Declarant Testifying at Trial and Subject to Cross-Examination Is Admissible If It Narrates, Describes, or Explains an Event Within Declarant's Personal Knowledge

People v. Thomas, 178 Ill. 2d 215 (1997)

Defendant was convicted of murder. After the shooting, a co-defendant's fiancée told the police that defendant and another co-defendant came to her home and that defendant told her that "he had shot a man in the face." The fiancée later testified at trial for the state but claimed that her prior statement was false and that she had lied to the police because she was upset with the defendant. The state impeached her with her prior inconsistent statement and the trial court admitted the statement as

> substantive evidence pursuant to 725 ILCS 5/115-10.1(c)(2). The Illinois Supreme Court noted that pursuant to section 5/115-10.1(c)(2), a prior inconsistent statement is admissible as substantive evidence where "certain prerequisites" are met if "the witness is subject to cross-examination concerning the statement, and the statement . . . narrates, describes, or explains an event or condition of which the witness had personal knowledge." Defendant contended that the statement was inadmissible in this case because the witness lacked personal knowledge of the murder and could not testify that defendant admitted to committing the murder.

The Illinois Supreme Court found that defendant waived the issue and that plain error doctrine did not apply because the evidence was not closely balanced. The Supreme Court concluded that even if the statement pertaining to defendant's admission were excluded, the witness' testimony about the defendant's and co-defendant's appearance that night as well as her other statements "strongly corroborated defendant's participation in the murder" and any error would be harmless beyond a reasonable doubt.

8. Witness' Prior Testimony Need Not Directly Contradict Trial Testimony to Be Considered Inconsistent

People v. Flores, 128 Ill. 2d 66 (1989)

Defendant was convicted of armed robbery and murder. An accomplice testified at the grand jury proceeding. The accomplice later testified at trial under a grant of immunity but stated that he could not remember the content of his grand jury testimony. The state introduced the witness' grand jury testimony and the trial court admitted it as substantive evidence pursuant to 725 ILCS 5/115-10.1. The defendant contended on appeal that the trial court erred in admitting the hearsay testimony because it was not "inconsistent" with his trial testimony. The Illinois Supreme Court disagreed, noting that

> [a] witness' prior testimony . . . does not have to directly contradict testimony given at trial to be considered inconsistent within the meaning of that term set out in section 115-10.1. People v. Hastings, 161 Ill. App. 3d 714, 719 (1st Dist. 1978); People v. Davis, 106 Ill. App. 3d 260, 263-64 (2nd Dist. 1982). Dean Wigmore covered the question: "where a witness now claims to be unable to recollect a matter, a former affirmation of it should be admitted as a contradiction." *See* 3A J. WIGMORE, EVIDENCE IN TRIALS AT COMMON LAW § 1018, at 1061 (Chadbourn rev. 1970).

The Supreme Court found that the trial court's finding that witness' "memory loss" was inconsistent with his prior testimony was not an abuse of discretion. The Supreme Court also considered whether the witness' memory loss deprived the defendant of his sixth amendment right to confront witnesses against him. The Supreme Court concluded that "[t]he confrontation clause is not violated by admitting a declarant's out-of-court statements, as long as the declarant is testifying as a witness and subject to full and effective cross-examination."

9. Prior Statements Inconsistent with Trial Testimony May Be Used as Substantive Evidence Under Certain Circumstances and 725 ILCS 5/115-10.1 Is Constitutional
People v. Orange, 121 Ill. 2d 364 (1988)

Defendant was convicted of murder, concealment of a homicidal death and aggravated arson. Defendant's brother was also arrested in connection with these crimes and subsequently provided a confession to the police which also incriminated defendant. The brother testified at defendant's trial and conceded that he had previously told the assistant state's attorney during a custodial interrogation that defendant was involved in the crimes. The brother alleged that he made this prior statement because he was trying to "put the blame" on defendant. The state subsequently introduced the statement in evidence during presentation of rebuttal evidence through the testimony of an assistant state's attorney who took the brother's statement. Defendant sought to cross-examine the assistant state's attorney, but the trial court would not allow such questioning. Defendant also requested to recall the brother, but the trial court rejected this request. Defendant contended on appeal that the trial court erred in limiting his examination of the assistant state's attorney. The Illinois Supreme Court disagreed, explaining that

> [d]uring cross-examination [the brother] was asked about his pretrial statement to the police, and its substantive use became clear at that point. The proper procedure was for defense counsel to make the desired inquiry on redirect examination. Addressing the substantive use of prior inconsistent statements, one commentator has noted, "[I]f a full foundation is provided—i.e., if the questioning covers the time, place, persons present, and content of the prior statement ***—an opportunity is obviously provided to opposing counsel to explore the prior inconsistent statement on redirect and to bring out any explanation the witness may have." (Graham, *Employing Inconsistent Statements for Impeachment and as Substantive Evidence: A Critical Review and Proposed Amendments of Federal Rules of Evidence 801(d)(1)(A), 613, and 607*, 75 MICH. L. REV. 1565, 1605 (1977).) Accordingly, defense counsel's opportunity for questioning [the brother] about the confession came during redirect examination. At that

> time, counsel asked [the brother] about the statement, and elicited from him the explanation that he had been trying to put the blame on the defendant. It is not clear from the record here what additional information [the brother] could have provided, had the court granted defense counsel's request to recall [the brother]. Counsel told the trial judge, "I haven't spoken to him about this so I can't tell you everything he would say, but I would like to cover some of the areas that were covered in his statement." The court denied the request, correctly believing that counsel had had "ample opportunity" to make that inquiry.

The defendant also challenged the constitutionality of 725 ILCS 5/115-10.1, contending that the statute violated the separation of powers. The Illinois Supreme Court rejected this argument and found Section 115-10.1 constitutional, stating:

> . . . the statute was clearly within the legislature's authority. *See* People v. Rolfingsmeyer, 101 Ill. 2d 137, 140 (1984) ("[I]t is clear that 'the legislature of a State has the power to prescribe new and alter existing rules of evidence or to prescribe methods of proof.'" quoting People v. Wells, 380 Ill. 347, 354 (1942).) That this court has previously refused to allow the substantive use of prior inconsistent statements [citation omitted] did not preclude the legislature from doing so.

10. Witness' Invocation of His or Her Fifth Amendment Privilege Against Self-Incrimination Is Not to Be Treated as a Memory Loss and Cannot, Therefore, Satisfy the Element of Inconsistency
People v. Redd, 135 Ill. 2d 252 (1990)

Defendant was convicted of rapes and murders of two minor victims. The brother-in-law of the victims' mother testified at the grand jury proceeding. He testified that he saw defendant leave the room for about 30 minutes and when he returned he had a dark red stain on his jacket and a dried dark stain on his hands. He was also called as a witness at trial but invoked the fifth amendment privilege against self-incrimination. The trial court admitted the witness' prior grand jury testimony as a prior inconsistent statement. Defendant contended that the trial court erred in admitting this testimony as substantive evidence. The Illinois Supreme Court concluded that

> the assertion of the fifth amendment privilege may not be treated as a memory loss for purposes of satisfying the requirement of inconsistency in section 115-10.1(a). When a witness is permitted to assert the privilege not to incriminate himself, he is not claiming to be unable to recollect prior affirmations of asserted facts. The witness is not asserting a "gap in [his] recollection concerning the content of a prior statement." People v. Flores, 128 Ill. 2d 66, 88 (1989). The witness is asserting only that he believes the answers to questions posed may tend to incriminate him.
>
> ***
>
> The assertion by [the witness] of his fifth amendment privilege also prevented defendant an opportunity to cross-examine [the witness] in any meaningful manner. The requirement of subsection (b) of section 115-10.1 that [the witness] be subject to cross-examination was not met when [the witness] refused to testify on direct examination or on cross-examination.

11. Relevant Evidence of Non-Identification (Failure to Identify) Is Admissible
People v. Tisdel, 201 Ill. 2d 210 (2002)

The trial court permitted the state's witnesses to testify that they had viewed pretrial lineups that did not contain the defendant and that they had not made any identifications. The defendant contended that the trial court erred and that he was deprived of a fair trial due to the admissibility of the non-identification testimony. The appellate court held that it was error for the trial court to allow the impermissible use of the non-identification testimony to corroborate or bolster the witnesses' subsequent identification of the accused. The Supreme Court reversed, abrogating its earlier decision of People v. Hayes, 139 Ill. 2d 89 (1990).

In *Hayes*, the Supreme Court held that it was error for the trial court to admit testimony that the witnesses viewed pictures of persons other than the defendant and had made no identification. The Supreme Court in *Hayes* concluded that such statements did not identify the defendant and, therefore, were not admissible under the "statements of identification" exception. Here, the Supreme Court concluded that the holding in *Hayes* read the term "statements of identification" too narrowly. According to the Supreme Court,

> [t]his type of nonidentification is crucial to the accuracy of the witness' identification because, in the typical case, a witness is shown a group of similar looking individuals and asked to pick out only the one who committed the crime. Consequently, the fact that the witness did not pick the other individuals in the lineup becomes as important as the fact that the witness did pick the defendant. Given the crucial role that nonidentification plays with regard to a lineup or photo array where a defendant is positively identified, it follows that the same considerations apply with regard to those lineups or photo arrays where a defendant is not identified. Indeed, it is logical to presume that the more lineups and photo arrays a witness views, the more likely that witness' identification is reliable and is not based upon suggestiveness.

Therefore, the Supreme Court concluded that "the *Hayes* court erred in limiting 'statements of identification' to a witness' actual identification of defendant." The Supreme Court cautioned, however, that admissibility of non-identification evidence is to be limited by considerations of relevancy. The Supreme Court concluded that the trial court did not err in allowing the state's witnesses to testify as to their non-identification of the defendant.

12. Prior Out-of-Court Identification of a Witness Later Unable to Explain Basis of Identification Due to Memory Loss Is Admissible
United States v. Owens, 484 U.S. 554 (1988)

The victim, a correctional counselor at a federal prison, was severely beaten. One week after he was injured he was unable to provide a name of the attacker due to memory impairment resulting from his injuries. A few days later, however, he identified the defendant from a photo array. The victim testified at trial that he remembered identifying the defendant but on cross-examination admitted that he never saw the assailant. There was evidence that the victim had previously identified someone other than the defendant as his attacker, but the victim could not remember ever having made this identification.

The United States Supreme Court held that neither the confrontation clause of the sixth amendment nor Federal Rule of Evidence 802 bars testimony of a prior out-of-court identification when the identifying witness is unable because of memory loss to explain the basis for the identification. The Supreme Court reasoned that the requirements of the confrontation clause are satisfied if the declarant is present at trial, takes an oath, and is subject to unrestricted cross-examination, and if the fact finder is given an opportunity to observe the declarant's demeanor. The Supreme Court concluded that although cross-examination may not impugn the testimony when memory loss is claimed, "successful cross-examination is not the constitutional guarantee." Moreover, the Supreme Court explained that the victim's testimony was not hearsay under Federal Rule of Evidence 802, which prohibits admissibility of hearsay, because the victim testified at trial to his prior statements, was subject to cross-examination and the jury had an opportunity to evaluate his demeanor. Applying the Federal Rule of Evidence 801(d)(1)(C), the court reasoned that since the victim had identified defendant after perceiving him, such evidence is not hearsay.

13. Third-Person Witness May Testify as to Declarant's Out-of-Court Identification Whether or Not the Declarant Testifies at Trial

People v. Lewis, 223 Ill. 2d 393 (2006)

The Illinois Supreme Court has made it very clear that a witness to an out-of-court identification may testify about that identification whether or not the out-of-court identifier testifies about his or her out-of-court identification at trial. Such testimony is admissible as substantive evidence.

Here, the defendant appealed his bench trial conviction of criminal drug conspiracy and delivery of a controlled substance. Defendant argued that the trial court improperly admitted testimony of a third person where the out-of-court declarant testified at trial but did not address her out-of-court identification in her direct examination, and was not cross-examined concerning the out-of-court identification. The appellate court affirmed, finding that the testimony of the third person was properly admitted under 725 ILCS 5/115-12. The Illinois Supreme Court affirmed the ruling of the appellate court.

A witness testified at the defendant's trial that she agreed to obtain crack cocaine for an acquaintance. The witness stated that she planned to purchase the drugs from neighbors who lived across the alley. She identified the neighbors as a man, a woman, and the defendant. On an earlier occasion, the woman indicated that she or the defendant could supply the witness with drugs. She gave the witness her and defendant's cell phone numbers. After agreeing to purchase crack cocaine for her acquaintance, the witness contacted the defendant, known to her by the nickname "Rail," negotiated a deal, and agreed to purchase the crack cocaine when her buyer arrived. When her acquaintance arrived, accompanied by an undercover officer, the witness met the defendant in the back of her home and made the exchange. She approached the car occupied by the buyer and the officer, delivered the drugs, and asked if the driver was a police officer. The undercover officer denied being a police officer and drove away. The following day the witness was arrested and interviewed by the officer.

The officer testified that he observed a man behind the witness's house and identified the defendant as that individual. When the officer interviewed the witness, she identified the person who sold her the crack cocaine as "Rail." The officer connected the nickname to the defendant, obtained a photograph, and recognized the image as the defendant. He showed the picture to the witness and testified that she identified the defendant as the person in the photograph who sold her the cocaine.

The defendant raised a hearsay objection to the officer's testimony about the out-of-court identification, arguing that the requirements of 725 ILCS 5/115-12 were not satisfied because the declarant must testify about her out-of-court identification before a third person may do so. The court noted an appellate court split over the interpretation of 725 ILCS 5/115-12. The statute reads as follows: "[a] statement is not rendered inadmissible by the hearsay rule if (a) the declarant testifies at the trial or hearing, and (b) the declarant is subject to cross-examination concerning the statement and (c) the statement is one of identification of a person made after perceiving him." Some courts had held that the section requires the declarant to testify first concerning the out-of-court identification before a third person may do so. Conversely, the appellate court below held that the declarant is not required to testify about her out-of-court identification evidence before a third person presents identification evidence. The Supreme Court resolved the conflict by examining the plain language of the statute and determined that the requirements were satisfied in this case. The statute contains no language that expressly determines the order of such testimony, and the court is not permitted to add a requirement to the statute.

The defendant argued next that the officer's testimony was not admissible because the witness was not subject to cross-examination concerning her out-of-court statement since the state did not address the out-of-court identification in her direct examination. The defendant was, therefore, prevented from exploring her out-of-court identification on cross-examination. The Supreme Court rejected this claim, reasoning that the witness was subject to cross-examination because she did take the witness stand and responded willingly to questions. While the scope of cross-examination is generally limited to matters raised on direct, when the identification of the accused is at issue, the defense is allowed considerable latitude in questioning the identifying witness. Additionally, the defense could have recalled the witness in order to question her about the identification following the officer's testimony.

14. Any Statement by the Accused, Unless Excluded by a Privilege or Other Exclusionary Rule, May Be Used Against Him or Her as an Admission
People v. Aguilar, 265 Ill. App. 3d 105 (3d Dist. 1994)

The Third District of the Illinois Appellate Court noted the difference between an "admission" as defined by Federal Rule of Evidence 801(d)(2) and the Illinois common law doctrine of "incriminating admission" as follows:

> The hearsay rule is not a basis for objection when the defendant's own statements are offered against the defendant; in such a case the defendant's statements are termed "admissions." [citation omitted]. Any statement by an accused person, unless excluded by the privilege against self-incrimination or other exclusionary rules, may be used against him as an admission. Illinois courts have relied on Federal Rule of Evidence 801(d)(2) in finding that a defendant's admissions are not excludable as hearsay. [. . .] There is no requirement that an admission be inculpatory or against interest when made or when offered, because the theory of the admissions exception is based upon the view that the admissibility of a party's own statement is a product of the adversary system. [. . .] Our supreme court relied on Rule 801(d)(2) as recently as 1992 when it noted that a statement may be admissible as an admission against a party, but not when it is offered to support a the defendant's own position. *See* People v. Pasch, 152 Ill. 2d 133, 197 (1992).
>
> It is important to understand where this definition of the term "admission" comes from because "admission" has been used in two different contexts. One is the definition that appears in Federal Rule of Evidence 801(d)(2) of an "admission by a party opponent" that a statement is not hearsay if it is a party's own statement offered against that party. This comports with the definition [. . .] that often appears in Illinois cases that any and every statement by an accused person, unless excluded by the privilege against self-incrimination or other exclusionary rules, may be used against him as an admission. [citations omitted].
>
> The other definition of admission mentioned above that "an admission is a statement or conduct from which guilt may be inferred, when taken in connection with other facts, but from which guilt does not necessarily follow," was a doctrine used by courts to distinguish certain statements of defendants that were incriminatory but were not confessions. This was done to avoid the strict admissibility requirements of confessions (e.g., the voluntariness requirement). Originally, when used in this context, the term our supreme court used was "incriminating admissions." *See* People v. Sovetsky, 323 Ill. 133 (1926); People v. Kircher, 309 Ill. 500 (1923). Later, the word "incriminating" was dropped and just the term "admission" was used. *See* People v. Stanton, 16 Ill. 2d 459 (1959); People v. Griswold, 405 Ill. 533 (1950). It is important to note that in all of these cases, the term "admission" was used to distinguish certain statements from confessions. In none of these cases does the court use it in reference to the hearsay rule. [. . .] The distinction between the two different uses of the term "admission" can also be seen in MCCORMICK'S HANDBOOK OF THE LAW OF EVIDENCE (2d ed. 1972). Chapter 26 of that work is entitled "Admissions of a Party Opponent," and contains the following

> definition of "admission": "Admissions are the words or acts of a party-opponent, or of his predecessor or representative, offered as evidence against him." (CLEARY ET AL., MCCORMICK'S HANDBOOK OF THE LAW OF EVIDENCE § 262 at 628 (2d ed. 1972).) Chapter 14 is entitled "Confessions," and contains the following definition of "admission": "An admission, on the other hand, is an acknowledgment of a fact or facts tending to prove guilt which falls short of an acknowledgement of all essential elements of the crime." (MCCORMICK § 144 at 310.) The author noted the distinction between admissions and confessions "has been undertaken primarily by courts seeking to avoid the application of stringent rules governing use of "confessions" to all statements made by an accused and offered at trial." (MCCORMICK § 144 at 309.) [. . .]
>
> ***
>
> Therefore, saying that an "admission" is a "statement or conduct from which guilt may be inferred, when taken in connection with other facts, but from which guilt does not necessarily follow," seems to be little more than a requirement that the statement be relevant.

15. Admission by Party-Opponent Is Not Excludable as Hearsay
People v. Simpson, 68 Ill. 2d 276 (1977)

Defendant was convicted of murdering his "paramour." On the night of the murder, the police observed defendant arguing with the victim. Later that night, defendant came to the house of his estranged wife. He looked disheveled and was carrying a woman's purse. His wife burned defendant's pants. At the police station, the police were interviewing defendant when his wife came into the room. Police officers asked her what defendant told her on the night of the murder. She stated that he told her he had shot the victim. In response to the wife's allegations, defendant stated "Yes, but I told you later I was lying." The trial court found that defendant's wife "could not testify" as to the confidential conversation she had with her husband on the night of the murder. An assistant state's attorney, who was present during defendant's questioning at the police station and heard his statement, could testify. The trial court found that the assistant state's attorney was permitted to testify about the statement because defendant, as the holder of the marital privilege, disclosed the confidential communication to a third party. Defendant argued that the statement was inadmissible as hearsay. The Illinois Supreme Court noted, however,

> that extrajudicial admissions made by a party opponent are not excludable as hearsay. People v. Newbury, 53 Ill. 2d 228, 234 (1972); MCCORMICK, EVIDENCE sec. 262, at 628 *et seq.* Compare FED. R. EVID. 801(d)(2) with FED. R. EVID. 804(b)(3).) The admission here was not that defendant shot [the victim], but that he had previously told his wife he had. We deem it clear that [the assistant state's attorney's] report of the wife's police station statement was admissible to explain the bare words of defendant's public admission, "Yes." Her statement gave meaning to the defendant's otherwise incomprehensible statement above, and merely revealed what the defendant thereby admitted to having said.

16. Self-Serving Out-of-Court Statements by the Accused Are Inadmissible Hearsay
People v. Pasch, 152 Ill. 2d 133 (1992)

Defendant was charged with murder and aggravated kidnapping after he shot and killed two people and held a third person hostage for 36 hours. The hostage negotiator testified at trial about statements defendant made to him during the negotiation. State objected to some of the statements claiming that they were inadmissible hearsay because they were self-serving. Defendant allegedly stated that he did not intentionally shoot at people, that he did not know that he was shooting at police officers, and that he did not know what he was doing because he was so "hopped up." Defendant also allegedly stated that one of the victims attacked him first and that he shot him in self-defense. Defendant sought to admit these statements to support a voluntary manslaughter instruction. The trial court excluded the evidence. Defendant argued on appeal that the statements should have been admitted as an admission. The Illinois Supreme Court rejected his position, noting that

> [a] statement may be admissible as an admission when it is offered by a defendant against a party, but not when it is offered to support the defendant's own position. People v. Berry, 172 Ill. App. 3d 256, 261 (1st Dist. 1988); M. GRAHAM, CLEARY & GRAHAM'S HANDBOOK OF ILLINOIS EVIDENCE § 802.1, at 595 (5th ed. 1990); FED. R. EVID. 801(d)(2). Therefore, because defendant's purported statement to [the hostage negotiator] that [one of the victims] struck him prior to the shooting was not being offered against a party, but was being offered to support defendant's position that he was guilty not of murder, but only of voluntary manslaughter, such statement was not admissible as an admission.
>
> Further, this purported statement not only was inadmissible as an admission, but was properly excluded as hearsay. Here, defendant attempted at trial to elicit, through [hostage negotiator's] testimony, an out-of-court statement made by defendant. Defendant wanted [the negotiator] to tell the jury that defendant told him that [the victim] had struck him and that that was why defendant shot [him]. Clearly, defendant wanted this evidence elicited at trial to be used as substantive evidence to prove the truth of defendant's own statement. Therefore, such statement was properly excluded by the trial court as hearsay.

17. "Dream" Statements by the Accused Are Not Admissions Because They Do Not Carry the Necessary Indicia of Trustworthiness

People v. Kidd, 147 Ill. 2d 510 (1992)

Defendant was convicted of murder and arson after 10 children died in an apartment building fire. Following the fire, a witness heard the defendant apologizing to two of the victims. It was not clear whether defendant was awake or asleep when he made these statements. The Illinois Supreme Court held that statements made by the defendant while asleep, offered as admissions, were not admissible. While the court noted that other jurisdictions allow such statements into evidence, it declined to follow these jurisdictions and, instead, agreed with those jurisdictions which condemn such statements and hold them inadmissible. The Supreme Court explained as follows:

> '[w]hat a dream means, if anything, presents an occurrence filled with mystery. As to the meaning of a dream, we can only conjecture.' State v. White, 271 N.C. 391, 394-95 (1967). While we do not doubt that dreams may in some respect relate to real experiences, their real meaning is open to a variety of interpretations. Dreams are imaginings and fantasy, and involve little logical thought. Furthermore, we are not aware of any scientific agreement, at present, that dreams can be explained in purely psychological, rather than physiological, terms. [Citation omitted]. Consequently, we hold that statements made by a declarant while asleep, and offered as admissions, do not carry the necessary indicia of trustworthiness required of competent evidence and are inadmissible.

In evaluating such evidence, the court set forth the following guidelines:

> We believe that the trial judge must make an initial factual determination regarding the admissibility of this evidence. That determination must, in part, consist of whether these statements were made while the declarant was asleep. For, given our holding today, if the declarant was asleep, the statements would not be trustworthy or reliable, and thus they would be inadmissible. We hold that in situations where the evidence is contradictory regarding whether the declarant is awake or asleep, the trial judge must make a preliminary finding of

fact that the defendant was awake for the statements to be admissible. In making its determination, the trial court should apply the burden of persuasion of more probably true than not.

18. Proof of *Corpus Delicti* of a Charged Offense May Not Rest Exclusively on Defendant's Extrajudicial Confession, Admission, or Other Statement
People v. Howard, 147 Ill. 2d 103 (1991)

Defendant argued that his conviction for armed robbery should be overturned because it was based solely on his own confession. The Illinois Supreme Court explained that

> [t]he *corpus delicti* of an offense has been defined as the occurrence of the injury or loss and its causation by criminal conduct. People v. Furby, 138 Ill. 2d 434, 446 (1990), citing 7 J. WIGMORE, EVIDENCE § 2072, at 524-25 (Chadbourn rev. ed. 1978); 1 W. LAFAVE & A. SCOTT, SUBSTANTIVE CRIMINAL LAW § 1.4, at 24 (1986).) Under the prevailing view, proof of the *corpus delicti* may not rest exclusively on a defendant's extrajudicial confession, admission, or other statement. *Furby*, 138 Ill. 2d at 446, citing 7 J. WIGMORE, EVIDENCE § 2071 (Chadbourn rev. ed. 1978); E. CLEARY, MCCORMICK ON EVIDENCE § 145 (3d ed. 1984).) Rather, under the rule applied in Illinois, the prosecution must present evidence apart from the defendant's own statements that tends to show the commission of the offense and that corroborates the facts related in the statement.

The Supreme Court found that witness testimony and physical evidence sufficiently corroborated the confession to sustain his conviction.

19. An Incriminating Statement Made in Defendant's Presence That Defendant Fails to Deny, Contradict, or Object to May Qualify as an Admission by Silence
People v. McCain, 29 Ill. 2d 132 (1963)

Defendant was convicted of robbery and armed robbery after he robbed and stabbed a taxi driver. The taxi driver appeared at a lineup at the police station and when he saw defendant, he walked over to him, placed his hand on his shoulder and stated that "[t]his is the man that held me up with a knife." The defendant did not respond in any way to the accusation. The state argued that the statement was properly admitted as an admission by silence. The Illinois Supreme Court disagreed, explaining that to be admissible as an admission by silence,

> it is necessary that the circumstances be such 'that the accused has heard the statement implicating him and has voluntarily refused to challenge the statement. People v. Nitti, 312 Ill. 73 (1924). While it affirmatively appears that defendant must have heard the statement, there is nothing in this record to indicate whether defendant remained silent or denied the accusation. Since the principle permitting admission is that the natural reaction of an innocent person would be to deny the accusation, and that silence is an admission of guilt, proof of defendant's silence is essential to the admission of the declaration. *Nitti*, 312 Ill. 73; People v. Smith, 25 Ill. 2d 219, 224 (1962).
>
> The People argue that the failure of the defendant to show a denial of the accusation renders proof of it competent, but the People misplace the burden. It is not defendant's responsibility to prove he denied the accusation-the People must establish his failure to do so, and it is precisely the absence of such proof that renders the admission of the statement here erroneous.

20. Admission by Silence Evidence Should Be Received with Caution and Only When It Affirmatively Appears That Defendant Was Addressed or Questioned About the Crime for Which He or She Is Subsequently Prosecuted
People v. Aughinbaugh, 36 Ill. 2d 320 (1967)

Defendant was convicted of robbery and armed robbery and alleged on appeal that the trial court violated his constitutional rights by testimony and comments about his silence at the time he was identified in a police lineup. The victim, an owner of the store defendant robbed, identified defendant by tapping him on his shoulder in a police lineup. Defendant had his back turned to the victim when he was identified. The victim testified that the defendant did not say or do anything when he was identified by the victim. The Illinois Supreme Court noted that

> [w]hile the tacit admission rule obtains in this State, and the silence of a defendant in the face of an accusation of guilt may be shown at his trial as evidence of guilt, such evidence should be received with caution and only when the conditions upon which it becomes admissible are clearly shown to exist. People v. Bennett, 3 Ill. 2d 357, 361 (1954). It must affirmatively appear that the defendant knew he was being asked about the crime for which he is on trial, for it is the assumption that one similarly situated would ordinarily deny the imputation of guilt which renders admissible defendant's failure to do so. *See* People v. Smith, 25 Ill. 2d 219, 224 (1962); *Bennett*, 3 Ill. 2d 357, 361.

Here, the Supreme Court found that there was insufficient evidence to show that defendant knew the crime he was arrested for or the purpose of his appearance in the lineup. The victim simply touched the defendant on the shoulder without any verbal accusation. The Supreme Court concluded that defendant's silence could not be considered a tacit admission of his guilt.

21. Statement by a Party's Agent If Made Within the Scope of Agency or Employment and During Existence of the Relationship May Be Used as an Admission Against the Party

Pietruszynski v. McClier Corp., 338 Ill. App. 3d 58 (1st Dist. 2003)

The First District of the Illinois Appellate Court recognized the "modern trend" in Illinois which does not require that an agent be authorized to speak on behalf of the principal. The court followed the reasoning in Pavlik v. Wal-Mart Stores, Inc., 323 Ill. App. 3d 1060 (1st Dist. 2001), and explained that

> [u]nder the traditional agency approach, the proponent of the statement must establish that (1) the declarant was an agent or employee, (2) the statement was made about a matter over which she had actual or apparent authority, and (3) she spoke by virtue of her authority as such agent or employee. Jenkins v. Dominick's Finer Foods, Inc., 288 Ill. App. 3d 827, 834 (1st Dist. 1997); Bafia v. City Int'l Trucks, Inc., 258 Ill. App. 3d 4 (1st Dist. 1994); Roberts v. Norfolk & Western Ry. Co., 229 Ill. App. 3d 706, 713-14 (4th Dist. 1992). In applying this rule, many courts found damaging statements to be outside the scope of authority, even in cases involving relatively high-level employees, since employees are seldom hired to make damaging statements. Halleck v. Coastal Building Maintenance Co., 269 Ill. App. 3d 887, 892 (1995); see *Jenkins*, 288 Ill. App. 3d at 834; *see also* M. GRAHAM, CLEARY & GRAHAM'S HANDBOOK OF ILLINOIS EVIDENCE § 802.9 at 770. (7th ed. 1999) (hereinafter Handbook). The modern trend in Illinois case law seemingly rejects the traditional agency approach in favor of the scope of employment approach espoused by Rule 801(d)(2)(D) of the Federal Rules of Evidence (Fed. R. Evid. 801(d)(2)(D)), which provides that statements by an employee concerning a matter within the scope of her employment constitute admissions by her employer if the statements are made during the existence of the employment relationship. Handbook § 802.9, at 770-74; *see, e.g.*, Vojas v. K mart Corp., 312 Ill. App. 3d 544 (5th Dist. 2000); Halleck v. Coastal Bldg. Maint. Co., 269 Ill. App. 3d 887, 647 N.E.2d 618 (2d Dist.

> 1995); Rinchich v. Village of Bridgeview, 235 Ill. App. 3d 614 (1st Dist. 1992); Miller v. J.M. Jones Co., 225 Ill. App. 3d 799 (4th Dist. 1992). Under the scope of employment approach, the proponent of the evidence need not establish that the employee's statement was specifically authorized by the employer. *See Vojas*, 312 Ill. App. 3d 544; *Halleck*, 269 Ill. App. 3d 887.
>
> ***
>
> Applying the traditional agency approach would create an impossible burden on the plaintiffs in this case [. . .]. We find it hard to envision a set of facts where a plaintiff would be able to prove that an employee was specifically authorized to make a statement detrimental to the employer's interests.

22. An Assistant State's Attorney's Statement During Trial Argument May Constitute Admission Against the State
People v. Cruz, 162 Ill. 2d 314 (1994)

Defendant and co-defendant were tried together and convicted of kidnapping, rape and murder of a ten-year-old victim. The jury was unable to reach a verdict on identical charges against another co-defendant, and defendant's convictions were reversed. Defendant was convicted at his second trial. Defendant sought to show that a third person committed the crime. The third person had previously confessed to the murder and indicated that he murdered the victim on a path, near where the victim's body was found. The state sought to show that defendant, rather than the third person, committed the murder. To show this, the state indicated that the murder did not occur on the path as indicated by the third person. Defendant then tried to introduce evidence from his first trial where the state argued in its opening statement that the murder did occur on the path. Defendant sought to examine the state's attorney who was assigned to his first trial, but the trial court denied his request. The Illinois Supreme Court noted that

> [r]elevant admissions of a party, whether consisting of a statement or conduct, are admissible when offered by the opponent as an exception to the hearsay rule. Gillson v. Gulf, Mobile & Ohio R.R. Co., 42 Ill. 2d 193, 197 (1969). [. . .] An attorney may act as an agent and as such make admissions against his or her principal. [citations omitted] And Illinois courts have implicitly stated that an attorney's statements during trial argument may constitute admissions. [citations omitted] What constitutes an admission, however, is a matter of case-by-case analysis.
>
> Clearly, according to these authorities, the statements at issue here constituted evidentiary admissions. There can be no question regarding the assistant State's Attorney's authority, and the statements were not merely conjectural as to where the murder occurred. As such, the statements' general admissibility is accepted. However, we have found no Illinois case on point concerning whether counsel's admissions during argument at an earlier trial are admissible as evidence at a subsequent trial of the same matter.

The Supreme Court concluded that the trial court did not abuse its discretion in refusing to admit the evidence from defendant's first trial because of "important policies" such as "considerations of diversion from issues, marginality, prejudicial inference, chilling effect on vigorous advocacy, exposure of work product, trial tactics or legal theory" as well as lack of binding authority on the issue.

23. Statement by One Co-Conspirator Is Admissible Against All Conspirators Where It Was Made During the Pendency and in Furtherance of the Conspiracy
People v. Kliner, 185 Ill. 2d 81 (1998)

The Illinois Supreme Court held that the victim's husband's testimony given at a grand jury hearing regarding statements made by the two defendants prior to and following the murder of his wife were admissible. The husband had hired the two defendants to murder his wife and pleaded guilty to murder, conspiracy, and solicitation. The Supreme Court explained,

> any declaration by one coconspirator is admissible against all conspirators where the declaration was made during the pendency of and in furtherance of the conspiracy. *See* People v. Goodman, 81 Ill. 2d 278, 283 (1980). The coconspirator hearsay exception does not extend to a statement which is merely a narrative of past occurrences and which does not further any objective of the conspiracy. *See* People v. Byron, 164 Ill. 2d 279, 290 (1995). Statements made in furtherance of a conspiracy include those that have the effect of advising, encouraging, aiding or abetting its perpetration. *See* M. GRAHAM, CLEARY & GRAHAM'S HANDBOOK OF ILLINOIS EVIDENCE § 802.10 (6th ed. 1994). Statements relating to attempts at concealment further the objective of the conspiracy, which implicitly includes escaping punishment. Moreover, subsequent efforts at concealment of the crime, where sufficiently proximate in time to the offense, are considered as occurring during the course of the conspiracy. *See* People v. Thomas, 178 Ill. 2d 215, 238 (1997).

The Supreme Court concluded that the statements were admissible as co-conspirator's admissions because they showed a plan for the murder, agreement for payment, and attempt to obtain payment following the murder. Moreover, some of the statements were made in an effort to conceal the murder, and, therefore were made in furtherance of the conspiracy. The balance of the statements related to defendants' efforts to secure payment. The object of the conspiracy was to obtain the proceeds from an insurance policy and at the time the statements were made, the goal had not yet been reached.

24. In Federal Courts, a Statement Made in Furtherance of a Conspiracy May Be Sufficient to Prove the Existence of a Conspiracy Without Requirement of Independent Non-Hearsay Evidence; However, This Is Not the Illinois Standard
Bourjaily v. United States, 483 U.S. 171 (1987)

The defendant was charged with conspiring to distribute cocaine and possession of cocaine. An informant for the FBI arranged to sell a kilogram of cocaine to a middleman who then sold the drugs to the defendant. The middleman called the informant and told him that a "friend" was interested in the drugs. The transaction occurred in a parking lot where the middleman agreed to transfer the drugs from the informant to his "friend." After the transaction was complete, the FBI arrested defendant with a kilogram of cocaine and over $20,000 in his car. The District Court found that the prosecution established by a preponderance of the evidence that a conspiracy involving the middleman and defendant existed and that the statements made during their telephone conversation were in furtherance of the conspiracy and were not hearsay pursuant to Federal Rule of Evidence 801(d)(2)(E).

In construing Federal Rule of Evidence 801(d)(2)(E), the United States Supreme Court held that the existence of the conspiracy may be shown by evidence of the challenged statement itself. The court reasoned that "a co-conspirator's statements could themselves be probative of the existence of a conspiracy and the participation of both the defendant and the declarant in the conspiracy." Here, the Supreme Court concluded that the co-conspirator's statements were corroborated by independent evidence and were sufficient to establish a conspiracy by preponderance of the evidence. Defendant also argued that the admissibility of the co-conspirator's statements violated his sixth amendment right to confrontation because the co-conspirator invoked his fifth amendment right not to testify and was therefore not available for cross-examination. The Supreme Court disagreed, noting that

> [t]he admissibility of co-conspirators' statements was first established in this Court over a century and a half ago in United States v. Gooding, 12 Wheat. 460, 6 L. Ed. 693 (1827) (interpreting statements of co-conspirator as *res gestae* and thus admissible against defendant), and the Court has repeatedly reaffirmed the exception as accepted practice. [. . .] In Delaney v. United States, 263 U.S. 586, 590 (1924), the Court rejected the very challenge petitioner brings today, holding that there can be no separate Confrontation Clause challenge to the admission of a co-conspirator's out-of-court statement. In so ruling, the Court relied on established precedent holding such statements competent evidence. We think that these cases demonstrate that co-conspirators' statements, when made in the course and in furtherance of the conspiracy, have a long tradition of being outside the compass of the general hearsay exclusion. Accordingly, we hold that the Confrontation Clause does not require a court to embark on an independent inquiry into the reliability of statements that satisfy the requirements of Rule 801(d)(2)(E).

25. Illinois Requires That the Existence of a Conspiracy Be Shown by Independent Non-Hearsay Evidence Prior to the Admissibility of Co-Conspirator's Statements
People v. Goodman, 81 Ill. 2d 278 (1980)

Defendant and co-defendant were jointly tried for a controlled substance violation. Defendant claimed on appeal that the trial court erred in admitting his co-defendant's hearsay statements against him. Co-defendant did not testify at their trial. Defendant alleged that admissibility of the statements violated his sixth amendment right to confront witnesses against him. The charges against the defendant and co-defendant stemmed from an undercover police operation. An undercover police officer arranged to buy cocaine from co-defendant who would obtain the substance from "an unidentified contact." The transaction took place in a bar. Defendant, co-defendant and the undercover officer were sitting together at a table. Co-defendant and the officer went outside to discuss the sale. The officer asked co-defendant whether he could test the substance. Co-defendant agreed but noted that he would need some money as security. Co-defendant then re-entered the bar with the money. Defendant claimed that co-defendant asked him to watch his money and defendant complied. Surveillance officers sitting nearby, however, testified that co-defendant talked to defendant, defendant nodded in agreement, co-defendant handed him money and defendant took it and placed it in his pocket. The undercover officer testified that co-defendant told him that his "contact lived in rural Okawville in a trailer and had disconnected his phone out of fear of a wiretap." The officer testified that defendant met this description because he lived in a trailer in Okawville and had recently disconnected his telephone. Defendant argued that there was "insufficient independent evidence to make a *prima facie* case of the existence of a conspiracy." The Illinois Supreme Court disagreed, noting that

> the declarations-of-coconspirators [. . .] are admissible against all conspirators upon an independent, *prima facie* evidentiary showing of a conspiracy or joint venture between the declarant and one of the other defendants, insofar as such declarations are made in furtherance of and during the pendency of the conspiracy, even in the absence of a conspiracy indictment. United States v. Nixon, 418 U.S. 683, 701 & n.14 (1974); Anderson v. United States, 417 U.S. 211, 218 (1974); People v. Davis, 46 Ill. 2d 554, 558-59 (1970); People v. Parson, 27 Ill. 2d 263 (1963); *see generally*, Levie, *Hearsay and Conspiracy, A Reexamination of the Co-Conspirators' Exception to the Hearsay Rule*, 52 MICH. L. REV. 1159 (1954); Comment, *The Hearsay Exception For Co-Conspirators' Declarations*, 25 U. CHI. L. REV. 530 (1958); Comment, *Reconstructing the Independent Evidence Requirement of the Coconspirator Hearsay Exception*, 127 U. PA. L. REV. 1439 (1979).) Defendant contends only that there was insufficient independent evidence to make a *prima facie* case of the existence of a conspiracy

> between [defendant] and [co-defendant] and that the coconspirators exception, as applied here, violates the ruling of the United States Supreme Court in Bruton v. United States, 391 U.S. 123 (1968).
>
> There was sufficient independent evidence of conspiracy. [Defendant] admitted he had been a very close friend of [co-defendant] for over 10 years. According to [the undercover officer], [co-defendant] announced that he had the cocaine in [defendant's] presence, negating defendant's claim of ignorance of the nature of the transaction. [Defendant] and [co-defendant] were seen in discussion after [the undercover officer] requested a test of the cocaine and offered $1,000 as security. [Defendant] was seen to affirmatively nod his head to [co-defendant] and to receive $1,000 in cash. (This money was marked and was found on [the defendant] when he was arrested.) This is evidence from which an agreement to sell cocaine could be inferred. Therefore, because a sufficient *prima facie* case of conspiracy was shown by independent evidence, the evidence was properly admitted. (It is preferable for the independent evidence of conspiracy to be introduced prior to the admission of a coconspirator's declarations (see United States v. James (5th Cir. 1979), 590 F.2d 575, 581-82), but there is no mandatory rule to this effect.)
>
> The admission of [co-defendant's] declarations, further, was not contrary to Bruton v. United States, 391 U.S. 123 (1968), [. . . because] defendant was able to cross-examine the officer who contended that the statements were made. The statements themselves were not devastating assertions about past facts but were, rather, only inferentially inculpatory assertions about contemporaneous events.

26. Statement of a Co-Conspirator Made During Subsequent Attempts to Conceal the Crime Is Admissible as an Admission

People v. Thomas, 178 Ill. 2d 215 (1997)

Defendant and two other individuals participated in the shooting death of the victim. After the shooting, defendant and one of the two co-conspirators went to the accomplice's fiancée's home. The fiancée gave the police a written statement. She stated that the defendant told her he had shot someone. Once the co-conspirator noticed that his fiancée was nervous, he got angry at defendant for telling her. At trial the fiancée denied knowing the content of the conversation between the co-conspirator and defendant and denied knowing why defendant was angry. On cross-examination, the witness testified that the statement to the police was a lie because she was mad at defendant and wanted to frame him. The trial court admitted the witness' statement as impeachment evidence only.

The Supreme Court noted that the statement qualified as an admission. The Supreme Court explained that

> the statement of one coconspirator is admissible against the others where the statement is made during the course of and in furtherance of the conspiracy. People v. Davis, 46 Ill. 2d 554 (1970). Although [the co-conspirator's] statements occurred after the completion of the robbery and murder, the statements constituted an attempt at concealment. Our appellate court has repeatedly held that the course of a conspiracy includes subsequent attempts at concealment of the crime where sufficiently proximate in time to the offense. People v. Columbo, 118 Ill. App. 3d 882, 948 (1983); People v. Meagher, 70 Ill. App. 3d 597, 603 (1979); People v. McInnis, 88 Ill. App. 3d 555, 566 (1980); People v. Eddington, 129 Ill. App. 3d 745, 773 (1984); *see also* People v. Parmly, 117 Ill. 2d 386, 393 (1987) (assuming, but not deciding, that conspiracy includes subsequent efforts at concealment). [Co-conspirator's] statement to defendant occurred immediately after the murder and expressed the desire to conceal the matter and prevent his fiancée's involvement. In addition, the statement was made

> prior to defendant's retrieving and disposing of the gun. Therefore, the statement was admissible against defendant as a coconspirator's statement.

Here, the Illinois Supreme Court found that the statement by the co-conspirator as introduced through his fiancée's testimony was admissible because it was "spontaneous, against his penal interest, and generally made under circumstances which indicate the statement was reliable."

Hearsay Rule

Rule 802. Hearsay Rule

Hearsay is not admissible except as provided by these rules, by other rules prescribed by the Supreme Court, or by statute as provided in Rule 101.

Adopted September 27, 2010, eff. January 1, 2011.

Author's Commentary

Illinois Rule of Evidence 802 codifies prior Illinois common law that requires the exclusion of hearsay evidence unless the out-of-court statement falls within a "recognized" common-law exception or one created by statute or supreme court rule. People v. Dabbs, 239 Ill. 2d 277 (2010).

Prior Illinois Case Law

1. Fundamental Purpose of the Hearsay Rule Is to Subject Source of an Assertion to Cross-Examination by Party Against Whom It Is Offered

People v. Carpenter, 28 Ill. 2d 116 (1963)

The presence or absence of the defendant is not relevant at all in determining whether a statement is hearsay, unless his or her presence and silence constitute an implied admission. Defendant was charged with sale of a controlled substance. He contended on appeal that the trial court erroneously permitted a witness to testify as to a conversation between the witness and co-defendant outside of the presence of the defendant. The Illinois Supreme Court disagreed, noting that the witness' testimony was not hearsay. The Supreme Court explained that

> [t]he fundamental purpose of the hearsay rule was and is to test the real value of testimony by exposing the source of the assertion to cross-examination by the party against whom it is offered. While the administration of an oath and the right of confrontation are also spoken of as necessary elements, the essential feature, without which testimonial offerings must be rejected, is the opportunity for cross-examination of the party whose assertions are offered to prove the truth of the act asserted. Wigmore on Evidence, 3rd ed. sec. 1361, *et seq*.; People v. Smuk, 12 Ill. 2d 360 (1957). If this requirement is met, with the exception of instances such as those where the silence of the defendant is claimed to constitute an implied admission, the presence or absence of the defendant is immaterial.
>
> The distinction between admissible testimony and that which is barred by the hearsay rule is well illustrated by Wigmore's example of the witness A testifying that 'B told me that event X occurred'. If A's testimony is offered for the purpose of establishing that B said this, it is clearly admissible-if offered to prove that event X occurred, it is clearly inadmissible, for the only probative value rests in B's knowledge-and B is not present to be cross-examined.

Hearsay Exceptions

Rule 803. Hearsay Exceptions; Availability of Declarant Immaterial

The following are not excluded by the hearsay rule, even though the declarant is available as a witness:

(1) Reserved. [Present Sense Impressions]

(2) Excited Utterance. A statement relating to a startling event or condition made while the declarant was under the stress of excitement caused by the event or condition.

(3) Then-Existing Mental, Emotional, or Physical Condition. A statement of the declarant's then-existing state of mind, emotion, sensation, or physical condition (such as intent, plan, motive, design, mental feeling, pain, and bodily health), but not including:

(A) a statement of memory or belief to prove the fact remembered or believed unless it relates to the execution, revocation, identification, or terms of declarant's will; or

(B) a statement of declarant's then-existing state of mind, emotion, sensation, or physical condition to prove the state of mind, emotion, sensation, or physical condition of another declarant at that time or at any other time when such state of the other declarant is an issue in the action.

(4) Statements for Purposes of Medical Diagnosis or Treatment. (A) Statements made for purposes of medical treatment, or medical diagnosis in contemplation of treatment, and describing medical history, or past or present symptoms, pain, or sensations, or the inception or general character of the cause or external source thereof insofar as reasonably pertinent to diagnosis or treatment but, subject to Rule 703, not including statements made to a health care provider consulted solely for the purpose of preparing for litigation or obtaining testimony for trial, or (B) in a prosecution for violation of sections 11-1.20, 11-1.30, 11-1.40, 11-1.50, or 11-1.60 of the Criminal Code of 1961 (720 ILCS 5/11-1.20, 11-1.30, 11-1.40, 11-1.50, or 11-1.60), or for a violation of the Article 12 statutes in the Criminal Code of 1961 that previously defined the same offenses, statements made by the victim to medical personnel for purposes of medical diagnoses or treatment including descriptions of the cause of symptom, pain or sensations, or the inception or general character of the cause or external source thereof insofar as reasonably pertinent to diagnosis or treatment.

(5) Recorded Recollection. A memorandum or record concerning a matter about which a witness once had knowledge but now has insufficient recollection to enable the witness to testify fully and accurately, shown to have been made or adopted by the witness when the matter was fresh in the witness' memory and to reflect that knowledge correctly.

(6) Records of Regularly Conducted Activity. A memorandum, report, record, or data compilation, in any form, of acts, events, conditions, opinions, or diagnoses, made at or near the time by, or from information transmitted by, a person with knowledge, if kept in the course of a regularly conducted business activity, and if it was the regular practice of that business activity to make the memorandum, report, record or data compilation, all as shown by the testimony of the custodian or other qualified witness, or by certification that complies with Rule 902(11), unless the source of information or the method or circumstances of preparation indicate lack of trustworthiness, but not including in criminal cases medical records. The term "business" as used in this paragraph includes business, institution, association, profession, occupation, and calling of every kind, whether or not conducted for profit.

(7) Absence of Entry in Records Kept in Accordance With the Provisions of Paragraph (6). Evidence that a matter is not included in the memoranda reports, records, or data compilations, in any form, kept in accordance with the provisions of paragraph (6), to prove the nonoccurrence or nonexistence of the matter, if the matter was of a kind of which a memorandum, report, record, or data compilation was regularly made and preserved, unless the sources of information or other circumstances indicate lack of trustworthiness.

(8) Public Records and Reports. Records, reports, statements, or data compilations, in any form, of public offices or agencies, setting forth (A) the activities of the office or agency, or (B) matters observed pursuant to duty imposed by law as to which matters there was a duty to report, excluding, however, police accident reports and in criminal cases medical records and matters observed by police officers and other law enforcement personnel, unless the sources of information or other circumstances indicate lack of trustworthiness.

(9) Records of Vital Statistics. Facts contained in records or data compilations, in any form, of births, fetal deaths, deaths, or marriages, if the report thereof was made to a public office pursuant to requirements of law.

(10) Absence of Public Record or Entry. To prove the absence of a record, report, statement, or data compilation, in any form, or the nonoccurrence or nonexistence of a matter of which a record, report, statement, or data compilation, in any form, was regularly made and preserved by a public office or agency, evidence in the form of a certification in accordance with Rule 902, or testimony, that diligent search failed to disclose the record, report, statement, or data compilation, or entry.

(11) Records of Religious Organizations. Statements of births, marriages, divorces, deaths, legitimacy, ancestry, relationship by blood or marriage, or other similar facts of personal or family history, contained in a regularly kept record of a religious organization.

(12) Marriage, Baptismal, and Similar Certificates. Statements of fact contained in a certificate that the maker performed a marriage or other ceremony or administered a sacrament, made by a clergyman, public official, or other person authorized by the rules or practices of a religious organization or by law to perform the act certified, and purporting to have been issued at the time of the act or within a reasonable time thereafter.

(13) Family Records. Statements of fact concerning personal or family history contained in family Bibles, genealogies, charts, engravings on rings, inscriptions on family portraits, engravings on urns, crypts, or tombstones, or the like.

(14) Records of Documents Affecting an Interest in Property. The record of a document purporting to establish or affect an interest in property, as proof of the content of the original recorded document and its execution and delivery by each person by whom it purports to have been executed, if the record is a record of a public office and an applicable statute authorizes the recording of documents of that kind in that office.

(15) Statements in Documents Affecting an Interest in Property. A statement contained in a document purporting to establish or affect an interest in property if the matter stated was relevant to the purpose of the document, unless dealings with the property since the document was made have been inconsistent with the truth of the statement or the purport of the document.

(16) Statements in Ancient Documents. Statements in a document in existence 20 years or more the authenticity of which is established.

(17) Market Reports, Commercial Publications. Market quotations, tabulations, lists, directories, or other published compilations, generally used and relied upon by the public or by persons in particular occupations.

(18) Reserved. [Learned Treatises]

(19) Reputation Concerning Personal or Family History. Reputation among members of a person's family by blood, adoption, or marriage, or among a person's associates, or in the community, concerning a person's birth, adoption, marriage, divorce, death, legitimacy, relationship by blood, adoption, or marriage, ancestry, or other similar fact of personal or family history.

(20) Reputation Concerning Boundaries or General History. Reputation in a community, arising before the controversy, as to boundaries of or customs affecting lands in the community, and reputation as to events of general history important to the community or State or nation in which located.

(21) Reputation as to Character. Reputation of a person's character among associates or in the community.

(22) Judgment of Previous Conviction. Evidence of a final judgment, entered after a trial or upon a plea of guilty, adjudging a person guilty of a crime punishable by death or imprisonment in excess of one year, to prove any fact essential to sustain the judgment, but not including, when offered by the Government in a criminal prosecution for purposes other than impeachment, judgments against persons other than the accused. The pendency of an appeal may be shown but does not affect admissibility.

(23) Judgment as to Personal, Family, or General History, or Boundaries. Judgments as proof of matters of personal, family or general history, or boundaries, essential to the judgment, if the same would be provable by evidence of reputation.

(24) Receipt or Paid Bill. A receipt or paid bill as *prima facie* evidence of the fact of payment and as *prima facie* evidence that the charge was reasonable.

Adopted September 27, 2010, eff. January 1, 2011; amended April 26, 2012, eff. immediately.

Committee Commentary

(1) Codification. [. . .] Rules 803(1) and 803(18) [have been reserved] because Illinois common law does not recognize either a present sense impression or a learned treatise hearsay exception.

ILL. R. EVID. Committee Commentary § 1, pg. 1.

(3) Modernization: Where there was no conflict with statutes or recent Illinois Supreme Court or Illinois Appellate Court decisions, and where it was determined to be beneficial and uniformly or almost uniformly accepted elsewhere, the Committee incorporated into the Illinois Rules of Evidence uncontroversial developments with respect to the law of evidence as reflected in the Federal Rules of Evidence and the 44 surveyed jurisdictions. [Some of t]he 14 instances of modernization of note are as follows:

(7) Rule 803(13). Family Records. The requirement that the declarant be unavailable and that the statement be made before the controversy or a motive to misrepresent arose, Sugrue v. Crilley, 329 Ill. 458, 160 N.E. 847 (1928), have been eliminated.

(8) Rule 803(14), (15), (19), (20), and (23). With respect to records of or statements in documents affecting an interest in property, reputation concerning personal or family history, and concerning boundaries or general history, and judgments as to personal, family or general history or boundaries, Illinois law in each area was sparse or nonexistent.

(9) Rules 803(16) and 901(b)(8). Statements in Ancient Documents. The 30-year limitation to real property, Reuter v. Stuckart, 181 Ill. 529, 54 N.E. 1014 (1899), is relaxed in favor of 20 years without subject matter restriction.
ILL. R. EVID. Committee Commentary § 3, pg. 2-3.

(4) Recommendations: The Committee recommended to the Illinois Supreme Court a limited number of changes to Illinois evidence law (1) where the particularized evidentiary principle was neither addressed by statute nor specifically addressed in a comprehensive manner within recent history by the Illinois Supreme Court, and (2) where prior Illinois law simply did not properly reflect evidentiary policy considerations or raised practical application problems when considered in light of modern developments and evidence rules adopted elsewhere with respect to the identical issue. The Committee identified, and the Illinois Supreme Court approved, recommendations in [the following area]: ***

(b) Rule 803(3) eliminates the requirements currently existing in Illinois law, that do not exist in any other jurisdiction, with respect to statements of then existing mental, emotional, or physical condition, that the statement be made by a declarant found unavailable to testify, and that the trial court find that there is a "reasonable probability" that the statement is truthful ***

The initial reference in Illinois to "unavailability" and "reasonable probability" occurred in People v. Reddock, 13 Ill. App. 3d 296, 300 N.E.2d 31 (1973), adopting the position taken by the North Carolina Supreme Court in State v. Vestal, 278 N.C. 561, 180 S.E.2d 755 (1971), when dealing with statements of intent by a declarant to prove conduct by the declarant consistent with that intent. Subsequent cases simply incorporated the two qualifications without analysis, evaluation, critique, or discussion. No reference has been made to the fact that the two requirements were initially adopted solely to deal with the Mutual Life Ins. v. Hillmon, 145 U.S. 285 (1892), issue as to whether a statement of an out-of-court declarant expressing her intent to perform a future act was admissible as evidence to prove the doing of the intended act. Interestingly, the North Carolina version of Rule 803(3) in the North Carolina Rules of Evidence is in substance the same as Rule 803(3), i.e., neither a requirement of "unavailability" nor "reasonable probability" is included. Rule 803(3) permits admissibility of declarations of intent to do an act as evidence to establish intent and as evidence to prove the doing of the intended act regardless of the availability of the declarant and without the court finding a reasonable probability that the statement is truthful. Consistent with prior Illinois law, Rule 803(3)(B) provides that the hearsay exception for admissibility of a statement of intent as tending to prove the doing of the act intended applies only to the statements of intent by a declarant to prove her future conduct, not the future conduct of another person.
ILL. R. EVID. Committee Commentary § 4, pg. 4-6.

(5) Structural Change: A hearsay exception in Illinois with respect to both business and public records is recognized in civil cases by Illinois Supreme Court Rule 236, excluding police accident reports, and in criminal cases by section 115 of the Code of Criminal Procedure (725 ILCS 5/115), excluding medical records and police investigative records. The Illinois Rules of Evidence in Rule 803(6), records of regularly conducted activity (i.e., business records), and in Rule 803(8), public records and reports, while retaining the exclusions described above, removes the difference between civil and criminal business and public records in favor of the traditional and otherwise uniformly accepted division between business records, Rule 803(6), and public records and reports, Rule 803(8), both applicable in civil and criminal cases.
ILL. R. EVID. Committee Commentary § 5, pg. 6-7.

(6) Referenced Statutes: Numerous existing statutes, the validity of which are not affected by promulgation of the Illinois Rules of Evidence, ILL. R. EVID. 101, relate in one form or another to the law of evidence. The Committee felt it was inappropriate, unnecessary and unwise to refer specifically to the abundance of statutory authority in an Appendix or otherwise. Reference is, however, made in the body of the text of the Illinois Rules of Evidence to certain statutes by citation or verbatim incorporation. Such references and the reasons therefor are as follows:

(6) Rule 803(4)(B): 725 ILCS 5/115-13, dealing with statements by the victim to medical personnel in sexual abuse prosecutions, is included verbatim in recognition that the statute admits statements to examining physicians while the generally applicable provisions of Rule 803(4)(A) do not.
ILL. R. EVID. Committee Commentary § 6, pg. 8-9.

AUTHOR'S COMMENTARY

Illinois Rule of Evidence 803(1) Reserved [Present Sense Impressions]

The Special Supreme Court Committee on Illinois Evidence reserved Rule 803(1), noting that "Illinois common law does not recognize [. . .] a present sense impression" exception to the hearsay rule. ILL. R. EVID. Committee Commentary § 1, pg. 1. Illinois continues not to follow Federal Rule of Evidence 803(1), which provides this exception. *See* Gino L. DiVito, *The Illinois Rules of Evidence: A Color-Coded Guide Containing the New Rules, the Committee's General and Specific Comments, a Comparison with the Federal Rules of Evidence, and Additional Commentary* (*Including the Federal Rules of Evidence as Amended Effective December 1, 2011*) (Jan. 1, 2012), at 101, http://www.tdrlawfirm.com/assets/downloads/Illinois_Rules_of_Evidence_Color-Coded_Guide.pdf. Illinois common law therefore remains the rule after the enactment of the Illinois Rules of Evidence.

Illinois Rule of Evidence 803(2) Excited Utterance

Illinois has adopted Federal Rule of Evidence 803(2), effective until its stylistic amendment on December 1, 2011, which provides the excited utterance exception to the hearsay rule, also known at Illinois common law as the "spontaneous declaration exception." Gino L. DiVito, *The Illinois Rules of Evidence: A Color-Coded Guide Containing the New Rules, the Committee's General and Specific Comments, a Comparison with the Federal Rules of Evidence, and Additional Commentary* (*Including the Federal Rules of Evidence as Amended Effective December 1, 2011*) (Jan. 1, 2012), at 101, http://www.tdrlawfirm.com/assets/downloads/Illinois_Rules_of_Evidence_Color-Coded_Guide.pdf. The exception provides for the admissibility of a "statement relating to a startling event or condition made while the declarant was under the stress of excitement caused by the event or condition." ILL. R. EVID. 803(2).

Illinois Rule of Evidence 803(3) Then-Existing Mental, Emotional, or Physical Condition

A declarant's out-of-court statements about his or her then-existing state of mind, such as intent, plan, motive, design, or feeling, are admissible to prove the truth of the matter asserted as an exception to the hearsay rule. ILL. R. EVID. 803(3). In the past, Illinois courts interpreted this exception to require

a) the declarant to be unavailable to testify;
b) there be a reasonable probability that the statements were truthful; and
c) the statements were relevant.

See e.g., People v. Caffey, 205 Ill. 2d 52 (2001) (excluding a hearsay statement of a co-conspirator indicating that he was looking for defendant because he wanted to buy drugs from him because the co-conspirator had "greater reason to lie about his motive for finding defendant than to tell the truth"); People v. Floyd, 103 Ill. 2d 541 (1984) (finding that although victim was an unavailable declarant, her statements indicating that she feared for her life were not relevant for a purpose other than to suggest that defendant was guilty of murder). Illinois Rule of Evidence 803(3), however, has changed prior Illinois common law by "eliminat[ing] the requirements [. . .] that the statement be made by a declarant found unavailable to testify, and that the trial court find that there is a 'reasonable probability' that the statement is truthful." ILL. R. EVID. Committee Commentary § 4, pg. 5. For additional discussion of this hearsay exception, see RALPH RUEBNER, ILLINOIS CRIMINAL TRIAL EVIDENCE 255-56 (4th ed. 2001).

Illinois Rule of Evidence 803(4) Statements for Purposes of Medical Diagnosis or Treatment

Illinois Rule of Evidence 803(4) retains the Illinois common law rule that allows admissibility of statements made by a patient to a treating physician disclosing the cause or external source of the patient's condition. *See* People v. Gant, 58 Ill. 2d 178 (1974). The Illinois Rule of Evidence 803(4), however, is narrower than the Federal Rule of Evidence 803(4), in that the Illinois Rule of Evidence does not allow admissibility of statements that narrate details of criminal conduct or criminal agency because they are not needed for medical diagnosis or treatment. Gino L. DiVito, *The Illinois Rules of Evidence: A Color-Coded Guide Containing the New Rules, the Committee's General and Specific Comments, a Comparison with the Federal Rules of Evidence, and Additional Commentary* (*Including the Federal Rules of Evidence as Amended Effective December 1, 2011*) (Jan. 1, 2012), at 104, http://www.tdrlawfirm.com/assets/downloads/Illinois_Rules_of_Evidence_Color-Coded_Guide.pdf [hereinafter DiVito, *Color-Coded Guide*]. Therefore, Illinois Rule of Evidence 803(4)(A) excludes statements that were made to a health care provider "solely for the purpose of preparing for litigation or obtaining testimony for trial." Illinois Rule of Evidence 803(4)(B) also differs from Federal Rule of Evidence 803(4). It codifies 725 ILCS 5/115-13, by "includ[ing] verbatim" a statute which allows admissibility of statements made by a victim of specified sexual offenses to medical personnel. ILL. R. EVID. Committee Commentary § 6, pg. 8-9. The statute and now Illinois Rule of Evidence 803(4)(B), allow such statements in evidence when made by the victim "for purposes of medical treatment," including "descriptions of the cause of symptom, pain or sensations, or the inception or general character of the cause or external source" as long as such descriptions are "reasonably pertinent to diagnosis or treatment." ILL. R. EVID. Committee Commentary § 6, pg. 8-9; DiVito, *Color-Coded Guide* at 104-106. Unlike Illinois Rule of

Evidence 803(4)(A), Illinois Rule of Evidence 803(4)(B) allows admissibility of a broader range of statements made to medical personnel where such statements were made by victims of sexual offenses. ILL. R. EVID. Committee Commentary § 6, pg. 8-9; DiVito, *Color-Coded Guide*, at 104-106.

Illinois Rule of Evidence 803(5) Recorded Recollection
The Illinois common law rule referred to this exception as "past recollection recorded statements." People v. Speed, 315 Ill. App. 3d 511 (4th Dist. 2000). It allowed the admissibility of a written document containing an-out-of court declaration if the proponent could establish the following foundation:

a) the witness has no recollection of the incident described in the record;
b) the document does not refresh the recollection of the witness;
c) the written document was prepared by the witness at the time of or soon after the incident that prompted him or her to record; and
d) the witness vouches for the truth and accuracy of the document.

People v. Beasley, 307 Ill. App. 3d 200 (1st Dist. 1999). Illinois Rule of Evidence 803(5) has changed the Illinois common law rule. It now allows a statement in evidence where the witness has "insufficient recollection to enable the witness to testify fully and accurately."

The reason for allowing a recorded recollection statement in evidence is its trustworthiness or reliability that is derived from the fact that it was prepared at or near the time of the event and while the witness' memory was clear and accurate. People v. Olson, 59 Ill. App. 3d 643 (4th Dist. 1978). The document should not be admitted if the witness does not recall preparing it, fails to demonstrate that the document was prepared at or near the time of the event, or fails to testify that the document was accurate when made. People v. Munoz, 31 Ill. App. 3d 689 (2d Dist. 1975). A recorded recollection statement may be read to the jury and admitted as an exhibit. *Olson*, 59 Ill. App. 3d at 647-48. Illinois has not adopted that portion of the Federal Rule of Evidence 803(5) that states that a recorded recollection statement "may be received as an exhibit only if offered by an adverse party." FED. R. EVID. 803(5) (effective Dec. 1, 2011). The rationale for not adopting this statement was explained by Justice DiVito as follows: "The second sentence [of the Federal Rule] is not adopted because Illinois allows a recorded recollection to be received into evidence at the request even of the proponent of the evidence. *See* People v. Olson, 59 Ill. App. 3d 643 (1978) for a discussion of authorities and a general recitation of the principles." Gino L. DiVito, *The Illinois Rules of Evidence: A Color-Coded Guide Containing the New Rules, the Committee's General and Specific Comments, a Comparison with the Federal Rules of Evidence, and Additional Commentary (Including the Federal Rules of Evidence as Amended Effective December 1, 2011)* (Jan. 1, 2012), at 106, http://www.tdrlawfirm.com/assets/downloads/Illinois_Rules_of_Evidence_Color-Coded_Guide.pdf. Police reports, which are generally inadmissible as substantive evidence because they are hearsay, may nevertheless be admitted under this exception if the necessary foundation requirements are satisfied.

Illinois Rule of Evidence 803(6) Records of Regularly Conducted Activity and Illinois Rule of Evidence 803(8) Public Records and Reports
The business records exception to the hearsay rule is deeply rooted in Illinois law. Prior to the adoption of the Illinois Rule of Evidence 803(6) it was codified in 725 ILCS 5/115-5 and regulated by Illinois Supreme Court Rule 236. Rule 236 and section 115-5 are consistent with and complement each other. While section 115-5 deals with criminal law, Illinois Supreme Court Rule 236 deals with civil law. According to Professor Graham, Rule 236 and section 115-5 are "subject to repeal" because they have been "replaced by" Illinois

Rule 803(6) and 803(8). MICHAEL H. GRAHAM, GRAHAM'S HANDBOOK OF ILLINOIS EVIDENCE ii (10th ed. 2010). Professor Graham further notes that unlike section 115-5 and Rule 236, the new Illinois Rules of Evidence 803(6) and 803(8) pertain to both civil and criminal cases. *See* GRAHAM at § 803.6. The Committee Commentary to the Illinois Rules of Evidence emphasizes that Rules 803(6) and 803(8) have "retain[ed] the exclusions [of] medical records and police investigative records" pursuant to section 115-5, as well as the exclusion of police accident reports pursuant to Illinois Supreme Court Rule 236. ILL. R. EVID. Committee Commentary § 5, pg. 6-7. Professor Graham echoes the commentary and notes that the new Illinois Rules of Evidence 803(6) and 803(8) "incorporate[d] [. . .] all of the operative provisions of" Illinois Supreme Court Rule 236 and section 115-5. GRAHAM at § 803.6, 803.8. Professor Graham explains that the changes made by Illinois Rules 803(6) and 803(8) to the pre-existing statutory provision and Illinois Supreme Court Rule are "solely as to organization; no substantive change with respect to admissibility of records of regularly conducted activities occurred." GRAHAM at § 803.6, 803.8.

Section 115-5 provides for the admissibility of a writing or a record in a criminal case that was created to memorialize "any act, transaction, occurrence, or event." The proponent must establish a foundation showing that it was "made in regular course of any business" and "it was the regular course of such business to make such memorandum or record at the time of such act, transaction, occurrence, or event or within a reasonable time thereafter." Records that are prepared during a criminal investigation and records prepared with view towards litigation are not routinely made and therefore are inadmissible under the business records exception to the hearsay rule. Similarly, police accident reports are inadmissible as records made in the regular course of business. ILL. S. CT. RULE 236(b). Statements contained in police reports may, however, be used for impeachment purposes and may qualify for admissibility as recorded recollection statements. *See* People v. Williams, 159 Ill. App. 3d 527 (1st Dist. 1987) (police dispatch card admissible to impeach defendant's testimony about time he had called police); People v. Strausberger, 151 Ill. App. 3d 832 (2d Dist. 1987) (admitting police accident report under past recollection recorded exception in a reckless homicide prosecution to establish why officer concluded that defendant was intoxicated on the night of the accident). Generally, medical and hospital records are not admissible as business records in a criminal trial, although the legislature has enacted a statutory exception in the form of 625 ILCS 5/11-501.4. Pursuant to section 11-501.4, test results of blood or urine conducted in the regular course of emergency medical treatment following a motor vehicle accident are admissible as a business record exception to the hearsay rule in prosecutions for driving under the influence or reckless homicide. People v. Jung, 192 Ill. 2d 1 (2000).

The proponent of evidence under section 5/115-5 needs a foundation witness who is familiar with the business and the record to authenticate the exhibit. Before the enactment of the Illinois Rules of Evidence, the common law required that a qualified witness possess personal knowledge of the event or its recordation. *See* People v. Small, 319 Ill. 437 (1925). Personal knowledge is no longer a requirement under Illinois Rule of Evidence 803(6). GRAHAM at § 803.6. However, lack of personal knowledge on the part of the foundation witness may affect the weight of the evidence.

Records and reports maintained by public officials or government agencies are generally admissible as an exception to the hearsay rule. Public records and reports are reliable because courts assume that public officers have no motive to falsify whatever they report or record, that they will perform their duties lawfully, and that public inspection of available public records will disclose any inaccuracies. Federal Rule of Evidence 803(8)(C) provides for the admissibility of "factual findings" and has been interpreted to also include "factually based conclusions or opinions." Beech Aircraft Corp. v. Rainey, 488 U.S. 153, 162 (1988). Unlike Federal Rule of Evidence 803(8)(C), which allows in a criminal case the admissibility of "factual findings from a legally authorized investigation" against the government, Illinois has chosen to disallow the use of such factual findings against the prosecution in Illinois Rule of Evidence 803(8). Gino L. DiVito, *The Illinois Rules of Evidence: A Color-Coded Guide Containing the New Rules, the Committee's General and Specific Comments, a Comparison with the Federal Rules of Evidence, and Additional Commentary* (*Including the Federal Rules of Evidence as Amended Effective December 1, 2011*) (Jan. 1, 2012), at 109, http://www.tdrlawfirm.com/assets/downloads/Illinois_Rules _of_Evidence_Color-Coded_Guide.pdf guide.

Illinois Rule of Evidence 803(7) Absence of Entry in Records Kept in Accordance with the Provisions of Paragraph (6)

Illinois Rule of Evidence 803(7) retains the Illinois common law rule that states that once evidence is admitted as a business record, the absence of an entry in the record is admissible to prove the nonexistence of a fact or an event. Easley v. Apollo Detective Agency, Inc., 69 Ill. App. 3d 920 (1st Dist. 1979). The proponent must establish that an entry would normally have been made. Illinois Rule of Evidence 803(7) is identical to the Federal Rule of Evidence 803(7) in effect until its stylistic amendment effective December 1, 2011. Gino L. DiVito, *The Illinois Rules of Evidence: A Color-Coded Guide Containing the New Rules, the Committee's General and Specific Comments, a Comparison with the Federal Rules of Evidence, and Additional Commentary* (*Including the Federal Rules of Evidence as Amended Effective December 1, 2011*) (Jan. 1, 2012), at 108, http://www.tdrlawfirm .com/assets/downloads/Illinois_Rules_of_Evidence_Color-Coded_Guide.pdf.

Illinois Rule of Evidence 803(10) Absence of Public Record or Entry

Illinois Rule of Evidence 803(10) retains the Illinois common law rule that states that once evidence is admitted as a public record, the absence of an entry in the record is admissible to prove the nonexistence of a fact or an event. People v. Love, 310 Ill. 558 (1923).

Illinois Rule of Evidence 803(13) Family Records

Illinois Rule of Evidence 803(13) allows admissibility of "[s]tatements of fact concerning personal or family history contained in family" records. The rule has eliminated the common law "requirement that the declarant be unavailable and that the statement be made before the controversy or a motive to misrepresent arose, Sugrue v. Crilley, 329 Ill. 458, 160 N.E. 847 (1928)." ILL. R. EVID. Committee Commentary § 3, pg. 2-3.

Illinois Rule of Evidence 803(16) Statements in Ancient Documents

Prior to the enactment of the Illinois Rules of Evidence, statements contained in ancient documents pertaining to real property were admissible as long as the documents were in existence for 30 years or more. *See* Johnston v. Masterson, 397 Ill. 168, 171 (1947); Reuter v. Stuckart, 181 Ill. 529 (1899); Gino L. DiVito, *The Illinois Rules of Evidence: A Color-Coded Guide Containing the New Rules, the Committee's General and Specific Comments, a Comparison with the Federal Rules of Evidence, and Additional Commentary* (*Including the Federal Rules of Evidence as Amended Effective December 1, 2011*) (Jan. 1, 2012), at 114, http://www.tdrlawfirm.com/assets/downloads/Illinois_Rules_of_Evidence_Color-Coded_ Guide.pdf [hereinafter DiVito, *Color-Coded Guide*]. Illinois Rule of Evidence 803(16) adopted the Federal Rule of Evidence 803(16), in effect prior to its stylistic amendment on December 1, 2011, and has removed the limitation to real property. DiVito, *Color-Coded Guide* at 114; ILL. R. EVID. Committee Commentary § 3, pg. 2-3. It now provides that such statements are admissible as long as the documents in which they are contained have been in existence for 20 years or more. DiVito, *Color-Coded Guide* at 114; ILL. R. EVID. Committee Commentary § 3, pg. 2-3.

Illinois Rule of Evidence 803(18) Reserved [Learned Treatises]
The Special Supreme Court Committee on Illinois Evidence has reserved Rule 803(18), because adoption of Federal Rule of Evidence 803(18) "would have represented a substantive change in Illinois law." Gino L. DiVito, *The Illinois Rules of Evidence: A Color-Coded Guide Containing the New Rules, the Committee's General and Specific Comments, a Comparison with the Federal Rules of Evidence, and Additional Commentary (Including the Federal Rules of Evidence as Amended Effective December 1, 2011)* (Jan. 1, 2012), at 114, http://www.tdrlawfirm.com/assets/downloads/Illinois_Rules_of_Evidence_Color-Coded_Guide.pdf. Federal Rule of Evidence 803(18), in effect December 1, 2011, allows admissibility of "[a] statement contained in a treatise [if it] is called to the attention of an expert witness on cross-examination or relied on by the expert on direct examination; and [. . .] the publication is established as reliable authority." Pursuant to the Illinois common law rule, a learned treatise is not admissible substantively as an exception to the hearsay rule. However, a learned treatise may be used in the cross-examination of an expert witness, which may also include questions concerning the views of recognized authorities in his or her particular field of expertise. People v. Anderson, 93 Ill. App. 3d 646 (1st Dist. 1981) (relying on Darling v. Charleston Cmty. Mem'l Hosp., 33 Ill. 2d 326, 335 (1965)). A learned treatise may be used to impeach the credibility of an expert witness and to rehabilitate his or her credibility following impeachment.

Illinois Rule of Evidence 803(22) Judgment of Previous Conviction
Illinois Rule of Evidence 803(22) allows admissibility of a final judgment, "entered after a trial or upon a plea of guilty," only if the underlying crime was "punishable by death or imprisonment in excess of one year." Illinois Rule of Evidence 803(22) was modeled on Federal Rule of Evidence 803(22), in effect until its stylistic amendment on December 1, 2011, except that Illinois Rule of Evidence 803(22) includes judgments based "upon a plea of nolo contendere," which Federal Rule of Evidence 803(22) explicitly excludes. Gino L. DiVito, *The Illinois Rules of Evidence: A Color-Coded Guide Containing the New Rules, the Committee's General and Specific Comments, a Comparison with the Federal Rules of Evidence, and Additional Commentary (Including the Federal Rules of Evidence as Amended Effective December 1, 2011)* (Jan. 1, 2012), at 116, http://www.tdrlawfirm.com/assets/downloads/Illinois_Rules_of_Evidence_Color-Coded_Guide.pdf [hereinafter DiVito, *Color-Coded Guide*]; FED. R. EVID. 803, Federal Advisory Committee Notes (1972 Proposed Rules). Justice DiVito notes that Illinois Rule of Evidence 803(22) had not adopted the language in Federal Rule of Evidence 803(22) referring to pleas of nolo contendere, suggesting that such pleas are not excluded at all in Illinois. DiVito, *Color-Coded Guide* at 116. Professor Graham, on the other hand, broadly states that a "judgment based upon a plea of nolo contendere is not admissible" in Illinois. MICHAEL H. GRAHAM, GRAHAM'S HANDBOOK OF ILLINOIS EVIDENCE at § 803.22 (10th ed. 2010). Each of these suggestions requires qualification.

While a judgment based upon a plea of nolo contendere is not admissible in federal civil and criminal proceedings pursuant to Federal Rules of Evidence 803(22) and 410, due to the "inconclusive and compromise nature of judgments based on nolo pleas," (FED. R. EVID. 410, Federal Advisory Committee Notes (1972 Proposed Rules)), evidence of a plea of nolo contendere is only inadmissible in Illinois in criminal proceedings pursuant to Illinois Rule of Evidence 410. Pursuant to the "unified scheme" of the Illinois Rules of Evidence and the "threshold requirement of relevance," the hearsay exception in Illinois Rule of Evidence 803(22) is limited by the operation of the relevancy provisions of Illinois

Rule of Evidence 410, resulting in an exclusion of pleas of nolo contendere from admissibility in "any criminal proceeding." ILL. R. EVID. 410; People v. Dabbs, 239 Ill. 2d 277 (2010). Pleas of nolo contendere also cannot be used to impeach the credibility of a witness per Illinois Rule of Evidence 609.

Federal Rule of Evidence 803(22) excludes "convictions of minor offenses [] not because the administration of justice in its lower echelons must be inferior, but because motivation to defend at this level is often minimal or nonexistent." FED. R. EVID. 803, Federal Advisory Committee Notes (1972 Proposed Rules). Minor offenses, such as traffic convictions, are excluded from subsequent civil actions because they constitute "unreliable hearsay." Ralph Ruebner & Anne M. Herbert, *Why Not Make All Traffic Convictions Inadmissible in Civil Cases?*, 83 ILL. B.J. 226 (1995). Such minor convictions are excluded from evidence because their admissibility in a subsequent civil proceeding "could conceivably turn a mechanical and summary traffic court hearing into the cornerstone of a significant civil action filed after the conclusion of the criminal proceeding." *Id.* at 231.

RELEVANT STATUTORY AUTHORITY

Criminal Sexual Assault: 720 ILCS 5/12-13

(Renumbered as 720 ILCS 5/11-1.20 by P.A. 96-1551, Art. 2, § 5, eff. July 1, 2011)

§ 11-1.20. Criminal Sexual Assault.

(a) A person commits criminal sexual assault if that person commits an act of sexual penetration and:

(1) uses force or threat of force;

(2) knows that the victim is unable to understand the nature of the act or is unable to give knowing consent;

(3) is a family member of the victim, and the victim is under 18 years of age; or

(4) is 17 years of age or over and holds a position of trust, authority, or supervision in relation to the victim, and the victim is at least 13 years of age but under 18 years of age.

(b) Sentence.

(1) Criminal sexual assault is a Class 1 felony, except that:

(A) A person who is convicted of the offense of criminal sexual assault as defined in paragraph (a)(1) or (a)(2) after having previously been convicted of the offense of criminal sexual assault or the offense of exploitation of a child, or who is convicted of the offense of criminal sexual assault as defined in paragraph (a)(1) or (a)(2) after having previously been convicted under the laws of this State or any other state of an offense that is substantially equivalent to the offense of criminal sexual assault or to the offense of exploitation of a child, commits a Class X felony for which the person shall be sentenced to a term of imprisonment of not less than 30 years and not more than 60 years. The commission of the second or subsequent offense is required to have been after the initial conviction for this paragraph (A) to apply.

(B) A person who is convicted of the offense of criminal sexual assault as defined in paragraph (a)(1) or (a)(2) after having previously been convicted of the offense of aggravated criminal sexual assault or the offense of predatory criminal sexual assault of a child, or who is convicted of the offense of criminal sexual assault as defined in paragraph (a)(1) or (a)(2) after having previously been convicted under the laws of this State or any other state of an offense that is substantially equivalent to the offense of aggravated criminal sexual assault or the offense of predatory criminal sexual assault of a child shall be sentenced to a term of natural life imprisonment. The commission of the second or subsequent offense is required to have been after the initial conviction for this paragraph (B) to apply.

(C) A second or subsequent conviction for a violation of paragraph (a)(3) or (a)(4) or under any similar statute of this State or any other state for any offense involving criminal sexual assault that is substantially equivalent to or more serious than the sexual assault prohibited under paragraph (a)(3) or (a)(4) is a Class X felony.

Effective July 1, 2011.

Aggravated Criminal Sexual Assault: 720 ILCS 5/12-14
(Renumbered as 720 ILCS 5/11-1.30 by P.A. 96-1551, Art. 2, § 5, eff. July 1, 2011)
§ 11-1.30. Aggravated Criminal Sexual Assault.

(a) A person commits aggravated criminal sexual assault if that person commits criminal sexual assault and any of the following aggravating circumstances exist during the commission of the offense or, for purposes of paragraph (7), occur as part of the same course of conduct as the commission of the offense:

(1) the person displays, threatens to use, or uses a dangerous weapon, other than a firearm, or any other object fashioned or used in a manner that leads the victim, under the circumstances, reasonably to believe that the object is a dangerous weapon;
(2) the person causes bodily harm to the victim, except as provided in paragraph (10);
(3) the person acts in a manner that threatens or endangers the life of the victim or any other person;
(4) the person commits the criminal sexual assault during the course of committing or attempting to commit any other felony;
(5) the victim is 60 years of age or older;
(6) the victim is a physically handicapped person;
(7) the person delivers (by injection, inhalation, ingestion, transfer of possession, or any other means) any controlled substance to the victim without the victim's consent or by threat or deception for other than medical purposes;
(8) the person is armed with a firearm;
(9) the person personally discharges a firearm during the commission of the offense; or
(10) the person personally discharges a firearm during the commission of the offense, and that discharge proximately causes great bodily harm, permanent disability, permanent disfigurement, or death to another person.

(b) A person commits aggravated criminal sexual assault if that person is under 17 years of age and: (i) commits an act of sexual penetration with a victim who is under 9 years of age; or (ii) commits an act of sexual penetration with a victim who is at least 9 years of age but under 13 years of age and the person uses force or threat of force to commit the act.

(c) A person commits aggravated criminal sexual assault if that person commits an act of sexual penetration with a victim who is a severely or profoundly intellectually disabled person.

(d) Sentence.

(1) Aggravated criminal sexual assault in violation of paragraph (2), (3), (4), (5), (6), or (7) of subsection (a) or in violation of subsection (b) or (c) is a Class X felony. A violation of subsection (a)(1) is a Class X felony for which 10 years shall be added to the term of imprisonment imposed by the court. A violation of subsection (a)(8) is a Class X felony for which 15 years shall be added to the term of imprisonment imposed by the court. A violation of subsection (a)(9) is a Class X felony for which 20 years shall be added to the term of imprisonment imposed by the court. A violation of subsection (a)(10) is a Class X felony for which 25 years or up to a term of natural life imprisonment shall be added to the term of imprisonment imposed by the court.

(2) A person who is convicted of a second or subsequent offense of aggravated criminal sexual assault, or who is convicted of the offense of aggravated criminal sexual assault after having previously been convicted of the offense of criminal sexual assault or the offense of predatory criminal sexual assault of a child, or who is convicted of the offense of aggravated criminal sexual assault after having previously been convicted under the laws of this or any other state of an offense that is substantially equivalent to the offense of criminal sexual assault, the offense of aggravated criminal sexual assault or the offense of predatory criminal sexual assault of a child, shall be sentenced to a term of natural life imprisonment. The commission of the second or subsequent offense is required to have been after the initial conviction for this paragraph (2) to apply.

Predatory Criminal Sexual Assault of a Child: 720 ILCS 5/12-14.1
(Renumbered as 720 ILCS 5/11-1.40 by P.A. 96-1551, Art. 2, § 5, eff. July 1, 2011)
§ 11-1.40. Predatory criminal sexual assault of a child.
(a) A person commits predatory criminal sexual assault of a child if that person commits an act of sexual penetration, is 17 years of age or older, and:

(1) the victim is under 13 years of age; or
(2) the victim is under 13 years of age and that person:

(A) is armed with a firearm;
(B) personally discharges a firearm during the commission of the offense;
(C) causes great bodily harm to the victim that:

(i) results in permanent disability; or
(ii) is life threatening; or

(D) delivers (by injection, inhalation, ingestion, transfer of possession, or any other means) any controlled substance to the victim without the victim's consent or by threat or deception, for other than medical purposes.

(b) Sentence.

(1) A person convicted of a violation of subsection (a)(1) commits a Class X felony, for which the person shall be sentenced to a term of imprisonment of not less than 6 years and not more than 60 years. A person convicted of a violation of subsection (a)(2)(A) commits a Class X felony for which 15 years shall be added to the term of imprisonment imposed by the court. A person convicted of a violation of subsection (a)(2)(B) commits a Class X felony for which 20 years shall be added to the term of imprisonment imposed by the court. A person convicted of a violation of subsection (a)(2)(C) commits a Class X felony for

which the person shall be sentenced to a term of imprisonment of not less than 50 years or up to a term of natural life imprisonment.

(1.1) A person convicted of a violation of subsection (a)(2)(D) commits a Class X felony for which the person shall be sentenced to a term of imprisonment of not less than 50 years and not more than 60 years.

(1.2) A person convicted of predatory criminal sexual assault of a child committed against 2 or more persons regardless of whether the offenses occurred as the result of the same act or of several related or unrelated acts shall be sentenced to a term of natural life imprisonment.

(2) A person who is convicted of a second or subsequent offense of predatory criminal sexual assault of a child, or who is convicted of the offense of predatory criminal sexual assault of a child after having previously been convicted of the offense of criminal sexual assault or the offense of aggravated criminal sexual assault, or who is convicted of the offense of predatory criminal sexual assault of a child after having previously been convicted under the laws of this State or any other state of an offense that is substantially equivalent to the offense of predatory criminal sexual assault of a child, the offense of aggravated criminal sexual assault or the offense of criminal sexual assault, shall be sentenced to a term of natural life imprisonment. The commission of the second or subsequent offense is required to have been after the initial conviction for this paragraph (2) to apply. Effective July 1, 2011.

Criminal Sexual Abuse: 720 ILCS 5/12-15
(Renumbered as 720 ILCS 5/11-1.50 by P.A. 96-1551, Art. 2, § 5, eff. July 1, 2011)
§ 11-1.50. Criminal sexual abuse.
(a) A person commits criminal sexual abuse if that person:

(1) commits an act of sexual conduct by the use of force or threat of force; or
(2) commits an act of sexual conduct and knows that the victim is unable to understand the nature of the act or is unable to give knowing consent.

(b) A person commits criminal sexual abuse if that person is under 17 years of age and commits an act of sexual penetration or sexual conduct with a victim who is at least 9 years of age but under 17 years of age.

(c) A person commits criminal sexual abuse if that person commits an act of sexual penetration or sexual conduct with a victim who is at least 13 years of age but under 17 years of age and the person is less than 5 years older than the victim.

(d) Sentence. Criminal sexual abuse for a violation of subsection (b) or (c) of this Section is a Class A misdemeanor. Criminal sexual abuse for a violation of paragraph (1) or (2) of subsection (a) of this Section is a Class 4 felony. A second or subsequent conviction for a violation of subsection (a) of this Section is a Class 2 felony. For purposes of this Section it is a second or subsequent conviction if the accused has at any time been convicted under this Section or under any similar statute of this State or any other state for any offense involving sexual abuse or sexual assault that is substantially equivalent to or more serious than the sexual abuse prohibited under this Section.

Effective July 1, 2011.

Aggravated Criminal Sexual Abuse: 720 ILCS 5/12-16
(Renumbered as 720 ILCS 5/11-1.60 by P.A. 96-1551, Art. 2, § 5, eff. July 1, 2011)
§ 11-1.60. Aggravated Criminal Sexual Abuse.

(a) A person commits aggravated criminal sexual abuse if that person commits criminal sexual abuse and any of the following aggravating circumstances exist (i) during the commission of the offense or (ii) for purposes of paragraph (7), as part of the same course of conduct as the commission of the offense:

(1) the person displays, threatens to use, or uses a dangerous weapon or any other object fashioned or used in a manner that leads the victim, under the circumstances, reasonably to believe that the object is a dangerous weapon;
(2) the person causes bodily harm to the victim;
(3) the victim is 60 years of age or older;
(4) the victim is a physically handicapped person;
(5) the person acts in a manner that threatens or endangers the life of the victim or any other person;
(6) the person commits the criminal sexual abuse during the course of committing or attempting to commit any other felony; or
(7) the person delivers (by injection, inhalation, ingestion, transfer of possession, or any other means) any controlled substance to the victim for other than medical purposes without the victim's consent or by threat or deception.

(b) A person commits aggravated criminal sexual abuse if that person commits an act of sexual conduct with a victim who is under 18 years of age and the person is a family member.

(c) A person commits aggravated criminal sexual abuse if:

(1) that person is 17 years of age or over and: (i) commits an act of sexual conduct with a victim who is under 13 years of age; or (ii) commits an act of sexual conduct with a victim who is at least 13 years of age but under 17 years of age and the person uses force or threat of force to commit the act; or
(2) that person is under 17 years of age and: (i) commits an act of sexual conduct with a victim who is under 9 years of age; or (ii) commits an act of sexual conduct with a victim who is at least 9 years of age but under 17 years of age and the person uses force or threat of force to commit the act.

(d) A person commits aggravated criminal sexual abuse if that person commits an act of sexual penetration or sexual conduct with a victim who is at least 13 years of age but under 17 years of age and the person is at least 5 years older than the victim.

(e) A person commits aggravated criminal sexual abuse if that person commits an act of sexual conduct with a victim who is a severely or profoundly intellectually disabled person.

(f) A person commits aggravated criminal sexual abuse if that person commits an act of sexual conduct with a victim who is at least 13 years of age but under 18 years of age and the person is 17 years of age or over and holds a position of trust, authority, or supervision in relation to the victim.

(g) Sentence. Aggravated criminal sexual abuse is a Class 2 felony.
Effective July 1, 2011.

Hearsay Exception; Statements by Victims of Sex Offenses to Medical Personnel: 725 ILCS 5/115-13

§ 115-13. In a prosecution for violation of Section 11-1.20, 11-1.30, 11-1.40, 11-1.50, 11-1.60, 12-13, 12-14, 12-14.1, 12-15 or 12-16 of the "Criminal Code of 1961," statements made by the victim to medical personnel for purposes of medical diagnosis or treatment including descriptions of the cause of symptom, pain or sensations, or the inception or general character of the cause or external source thereof insofar as reasonably pertinent to diagnosis or treatment shall be admitted as an exception to the hearsay rule.

Certain Hearsay Exceptions: 725 ILCS 5/115-10

§ 115-10. Certain hearsay exceptions.

(a) In a prosecution for a physical or sexual act perpetrated upon or against a child under the age of 13, or a person who was a moderately, severely, or profoundly intellectually disabled person as defined in this Code and in Section 2-10.1 of the Criminal Code of 1961 at the time the act was committed, including but not limited to prosecutions for violations of Sections 11-1.20 through 11-1.60 or 12-13 through 12-16 of the Criminal Code of 1961 and prosecutions for violations of Sections 10-1 (kidnapping), 10-2 (aggravated kidnapping), 10-3 (unlawful restraint), 10-3.1 (aggravated unlawful restraint), 10-4 (forcible detention), 10-5 (child abduction), 10-6 (harboring a runaway), 10-7 (aiding or abetting child abduction), 11-9 (public indecency), 11-11 (sexual relations within families), 11-21 (harmful material), 12-1 (assault), 12-2 (aggravated assault), 12-3 (battery), 12-3.2 (domestic battery), 12-3.3 (aggravated domestic battery), 12-3.05 or 12-4 (aggravated battery), 12-4.1 (heinous battery), 12-4.2 (aggravated battery with a firearm), 12-4.3 (aggravated battery of a child), 12-4.7 (drug induced infliction of great bodily harm), 12-5 (reckless conduct), 12-6 (intimidation), 12-6.1 or 12-6.5 (compelling organization membership of persons), 12-7.1 (hate crime), 12-7.3 (stalking), 12-7.4 (aggravated stalking), 12-10 (tattooing body of minor), 12-11 (home invasion), 12-21.5 (child abandonment), 12-21.6 (endangering the life or health of a child) or 12-32 (ritual mutilation) of the Criminal Code of 1961 or any sex offense as defined in subsection (B) of Section 2 of the Sex Offender Registration Act, the following evidence shall be admitted as an exception to the hearsay rule:

(1) testimony by the victim of an out-of-court statement made by the victim that he or she complained of such act to another; and

(2) testimony of an out-of-court statement made by the victim describing any complaint of such act or matter or detail pertaining to any act which is an element of an offense which is the subject of a prosecution for a sexual or physical act against that victim.

(b) Such testimony shall only be admitted if:

(1) The court finds in a hearing conducted outside the presence of the jury that the time, content, and circumstances of the statement provide sufficient safeguards of reliability; and

(2) The child or moderately, severely, or profoundly intellectually disabled person either:

(A) testifies at the proceeding; or

(B) is unavailable as a witness and there is corroborative evidence of the act which is the subject of the statement; and

(3) In a case involving an offense perpetrated against a child under the age of 13, the out-of-court statement was made before the victim attained 13 years of age or within 3 months after the commission of the offense, whichever occurs later, but the statement may be admitted regardless of the age of the victim at the time of the proceeding.

(c) If a statement is admitted pursuant to this Section, the court shall instruct the jury that it is for the jury to determine the weight and credibility to be given the statement and that, in making the determination, it shall consider the age and maturity of the child, or the intellectual capabilities of the moderately, severely, or profoundly intellectually disabled person, the nature of the statement, the circumstances under which the statement was made, and any other relevant factor.

(d) The proponent of the statement shall give the adverse party reasonable notice of his intention to offer the statement and the particulars of the statement.

(e) Statements described in paragraphs (1) and (2) of subsection (a) shall not be excluded on the basis that they were obtained as a result of interviews conducted pursuant to a protocol adopted by a Child Advocacy Advisory Board as set forth in subsections (c), (d), and (e) of Section 3 of the Children's Advocacy Center Act or that an interviewer or witness to the interview was or is an employee, agent, or investigator of a State's Attorney's office.

Effective January 1, 2012.

Business Records as Evidence: 725 ILCS 5/115-5

§ 115-5. Business records as evidence.

(a) Any writing or record, whether in the form of an entry in a book or otherwise, made as a memorandum or record of any act, transaction, occurrence, or event, shall be admissible as evidence of such act, transaction, occurrence, or event, if made in regular course of any business, and if it was the regular course of such business to make such memorandum or record at the time of such act, transaction, occurrence, or event or within a reasonable time thereafter.

All other circumstances of the making of such writing or record, including lack of personal knowledge by the entrant or maker, may be shown to affect its weight, but such circumstances shall not affect its admissibility.

The term "business," as used in this Section, includes business, profession, occupation, and calling of every kind.

(b) If any business, institution, member of a profession or calling, or any department or agency of government, in the regular course of business or activity has kept or recorded any memorandum, writing, entry, print, representation or combination thereof, of any act, transaction, occurrence, or event, and in the regular course of business has caused any or all of the same to be recorded, copied, or reproduced by any photographic, photostatic, microfilm, micro-card, miniature photographic, optical imaging, or other process which accurately reproduces or forms a medium for so reproducing the original, the original may be destroyed in the regular course of business unless its preservation is required by law. Such reproduction, when satisfactorily identified, is as admissible in evidence as the original itself in any proceeding whether the original is in existence or not and an enlargement or facsimile of such reproduction is likewise admissible in evidence if the original reproduction is in existence and available for inspection under direction of court. The introduction of a reproduced record, enlargement, or facsimile does not preclude admission of the original. This Section shall not be construed to exclude from evidence any document or copy thereof which is otherwise admissible under the rules of evidence.

(c) No writing or record made in the regular course of any business shall become admissible as evidence by the application of this Section if:

(1) Such writing or record has been made by anyone in the regular course of any form of hospital or medical business; or

(2) Such writing or record has been made by anyone during an investigation of an alleged offense or during any investigation relating to pending or anticipated litigation of any kind, except during a hearing to revoke a sentence of probation or conditional discharge or an order of court supervision that is based on a technical violation of a sentencing order when the hearing involves a probationer or defendant who has transferred or moved from the county having jurisdiction over the original charge or sentence. For the purposes of this subsection (c), "technical violation" means a breach of a sentencing order but does not include an allegation of a subsequent criminal act asserted in a formal criminal charge.
Effective January 1, 2000.

Records of the Coroner's Medical or Laboratory Examiner as Evidence: 725 ILCS 5/115-5.1

§ 115-5.1. In any civil or criminal action the records of the coroner's medical or laboratory examiner summarizing and detailing the performance of his or her official duties in performing medical examinations upon deceased persons or autopsies, or both, and kept in the ordinary course of business of the coroner's office, duly certified by the county coroner or chief supervisory coroner's pathologist or medical examiner, shall be received as competent evidence in any court of this State, to the extent permitted by this Section. These reports, specifically including but not limited to the pathologist's protocol, autopsy reports and toxicological reports, shall be public documents and thereby may be admissible as *prima facie* evidence of the facts, findings, opinions, diagnoses and conditions stated therein.

A duly certified coroner's protocol or autopsy report, or both, complying with the requirements of this Section may be duly admitted into evidence as an exception to the hearsay rule as *prima facie* proof of the cause of death of the person to whom it relates. The records referred to in this Section shall be limited to the records of the results of postmortem examinations of the findings of autopsy and toxicological laboratory examinations.

Persons who prepare reports or records offered in evidence hereunder may be subpoenaed as witnesses in civil or criminal cases upon the request of either party to the cause. However, if such person is dead, the county coroner or a duly authorized official of the coroner's office may testify to the fact that the examining pathologist, toxicologist, or other medical or laboratory examiner is deceased and that the offered report or record was prepared by such deceased person. The witness must further attest that the medical report or record was prepared in the ordinary and usual course of the deceased person's duty or employment in conformity with the provisions of this Section.

Effective July 13, 1982.

PRIOR ILLINOIS CASE LAW

1. Statement Related to a Startling Event Made While Declarant Was Under the Stress of Excitement Caused by the Event Is Admissible as an Excited Utterance

People v. Thomas, 178 Ill. 2d 215 (1997)

Defendant and two other individuals participated in the shooting death of the victim. After the shooting, defendant and one of the two accomplices went to the accomplice's fiancée's home. The fiancée gave the police a written statement. She stated that the defendant told her he had shot someone. Once the accomplice noticed that his fiancée was nervous, he got angry at defendant for telling her. At trial the fiancée denied knowing the content of the conversation between the accomplice and defendant and denied knowing why defendant was angry. On cross-examination, the witness testified that the statement to the police was a lie because she was mad at defendant and wanted to frame him. The trial court admitted the witness' statement as impeachment evidence only.

The Supreme Court noted that the statement qualified as an excited utterance, since the accomplice had just found out that defendant had told his fiancée about the murder. The Supreme Court explained that "[a] statement related to a startling event made while the declarant was under the stress of excitement caused by the event is admissible despite its hearsay nature on the theory that the declarant lacks an opportunity to fabricate."

2. Courts Evaluate the Totality of Circumstances to Determine Whether a Statement Qualifies Under the Excited Utterance Exception to the Hearsay Rule
People v. Sutton, 233 Ill. 2d 89 (2009)

Defendant was convicted of murder after he shot and wounded a victim and robbed, sexually assaulted and killed the victim's girlfriend. The police found the victim "bleeding and staggering" on the street shortly after the shooting. He had knocked on several doors and had asked residents to call the police. Once police officers arrived, he gave them a description of the assailant. The police took him to the hospital in an ambulance about 20 minutes after the shooting. While the officers continued to question the victim in the ambulance, the medics tried to calm him down, treated his injuries and tried to stop his bleeding. The victim spent almost a week in the hospital during which time he could not independently recall anything about the incident. In an attempt to remember the incident, he underwent several hypnotherapy sessions. Hypnotherapy helped him remember portions of the events and he was able to identify the defendant in a lineup several years after the shooting.

Prior to trial, defendant filed a motion to exclude the victim's statements made to the police shortly after the incident and those made by him in the ambulance. The appellate court found that the victim's statements made to the police shortly after the crime were non-testimonial. It also held that these statements were admissible under the spontaneous declaration exception to the hearsay rule. The appellate court also found that the victim's statements to the police once he was on his way to the hospital were testimonial but nevertheless admissible because he testified at trial and was available for cross-examination. On appeal to the Illinois Supreme Court, the defendant challenged the appellate court's finding that the victim's statements to the police following the shooting were not testimonial and that he was available for cross-examination. The Illinois Supreme Court explained that

> [f]or a hearsay statement to be admissible under the spontaneous declaration exception, there must be an occurrence sufficiently startling to produce a spontaneous and unreflecting statement, there must be an absence of time for the declarant to fabricate the statement, and the statement must relate to the circumstances of the occurrence. People v. Williams, 193 Ill. 2d 306, 352 (2000). Courts employ a totality of the circumstances analysis in determining whether a hearsay statement is admissible under the spontaneous declaration exception. *Williams*, 193 Ill. 2d at 352, 250 Ill. Dec. 692, 739 N.E.2d 455. The totality of the circumstances analysis involves consideration of several factors, including time, the mental and physical condition of the declarant, the nature of the event, and the presence or absence of self-interest. *Williams*, 193 Ill. 2d at 352, quoting People v. House, 141 Ill. 2d 323, 382 (1990).
>
> ***
>
> The period of time that may pass without affecting the admissibility of a statement varies greatly. *Williams*, 193 Ill. 2d at 353. The critical inquiry with regard to time is "'whether the statement was made while the excitement of the event predominated.'" People v. Smith, 152 Ill. 2d 229, 260 (1992), quoting M. GRAHAM, CLEARY & GRAHAM'S HANDBOOK OF ILLINOIS EVIDENCE § 803.3, at 627 (5th ed. 1990).

Here, the Supreme Court found that the victim lacked the time to fabricate a description of the defendant because of the circumstances surrounding his statements. The Supreme Court observed that the police arrived and found the victim bleeding from his head and staggering down the street, telling them that he and his girlfriend had been shot. The Supreme Court found it "inconceivable" that he would have spent the minutes between the shooting and the officers' arrival to fabricate a statement about what had occurred. The Supreme Court therefore found that the victim's statements made to the police officers shortly after the shooting were admissible under the spontaneous declaration exception to the hearsay rule. The Supreme Court noted that the statements made to the police on the victim's way to the hospital also qualified as spontaneous declarations although they were made 20 minutes after the shooting. The Supreme Court observed that the "passage of time between the crime and his statements did not destroy the spontaneity of those statements" because they were made while he was being treated by the medics and while he was in a "highly emotional" state of mind. The court concluded that the witness had no time to fabricate his statements due to his "mental and physical condition, the nature of the event, and the absence of self-interest."

The Supreme Court determined that the statements made at the scene of the shooting were non-testimonial, while the statements made on the way to the hospital were testimonial. It explained that the officers initially learned about the shooting from 911 calls made by neighbors, whose doors were knocked on by the "bleeding and staggering" victim. The court concluded that the purpose of the initial police questioning was to obtain information about the ongoing emergency. On the way to the hospital, however, the immediate ongoing emergency was over and the court determined that the purpose of the questioning in the ambulance was to ascertain past events and investigate in greater detail the circumstances surrounding the shooting.

Although the Supreme Court found that the statements made in the ambulance were testimonial, it nevertheless admitted them because the witness was available for cross-examination. Defendant argued that because the victim had undergone hypnosis and other memory retrieval therapies, he should not be considered an available witness. The court disagreed, noting that even though testimony influenced by hypnosis is *per se* inadmissible, the rule against admissibility of hypnotically induced statements does not affect statements made prior to hypnosis. The court concluded that the witness was competent to testify concerning events occurring prior to hypnosis and other memory retrieval therapies.

3. Child's Statement May Qualify as an Excited Utterance Although Significant Amount of Time Had Passed Since the Startling Event and the Statement Was in Response to a Question

People v. Smith, 152 Ill. 2d 229 (1992)

Defendant on trial for murder and aggravated criminal sexual assault argued that a four-year-old child's hearsay statements should not have been allowed in evidence. Immediately following the murder of her babysitter, police asked the minor who had witnessed the crime about what happened. The minor implicated defendant in the crime. Although the minor did not testify at trial, the police officer who interviewed her testified about statements she made 10 minutes after the murder. The trial court admitted the officer's testimony under the excited utterance hearsay exception. Defendant challenged the admissibility of the statements, but the Illinois Supreme Court found that the trial court properly admitted them under this exception. The Supreme Court explained that

> [t]o secure admission of a "spontaneous declaration" or "excited utterance," the proponent of the evidence must demonstrate: (1) the occurrence of an event or condition sufficiently startling to produce a spontaneous and unreflecting statement; (2) absence of time to fabricate;

> and (3) a statement relating to the circumstances of the occurrence. People v. Poland, 22 Ill. 2d 175, 181 (1961).

The Supreme Court further explained that a child's out-of-court statements are admissible

> under the excited utterance exception despite (1) the significant passage of time between the assault and the statement, and (2) the fact that the statement was made in response to a question [because the] court found the statement to be "the product of the event, rather than the child's deliberation." People v. Nevitt, 135 Ill. 2d 423 (1990).

The Supreme Court found that the child was exposed to a startling event. Although she did not see defendant brutally stab her babysitter, she could hear her screams from the next room. Moreover, the Supreme Court noted that the child did not have enough time to fabricate her statement because the officer arrived at the scene within 10 minutes of the victim's screams. The Supreme Court observed that although the child responded to the officer's questions, such prompting did not "destroy the spontaneity" of her statement. Finally, the Supreme Court concluded that although the child's statement may have merely indicated that the defendant had been at the apartment at some point on the evening of the crime, the evidence was admitted to show why defendant had been arrested and not necessarily that defendant had committed the crime.

4. Out-of-Court Statement Is Admissible Pursuant to the State of Mind Exception When It Tends to Show the Declarant's State of Mind at the Time of the Utterance
People v. Cloutier, 178 Ill. 2d 141 (1997)

Defendant was convicted of first degree murder and aggravated criminal sexual assault after he assaulted and strangled a woman in the back seat of her car. He then assaulted two more women. He pulled each one into the car, made them take off their clothes, and forced the women to observe the victim's dead body in the back seat. Both women escaped and gave statements to a detective. The state introduced the women's accounts of the assaults through the detective's testimony at trial. The jury found defendant eligible for the death penalty and both women testified at the aggravation and mitigation hearing. Defendant contended on appeal that the women's out-of-court statements as presented by the detective were inadmissible hearsay. The Illinois Supreme Court agreed, noting that the state was incorrect in arguing that the evidence was admissible under the state of mind exception. The state claimed that the evidence showed that defendant wanted to scare the women by showing them the victim's body so that they would "submit to his wishes." The Supreme Court disagreed, explaining that the state misunderstood the state of mind exception:

> Under that exception, an out-of-court statement of a declarant is admissible when that statement tends to show the declarant's state of mind at the time of the utterance. People v. Lawler, 142 Ill. 2d 548, 558 (1991). In order to be admissible, the declarant's state of mind must be relevant to a material issue in the case. People v. Nyberg, 275 Ill. App. 3d 570, 580 (1995). In this case, defendant was not the declarant: the declarants were [the two women]. Their state of mind when they spoke with [the detective] has no bearing on defendant's state of mind when he killed the victim.

5. A State of Mind Statement May Be Admitted to Prove Declarant's Intent and That He or She Acted in Accordance with That Intent
People v. Bartall, 98 Ill. 2d 294 (1983)

Defendant fired two shots out of his car and killed a woman standing nearby. The trial court admitted evidence of an incident that occurred one day after this shooting. A witness testified that as she was driving down a street, a car swerved near her vehicle and saw defendant who pointed a gun at her head. She then heard multiple gun shots. Defendant was arrested shortly thereafter. A technician later determined that the bullets from the murder and from the subsequent shooting came from the same gun. Defendant's girlfriend testified at trial that defendant told her he would shoot out the tires of the witness' vehicle. The trial judge sustained the state's objection to the girlfriend's testimony about his out-of-court statement. Defendant contended that the trial court erroneously excluded his statement because it fell within the state of mind exception to the hearsay rule. Although the Illinois Supreme Court agreed with defendant that his statement "was admissible to prove his intent in the [later] attack and to prove that he acted in accordance with that intent," it found that the trial court's exclusion of the statement was harmless beyond a reasonable doubt.

6. Out-of-Court Statements Made by a Patient to a Physician for Purposes of Medical Treatment Are Admissible as Exception to Hearsay Rule
People v. Gant, 58 Ill. 2d 178 (1974)

Defendant was charged with attempted murder, aggravated battery, burglary and armed violence. Defendant had shot his girlfriend. While in the emergency room, the victim spoke to a physician. The physician initially thought that the victim's injuries were caused by a blunt object, but not by a gun shot. The physician asked the victim what happened so that he could better understand the "wound problem." The victim told him that a man had entered her room and then "something hit her on the head, and at the same time" she heard a gun go off. She also told the physician that she knew the man. The victim was reluctant to testify against defendant because she "loved" him. The Illinois Supreme Court noted that the statement was admissible through testimony of the physician as substantive evidence. The Supreme Court explained that

> '[s]tatements of a presently existing bodily condition made by a patient to a doctor consulted for treatment are almost universally admitted as evidence of the facts stated ***. Although statements to physicians are not likely to be spontaneous, since they are usually made in response to questions, their reliability is assured by the likelihood that the patient believes that the effectiveness of the treatment he receives may depend largely upon the accuracy of the information he provides the physician.*** 'The exception might be taken one step further to encompass statements made to a physician concerning the cause or the external source of the condition to be treated.' McCormick, Handbook of the Law of Evidence 690–691 (2d ed. 1972); *see also* Annot., 37 A.L.R.3d 778, 802 (1971); Jensen v. Elgin, Joliet and Eastern Ry. Co., 24 Ill. 2d 383, 388 (1962).

7. Sexual Abuse Victim's Statements Made to Medical Personnel for Purpose of Diagnosis or Treatment Are Admissible Pursuant to 725 ILCS 5/115-13 as Exception to Hearsay Rule
People v. Falaster, 173 Ill. 2d 220 (1996)

Defendant was convicted of aggravated criminal sexual assault, criminal sexual assault and unlawful distribution of harmful material pursuant to 720 ILCS 5/12-13 and 720 ILCS 5/12-14 for the abuse of his minor daughter. A nurse who obtained the victim's history before a physical examination testified for the state. She testified that the victim reported she had been abused by the defendant since she was eight years old.

Defendant contended on appeal that the trial court erroneously permitted the nurse to provide hearsay evidence of the victim's identification of the defendant as the perpetrator pursuant to 725 ILCS 5/115-13. Section 115-13 permits admissibility of sexual abuse victim's statements made to "medical personnel for purposes of medical diagnosis or treatment including descriptions of the cause of symptom, pain or sensations, or the inception or general character of the cause or external source thereof insofar as reasonably pertinent to diagnosis or treatment as an exception to the hearsay rule." The defendant argued that section 115-13 did not apply because the victim was not seeking medical diagnosis or treatment when she made the identification statements. Rather, defendant claimed, she was undergoing the examination for the sole purpose of "developing evidence for use in a subsequent prosecution." The Illinois Supreme Court disagreed, observing that section 115-13 "does not distinguish between examining physicians and treating physicians."

Defendant also argued that the victim's statement identifying him as the abuser was inadmissible because it was irrelevant to diagnosis and treatment. The Illinois Supreme Court rejected this argument as well, noting that

> at least in the family setting, a victim's identification of a family member as the offender is closely related to the victim's diagnosis and treatment in cases involving allegations of sexual abuse, and thus we agree with those decisions that have permitted the admission of such hearsay evidence. People v. Morgan, 259 Ill. App. 3d 770, 781-82 (1994); *see also* United States v. Renville, 779 F.2d 430, 437 (8th Cir. 1985) ("[C]hild abuse involves more than physical injury; the physician must be attentive to treating the emotional and psychological injuries which accompany this crime. [Citations.] The exact nature and extent of the psychological problems which ensure from child abuse often depend on the identity of the abuser"). [. . .] We believe that the nurse's testimony relating the minor's identification of the defendant as the abuser was properly admitted under the terms of section 115-13.

8. Hearsay Statements of Child Sex Abuse Victim Admitted Pursuant to 725 ILCS 5/115-10 Must Be Judicially Determined to Be Reliable

People v. Kitch, 239 Ill. 2d 452 (2011)

Defendant was charged with predatory criminal sexual assault of a child pursuant to 720 ILCS 5/12-14.1 and aggravated criminal sexual abuse pursuant to 720 ILCS 5/12-16. The state informed the trial court before trial that it intended to introduce hearsay statements of the two minor victims about the abuse pursuant to 725 ILCS 5/115-10. Defendant objected to the admissibility of the statements. The trial court conducted a hearing where a sheriff and one of his employees testified as to the statements the victims made to them during an interview. The statements were transcribed by the sheriff and his employee. The trial court admitted the statements on the condition that the children would testify. Both children testified at trial consistently with their earlier statements but defendant argued on appeal that neither child testified in sufficient detail to have "'appeared' for cross-examination within the meaning of the confrontation clause." The Illinois Supreme Court noted that defendant forfeited this argument because he failed to object at trial or raise the issue in a post-trial motion. The Supreme Court observed that defendant "only [argued] that the hearsay statements were not sufficiently reliable, an apparent reference to section 115-10(b)(1), which requires a judicial determination that "the time, content, and circumstances of the statement provide sufficient safeguards of reliability" (725 ILCS 5/115-10(b)(1) (West 2004)). The Supreme Court reviewed the issue for plain error and determined that the victims' trial testimony on direct examination was sufficient to establish the elements of the relevant counts and that the victims were fully cross-examined by defense counsel and thoroughly answered all questions put to them.

See also People v. Cookson, 215 Ill. 2d 194 (2005) (finding that the time, content, and circumstances of the out-of-court statement of a child victim must provide sufficient safeguards of reliability to be admissible pursuant to 725 ILCS 5/115-10).

9. Trial Court Should Give an Instruction Pertaining to Facts the Jury Must Consider in Determining Weight and Credibility of Hearsay Statements Made by a Child Victim of Sexual Abuse

People v. Sargent, 239 Ill. 2d 166 (2010)

Defendant was convicted of predatory criminal sexual assault of one of his minor stepsons and three counts of predatory criminal sexual assault and two counts of aggravated criminal sexual abuse of a younger stepson. At trial, the state introduced the hearsay statements of the two victims and the trial court failed to tender to the jury an instruction governing the hearsay evidence. Defendant argued on appeal that the trial court erred in failing to instruct the jury pursuant to 725 ILCS 5/115-10 which requires that

> the court shall instruct the jury that it is for the jury to determine the weight and credibility to be given the statement and that, in making the determination, it shall consider the age and maturity of the child [. . .] the nature of the statement, the circumstances under which the statement was made, and any other relevant factor.

The Illinois Supreme Court rejected defendant's argument, noting that defendant waived it because he failed to raise his objection at trial or in a post-trial motion. The Supreme Court also refused to consider the argument under plain error review because defendant failed to prove either prong of the plain error review. The Supreme Court explained that although "sending the case to the jury without such an instruction was a clear and obvious error," the evidence was not closely balanced and the absence of the jury instructions did not "severely threaten the fairness" of the trial.

See also People v. Becker, 239 Ill. 2d 215 (2010) (finding that where child victim's hearsay statements are admitted as evidence pursuant to 725 ILCS 5/115-10, expert witnesses may not testify as to reliability of those statements).

10. Unavailable Child Declarant's Statements Pertaining to an Element of the Charged Offense Are Admissible Under 725 ILCS 5/115-10 If Found to Possess Sufficient Indicia of Reliability

People v. Williams, 193 Ill. 2d 306 (2000)

A child witnessed the murder of his family, was kidnapped by the defendant, and murdered within 24 hours of his family's murder. During the period of time when the child-victim was kidnapped, the defendant placed him in the care of her friend. During this period, the child-victim told the friend, at intervals between 6 and 11 hours after his family's murder, that his mother and sister were dead, as well as other details of the crime, including naming the defendant and three others as the actors. The state offered the friend's testimony pursuant to 725 ILCS 5/115-10. The trial court ruled that the child's out-of-court statements, as retold by the friend, were admissible under section 115-10, as well as under the common law spontaneous declaration exception. On appeal, the defendant challenged the admissibility of the testimony, claiming that it did not meet the statutory requirement that it "pertain[] to an act which is an element of an offense which is the subject of a prosecution for a sexual or physical act perpetrated upon or against a child."

The Illinois Supreme Court held that the child-victim's statements did relate to an element of the crime, specifically, the charge of aggravated kidnapping, since the statements "explained how and why [the child-victim] came to be confined by defendant and established that the confinement was without the consent of his mother," an element of aggravated kidnapping. The defendant also argued that the testimony did not "bear adequate 'indicia of reliability.'" The Illinois Supreme Court noted that pursuant to section 115-10, "a hearsay statement by a child declarant may not be admitted unless the circuit court first finds in a hearing conducted outside the presence of the jury that the time, content, and circumstances of the statement provide sufficient safeguards of reliability." The Illinois Supreme Court concluded that the trial court did not abuse its discretion in admitting the statements since the trial court was in the best position to assess whether they possessed indicia of trustworthiness.

11. Trial Court Must Conduct a Hearing to Determine Reliability of Out-of-Court Statements of Victim Child Pursuant to 725 ILCS 5/115-10

People v. Mitchell, 155 Ill. 2d 344 (1993)

Defendant was convicted of aggravated criminal sexual assault. The victim gave inconsistent testimony at trial about the assault, indicating that the defendant only touched her leg but later claiming that he touched her in "a bad place." The trial court failed to conduct a hearing pursuant to 725 ILCS 5/115-10 to determine whether the victim's out-of-court statements were sufficiently reliable. A detective subsequently testified as to the child's statements. The Illinois Supreme Court found that the victim's statements as introduced by the detective were highly prejudicial to the defendant because the testimony was largely inconsistent and contradictory. The Supreme Court agreed with the appellate court that the "failure to conduct such a hearing was error, compounded by the fact that [the victim's] testimony was ambiguous, inconsistent and contradictory in a case in which credibility of the witnesses and reliability of their testimony was particularly important."

12. 725 ILCS 5/115-10 Permits Admissibility of Out-of-Court Videotaped Statement of a Child Victim

People v. Bowen, 183 Ill. 2d 103 (1998)

Defendant was charged with aggravated criminal sexual assault. The victim gave a videotaped statement pertaining to the events of the alleged abuse and later testified at trial. Defendant argued that admissibility of the videotape violated 725 ILCS 5/115-10. The Illinois Supreme Court held that an out-of-court videotape of the child's previous statements was admissible as corroborative evidence of the child's in-court testimony. The court reasoned that, "with regard to the impact on the defendant's rights, there is little difference between introducing the statement on videotape and allowing it to be recounted in detail through the testimony of a third party." The Supreme Court noted that "[u]nlike typical hearsay, videotaping enables the trier of fact to observe firsthand the nature and suggestiveness of the questions posed to the child; the substance and subtleties of the child's responses; and the child's demeanor in giving those responses." Nonetheless, since the trial court failed to instruct the jury to specifically address and evaluate the credibility and weight of the victim's statement, to consider the age and maturity of the child, or the circumstances under which it was made, the Supreme Court concluded that this failure to instruct was plain error where the evidence was closely balanced and the trial court failed to conduct a pretrial hearing as to the statement's reliability.

13. Under Prior Illinois Common Law, Pursuant to the Past Recollection Recorded Exception to the Hearsay Rule, a Witness Must Lack Present Recollection of the Event at Trial

People v. Beasley, 307 Ill. App. 3d 200 (1st Dist. 1999)

Defendant was charged with aggravated criminal sexual assault, criminal sexual assault and unlawful restraint. The physician who treated the victim after the assault testified for the defense. He stated that although he had no recollection of treating the victim, he kept a record of all patients he treated. He briefly saw the record which contained his signature and again testified that he did not remember details pertaining to the victim but that he could testify based on his report. The state objected to the physician's testimony, arguing that defense could not question him about specific parts of the report since he did not remember it. The trial court ultimately found that the physician had no independent recollection of the record and granted the state's objection. Defense made an offer of proof which indicated that the medical record contained various statements, including ones by the victim where she stated how she was assaulted and the physician's findings pertaining to the victim's injuries. The report noted that the victim suffered "relatively minor" injuries, but the defense was precluded from introducing this fact to the jury because the trial court precluded the physician from testifying as to the contents of his report. The jury found defendant guilty and defendant appealed, contending that the medical report should have been admitted under the past recollection recorded exception to the hearsay rule. The First District of the Illinois Appellate Court noted,

> to fall within the past-recollection-recorded exception, the evidence must meet four requirements: (1) the witness had firsthand knowledge of the recorded event; (2) the written statement was made at or near the time of the event and while the witness had a clear and accurate memory of it; (3) the witness lacks present recollection of the event; and (4) the witness can vouch for the accuracy of the written statement. Salcik v. Tassone, 236 Ill. App. 3d 548, 554 (1st Dist. 1992).

The appellate court found, however, that defendant waived the past recollection recorded claim because he did not raise it at trial or in a post-trial motion. The court explained,

> [f]irst, defendant never specifically asked the trial court to admit the medical record as a past recollection recorded. Instead, he attempted to use the report only to refresh [the physician's] memory, which it did not do. When he did attempt to admit the report in evidence, he never suggested past-recollection recorded. Second, defendant never included the issue in his post-trial memorandum. Although he there stated that the trial court "erred in denying the admission of [the physician's] medical report," he failed to elaborate why doing so was error. Our courts have consistently stated that an issue must be specifically stated in a post-trial motion in order to properly preserve the issue on appeal. People v. Enoch, 122 Ill. 2d 176, 186 (1988).

14. All Foundation Requirements Must Be Met for a Document to Be Admitted as Past Recollection Recorded

People v. Speed, 315 Ill. App. 3d 511 (4th Dist. 2000)

Defendant was charged with domestic battery. At trial, the prosecution offered a written account of the alleged incident prepared by the victim at the police station shortly after the incident. The state offered the document as the victim's past recollection recorded. The appellate court held that the victim's

> statement was not properly admitted into evidence as her past recollection recorded. [The victim] did not vouch for the accuracy of her written statement as of the time she made it. The first three requirements for admissibility as past recollection recorded were fulfilled: (1) [The victim] had firsthand knowledge of the events recorded in the statement; (2) the statement failed to refresh her recollection; and (3) the statement was written very shortly after the incident occurred. However, [the victim] did not testify that the statement was accurate when written.

The court concluded that the victim's failure to testify as to the accuracy of her statement was fatal to admissibility of the statement as past recollection recorded. The court instead suggested that the document was admissible as the victim's prior inconsistent statement. The defendant challenged this theory arguing that the victim's present inability to remember should not be "testimony" inconsistent with her prior statement. The court held that "a witness' prior testimony does not have to directly contradict testimony given at trial to be considered 'inconsistent.' [. . .] Where a witness now claims to be unable to recollect a matter, a former affirmation of it should be admitted [in evidence]."

15. Police Reports, Although Generally Inadmissible as Substantive Evidence Because They Are Hearsay, Are Admissible as Past Recollection Recorded If the Necessary Foundation Requirements Are Met
People v. Andrews, 101 Ill. App. 3d 808 (1st Dist. 1981)

Two defendants were found guilty of robbery. The investigating police officers wrote a report that identified the clerk and another man as witnesses. The man, however, testified that his brother's name erroneously appeared in the report, and that it was he who saw the robbery in progress. The investigating police officers testified at trial but had no recollection of who they interviewed after the robbery. Defense counsel sought to enter the officers' report in evidence as past recollection recorded, but the trial court denied the request. The defense appealed, and the appellate court found that

> [t]he trial court refused to admit the report into evidence, because "the report itself comes from sources quite possibly other than the witnesses that are sought to be impeached." Defendants-appellants maintain that this ruling was erroneous and we agree. The most effective and most frequently used attack upon the credibility of witnesses is proof of a prior inconsistent statement. The question here is, was the police report competent evidence of such prior statements. Illinois courts do not admit police reports into evidence as substantive evidence of the facts related therein. Such reports, however, may be used for the limited purpose of impeachment. (People v. Morris (1978), 65 Ill. App. 3d 155, 22 Ill. Dec. 63, 382 N.E.2d 383.) Here the report was offered not as substantive evidence, but to impeach by showing what was said to the investigating officers. The rule permitting the introduction of past recollection recorded has four requirements which must be met: "(1) the witness must have had firsthand knowledge of the event, (2) the written statement must be an original memorandum made at or near the time of the event and while the witness had a clear and accurate memory of it, (3) the witness must lack a present recollection of the event, and (4) the witness must vouch for the accuracy of the written memorandum." People v. Skidmore, 56 Ill. App. 3d 862, 865 (1978); People v. Munoz, 31 Ill. App. 3d 689, 693 (1975); McCormick, Evidence § 299 at 712 (2d ed. 1972). This record has evidence supporting each of these requirements. Both officers at the time of making the report had firsthand knowledge of what the witnesses had told them. The report was made shortly after the interviews while they still had a clear memory of what was said, but at the time of trial they did not. Lastly, both testified that the report was accurate when written. The report was admissible as past recollection recorded.

16. Past Recollection Recorded May Be Read to the Jury and Admitted as an Exhibit
People v. Olson, 59 Ill. App. 3d 643 (4th Dist. 1978)

Defendant was convicted of two counts of delivery of a controlled substance. At the trial for the first count, the individual who conducted the analysis of the controlled substance testified about the procedures employed. The witness could not recall specifically analyzing the substance at issue, although he could testify from notes he took while analyzing it. Defendant objected to the witness' testimony but the trial court overruled his objections. At the trial for the second count, an analyst testified that she tested the substance, but that she could not independently recall testing the substance. She relied on her notes in the original laboratory report to provide testimony at trial. Defendant objected to this testimony as hearsay, but the trial court overruled his objection. Defendant appealed. The Fourth District of the Illinois Appellate Court explained that

> [i]f the witness has exhausted his memory and is unable to recall an event even after counsel has attempted to refresh the witness' memory with a document, the document itself may be admissible under the doctrine of past recollection recorded. In such an event, the court should be primarily concerned with the reliability of the writing which the witness must swear is a record of his past recollection. (McCORMICK, §§ 299-303, at 712-16; 3 WIGMORE, §§ 734-55, at 77-125; CLEARY, § 17.32, at 299.) McCormick notes that, while a few courts hold that the writing itself is not admissible as an exhibit, a majority of courts hold that the writing is admissible to prove the truth of matters asserted in it. (McCORMICK, § 299, at 712-13.) This majority rule was followed by our supreme court in People v. Harrison, 384 Ill. 201, 206 (1943), where the court held: "The rule is that where there has been a writing made by a witness, or made at his direction at the time of the fact, for the purpose of preserving the memory of it, if at the time of testifying he can recall nothing further than that he had accurately reduced the whole transaction to writing, the latter may be admitted in evidence." People v. Greenspawn, 346 Ill. 484 (1931).
>
> ***
>
> In the instant case, the State's criminologists [. . .] testified that they exhausted their independent memories on the stand and were testifying directly from their notes. In having the witnesses testify from their notes, the State was not refreshing the witnesses' present memories, but was introducing evidence of the witnesses' recorded past recollection without actually presenting the record to the jury. Neither the State nor the defendant offered the record as an exhibit. The doctrine of past recollection recorded does not require that the actual record be admitted into evidence if an adverse party fails to move for its admission, however, the record's contents may still be read to the jury by the witness. People v. Vance, 53 Ill. App. 3d 573, 580-582 (1977); People v. Jenkins, 10 Ill. App. 3d 166, 172 (1973); Stanton v. Pennsylvania R. R. Co., 32 Ill. App. 2d 406, 408-10 (1961). In fact, in the Federal courts, the record cannot be admitted as an exhibit unless offered by an adverse party. FED. R. EVID. 803(5). In the instant case, because the requirements of *Harrison* were met and because the defendant did not ask that the notes taken by [the analysts] be admitted into evidence, we find no error in the denial of the motions to strike the testimony of those witnesses.

17. The Illinois Common Law Business Records Exception Required the Witness to Have Personal Knowledge of the Fact Recorded and That a Record Was Kept in the Usual Course of Business

People v. Small, 319 Ill. 437 (1925)

Defendant was an Illinois state treasurer and was charged with misappropriating a large sum of public funds by placing the money into a "safe fund" in his control. State alleged that defendant kept a personal account book and other records that detailed the amounts of money stolen from the state, but that he subsequently destroyed these records when charges were brought against him. Defendant claimed on appeal that insufficient foundation was laid for admissibility of certain records pertaining to a company he allegedly used to conceal the stolen money. The Illinois Supreme Court agreed, noting that the employee of the company who testified had no connection to it or its records during the relevant period of time. The Supreme Court explained that the employee could not testify that "these records were kept in due course of business and that they were correctly kept." The Supreme Court explained that

> [i]n order to render an account book admissible, it is essential that proof as satisfactory as the transactions are under the circumstances reasonably susceptible of shall be given that the entries made are correctly recorded. Chisholm v. Beaman Machine Co., 160 Ill. 101 (1895); House v. Beak, 141 Ill. 290 (1892). Before a record can be admitted there must be proof by one who knows that it was made in the usual course of business, in accordance with a uniform practice to make them, when the transaction occurred, and to record the transaction precisely as it occurred. [citation omitted]. Where the record is made in due course of business and according to methods proven accurate by many years' test, it is competent. Pittsburgh, Cincinnati, Chicago & St. Louis Railway Co. v. City of Chicago, 242 Ill. 178 (1900).

18. Record of Regularly Conducted Activity Is Admissible as Exception to Hearsay Rule As Long As It Was the Regular Practice of That Business Activity to Make Such Record as Shown by the Testimony of a Qualified Witness

People v. Jackson, 41 Ill. 2d 102 (1968)

Defendant was convicted of murder and claimed that he had been beaten by police officers while in custody. The state introduced the defendant's inmate record that is created when a prisoner is processed upon his or her arrival in jail. A receiving clerk testified as to the record, explaining that the "medical notations indicated that defendant's condition was good" at the time he was processed. The clerk did not know the processing procedures when defendant was admitted, but that the defendant's inmate card was the same as those the jail currently used. Defendant contended on appeal that his inmate card was improperly admitted at trial because it was a medical record. The Illinois Supreme Court disagreed, noting that the card was

> kept pursuant to long standing practice and the statutory requirement that the warden keep an exact calendar of persons committed to jail, their place of abode, the time, cause and authority of their commitment, and 'a description of the person,' and the time and manner of discharge. ILL. REV. STAT. 1967, chap. 75, par. 7.
>
> Defendant's inmate history card was, therefore, considerably more than the diagnostic medical record intended to be excluded without doctor identification by the Supreme Court rule [236]. In fact the medical portion is essentially descriptive of the prisoner's appearance, and in view of the contents, mode of preparation and purport, the card should not come within the purview of the medical records exclusion. Quite the contrary, the same justification exists here for admitting the card as exists for records made in the regular course of business. People v. Small, 319 Ill. 437 (1925). [The rule] was intended to make unnecessary the original entrants' production at the trial because of their numbers or anonymity, or for reasons which made their production impracticable *** [and] to be sufficient if the custodian of the records, or some person familiar with the business and its mode of operation, would testify at the trial as to the manner in which the record was prepared ***. 5 WIGMORE ON EVIDENCE (3d ed. 1940) p. 391.
>
> It is our view, therefore, that defendant's county jail inmate card was properly admitted in evidence; and furthermore, since the medical notation was merely cumulative evidence refuting the alleged physical coercion, the admission of the card should not be deemed reversible error.

19. Record Prepared with a View Toward Litigation or in a Criminal Investigation Is Not Routine and Therefore Is Inadmissible as a Record of Regularly Conducted Activity

People v. Smith, 141 Ill. 2d 40 (1990)

Defendant was convicted of murder in the death of a prison warden. Defendant argued on appeal that a prison incident report was improperly admitted into evidence at trial under the business records exception to the hearsay rule. State's theory at trial was that defendant was a member of the King Cobra street gang and that the leader of the gang had the warden killed in retaliation for his strict disciplinary actions against gang members in the prison. State introduced a prison incident report that detailed the gang leader's altercation with the victim. A reviewing officer who signed the report testified that the report was kept in the ordinary course of business immediately after the incident. The Illinois Supreme Court noted that pursuant to 725 ILCS 5/115-5

> (c) No writing or record made in the regular course of any business shall become admissible as evidence by the application of this Section if: ***
>
> > (2) Such writing or record has been made by anyone during an investigation of an alleged offense or during any investigation relating to pending or anticipated litigation of any kind.
>
> Thus writings or records relating to a police investigation are generally excluded from the business records exception to the rule against hearsay, even though they may be kept "in the regular course" of law enforcement "business." [citations omitted]. This exclusion certainly extends to reports or records of observations of police officers or other law enforcement personnel at the scene of a crime or apprehension of the accused. M. GRAHAM, CLEARY & GRAHAM'S HANDBOOK OF ILLINOIS EVIDENCE § 803.13 (5th ed. 1990). The information contained in such reports or records may well call into question the motivation, the recall, or the soundness of conclusions of the author of the report or the person providing the information contained in the report. [citations omitted]. Such reports or records, by themselves, thus generally lack the earmarks of trustworthiness and reliability which are the true basis for the business records exception to the rule against hearsay and which business records are assumed to ordinarily have.

The Illinois Supreme Court observed that the incident report lacked the necessary "trustworthiness and reliability generally attendant to regularly kept business records," although the Department of Corrections was by law required to keep such reports. The report was created with the goal of determining appropriate disciplinary action. The Supreme Court concluded "that prison incident reports are not admissible under the business records exception to the rule against hearsay when offered to prove the particulars of disciplinary infractions or of confrontations between prison employees, or law enforcement personnel and prison inmates."

20. Record That Qualifies as a Business Record Is Admissible Even If Generated by a Computer and Used in a Criminal Investigation

People v. Holowko, 109 Ill. 2d 187 (1985)

Defendant was charged with harassment by telephone. The police placed a "trap" on a telephone to determine the number from which the harassing telephone calls were made. Prior to trial, defendant filed a motion *in limine* based on 725 ILCS 5/115-5 seeking to exclude recordings of telephone numbers of the incoming calls to the traced telephone. The state contended that section 115-5 was inapplicable and the records made by the "trap" machine were admissible because it had "no capacity to intentionally falsify information." Defendant claimed that the records were made in the course of a criminal investigation and were therefore inadmissible.

The Illinois Supreme Court held that the printout of results of computerized telephone tracing equipment was admissible even though the trap was installed during an investigation initiated by a police request. The court concluded that

> the printout of results of computerized telephone tracing equipment is not hearsay evidence of the type contemplated by section 115-5(c)(2), but "represents a self-generated record of its operations, much like a seismograph can produce a record of geophysical occurrences, a flight recorder can produce a record of physical conditions onboard an aircraft, and an electron microscope can produce a micrograph, which is a photograph of things too small to be viewed by the human eye." (State v. Armstead (La. 1983), 432 So. 2d 837, 840.) We hold, therefore, that their admission into evidence requires only foundation proof of the method of the recording of the information and the proper functioning of the device by which it was effected and that section 115-5(c)(2) is not applicable.

21. Computer Records Are Admissible as Records of Regularly Conducted Activity If Foundation Requirements Are Satisfied

People v. Hagan, 145 Ill. 2d 287 (1991)

Defendant was convicted of forgery and attempted theft by deception of over $100,000. He sought to lease commercial space from a firm. The firm requested that he submit a summary of his bank accounts. Defendant requested such a summary from his banker. The banker indicated that his bank accounts contained very low sums of money. She then wrote and signed a letter that did not contain defendant's account balances and included a separate note that provided the balance for defendant's information. Defendant took the letter that did not contain the balances and added information pertaining to his balances that was much higher than the actual amount in his bank accounts. Defendant then faxed the letter containing the banker's signature to the firm from Mailboxes, Etc. store. Employee of Mailboxes who was in charge of the facsimile machine testified at trial that she saw defendant fax various documents at the store. She noted that the store's facsimile machine "timely" records the dates and times it prints on documents it faxes. Defendant argued on appeal that he was prejudiced by the admissibility of this evidence, because the authenticity of the faxed letter was not established and was inadmissible hearsay. In determining whether the faxed documents were authenticated, the Illinois Supreme Court looked to the

> guidelines for determining the admissibility of computer printouts of business records stored on electronic computing equipment. [S]uch printouts are admissible where it is shown that:
>
> (1) the electronic computing equipment is recognized as standard equipment;
> (2) the entries are made in the regular course of business at or reasonably near the time of the occurrence of the event recorded; and
> (3) the foundation testimony satisfies the court that the sources of information, method and time of preparation indicated its trustworthiness and justify its admission.
>
> We are concerned here with the third prong of the test [. . .] because defendant's objection is based on the foundation requirement. Accordingly, it was necessary that the sources of information, method and time of preparation indicated the trustworthiness and justify the admission of the "faxed" letter. Evidence which can establish the foundation requirement, by establishing the trustworthiness of such a document, includes testimony by a person who can explain a business' procedures for compiling information and methods for checking for mechanical and human error; explain the operation of the machine and testify that the machine properly did what it was supposed to do; and testify as to the mechanical reliability of the machine.

The Supreme Court observed that state fulfilled the foundation requirements for the facsimile document. The Mailboxes employee testified in detail about the store's procedures for faxing documents and that the machine was programmed to indicate the date, time and store's name on each document sent. The Supreme Court also rejected defendant's argument that the faxed letter and transmittal sheet were inadmissible hearsay, finding that defendant failed to preserve this issue for appeal.

For confrontation issues that may arise whenever an expert relies on third party's testimonial statements as basis in forming his or her opinion, see Chapter 7 and the following cases:

Melendez-Diaz v. Massachusetts, 129 S. Ct. 2527 (2009) (holding that prosecution may not introduce a forensic laboratory report created for use at trial absent offering live witness competent to testify to the truth of the content of the report).

Bullcoming v. New Mexico, 131 S. Ct. 2705 (2011) (finding that blood-alcohol analysis report may not be introduced against the accused at trial unless the witness who made the report is unavailable and accused had a prior opportunity to cross-examine him or her).

Williams v. Illinois, 132 S. Ct. 2221 (2012) (concluding that expert's testimony about non-testifying third party's findings is not "hearsay" and does not implicate defendant's sixth amendment confrontation rights).

People v. McClanahan, 191 Ill. 2d 127 (2000) (finding statute permitting state in drug prosecutions to use lab reports in lieu of actual testimony of the laboratory technician who prepared them as *prima facie* evidence of the contents of the substance at issue violates the confrontation clause).

22. Absent Stipulation by Parties, Medical or Hospital Records Are Generally Not Admissible as Business Records in a Criminal Trial Unless Person Who Prepared the Record Testifies at Trial and Is Subject to Cross-Examination
People v. Giovanetti, 70 Ill. App. 3d 275 (1st Dist. 1979)

Defendant was a bouncer at a night club and was convicted of voluntary manslaughter after fatally beating a patron. An emergency room physician testified at trial that although he had no independent recollection of the victim's treatment, he had a copy of the emergency room record. The record stated that the victim walked into the emergency room. The victim later suffered cardiac arrest and died a short time after. The record showed that the victim was "in very serious condition" and that he had various injuries on his upper body. Defense sought to elicit from the physician the fact that a nurse who admitted the victim to the emergency room noted in his chart that the victim was coherent and calm and that he made some statements potentially exculpatory to defendant. The trial court denied defendant's request. The appellate court affirmed, noting,

> [d]efendant's reliance upon the business records exception to the hearsay rule (ILL. REV. STAT. 1975, ch. 110A, par. 236; ch. 38, par. 115-5(c)(1)) for admissibility of the hospital records is [. . .] misplaced, inasmuch as both the Supreme Court Rules and the Code of Criminal Law and Procedure specifically exclude medical records from introduction in evidence as business records.
>
> ***
>
> A similar claim of error was made and rejected in People v. Aristole, 131 Ill. App. 2d 175 (1971), because the physician through whom the defendant in that case sought to elicit the medical history was not involved in its preparation. Further, in Slater v. Missionary Sisters of Sacred Heart, 20 Ill. App. 3d 464 (1974), it was held that hospital records are not admissible without the testimony of the persons who made the entries which comprise the medical records, and in Le Master v. Chicago R. I. & P. R.R., 35 Ill. App. 3d 1001 (1976), the court held that a hospital record was admissible only if those persons who made entries in it testify to their correctness, even where the witness was the treating physician who had read the history and made one of the entries therein.

***

> Defendant also seeks support for his position from People v. Walton, 43 Ill. App. 3d 74 (1976); People v. Jackson, 41 Ill. 2d 102 (1968), and Wright v. Upson, 303 Ill. 120 (1922). In People v. Walton, no objection to the testimony of the treating physician as to the medical records was made and [. . .] the witness was the doctor who treated the victim in any event. In People v. Jackson, a jail inmate admittance card was received in evidence, which contained a notation that defendant's condition was good, as well as his non-medical history, picture, finger prints and reason for admission, pursuant to statutory requirement. The Supreme Court noted that the defendant's inmate history card was considerably more than the diagnostic medical record intended to be excluded without doctor identification by the Supreme Court Rule. The court also observed that the medical portion was merely descriptive of the prisoner's appearance. [citation omitted]. In Wright v. Upson, the Supreme Court held that admission of the medical record in that case was error because only one of the two nurses who made the entries was called to testify as to their correctness and there was no showing that the other nurse or nurses were deceased or out of the jurisdiction. [citation omitted]. Under the authorities cited by defendant, the exclusion of the medical records in the instant case was not error.

23. Autopsy Reports May Be Admitted into Evidence as *Prima Facie* Proof of the Cause of Death Under the Public Records Exception to the Hearsay Rule

People v. Leach, 405 Ill. App. 3d 297 (1st Dist. 2010) *appeal allowed*, 239 Ill. 2d 572 (2011)

Defendant was convicted at a bench trial of the murder of his wife. He appealed, arguing that the court erroneously admitted a medical examiner's hearsay evidence based on autopsy findings by a retired pathologist. The medical examiner testified at trial that she examined the retired pathologist's findings following his autopsy of the victim and concluded that the victim had been strangled. Defendant contended that the medical examiner's testimony pertaining to the pathologist's findings violated his confrontation rights. The state argued that the results of the pathologist's autopsy were properly admitted as a business record exception to the hearsay rule pursuant to 725 ILCS 5/115-5.1. The First District of the Illinois Appellate Court observed that business records have been recognized "as historically nontestimonial." The court noted that

> [e]mbraced within the rubric of nontestimonial hearsay is the public records exception, records required by statute or authorized to be maintained by the nature of the office, evidencing matters properly required to be maintained and recorded. People v. Hester, 88 Ill. App. 3d 391 (1980). Like business records, the exception is based on the assumption that public officers will perform their duties, that they lack motive to falsify, and that public inspection to which many such records are subject will disclose inaccuracies. M. GRAHAM, CLEARY & GRAHAM'S HANDBOOK OF ILLINOIS EVIDENCE § 803.12 (8th ed. 2004). Records of the medical examiner are a species of "public documents," generally admissible at common law even in the absence of statutory authority. Steward v. Crissell, 289 Ill. App. 3d 66, 69 (1997). Moreover, autopsy reports are clearly recognized under the codification of the common law exception [in s]ection 115-5.1 of the Code of Criminal Procedure of 1963 [which] provides: ***
>
> A duly certified coroner's protocol or autopsy report, or both, complying with the requirements of this Section may be duly admitted into evidence as an exception to the hearsay rule as *prima facie* proof of the cause of death of the person to whom it relates.

Defendant further argued that the pathologist's conclusions about the victim's autopsy were testimonial because the pathologist worked with law enforcement authorities and performed autopsies "for purposes of investigating crimes, in anticipation of future prosecutions." The appellate court disagreed, indicating that a medical examiner merely establishes manner and cause of death of a victim and does not perform a law enforcement function. Even if the findings were testimonial, the court noted that the hearsay "rule is not implicated, [. . .] where statements otherwise inadmissible as hearsay are used by experts for the purpose of explaining the bases for their opinions."

24. Blood or Urine Tests Are Admissible Under the Business Record Exception to the Hearsay Rule in Prosecutions for Driving While Intoxicated or Reckless Homicide Pursuant to 625 ILCS 5/11-501.4-1
People v. Jung, 192 Ill. 2d 1 (2000)

The defendant was the driver of an automobile involved in a collision with another vehicle. He was taken to the hospital for treatment and medical care. The hospital staff took a blood sample, had it analyzed, and upon a police officer's arrival at the hospital, the lab technician gave the officer the results of the defendant's blood-work pursuant to 625 ILCS 5/11-501.4-1. Section 11-501.4-1 of the Illinois Motor Vehicle Code allows for admissibility of test results of blood or urine conducted in the regular course of emergency medical treatment following a motor vehicle accident

> as a business record exception to the hearsay rule only in prosecutions for any violation of Section 11-501 of this Code [625 ILCS 5/11-501] or a similar provision of a local ordinance, or in prosecutions for reckless homicide brought under the Criminal Code of 1961 [720 ILCS 5/1-1 *et seq*.].

Here, the blood test results revealed that the defendant was legally intoxicated, and he was subsequently arrested for driving under the influence of alcohol. The trial court ruled the statute authorizing the release of the blood test results unconstitutional. The Illinois Supreme Court disagreed, reasoning that since "life, limb and property are seriously threatened by drunken driving and given the all too common reality that a driver involved in a motor vehicle accident may be intoxicated, waiver of a driver's privacy interest in his blood or urine test results in this situation is reasonable and does not violate his constitutional right to privacy."

25. Absence of Entry in Records of Regularly Conducted Business Activity Is Admissible If Accompanied by Testimony That Such Entry Would Have Normally Been Made
Easley v. Apollo Detective Agency, Inc., 69 Ill. App. 3d 920 (1st Dist. 1979)

Plaintiff sued a security company for willful and wanton misconduct in hiring a security guard who broke into her home with a pass key. Plaintiff called the personnel director and manager for the defendant to testify at trial. The director testified that it is the practice of the defendant to check every employee's application for prior and current addresses, references, and other information. He stated that after the information is confirmed or not, he or a secretary makes a mark indicating that a guard's personal information and references had been checked. He also testified that the security guard's application had not been so checked because no marks were made on his application. The court noted that defendant complained

> of the admission of the files for what they do not contain, that is, any notation that anyone from [defendant's office] ever called the prior employers, along with testimony that such a notation would normally have been made. The files having once been admitted as business records, we believe that the absence of an entry therein could properly be admitted if accompanied by testimony that an entry would normally have been made. This is both the majority common law rule (MCCORMICK ON EVIDENCE § 307 at 722 (2d ed. E. Cleary 1972)) and the federal rule (FED. R. EVID. 803(7)), and the only Illinois case we have found on the subject so holds. (Lawrence v. Stiles (1885), 16 Ill. App. 489.) We therefore hold that evidence of the absence of an entry in the records was properly admitted. While [defendant] argues that there is

> evidence that one prior employer [. . .] did not on one other occasion follow its procedure, this would go to weight, not admissibility.

26. Public Records Kept by Persons Required Either by Statute or Nature of Their Office to Maintain Them in Connection with the Performance of Their Official Duties Are Admissible in Evidence Exception to Hearsay Rule
People *ex rel.* Wenzel v. Chicago & N. W. Ry. Co., 28 Ill. 2d 205 (1963)

A railroad objected to taxes levied against its property, contending that the Department of Revenue deliberately under-assessed the property value. Department of Revenue records showed supervised, systematic, and careful selection and analysis of data pertaining to the "sales-assessment method by which Department determine[d] the ratio between the full and assessed values of real estate." The railroad objected to the admissibility of these studies, claiming that they were inadmissible hearsay because every person who participated in their compilation did not testify at trial. The Illinois Supreme Court disagreed, noting that

> [a]t common law it has long been settled as an exception to the hearsay rule that records kept by persons in public office, which they are required either by statute or the nature of their office to maintain in connection with the performance of their official duties, are admissible in evidence and are evidence of those matters which are properly required to be maintained and recorded therein. (Lane v. Bommelmann, 17 Ill. 95; Carlin v. Chicago and Western Indiana Railroad Co., 297 Ill. 184; Bell v. Bankers Life & Casualty Co., 327 Ill. App. 321; 32 C.J.S. Evidence § 644; 5 Wigmore on Evidence, 3rd ed. §§ 1631, 1670; CLEARY, HANDBOOK OF ILLINOIS EVIDENCE, sec. 13.37.) This exception, as pointed out by Professor Cleary, is 'based upon the assumptions that public officers will perform their duties and are without motive to falsify, and that public inspection, to which some such records are subject, will disclose inaccuracies.' Based upon the exception, as well as the evidence which shows a supervised, systematic and careful selection and analysis of data in each year, we conclude that the [. . .] studies were admissible without the need of calling as witnesses all persons who had in some manner contributed to them.

27. Facts Contained in the Records of Vital Statistics Are Admissible If Made to a Public Office Pursuant to Requirements of Law
People v. Fiddler, 45 Ill. 2d 181 (1970)

Defendant was convicted of murder. The only direct evidence offered by state as to the cause of death of the victim was a certified copy of a coroner's certificate issued by the county clerk. Only a portion of the certificate was read to the jury, stating that "[i]n the medical opinion of the Coroner's office, *** the cause of death was ligature strangulation." The trial court permitted this evidence although it noted that it was hearsay. The Illinois Supreme Court found that the opinion of an examining physician as to the cause of death was inadmissible as a fact contained in the records of vital statistics because it

> is not a 'fact' which is to be admissible as *[p]rima facie* evidence. In this case the determination of the cause of death was not made by an attending physician but only after an autopsy was performed. [. . .] The determination of the cause of death, therefore, may be the result of a complex value judgment which the examining doctor made upon the conclusion of the autopsy. [citation omitted] The doctor's opinion as to the cause of death is not converted into a fact by the process of including it in a certified copy of the coroner's death certificate.

28. Absence of a Public Record or Entry Is Admissible as Exception to Hearsay Rule
People v. Love, 310 Ill. 558 (1923)

Defendants were the president and secretary of a corporation. They were charged with violation of Illinois securities laws after failing to file certificates for sale of securities. The state conducted a search of secretary of state's records and found that no certificate filing had been made on behalf of the defendants. State used the absence of the filing as *prima facie* evidence to show that defendants did not file the necessary documents pursuant to Illinois securities law. The applicable statute effective at the time stated that a certificate under the seal of state, duly signed by the secretary of state, showing compliance or noncompliance with the provisions of the Illinois Securities Law, respecting the securities in question or respecting compliance or noncompliance with the provisions of the act by any issuer, solicitor, agent, broker, dealer or owner, shall constitute *prima facie* evidence of such compliance or of such noncompliance with the provisions of this act. [Illinois Securities Law, §§ 9, 29]

Defendants argued that such evidence was inadmissible because it denied the right to confront witnesses against them. The Illinois Supreme Court disagreed, noting that

> [t]he certificate required by the act does not call for the secretary's conclusions concerning the guilt or innocence of one accused of a breach of the law, but is a certificate of the condition of the records in his office concerning the documents required to be filed and is to be taken as *prima facie* evidence of such state of his records. [. . .] [T]he section [is not] void as depriving the accused of a right to meet witnesses face to face. Such doctrine has no application to documentary evidence of this character. Sokel v. People, 212 Ill. 238; Tucker v. People, 122 Ill. 583. The certificate of the secretary of state is an official act under the seal of the state, required of a public officer by the statute, certifying to what the records of his office show. [. . .] The act is not open to the constitutional objections urged.

29. Records of Religious Organizations Are Admissible as Exception to Hearsay Rule
Matter of Severson's Estate, 107 Ill. App. 3d 634 (2d Dist. 1982)

Petitioner argued that she was the sole heir of decedent's estate. The executor of the estate challenged this contention, arguing that the decedent was not the sister of petitioner's father. The executor introduced a baptismal record pertaining to the decedent. The appellate court admitted the record and noted that

> [t]he record is entitled as the Church Book for birth clinic for the Christiania Parish, recording matters that transpired in the late 1800's in Norway (Exhibit No. 29). We conclude that it was admitted properly pursuant to Supreme Court Rule 236 (73 Ill. 2d R. 236). The writing or record memoralizing or recording any act made "in the regular course of business" at or within a reasonable time after the event is admissible without introducing all the circumstances to the making; and the hearsay nature of the entry affects its weight, not admissibility. "Business" is defined in the rule to include a "calling of every kind." We consider the rule broad enough to cover regular entries in church records. See Ill. Ann. Stat., ch. 110A, par. 236, Historical and Practice Notes, at 187 (Smith-Hurd Supp. 1981-82.) *See also* FED. R. EVID. 803(11).
>
> The document appears to be a baptismal register and the entry as to [the decedent] reasonably appears to have been made in the regular course of church business; timely to the event recorded; and to be of the kind which the church regularly kept. It was found in the custody of a hospital priest who permitted the genealogical investigator to examine the entry. The church book covered the period from November 17, 1885, to May 26, 1890, inclusive. The year 1888 appears on the top of the page containing the entry for [decedent]. It bears the number 234; the

> entry beneath it, though lined out, clearly bears entry number 235. (In making a photocopy the priest blanked out other entries on the page that had no relation to [decedent].) The fact that the entry was dated (born-16th; baptized 23rd) and numbered indicates that the entry was recorded in sequence. It thus appears that the church book is a register or record comprising in a single volume a series of homogenous statements recorded by entries made and regularly kept in official custody. (See 5 WIGMORE, EVIDENCE Sec. 1636, at 646 (Chadbourn Rev. Ed. 1974). The fact that the handwriting of the entrant, presumably the clergyman now deceased, was not proved is an additional circumstance but affects the weight only. It may be noted in this connection that the writing in entries 234 and 235 appear to be in the same hand. That the columnar entries containing the names of the parents are regularly kept is inferentially established by the column headings appearing in type at the top of the page of the register. The hearsay nature of this portion of the recording again affects its weight but not its admissibility pursuant to Supreme Court Rule 236. The case of Dailey v. Brother. of R. R. Trainmen, 311 Ill. 184 (1924), cited by [petitioner], holds that a baptismal register is admissible only to show the fact, date and place of baptism (311 Ill. 184, 189). However, the conclusion is based on the reasoning that these facts alone are within the personal knowledge of the clergyman. Under Supreme Court Rule 236(a) which post-dates such rulings, it would appear that all contents regularly kept of record by religious organizations would be admissible, as an exception to the hearsay rule.

30. Marriage, Baptismal, and Similar Certificates Are Not Excluded by Hearsay Rule

In re Curby's Estate, 334 Ill. App. 212 (2d Dist. 1948)

The petitioner requested to be appointed an administrator of the deceased, alleging that he was her son. Other family members argued that the petitioner was not the son of the deceased because he was not properly adopted by the decedent. A baptismal record of a local church was introduced in evidence. It confirmed that the petitioner was not the decedent's son. The appellate court found that the record was properly admitted in evidence to show that the decedent was not the petitioner's mother.

31. Family Records Are Admissible as Exception to Hearsay Rule

Dailey v. Grand Lodge, Bhd. of R.R. Trainmen, 311 Ill. 184 (1924)

The Illinois Supreme Court noted that

> [t]here is a class of records, not kept by public officials as a part of official duty, with the attending sanction, nor authorized by statute to be proved by a certified copy, and therefore not coming within any provision of the act on evidence and depositions, but which are admissible in evidence to prove the fact recorded. These records are of such a character and made under such conditions as to create confidence in their truth, and they are universally acted upon as evidence of the facts recorded. Entries in family Bibles are not made by any official, nor as a public official duty, but are evidence of the facts recorded, and entries in church registers, kept in accordance with church law or usage, are for similar reasons evidence of the facts therein stated. The duty of the church official to record the fact, its character in connection with a religious ceremony, and its general nature, create confidence in its truth recognized by the courts.

32. Historically, Statements in Ancient Documents in Existence 30 Years or More Were Admissible

Reuter v. Stuckart, 181 Ill. 529 (1899)

Husband of the decedent filed suit and petitioned the court to declare his wife as the sole owner of a specific property as a result of her adverse possession of the property. Another individual challenged this action, claiming that his father was the owner of the property. This person offered a deed that was more than 30 years old and which contained his father's name on it. The Illinois Supreme Court noted that

> [w]hen this deed was introduced in evidence upon the trial of the cause, it was more than 30 years old, and must therefore be regarded as an ancient deed. It is true that, when the original bill in this case was filed [. . .] the deed was not 30 years old; but the rule is that documents more than 30 years old at the date of the trial are 'ancient,' although less than 30 years old at the date of the commencement of the suit. [citation omitted]. In Applegate v. Mining Co., 117 U.S. 255 (1886), the supreme court of the United States say: 'The rule is that an ancient deed may be admitted in evidence, without direct proof of its execution, if it appears to be of the age of at least 30 years, when it is found in proper custody, and either possession under it is shown, or some other corroborative evidence of its authenticity, freeing it from all just grounds of suspicion.' In Whitman v. Heneberry, 73 Ill. 109 (1874), we held that deeds more than 30 years old are ancient deeds, and may be admitted in evidence without proof of execution; but that, before they can be so admitted, it must appear that the instrument comes from such custody as to show a reasonable presumption of its genuineness, and that facts and circumstances must be proven which will establish the fact that the instrument has been in existence the length of time indicated by its date. Some of the authorities differ as to whether it is necessary to show that possession was taken under the deed. It seems to be settled, however, by the weight of authority, that such possession, if necessary to be shown, need not be for the full period of 30 years, but may be for a less period, if there are other circumstances tending to show the genuineness of the instrument. In Whitman v. Heneberry, supra, it was said that indorsements or memoranda upon the deed, when they are of such character as to satisfy a cautious and discriminating mind that they would not be there if the paper were a forgery, have been considered as circumstances indicating that the deed is genuine. It was there said that, if the deed has been on record for over 30 years, that circumstance is a strong fact in favor of its genuineness. Greenleaf, in his work on Evidence, says that an ancient deed—that is to say, one more than 30 years old—is presumed to be genuine without express proof of its execution, if it is found in the proper custody, and is free from just grounds of suspicion, and is corroborated by evidence of ancient or modern corresponding enjoyment, or by other equivalent or explanatory proof. In such case, the witnesses to the deed are presumed to be dead, and the deed is presumed to have constituted a part of the actual transfer of the property mentioned in it. [1 GREENLEAF EVID. (15th Ed.) §§ 21, 144.]

33. City and Telephone Directories Are Not Excluded by Hearsay Rule and Illinois Rule of Evidence 803(17)

People v. Cowper, 145 Ill. App. 3d 1074 (2d Dist. 1986)

The appellate court recognized that telephone and city directories are admissible in Illinois and are not excluded by the hearsay rule. A detective testified, over hearsay objection, concerning the lack of a listing for an individual in police computer records or in telephone and city directories. The court initially noted that a specific objection on hearsay grounds waived any objection as to foundation for the computer records. The court allowed the evidence as an exception to the hearsay rule where evidence of the inability to find a listing for an individual was determined after a diligent search. The appellate court reasoned that telephone and city directories fall within a special exception to the hearsay rule. The court noted that defense counsel thoroughly cross-examined the detective as to the records employed. Lastly, the court concluded that inquiries that are unavailing may be proven by hearsay evidence, as an exception to the general rule, where such inquiries are not capable of proof by other means. The appellate court explained its reasoning:

> [a]s to whether the evidence in question was hearsay. [W]e agree the evidence was admissible as non-hearsay in that it was evidence of the inability of [the detective] to find a listing for [the individual] after diligent search, which, in turn, provided circumstantial evidence of his nonexistence. (MCCORMICK, EVIDENCE § 249, at 594 (2d ed. 1972).) Telephone and city directories themselves fall within a special exception to the hearsay rule, and are admissible as substantive evidence of the truth of assertions they contain. (MCCORMICK, EVIDENCE § 321, at 744 (2d ed. 1972).) We note defense counsel thoroughly cross-examined [the detective], lessening the effect of this circumstantial evidence by establishing the telephone directory does not include persons who have no phone or who wish to remain unlisted, that the city directory does not include persons who are not residents or who have recently moved to Elgin, and the police computer records would not have a record of persons who had not had contact with the police. [The detective] was available for cross-examination, too, as to the extent of his diligence in seeking a listing for [the individual], and as to the method and manner in which his search for such listing was conducted. *Cf.* People v. McClinton, 59 Ill. App. 3d 168, 175 (1978), (where officer did not personally check weapon through firearms registration section to ascertain ownership status).

34. Reputation Concerning Personal or Family History Is Admissible
Miller v. White, 80 Ill. 580 (1875)

A landlord obtained an eviction notice against her tenant. The tenant argued that she was a sub-tenant and that the notice was ineffective against her. The landlord sought to show at trial that the tenant was not a sub-tenant because she was married to the original tenant and he resided with her. The landlord introduced evidence through testimony of various witnesses that the tenant lived with the original tenant "as man and wife" and that they held each other out as husband and wife to the community. The landlord sought to show by "general reputation in the neighborhood" that the tenants were cohabitating and possibly married. The trial court refused to admit this evidence. The Illinois Supreme Court disagreed, noting that

> the [trial] court, in rejecting this testimony, erred. We do not now remember but two cases in which proof of actual marriage is required—the one is in a prosecution for bigamy, the other in an action for criminal conversation. In other cases, the presumption of marriage may be indulged from cohabitation, name, reputation and other circumstances.

35. Any Person, Even a Minor, Is Competent to Testify as to His or Her Own Age
People v. Harvey, 9 Ill. App. 3d 944 (1st Dist. 1973)

Defendant was convicted of indecent liberties with a child following a bench trial. The offense of indecent liberties with a child required the state to show that the accused was 17 years or older at the time he committed the crime and that the victim was 16 years or younger at that time. The parties stipulated that defendant was 17 years old at the time of trial. The trial occurred nine months after the alleged offense took place. Defendant's mother testified about defendant's date of birth. At the mitigation and aggravation hearing, defendant testified that he was 18 years old at the time of the hearing. On appeal, defendant claimed that state failed to establish all elements of the offense because it did not present evidence of defendant's age and the age of the victim. The appellate court disagreed, noting that defendant's mother's testimony established his date of birth and that "by simple computation" the defendant would have been 17 years or older at the time of the offense. The appellate court also found

> [t]he cases cited by defendant in support of his argument [. . .] distinguishable. People v. Rogers, 415 Ill. 343 (1953), the only attempt to prove the age of defendant, came through the

testimony of a police officer who testified that the defendant had admitted to him that he was 35 years of age. Wistrand v. People, 213 Ill. 72 (1904), the attempted proof of age, came by way of the introduction of defendant's confession which contained a statement that he was 44 years of age. The court stated you cannot prove the age of a defendant by his confession. These cases stand for the proposition that a defendant's age cannot be established by an extra-judicial verbal confession or admission alone. People v. Rogers, 415 Ill. 343 (1953).

***

In view of defendant's mother's testimony as to the defendant's exact date of birth in the instant case, these two cases are clearly distinguishable.

***

With regard to the age of the victim, the defendant notes that the statute under which he was convicted requires that the victim be 16 years or younger. He argues that there was no competent evidence adduced at trial to establish the victim's age. Even though the victim testified on direct examination by the State that he was 9 years old, defendant argues that such testimony was hearsay. We do not agree.

***

The rule in Illinois is that an individual, even though a minor, is competent to testify as to his own age. Raymond v. People, 226 Ill. 433 (1907); People v. Pennell, 315 Ill. 124 (1924). In *Pennell* the court said [. . .]:

> *** It is, of course, recognized in all cases where one testifies as to his own age that in a sense his testimony is hearsay, but that fact does not of itself affect the competency nor the weight of that testimony. Raymond v. People, 226 Ill. 433; Mash v. People, 220 Ill. 86.

36. Reputation Concerning Boundaries or General History Arising Before the Controversy Is Admissible

People v. Morgan, 301 Ill. App. 3d 1026 (2d Dist. 1998)

Defendant was convicted of unlawful possession of a controlled substance and unlawful delivery of a controlled substance within 1,000 feet of a public park. Defendant alleged that the state did not prove beyond a reasonable doubt that the park near which defendant allegedly completed the controlled substance transaction was a public park. Defendant claimed that the officer who testified that the park was public was not qualified to testify as to this fact. The Second District of the Illinois Appellate Court disagreed, noting that the officer was qualified because he

> was a 10-year veteran of the [. . .] police department who was familiar with the nature of [the park] and had made over 100 arrests there. It is generally understood that persons living and working in the community are familiar with various public places in the neighborhood, such as the location of streets, buildings, and the boundaries of counties and town lots. *See* People v. Jones, 6 Ill. 2d 252, 254 (1955). Such testimony is justified by the same circumstantial assurances of trustworthiness inherent in other types of common knowledge by repute. [citations omitted].
>
> We therefore reject the defendant's assertion that the State was obligated to produce recorded plats of survey to establish that [the park] was a legally dedicated city park. Rather, we hold that the State here sustained its evidentiary burden under the statute. Indeed, we note that the defendant himself referred to [the park] as a "park" and admitted playing basketball there while he was waiting for his car to be returned. Therefore, based on the totality of the evidence, we conclude that the defendant was proved guilty of the offense beyond a reasonable doubt.

37. Reputation as to Person's Character in the Community Is Admissible

People v. Meyer, 176 Ill. 2d 372 (1997)

Defendant was convicted of aggravated battery. At the mitigation and aggravation stage of sentencing various witnesses testified as to the reputation of defendant's character in the community. The Illinois Supreme Court noted that

> [f]riends of the defendant [. . .] also testified. All three described the defendant's good character and reputation within the community. [. . .] In addition to the testimony of the witnesses, 20 letters were submitted by individuals from throughout the defendant's community. These letters chronicle examples of the defendant's generosity and willingness to assist friends and neighbors in need. The letters contain many descriptions of the defendant's good character and reputation.

38. Evidence of a Final Judgment of a Previous Conviction for a Crime Punishable by Death or Imprisonment in Excess of One Year Is Admissible

Am. Family Mut. Ins. Co. v. Savickas, 193 Ill. 2d 378 (2000)

Defendant was convicted of first degree murder and was consequently sued in a civil wrongful death suit by survivors of the victim. Defendant's insurer contended that it should not be required to defend or indemnify him because the criminal prosecution established that defendant intended the victim's death, an exclusion in the insurance policy. The Illinois Supreme Court explained that

> a criminal conviction now acts as a bar and collaterally estops the retrial of issues in a later civil trial that were actually litigated in the criminal trial. [. . .] As the authorities have noted, the differences between civil and criminal litigation all favor the criminal defendant. [citation omitted]. First and foremost, the State must prove the defendant guilty beyond a reasonable doubt by a unanimous verdict, a greater burden than that faced by any civil litigant. The defendant may remain silent and the State is prohibited from commenting on his silence. Moreover, the defendant has the right to counsel and to a record paid for by the State on appeal. [citation omitted] These differences militate, if anything, in favor of according estoppel effect to criminal convictions because of the greater safeguards in favor of their reliability. It surely could not inspire faith in our judicial system to hold that a criminal conviction, upon which society may deprive a defendant of his liberty, or indeed his very life, is not worthy of the same preclusive effect as may be accorded an ordinary civil judgment.

39. Receipt or Paid Bill Is Admissible as *Prima Facie* Evidence of the Fact of Payment and Is Not Excluded by Hearsay Rule

People v. Davis, 269 Ill. 256 (1915)

Defendant, an attorney, was charged with embezzling funds from his client. Defendant presented evidence of receipts he had kept while he represented his client and her estate, but the trial court would not allow him to present all of the receipts. The Supreme Court noted that proof of receipts may be admitted to prove truth of its content. The court explained that

> the trial court erred in refusing to permit the introduction of certain receipts offered by [defendant] while on the stand. At the time they were offered it was contended by counsel that such receipts corroborated [defendant] as to how he had paid out money for many of the items of disbursements. As between principal and agent, receipts given to the agent for payments made by him in his principal's business are competent evidence of the amounts paid. [citations omitted] A written receipt, if properly identified, is *prima facie* evidence of the truth of the recitals which it contains. JONES ON EVIDENCE (2d Ed.) § 492. As we understand the offer of proof as to these receipts, the court should have admitted them in evidence.

40. Evidence of a Paid Medical Bill Is *Prima Facie* Evidence That the Amount of the Bill Was Reasonable

Wills v. Foster, 229 Ill. 2d 393 (2008)

Plaintiff sought to recover for injuries after being involved in a car accident with the defendant. Part of plaintiff's medical bills was paid by Medicaid and Medicare. Defendant wanted to prevent plaintiff from introducing anything but evidence of the paid bills. The Illinois Supreme Court noted that

> [i]n Illinois, a paid bill constitutes *prima facie* evidence of reasonableness. In a case in which the plaintiff seeks to admit a bill that has not been paid in whole or in part, he or she must establish reasonableness by other means—such as by introducing the testimony of someone having knowledge of the services rendered and the reasonable and customary charge for such services.

41. Ingredients Label on a Medicine Container Is a Trade Inscription and Is Admissible as Exception to Hearsay Rule

People v. Shevock, 335 Ill. App. 3d 1031 (4th Dist. 2003)

The appellate court affirmed a jury verdict finding the defendant guilty of unlawful possession of a methamphetamine manufacturing chemical with the intent to manufacture methamphetamine. Among the many items found in the defendant's lab, a motel room, were 23 boxes of Sudafed antihistamine medication. The police also found a chunky substance wrapped in tinfoil, later identified as methamphetamine. A state police special agent testified that the amount of Sudafed in the defendant's possession would yield between 33 and 51 grams of methamphetamine. The label of a box of Sudafed, stating its active ingredient was pseudoephedrine, was admitted over the defendant's objection. On appeal, the defendant argued that the trial judge erred in admitting the box label as proof that Sudafed actually contained ephedrine or pseudoephedrine because it was so stated on the label. Ultimately, the evidence was used to prove that the defendant possessed 5,520 milligrams of ephedrine or pseudoephedrine. The defendant argued that the label on the box constituted hearsay and did not fit under the business records exception or any other recognized exception to the rule against hearsay. He also argued that the state failed to present any witness to authenticate the pills, interpret the labels, or testify that Sudafed pills were a necessary ingredient of a methamphetamine recipe.

The appellate court allowed the label as a trade inscription exception to the hearsay rule. The state argued that this case was analogous to a Second District case, *In re* T.D., 115 Ill. App. 3d 872 (2d Dist. 1983). In that case, the appellate court allowed the use of a label on a glue container to prove the glue contained a chemical that was a hazardous substance. There, the court found that the container did not fit the business records exception to the hearsay rule because no one identified the label, nor was there testimony that the label was produced in the routine course of business. However, the court found the label admissible because it was sufficiently reliable and trustworthy—reliability or trustworthiness was derived from state and federal laws that require such a label, subject to penalty, because the chemical in question was hazardous. Moreover, since the product had been purchased by the defendant and it was in its original package, there was reduced opportunity for tampering or adulteration.

Here, the appellate court applied the rationale adopted in *In re* T.D. The court first determined that because the Sudafed boxes were unopened when they were confiscated from the defendant, the opportunity for tampering or adulteration was reduced. The court further relied on the Illinois labeling act, which requires that drugs with more than two ingredients to list each active ingredient, subject to penalty. The labels found on the Sudafed boxes were properly admitted in evidence as within an exception to the rule against hearsay as substantive proof that Sudafed contained pseudoephedrine.

Rule 804. Hearsay Exceptions; Declarant Unavailable

(a) Definition of Unavailability. "Unavailability as a witness" includes situations in which the declarant-

(1) is exempted by ruling of the court on the ground of privilege from testifying concerning the subject matter of the declarant's statement; or
(2) persists in refusing to testify concerning the subject matter of the declarant's statement despite an order of the court to do so; or
(3) testifies to a lack of memory of the subject matter of the declarant's statement; or
(4) is unable to be present or to testify at the hearing because of death or then-existing physical or mental illness or infirmity; or
(5) is absent from the hearing and the proponent of a statement has been unable to procure the declarant's attendance (or in the case of a hearsay exception under subdivision (b)(2), (3), or (4), the declarant's attendance or testimony) by process or other reasonable means.

A declarant is not unavailable as a witness if exemption, refusal, claim of lack of memory, inability, or absence is due to the procurement or wrongdoing of the proponent of a statement for the purpose of preventing the witness from attending or testifying.

(b) Hearsay Exceptions. The following are not excluded by the hearsay rule if the declarant is unavailable as a witness:

(1) Former Testimony. Testimony given as a witness (A) at another hearing of the same or a different proceeding, or in an evidence deposition taken in compliance with law in the course of the same or another proceeding, if the party against whom the testimony is now offered, or, in a civil action or proceeding, a predecessor in interest, had an opportunity and similar motive to develop the testimony by direct, cross, or redirect examination, or (B) in a discovery deposition as provided for in Supreme Court Rule 212(a)(5).
(2) Statement Under Belief of Impending Death. In a prosecution for homicide, a statement made by a declarant while believing that the declarant's death was imminent, concerning the cause or circumstances of what the declarant believed to be impending death.
(3) Statement Against Interest. A statement which was at the time of its making so far contrary to the declarant's pecuniary or proprietary interest, or so far tended to subject the declarant to civil or criminal liability, or to render invalid a claim by the declarant against another, that a reasonable person in the declarant's position would not have made the statement unless believing it to be true. A statement tending to expose the declarant to criminal liability and offered in a criminal case is not admissible unless corroborating circumstances clearly indicate the trustworthiness of the statement.
(4) Statement of Personal or Family History.
(A) A statement concerning the declarant's own birth, adoption, marriage, divorce, legitimacy, relationship by blood, adoption, or marriage, ancestry, or other similar fact of personal or family history, even though declarant had no means of acquiring personal knowledge of the matter stated; or
(B) a statement concerning the foregoing matters, and death also, of another

person, if the declarant was related to the other by blood, adoption, or marriage or was so intimately associated with the other's family as to be likely to have accurate information concerning the matter declared.

(5) Forfeiture by Wrongdoing. A statement offered against a party that has engaged or acquiesced in wrongdoing that was intended to, and did, procure the unavailability of the declarant as a witness.

Adopted September 27, 2010, eff. January 1, 2011.

Committee Commentary

(3) Modernization: Where there was no conflict with statutes or recent Illinois Supreme Court or Illinois Appellate Court decisions, and where it was determined to be beneficial and uniformly or almost uniformly accepted elsewhere, the Committee incorporated into the Illinois Rules of Evidence uncontroversial developments with respect to the law of evidence as reflected in the Federal Rules of Evidence and the 44 surveyed jurisdictions. [One of t]he 14 instances of modernization of note [is] as follows: ***

(10) Rule 804(b)(3). Statement Against Interest. Rule 804(b)(3) makes applicable to the prosecution as well as the defense the requirement that in a criminal case a statement tending to expose the declarant to criminal liability is not admissible as a hearsay exception unless corroborating circumstances clearly indicate the trustworthiness of the statement.

ILL. R. EVID. Committee Commentary § 3, Pg. 2-3.

AUTHOR'S COMMENTARY

Illinois had by case law adopted Federal Rule of Evidence 804(a), effective until its stylistic amendment on December 1, 2011, which provides the definition of "unavailability." People v. Johnson, 118 Ill. 2d 501 (1987). The new Illinois Rule of Evidence 804(a) has also adopted the federal definition. *See* Gino L. DiVito, *The Illinois Rules of Evidence: A Color-Coded Guide Containing the New Rules, the Committee's General and Specific Comments, a Comparison with the Federal Rules of Evidence, and Additional Commentary* (*Including the Federal Rules of Evidence as Amended Effective December 1, 2011*) (Jan. 1, 2012) [hereinafter DiVito, *Color-Coded Guide*], at 119, http://www.tdrlawfirm.com/assets/downloads/Illinois_Rules_of_Evidence_Color-Coded_Guide.pdf.

Previously under Illinois common law, a transcript or videotape of testimony at a former trial, judicial proceeding or evidence deposition of an unavailable witness could be admitted as substantive evidence at a subsequent trial of the *same* cause under the former testimony exception to the hearsay rule. People v. Zehr, 103 Ill. 2d 472 (1984). Illinois Rule of Evidence 804(b)(1) is broader than the common law rule and allows the testimony of an unavailable witness to be admitted "at another hearing of the *same or a different* proceeding, or in an evidence deposition taken in compliance with law in the course of the *same or another* proceeding" (emphasis added). Illinois Rule of Evidence 804(b)(1) also reflects the fact that in Illinois "depositions are not admissible unless permitted by [another] rule" and therefore differs slightly from Federal Rule of Evidence 804(b)(1), in effect prior to its stylistic amendment on December 1, 2011. DiVito, *Color-Coded Guide*, at 120. Illinois Rule of Evidence 804(b)(1)(A) specifically states that the testimony of an unavailable witness is admissible when given "in an *evidence* deposition," while the Federal Rule speaks only about a "deposition" and makes no distinction between discovery and evidence depositions. (emphasis added). DiVito, *Color-Coded Guide*, at 120-21. Although Professor Graham does not mention this difference between Illinois Rule of Evidence 804(b)(1)(A) and Federal Rule of Evidence 804(b)(1), he does note that Illinois Supreme

Court Rules 202, 212, and 414 "also specify avenues of admissibility of evidence depositions." MICHAEL H. GRAHAM, GRAHAM'S HANDBOOK OF ILLINOIS EVIDENCE § 804.1 (10th ed. 2010). The Illinois Rule of Evidence 804(b) also contains section (1)(B), which the federal rule does not have, and states that the testimony of an unavailable witness "in a discovery deposition as provided for in Supreme Court Rule 212(a)(5)" is admissible in civil cases. GRAHAM at § 804.1.

Under prior Illinois common law principles, dying declarations were admissible as an exception to the hearsay rule. Dying declarations were limited to statements made by a homicide victim about the cause and circumstances of the homicide. People v. Odum, 27 Ill. 2d 237 (1963). The new Illinois Rule of Evidence 804(b)(2) has adopted the common law standard and permits admissibility of a statement under belief of impending death. The Illinois rule is almost identical to Federal Rule of Evidence 804(b)(2), effective until its stylistic amendment on December 1, 2011, but unlike the federal rule, statements under belief of impending death may only be used in a homicide prosecution in Illinois and are not to be used in a civil action. DiVito, *Color-Coded Guide*, at 121.

Under Illinois common law, a statement against interest was admissible as an exception to the hearsay rule if the proponent of the evidence was able to establish that the out-of-court statement was against the declarant's pecuniary, proprietary, or penal interest when made, the declarant had knowledge of the facts declared and the declarant lacked a motive to falsify. People v. Lettrich, 413 Ill. 172 (1952). The exception did not require the unavailability of the declarant. GRAHAM at § 804.3. The statement against penal interest exception to the Illinois common law hearsay rule generally did not permit admissibility of an out-of-court declaration of a third person stating that he or she, and not the defendant, had committed the crime. *See Lettrich*, 413 Ill. 172. However, such statements have been allowed in evidence under a constitutional due process "indicia of trustworthiness" standard. Chambers v. Mississippi, 410 U.S. 284 (1973).

The new Illinois Rule of Evidence 804(b)(3) requires that the proponent of the evidence establish the unavailability of the declarant as a witness. Illinois Rule of Evidence 804(b)(3) adopted almost verbatim the Federal Rule of Evidence 804(b)(3), in existence before its stylistic amendment on December 1, 2011. DiVito, *Color-Coded Guide* at 122. Federal Rule of Evidence 804(b)(3) stated in relevant part that "[a] statement tending to expose the declarant to criminal liability and *offered to exculpate the accused* is not admissible unless corroborating circumstances clearly indicate the trustworthiness of the statement." Illinois Rule of Evidence 804(b)(3) goes further. ILL. R. EVID. Committee Commentary § 3, pg. 2-3; DiVito, *Color-Coded Guide* at 122. Either the accused or the prosecution may offer it in evidence. ILL. R. EVID. Committee Commentary § 3, pg. 2-3; DiVito, *Color-Coded Guide* at 122. It states that "[a] statement tending to expose the declarant to criminal liability and *offered in a criminal case* is not admissible unless corroborating circumstances clearly indicate the trustworthiness of the statement." ILL. R. EVID. 804(b)(3); DiVito, *Color-Coded Guide* at 122.

Prior to the enactment of Illinois Rule of Evidence 804(b)(5), Illinois recognized the common law doctrine of forfeiture by wrongdoing which did not require a determination of reliability before statements of an unavailable declarant could be admitted at trial. People v. Hanson, 238 Ill. 2d 74 (2010). The Illinois legislature subsequently enacted two statutory provisions—725 ILCS 5/115-10.6 and 725 ILCS 5/115-10.7—that address the doctrine. Contrary to the common law doctrine of forfeiture by wrongdoing, section 115-10.6(e)(2) requires the court to determine at a pretrial hearing whether the proponent of the evidence established by a preponderance of the evidence "that the time, content and circumstances of the statements provide sufficient safeguards of reliability." Section 115-10.6(g), however, emphasizes that it was not intended to "preclude[] or change[] the application of the existing common law doctrine of forfeiture by wrongdoing." Contrary to section 115-10.6, but in agreement with the common law rule, the new Illinois Rule of Evidence 804(b)(5) does not require a determination of reliability to be made before statements may be admitted. People v. Peterson, 2011 IL App (3d) 100513, *appeal denied, judgment vacated,* 2011 WL 6185448 (Ill. Nov. 30, 2011) (order directing appellate court to address appeal on the merits) (Carter, J., partially dissenting); People v. Stechly, 225 Ill. 2d 246 (2007); GRAHAM at § 804.5, § 804.9 (noting that the Illinois Supreme Court in *Stechly* had not imposed "a further requirement that a 'sufficient safeguards of reliability' finding be made with respect to the statement itself"); DiVito, *Color-Coded Guide* at 125. In a civil or a criminal case, Illinois Rule of Evidence 804(b)(5) allows admissibility of any out-of-court statement against any party who engaged in wrongdoing that was intended to and procured the unavailability of the declarant as a trial witness. DiVito, *Color-Coded Guide* at 125.

RELEVANT ILLINOIS SUPREME COURT RULES

Illinois Supreme Court Rule 202. Purposes for Which Depositions May Be Taken in a Pending Action

Any party may take the testimony of any party or person by deposition upon oral examination or written questions for the purpose of discovery or for use as evidence in the action. The notice, order, or stipulation to take a deposition shall specify whether the deposition is to be a discovery deposition or an evidence deposition. In the absence of specification a deposition is a discovery deposition only. If both discovery and evidence depositions are desired of the same witness they shall be taken separately, unless the parties stipulate otherwise or the court orders otherwise upon notice and motion. If the evidence deposition of a witness is to be taken within 21 days of trial, a discovery deposition is not permitted unless the parties stipulate otherwise or the court orders otherwise upon notice and motion.

Amended June 1, 1995, effective January 1, 1996.

Committee Comments

This rule is former Rule 19 with minor language changes but no changes of substance. The rule preserves the distinction that has been made in Illinois between a deposition taken for discovery purposes and one taken for evidence. See Rule 212, dealing with the use of discovery depositions and evidence depositions at the trial.

Pursuant to the amended language of this rule, an evidence deposition may be taken within 21 days of trial without a discovery deposition. This change is to ensure that there will no longer be delays in commencing a trial because an attorney wanted a separate discovery deposition prior to taking an evidence deposition shortly before trial without leave of court or stipulation.

Illinois Supreme Court Rule 212. Use of Depositions

(a) Purposes for Which Discovery Depositions May Be Used. Discovery depositions taken under the provisions of this rule may be used only:

(1) for the purpose of impeaching the testimony of the deponent as a witness in the same manner and to the same extent as any inconsistent statement made by a witness;
(2) as an admission made by a party or by an officer or agent of a party in the same manner and to the same extent as any other admission made by that person;
(3) if otherwise admissible as an exception to the hearsay rule;

(4) for any purpose for which an affidavit may be used; or

(5) upon reasonable notice to all parties, as evidence at trial or hearing against a party who appeared at the deposition or was given proper notice thereof, if the court finds that the deponent is neither not a controlled expert witness nor a party, the deponent's evidence deposition has not been taken, and the deponent is unable to attend or testify because of death or infirmity, and if the court, based on its sound discretion, further finds such evidence at trial or hearing will do substantial justice between or among the parties.

(b) Use of Evidence Depositions. The evidence deposition of a physician or surgeon may be introduced in evidence at trial on the motion of either party regardless of the availability of the deponent, without prejudice to the right of either party to subpoena or otherwise call the physician or surgeon for attendance at trial. All or any part of other evidence depositions may be used for any purpose for which a discovery deposition may be used, and may be used by any party for any purpose if the court finds that at the time of the trial:

(1) the deponent is dead or unable to attend or testify because of age, sickness, infirmity or imprisonment;

(2) the deponent is out of the county, unless it appears that the absence was procured by the party offering the deposition, provided, that a party who is not a resident of this State may introduce his own deposition if he is absent from the county; or

(3) the party offering the deposition has exercised reasonable diligence but has been unable to procure the attendance of the deponent by subpoena; or finds, upon notice and motion in advance of trial, that exceptional circumstances exist which make it desirable, in the interest of justice and with due regard for the importance of presenting the testimony of witnesses orally in open court, to allow the deposition to be used.

(c) Partial Use. If only a part of a deposition is read or used at the trial by a party, any other party may at that time read or use or require him to read any other part of the deposition which ought in fairness to be considered in connection with the part read or used.

(d) Use After Substitution, Dismissal, or Remandment. Substitution of parties does not affect the right to use depositions previously taken. If any action in any court of this or any other jurisdiction of the United States is dismissed and another action involving the same subject matter is afterward brought between the same parties or their representatives or successors in interest, or if any action is remanded by a court of the United States to a court of this State, all depositions lawfully taken and duly filed in the former action, or before remandment, may be used as if taken in the later action, or after remandment.

Amended February 19, 1982, effective April 1, 1982; amended May 28, 1982, effective July 1, 1982; amended March 1, 2001, effective immediately; amended March 28, 2002, effective July 1, 2002; amended December 8, 2010, effective January 1, 2011.

Committee Comments

(January 1, 2011)

Paragraph (a)

The Committee was prompted to examine this issue by the decision in Berry v. American Standard, Inc., 382 Ill. App. 3d 895 (5th Dist. 2008). The Committee believes that a trial court should have the discretion under subparagraph (a)(5) to permit the use of a party's discovery deposition at trial. It appears that there may be rare, but compelling, circumstances under which a party's discovery deposition should be permitted to be used. In the Committee's view, *Berry* presents such circumstances. Given that in most cases counsel will have the opportunity to preserve a party's testimony via an evidence deposition, it is expected that the circumstances that would justify use of a discovery deposition would be extremely limited.

This amendment applies to cases filed on or after the effective date.

Illinois Supreme Court Rule 414. Evidence Depositions

(a) If it appears to the court in which a criminal charge is pending that the deposition of any person other than the defendant is necessary for the preservation of relevant testimony because of the substantial possibility it would be unavailable at the time of hearing or trial, the court may, upon motion and notice to both parties and their counsel, order the taking of such person's deposition under oral examination or written questions for use as evidence at a hearing or trial.

(b) The taking of depositions shall be in accordance with rules providing for the taking of depositions in civil cases, and the order for the taking of a deposition may provide that any designated books, papers, documents or tangible objects, not privileged, be produced at the same time and place.

(c) If a witness is committed for failure to execute a recognizance to appear to testify at a hearing or trial, the court, on written motion of the witness and upon notice to the State and defense counsel, may order that his deposition be taken, and after the deposition has been subscribed, the court may discharge the witness.

(d) Rule 207—Signing and Filing Depositions—shall apply to the signing and filing of depositions taken pursuant to this rule.

(e) The defendant and defense counsel shall have the right to confront and cross-examine any witness whose deposition is taken. The defendant and defense counsel may waive such right in writing, filed with the clerk of the court.

(f) If the defendant is indigent, all costs of taking depositions shall be paid by the county wherein the criminal charge is initiated. If the defendant is not indigent the costs shall be allocated as in civil cases.

Effective October 1, 1971.

Committee Comments

The committee chose not to include depositions for discovery purposes, but did decide to follow the unmistakable trend and provide for depositions to preserve testimony. This rule allows both the State and defense counsel to take such depositions and use the testimony as evidence at a hearing or trial in situations where the potential witness will be unable to appear at hearing or trial for any reason. The deposition is not taken by right but is subject to court approval. Notice should be taken of the fact that depositions may be taken by written questions as well as by oral examination.

Paragraph (c) provides for the taking of a deposition in circumstances which most other jurisdictions have recognized as a necessary use of depositions. In order to prevent unnecessary incarceration, a judge may permit the deposition of a witness committed for failure to execute a recognizance to appear.

Paragraphs (e) and (f) protect the defendant's constitutional rights. Paragraph (e) protects his rights of confrontation and cross-examination, and paragraph (f) assures equal protection to those indigents whose defense requires the taking of a deposition.

Relevant Statutory Authority

Hearsay Exception for Intentional Murder of a Witness: 725 ILCS 5/115-10.6

§ 115-10.6. Hearsay exception for intentional murder of a witness.

(a) A statement is not rendered inadmissible by the hearsay rule if it is offered against a party that has killed the declarant in violation of clauses (a)(1) and (a)(2) of Section 9-1 of the Criminal Code of 1961 intending to procure the unavailability of the declarant as a witness in a criminal or civil proceeding.

(b) While intent to procure the unavailability of the witness is a necessary element for the introduction of the statements, it need not be the sole motivation behind the murder which procured the unavailability of the declarant as a witness.

(c) The murder of the declarant may, but need not, be the subject of the trial at which the statement is being offered. If the murder of the declarant is not the subject of the trial at which the statement is being offered, the murder need not have ever been prosecuted.

(d) The proponent of the statements shall give the adverse party reasonable written notice of its intention to offer the statements and the substance of the particulars of each statement of the declarant. For purposes of this Section, identifying the location of the statements in tendered discovery shall be sufficient to satisfy the substance of the particulars of the statement.

(e) The admissibility of the statements shall be determined by the court at a pretrial hearing. At the hearing, the proponent of the statement bears the burden of establishing three criteria by a preponderance of the evidence:

(1) first, that the adverse party murdered the declarant and that the murder was intended to cause the unavailability of the declarant as a witness;
(2) second, that the time, content, and circumstances of the statements provide sufficient safeguards of reliability;
(3) third, the interests of justice will best be served by admission of the statement into evidence.

(f) The court shall make specific findings as to each of these criteria on the record before ruling on the admissibility of said statements.

(g) This Section in no way precludes or changes the application of the existing common law doctrine of forfeiture by wrongdoing. Effective December 8, 2008.

Admissibility of a Prior Statement of an Unavailable Witness Whose Absence Was Wrongfully Procured: 725 ILCS 5/115-10.7

§ 115-10.7. Admissibility of prior statements of an unavailable witness whose absence was wrongfully procured.

(a) Legislative intent. The Illinois General Assembly finds that no party to a criminal case who wrongfully procures the unavailability of a witness should be allowed to benefit from such wrongdoing by depriving the trier of fact of relevant testimony.

(b) A statement of a witness is not excluded at the trial or hearing of any defendant by the hearsay rule or as a violation of any right to confront witnesses if the witness was killed, bribed, kidnapped, secreted, intimidated, or otherwise induced by a party, or one for whose conduct such party is legally responsible, to prevent the witness from being available to testify at such trial or hearing.

(c) The party seeking to introduce the statement shall disclose the statement sufficiently in advance of trial or hearing to provide the opposing party with a fair opportunity to meet it. The disclosure shall include notice of an intent to offer the statement, including the identity of the declarant.

(d) Prior to ruling on the admissibility of a statement under this Section, the court shall conduct a hearing outside the presence of the jury. During the course of the hearing the court may allow the parties to proceed by way of proffer. Except in cases where a preponderance of the evidence establishes that the defendant killed the declarant, the party seeking to introduce the statement shall be required to show by a preponderance of the evidence that the party who caused the unavailability of the witness did so with the intent or motive that the witness be unavailable for trial or hearing. The court is not required to find that the conduct or wrongdoing amounts to a criminal act.

(e) Nothing in this Section shall be construed to prevent the admissibility of statements under existing hearsay exceptions.

Effective August 11, 2009.

PRIOR ILLINOIS CASE LAW

1. Former Testimony Is Admissible as Exception to Hearsay Rule As Long As Declarant Is Unavailable, and Not Merely Reluctant to Testify

People v. Johnson, 118 Ill. 2d 501 (1987)

Defendant was charged with aggravated indecent liberties with a child. The trial court held a competency hearing before trial to determine whether the five-year-old victim and her seven-year-old brother were competent to testify. The victim was quite unresponsive but her brother was "more verbal." The trial court found the brother competent to testify but reserved its ruling on the victim's competency until after she testified at trial. At trial, the judge removed the spectators and jury from the courtroom and ordered that the children's testimony be recorded on video. The victim began testifying but became unresponsive as soon as she was asked about the day she got "hurt." The trial judge moved the defendant to another room where he contemporaneously watched the child's testimony on a television. The victim managed to testify that the defendant committed the crime but was mostly unresponsive to all other questions. The victim was also unresponsive on cross-examination and provided contradictory answers on redirect examination. The victim's brother testified with the defendant present in the courtroom. Defendant challenged the propriety of the videotapes on appeal, arguing that they violated his right to confront witnesses against him. The appellate court found that both witnesses were unavailable due to their "reluctance to testify," and that the videotaping procedure was therefore proper. The Illinois Supreme Court held that the reluctance of a witness to testify at the trial does not constitute unavailability. The Supreme Court considered the "unavailability" definition of the Federal Rule of Evidence 804 and "embrace[d] the general principles reflected therein." The court explained:

> Rule 804 of the Federal Rules of Evidence provides that certain hearsay is not inadmissible if the declarant is unavailable as a witness. The rule includes the following:
>
> (a) Definition of unavailability.- "Unavailability as a witness' includes situations in which the declarant-
>
> > (1) is exempted by ruling of the court on the ground of privilege from testifying concerning the subject matter of his statement; or
> >
> > (2) persists in refusing to testify concerning the subject matter of his statement despite an order of the court to do so; or

> (3) testifies to a lack of memory of the subject matter of his statement; or
> (4) is unable to be present or to testify at the hearing because of death or then existing physical or mental illness or infirmity; or
> (5) is absent from the hearing and the proponent of his statement has been unable to procure his attendance (or in the case of a hearsay exception under subdivision (b)(2), (3), or (4), his attendance or testimony) by process or other reasonable means.
>
> A declarant is not unavailable as a witness if his exemption, refusal, claim of lack of memory, inability, or absence is due to the procurement or wrongdoing of the proponent of his statement for the purpose of preventing the witness from attending or testifying.

While we do not necessarily adopt Rule 804 as an exhaustive definition of "unavailable" under Illinois law, we do embrace the general principles reflected therein. The general thrust of the rule makes clear that "unavailability" is a narrow concept, subject to a rigorous standard. The reasons for unavailability which are acceptable under Federal Rule 804—privilege, persistent contemptuous refusal to testify, failure of memory, death or illness, etc.—are substantial and therefore legally cognizable.

As we see it, the mere unwillingness of an otherwise available witness to testify simply does not rise to the high level of the Federal Rule 804 standards. Hence, it cannot constitute excusable unavailability for purposes of our [Supreme Court] Rule 414. The reasons for this view should be obvious. There is no question that testifying in open court can be a difficult experience, especially for victims of serious crimes. However, our legal system makes public testimony in front of the fact finder an important element of the truth seeking process. Any departure from this preference must be based upon a showing of special need. It follows that a witness' mere reluctance to testify cannot be accepted as a good enough reason to permit the use of out-of-court testimony.

2. It Is Within the Trial Court's Discretion to Permit Use of Videotape Deposition of Witness Who Is Likely to Be Unavailable at Trial

People v. Zehr, 103 Ill. 2d 472 (1984)

Defendant was convicted of home invasion, burglary and aggravated battery. The state filed a motion before trial to videotape the victim's evidence deposition. State claimed that the victim had medical issues and might be unavailable at trial. Defendant argued that state failed to show "good cause" for obtaining videotaped deposition testimony from the victim and that the videotaped deposition was not admissible in evidence because the state failed to establish that the victim would be unable to testify at trial. In a majority opinion, the Illinois Supreme Court rejected the claim, explaining that

> [t]he taking of evidence depositions in criminal cases is governed by the rules relevant to evidence depositions in civil cases. 87 Ill. 2d R. 414(b). The provision here pertinent is:
>
> > "The testimony shall be taken stenographically or by sound-recording device, and upon agreement of the parties, or by order of the court for good cause shown, may be taken by audio-visual recording device. The testimony shall be transcribed at the request of any party." 87 Ill. 2d R. 206(e).

Rule 206(e) permits the taking and use of depositions by the usual court reporting methods (in written or audio form) but requires the agreement of the parties or "order of the court for good cause shown" for the use of a videotape recording device. The only reason offered by the People for its use was to enable the jury to view the witness' demeanor. Although, as noted by the appellate court, the jury may possibly be in a better position to observe the witness' demeanor by means of videotape, that reason would be present in virtually every case where a witness is unavailable. It is the opinion of Justices Ward and Clark and the author of this opinion that witness demeanor alone, as a reason for the use of videotape, would render the "good cause" requirement in the rule meaningless, and that while the viewing of a witness by the jury may possibly be of importance in some cases, the circumstances here do not show the "good cause" required by the rule. A majority of the court, however, holds that the determination of the question whether to permit use of the videotaped deposition was within the discretion of the circuit court and that the record shows no abuse of discretion. The holding of the appellate court with respect to the use of the deposition was therefore in error.

Three justices of the Illinois Supreme Court expressed the view that the purported need for a jury to observe the witness' demeanor is not sufficient good cause for allowing the use of a videotaped deposition instead of the traditional written or audio form.

3. Witness Who Testifies to a Lack of Memory, Genuine or Not, Is Unavailable and Former Testimony Is Admissible

People v. Ramey, 152 Ill. 2d 41 (1992)

Defendant was convicted of murder, armed robbery and armed violence. At his sentencing hearing the state introduced evidence that defendant was involved in the murder of an individual other than the victim in the present case. A witness who testified against defendant at the first murder trial invoked his fifth amendment right at the sentencing hearing and refused to testify. The witness had befriended defendant while they were both incarcerated. The trial court found that the witness had no basis on which to refuse to testify and ordered him to testify. The witness then claimed that he could not remember the content of his prior testimony. State presented the witness' testimony through the prosecutor who worked on defendant's first trial. Defense, however, was not allowed to cross-examine the prosecutor with respect to the witness' earlier testimony that he hoped for leniency in exchange for testifying. Defendant argued on appeal that the use of the witness' testimony from the earlier trial denied him the right to confrontation. The Illinois Supreme Court disagreed.

The Supreme Court found that the lack of memory, either genuine or feigned, constitutes unavailability so that the witness' former testimony may be admitted. The court rejected the defendant's argument that the Supreme Court in People v. Johnson, 118 Ill. 2d 501 (1987), resolved this issue and required exclusion. The Illinois Supreme Court did not equate reluctance to testify with lack of memory. Moreover, the court rejected the defendant's argument that lack of memory constitutes unavailability only when the lapse is sincere. It explained that

> [c]ontrary to defendant's assertion that lack of memory must be sincere for purposes of unavailability of a witness, all that is needed for the application of that definition of unavailability is "a claim" of lack of memory, whether genuine or not. The plain language of Federal Rule 804 (" 'Unavailability as a witness' includes situations in which the declarant *** testifies to a lack of memory" and "[a] declarant is not unavailable *** if his *** claim of lack of memory *** is due to the procurement or wrongdoing of the proponent of his statement" (emphasis added)) clearly reveals that lack of memory, whether genuine or feigned, constitutes unavailability for purposes of introducing his hearsay statement.

See also Hardy v. Cross, 132 S. Ct. 490 (2011) (finding that a witness is unavailable for purposes of sixth amendment confrontation clause if prosecution fails to obtain the witness' presence at trial after making a good-faith effort).

For a discussion on the admissibility of out-of-court testimonial statements, see:

Crawford v. Washington, 541 U.S. 36 (2004) (holding that out-of-court testimonial statements are inadmissible unless witness is unavailable and defendant had a prior opportunity to cross-examine witness, regardless of whether such statements are found to be reliable).

People v. Torres, 2012 IL 111302 (holding that preliminary hearing testimony of an unavailable witness is admissible at trial only if the defendant had a prior and fair opportunity to fully explore the "witness' opportunity to observe, interest, bias, prejudice and motive").

People v. Sutherland, 223 Ill. 2d 187 (2006) (holding that prior testimony of an unavailable witness is admissible if there was ample opportunity for cross-examination at prior trial or hearing).

Davis v. Washington, 547 U.S. 813 (2006) (finding that statements made by victim during police investigation for the primary purpose of meeting an ongoing emergency are not testimonial under the confrontation clause of the sixth amendment and are admissible).

Michigan v. Bryant, 131 S. Ct. 1143 (2011) (finding that statements made by mortally wounded victim to police officers attempting to meet an ongoing emergency are not testimonial).

People v. Stechly, 225 Ill. 2d 246 (2007) (defining a testimonial statement as one made in a solemn fashion intended to establish a particular fact).

4. Co-Defendant's Exculpatory Testimony at a Suppression Hearing Not Admissible Under Former Testimony Exception to Hearsay Rule Because State Did Not Have Adequate Opportunity for Cross-Examination

People v. Rice, 166 Ill. 2d 35 (1995)

Defendant was convicted of possession of a controlled substance with intent to deliver. At a joint trial of defendant and co-defendant, defendant's counsel called co-defendant as a witness. Co-defendant invoked his fifth amendment privilege against self-incrimination and refused to testify. Defense moved to admit his prior testimony at a suppression hearing. At the suppression hearing co-defendant admitted that he, and not the defendant, had possession of the controlled substance. The trial judge denied the defense motion, explaining that the issues at trial were different from those at the suppression hearing and that state did not have a meaningful opportunity to cross-examine co-defendant when he gave the prior testimony.

The Illinois Supreme Court found that co-defendant's self-implicating testimony at a suppression hearing was not admissible under the former testimony exception to the hearsay rule. The Supreme Court explained that

> the testimony of a witness at a prior hearing is admissible in evidence at trial where the witness is unavailable and when ample opportunity to cross-examine existed at the prior hearing. People v. Horton, 65 Ill. 2d 413, 416 (1976); People v. Tennant, 65 Ill. 2d 401, 411 (1976). It is the second element which serves as the focal point of the dispute in this case. As this court has stated, determining whether ample opportunity to cross-examine at the prior hearing exists does not lend itself to a *per se* determination, but must be decided on the circumstances of each case. *See Horton*, 65 Ill. 2d at 417.
>
> In applying the former testimony exception to testimony elicited at a preliminary hearing, this court has recognized the distinction between the opportunity to cross-examine afforded at trial and at a preliminary hearing. " 'A preliminary hearing is ordinarily a much less searching exploration into the merits of a case than a trial, simply because its function is the more limited one of determining whether probable cause exists to hold the accused for trial.' " [citations omitted]. Cross-examination at a preliminary hearing is subject to the general rule that questioning may not extend beyond the scope of the direct examination and such further

> interrogation as necessary to show interest, bias, prejudice, or motive of the witness, to the extent that these factors are relevant to the question of probable cause.
>
> In view of the limited nature of the evidence that may be introduced at a preliminary hearing, this court has stated that whether adequate opportunity to cross-examine existed at a preliminary hearing "may not depend in its entirety on what transpired at that hearing." *Horton*, 65 Ill. 2d at 417. "Adequate opportunity to cross-examine means an opportunity to effectively cross-examine ***." *Horton*, 65 Ill. 2d at 417. Merely providing some opportunity to cross-examine at a preliminary hearing does not necessarily establish that the party had an adequate opportunity. *Horton*, 65 Ill. 2d at 417. Because a suppression hearing is even more limited in focus than a preliminary hearing, the reasoning in *Horton* is equally applicable to the present case.

The Supreme Court reasoned that the state did not have an ample opportunity to cross-examine him due to the limited nature of the evidence introduced at the suppression hearing. In addition, the motive and focus of the cross-examination were quite different at the suppression hearing (conduct of co-defendant) than at trial (guilt or innocence of defendant). Therefore, because the issues were not similar, the court held that the state did not have a meaningful opportunity to effectively cross-examine the co-defendant at the suppression hearing and his prior testimony was inadmissible.

Defendant also sought to admit the co-defendant's statement as a statement against penal interest. The Illinois Supreme Court listed the requirements for the admissibility of a statement against penal interest: "(1) the declarant must be unavailable, (2) the declarant's statement must have been against penal interest, and (3) corroborating circumstances support the trustworthiness of the statement." The court found that co-defendant's testimony at the suppression hearing implicating himself was not admissible under the statement against penal interest exception to the hearsay rule because although the first two requirements for admissibility were fulfilled, the defendant failed to satisfy the third. The Supreme Court explained that

> the focus and purpose of the State's cross-examination of codefendant at the suppression hearing was limited, and thus the State was not able to fully test the testimony's reliability. It therefore cannot be said that the fact codefendant was subject to cross-examination assures the testimony's reliability. 5 J. WIGMORE, EVIDENCE § 1387, at 90 (Chadbourn rev. ed. 1974). [. . .]
>
> ***
>
> Moreover, the absence of several other factors further supports our conclusion that codefendant's testimony was not sufficiently trustworthy to be admitted. Codefendant's testimony was not a spontaneous statement to a close acquaintance, [. . .] but was elicited through questioning at the pretrial motion to suppress, held approximately 22 months after the seizure at issue. Further, we note that codefendant had a motive to testify falsely. Codefendant stood to benefit at the suppression hearing by making the statement in question because, if his testimony had been believed, his motion would have been granted and the evidence against him suppressed. Additionally, codefendant's statement that he placed the bag in his pants two hours prior to being stopped was not corroborated by any other evidence. Because we believe that there was insufficient indicia of reliability of codefendant's testimony at the suppression hearing, we find it inadmissible at trial.

5. Statements Concerning Cause or Circumstances of Impending Death Made by Victim Under Belief of Impending Death Are Admissible as Exception to Hearsay Rule

People v. Odum, 27 Ill. 2d 237 (1963)

Defendant was convicted of murder. He contended on appeal that the trial court improperly admitted a dying declaration of the victim via the testimony of two police officers. The officers stated that they spoke with the victim and that he was in a very serious condition after he was shot three times. They told him that he was badly injured and asked him who shot him. The victim said that three men attacked him and that he was to testify against one of the men whose name was "Otis or Odum." The Illinois Supreme Court noted that none of the police officers who testified at trial "told the same story." The Supreme Court therefore urged caution in the admissibility of such statements, and noted that

> [t]he law with respect to dying declarations has been firmly established in this State. They are defined as statements of fact by the victim concerning the cause and circumstances of a homicide. To make them admissible into evidence as dying declarations, an exception to the rule against hearsay evidence, it must appear that they are made by the victim under the fixed belief and moral conviction that death is impending and certain to follow almost immediately, without opportunity for repentance and in the absence of all hope of avoidance, when he has despaired of life and looks to death as inevitable and at hand. People v. Tilley, 406 Ill. 398, 403 (1950); People v. Hubbs, 401 Ill. 613 (1948); People v. Savant, 301 Ill. 225 (1921).
>
> The reasons for this stringent rule were stated in Starkey v. People, 17 Ill. 17, 20 (1855), 'The statements of the deceased as to the cause of the injury from which death finally results, when dying declarations within the meaning of the law, are admitted in evidence on the ground of necessity, and the rule under which they are admitted, forms an exception in the law of evidence. The accused, under the rule has not the benefit of 'meeting the witness against him face to face;' a constitutional right in all criminal trials with this solitary exception. He is deprived of the security of an oath attended with consequences of temporal punishment for perjury. He is deprived of the great safeguard against misrepresentation and misapprehension-the power of cross-examination. The evidence is hearsay in its character; the statements are liable to be misunderstood and to be misrepeated upon the trial, and the evidence goes to the jury with surroundings tending to produce upon the mind emotions of deep sympathy for the deceased, and of involuntary resentment against the accused.'

The Supreme Court observed that none of the medical personnel that visited the victim told him that he was dying, and there was no evidence introduced at trial showing that the victim believed he was facing imminent death. The Supreme Court concluded that the evidence was insufficient to permit the victim's statement to be introduced as a dying declaration because the medical personnel did not advise the badly wounded victim that his death was imminent and he did not show an abandonment of hope.

6. Dying Declaration Is Admissible If Trial Court First Determines Beyond a Reasonable Doubt That It Was Made *in Extremis*
People v. Beier, 29 Ill. 2d 511 (1963)

Defendant was charged with murder of her husband. The husband had been shot but was conscious. Defendant told bystanders that her husband shot her, but her husband disputed it and claimed that she had shot him. Defendant testified at trial that she could not remember anything about the shooting. A police officer testified that after the victim was brought to the hospital, he stated that his wife had shot him. Defense objected to this testimony but the trial court overruled it. The Illinois Supreme Court held that the trial court erroneously overruled the defense objection because it was not clear that the victim made the statement under the belief of impending death, explaining that

> [t]he belief of the dying man that death is impending furnishes the guaranty of truthfulness which makes his declaration admissible in evidence. The rule is that such a declaration must be

> made under the fixed belief and moral conviction of the person making it that his death is impending and certain to follow almost immediately, without opportunity for repentance and in the absence of all hope of avoidance, when he has despaired of life and looks to death as at hand. People v. Maria, 359 Ill. 231 (1935). As this court said in the *Maria* case, 'In the first instance the court must be satisfied, beyond a reasonable doubt, that the statement was made *in extremis*, and unless it was so made it should not be allowed to go to the jury.'

7. Trial Court Must Examine All Facts Existing and Surrounding the Individual Making the Dying Declaration to Determine Whether the Declarant Understood What He or She Was Doing and Could Give a Correct Account

People v. Tilley, 406 Ill. 398 (1950)

The Illinois Supreme Court found that victim's statements were admissible as dying declarations where she requested last rites, which she knew were given only to those in danger of dying. The Supreme Court explained that the trial court must determine whether the declaration qualifies under the dying declaration exception to the hearsay rule. In making that determination, the trial court should consider the following:

> it must appear that [the declarations] are made by the victim under the fixed belief and moral conviction that death is impending and certain to follow almost immediately, without opportunity for repentance and in the absence of all hope of avoidance, when he has despaired of life and looks to death as inevitable and at hand. [. . .]
>
> The declarant must be in possession of his mental faculties sufficiently to understand what he is doing and to be able to give a true and correct account of the facts to which the statement relates. [. . .] Courts will look to all the facts existing and surrounding the party giving the dying declaration at the time, before and after the declarations are made forming the *res gestae* and tending to show his true state of mind. [citation omitted].
>
> Finally, the court, upon a preliminary hearing outside the presence of the jury, must first be convinced beyond all reasonable doubt that all the elements of a true dying declaration are present, before such statements may be heard and considered by the jury.

The Supreme Court concluded that the request showed that the victim knew death was imminent and that she had abandoned hope.

8. Out-of-Court Declaration of a Third Person That He or She, and Not Defendant, Committed the Crime Is Inadmissible as Statement Against Interest Unless Justice Requires Such Result Generally

People v. Lettrich, 413 Ill. 172 (1952)

After the murder of a 10-year-old girl, the police questioned defendant extensively at the police station. Defendant claimed that he did not know anything about the murder and that he did not commit it. Defendant testified that one officer gave him four polygraph examinations after recounting the details of the crime, and that defendant eventually said, "All right, I did it." Defendant later repudiated his confession. The Illinois Supreme Court observed that there was "not a scintilla of evidence to connect" defendant with the crime, except for his repudiated confession. The court also noted that another person confessed to the crime but that the trial court refused to admit the evidence. The Supreme Court explained that although a statement against penal interest of a non-party and unavailable declarant is admissible, an out-of-court declaration of a third person that he or she and not the defendant committed the crime is inadmissible under this exception to the hearsay rule. The Supreme Court explained that

> [t]he practicality of this rule is obvious. General admission of such statements could seriously handicap the administration of justice in tempting everyone accused of crime to introduce perjured testimony that a third party, then deceased or beyond the jurisdiction of the court, had declared that he, and not the accused, had committed the crime. The rule is sound and should not be departed from except in cases where it is obvious that justice demands a departure. But it would be absurd, and shocking to all sense of justice, to indiscriminately apply such a rule to prevent one accused of a crime from showing that another person was the real culprit merely because that other person was deceased, insane or outside the jurisdiction of the court.
>
> ***
>
> We think under the special circumstances of the instant case justice demands a departure from the rule. The State is here relying upon a confession, which the defendant alleges was procured by duress and fear. That confession does not coincide with many of the known facts and cannot be entirely true. Any suspicion that the offered declarations of the third party in this case is testimony induced by the accused will not even be considered. Where the State is relying solely upon the repudiated confession of the defendant, and that confession in material respects does not conform to the known facts, it seems that justice requires that the jury consider every circumstance which reflects upon the reliability of that confession, and a confession of a third person that he perpetrated the offense is such a circumstance.

For additional case law pertaining to the statement against penal interest exception to the hearsay rule, see:

Chambers v. Mississippi, 410 U.S. 284 (1973) (finding that a third person's confession to the charged crime may be admissible as statement against penal interest if it bears substantial assurance of trustworthiness).

People v. Bowel, 111 Ill. 2d 58 (1986) (holding that *Chambers* factors are to be considered for indicia of trustworthiness of a statement and not as conditions of admissibility).

People v. Tenney, 205 Ill. 2d 411 (2002) (finding that exclusion of a reliable confession inculpating declarant and exculpating defendant is prejudicial error).

People v. Caffey, 205 Ill. 2d 52 (2001) (noting that declarant who asserts fifth amendment right not to testify is unavailable for purposes of statement against interest exception to the hearsay rule).

9. Statement Against Penal Interest Exception Under the Federal Rules of Evidence Does Not Permit Admissibility of Non-Self-Inculpatory Statements, Even If Made Within Broader Narrative That Is Generally Self-Inculpatory

Williamson v. United States, 512 U.S. 594 (1994)

The United States Supreme Court interpreted Federal Rule of Evidence 804(b)(3). At trial, the district court admitted a statement introduced by prosecution and made by a participant in the crime that implicated him and the defendant. The Supreme Court found that the district court erred in admitting this statement. The Supreme Court first determined the meaning of "statement" as used in the rules. The Supreme Court explained that

> [o]ne possible meaning, "a report or narrative," Webster's Third New International Dictionary 2229, defn. 2(a) (1961), connotes an extended declaration. Under this reading, [co-participant's] entire confession—even if it contains both self-inculpatory and non-self-inculpatory parts—would be admissible so long as in the aggregate the confession sufficiently inculpates him. Another meaning of "statement," "a single declaration or remark," would make Rule 804(b)(3) cover only those declarations or remarks within the confession that are individually self-inculpatory.

The Supreme Court adopted the latter interpretation, explaining that

> [a]lthough the text of the Rule does not directly resolve the matter, the principle behind the Rule, so far as it is discernible from the text, points clearly to the narrower reading. Rule 804(b)(3) is founded on the commonsense notion that reasonable people, even reasonable people who are not especially honest, tend not to make self-inculpatory statements unless they believe them to be true. This notion simply does not extend to the broader definition of "statement." The fact that a person is making a broadly self-inculpatory confession does not make more credible the confession's non-self-inculpatory parts. One of the most effective ways to lie is to mix falsehood with truth, especially truth that seems particularly persuasive because of its self-inculpatory nature.
>
> ***
>
> Congress certainly could, subject to the constraints of the Confrontation Clause, make statements admissible based on their proximity to self-inculpatory statements. But we will not lightly assume that the ambiguous language means anything so inconsistent with the Rule's underlying theory. *See* Cooter & Gell v. Hartmarx Corp., 496 U.S. 384, 394-395 (1990). In our view, the most faithful reading of Rule 804(b)(3) is that it does not allow admission of non-self-inculpatory statements, even if they are made within a broader narrative that is generally self-inculpatory. The district court may not just assume for purposes of Rule 804(b)(3) that a statement is self-inculpatory because it is part of a fuller confession, and this is especially true when the statement implicates someone else. "[T]he arrest statements of a codefendant have traditionally been viewed with special suspicion. Due to his strong motivation to implicate the defendant and to exonerate himself, a codefendant's statements about what the defendant said or did are less credible than ordinary hearsay evidence." Lee v. Illinois, 476 U.S. 530, 541 (1986) (internal quotation marks omitted); *see also* Bruton v. United States, 391 U.S. 123, 136, 88 S. Ct. 1620, 1628, 20 L. Ed. 2d 476 (1968); Dutton v. Evans, 400 U.S. 74, 98 (1970) (Harlan, J., concurring in result).

The Supreme Court, however, did not create a *per se* rule. A statement concerning another may still be self-inculpatory and therefore admissible. The trial court must evaluate each statement individually in context of the entire statement, in other words, in light of all the surrounding circumstances. The Court remanded to the district court for a determination as to whether each statement in the confession was "truly self-inculpatory."

10. Proponent of Statement Under Doctrine of Forfeiture by Wrongdoing Has the Burden of Showing All Elements of the Doctrine by Preponderance of the Evidence
People v. Peterson, 2011 IL App (3d) 100513, *appeal denied, judgment vacated*, 2011 WL 6185448 (Ill. Nov. 30, 2011) (order directing appellate court to address appeal on the merits)

The state sought to admit various hearsay statements of defendant's deceased ex-wife and missing wife, one of whom was murdered and the other one disappeared, under 725 ILCS 5/115-10.6 and the common law doctrine of forfeiture by wrongdoing. The state claimed that defendant murdered his ex-wife to prevent her from testifying at a distribution of marital property proceeding, and procured his wife's unavailability to preclude her from testifying at their future divorce proceedings and at his trial for his ex-wife's murder. The Third District of the Illinois Appellate Court noted that pursuant to section 115-10.6,

> the proponent of the statement bears the burden of establishing by a preponderance of the evidence: (1) that the adverse party murdered the declarant and that the murder was intended to cause the unavailability of the declarant as a witness; (2) that the time, content, and circumstances of the statements provide "sufficient safeguards of reliability"; and (3) that "the interests of justice will best be served by admission of the statement into evidence." 725 ILCS

> 5/115-10.6(e) (West 2008). The circuit court must make "specific findings as to each of these criteria on the record" before ruling on the admissibility of the statements at issue. 725 ILCS 5/115-10.6(f) (West 2008). The statute provides that it "in no way precludes or changes the application of the existing common law doctrine of forfeiture by wrongdoing." 725 ILCS 5/115-10.6(g) (West 2008). The common law doctrine of forfeiture by wrongdoing provides a hearsay exception for statements made by an unavailable witness where the defendant intentionally made the witness unavailable in order to prevent her from testifying. People v. Hanson, 238 Ill. 2d 74 (2010); People v. Stechly, 225 Ill. 2d 246, 272-73 (2007).

The trial court conducted a hearing pursuant to the statute and found that the state established by the preponderance of the evidence that defendant murdered the witnesses to keep them from testifying against him, and that their statements were sufficiently reliable to be admissible. It admitted several statements but excluded others because it found that they failed to meet the reliability requirement:

> the court found that, pursuant to the statute, 6 of the 14 proffered hearsay statements contained sufficient "safeguards of reliability" and that the interests of justice would be served by the admission of those statements into evidence. The court found the following six statements admissible under the statute: (1) portions of a letter that [the deceased ex-wife] wrote to the Will County State's Attorney's office which described a confrontation that [the deceased ex-wife] allegedly had with the defendant on July 5, 2002, while the divorce proceedings were pending; (2) A REDACTED VERSION [o]f a handwritten statement that [the deceased ex-wife] gave to the Bolingbrook police describing the alleged July 5, 2002, incident; (3) a statement that [his deceased ex-wife] allegedly made to her sister [. . .]; (4)a statement that [the deceased ex-wife] allegedly made in late 2003 to [a friend] who attended nursing classes with [the deceased ex-wife] at Joliet Junior College; (5) another statement that [the deceased ex-wife] allegedly made to [a friend]; and (6) a statement that [the missing wife] allegedly made to her pastor [. . .] regarding an encounter that she allegedly had with her husband on the night [the deceased wife] died.
>
> ***
>
> The circuit court ruled that the remaining eight hearsay statements proffered by the State did not meet the statutory standard of reliability and that the interests of justice would not be served by the admission of those statements. The court excluded the following statements under the statute: (1) statements that [the deceased ex-wife] allegedly made to her other sister [. . .]; (2) a statement that [the deceased ex-wife] allegedly made to her attorney [. . .]; (3) statements that [the deceased ex-wife] allegedly made to her friend, [. . .] regarding the alleged July 5, 2002, incident; (4) a statement that [the deceased ex-wife] allegedly made to [. . .] one of her former coworkers; (5) statements that [the missing wife] allegedly made to [a person] she had met at Joliet Junior College in 2002; (6) a statement that [missing wife] allegedly made to her friend [. . .] in the fall of 2007 regarding her alleged encounter with the defendant on the night [the deceased ex-wife] died; (7) portions of an audiotaped statement made by [the deceased ex-wife] to an insurance agent; and (8) portions of statements that [the deceased ex-wife] made under oath during an examination conducted by a Country Insurance agent on August 6, 2003.

The state petitioned the court to conduct an evaluation of the statements under the common law doctrine of forfeiture by wrongdoing which does not require a determination of reliability, pursuant to People v. Hanson, 238 Ill. 2d 74 (2010), which was decided four days before state filed its motion. The defendant argued that the state's motion was untimely. The trial court did not consider defendant's argument and rather found that "the statute codified the common law and that the statute therefore takes precedence over the common law unless the statute is declared unconstitutional or otherwise invalidated." The Third District found that it did not have jurisdiction to consider the case because of the state's untimely motion. Only if the state could show that there had been a "material change in the facts that could not have been presented earlier with *due diligence*," would the court have jurisdiction to consider the motion. State argued that the Supreme Court's decision in *Hanson* constituted such a material change in the facts, because it recognized that no finding of reliability is necessary for admissibility of statements under the common law forfeiture by wrongdoing doctrine. The court disagreed, noting that even

> [a]ssuming arguendo that a change in the governing law could trigger the [. . .] exception for a "material change in facts"—a question which we do not decide—the State cannot show that any change in the applicable law occurred here. The common law doctrine of forfeiture by wrongdoing was recognized by the United States Supreme Court as early as 1878. *Hanson*, 238 Ill. 2d at 96. In 1997, the doctrine was codified at the federal level by Federal Rule of Evidence 804(b)(6) as an exception to the general rule against hearsay. FED. R. EVID. 804(b)(6); *Hanson*, 238 Ill. 2d at 96; Giles v. California, 554 U.S. 353, 367 (2008). Rule 804(b)(6) provides a hearsay exception for "[a] statement offered against a party that has engaged or acquiesced in wrongdoing that was intended to, and did, procure the unavailability of the declarant as a witness." FED. R. EVID. 804(b)(6). The rule does not condition the admissibility of such statements upon a showing that the statements are trustworthy or reliable. FED. R. EVID. 804(b)(6); United States v. White, 116 F.3d 903, 912-13 (D.C. Cir. 1997). In a case decided more than three years before *Hanson*, our supreme court adopted the common law doctrine as the law of Illinois and expressly recognized that the doctrine was "coextensive with" Federal Rule 804(b)(6), which was a "codifi[cation]" or "legislative enactment" of the doctrine. People v. Stechly, 225 Ill. 2d 246, 272-73 (2007) (citing Davis v. Washington, 547 U.S. 813, 833 (2006)).
>
> ***
>
> Thus, contrary to the State's argument, it was clear long before *Hanson* that the common law doctrine of forfeiture by wrongdoing was a general hearsay exception in Illinois and that the admission of hearsay statements under the doctrine did not depend upon a showing of reliability. *See Stechly*, 225 Ill. 2d at 272-73; see also MICHAEL H. GRAHAM, GRAHAM'S HANDBOOK OF ILLINOIS EVIDENCE § 804.5, at 985 (10th ed. 2011).

In a partially dissenting opinion, one judge noted that the new Illinois Rule of Evidence 804(b)(5) does not contain a requirement of reliability, and that the majority erred in not admitting the hearsay statements pursuant to the Illinois Rule which codified the common law rule.

See also People v. Hanson, 238 Ill. 2d 74 (2010) (finding that a statement offered against a party who procured the unavailability of declarant as a witness is admissible under the forfeiture by wrongdoing doctrine).

And see Giles v. California, 554 U.S. 353 (2008) (finding that a defendant must have an intent to procure unavailability of witness for forfeiture by wrongdoing doctrine to apply).

Rule 805. Hearsay within Hearsay

Hearsay included within hearsay is not excluded under the hearsay rule if each part of the combined statements conforms with an exception to the hearsay rule provided in these rules.

Adopted September 27, 2010, eff. January 1, 2011.

AUTHOR'S COMMENTARY

Illinois Rule of Evidence 805 codifies the Illinois common law rule (People v. Thomas, 178 Ill. 2d 215 (1997)), and is identical to the Federal Rule of Evidence 805 in effect until its December 1, 2011, stylistic amendment. *See* Gino L. DiVito, *The Illinois Rules of Evidence: A Color-Coded Guide Containing the New Rules, the Committee's General and Specific Comments, a Comparison with the Federal Rules of Evidence, and Additional Commentary (Including the Federal Rules of Evidence as Amended Effective December 1, 2011)* (Jan. 1, 2012), at 126, http://www.tdrlawfirm.com/assets/downloads/Illinois_Rules_of_Evidence_Color-Coded_Guide.pdf [hereinafter DiVito, *Color-Coded Guide*].

The Federal Rule has since been amended in style but not in substance, and states that "[h]earsay within hearsay is not excluded by the rule against hearsay if each part of the combined statements conforms with an exception to the rule." FED. R. EVID. 805 (eff. Dec. 1, 2011); Federal Advisory Committee Notes to FED. R. EVID. 805 (noting that "changes are intended to be stylistic only. There is no intent to change any result in any ruling on evidence admissibility").

PRIOR ILLINOIS CASE LAW

1. There Is No Hearsay Within Hearsay Problem If Each Part of the Combined Statement Falls Under an Exception to Hearsay Rule

People v. Thomas, 178 Ill. 2d 215 (1997)

Defendant and two other individuals participated in the shooting death of the victim. After the shooting, defendant and one of the two accomplices went to the accomplice's fiancée's home. The fiancée gave the police a written statement. She stated that the defendant told her he had shot someone. Once the accomplice noticed that his fiancée was nervous, he got angry at defendant for telling her about the shooting. At trial, the fiancée denied knowing the content of the conversation between the accomplice and defendant and denied knowing why defendant was angry. On cross-examination, the fiancée testified that the statement to the police was a lie because she was mad at defendant and wanted to frame him. The trial court admitted the fiancée's prior statement as impeachment evidence only. Defendant argued that the fiancée's statements were inadmissible as hearsay within hearsay. The first statement was the accomplice's statement to the defendant that the fiancée had overheard. The second statement was the fiancée's statement to the police. The Supreme Court disagreed, noting that each statement fell within an exception to the hearsay rule.

The first statement was admissible as a co-conspirator's statement even though the statement occurred after the completion of the crime because it was an attempt at concealment. It was also made before the defendant had retrieved and disposed of the gun used in the offense. The court noted that the statement also qualified as an excited utterance, since the accomplice had just found out that defendant had told his fiancée about the murder. The Supreme Court explained that "[a] statement related to a startling event made while the declarant was under the stress of excitement caused by the event is admissible despite its hearsay nature on the theory that the declarant lacks an opportunity to fabricate." The second statement was admissible under 725 ILCS 5/115-10.1 as a prior inconsistent statement. The personal knowledge requirement was satisfied because the fiancée overheard the conversation between the defendant and the accomplice.

Finally, the Supreme Court concluded that the use of the statements as substantive evidence would not deny defendant his constitutional right to confront witnesses because the witness testified at trial and the statement was admissible under a firmly rooted exception to the hearsay rule.

Credibility of Declarant

Rule 806. Attacking and Supporting Credibility of Declarant

When a hearsay statement, or a statement defined in Rule 801(d)(2)(C), (D), (E), or (F), has been admitted in evidence, the credibility of the declarant may be attacked, and if attacked may be supported, by any evidence which would be admissible for those purposes if declarant had testified as a witness. Evidence of a statement or conduct by the declarant at any time, inconsistent with the declarant's hearsay statement, is not subject to any requirement that the declarant may have been afforded an opportunity to deny or explain. If the party against whom a hearsay statement has been admitted calls the declarant as a witness, the party is entitled to examine the declarant on the statement as if under cross-examination.

Adopted September 27, 2010, eff. January 1, 2011.

Committee Commentary

(3) Modernization: Where there was no conflict with statutes or recent Illinois Supreme Court or Illinois Appellate Court decisions, and where it was determined to be beneficial and uniformly or almost uniformly accepted elsewhere, the Committee incorporated into the Illinois Rules of Evidence uncontroversial developments with respect to the law of evidence as reflected in the Federal Rules of Evidence and the 44 surveyed jurisdictions. [One of t]he 14 instances of modernization of note [is] as follows: ***

> **(11) Rule 806.** Attacking and Supporting Credibility of Declarant. Rule 806 dispenses with the requirement of an opportunity to deny or explain an inconsistent statement or conduct of an out-of-court declarant under all circumstances when a hearsay statement is involved. Whether Illinois law had already dispensed with the requirement with respect to a deposition was unclear.
>
> ILL. R. EVID. Committee Commentary § 3, pg. 2-3.

AUTHOR'S COMMENTARY

Illinois common law principles generally allowed a party to challenge the credibility of a hearsay declarant. One appellate court has found that a non-testifying declarant of an excited utterance could not be impeached by a prior conviction. People v. Johnson, 271 Ill. App. 3d 962 (4th Dist. 1995). The court reasoned that the reliability of an excited utterance does not depend on the credibility of the declarant. *Id.* Professor Graham, however, has cautioned that this "novel position" is "contrary" to Illinois Rule of Evidence 806. MICHAEL H. GRAHAM, GRAHAM'S HANDBOOK OF ILLINOIS EVIDENCE § 806.1 (10th ed. 2010).

PRIOR ILLINOIS CASE LAW

1. Credibility of a Declarant of a Hearsay Statement May Be Attacked

People v. Edgeston, 157 Ill. 2d 201 (1993)

Defendant was convicted of murder in the shooting death of the victim. The victim was shot in the back. Defendant testified that he was with an acquaintance on the night of the shooting. He stated that the victim was harassing him that night and that there had previously been "bad blood" between them. He claimed, however, that he did not shoot the victim. He stated that as the victim was taunting him, he tore off the victim's necklace and ran from the victim. As he ran away, the defendant allegedly heard a shot being fired and saw his acquaintance catch up to him with a shotgun in his hand. The trial court admitted the victim's dying declaration stating that defendant was the shooter. The defendant contended that the victim's dying declaration could not sustain his murder conviction because it should be "entitled to very little weight." The defendant argued that the victim was shot in the back and therefore could not have seen the shooter. Defendant claimed that his acquaintance was the shooter, but that the victim could not have named him as the shooter because he did not know his name. The Illinois Supreme Court noted that

> although a dying declaration is considered secondary evidence, the weight it is to be accorded is strictly a function of the jury. People v. Tilley, 406 Ill. 398, 408 (1950). In determining the credibility or weight to be given such a declaration, the jury should consider the circumstances under which it was made, the physical and mental condition of the declarant, and the method and manner in which it is received. *Tilley*, 411 Ill. at 476-77. Additionally, where a dying declaration is offered in evidence, it is permissible for the defendant to show that the deceased, in making the statements, "entertained feelings of malice and hostility towards the accused." Nordgren v. People, 211 Ill. 425, 436 (1904).

The Supreme Court concluded that "the jury was fully apprised of the circumstances surrounding [the victim's] dying declaration, and the record contains evidence which, if believed by the jury, would substantially corroborate the declaration."

2. Defendant May Not Impeach Non-Testifying Declarant of Excited Utterance Through Prior Conviction

People v. Johnson, 271 Ill. App. 3d 962 (4th Dist. 1995)

In a case of first impression, the court held that a non-testifying declarant of an excited utterance cannot be impeached by a prior conviction. The court noted that the reliability of an excited utterance does not depend on the credibility of the declarant. Instead, the statement is admitted based on the circumstances surrounding its making, in particular, the fact that declarant was speaking spontaneously and did not have time to fabricate a lie. The court explained that it did

> not consider a declarant of an excited utterance to be a witness capable of impeachment by a prior conviction. Impeachment by a prior conviction questions the veracity of the witness; however, the veracity of a excited utterance does not depend upon the declarant. An out-of-court statement will be admitted under the excited utterance exception to the hearsay rule if it meets three criteria: (1) the occurrence of an event or condition sufficiently startling to produce a spontaneous and unreflecting statement; (2) absence of time to fabricate; and (3) a statement relating to the circumstances of the occurrence. People v. Smith, 152 Ill. 2d 229, 258 (1992). The reason these statements are admitted is that the declarant is speaking "spontaneously," without the opportunity to fabricate a lie. As noted by the supreme court, excited utterances are admissible as exceptions to the hearsay rule because statements prompted by shocking or startling events have a reduced probability of fabrication and are "particularly trustworthy" since they are a product of sense and not thoughtful, self-interested reflection. People v. Poland, 22 Ill. 2d 175, 180-81 (1961); People v. M.S., 247 Ill. App. 3d 1074, 1089 (1993). Or, stated in another manner:
>
> > 'Since this utterance is made under the immediate and uncontrolled domination of the senses, rather than reason and reflection, and during the brief period when consideration of self-interest could not have been fully brought to bear, the utterance may be taken as expressing the real belief of the speaker as to the facts just observed by him.' People v. Damen (1963), 28 Ill. 2d 464, 471 (1963).

An excited utterance rests upon the circumstances under which it was uttered, not upon the reliability of the declarant. People v. Wright, 234 Ill. App. 3d 880, 892 (1992). Indeed, the declarant need not be competent as a witness. People v. Merideth, 152 Ill. App. 3d 304, 312 (1987); People v. Harris, 134 Ill. App. 3d 705, 711 (1985). An excited utterance may be characterized as an event speaking through the declarant and not the person speaking about the event. [citation omitted]. Since the declarant's credibility is immaterial to the veracity of an excited utterance, the declarant's prior criminal convictions are also irrelevant to the veracity of an excited utterance. Accordingly, we hold that a nontestifying declarant of an excited utterance may not be impeached by a prior conviction.

We are aware that other jurisdictions allow the impeachment of an excited utterance declarant. [citations omitted] Although Federal courts allow impeachment by prior convictions in cases such as this because it is authorized by Rule 806 of the Federal Rules of Evidence, the advisory committee notes to Federal Rule 803(2) support our holding:

The theory of [excited utterances] is simply that circumstances may produce a condition of excitement which temporarily stills the capacity of reflection and produces utterances free of conscious fabrication. (Emphasis added.) FED. R. EVID. 803(2), 28 U.S.C., Notes of Advisory Committee on Proposed Rules, at 778 (1988).

We point out that our holding is very narrow because it applies only to impeachment of a nontestifying excited utterance declarant by prior conviction. For example, an excited utterance may be impeached by other means, such as the nontestifying declarant's subsequent inconsistent statement. People v. Smith, 127 Ill. App. 3d 622, 630 (1984). Parties must be given latitude to controvert an excited utterance, particularly since the exception has been criticized on the ground that excitement impairs accuracy of observation as well as eliminating conscious fabrication. *See* FED. R. EVID. 803, 28 U.S.C., Notes of the Advisory Committee on Proposed Rules, at 778 (1988).

Chapter 7

Constitutional Rights of the Accused

Constitutional Right to Testify, Call Witnesses, and Present a Defense

Recanted, False, and Perjured Testimony

Constitutional Right Under the Sixth Amendment to Confront Witnesses, Including Expert Witnesses

Chapter 7

Constitutional Rights of the Accused

Constitutional Right to Testify, Call Witnesses, and Present a Defense

AUTHOR'S COMMENTARY

Pursuant to the due process clause of the fourteenth amendment and the confrontation clause and compulsory process clause of the sixth amendment to the United States Constitution, a criminal defendant is guaranteed "a meaningful opportunity to present a complete defense" and to call witnesses on his or her behalf. Holmes v. South Carolina, 547 U.S. 319 (2006); *see also* Washington v. Texas, 388 U.S. 14 (1967). A criminal defendant has a due process right to testify in his or her behalf at trial. Rock v. Arkansas, 483 U.S. 44 (1987). Similarly, according to Article I, section 8 of the Illinois Constitution,

> [i]n criminal prosecutions, the accused shall have the right to appear and defend in person and by counsel; to demand the nature and cause of the accusation and have a copy thereof; to be confronted with the witnesses against him or her and to have process to compel the attendance of witnesses in his or her behalf.

Defendant may, however, waive the right to testify, and Illinois courts do not require the trial court to inform defendant of this right or to ensure that he or she waives it knowingly or intelligently. People v. Smith, 176 Ill. 2d 217 (1997).

RELEVANT ILLINOIS SUPREME COURT RULES

Illinois Supreme Court Rule 402. Pleas of Guilty or Stipulations Sufficient to Convict

In hearings on pleas of guilty, or in any case in which the defense offers to stipulate that the evidence is sufficient to convict, there must be substantial compliance with the following:

(a) Admonitions to Defendant. The court shall not accept a plea of guilty or a stipulation that the evidence is sufficient to convict without first, by addressing the defendant personally in open court, informing him of and determining that he understands the following:

(1) the nature of the charge;

(2) the minimum and maximum sentence prescribed by law, including, when applicable, the penalty to which the defendant may be subjected because of prior convictions or consecutive sentences;

(3) that the defendant has the right to plead not guilty, or to persist in that plea if it has already been made, or to plead guilty; and

(4) that if he pleads guilty there will not be a trial of any kind, so that by pleading guilty he waives the right to a trial by jury and the right to be confronted with the witnesses against him; or that by stipulating the evidence is sufficient to convict, he waives the right to a trial by jury and the right to be confronted with any witnesses against him who have not testified.

(b) Determining Whether the Plea Is Voluntary. The court shall not accept a plea of guilty without first determining that the plea is voluntary. If the tendered plea is the result of a plea agreement, the agreement shall be stated in open court. The court, by questioning the defendant personally in open court, shall confirm the terms of the plea agreement, or that there is no agreement, and shall determine whether any force or threats or any promises, apart from a plea agreement, were used to obtain the plea.

(c) Determining Factual Basis for Plea. The court shall not enter final judgment on a plea of guilty without first determining that there is a factual basis for the plea.

(d) Plea Discussions and Agreements. When there is a plea discussion or plea agreement, the following provisions, in addition to the preceding paragraphs of this rule, shall apply:

(1) The trial judge shall not initiate plea discussions.

(2) If a tentative plea agreement has been reached by the parties which contemplates entry of a plea of guilty in the expectation that a specified sentence will be imposed or that other charges before the court will be dismissed, the trial judge may permit, upon request of the parties, the disclosure to him of the tentative agreement and the reasons therefor in advance of the tender of the plea. At the same time he may also receive, with the consent of the defendant, evidence in aggravation or mitigation. The judge may then indicate to the parties whether he will concur in the proposed disposition; and if he has not yet received evidence in aggravation or mitigation, he may indicate that his concurrence is conditional on that evidence being consistent with the representations made to him. If he has indicated his concurrence or conditional concurrence, he shall so state in open court at the time the agreement is stated as required by paragraph (b) of this rule. If the defendant thereupon pleads guilty, but the trial judge later withdraws his concurrence or conditional concurrence, he shall so advise the parties and then call upon the defendant either to affirm or to withdraw his plea of guilty. If the defendant thereupon withdraws his plea, the trial judge shall recuse himself.

(3) If the parties have not sought or the trial judge has declined to give his concurrence or conditional concurrence to a plea agreement, he shall inform the defendant in open court at the time the agreement is stated as required by paragraph (b) of this rule that the court is not bound by the plea agreement, and that if the defendant persists in his plea the disposition may be different from that contemplated by the plea agreement.

(e) Transcript. In cases in which the defendant is charged with a crime punishable by imprisonment in the penitentiary, the proceedings required by this rule to be in open court shall be taken verbatim, and upon order of the trial court transcribed, filed, and made a part of the common law record.

(f) Plea Discussions, Plea Agreements, Pleas of Guilty Inadmissible Under Certain Circumstances. If a plea discussion does not result in a plea of guilty, or if a plea of guilty is not accepted or is withdrawn, or if judgment on a plea of guilty is reversed on direct or collateral review, neither the plea discussion nor any resulting agreement, plea, or judgment shall be admissible against the defendant in any criminal proceeding.

Adopted June 26, 1970, effective September 1, 1970; amended effective September 17, 1970; amended January 5, 1981, effective February 1, 1981; amended May 20, 1997, effective July 1, 1997.

Committee Comments

(Revised May 1997)

The procedure on pleas of guilty was previously dealt with briefly in former Rule 401, paragraph (b). More extended and specific treatment of this subject is now required for at least two reasons. For one, the Supreme Court of the United States has recently held that it is a violation of due process to accept a guilty plea in State criminal proceedings without an affirmative showing, placed on the record, that the defendant voluntarily and understandingly entered his plea of guilty. (*Boykin v. Alabama* (1969), 395 U.S. 238.) For another, increased attention has recently been given to the long-standing practice of pleading guilty as a consequence of a prior agreement between the prosecution and defense concerning the disposition of the case; it is generally conceded that "plea discussions" and "plea agreements" are often appropriate, but that such procedures should not be concealed behind an in-court ceremony at which the defendant sometimes seems to think that he is expected to state falsely that no promises were made to him. (See American Bar Association Project on Minimum Standards for Criminal Justice, Standards Relating to Pleas of Guilty (Approved Draft 1968); Enker, *Perspectives on Plea Bargaining*, in The President's Commission on Law Enforcement and Administration of Justice, Task Force Report (1967): The Courts.) Two major objectives of new Rule 402 are: (1) to insure compliance with the *Boykin* requirements; and (2) to give visibility to the plea-agreement process and thus provide the reviewing court with a record containing an accurate and complete account of all relevant circumstances surrounding the guilty plea. *See* United States v. Jackson (7th Cir. 1968), 390 F.2d 130.

Paragraph (a) sets forth the admonitions which must be given to the defendant to insure that his guilty plea is intelligently and understandingly made, as required by *Boykin*. Subparagraph (1) requires that the defendant be informed of the nature of the charge, as now also required by section 113-1 of the Code of Criminal Procedure of 1963. Subparagraph (2) requires that the defendant also be informed of the minimum and maximum sentences prescribed by law; this deviation from section 113-4(c) of the Code, which only expressly requires explanation of the "maximum penalty provided by law," is based upon the assumption that notice of both the minimum and maximum will give the defendant a more realistic picture of what might happen to him. (See ABA Standards Relating to Pleas of Guilty 28 (Approved Draft 1968).) Subparagraphs (3) and (4) cover the requirements enumerated in *Boykin*, namely, that the record on a guilty plea affirmatively show a waiver of "three important federal rights": the privilege against self-incrimination; the right to trial by jury; and the right to confront one's accusers.

The 1997 amendment was added to require that admonitions be given in cases in which the defense offers to stipulate to the sufficiency of the evidence to convict. See *People v. Horton*, 143 Ill. 2d 11 (1991).

Paragraph (b) requires a determination that the guilty plea is voluntary by inquiry of the defendant as to whether any force or threats or promises were made to him. This is now accepted practice, see, *e.g., People v. Darrah* (1965), 33 Ill. 2d 175, 210 N.E.2d 478, although not expressly required by Code section 113-4. In contrast to current practice, paragraph (b) also requires that if the tendered plea is the result of a plea agreement, then the agreement must be stated in open court. It is important to give visibility to the plea-agreement process in this way, as otherwise the defendant may feel required to state falsely that no promises were made and the plea may later be subject to collateral attack.

Paragraph (c) requires that the court determine there is a factual basis for the plea. Such inquiry is not uncommon in current practice, but heretofore has not been specifically required by law. The language of paragraph (c) is based upon the recent revision of Rule 11 of the Federal Rules of Criminal Procedure, and, as is true under the Federal rule, no particular kind of inquiry is specified; the court may satisfy itself by inquiry of the defendant or the attorney for the government, by examination of the presentence report, or by any other means which seem best for the kind of case involved. For a statement of the value of such a procedure, see ABA Standards Relating to Pleas of Guilty 30-34 (Approved Draft 1968).

Underlying paragraph (d), concerning plea discussions and plea agreements, is the notion that it is sometimes permissible for a defendant to plead guilty pursuant to a prior agreement that the prosecution will obtain, seek, or not oppose a certain disposition. For one assessment of various reasons upon which such practices may be legitimately based, see ABA Standards Relating to Pleas of Guilty 36-52 (Approved Draft 1968).

Subparagraph (1) of paragraph (d) prohibits the trial judge from initiating plea discussions. Under subparagraph (d)(2), the judge, if he considers it appropriate, may be advised, in advance of the plea, of the tentative plea agreement and indicate his conditional concurrence or (if, with consent of the defendant, he then receives evidence in aggravation or mitigation) concurrence. Such concurrence or conditional concurrence is to be stated for the record when the plea is received, but if the judge later determines before sentencing that a more severe disposition is called for he must so advise the defendant and give him an opportunity to withdraw the plea. If the defendant does withdraw his plea under these circumstances, it would be inappropriate for the same judge to be involved in the trial of the case, so he is required to recuse himself. If, however, the defendant elects not to withdraw his plea, the judge is not required to recuse himself. Under subparagraph (3), where there is a plea agreement but no concurrence or conditional concurrence by the judge (either because the parties have not sought it or the judge has declined to give it), the judge is required to advise the defendant that he is not bound by the agreement stated in court at the time of the plea. This caution will remove any possibility of an inference by the defendant that the judge's awareness of the agreement indicates concurrence in it. See *People v. Baldridge* (1960), 19 Ill. 2d 616, 169 N.E.2d 353.

Paragraph (e) is derived from former Rule 401. It was amended in 1981 to leave within the court's discretion the question of whether the proceedings shall be transcribed. The requirement that they shall be taken verbatim remains.

Paragraph (f) adopts the prevailing view that once a guilty plea has been annulled by withdrawal or other means, it should not be subsequently admissible against the defendant in criminal proceedings. (See *People v. Haycraft* (1966), 76 Ill. App. 2d 149, 221 N.E.2d 317.) It follows that a plea discussion which has not resulted in a still-effective guilty plea should likewise be inadmissible, for otherwise defendants could engage in plea discussions only at their peril.

Relevant Statutory Authority

Plea: 725 ILCS 5/113-4

§ 113-4. Plea. (a) When called upon to plead at arraignment the defendant shall be furnished with a copy of the charge and shall plead guilty, guilty but mentally ill, or not guilty.

(b) If the defendant stands mute a plea of not guilty shall be entered for him and the trial shall proceed on such plea.

(c) If the defendant pleads guilty such plea shall not be accepted until the court shall have fully explained to the defendant the consequences of such plea and the maximum penalty provided by law for the offense which may be imposed by the court. After such explanation if the defendant understandingly persists in his plea it shall be accepted by the court and recorded.

(d) If the defendant pleads guilty but mentally ill, the court shall not accept such a plea until the defendant has undergone examination by a clinical psychologist or psychiatrist and the judge has examined the psychiatric or psychological report or reports, held a hearing on the issue of the defendant's mental condition and is satisfied that there is a factual basis that the defendant was mentally ill at the time of the offense to which the plea is entered.

(e) If a defendant pleads not guilty, the court shall advise him at that time or at any later court date on which he is present that if he escapes from custody or is released on bond and fails to appear in court when required by the court that his failure to appear would constitute a waiver of his right to confront the witnesses against him and trial could proceed in his absence.

Effective September 17, 1981.

Prior Illinois Case Law

1. Pursuant to the Sixth Amendment of the United States Constitution, a Criminal Defendant Has the Right to Present a Defense by Calling Witnesses on His or Her Behalf

Washington v. Texas, 388 U.S. 14 (1967)

Defendant has a constitutional right to call witnesses and to present a defense at his or her trial pursuant to the sixth amendment of the United States Constitution as incorporated in the due process clause of the fourteenth amendment. The United States Supreme Court explained that

> [t]he right to offer the testimony of witnesses, and to compel their attendance, if necessary, is in plain terms the right to present a defense, the right to present the defendant's version of the facts as well as the prosecution's to the jury so it may decide where the truth lies. Just as an accused has the right to confront the prosecution's witnesses for the purpose of challenging their testimony, he has the right to present his own witnesses to establish a defense. This right is a fundamental element of due process of law.

The United States Supreme Court held that a violation of the right to present witnesses occurs when a witness is not permitted to testify and the defendant demonstrates that

> a. the witness is "physically and mentally capable of testifying to events that he had personally observed";
> b. the witness' testimony is relevant; and
> c. the witness' testimony is material to defense;

The Supreme Court noted in a footnote that "[n]othing in this opinion should be construed as disapproving testimonial privileges, such as the privilege against self-incrimination," indicating that a witness who invokes the constitutional protection against self-incrimination enjoys a superior right not to testify.

2. Defendant Has the Right to Present His or Her Version of the Facts to Establish a Defense

People v. Manion, 67 Ill. 2d 564 (1977)

Defendant was convicted of armed robbery of a store. Several witnesses identified him as the perpetrator after they saw a man in dark pants and a brown shirt running away from the store. An assistant manager of the store testified at trial that a cashier at the store told him she had been robbed. He then ran out of the store after the robber. The manager saw a man running away who was wearing a brown shirt and dark pants and was unshaven. While chasing the man, the manager described that he saw him turn back and point a gun at him, then "duck[]" near a car and reemerge shortly thereafter. The manager then alerted police officers who were in the area, who continued the chase until they caught the man. The manager found a brown shirt near the car where the man had "ducked." Defendant was arrested wearing a white shirt and dark pants. An assistant manager's trainee testified that he chased the man who was wearing a brown shirt, dark pants and a blue and white baseball cap, and stated that he lost sight of the man for "only three to four seconds during the chase," after which he saw the man wearing a white shirt and dark pants. Defendant, a Chicago police officer suspended for not living in the city, testified that he wore a white shirt and dark pants on the day of the incident. He said he went to the store with his five children. Defendant stated that he bought some items at the store and left. Once in the parking lot, he decided to go back to the store to pick up one more item. As he was getting out of the car, defendant heard a commotion and saw two men chasing a third man out of the store. Defendant retrieved his gun because he thought the man was a shoplifter and started pursuing him. He said the man was running toward a grocery store nearby. Defendant said that he picked up a brown shirt that he found on the ground and waved it to attract the attention of the police officers nearby. He was eventually prevented from chasing after the man when the police stopped him. He told them that they had the "wrong man." The trial court prevented defendant from explaining how he had acted in other situations while he was off-duty and when "immediate action" was required. He was, however, permitted to testify about his actions during the charged incident and was therefore able to explain that he was acting pursuant to a requirement of an off-duty police officer to act when witnessing a crime. Defendant contended on appeal that the trial court's exclusion of some of his testimony violated his right to present a defense and warranted reversal. The Illinois Supreme Court disagreed, noting that

> [w]ithout question, as the defendant states, an accused has "the right to present a defense, the right to present the defendant's version of the facts as well as the prosecution's to the jury so it may decide where the truth lies." Washington v. Texas, 388 U.S. 14, 19 (1967). In addition, it is clear that, consistent with the right to present a defense, there is the right of an accused to show, by competent evidence, facts which tend to prove that he did not flee from the scene of the crime from a consciousness of guilt. People v. Autman, 393 Ill. 262 (1946).
>
> ***
>
> Here, however, defendant was not denied an opportunity to present crucial matters explaining his actions. The exclusion of testimony as to defendant's prior off-duty arrests did not prevent him from furnishing an explanation for his apparent flight through the parking lot with a gun in his hand subsequent to the robbery. Rather, defendant was allowed to testify that he was chasing a man he believed to be a shoplifter when he himself was arrested. And he was allowed to assert that he was an 18-year veteran of the Chicago Police Department and that the department's policy is that an officer is on duty 24 hours a day and is expected to take immediate action if he is a witness to a crime. Such testimony sufficiently allowed the jury to infer that the accused was acting pursuant to that policy, at the scene of the crime, even though he was suspended, and that he was doing so with an innocent state of mind.

3. Defendant Has a Due Process Right to the Disclosure of Evidence That Is Favorable to the Defense and Material to the Determination of Defendant's Guilt
Smith v. Cain, 132 S. Ct. 627 (2012)

Defendant was convicted of first degree murder for the shooting death of five people based on claims by a single eyewitness that he was the perpetrator. No other evidence linked defendant to the crime. Evidence showed that three armed individuals broke into the victims' house and started shooting, killing five. Defendant sought post-conviction relief and requested police files from investigation pertaining to his case. The files revealed that the eyewitness told an investigating officer on the night of the murders that he "couldn't see faces" of the perpetrators and would not be able to make an identification if he saw them. Defendant requested that his conviction be vacated because prosecution's failure to disclose the investigating officer's notes constituted a *Brady* violation. Under Brady v. Maryland, 373 U.S. 83 (1963), "the State violates a defendant's right to due process if it withholds evidence that is favorable to the defense and material to the defendant's guilt or punishment." The state argued that it did not commit a *Brady* violation because the eyewitness' statements were not material to the determination of defendant's guilt. The United Supreme Court explained that evidence is considered "material" under *Brady*

> when there is a reasonable probability that, that, had the evidence been disclosed, the result of the proceeding would have been different. [citation omitted]. A reasonable probability does not mean that the defendant 'would more likely than not have received a different verdict with the evidence,' only that the likelihood of a different result is great enough to 'undermine[] confidence in the outcome of the trial.' [citation omitted].
>
> ***
>
> We have observed that evidence impeaching an eyewitness may not be material if the State's other evidence is strong enough to sustain confidence in the verdict. *See* United States v. Agurs, 427 U.S. 97, 112-113, and n. 21 (1976). That is not the case here. [The eyewitness'] testimony was the only evidence linking [defendant] to the crime. And [the eyewitness'] undisclosed statements directly contradict his testimony: [the eyewitness] told the jury that he had "[n]o doubt" that [defendant] was the gunman he stood "face to face" with on the night of the crime, but [the investigative officer's] notes show [the eyewitness] saying that he "could not ID anyone because [he] couldn't see faces" and "would not know them if [he] saw them." [citation omitted]. [The eyewitness'] undisclosed statements were plainly material.

4. Defendant's Right to Call Witnesses May Be Conditioned on Compliance with Discovery Obligations

Taylor v. Illinois, 484 U.S. 400 (1988)

A defendant's right to call witnesses and to present a defense at his or her trial is a fundamental right, but it is not absolute. The United States Supreme Court has held that the right to present a witness may be conditioned on his or her compliance with discovery obligations. The Supreme Court explained that

> [t]he principle that undergirds the defendant's right to present exculpatory evidence is also the source of essential limitations on the right. The adversary process could not function effectively without adherence to rules of procedure that govern the orderly presentation of facts and arguments to provide each party with a fair opportunity to assemble and submit evidence to contradict or explain the opponent's case. The trial process would be a shambles if either party had an absolute right to control the time and content of his witnesses' testimony. Neither may insist on the right to interrupt the opposing party's case, and obviously there is no absolute right to interrupt the deliberations of the jury to present newly discovered evidence. The State's interest in the orderly conduct of a criminal trial is sufficient to justify the imposition and enforcement of firm, though not always inflexible, rules relating to the identification and presentation of evidence.
>
> The defendant's right to compulsory process is itself designed to vindicate the principle that the 'ends of criminal justice would be defeated if judgments were to be founded on a partial or speculative presentation of the facts.' [Citation omitted]. Rules that provide for pretrial

> discovery of an opponent's witnesses serve the same high purpose. Discovery, like cross examination, minimizes the risk that a judgment will be predicated on incomplete, misleading, or even deliberately fabricated testimony. The 'State's interest in protecting itself against an eleventh-hour defense' is merely one component of the broader public interest in a full and truthful disclosure of critical facts.

5. Exclusion of Evidence That a Third Party Committed the Offense with Which Defendant Is Charged May Deny Defendant a Meaningful Opportunity to Present a Defense

Holmes v. South Carolina, 547 U.S. 319 (2006)

A jury convicted the defendant of murder, first degree criminal sexual conduct, first degree burglary, and robbery. He was sentenced to death. On post-conviction he was granted a new trial. At his second trial, the prosecution relied heavily on several items of forensic evidence, including a palm print, fibers, fluids, and DNA that matched the defendant's and was found at the victim's house. At trial, the defendant suggested that the forensic evidence had been contaminated and that police officers had attempted to frame him. An expert testified for the defense, criticizing the procedures used by the police in handling the fiber and DNA evidence. Another defense witness supported his claim that the palm print had been planted by the police. The defendant sought to introduce evidence that another person was responsible for the attack. At a pretrial hearing, the defense presented several witnesses, one placing the other individual in the victim's neighborhood on the morning of the crime. Two witnesses testified that that person had made incriminating statements regarding the commission of the crime. That same person testified at the hearing but he denied making the incriminating statements and provided an alibi. Another witness refuted the alibi. The trial court excluded the evidence, reasoning that such evidence is admissible if it "raise[s] a reasonable inference or presumption as to [the defendant's] own innocence" but is not admissible if it merely "cast[s] a bare suspicion upon another" or "raise[s] a conjectural inference as to the commission of the crime by another." The South Carolina Supreme Court affirmed the trial court's ruling, reasoning that the defendant could not overcome the strong forensic evidence against him to raise a reasonable inference as to his innocence.

On appeal to the United States Supreme Court, the defendant argued that the exclusion of the evidence violated his sixth amendment right to have a meaningful opportunity to present a defense. The Supreme Court agreed that the exclusion of third-party guilt evidence denied the defendant a fair trial. The Supreme Court acknowledged that nearly every state, including Illinois, has a rule of evidence that an accused may introduce evidence of the guilt of another, but that such evidence may be excluded where it does not sufficiently connect the other person to the crime. Under those circumstances the evidence is "speculative or remote, or does not tend to prove or disprove a material fact at issue at the defendant's trial." The Supreme Court noted that in the present case, the South Carolina Supreme Court had excluded the evidence because there was "strong evidence" of the defendant's guilt and particularly strong forensic evidence which the defendant's proffered evidence could not overcome. The United States Supreme Court rejected the South Carolina Supreme Court's analysis because it

> applied the rule that "where there is strong evidence of [a defendant's] guilt, especially where there is strong forensic evidence, the proffered evidence about a third party's alleged guilt" may (or perhaps must) be excluded. [citation omitted]. Under this rule, the trial judge does not focus on the probative value or the potential adverse effects of admitting the defense evidence of third-party guilt. Instead, the critical inquiry concerns the strength of the prosecution's case: If the prosecution's case is strong enough, the evidence of third-party guilt is excluded even if

> that evidence, if viewed independently, would have great probative value and even if it would not pose an undue risk of harassment, prejudice, or confusion of the issues.
>
> Furthermore, as applied in this case, the South Carolina Supreme Court's rule seems to call for little, if any, examination of the credibility of the prosecution's witnesses or the reliability of its evidence. Here, for example, the defense strenuously claimed that the prosecution's forensic evidence was so unreliable (due to mishandling and a deliberate plot to frame petitioner) that the evidence should not have even been admitted. The South Carolina Supreme Court responded that these challenges did not entirely "eviscerate" the forensic evidence and that the defense challenges went to the weight and not to the admissibility of that evidence. [citation omitted] Yet, in evaluating the prosecution's forensic evidence and deeming it to be "strong"—and thereby justifying exclusion of petitioner's third-party guilt evidence—the South Carolina Supreme Court made no mention of the defense challenges to the prosecution's evidence.
>
> Just because the prosecution's evidence, if credited, would provide strong support for a guilty verdict, it does not follow that evidence of third-party guilt has only a weak logical connection to the central issues in the case. And where the credibility of the prosecution's witnesses or the reliability of its evidence is not conceded, the strength of the prosecution's case cannot be assessed without making the sort of factual findings that have traditionally been reserved for the trier of fact and that the South Carolina courts did not purport to make in this case.

The Supreme Court reversed the South Carolina ruling because the rule pronounced by the South Carolina Supreme Court was arbitrary. The Supreme Court stated that

> [t]he rule applied in this case is no more logical than its converse would be, i.e., a rule barring the prosecution from introducing evidence of a defendant's guilt if the defendant is able to proffer, at a pretrial hearing, evidence that, if believed, strongly supports a verdict of not guilty. In the present case, for example, the petitioner proffered evidence that, if believed, squarely proved that [another person], not petitioner, was the perpetrator. It would make no sense, however, to hold that this proffer precluded the prosecution from introducing its evidence, including the forensic evidence that, if credited, provided strong proof of the petitioner's guilt.
>
> The point is that, by evaluating the strength of only one party's evidence, no logical conclusion can be reached regarding the strength of contrary evidence offered by the other side to rebut or cast doubt. Because the rule applied by the State Supreme Court in this case did not heed this point, the rule is "arbitrary" in the sense that it does not rationally serve the end that the *Gregory* rule and other similar third-party guilt rules were designed to further. Nor has the State identified any other legitimate end that the rule serves. It follows that the rule applied in this case by the State Supreme Court violates a criminal defendant's right to have a meaningful opportunity to present a complete defense. Crane v. Kentucky, 106 S. Ct. 2142 (1986), (quoting California v. Trombetta, 467 U.S. 479 (1984)).

The Supreme Court explained that although

> "[s]tate and federal rulemakers have broad latitude under the Constitution to establish rules excluding evidence from criminal trials[,]" (United States v. Scheffer, 523 U.S. 303, 308 (1998); *see also* Crane v. Kentucky, 476 U.S. 683, 689-690 (1986); Marshall v. Lonberger, 459 U.S. 422, 438, n. 6 (1983); Chambers v. Mississippi, 410 U.S. 284, 302-303 (1973); Spencer v. Texas, 385 U.S. 554, 564 (1967)), [t]his latitude [. . .] has limits. "Whether rooted directly in the Due Process Clause of the Fourteenth Amendment or in the Compulsory Process or Confrontation Clauses of the Sixth Amendment, the Constitution guarantees criminal defendants 'a meaningful opportunity to present a complete defense.' " [citation omitted] This right is abridged by evidence rules that "infring[e] upon a weighty interest of the accused" and

are " 'arbitrary' or 'disproportionate to the purposes they are designed to serve.' " [citation omitted].

6. Third Person's Confession to the Charged Crime May Be Admissible as Statement Against Penal Interest If It Bears Substantial Assurance of Trustworthiness

Chambers v. Mississippi, 410 U.S. 284 (1973)

Defendant was charged with the murder of a police officer. Police officers were attempting to arrest someone at a bar but a crowd gathered and prevented them from effecting the arrest. The situation got out of hand and several shots were fired. One officer was shot in the back several times. Before he died he turned around and fired several shots, some of which were not aimed but a few that were specifically aimed at and hit defendant. Another individual later confessed to shooting the officer but recanted his confession one month later. Defendant sought to call the third party to testify, requested to introduce the third party's confession at trial, and petitioned the trial court to allow him to call witnesses to whom the third person confessed, but the trial court prevented him from doing so, applying state rules of evidence that exclude hearsay statements. The United States Supreme Court noted that the hearsay statements should have been admitted in evidence, reasoning that

> [t]he hearsay statements involved in this case were originally made and subsequently offered at trial under circumstances that provided considerable assurance of their reliability. First, each of [the third person's] confessions was *made spontaneously to a close acquaintance shortly after the murder had occurred.* [emphasis added]. Second, each one was *corroborated by some other evidence* in the case—[his] sworn confession, the testimony of an eyewitness to the shooting, the testimony that [he] was seen with a gun immediately after the shooting, and proof of his prior ownership of a .22-caliber revolver and subsequent purchase of a new weapon. [emphasis added]. The sheer number of independent confessions provided additional corroboration for each. Third, whatever may be the parameters of the penal-interest rationale, each confession here was in a very real sense *self-incriminatory and unquestionably against interest. See* United States v. Harris, 403 U.S. 573, 584 (1971); Dutton v. Evans, 400 U.S., 74, 89 (1970). [emphasis added]. [The third party] stood to benefit nothing by disclosing his role in the shooting to any of his three friends and he must have been aware of the possibility that disclosure would lead to criminal prosecution. Indeed, after telling [a friend] of his involvement, he subsequently urged [the friend] not to 'mess him up.' Finally, if there was any question about the truthfulness of the extrajudicial statements, [the third party] was present in the courtroom and was under oath. He *could have been cross-examined* by the State, and his demeanor and responses weighed by the jury. See California v. Green, 399 U.S. 149 (1970). [emphasis added].
>
> ***
>
> Few rights are more fundamental than that of an accused to present witnesses in his own defense. [citations omitted]. In the exercise of this right, the accused, as is required of the State, must comply with established rules of procedure and evidence designed to assure both fairness and reliability in the ascertainment of guilt and innocence. Although perhaps no rule of evidence has been more respected or more frequently applied in jury trials than that applicable to the exclusion of hearsay, exceptions tailored to allow the introduction of evidence which in fact is likely to be trustworthy have long existed. The testimony rejected by the trial court here bore persuasive assurances of trustworthiness and thus was well within the basic rationale of the exception for declarations against interest. That testimony also was critical to [the defendant's] defense. In these circumstances, where constitutional rights directly affecting the ascertainment of guilt are implicated, the hearsay rule may not be applied mechanistically to defeat the ends of justice.

> We conclude that the exclusion of this critical evidence, coupled with the State's refusal to permit [defendant] to cross-examine [the third person], denied him a trial in accord with traditional and fundamental standards of due process.

7. *Chambers* Factors Are to Be Considered for Indicia of Trustworthiness of a Statement and Not as Conditions of Admissibility

People v. Bowel, 111 Ill. 2d 58 (1986)

Defendant was convicted of theft and robbery. Defendant and three other men were standing on a street corner when two women walked down the street. One of the men ran up behind one of the women, took her purse and ran away. Defendant claimed that he was not the person who took the woman's purse and that another man in his party committed the crime. He sought to introduce this man's incriminating statement overheard by a third party as a statement against penal interest.

There was some disagreement among the parties as to whether all of the four indicia of reliability enumerated in Chambers v. Mississippi, 410 U.S. 284 (1973), are necessary before a statement may be admitted as an exception to the hearsay rule. The Supreme Court in *Chambers*

> stated that there were sufficient indicia of trustworthiness in that (1) the statement was made spontaneously to a close acquaintance shortly after the crime occurred; (2) the statement was corroborated by other evidence; (3) the statement was self-incriminating and against the declarant's interest; and (4) there was adequate opportunity for cross-examination of the declarant.

The Illinois Supreme Court observed that

> The four factors [. . .] are to be regarded simply as indicia of trustworthiness and not as requirements of admissibility. The question to be considered in judging the admissibility of a declaration of this character is whether the declaration was made under circumstances that provide "considerable assurance" of its reliability by objective indicia of trustworthiness. Chambers v. Mississippi, 410 U.S. 284, 300-01 (1973); People v. Tate, 87 Ill. 2d 134, 144 (1981).

The Supreme Court found that the statement was properly excluded by the trial court because it lacked indicia of reliability as it was unclear what portion of the alleged conversation the third party heard or how far he was from the declarant. The Supreme Court noted that the declarant was not available to testify and the state could therefore not cross-examine him.

8. Exclusion of a Reliable Confession Inculpating Declarant and Exculpating Defendant Is Prejudicial Error

People v. Tenney, 205 Ill. 2d 411 (2002)

The Illinois Supreme Court reversed and remanded a capital murder conviction because the trial judge improperly excluded a statement against penal interest that was offered by the defense. The defendant was tried on one count of knowing murder and one count of felony murder based on residential burglary. The defendant's theory of the case was that four other individuals committed the crime. One of these individuals was previously charged, tried, and convicted of the murder. On the state's attorney's motion, however, his conviction was vacated when the defendant was charged with the murder. Defendant presented most of the evidence the state had used against the third person at his trial, including his admission to a jail inmate, a stranger, that he had shot the victim in the head. The jail inmate gave similar testimony for the defendant. The defendant also offered a transcript of the testimony of another state's witness in the third party's trial who was not available to testify in this case. The trial judge excluded the evidence in which the third person inculpated himself and exculpated the defendant. The trial judge was persuaded that the defense, with the cooperation of the state's attorney, diligently and in good faith attempted to find the third person and the other missing witness but without success.

The Illinois Supreme Court found the exclusion to be reversible error under the guidelines of Chambers v. Mississippi, 410 U.S. 284 (1973). *Chambers* identified four factors to help determine the reliability of a hearsay statement:

> (1) the statement was spontaneously made to a close acquaintance shortly after the crime occurred; (2) the statement is corroborated by some other evidence; (3) the statement is self-incriminating and against the declarant's interest; and (4) there was adequate opportunity for cross-examination of the declarant. The *Chambers* factors are merely guidelines to admissibility rather than hard and fast requirements; the presence of all four factors is not a condition of admissibility. Rather, the question to be considered in deciding the admissibility of such an extrajudicial statement is whether it was made under circumstances which provide 'considerable assurance' of its reliability by objective indicia of trustworthiness.

The Supreme Court analyzed these factors in the order of their significance in this trial. It first concluded that the third party's statement satisfied the third factor because "his statement was self-incriminating and against his penal interest." The second factor was also satisfied because the state's independent evidence corroborated the statement. The independent evidence at defendant's trial showed that the victim's house was burglarized and property was removed from it; the victim was alone; and the victim was shot. Moreover, the declarant's prior testimony was under oath and was subjected to cross-examination. The first *Chambers* factor, however, was not satisfied because the third party made his statement nine months after the murder. Nor was the fourth *Chambers* factor satisfied since the third party did not testify at his own trial, and he was not available at the defendant's trial for cross-examination. Nonetheless, since the prosecution used the third party's out-of-court statement against him at his own trial via the same witness, and obtained a conviction against him, it was contradictory for the prosecution to now oppose the statement as unreliable. The Supreme Court concluded that based on the totality of circumstances, the exclusion of the third person's confession denied defendant a fair trial.

9. Declarant Who Asserts Fifth Amendment Right Not to Testify Is Unavailable for Purposes of Statement Against Interest Exception to the Hearsay Rule
People v. Caffey, 205 Ill. 2d 52 (2001)

Defendant was convicted of first degree murder and aggravated kidnapping in the killing of a pregnant woman and two of her children. The woman was shot and stabbed in her home and her nine month old fetus was cut out of her uterus. Her minor daughter was killed in the home and her minor son was taken and killed later when he indicated he could recognize the perpetrators. A woman who was charged with obstruction of justice with respect to these crimes refused to testify on defendant's behalf at trial and invoked the fifth amendment. The woman had previously given statements to the police that defendant's girlfriend came to her home on the night of the murders and said that she had just given birth to defendant's baby. The witness helped bandage the baby and drove the girlfriend home. When they arrived defendant was home. The witness then told him that his girlfriend went into labor at her home and that she drove her to the hospital. The witness also stated that she took the girlfriend home after she gave birth because she did not have health insurance. The witness alleged that defendant's girlfriend gave her a bloody jacket which she then gave to defendant as a "Daddy's Day present." The bloody jacket was taken from the victim's residence earlier that night. Defendant sought the admissibility of these statements under the statement against interest exception to the hearsay rule. The Illinois Supreme Court noted that

> [g]enerally, an unsworn extrajudicial declaration that the declarant committed the crime, and not the defendant on trial, is inadmissible hearsay, even though the declaration is against the declarant's penal interest. People v. Bowel, 111 Ill. 2d 58, 66 (1986). However, where constitutional rights that directly affect the ascertainment of guilt are implicated, the hearsay rule may not be mechanically applied to defeat the ends of justice. Therefore, where hearsay testimony bears persuasive assurances of trustworthiness and is critical to the accused's defense, its exclusion deprives the defendant of a fair trial in accord with due process. People v. Thomas, 171 Ill. 2d 207, 215-16 (1996), citing Chambers v. Mississippi, 410 U.S. 284, 302 (1973). Such testimony may be admissible under the statement-against-penal-interest exception to the hearsay rule. *Bowel*, 111 Ill. 2d at 66. *Chambers* established four factors to help determine the reliability of a hearsay statement: (1) the statement was spontaneously made to a close acquaintance shortly after the crime occurred; (2) the statement is corroborated by other evidence; (3) the statement is self-incriminating and against the declarant's interests; and (4) there was adequate opportunity for cross-examination of the declarant. *Chambers*, 410 U.S. at 300-01. The presence of all four factors is not a condition of admissibility. Rather, the question to be considered in deciding the admissibility of such an extrajudicial statement is whether it was made under circumstances which provide considerable assurance of its reliability by objective indicia of trustworthiness. *Thomas*, 171 Ill. 2d at 216.

The Supreme Court observed that the witness' statements here were not spontaneous and were not made to a close acquaintance. Instead, the statements were made some time after the crime to police officers conducting an investigation into the murders. The Supreme Court also noted that the witness did not confess to the same crimes as those with which defendant was charged, but rather implicated defendant's girlfriend in the crimes connected to those defendant allegedly committed. Although the Supreme Court found that certain evidence corroborated the witness' statements, it concluded that the statements were not against the witness' interest. The Supreme Court invoked Federal Rule of Evidence 804(a) and noted that the witness was unavailable for purposes of cross-examination because she invoked the fifth amendment at trial. The Supreme Court explained that "[t]he exercise of privilege to avoid testifying, as in the case before us, is a classic example of a witness being available in person but not [the witness'] testimony." The Supreme Court rejected defendant's argument that the witness was available for cross-examination because state could have granted her immunity. The Supreme Court determined that defendant does not have the right to force the state to offer immunity to a witness who has invoked the fifth amendment. The court concluded that the witness' statements were properly excluded for lack of reliability because defendant failed to establish three out of the four *Chambers* factors.

10. Evidence That a Third Party Committed the Crime Is Admissible If It Tends to Make the Question of Guilt More or Less Probable and Where Such Evidence Is Not Speculative

People v. Lewis, 165 Ill. 2d 305 (1995)

The trial court precluded evidence of police investigation of another suspect in the robbery and murder of the victim. Defendant argued that exclusion of the evidence denied him a fair trial as the other suspect's appearance matched the description of the offender. The trial court rejected the evidence, noting that it was not reliable. The Illinois Supreme Court agreed with the trial court, noting:

> Certainly, "[a]n accused . . . may attempt to prove that someone else committed the crime with which he is charged [citation], but this right is not without limitations." People v. Ward, 101 Ill. 2d 443, 455 (1984). Generally, the test for admissibility of evidence is whether such evidence tends to prove the particular offense charged. People v. Peter, 55 Ill. 2d 443, 459 (1973). "[W]hether what is offered as evidence will be admitted or excluded depends upon whether it tends to make the question of guilt more or less probable." *Ward*, 101 Ill. 2d at 455. Where the offered evidence is uncertain or speculative, the trial court, in its discretion, may properly reject it. *Ward*, 101 Ill. 2d at 455-56, *see also* People v. Dukett, 56 Ill. 2d 432, 450 (1974).

Here, the Supreme Court found that nothing connected the other suspect to the crime, and that the evidence was purely speculative and thus properly excluded at trial.

11. Defendant Has a Constitutional Right to Testify on His or Her Behalf
Rock v. Arkansas, 483 U.S. 44 (1987)

Defendant was charged with manslaughter for the shooting death of her husband. She could not remember many details of the incident and submitted to hypnosis twice in hopes of refreshing her memory. During the hypnosis sessions the defendant could not remember any additional details other than those she had already provided to the police. After the hypnosis ended, however, she was able to recall that while fighting with her husband on the night of the shooting she was holding the gun but did not have her finger on the trigger and that the gun fired after her husband grabbed her arm. A gun expert evaluated the gun and determined that the gun was defective and could fire even without someone pulling the trigger. State subsequently filed a motion to exclude all hypnotically-induced testimony at trial and the trial court granted the motion pursuant to a state rule of evidence. The United States Supreme Court explained that

> [t]he right to testify on one's own behalf at a criminal trial has sources in several provisions of the Constitution. It is one of the rights that "are essential to due process of law in a fair adversary process." Faretta v. California, 422 U.S. 806, 819, n. 15 (1975). The necessary ingredients of the Fourteenth Amendment's guarantee that no one shall be deprived of liberty without due process of law include a right to be heard and to offer testimony:
>
>> "A person's right to reasonable notice of a charge against him, and *an opportunity to be heard in his defense*—a right to his day in court-are basic in our system of jurisprudence; and these rights include, as a minimum, a right to examine the witnesses against him, to offer testimony, and to be represented by counsel." (Emphasis added.) *In re* Oliver, 333 U.S. 257, 273 (1948).
>
> ***
>
> The right to testify is also found in the Compulsory Process Clause of the Sixth Amendment, which grants a defendant the right to call "witnesses in his favor," a right that is guaranteed in the criminal courts of the States by the Fourteenth Amendment. Washington v. Texas, 388 U.S. 14, 17-19 (1967). Logically included in the accused's right to call witnesses whose testimony is "material and favorable to his defense," United States v. Valenzuela-Bernal, 458 U.S. 858, 867 (1982), is a right to testify himself, should he decide it is in his favor to do so. In fact, the most important witness for the defense in many criminal cases is the defendant himself.
>
> ***
>
> The opportunity to testify is also a necessary corollary to the Fifth Amendment's guarantee against compelled testimony. In Harris v. New York, 401 U.S. 222, 230 (1971), the Court stated: "Every criminal defendant is privileged to testify in his own defense, or to refuse to do so." *Id.*, at 225.

The Supreme Court concluded that the *per se* state rule prohibiting defendant's hypnotically refreshed testimony arbitrarily excluded material portions of her testimony and was not justified in limiting the her constitutional right to testify.

12. Defendant Ultimately Has the Right to Decide Whether He or She Will Take the Stand Although Such Decision Can Be Made with Attorney's Advice
People v. Patrick, 233 Ill. 2d 62 (2009)

The Illinois Supreme Court considered a consolidated appeal by two defendants. The first defendant was on trial for first degree murder. During trial the defendant filed a motion *in limine* seeking to bar the state from presenting evidence of his prior convictions. Defendant had three prior convictions for possession of a controlled substance. The judge refused to rule on the motion prior to defendant's testimony. Defendant testified and the state impeached him with his prior convictions for possession of a controlled substance. Defendant raised a theory of self-defense and was convicted of second degree murder. The defendant argued on appeal that the trial court erred by refusing to rule on his motion until after he testified. The Illinois Supreme Court agreed and explained that

> [a] criminal defendant's right to testify on his own behalf, or not to testify at all, is rooted in the fifth, sixth, and fourteenth amendments of the United States Constitution. Rock v. Arkansas, 483 U.S. 44, 51-53 (1987). A defendant's decision whether to testify is an important tactical determination. Brooks v. Tennessee, 406 U.S. 605, 612 (1972). A defendant who chooses to testify faces serious risks of impeachment and may open the door to otherwise inadmissible evidence. *Brooks*, 406 U.S. at 609. The decision to testify ultimately belongs to the defendant but is generally made after consultation with counsel. People v. Medina, 221 Ill. 2d 394, 403 (2006). Making the important decision to testify without an opportunity to evaluate the actual strength of the State's evidence restricts the defense in planning its case. *Brooks*, 406 U.S. at 612.

Here, the defendant argued self-defense and the Supreme Court emphasized that it was important for him to know whether his prior convictions could be used for impeachment before he took the stand. Moreover, the prosecutor repeatedly argued that the jury should not believe "a three-time convicted felon." The Supreme Court held that, unless some compelling reason to delay the ruling exists, the trial court should rule on a defendant's motion to bar prior convictions before he or she testifies. The Supreme Court further explained that situations requiring the defendant to testify prior to the court making its decision would be exceedingly rare. The court found that the trial judge did not articulate any justification for delaying the ruling, and its decision was "arbitrary and without reason." The Supreme Court held that the trial court's failure to rule on the defendant's motion *in limine* on the admissibility of prior convictions, when it had sufficient information to make the ruling, constituted an abuse of discretion. The Supreme Court remanded for a new trial.

The second defendant was charged with attempted first degree murder, armed violence and aggravated battery. He sought to bar use of his four prior convictions, three of which were for armed violence, aggravated battery, and a controlled substance offense as impeachment evidence. The trial judge granted the defendant's motion *in limine* in part by excluding one of his four convictions but reserved ruling on the other three convictions that included armed violence, aggravated battery, and a controlled substance offense until defendant testified. Defendant chose not to testify at trial. The Supreme Court concluded that the defendant failed to preserve the issue of trial court's failure to consider his motion *in limine* because he did not testify at trial.

13. Although the Accused Has the Right to Choose to Testify or Not to Testify, Trial Court Is Not Required to Admonish Him or Her Regarding this Right

People v. Medina, 221 Ill. 2d 394 (2006)

The Illinois Supreme Court affirmed that a defendant's decision whether to testify or not to testify is a tactical decision that belongs to the accused. The Supreme Court explained that

> [a]lthough a criminal defendant has a constitutional right to testify in his own defense, this court has held that no procedures [similar to those required for waiver of jury trial and guilty pleas] require that the trial court admonish a defendant regarding his right to testify. People v. Smith, 176 Ill. 2d 217, 234-35 (1997). In so holding, this court cited, approvingly, the reasoning of United States v. Martinez, 883 F.2d 750, 760 (9th Cir. 1989), vacated on other grounds, 928 F.2d 1470 (9th Cir. 1991). In support of this court's conclusion that "the trial court is not required to advise a defendant of his right to testify, to inquire whether he knowingly and intelligently waived that right, or to set of record defendant's decision on this matter," this court quoted from *Martinez*, setting forth the seven reasons given in *Martinez* en route to the same result. *Smith*, 176 Ill. 2d at 235. As we find reasons three through seven pertinent to our present disposition, we too quote that portion of *Martinez*:
>
>> Third, by advising the defendant of his right to testify, the court could influence the defendant to waive his right not to testify, 'thus threatening the exercise of this other, converse, constitutionally explicit and more fragile right.' [Citation.] Fourth, a court so advising a defendant might improperly intrude on the attorney-client relation, protected by the Sixth Amendment. [Citation.] Fifth, there is danger that the judge's admonition would introduce error into the trial. [Citation.] Sixth, it is hard to say when the judge should appropriately advise the defendant—the judge does not know the defendant is not testifying until the defense rests, not an opportune moment to conduct a colloquy. [Citation.] Seventh, the judge should not interfere with defense strategy. [Citation.]" (Emphases in original.) *Martinez,* 883 F.2d at 760.

14. Defendant May Waive His or Her Right to Testify and Waiver Will Be Presumed If Defendant Fails to Testify or to Notify Trial Court of His or Her Desire to Testify

People v. Smith, 176 Ill. 2d 217 (1997)

Defendant was convicted of first degree murder, aggravated criminal sexual assault and home invasion. Defendant argued on appeal that error occurred because he did not testify at his second stage capital sentencing hearing and the record failed to show that he had waived his right to testify. The Illinois Supreme Court disagreed, explaining that at no time did defendant express his wish to testify during the hearing. The Supreme Court noted that

> Illinois courts have consistently found [. . .] that when a defendant contends on appeal that he was precluded from testifying at trial, his conviction cannot be reversed on the basis that he was prevented from exercising that right unless he contemporaneously asserted his right to testify by informing the trial court that he wished to do so. *See* People v. Thompkins, 161 Ill. 2d 148, 177-78 (1994); People v. Brown, 54 Ill. 2d 21, 24 (1973).
>
> ***
>
> Indeed, a vast majority of the states considering this question have held that a defendant's waiver of his right to testify is presumed if, as in the present case, he fails to testify or notify the court of his desire to do so.
>
> ***
>
> Additionally, a majority of jurisdictions, and our own appellate court, have found that a trial court has no duty to advise a defendant, represented by counsel, of his right to testify, nor is the court required to ensure that an on-the-record waiver has occurred.

The Supreme Court concluded that no error occurred in the present case because the trial court is "not required to advise a defendant of his right to testify, to inquire whether he knowingly and intelligently waived that right, or to set of record defendant's decision on this matter."

See also People v. Davis, 378 Ill. App. 3d 1 (1st Dist. 2007) (quoting *Smith* and noting that "[a]lthough the right to testify is a fundamental right, the Illinois Supreme Court has held that a trial court has no duty to inform a defendant about the right to testify or to obtain an "on-the-record waiver").

But see People v. Whiting, 365 Ill. App. 3d 402 (2d Dist. 2006) (finding that defendant did not knowingly and voluntarily waive her right to testify where she told her trial counsel of her wish to testify, and consequently fired counsel and raised the issue with new counsel prior to sentencing).

Recanted, False, and Perjured Testimony

AUTHOR'S COMMENTARY

Prosecutor who knowingly uses false or perjured testimony to obtain a conviction violates the accused's constitutional guarantees of the due process clause of the fourteenth amendment of the United States Constitution and Article I, section 2 of the Illinois Constitution. U.S. CONST. amend. XIV, § 1; ILL. CONST. Art. I, s. 2; Napue v. People of State of Ill., 360 U.S. 264 (1959); People v. Jimerson, 166 Ill. 2d 211 (1995).

Illinois reviewing courts universally distrust recanted testimony because it is highly unreliable. People v. Fields, 135 Ill. 2d 18 (1990). There is a presumption that a witness' trial testimony was truthful and the recantation false. People v. Marquis, 344 Ill. 261 (1931). The defendant may present affidavits or testimony showing that a prosecution witness' trial testimony was a lie. People v. Jennings, 48 Ill. 2d 295 (1971). The defendant must establish by clear and convincing evidence that the testimony was (1) perjured, (2) not merely false, and (3) willfully and purposely given. *Id.* Where the perjured testimony is merely cumulative and other evidence exists to support the conviction, the conviction will stand, but where the conviction rests solely on the perjured testimony of a prosecution witness, the conviction should be vacated. *Id.* For additional discussion of recanted, false and perjured testimony, see RALPH RUEBNER, ILLINOIS CRIMINAL TRIAL EVIDENCE 209-210 (4th ed. 2001).

PRIOR ILLINOIS CASE LAW

1. Prosecutor's Knowing Use of False or Perjured Testimony to Convict Defendant Violates the Constitutional Guarantees of the Due Process Clause of the Fourteenth Amendment

Napue v. People of State of Ill., 360 U.S. 264 (1959)

Defendant and several other men participated in an armed robbery that resulted in the shooting death of an off duty police officer. One of the defendant's accomplices was convicted and sentenced to 199 years for the crime. The accomplice testified against defendant. After defendant was convicted of murder, the assistant state's attorney who prosecuted defendant and the accomplice submitted a petition on behalf of the accomplice for a reduction of his sentence due to his testimony against the defendant. Defendant found out about the petition and filed a post-conviction petition alleging that the accomplice falsely testified that he was not promised leniency in exchange for his testimony. Although the Illinois Supreme Court found that the assistant state's attorney promised consideration for the accomplice's testimony and that he knew that the accomplice testified falsely, it nevertheless held that defendant was not entitled to relief because the jury had been informed at trial that a public defender would "do what he could" for the accomplice. The United States Supreme Court granted certiorari, reversed the Illinois Supreme Court, and explained that

> a conviction obtained through use of false evidence, known to be such by representatives of the State, must fall under the Fourteenth Amendment, Mooney v. Holohan, 294 U.S. 103 (1935); Pyle v. State of Kansas, 317 U.S. 213 (1942); [citations omitted]. The same result obtains when the State, although not soliciting false evidence, allows it to go uncorrected when it appears. Alcorta v. State of Texas, 355 U.S. 28 (1957); [citations omitted].
>
> The principle that a State may not knowingly use false evidence, including false testimony, to obtain a tainted conviction, implicit in any concept of ordered liberty, does not cease to apply merely because the false testimony goes only to the credibility of the witness. The jury's estimate of the truthfulness and reliability of a given witness may well be determinative of guilt or innocence, and it is upon such subtle factors as the possible interest of the witness in testifying falsely that a defendant's life or liberty may depend. As stated by the New York Court of Appeals in a case very similar to this one, People v. Savvides, 1 N.Y.2d 554, 557 (1956):
>
>> It is of no consequence that the falsehood bore upon the witness' credibility rather than directly upon defendant's guilt. A lie is a lie, no matter what its subject, and, if it is in any way relevant to the case, the district attorney has the responsibility and duty to correct what he knows to be false and elicit the truth. *** That the district attorney's silence was not the result of guile or a desire to prejudice matters little, for its impact was the same, preventing, as it did, a trial that could in any real sense be termed fair.'

The Supreme Court explained that had the jury been informed of the assistant state's attorney's promises to the accomplice, it could "have concluded that [the accomplice] had fabricated testimony in order to curry" favor with him. The Supreme Court concluded that "the false testimony used by the State in securing the conviction of petitioner may have had an effect on the outcome of the trial."

2. Defendant May Be Entitled to New Trial due to Violation of Due Process and Fair Trial Rights If Key State Witness Testifies Falsely

People v. Jimerson, 166 Ill. 2d 211 (1995)

The Illinois Supreme Court remanded for a new trial, finding that defendant's due process rights were violated where the state allowed the use of perjured testimony to convict defendant. In this case, the state's primary witness against defendant repeatedly falsely testified at defendant's trial that she was not promised anything in exchange for her testimony against defendant. In exchange for her testimony, the state had agreed to drop murder and rape charges against her. The state nonetheless failed to correct the witness' testimony at trial. The Supreme Court noted that

> if a prosecutor knowingly permits perjured testimony to be used in a criminal prosecution, "it is incontrovertible that defendant's trial lacked the fundamental fairness implicit in constitutional guarantees of due process of law, thus entitling him to a new trial." People v. McKinney, 31 Ill. 2d 246, 247 (1964) (citing Napue v. People of State of Ill., 360 U.S. 264 (1959), and People v. Lueck, 24 Ill. 2d 554 (1962)).

In finding defendant was entitled to a new trial, the Supreme Court held that the evidence clearly supported a finding that the witness had been given promises of leniency in exchange for her testimony. The state's answer to discovery indicated it would drop charges against her.

The state's brief on appeal, in three separate instances, admitted it had a deal with the witness. Finally, the charges of murder and rape were ultimately dismissed against the witness. Accordingly, the court found this error reversible and not harmless, since the witness was crucial to the state's case because she was the only individual who linked defendant to the crime.

See also People v. Nash, 36 Ill. 2d 275 (1966) (defendant was not denied due process of law where key state witness falsely testified that he had not been offered leniency in exchange for testimony because evidence later introduced contradicted the witness' false testimony).

3. Expert Witness' False Testimony About Qualifications May Constitute a Violation of Due Process and May Entitle Defendant to a New Trial
People v. Cornille, 95 Ill. 2d 497 (1983)

The defendant may present affidavits or testimony showing that a prosecution witness' trial testimony was a lie. The claim of perjury can be raised in a post-trial motion for new trial or in collateral remedy proceedings.

Here, the defendant was convicted of arson. The evidence against him was not unequivocal and the experts testifying at his trial disagreed significantly about the cause of the fire. State's expert arson-investigator who provided "crucial testimony" at trial later admitted in a newspaper interview that he had fabricated his qualifications as an expert at the defendant's trial and at other criminal trials. The expert's testimony was crucial to the state's case because he claimed that his special superior method of sampling the charred floor surrounding the origin of the fire allowed him to determine that an accelerant was used testimony other experts were unable to provide. The Illinois Supreme Court noted that

> [t]o establish a violation of due process the defendant must demonstrate that some action of the State was inconsistent "with the fundamental principles of liberty and justice which lie at the base of all our civil and political institutions" (Herbert v. Louisiana, 272 U.S. 312, 316 (1926), and which reflect "the community's sense of fair play and decency" (Rochin v. California, 342 U.S. 165, 173 (1952). "Perjury is the mortal enemy of justice" (People v. Shannon, 28 Ill. App. 3d 873, 878 (1975)), and it has long been recognized that the deprivation of an individual's liberty based upon false testimony is contrary to fundamental principles of fairness in a civilized society (*see, e.g.*, Mooney v. Holohan, 294 U.S. 103, 112 (1935) (*per curiam*); Napue v. Illinois (1959), 360 U.S. 264, 269 (1959). Every major civil and common law jurisdiction has provided some means of redress for persons unjustly convicted on false testimony. *See, e.g.*, Murray, *Convictions Obtained by Perjured Testimony: A Comparative View*, 27 OHIO ST. L.J. 102 (1966) (reviewing remedies provided by the United States, Great Britain, France, Germany, Spain, and Mexico). As the Supreme Court observed in granting a new trial under its supervisory authority, "The government of a strong and free nation does not need convictions based upon such testimony." Mesarosh v. United States, 352 U.S. 1, 14 (1956); *see also* Communist Party of the United States v. Subversive Activities Control Board, 351 U.S. 115 (1956).

The Supreme Court explained that

> [t]he convincing evidence of [the expert's] false testimony makes this case unique [because] [t]he prosecution admit[ted], and the circuit court found, that [the defendant] has established beyond doubt that false testimony was given at his trial. Beyond that, the witness who allegedly gave the false testimony has been charged by information with perjury in connection with his testimony at that trial. It is antithetical to our system of justice to refuse to grant a new

> trial for a defendant when it is convincingly established that he was convicted on the basis of false testimony.

The Supreme Court concluded that although the state used the testimony without knowing that it was false, the presentation of the perjured statements nevertheless violated defendant's right to due process. The Supreme Court reasoned that it would have been easy for the state to confirm the witness' credentials and that such "lack of diligence" constituted a violation of due process.

But see People v. Nowicki, 385 Ill. App. 3d 53 (1st Dist. 2008) (finding no violation of defendant's due process rights where occurrence witness falsely testified that he had served "three tours in Vietnam" and was a "beret" because state did not know of the perjury and did not have an opportunity or time to confirm witness' credentials).

4. Recanted Testimony Is Generally Considered Unreliable
People v. Fields, 135 Ill. 2d 18 (1990)

Defendants were charged with murders of two gang members. One witness testified that he saw the gunmen wearing ski masks shoot two individuals outside of a housing complex. The gunmen then took off their ski masks and the witness was able to see their faces. He immediately recognized one of them and later identified the other during a police lineup.

At the defendants' second stage death penalty hearing, the defense called the witness to testify in mitigation. The witness recanted his testimony, stating that he had never seen the shooters' faces and that the police urged him to falsely identify the defendants. The jury found that there were insufficient mitigating circumstances to prevent imposition of the death penalty. The trial court sentenced the defendants to death. Defendants contended on appeal that the testimony of the witness identifying them as shooters should be disregarded because the witness recanted his testimony at the death sentencing hearing. The Illinois Supreme Court disagreed, noting that

> [i]t is well settled that recantation of trial testimony is generally regarded as unreliable. People v. Marquis, 344 Ill. 261, 265 (1931); People v. Worthen, 105 Ill. App. 3d 386 (1982). It is for the trial judge to determine the credibility of the recantation testimony after having observed the demeanor of the witness. People v. Montgomery, 93 Ill. App. 3d 498 (1981).

The Supreme Court observed that the witness had been confined in a juvenile detention facility prior to the sentencing hearing and that one of the defendants' lawyers came to visit him at the facility. The witness admitted that it was then that he for the first time claimed that he had lied at trial. The witness further stated that he would be released from the facility shortly after the sentencing hearing and that he was scared for his family's safety. The witness also stated that he saw members of the defendants' gang in the courtroom while he testified. The Supreme Court concluded that the trial judge had the best opportunity to evaluate the witness' testimony and that it could not be said that the trial court erred in rejecting his recantation.

5. There Is a Presumption That Witness' Trial Testimony Was True and Recantation Was False
People v. Marquis, 344 Ill. 261 (1931)

Defendant was convicted of murdering his son. His daughter testified before the grand jury and at trial that after defendant shot his son, he stated: "I told you I would do that some day and I am going to kill another one before I die." In his motion for new trial defendant attached an affidavit by his daughter which stated that she lied during the grand jury proceeding and at trial. She claimed that when she first testified she was 15 years old and had found out she was pregnant. She stated that her fear of her father finding out the identity of the father of her child caused her to be "partially deranged." She further noted that she could now clearly recall what happened on the day of the shooting and that her father never made the statement to which she testified earlier. In consideration of the daughter's recanted testimony, the Illinois Supreme Court observed that

> [r]ecantation by a witness of his testimony on a trial does not necessarily entitle a defendant to a new trial. Recanting testimony is regarded as very unreliable, and a court will usually deny a new trial based on that ground where it is not satisfied that such testimony is true. Especially is this true where the recantation relied on involves a confession of perjury. The recanting testimony of witnesses will not ordinarily be regarded as sufficient ground for a new trial except in extraordinary and unusual cases. [citation omitted] The affidavit of a recanting witness is not entitled to so much weight as to justify the conclusion that the evidence given by him was corrupt and willfully false. The conclusion of the jury would rather warrant the presumption that his testimony was truthful and his affidavit false.

The Supreme Court explained that in this case the evidence showed that the recanted testimony was unreliable. Specifically, the Supreme Court noted that it was highly unlikely that a father involved in an accidental shooting with his son would fail to explain himself to his other family members. Moreover, the physical evidence failed to support defendant's testimony that the gun accidentally went off. The Supreme Court concluded that the trial court properly denied defendant's motion for a new trial.

6. Defendant Must Establish That Testimony Was Perjured and Willfully Given
People v. Jennings, 48 Ill. 2d 295 (1971)

The Illinois Supreme Court stated that defendant seeking relief from a final judgment must initially establish by clear and convincing evidence that the testimony was (1) perjured, (2) not merely false, and (3) willfully and purposefully given. Where the perjured testimony is merely cumulative and other evidence exists to support the conviction, the conviction will stand. Here, defendant contended that a witness perjured himself at trial by stating that he was the first responding officer at the scene of the crime. Defendant was an off-duty police officer who physically abused a suspect. The police officer who responded to the altercation testified at defendant's trial that he was the first police officer to respond. Defendant argued that the officer was not the first one at the scene. The Illinois Supreme Court rejected the defendant's argument, explaining that

> perjured testimony that warrants relief from a final judgment must be shown by clear and convincing evidence to have been not merely false, but to have been wilfully and purposely given, and to have been material to the issue tried and not merely cumulative, and that it probably controlled the determination.

Here, the Supreme Court found that the defendant failed to provide any factual allegations that would support his claim of perjury. Moreover, the defendant, through reasonable diligence, could have presented this argument at trial because he had first-hand knowledge of the identity of the first responding officer at the scene. The Supreme Court concluded that even if the officer provided perjured testimony, such testimony was not controlling of the result of the trial.

7. Defendant May Be Entitled to an Evidentiary Hearing on Validity of Witness' Recanted Testimony If Judge Who Hears the Petition Did Not Preside Over Trial
People v. Hernandez, 298 Ill. App. 3d 36 (1st Dist. 1998)

If the trial judge also hears the post-conviction petition, the judge may dismiss the petition without holding an evidentiary hearing since the judge can assess the witness' credibility based on the witness' trial testimony. If the judge who hears the post-conviction petition did not preside over the trial, an evidentiary hearing will usually be necessary.

But see People v. Broughton, 344 Ill. App. 3d 232 (1st Dist. 2003) (finding that where recanted testimony, even if true, was not exculpatory and did not provide defendant with an alibi, no evidentiary hearing was necessary).

Constitutional Right Under the Sixth Amendment to Confront Witnesses, Including Expert Witnesses

AUTHOR'S COMMENTARY

The sixth amendment of the United States Constitution and Article I, section 8 of the Illinois Constitution protect the accused's right to confront witnesses against him or her. These constitutional provisions also protect the accused's right to confront witnesses against him or her by cross-examining them about any possible bias, interest, or motive to testify falsely. Davis v. Alaska, 415 U.S. 308 (1974); People v. Gonzalez, 104 Ill. 2d 332 (1984).

The sixth amendment of the United States Constitution states that "[i]n all criminal prosecutions, the accused shall enjoy the right . . . to be confronted with the witnesses against him." The fourteenth amendment of the United States Constitution makes this fundamental right applicable to the states. Pointer v. Texas, 380 U.S. 400 (1965).

Article I, section 8 of the Illinois Constitution also guarantees an accused in criminal prosecutions the right "to be confronted with witnesses against him or her." Prior to the 1994 amendment to the Illinois Constitution, the clause required a witness to confront defendant "face to face." This face to face requirement is no longer the law. On November 8, 1994, the Illinois Constitution was amended to delete the requirement that a defendant is entitled to confront the witnesses against him or her face to face. ILL. CONST. (1970, amended 1994). In conjunction with the new constitutional mandate omitting face to face confrontation, the legislature enacted 725 ILCS 5/106B-5. Section 106B-5 allows a sexual crime victim who is a minor or a person with an intellectual or developmental disability to testify against the accused via closed circuit television. The statutory provision was created to protect especially vulnerable victims from suffering "serious emotional distress" when they are required to testify against the accused at trial. 725 ILCS 5/106B-5.

The sixth amendment confrontation clause prohibits the admissibility in evidence of a confession or an admission of a non-testifying co-defendant that implicates the defendant at their joint trial. Bruton v. United States, 391 U.S. 123 (1968). Under Illinois' common law hearsay rules of evidence, such evidence is also inadmissible at a defendant's separate trial. People v. Johnson, 116 Ill. 2d 13 (1987). Out-of-court testimonial statements of an unavailable witness are only admissible against the defendant if he or she had a prior opportunity to cross-examine the now unavailable witness who was the out-of-court declarant. Crawford v. Washington, 541 U.S. 36 (2004).

Illinois Rule of Evidence 702, which addresses the admissibility of expert testimony, codifies Illinois common law principle as articulated by the Illinois Supreme Court in Donaldson v. Cent. Illinois Pub. Serv. Co., 199 Ill. 2d 63 (2002). Experts may generally rely on inadmissible hearsay to explain the basis of their opinion. People v. Lovejoy, 235 Ill. 2d 97 (2009). However, confrontation issues may arise whenever the expert relies on third party's testimonial statements as a basis in forming an opinion. Melendez-Diaz v. Massachusetts, 129 S. Ct. 2527 (2009). The United States Supreme Court recently held that an expert's testimony indicating that there was a match between defendant's DNA profile and the semen taken from the victim, which was analyzed by a non-testifying third party, did not violate the confrontation clause. Williams v. Illinois, 132 S. Ct. 2221 (2012).

Relevant Statutory Authority

Testimony by Sexual Crime Victim Who Is a Child or a Person with an Intellectual or Developmental Disability: 725 ILCS 5/106B-5

Sec. 106B-5. Testimony by a victim who is a child or a moderately, severely, or profoundly intellectually disabled person or a person affected by a developmental disability.

(a) In a proceeding in the prosecution of an offense of criminal sexual assault, predatory criminal sexual assault of a child, aggravated criminal sexual assault, criminal sexual abuse, or aggravated criminal sexual abuse, a court may order that the testimony of a victim who is a child under the age of 18 years or a moderately, severely, or profoundly intellectually disabled person or a person affected by a developmental disability be taken outside the courtroom and shown in the courtroom by means of a closed circuit television if:

(1) the testimony is taken during the proceeding; and
(2) the judge determines that testimony by the child victim or moderately, severely, or profoundly intellectually disabled victim or victim affected by a developmental disability in the courtroom will result in the child or moderately, severely, or profoundly intellectually disabled person or person affected by a developmental disability suffering serious emotional distress such that the child or moderately, severely, or profoundly intellectually disabled person or person affected by a developmental disability cannot reasonably communicate or that the child or moderately, severely, or profoundly intellectually disabled person or person affected by a developmental disability will suffer severe emotional distress that is likely to cause the child or moderately, severely, or profoundly intellectually disabled person or person affected by a developmental disability to suffer severe adverse effects.

(b) Only the prosecuting attorney, the attorney for the defendant, and the judge may question the child or moderately, severely, or profoundly intellectually disabled person or person affected by a developmental disability.

(c) The operators of the closed circuit television shall make every effort to be unobtrusive.

(d) Only the following persons may be in the room with the child or moderately, severely, or profoundly intellectually disabled person or person affected by a developmental disability when the child or moderately, severely, or profoundly intellectually disabled person or person affected by a developmental disability testifies by closed circuit television:

(1) the prosecuting attorney;
(2) the attorney for the defendant;
(3) the judge;
(4) the operators of the closed circuit television equipment; and
(5) any person or persons whose presence, in the opinion of the court, contributes to the well-being of the child or moderately, severely, or profoundly intellectually disabled person or person affected by a developmental disability, including a person who has dealt with the child in a therapeutic setting concerning the abuse, a parent or guardian of the child or moderately, severely, or profoundly intellectually disabled person or person affected by a developmental disability, and court security personnel.

(e) During the child's or moderately, severely, or profoundly intellectually disabled person's or person affected by a developmental disability's testimony by closed circuit television, the defendant shall be in the courtroom and shall not communicate with the jury if the cause is being heard before a jury.

(f) The defendant shall be allowed to communicate with the persons in the room where the child or moderately, severely, or profoundly intellectually disabled person or person affected by a developmental disability is testifying by any appropriate electronic method.

(g) The provisions of this Section do not apply if the defendant represents himself *pro se*.

(h) This Section may not be interpreted to preclude, for purposes of identification of a defendant, the presence of both the victim and the defendant in the courtroom at the same time.

(i) This Section applies to prosecutions pending on or commenced on or after the effective date of this amendatory Act of 1994.

(j) For the purposes of this Section, "developmental disability" includes, but is not limited to, cerebral palsy, epilepsy, and autism.

Amended by P.A. 97-0227, effective January 1, 2012.

Discharge Hearing: 725 ILCS 5/104-25

§ 104-25. Discharge hearing.

(a) As provided for in paragraph (a) of Section 104-23 and subparagraph (1) of paragraph (b) of Section 104-23 a hearing to determine the sufficiency of the evidence shall be held. Such hearing shall be conducted by the court without a jury. The State and the defendant may introduce evidence relevant to the question of defendant's guilt of the crime charged.

The court may admit hearsay or affidavit evidence on secondary matters such as testimony to establish the chain of possession of physical evidence, laboratory reports, authentication of transcripts taken by official reporters, court and business records, and public documents.

(b) If the evidence does not prove the defendant guilty beyond a reasonable doubt, the court shall enter a judgment of acquittal; however nothing herein shall prevent the State from requesting the court to commit the defendant to the Department of Human Services under the provisions of the Mental Health and Developmental Disabilities Code.

(c) If the defendant is found not guilty by reason of insanity, the court shall enter a judgment of acquittal and the proceedings after acquittal by reason of insanity under Section 5-2-4 of the Unified Code of Corrections shall apply.

(d) If the discharge hearing does not result in an acquittal of the charge the defendant may be remanded for further treatment and the one year time limit set forth in Section 104-23 shall be extended as follows:

(1) If the most serious charge upon which the State sustained its burden of proof was a Class 1 or Class X felony, the treatment period may be extended up to a maximum treatment period of 2 years; if a Class 2, 3, or 4 felony, the treatment period may be extended up to a maximum of 15 months;
(2) If the State sustained its burden of proof on a charge of first degree murder, the treatment period may be extended up to a maximum treatment period of 5 years.

(e) Transcripts of testimony taken at a discharge hearing may be admitted in evidence at a subsequent trial of the case, subject to the rules of evidence, if the witness who gave such testimony is legally unavailable at the time of the subsequent trial.

(f) If the court fails to enter an order of acquittal the defendant may appeal from such judgment in the same manner provided for an appeal from a conviction in a criminal case.

(g) At the expiration of an extended period of treatment ordered pursuant to this Section:

(1) Upon a finding that the defendant is fit or can be rendered fit consistent with Section 104-22, the court may proceed with trial.

(2) If the defendant continues to be unfit to stand trial, the court shall determine whether he or she is subject to involuntary admission under the Mental Health and Developmental Disabilities Code or constitutes a serious threat to the public safety. If so found, the defendant shall be remanded to the Department of Human Services for further treatment and shall be treated in the same manner as a civilly committed patient for all purposes, except that the original court having jurisdiction over the defendant shall be required to approve any conditional release or discharge of the defendant, for the period of commitment equal to the maximum sentence to which the defendant would have been subject had he or she been convicted in a criminal proceeding. During this period of commitment, the original court having jurisdiction over the defendant shall hold hearings under clause (i) of this paragraph (2). However, if the defendant is remanded to the Department of Human Services, the defendant shall be placed in a secure setting unless the court determines that there are compelling reasons why such placement is not necessary.

If the defendant does not have a current treatment plan, then within 3 days of admission under this subdivision (g)(2), a treatment plan shall be prepared for each defendant and entered into his or her record. The plan shall include (i) an assessment of the defendant's treatment needs, (ii) a description of the services recommended for treatment, (iii) the goals of each type of element of service, (iv) an anticipated timetable for the accomplishment of the goals, and (v) a designation of the qualified professional responsible for the implementation of the plan. The plan shall be reviewed and updated as the clinical condition warrants, but not less than every 30 days.

Every 90 days after the initial admission under this subdivision (g)(2), the facility director shall file a typed treatment plan report with the original court having jurisdiction over the defendant. The report shall include an opinion as to whether the defendant is fit to stand trial and whether the defendant is currently subject to involuntary admission, in need of mental health services on an inpatient basis, or in need of mental health services on an outpatient basis. The report shall also summarize the basis for those findings and provide a current summary of the 5 items required in a treatment plan. A copy of the report shall be forwarded to the clerk of the court, the State's Attorney, and the defendant's attorney if the defendant is represented by counsel.

The court on its own motion may order a hearing to review the treatment plan. The defendant or the State's Attorney may request a treatment plan review every 90 days and the court shall review the current treatment plan to determine whether the plan complies with the requirements of this Section. The court may order an independent examination on its own initiative and shall order such an evaluation if either the recipient or the State's Attorney so requests and has demonstrated to the court that the plan cannot be effectively reviewed by the court without such an examination. Under no circumstances shall the court be required to order an independent examination pursuant to this Section more than once each year. The examination shall be conducted by a psychiatrist or clinical psychologist as defined in Section 1-103 of the Mental Health and Developmental Disabilities Code who is not in the employ of the Department of Human Services.

If, during the period within which the defendant is confined in a secure setting, the court enters an order that requires the defendant to appear, the court shall timely transmit a copy of the order or writ to the director of the particular Department of Human Services facility where the defendant resides authorizing the transportation of the defendant to the court for the purpose of the hearing.

(i) 180 days after a defendant is remanded to the Department of Human Services, under paragraph (2), and every 180 days thereafter for so long as the defendant is confined under the order entered thereunder, the court shall set a hearing and shall direct that notice of the time and place of the hearing be served upon the defendant, the facility director, the State's Attorney, and the defendant's attorney. If requested by either the State or the defense or if the court determines that it is appropriate, an impartial examination of the defendant by a psychiatrist or clinical psychologist as defined in Section 1-103 of the Mental Health and Developmental Disabilities Code who is not in the employ of the Department of Human Services shall be ordered, and the report considered at the time of the hearing. If the defendant is not currently represented by counsel the court shall appoint the public defender to represent the defendant at the hearing. The court shall make a finding as to whether the defendant is:

(A) subject to involuntary admission; or

(B) in need of mental health services in the form of inpatient care; or

(C) in need of mental health services but not subject to involuntary admission nor inpatient care.

The findings of the court shall be established by clear and convincing evidence and the burden of proof and the burden of going forward with the evidence shall rest with the State's Attorney. Upon finding by the court, the court shall enter its findings and an appropriate order.

(ii) The terms "subject to involuntary admission", "in need of mental health services in the form of inpatient care" and "in need of mental health services but not subject to involuntary admission nor inpatient care" shall have the meanings ascribed to them in clause (d)(3) of Section 5-2-4 of the Unified Code of Corrections.

(3) If the defendant is not committed pursuant to this Section, he or she shall be released.

(4) In no event may the treatment period be extended to exceed the maximum sentence to which a defendant would have been subject had he or she been convicted in a criminal proceeding. For purposes of this Section, the maximum sentence shall be determined by Section 5-8-1 (730 ILCS 5/5-8-1) or Article 4.5 of Chapter V of the "Unified Code of Corrections", excluding any sentence of natural life.
Effective July 1, 2009.

PRIOR ILLINOIS CASE LAW

1. Defendant's Failure to Appear for Trial Could Result in Waiver of the Right to Confront Witnesses

People v. Phillips, 242 Ill. 2d 189 (2011)

Defendant was charged with attempted first degree murder, armed violence and aggravated battery. The back of defendant's bail bond slip noted that if he failed to appear in court, his "failure to appear would constitute a waiver of [his] rights to confront the witnesses against [him]." Defendant signed the front of the slip. Although defendant was present in court for arraignment prior to posting bond, there was no evidence that the trial court provided any additional admonishments beside those noted on the bond slip to defendant about waiver. Defendant appeared during his entire trial but was not present when the jury read the verdict. He was sentenced *in absentia*. Defendant appealed, noting that he did not furnish a valid waiver of his right to be present at trial because the bond court judge did not admonish him properly. State argued that defendant's signature on the back of the bail bond slip constituted valid waiver. The Illinois Supreme Court disagreed, noting that

> [a]s a constitutional matter, a defendant has a right to be present at all stages of his trial, including sentencing. Snyder v. Massachusetts, 291 U.S. 97, 105-06 (1934). A defendant's voluntary absence from trial may be construed as an effective waiver of his constitutional right to be present and he may be tried and sentenced *in absentia*, even if he is not specifically warned that this is a possible consequence of his absence. Taylor v. United States, 414 U.S. 17, 18-20 (1973). As recognized by the appellate court, however, a defendant in Illinois has a statutory right under [725 ILCS 5/113-4(e)] to be admonished as to the possible consequences of failing to appear in court when required.
>
> ***
>
> [S]ection 113-4(e) admonishment serves as the procedural mechanism to effect a formal waiver of a defendant's right to be present. People v. Garner, 147 Ill. 2d 467, 483 (1992). Consequently, before a trial may proceed *in absentia*, the court must inform the defendant of his right to be present and the defendant must have knowingly and intelligently waived that right. *Garner*, 147 Ill. 2d at 483. Absent such a knowing and intelligent waiver, the defendant's statutory right to be informed that he could be tried in his absence is violated. *Garner*, 147 Ill. 2d at 483. This court also held that it is the intent of the legislature that section 113-4(e) admonishments be given at the time of arraignment and explained that the admonishment is most effective at that time when the defendant is also being informed of other significant protections, such as the right to counsel and the right to a jury trial. *Garner*, 147 Ill. 2d at 481.
>
> ***
>
> We find that section 113-4(e) unambiguously requires the trial court to admonish a defendant in open court and reject the State's claim that defendant waived his right to be admonished by a trial judge based upon the signed bond slip in this case. Defendant was required to sign the bond slip as a condition of his release from jail, which is a far different circumstance than a defendant voluntarily relinquishing a known statutory right in court. We [. . .] conclude that a warning provided outside the presence of the court through language contained on a bond slip does not constitute a blanket waiver precluding the need for any section 113-4(e) admonishment by the trial judge.

2. Sixth Amendment of the United States Constitution Protects the Accused's Right to Confront Witness by Cross-Examination About Any Bias, Interest, or Motive to Testify Falsely

Davis v. Alaska, 415 U.S. 308 (1974)

At defendant's trial for burglary and grand larceny of a safe, a prosecution witness testified that he saw the defendant prying open a safe with a crowbar. The witness was 16 years old at the time he witnessed defendant's actions and had turned 17 years old by the time of trial. Prosecution sought to bar evidence of the witness' juvenile record. At the time of trial the witness was on probation for the commission of two burglaries. Defendant sought to use the witness' juvenile adjudication to show his bias (but not to impeach his general character), claiming that the witness may have incorrectly identified the defendant in his haste to avoid any appearance of wrongdoing himself. The defendant intended to show that the witness feared revocation of his probation if the police thought he had been involved in the instant burglary. The trial court granted the prosecution's motion to preclude introduction of witness' juvenile record pursuant to a state statute that protects the confidentiality of juvenile records. During cross-examination defense counsel asked the witness whether he was apprehensive about the police possibly believing that he had committed the crime, and the witness responded in the negative. Defense counsel was attempting to show that the witness may have had motive to lie to the police about defendant's involvement in the burglary because of his prior juvenile adjudications for burglary. The United States Supreme Court noted that the witness' answer to defense questioning was "self-serving" and may not have been entirely truthful considering that while the witness was reporting a burglary he had prior juvenile adjudications for two burglaries. The Supreme Court explained that one

> particular attack on the witness' credibility is effected by means of cross-examination directed toward revealing possible biases, prejudices, or ulterior motives of the witness as they may relate directly to issues or personalities in the case at hand. The partiality of a witness is subject to exploration at trial, and is 'always relevant as discrediting the witness and affecting the weight of his testimony.' 3A J. WIGMORE, EVIDENCE § 940, p. 775 (Chadbourn rev. 1970). We have recognized that the exposure of a witness' motivation in testifying is a proper and important function of the constitutionally protected right of cross-examination. Greene v. McElroy, 360 U.S. 474, 496 (1959).

The Supreme Court observed that it was not clear that the jury would have believed the defendant's argument without the additional evidence that the witness was biased. The "accuracy and truthfulness of [the witness'] testimony were key elements in the State's case against [the defendant]" and the Supreme Court reasoned that the defendant should have been able to expose other facts from which the jury could have evaluated the witness' credibility. The Supreme Court concluded that the defendant was denied the right to effectively confront the witness against him, explaining that defendant

> sought to introduce evidence of [the witness'] probation for the purpose of suggesting that [he] was biased and, therefore, that his testimony was either not to be believed in his identification of [the defendant] or at least very carefully considered in that light. Serious damage to the strength of the State's case would have been a real possibility had [defendant] been allowed to pursue this line of inquiry. In this setting we conclude that the right of confrontation is paramount to the State's policy of protecting a juvenile offender. Whatever temporary embarrassment might result to [the witness] or his family by disclosure of his juvenile record—if the prosecution insisted on using him to make its case—is outweighed by [defendant's] right to probe into the influence of possible bias in the testimony of a crucial identification witness.

See also Olden v. Kentucky, 488 U.S. 227 (1988) (finding that black defendant accused of raping a white woman should have been allowed to impeach the woman with evidence of her relationship with a black man to show that she had motive to lie to protect this relationship).

3. Article I Section 8 of the Illinois Constitution Protects Defendant's Right to Cross-Examine a Witness as to Bias, Prejudice, or Motive
People v. Gonzalez, 104 Ill. 2d 332 (1984)

Defendant was on trial for murder. He sought to show that he withdrew from gang membership after he became a father and that a key witness against him was a gang member who threatened to "get" him if he did not re-join the gang. The trial court prevented all references to gang affiliation of the witness. The Illinois Supreme Court determined that this limitation violated defendant's constitutional right to confront witnesses against him pursuant to the sixth and fourteenth amendments of the United States Constitution and Article 1, section 8 of the Illinois Constitution. The Supreme Court held that defendant was entitled to cross-examine the witness about possible bias, prejudice or motive.

> We hold that the trial court's ruling that "[t]here is to be no reference to gang affiliations in this case" improperly limited the defendant in cross-examining [the gang member] as to his bias or motive to testify falsely. The right to cross-examine a witness as to his biases, prejudices, or ulterior motives is protected by both the Federal and Illinois constitutions. U.S. Const., amends. VI, XIV; Ill. Const. 1970, art. I, sec. 8; *see* Davis v. Alaska, 415 U.S. 308, 315-17 (19740. As the Supreme Court noted in Davis v. Alaska, 415 U.S. 308 (1974), "[t]he partiality of a witness is subject to exploration at trial, and is 'always relevant as discrediting the witness and affecting the weight of his testimony.' [Citation.] *** [T]he exposure of a witness' motivation in testifying is a proper and important function of the constitutionally protected right of cross-examination." This court has held that the widest latitude should be given the defense on cross-examination when trying to establish a witness' bias or motive. People v. Wilkerson, 87 Ill. 2d 151, 156 (1981).

See also People v. Blue, 205 Ill. 2d 1 (2001) (finding that the trial court may limit defendant's ability to cross-examine witnesses against him after it has permitted sufficient cross-examination to satisfy the confrontation clause).

4. The Sixth Amendment Confrontation Clause Guarantees an Opportunity for Effective Cross-Examination But Not Cross-Examination That Is Effective in Whatever Way and to Whatever Extent the Defense May Wish
People v. Klepper, 234 Ill. 2d 337 (2009)

Defendant was charged with disorderly conduct for falsely telling a police officer that his neighbor had attempted to hit him with his car. A witness testified that she observed defendant calling the police after his neighbor passed him by in his car without incident. The neighbor also denied that he had tried to run over the defendant in his vehicle. Trial court permitted brief testimony showing that defendant and his neighbor had an ongoing "feud," but did not allow defense counsel to extensively explore the topic on cross-examination. Defendant alleged that the witness who testified to seeing the incident from her kitchen window also had past disagreements with him. He contended that he should have had more opportunity to explore this bias. The Illinois Supreme Court disagreed and explained:

> The confrontation clause of the sixth amendment of the United States Constitution (U.S. Const., amend. VI) guarantees a defendant the right to cross-examine a witness against him for the purpose of showing the witness' bias, interest or motive to testify falsely. Davis v. Alaska, 415 U.S. 308 (1974); People v. Kirchner, 194 Ill. 2d 502, 536 (2000); People v. Harris, 123 Ill. 2d 113, 144 (1988). The exposure of a witness' motivation is an important function of the constitutionally protected right of cross-examination. Greene v. McElroy, 360 U.S. 474 (1959); *Harris*, 123 Ill. 2d at 144. However, a trial judge may impose limits on a defense counsel's

> inquiry into the potential bias of a prosecution witness without offending defendant's sixth amendment right. Delaware v. Van Arsdall, 475 U.S. 673, 679 (1986); *Harris*, 123 Ill. 2d at 144. A trial judge retains wide latitude to impose reasonable limits based on concerns about harassment, prejudice, confusion of the issues, the witness' safety, or interrogation that is repetitive or of little relevance. *Delaware v. Van Arsdall*, 475 U.S. at 679; *Harris*, 123 Ill. 2d at 144. As the United States Supreme Court observed in Delaware v. Fensterer, 474 U.S. 15, 20 (1985), 'the Confrontation Clause guarantees an opportunity for effective cross-examination, not cross-examination that is effective in whatever way, and to whatever extent, the defense might wish.' *Harris*, 123 Ill. 2d at 144, quoting *Fensterer*, 474 U.S. at 20. *** [T]he question in each case must finally be whether defendant's inability to make the inquiry created a substantial danger of prejudice by depriving him of the ability to test the truth of the witness's direct testimony. *** Thus, if a review of the entire record reveals that the fact-finder has been made aware of adequate factors concerning relevant areas of impeachment of a witness, no constitutional question arises merely because the defendant has been prohibited on cross-examination from pursuing other areas of inquiry. *Harris*, 123 Ill. 2d at 145.

The Supreme Court determined that the record showed that the fact-finder was well-informed about any witness bias and that any potential bias was sufficiently revealed on cross-examination and during defendant's own testimony. Additionally, a police officer who had previously responded to incidents between defendant and the neighbor who allegedly tried to hit him with his car testified about his observations. The court observed that further cross-examination of the witness who allegedly saw the incident would not have changed the outcome of the case because there was other evidence establishing defendant's guilt. The Supreme Court concluded that any bias was well-explored and that the trial court "acted within its wide latitude in limiting cross-examination."

5. Out-of-Court Testimonial Statements Are Inadmissible Unless Witness Is Unavailable and Defendant Had a Prior Opportunity to Cross-Examine Witness, Regardless of Whether Such Statements Are Found to Be Reliable

Crawford v. Washington, 541 U.S. 36 (2004)

Defendant stabbed a man who allegedly tried to rape his wife. Defendant and his wife were interviewed by the police and gave statements. In his statement defendant claimed that he stabbed the victim in self-defense after he saw the victim "fiddlin' around" in his pocket and pull something out just before the fight commenced. At trial, the state introduced a tape-recorded statement that defendant's wife made to the police shortly after the stabbing, stating that the hands of the victim were empty when he was stabbed by her husband. Defendant's wife invoked the state marital privilege statute and did not testify at trial. The state relied heavily on her tape-recorded statement given to police, and the jury convicted defendant of assault and attempted murder.

The United States Supreme Court held that where testimonial statements are at issue, the defendant must have had a prior opportunity to cross-examine the unavailable witness in order for his or her prior testimony to satisfy the confrontation clause of the sixth amendment. In so holding, the Supreme Court abrogated the rule established years earlier by Ohio v. Roberts, 448 U.S. 56 (1980), that allowed admissibility of an unavailable witness' statement against a defendant if it bore "adequate indicia of reliability," and that was determined by whether it fell within a firmly rooted hearsay exception or it bore "particularized guarantees of trustworthiness." According to the Supreme Court, the *Roberts* test was too unpredictable. The Supreme Court explained that the test was "too broad" in that it applied

> the same mode of analysis whether or not the hearsay consist[ed] of *ex parte* testimony. This often result[ed] in close constitutional scrutiny in cases that [we]re far removed from the core

> concerns of the Clause. At the same time, however, the test [was] too narrow: It admit[ted] statements that [did] consist of *ex parte* testimony upon a mere finding of reliability. This malleable standard often fail[ed] to protect against paradigmatic confrontation violations.
>
> ***
>
> Admitting statements deemed reliable by a judge is fundamentally at odds with the right of confrontation. To be sure, the Clause's ultimate goal is to ensure reliability of evidence, but it is a procedural rather than a substantive guarantee. It commands, not that evidence be reliable, but that reliability be assessed in a particular manner: by testing in the crucible of cross-examination. The Clause thus reflects a judgment, not only about the desirability of reliable evidence (a point on which there could be little dissent), but about how reliability can best be determined. *Cf.* 3 BLACKSTONE, COMMENTARIES, at 373 ("This open examination of witnesses . . . is much more conducive to the clearing up of truth"); M. HALE, HISTORY AND ANALYSIS OF THE COMMON LAW OF ENGLAND 258 (1713) (adversarial testing "beats and bolts out the Truth much better").
>
> The *Roberts* test allows a jury to hear evidence, untested by the adversary process, based on a mere judicial determination of reliability. It thus replaces the constitutionally prescribed method of assessing reliability with a wholly foreign one. In this respect, it is very different from exceptions to the Confrontation Clause that make no claim to be a surrogate means of assessing reliability.
>
> ***
>
> The [*Roberts*] framework is so unpredictable that it fails to provide meaningful protection from even core confrontation violations. [. . .] Reliability is an amorphous, if not entirely subjective, concept. [. . .] Whether a statement is deemed reliable depends heavily on which factors the judge considers and how much weight he accords each of them. Some courts wind up attaching the same significance to opposite facts.
>
> ***
>
> The unpardonable vice of the *Roberts* test, however, is not its unpredictability, but its demonstrated capacity to admit core testimonial statements that the Confrontation Clause plainly meant to exclude. *** To add insult to injury, some of the courts that admit untested testimonial statements find reliability in the very factors that make the statements testimonial. *** Other courts routinely rely on the fact that a prior statement is given under oath in judicial proceedings. (citations omitted). That inculpating statements are given in a testimonial setting is not an antidote to the confrontation problem, but rather the trigger that makes the Clause's demands most urgent. It is not enough to point out that most of the usual safeguards of the adversary process attend the statement, when the single safeguard missing is the one the Confrontation Clause demands.

The Supreme Court therefore held that where testimonial statements are involved, the only "indicium of reliability" is confrontation and, accordingly, the sixth amendment demands "unavailability and a prior opportunity for cross-examination." The Supreme Court declined to define what constituted a "testimonial" statement, but described it as one made under circumstances that would "lead an objective witness reasonably to believe that the statement would be available for use at a later trial." However, the Court did state, "[w]hatever else the term covers, it applies at a minimum to prior testimony at a preliminary hearing, before a grand jury, or at a formal trial; and to police interrogations."

6. Prior Testimony of an Unavailable Witness Is Admissible If There Was Ample Opportunity for Cross-Examination at Prior Trial or Hearing
People v. Sutherland, 223 Ill. 2d 187 (2006)

The defendant argued that the trial court had erred in denying his motion to bar at a retrial the admissibility of a witness' testimony from the first trial. Although the witness testified at the first trial and was later deposed by the defendant's attorney, he died prior to retrial. The witness was a crime-scene technician who previously testified about how the victim's body was found, in what condition the body was discovered, and about the injuries the victim suffered. The witness also testified about shoe prints recovered at the crime scene and other evidence found nearby. The trial court denied the defendant's motion to bar the deceased witness' testimony, stating that the witness was subject to unlimited cross-examination at the first trial.

The Illinois Supreme Court reviewed the trial court's ruling for an abuse of discretion. The Supreme Court explained that the prior testimony of a witness is admissible at trial

> where the witness is unavailable and when ample opportunity to cross-examine existed at the prior hearing." People v. Rice, 166 Ill. 2d 35, 39 (1995). Whether ample opportunity to cross-examine existed must be decided on a case-by-case basis. *Rice*, 166 Ill. 2d at 39. [. . .] [In *Rice*, the court] explained:
>
> > "For an opportunity to cross-examine to be considered meaningful, and therefore adequate and effective, the motive and focus of the cross-examination at the time of the initial proceeding must be the same or similar to that which guides the cross-examination during the subsequent proceeding." *Rice*, 166 Ill. 2d at 41 .[. . .]
> >
> > Here, no question exists that defendant had the opportunity at his first trial to cross-examine [the witness] and that the "motive and focus" of that cross-examination is the same as that which would have guided cross-examination at defendant's retrial. Under *Rice*, the trial court did not abuse its discretion by denying defendant's motion to bar [the witness'] testimony. *See also* People v. Hawkins, 326 Ill. App. 3d 992, 1003 (2001) (holding that prior testimony of deceased witness should have been admitted where the "motive and focus of the cross-examination at the time of the initial proceeding are exactly the same as they are today, i.e., the guilt or innocence of [the accused]"); People v. Taylor, 287 Ill. App. 3d 800, 810 (1997) (holding that posttrial motion testimony of unavailable witness was properly admitted at defendant's retrial where "[t]he testimony was given at a proceeding that afforded a meaningful opportunity to cross-examine [the unavailable witness] on the issue of guilt or innocence").

See also People v. Rice, 166 Ill. 2d 35 (1995) (finding co-defendant's exculpatory testimony at a suppression hearing not admissible under former testimony exception to the hearsay rule because state did not have adequate opportunity for cross-examination).

7. Preliminary Hearing Testimony of an Unavailable Witness Is Admissible at Trial Only If Defendant Had a Prior and Fair Opportunity to Fully Explore the Witness' Opportunity to Observe, Interest, Bias, Prejudice, and Motive

People v. Torres, 2012 IL 111302

Defendant was convicted of first degree murder following a bench trial. The victim was shot and killed at a bar. The bartender, a key witness, testified at the preliminary hearing that defendant "frequented" the bar. He stated that defendant and the victim were in the bar and were talking shortly before the shooting. He stated that he was not in the bar when the shooting occurred because he went to retrieve something from the back of the bar. He testified that he found the victim lying on the floor and bleeding from his head, and that when he walked outside he saw a person running away.

At the preliminary hearing, the defense counsel was able to conduct only a "very brief cross-examination" of the bartender. Counsel asked the bartender whether he knew the victim's father, but the state objected and the trial court sustained the objection. Defense counsel explained that he was attempting to elicit bias or prejudice of the witness, and the judge allowed him to "go ahead" with the questioning. The bartender subsequently stated that he did not know the victim's father, and defense counsel asked no further questions pertaining to his bias or possible prejudice. On further cross-examination, the bartender conceded that he never saw defendant with a gun and did not see him shoot the victim.

The defendant did not show up for arraignment and evaded arrest on the murder charges for over 20 years. The bartender was deported to Mexico shortly after defendant fled. After defendant's arrest and prior to trial, the state filed a motion *in limine* requesting that the trial court admit the bartender's preliminary hearing testimony. Defendant's new counsel argued that the testimony was inadmissible because the previous defense counsel did not have an opportunity to conduct an adequate cross-examination of the bartender at the preliminary hearing. He contended that prior counsel did not have "certain material information" such as the bartender's statements to the police shortly after the crime. Defense counsel alleged that the statements were inconsistent with the bartender's preliminary hearing testimony. Specifically, counsel noted that

> (1) [the bartender] told police that [the victim] had arrived at the tavern at 3:30 p.m., whereas he testified at the preliminary hearing that [the victim] arrived around 5 p.m.; (2) [he] told police that the defendant bought [the victim] a beer, something he failed to state at the preliminary hearing; and (3) [he] told the officers that [the victim], while in the tavern, had tried to kiss a girl, who became angry and left with another man.

The trial court granted the state's motion *in limine* and admitted the bartender's preliminary hearing testimony while noting that "it would allow defense counsel to bring those [prior inconsistent] statements out [. . .] without having to lay a foundation, either by way of cross-examination of the police officers who had made the relevant police reports or through a stipulation by the parties." In a bench trial, the trial court found defendant guilty of murder and defendant appealed, alleging, *inter alia*, that he did not have a sufficient opportunity to cross-examine the bartender at the preliminary hearing and that the trial court erred in admitting his testimony. The appellate court agreed with the defendant and reversed his conviction, explaining that the bartender's preliminary hearing testimony was inadmissible because defense counsel did not have adequate opportunity to cross-examine him. The appellate court noted, however, that its holding was "evidentiary in nature" and that it did not reach the defendant's confrontation clause claim. The Illinois Supreme Court affirmed but noted that the "constitutional considerations [were] inextricably intertwined with the question of admissibility." It explained that "the requirement of a prior, 'adequate opportunity to cross-examine' the absent witness is at once both an evidentiary and constitutional requisite for admission of former testimony. This is not, as the appellate court suggests, strictly an evidentiary matter." The Supreme Court observed that

> the requirements for admission of former testimony are twofold: the witness from the prior hearing must be unavailable at trial and the defendant must have had an adequate opportunity to effectively cross-examine the witness at the prior hearing. People v. Sutherland, 223 Ill. 2d 187, 273 (2006); People v. Rice, 166 Ill. 2d 35, 41 (1995).
>
> ***
>
> As this court and the Supreme Court have recognized, prior testimony from a preliminary hearing may be admissible at a subsequent trial so long as the two requirements for admission are met. *See* People v. Tennant, 65 Ill. 2d 401, 411 (1976); People v. Horton, 65 Ill. 2d 413, 417 (1976); Crawford v. Washington, 541 U.S. 36, 58 (2004) (citing approvingly Ohio v. Roberts, 448 U.S. 56 (1980), *overruled on other grounds by Crawford*). This court has

> indicated that determination is undertaken on a case-by-case basis. *Sutherland*, 223 Ill. 2d at 273; *Horton*, 65 Ill. 2d at 416. As in any other instance, the proponent of evidence bears the burden of proving the necessary elements for admissibility. *See* People v. Cookson, 215 Ill. 2d 194, 204 (2005).

The Supreme Court first observed that the state produced no evidence pertaining to the bartender's deportation and that defense had agreed to the fact that the witness had been deported. The Supreme Court explained that it would "view the parties' agreement regarding [the] deportation as the equivalent of a stipulation to that fact." The Supreme Court then considered whether defendant had a sufficient opportunity to cross-examine the witness at the preliminary hearing. The Supreme Court considered the precedent and noted that

> [i]n *Rice* and *Sutherland*, in the course of considering whether an adequate opportunity existed for cross-examination of the witness at the prior proceeding, this court looked, *inter alia*, to the "motive and focus" of the examination conducted at the first proceeding, and that which would have been conducted at the second. In *Sutherland*, this court quoted from *Rice*:
>
> > "For an opportunity to cross-examine to be considered meaningful, and therefore adequate and effective, the motive and focus of the cross-examination at the time of the initial proceeding must be the same or similar to that which guides the cross-examination during the subsequent proceeding." *Sutherland*, 223 Ill. 2d at 273 (quoting *Rice*, 166 Ill. 2d at 41).

Although the Supreme Court agreed with the state that defense counsel had the same "motive and focus" to cross-examine the witness at the preliminary hearing as he would have had at trial, it emphasized that "the motive-and-focus test [could not] be [the] *sole* guide to a resolution in this instance." The Supreme Court noted that

> [f]airness, and indeed defendant's right to confrontation, demand an opportunity for adequate cross-examination of the witness at the preliminary hearing if that testimony is to be subsequently admitted against the defendant at trial.
>
> Beyond the freedom to fully question the witness regarding critical areas of observation and recall, to test him for any bias and prejudice, and to otherwise probe for matters affecting his credibility, what counsel *knows* while conducting the cross-examination may, in a given case, impact counsel's ability and opportunity to effectively cross-examine the witness at the prior hearing.

The Supreme Court explained that additional cross-examination of the witness would have benefited defendant. It specifically noted that

> [d]efense counsel, at the preliminary hearing, was not privy to the inconsistent statements [the witness] gave to police, statements that counsel might have used to confront [him] and see if further changes in [his] version of events might be forthcoming. In addition, counsel apparently did not know about [the witness'] status as an alien, or the circumstances of his departure from this country. Defendant suggests—and we agree—that the looming threat of deportation might have furnished a formidable incentive for [the witness] to curry favor with the State. Moreover, [the witness'] testimony was not cumulative of any other witnesses; only his testimony placed defendant in the bar at the time of the shooting.

The Supreme Court concluded that these limitations prevented defense counsel from adequately cross-examining the witness. The Supreme Court found that the error was prejudicial and held that "for the preliminary hearing testimony of an unavailable witness to be subsequently admissible at trial, the trial court must have allowed defense counsel to fully explore the highly relevant areas of the witness' opportunity to observe, interest, bias, prejudice, and motive."

8. Testimonial Statement Is One Made in a Solemn Fashion Intended to Establish a Particular Fact

People v. Stechly, 225 Ill. 2d 246 (2007)

Defendant was convicted of predatory criminal sexual assault of a child, criminal sexual assault and aggravated criminal sexual abuse after a stipulated bench trial. Defendant had sexually abused his girlfriend's five-year-old daughter. Prior to trial, the court conducted a hearing pursuant to 725 ILCS 5/115-10 to determine the reliability of the minor victim's statements. After the hearing, the trial court found that the child's statements were sufficiently reliable and held that they should be admitted as long as either the child testified at trial or is determined to be unavailable and there is evidence to corroborate her account of the assault. The state filed a motion *in limine* for a judicial determination of the child's unavailability at trial. A clinical child psychologist testified at the hearing and opined that the victim "would likely experience trauma symptoms" if she were made to testify against defendant. The trial court found the victim to be unavailable. Defendant was initially tried before a jury. The victim's babysitter testified that she was the first person whom the victim told about the abuse. She stated that the victim only identified the perpetrator as "Bob" and that more than one individual named "Bob" babysat her. The jury trial resulted in a mistrial. Defendant waived his right to a second jury trial and requested a bench trial. The trial court found defendant guilty. Defendant appealed his conviction and the appellate court affirmed the trial court's judgment. During the pendency of his appeal the United States Supreme Court decided Crawford v. Washington, 541 U.S. 36 (2004). Defendant filed a supplemental petition for leave to appeal based on *Crawford* and the Illinois Supreme Court granted the petition. Defendant argued that state failed to meet its burden of establishing that the victim's hearsay statements were sufficiently reliable and that the trial court erred in determining that the child witness was unavailable. Defendant also offered a new argument, contending on the basis of *Crawford* that admissibility of the victim's hearsay statements violated his sixth amendment right to confront the witness. State argued that defendant waived his last argument and that he had forfeited the right to confrontation by procuring the unavailability of the victim by his wrongful conduct.

The Illinois Supreme Court found that defendant had not waived his claim because "*Crawford* announced a new rule . . . for the conduct of criminal prosecutions." The new rule applied "retroactively to all cases . . . pending on direct review or not yet final." The Supreme Court remanded the case for a determination whether defendant exhibited the intent to procure the unavailability of the victim by his wrongful conduct and therefore had forfeited his right to confront her.

The Supreme Court also considered whether the victim's statements were admissible at trial by considering *Crawford*, where the United States Supreme Court held that "a testimonial statement of a witness who does not testify at trial is never admissible unless (1) the witness is unavailable to testify, and (2) the defendant had a prior opportunity for cross-examination." The Illinois Supreme Court noted that there are

> two components to a "testimonial" statement. First, it must be made in solemn fashion. [. . .] The second requirement is that the statement must be intended to establish a particular fact. With respect to this requirement, the focus is on whether, at the time the statement was made, the witness was acting in a manner analogous to a witness at trial, describing or giving information regarding events which had previously occurred.

The Illinois Supreme Court indicated that in the police interrogation context, the intent of the officers is controlling. Therefore, wherever officers intend to obtain information for purposes of prosecution, the statements are testimonial. The Supreme Court explained that to determine whether a statement is testimonial outside of a police interrogation context it is necessary to determine

> the declarant's intent: Would the objective circumstances have led a reasonable person to conclude that their statement could be used against the defendant? [. . .] The fact that the instant case involves a child declarant complicates the issue, however. [. . .] Application of the objective approach to child witnesses raises the question of whether the child's age ought to be taken into account. [. . .] [W]e believe that the better view is to treat the child's age as one of the objective circumstances to be taken into account in determining whether a reasonable person in his or her circumstances would have understood that his or her statement would be available for use at a later trial.
>
> ***
>
> [W]e believe it would be fruitless to attempt to provide an exhaustive list of factors which may potentially enter into the "testimonial" calculus and the weight to be accorded them. Each case must be resolved on its own merits, and a pertinent factor in one case may not carry much weight in another. In this case, because the parties differ on the issue of whether the age of a child declarant may ever be taken into consideration, and because there is a divergence of opinion on the topic amongst the courts of our sister states, we have held that factor may be considered. This is not to say that age will necessarily be determinative in every case. We have simply held that it is among the circumstances potentially relevant to evaluating whether the objective circumstances of the statement would have led a reasonable declarant to understand that his or her statement could be used in a subsequent prosecution of the defendant.

The Illinois Supreme Court evaluated the testimony of the victim's mother and a child-abuse clinical specialist whom the victim saw in the emergency room to determine whether her statements were testimonial. The mother testified that the victim told her that "Bob had done something to her." The clinical specialist testified that she conducted an interview with the victim in which the victim said that she was in the hospital "because of what Bob had done to her," accused "Bob" of doing something to her she did not like, and stated that she was "mad" at him. The clinical specialist conducted another interview with the victim while two police officers watched it behind a one-way mirror. The Supreme Court concluded that the victim's statements to the clinical specialist were testimonial because the specialist was aware that abuse may have occurred and in the second interview was acting as an agent of law enforcement. The Supreme Court found, however, that the victim's statements to her mother were not testimonial in nature because the mother was simply attempting to discern why her daughter was not feeling well, and was not "attempting to gather evidence for a future prosecution."

The Supreme Court also determined that the trial court did not abuse its discretion in finding the victim to be unavailable and the victim's statements to her mother to be reliable at the section 115-10 hearing. The Supreme Court noted that

> the reliability and unavailability requirements of section 115-10 were met. A trial court's rulings on evidentiary matters will not be reversed absent a clear abuse of discretion. Fear and youth are factors to be considered in determining whether a child witness is unavailable. Reliability is judged based on the totality of the circumstances, but relevant factors include consistent repetition, use of terminology unexpected of a child of similar age, and lack of motive to fabricate. There was ample evidence supporting the circuit court's rulings regarding reliability and unavailability, and we find no abuse of discretion in the circuit court's ruling admitting [the victim's] statement under section 115-10.

9. Statements by Child Victim to a Child Advocate Acting on Behalf of the Police Are Testimonial

In re Rolandis G., 232 Ill. 2d 13 (2008)

Defendant, a juvenile, was adjudicated delinquent after the trial court found him guilty of aggravated criminal sexual assault. At trial, the victim testified about preliminary background information but refused to answer specific questions about the assault. Pursuant to 725 ILCS 5/115-10, the trial court found the victim unavailable and admitted the out-of-court statements made by the victim to his mother, a child abuse investigator, and a police detective as exceptions to the hearsay rule. Under the statute, the trial court held that in order to admit these statements either the declarant must be available to testify at the proceeding or the declarant is unavailable to testify and the state introduces corroborating evidence of the act which is the subject of the statement. The appellate court reversed, holding that the victim was unavailable although he provided some preliminary testimony and that the statements made to the police detective and the child abuse investigator were testimonial, and therefore should have been excluded. Moreover, the appellate court held section 115-10 unconstitutional as applied to the extent that it permitted the introduction of the victim's statements to the police detective and child abuse investigator in violation of the confrontation clause, where the defendant did not have an opportunity to cross-examine the victim due to his unavailability. However, the out-of-court statements which were made by the victim to his mother were non-testimonial, thus falling outside the scope of *Crawford*, and were admissible because the state introduced sufficient corroborating evidence under section 115-10.

On appeal to the Illinois Supreme Court, the state argued that the victim's statements to the child abuse investigator were not testimonial because neither the victim nor the investigator were acting "to produce a statement for future trial." Relying on its decision in People v. Stechly, 225 Ill. 2d 246 (2007), the Supreme Court noted that

> a testimonial statement is one which is (1) made in a solemn fashion, and (2) intended to establish a particular fact. In general, a statement is testimonial if the declarant is acting in a manner analogous to a witness at trial, describing or giving information regarding events that have already occurred. *Stechly*, 225 Ill. 2d at 281-82. Of course, this framework begs the question, "Whose intent is determinative-the questioner or the declarant?" [T]he *Stechly* plurality concluded that, when the statement under consideration is the product of questioning, either by the police or someone acting on the behalf of law enforcement, it is the objective intent of the questioner that is determinative. *Stechly*, 225 Ill. 2d at 284-85. However, where statements are not the product of law enforcement interrogation, the proper focus is on the intent of the declarant and the inquiry should be whether the objective circumstances would lead a reasonable person to conclude that his statement could be used against the defendant. *Stechly*, 225 Ill. 2d at 288-89.

The Illinois Supreme Court observed that the victim's interview with the investigator took place "on behalf of the police" and was "intended to gather information and establish past acts for future prosecution." The Supreme Court affirmed the appellate court and held that the victim's statements to the child abuse investigator and to the police detective were testimonial in nature and therefore were improperly admitted at trial in violation of defendant's right to confrontation. The state argued that "child abuse victims are often unavailable to testify because of their tender years" and that due to this concern the United States Supreme Court's decision in Crawford v. Washington, 541 U.S. 36 (2004), "is incompatible with the realities of child abuse prosecutions." The Illinois Supreme Court declined to accept this argument, relying on Davis v. Washington, 547 U.S. 813 (2006), noting that

> the Court in *Davis*, when faced with a similar argument in regard to victims of domestic violence, stated, 'We may not, however, vitiate constitutional guarantees when they have the effect of allowing the guilty to go free.' *Davis*, 547 U.S. at 832-33. Thus here, too, we may not abridge constitutional guarantees simply because they are a hindrance to the prosecution of child sexual abuse crimes.

10. Statements Made by Victim During Police Investigation for the Primary Purpose of Meeting an Ongoing Emergency Are Not Testimonial Under the Confrontation Clause of the Sixth Amendment and Are Admissible
Davis v. Washington, 547 U.S. 813 (2006)

The Supreme Court considered two consolidated cases. In the first case, a woman called 911 after her ex-boyfriend, against whom she had a no-contact order, entered her home and hit her. She dialed 911 during the domestic dispute but hung up the phone before speaking with an operator. The operator reversed the call and spoke with her. She described the context of the assault and the operator said the police were on their way but that they were going to check the area for defendant before coming to speak with her. Four minutes later, the police arrived and saw the victim, who was shaken and had fresh injuries on her forearm and her face. She was making frantic efforts to gather her belongings and her children to leave the residence. The state introduced the victim's 911 call in evidence. Defendant argued that the trial court erroneously admitted the 911 tape.

In the second case, police responded to a reported domestic disturbance and upon arrival found the victim sitting alone on the porch looking timid and frightened. She told the officers that nothing was wrong and gave them permission to enter the house. An officer noticed a gas heating unit in the corner with flames shooting out of the front of it and pieces of glass all over the floor in front of it. Defendant, who was present, told the officers that he and the victim had been arguing but everything was fine by then and the argument never became physical. The officers took the victim aside, refused to allow defendant to be in the same room, and questioned her about the events. Defendant became angry when an officer told him that he had to stay away while they investigated what had happened with the victim. The victim told the officers that defendant had physically attacked her and threw her down into the glass, which came from the heater that he broke, and that he punched her twice in the chest. After hearing the victim's side of the story, the officers had her fill out and sign a battery affidavit. The victim wrote the following: "Broke our furnace & shoved me down on the floor into the broken glass. Hit me in the chest and threw me down. Broke our lamps & phone. Tore up my van where I couldn't leave the house. Attacked my daughter." The state charged defendant with domestic battery and violation of his probation. The state subpoenaed the victim, but she did not appear as a witness at trial. The state called the officer who had questioned the victim to testify. Defendant repeatedly objected to the introduction of all of the evidence involving victim's oral and written statements. The prosecutor argued that the affidavit was written and signed under oath. Defense counsel responded "[t]hat [it] doesn't give us the opportunity to cross-examine [the] person who allegedly drafted it."

The United States Supreme Court explained that

> [w]ithout attempting to produce an exhaustive classification of all conceivable statements—or even all conceivable statements in response to police interrogation—as either testimonial or nontestimonial, it suffices to decide the present cases to hold as follows: Statements are nontestimonial when made in the course of police interrogation under circumstances objectively indicating that the primary purpose of the interrogation is to enable police assistance to meet an ongoing emergency. They are testimonial when the circumstances objectively indicate that there is no such ongoing emergency, and that the primary purpose of

> the interrogation is to establish or prove past events potentially relevant to later criminal prosecution.

The Supreme Court explained, however, that a conversation that begins as an attempt to determine the need for emergency assistance could nevertheless create testimonial statements, subject to the confrontation clause, once the emergency assistance purpose had been accomplished.

With respect to the first case, the Supreme Court found that the victim's statements to the 911 operator were not testimonial, but that any statements to the police officers once they arrived on the scene were testimonial. The Supreme Court recognized that a person who makes a statement to a 911 operator, while the event is happening, or shortly thereafter, is usually in a state of panic or excitement which is very different from a person who is being interrogated at a police station hours after an event. The Supreme Court explained that there was a difference between the scenario present in Crawford v. Washington, 541 U.S. 36 (2004) and here. It noted that

> [t]he difference between the interrogation [here] and the one in *Crawford* is apparent on the face of things. [Here, the victim] was speaking about events as they were actually happening, rather than "describ[ing] past events," Lilly v. Virginia, 527 U.S. 116, 137 (1999) (plurality opinion). [The witness's] interrogation [in *Crawford*], on the other hand, took place hours after the events she described had occurred. Moreover, any reasonable listener would recognize that [the victim here, unlike the one in *Crawford*], was facing an ongoing emergency. Although one might call 911 to provide a narrative report of a crime absent any imminent danger, [the victim's] call was plainly a call for help against *bona fide* physical threat. Third, the nature of what was asked and answered [here], again viewed objectively, was such that the elicited statements were necessary to be able to resolve the present emergency, rather than simply to learn (as in *Crawford*) what had happened in the past. That is true even of the operator's effort to establish the identity of the assailant, so that the dispatched officers might know whether they would be encountering a violent felon. *See, e.g.*, Hiibel v. Sixth Judicial Dist. Court of Nev., Humboldt Cty., 542 U.S. 177, 186 (2004). And finally, the difference in the level of formality between the two interviews is striking. *Crawford* was responding calmly, at the station house, to a series of questions, with the officer-interrogator taping and making notes of her answers; [here, the victim's] frantic answers were provided over the phone, in an environment that was not tranquil, or even (as far as any reasonable 911 operator could make out) safe.
>
> ***
>
> We conclude from all this that the circumstances of [victim's] interrogation objectively indicate its primary purpose was to enable police assistance to meet an ongoing emergency. She simply was not acting as a witness; she was not testifying.

With respect to the second case, the Supreme Court held that the domestic battery victim's statements given to the police in an affidavit were testimonial and therefore inadmissible at defendant's trial. The Supreme Court stated that it was clear that the officer was interrogating victim with the primary purpose of investigating a possible crime. The Supreme Court observed that

> [d]etermining the testimonial or nontestimonial character of the statements that were the product of the interrogation [here] is a much easier task, since they were not much different from the statements we found to be testimonial in *Crawford*. It is entirely clear from the circumstances that the interrogation was part of an investigation into possibly criminal past conduct [. . .]. There was no emergency in progress; the interrogating officer testified that he had heard no arguments or crashing and saw no one throw or break anything. When the

> officers first arrived, [the victim] told them that things were fine, and there was no immediate threat to her person. When the officer questioned [the victim] for the second time, and elicited the challenged statements, he was not seeking to determine [. . .] "what is happening," but rather "what happened." Objectively viewed, the primary, if not indeed the sole, purpose of the interrogation was to investigate a possible crime—which is, of course, precisely what the officer *should* have done.
>
> It is true that the *Crawford* interrogation was more formal. It followed a *Miranda* warning, was tape-recorded, and took place at the station house. While these features certainly strengthened the statements' testimonial aspect—made it more objectively apparent, that is, that the purpose of the exercise was to nail down the truth about past criminal events—none was essential to the point. It was formal enough that [the victim's] interrogation was conducted in a separate room, away from her husband (who tried to intervene), with the officer receiving her replies for use in his "investigat[ion]." [. . .] Such statements under official interrogation are an obvious substitute for live testimony, because they do precisely what a witness does on direct examination; they are inherently testimonial.

The Supreme Court observed that the charge against the defendant in the second case, domestic battery, is "notoriously susceptible" to intimidation or coercion against the victim to ensure that he or she does not testify. The Supreme Court noted that if the accused attempts to coerce silence from a potential witness then the sixth amendment provides a remedy of forfeiture which is based on equitable grounds. The Supreme Court noted that it took "no position on the standards necessary to demonstrate such forfeiture, but federal courts using Federal Rule of Evidence 804(b)(6), which codifies the forfeiture doctrine, have generally held the government to the preponderance-of-the-evidence standard. State courts tend to follow the same practice." The Supreme Court remanded the case to determine whether the defendant had forfeited his right to confrontation by virtue of his own wrongdoing.

11. Statements Made by Victim to Police Officers Attempting to Meet an Ongoing Emergency Are Not Testimonial and Their Admissibility Does Not Violate Defendant's Right to Confrontation
Michigan v. Bryant, 131 S. Ct. 1143 (2011)

The police found the victim lying next to his car in a gas station parking lot with a gunshot wound to his abdomen. The police asked him "what had happened, who had shot him, and where the shooting had occurred." The victim indicated that defendant shot him through a door in his house and the victim then drove himself to the gas station where the police found him. The victim was taken to a hospital and died a few hours later. The police found a hole through defendant's back door, the victim's identification documents at defendant's house and blood on defendant's back porch. The officers who found the victim testified as to his statements. Defendant claimed that the victim's statements to the police officers were testimonial and therefore inadmissible. The United States Supreme Court noted that unlike the circumstances in Davis v. Washington, 547 U.S. 813 (2006),

> [w]e now face a new context: a nondomestic dispute, involving a victim found in a public location, suffering from a fatal gunshot wound, and a perpetrator whose location was unknown at the time the police located the victim. Thus, we confront for the first time circumstances in which the "ongoing emergency" discussed in *Davis* extends beyond an initial victim to a potential threat to the responding police and the public at large. This new context requires us to provide additional clarification with regard to what *Davis* meant by "the primary purpose of the interrogation is to enable police assistance to meet an ongoing emergency."

***

> To determine whether the "primary purpose" of an interrogation is "to enable police assistance to meet an ongoing emergency," *Davis*, 547 U.S., at 822, which would render the resulting statements nontestimonial, we objectively evaluate the circumstances in which the encounter occurs and the statements and actions of the parties.
>
> ***
>
> The circumstances in which an encounter occurs—e.g., at or near the scene of the crime versus at a police station, during an ongoing emergency or afterwards—are clearly matters of objective fact. The statements and actions of the parties must also be objectively evaluated. That is, the relevant inquiry is not the subjective or actual purpose of the individuals involved in a particular encounter, but rather the purpose that reasonable participants would have had, as ascertained from the individuals' statements and actions and the circumstances in which the encounter occurred.

The Supreme Court explained that the existence of an ongoing emergency is an important factor in determining whether a declarant's statement is non-testimonial. Another factor to consider, the Supreme Court noted, is the "informality" of the encounter between a victim and the police. Here, the Supreme Court found that the police interaction with the victim took place in a public place in a "disorganized fashion." The Supreme Court then evaluated the statements and actions of the parties and found that

> [n]othing [the victim] said to the police indicated that the cause of the shooting was a purely private dispute or that the threat from the shooter had ended. The record reveals little about the motive for the shooting. [. . .] The police did not know, and [the victim] did not tell them, whether the threat was limited to him. The potential scope of the dispute and therefore the emergency in this case thus stretches more broadly than those at issue in *Davis* [. . .] and encompasses a threat potentially to the police and the public. [. . .] An emergency does not last only for the time between when the assailant pulls the trigger and the bullet hits the victim. If an out-of-sight sniper pauses between shots, no one would say that the emergency ceases during the pause. That is an extreme example and not the situation here, but it serves to highlight the implausibility, at least as to certain weapons, of construing the emergency to last only precisely as long as the violent act itself. [. . .] At no point during the questioning did either [the victim] or the police know the location of the shooter.

After establishing that the statements were made during an ongoing emergency, the Supreme Court turned to whether the statements were made for the purpose of allowing police to meet that emergency. It concluded that the statements were made for such purpose as evidenced by the victim's deteriorating condition and the fact that the police needed to find the shooter as soon as possible. The Supreme Court held that the statements were not testimonial hearsay and were not barred by the confrontation clause of the sixth amendment.

See also People v. Sutton, 233 Ill. 2d 89 (2009) (finding that statements made by victim who was "bleeding and staggering" on the street shortly after a shooting were non-testimonial, but treating statements made by the victim to the police in an ambulance on his way to the hospital as testimonial).

12. Testimonial and Non-Testimonial Statements Are Admissible Under the Forfeiture by Wrongdoing Doctrine

People v. Hanson, 238 Ill. 2d 74 (2010)

Defendant was convicted of first degree murder, armed robbery, aggravated kidnapping and identity theft in the deaths of his sister, her husband, and his parents. The police spoke with defendant's surviving sister who stated that she received a call from her now-deceased sister indicating that defendant was attempting to gain credit in their parents' names. The now-deceased sister also allegedly stated that defendant threatened to kill her if she ever told their father about defendant's actions. Defendant filed a motion *in limine* before trial seeking to exclude his sister's statements to the police about her belief that he was the perpetrator as inadmissible hearsay. The trial court denied his motion. The trial court granted the state's motion to admit testimony from defendant's surviving sister regarding her telephone conversation with her other sister who was murdered. Defendant's surviving sister testified at trial about her telephone conversation with her deceased sister and about her suspicion that defendant committed the murders.

Defendant argued on appeal that the trial court erred in admitting evidence of his sisters' telephone conversation about his threats before the murders. State contended that it had proved by a preponderance of the evidence that the defendant forfeited his right to cross-examine the deceased sister about her statements because he killed her in order to keep her from testifying against him. Defendant argued that the statements were inadmissible here because the forfeiture by wrongdoing doctrine requires the statements to be testimonial and to have some measure of reliability. The Illinois Supreme Court explained that

> [t]he doctrine of forfeiture by wrongdoing is a common law doctrine. As early as 1878, the United States Supreme Court acknowledged that if "a witness is absent by [a defendant's] own wrongful procurement, he cannot complain if competent evidence is admitted to supply the place of that which he has kept away." Reynolds v. United States, 98 U.S. 145, 158 (1878). The doctrine was later codified, at the federal level, by Federal Rule of Evidence 804(b)(6) as an exception to the general hearsay rule. FED. R. EVID. 804(b)(6). More recently, the Supreme Court, in Crawford v. Washington, recognized that the forfeiture by wrongdoing doctrine, in addition to serving as an exception to the hearsay rule, also "extinguishes confrontation claims on essentially equitable grounds." Crawford v. Washington, 541 U.S. 36, 62 (2004). [. . .]
>
> ***
>
> The doctrine of forfeiture by wrongdoing is not limited to evidentiary questions that raise *Crawford* concerns. Rather, Rule 804(b)(6) is a general exception to the hearsay rule. We have already expressed that the rule is coextensive with the common law doctrine. *Stechly*, 225 Ill. 2d at 272-73. This conclusion is based on the Supreme Court's acknowledgment that Rule 804(b)(6) codifies the forfeiture doctrine. Davis v. Washington, 547 U.S. 813, 833 (2006). [W]e now expressly recognize that the doctrine serves both as an exception to the hearsay rule and to extinguish confrontation clause claims.
>
> ***
>
> Traditionally, most hearsay exceptions allow the admission of nontestimonial evidence. *Crawford*, 541 U.S. at 56. Defendant provides no argument, other than a possible lack of reliability, for why the forfeiture by wrongdoing doctrine should not also permit nontestimonial statements. As we next discuss, lack of reliability is an insufficient rationale. Therefore, we hold that the doctrine may be applied to admit both testimonial and nontestimonial statements.

The Supreme Court then addressed the defendant's contention that the victim's statement was inadmissible because he could not test its reliability. The Supreme Court indicated that defendant "misapprehend[ed]" the purpose of the forfeiture by wrongdoing doctrine. It explained that defendant would have had a chance to test the reliability of his sister's statement had he not made her unavailable for trial by killing her. The Supreme Court also stated that defendant had sufficient opportunity to question the reliability of his other sister's testimony because she was an available witness at trial and was subject to cross-examination. The Supreme Court concluded that

> the forfeiture by wrongdoing doctrine by its application obviates the need to consider reliability. Under the doctrine, defendant had the opportunity to challenge the reliability of [his surviving sister's] testimony through cross-examination. Further, by his own wrongdoing, defendant forfeited his right to challenge the reliability of [of his deceased sisters] statements to [his surviving sister]. Accordingly, we hold that so long as the declarant's statements are relevant and otherwise admissible, statements admitted under the forfeiture by wrongdoing doctrine need not reflect additional indicia of reliability. Additionally, based on the testimony elicited at the hearing, discussed above, we cannot say that the circuit court's finding that defendant caused [his deceased sister] to be unavailable was arbitrary or unreasonable. The circuit court, therefore, did not abuse its discretion in granting the State's motion to allow [the surviving sister's] testimony.

13. Reviewing Court Must First Consider Whether a Statement Is Admissible per Statutory Requirements Before Evaluating a *Crawford* Confrontation Objection
In re E.H., 224 Ill. 2d 172 (2006)

The state brought a petition for adjudication of wardship against the minor for alleged improper sexual conduct with two children she babysat. The trial court determined that pursuant to 725 ILCS 5/115-10, the victims' statements made to their grandmother following the inappropriate conduct were admissible. The appellate court held that *Crawford* clearly rejected the admissibility of the type of statements that the Illinois statute permitted, finding section 115-10 to be unconstitutional. The court determined that the out-of-court statements made by the child victim of sexual abuse to her grandmother were accusatory statements and therefore testimonial, invoking the protections of the confrontation clause. The appellate court concluded that the admissibility of statements under the section 115-10 hearsay exception violated her rights under the confrontation clause because she never had an opportunity to cross-examine her accuser.

On appeal, the Illinois Supreme Court held that a reviewing court should consider first whether a statement is admissible as an evidentiary matter per statutory requirements before a *Crawford* confrontation objection is evaluated. In this case, the appellate court should have decided whether the trial court had erred in ruling that the child's statements were admissible pursuant to 725 ILCS 5/115-10. If that ruling was erroneous, the court should have decided next whether the error was harmless. Only after determining that the error was not harmless should the court have entertained the constitutional challenge. The Illinois Supreme Court reversed and remanded, stating that

> cases should be decided on nonconstitutional grounds whenever possible, reaching constitutional issues only as a last resort. [. . .] [T]he appellate court went on, having already decided the case before it, to evaluate the facial constitutionality of section 115-10 and declare the entire statute unconstitutional. Not only did this latter ruling violate the prohibition against deciding constitutional issues without first exhausting all potential nonconstitutional grounds for resolving the case, it was entirely unnecessary to decide the case before it. As we recently stated, courts "should not compromise the stability of the legal system by declaring legislation unconstitutional when a particular case does not require it."

14. Witness Is Unavailable for Purposes of Sixth Amendment Confrontation Clause If Prosecution Fails to Obtain the Witness' Presence at Trial After Making a Good-Faith Effort
Hardy v. Cross, 132 S. Ct. 490 (2011)

Defendant was charged with kidnapping and sexually assaulting a victim at knifepoint. Although the victim was fearful of testifying against defendant, she did testify and was fully cross-examined by the state. The jury found defendant not guilty of kidnapping and was unable to reach a verdict on the sexual assault charges. State decided to retry defendant. The victim indicated that although she was still afraid, she was willing to testify at the retrial. The state then became unable to reach the victim despite efforts to locate her. State's investigator repeatedly contacted the victim's mother, father, family members, her ex-boyfriend, and conducted checks of local hospitals, jails and morgues over a period of almost one month prior to retrial. The victim's mother told the investigator that the victim had called her and told her that she would not testify. Her mother did not know where the victim was or how to contact her. The state moved to have the victim's testimony admitted as former testimony and the trial court, finding that the victim was unavailable, granted the motion. The jury acquitted defendant of aggravated sexual assault but convicted him of criminal sexual assault. The appellate court agreed with the trial court's finding that the victim was unavailable because the state "conducted a good-faith, diligent search to locate" the victim. The Illinois Supreme Court denied defendant's petition for leave to appeal and the United States Supreme Court denied his petition for writ of certiorari. Defendant then filed a petition for a writ of habeas corpus. The United States District Court for the Northern District of Illinois denied the petition but the United States Court of Appeals for the Seventh Circuit reversed. The Seventh Circuit found that the Illinois appellate court "was unreasonable in holding that the State had made a sufficient effort to secure [the victim's] presence at the retrial."

The United States Supreme Court reversed the Seventh Circuit, finding that the Illinois appellate court's finding was not unreasonable. The Supreme Court observed that the state made repeated inquiries with the victim's family. Although the investigator did not question the victim's current boyfriend or friends in the area, the Supreme Court found that this was reasonable because the investigator did not have any reason to believe that any of these individuals would know where the victim was. The Supreme Court also found that the state appellate court was not unreasonable in holding that the prosecution's efforts to locate the witness were sufficient despite the state's failure to serve the victim with a subpoena when she indicated she was fearful about testifying at the retrial. The Supreme Court noted that the victim was afraid before testifying at the first trial but that she nevertheless testified. The Court explained that it had never before "held that the prosecution must have issued a subpoena if it wishes to prove that a witness who goes into hiding is unavailable for Confrontation Clause purposes, and the issuance of a subpoena may do little good if a sexual assault witness is so fearful of an assailant that she is willing to risk his acquittal by failing to testify at trial." The Supreme Court observed that "when a witness disappears before trial, it is always possible to think of additional steps that the prosecution might have taken to secure the witness' presence, but the Sixth Amendment does not require the prosecution to exhaust every avenue of inquiry, no matter how unpromising."

See also United States v. Owens, 484 U.S. 554 (1988) (noting that a prior out-of-court identification of a witness who is later unable to explain the basis of identification due to memory loss is admissible).

15. Violations of *Crawford v. Washington* Are Subject to Harmless Error Analysis
People v. Patterson, 217 Ill. 2d 407 (2005)

A jury convicted the defendant of first degree murder, concealment of a homicidal death, and arson. The defendant's girlfriend testified at a grand jury hearing but refused to testify at trial by invoking her privilege against self-incrimination. The judge declared her to be unavailable. Pursuant to 725 ILCS 5/115-10.2, the trial court allowed the prosecution to read her grand jury testimony to the jury. On appeal, the defendant argued that the admissibility of his girlfriend's grand jury testimony violated his right under the confrontation clause. The appellate court determined that under Crawford v. Washington, 541 U.S. 36 (2004), the trial court erred in admitting the grand jury testimony of defendant's girlfriend. However, the appellate court ruled that the error was harmless beyond a reasonable doubt and upheld the defendant's convictions.

The Illinois Supreme Court agreed that admitting the grand jury testimony violated the defendant's right under the confrontation clause. The critical inquiry in the case, however, was whether a *Crawford* violation was subject to harmless-error review. The Supreme Court first discussed the United States Supreme Court decision of Chapman v. California, 386 U.S. 18 (1967), which had held that a "constitutional error does not automatically require reversal of a conviction." The Illinois Supreme Court distinguished structural defects from ordinary trial errors. A structural defect, such as the absence of an attorney or a trial before an impartial judge, warrants reversal of a conviction because it affects the entire trial from beginning to end. It clouds the judgment of the trier of fact and results in substantial prejudice to the accused. The court defined trial errors as errors which occur during the state's presentation of the case to the jury "which may therefore be quantitatively assessed in the context of other evidence presented in order to determine whether its admission was harmless beyond a reasonable doubt." The court concluded that a confrontation clause violation is a trial error, and not a structural defect, that is subject to a harmless error analysis.

The Illinois Supreme Court recognized that prior to *Crawford*, confrontation clause violations were subject to harmless error review. The court also noted that the United States Supreme Court in *Crawford* declined to address the harmless error problem. The defendant claimed that the *Crawford* decision impliedly overruled previous decisions that had held that a confrontation clause violation may be subjected to harmless error review. The Illinois Supreme Court rejected this argument, stating that if the United States Supreme Court wishes to overturn a previous decision, it does so explicitly. Since *Crawford* was not an explicit rejection of the harmless error standard, the Illinois Supreme Court refused to find an implicit rejection of harmlessness. It concluded, therefore, that a *Crawford* violation may be subjected to a harmless error analysis.

Turning to whether the use of the girlfriend's grand jury testimony was harmless beyond a reasonable doubt, the court applied the test it announced in People v. Wilkerson, 87 Ill. 2d 151 (1981), in which the Illinois Supreme Court had listed

> three different approaches for measuring error under this harmless-constitutional-error test: (1) focusing on the error to determine whether it might have contributed to the conviction, (2) examining the other evidence in the case to see if overwhelming evidence supports the conviction, and (3) determining whether the improperly admitted evidence is merely cumulative or duplicates properly admitted evidence.

Applying this standard, the Illinois Supreme Court found that the other admissible evidence was overwhelming to sustain the convictions. The court noted that the grand jury testimony was merely duplicative of other perfectly admissible evidence and that the overwhelming evidence proved the defendant guilty beyond a reasonable doubt. Therefore, the error in admitting the grand jury testimony, while in violation of the defendant's right under the confrontation clause, was harmless beyond a reasonable doubt.

See also People v. McClanahan, 191 Ill. 2d 127 (2000) (reviewing court must be convinced beyond a reasonable doubt that error is harmless where claimed error impacts a federal constitutional right).

16. Defendant Must Have an Intent to Procure Unavailability of Witness for Forfeiture by Wrongdoing Doctrine to Apply
Giles v. California, 554 U.S. 353 (2008)

The defendant appealed his first degree murder conviction, arguing that the trial court improperly admitted statements made by his ex-girlfriend to police in violation of his sixth amendment right of confrontation. The statements were presented by the prosecution to rebut his claim of self-defense in the ex-girlfriend's murder. By causing his ex-girlfriend's unavailability, the California Supreme Court held that defendant had extinguished his right to confrontation under the doctrine of forfeiture by wrongdoing. The California Supreme Court also held that forfeiture by wrongdoing applies even if there is no evidence that the defendant had engaged in his wrongful conduct with the intent to eliminate the availability of the witness. Regardless of whether the defendant intended to prevent the witness from testifying, the court concluded that the defendant would benefit from his own wrongdoing if the witness' statements could not be used against him at trial.

The United States Supreme Court granted certiorari to decide whether the element of intent to cause a witness' absence at trial is necessary to trigger the application of the doctrine of forfeiture by wrongdoing. In a 6-3 decision written by Justice Scalia, the Court held that forfeiture by wrongdoing only applies to situations where the "defendant engaged in conduct designed to prevent the witness from testifying." In reaching its determination the majority referred to the first Supreme Court case that applied the forfeiture by wrongdoing doctrine, United States v. Reynolds, 98 U.S. 145 (1879). In *Reynolds*, the Supreme Court held that where a witness' absence results from the accused's own "wrongful procurement," he cannot complain that his constitutional rights have been violated. The Supreme Court determined that pursuant to the holding in *Reynolds* and other common law precedent, intent was a necessary element of the forfeiture by wrongdoing exception. The Supreme Court explained that under the common law rule,

> unconfronted testimony would not be admitted without a showing that the defendant intended to prevent a witness from testifying. In cases where the evidence suggested that the defendant had caused a person to be absent, but had not done so to prevent the person from testifying-as in the typical murder case involving accusatorial statements by the victim-the testimony was excluded unless it was confronted or fell within the dying-declarations exception. Prosecutors do not appear to have even argued that the judge could admit the unconfronted statements because the defendant committed the murder for which he was on trial.
>
> ***
>
> The State and the dissent note that common-law authorities justified the wrongful-procurement rule by invoking the maxim that a defendant should not be permitted to benefit from his own wrong. *See, e.g.*, G. GILBERT, LAW OF EVIDENCE 140-141 (1756) (if a witness was "detained and kept back from appearing by the means and procurement" testimony would be read because a defendant "shall never be admitted to shelter himself by such evil Practices on the Witness, that being to give him Advantage of his own Wrong"). But as the evidence amply shows, the "wrong" and the "evil Practices" to which these statements referred was conduct designed to prevent a witness from testifying. The absence of a forfeiture rule covering this sort of conduct would create an intolerable incentive for defendants to bribe, intimidate, or even kill witnesses against them. There is nothing mysterious about courts' refusal to carry the rationale further. The notion that judges may strip the defendant of a right that the Constitution deems essential to a fair trial, on the basis of a prior judicial assessment that the defendant is guilty as charged, does not sit well with the right to trial by jury. It is akin, one might say, to

> "dispensing with jury trial because a defendant is obviously guilty." *Crawford*, 541 U.S., at 62, 124 S. Ct. 1354.
>
> Not only was the State's proposed exception to the right of confrontation plainly not an "exceptio[n] established at the time of the founding," *id.*, at 54, 124 S. Ct. 1354; it is not established in American jurisprudence since the founding. American courts never-prior to 1985-invoked forfeiture outside the context of deliberate witness tampering.
>
> ***
>
> In 1997, this Court approved a Federal Rule of Evidence, entitled "Forfeiture by wrongdoing," which applies only when the defendant "engaged or acquiesced in wrongdoing that was intended to, and did, procure the unavailability of the declarant as a witness." FED. RULE EVID. 804(b)(6). We have described this as a rule "which codifies the forfeiture doctrine." Davis v. Washington, 547 U.S. 813, 833 (2006). Every commentator we are aware of has concluded the requirement of intent "means that the exception applies only if the defendant has in mind the particular purpose of making the witness unavailable." 5 C. MUELLER & L. KIRKPATRICK, FEDERAL EVIDENCE § 8:134, p. 235 (3d ed. 2007); 5 J. WEINSTEIN & M. BERGER, WEINSTEIN'S FEDERAL EVIDENCE § 804.03 [7] [b], p. 804-32 (J. McLaughlin ed., 2d ed. 2008); 2 K. BROUN, MCCORMICK ON EVIDENCE 176 (6th ed. 2006). The commentators come out this way because the dissent's claim that knowledge is sufficient to show intent is emphatically not the modern view. See 1 W. LAFAVE, SUBSTANTIVE CRIMINAL LAW § 5.2, p. 340 (2d ed. 2003).

The Supreme Court, relying on Davis v. Washington, 547 U.S. 813 (2006), noted that there is no requirement of prior confrontation of the unavailable witness because "one who obtains the absence of a witness by wrongdoing forfeits the constitutional right to confrontation."

Justice Breyer's dissent argued that the majority's formulation created a stronger standard than required for application of the forfeiture by wrongdoing exception by restricting its application to situations where it is the defendant's purpose rather than intent to cause the witness' unavailability. By killing his ex-girlfriend, the dissent argued, the defendant knew that she would be unavailable to testify against him, and that knowledge was sufficient to show that he intended to cause her unavailability. Further, the dissent maintained that injecting a strict element of intent into the forfeiture analysis frustrates the ethical objective of the doctrine because it still allows the accused to profit from his wrongdoing.

17. Confrontation Clause Does Not Grant an Absolute Right to Face-to-Face Confrontation of a Minor Victim of Abuse Who May Testify Outside of Defendant's Physical Presence

Maryland v. Craig, 497 U.S. 836 (1990)

Defendant was charged with child abuse, first and second degree sexual offenses, perverted sexual practice, assault, and battery of a six-year-old girl. The prosecution requested that the victim testify by one-way closed circuit television due to the "serious emotional distress" the child may suffer if required to testify in the courtroom. Defendant objected to the use of the procedure but the trial court granted the state's request.

The United States Supreme Court stated that a criminal defendant does not have an absolute right to face-to-face confrontation with the witnesses against him or her at trial. It explained that

> [t]he central concern of the Confrontation Clause is to ensure the reliability of the evidence against a criminal defendant by subjecting it to rigorous testing in the context of an adversary proceeding before the trier of fact. The word "confront," after all, also means a clashing of forces or ideas, thus carrying with it the notion of adversariness. [. . .] [T]he right guaranteed by the Confrontation Clause includes not only a 'personal examination,' but also (1) insures

> that the witness will give his statements under oath-thus impressing him with the seriousness of the matter and guarding against the lie by the possibility of a penalty for perjury; (2) forces the witness to submit to cross-examination, the 'greatest legal engine ever invented for the discovery of truth'; [and] (3) permits the jury that is to decide the defendant's fate to observe the demeanor of the witness in making his statement, thus aiding the jury in assessing his credibility.
>
> ***
>
> The combined effect of these elements of confrontation-physical presence, oath, cross-examination, and observation of demeanor by the trier of fact-serves the purposes of the Confrontation Clause by ensuring that evidence admitted against an accused is reliable and subject to the rigorous adversarial testing that is the norm of Anglo-American criminal proceedings.
>
> ***
>
> [W]e have never insisted on an actual face-to-face encounter at trial in every instance in which testimony is admitted against a defendant. Instead, we have repeatedly held that the Clause permits, where necessary, the admission of certain hearsay statements against a defendant despite the defendant's inability to confront the declarant at trial. [. . .] Thus, in certain narrow circumstances, "competing interests, if 'closely examined,' may warrant dispensing with confrontation at trial."

The Supreme Court found that actual face-to-face confrontation may be excused in prosecution of sexual offenses involving children. A procedure for the use of a one-way closed circuit television for the receipt of testimony of a child victim may pass constitutional challenges where the trial judge makes specific findings that this procedure is necessary in this case to protect the child from specific trauma occasioned by the presence of the defendant in the courtroom. The Supreme Court specified that although the procedure here prevented the child witness from seeing the accused, it

> preserve[d] all of the other elements of the confrontation right: The child witness must be competent to testify and must testify under oath; the defendant retains full opportunity for contemporaneous cross-examination; and the judge, jury, and defendant are able to view (albeit by video monitor) the demeanor (and body) of the witness as he or she testifies. Although we are mindful of the many subtle effects face-to-face confrontation may have on an adversary criminal proceeding, the presence of these other elements of confrontation-oath, cross-examination, and observation of the witness' demeanor-adequately ensures that the testimony is both reliable and subject to rigorous adversarial testing in a manner functionally equivalent to that accorded live, in-person testimony.

In making his or her ruling, the judge must be satisfied that the emotional distress or trauma which the child would experience in the presence of the defendant, face to face, is serious, more than mere nervousness, excitement, or some reluctance to testify.

18. The Right to Confront Witnesses Includes the Right to Hear and View Them as They Testify

People v. Lofton, 194 Ill. 2d 40 (2000)

The defendant was tried for predatory criminal sexual assault of a child. Pursuant to 725 ILCS 5/106B-5, the five year old victim was allowed to testify with her back to the defendant so that she would not see him. Additionally, podiums were placed in front of her so defendant could not see her. The appellate court held that this was improper because it violated defendant's right to confront witnesses against him. The appellate court explained that the trial court did not comport with the procedures set out in section 106B-5 which "have been found to pass constitutional muster." Section 106-5 requires the use of a closed-circuit television to transmit the testimony of the child witness after the trial court has determined that a child witness could suffer "serious emotional distress" if made to testify in defendant's presence. The appellate court noted that the trial court's procedure "had no basis in law and was violative of defendant's right to confrontation." The Illinois Supreme Court affirmed, explaining that

> although the confrontation clause generally requires face-to-face confrontation, the requirement is not absolute, the Supreme Court having carved out a narrow exception when denial of face-to-face confrontation is necessary to further an important public policy and the necessities of the case require. In the instant case the trial court's innovation falls far outside the narrow and limited exception created by Maryland v. Craig, 497 U.S. 836 (1990). When a child witness testifies pursuant to section 106B-5, which, as we have said, is similar to the statutory scheme allowed in *Craig*, the child testifies under oath, is subject to contemporaneous cross-examination, and "must testify under the watchful eyes of the parties and the fact finder." [citation omitted] The right to confront witnesses includes the right to hear and to view them as they testify.

The Illinois Supreme Court, however, concluded that the defendant was precluded from observing the victim during her testimony and this could have prejudiced his ability to aid counsel in effective cross-examination of the victim. Therefore, this procedure impinged upon the truth seeking purpose of the confrontation clause. The court further noted that the arrangement was neither authorized by statute nor the common law, it failed to ensure the reliability of the evidence, and it was, therefore, incompatible with the confrontation clause. Lastly, because the state did not argue that the error was harmless, it failed to meet its burden of proof on that issue, and the court declined to find the error harmless.

But see Bourjaily v. United States, 483 U.S. 171 (1987) (noting that hearsay statements of a non-testifying co-conspirator may be admitted against the accused despite the lack of a face-to-face encounter).

19. Sixth Amendment Confrontation Clause of the United States Constitution Prohibits the Admissibility of a Confession or an Admission of a Non-testifying Co-Defendant That Implicates the Defendant at Their Joint Trial
Bruton v. United States, 391 U.S. 123 (1968)

Defendant and co-defendant were convicted of federal charge of armed postal robbery. A postal inspector testified for prosecution that co-defendant confessed to the crime. The postal inspector claimed that co-defendant confessed that he and defendant had committed the crime. Co-defendant did not testify at trial. The trial court gave a limiting instruction to the jury to disregard the inadmissible hearsay evidence insofar as it incriminated defendant.

The United States Supreme Court found that such limiting instruction was insufficient to prevent the jury from using the improperly admitted evidence to determine defendant's guilt. It also determined that use of co-defendant's confession at the joint trial violated defendant's sixth amendment right to confrontation of witnesses against him since co-defendant did not testify. The Supreme Court held that "because of the substantial risk that the jury, despite instructions to the contrary, looked to the incriminating extrajudicial statements in determining petitioner's guilt, admission of [co-defendant's] confession in this joint trial violated [defendant's] right of cross-examination secured by the Confrontation Clause of the Sixth Amendment." The Supreme Court explained that the giving of a limiting instruction was insufficient in this case because

> there are some contexts in which the risk that the jury will not, or cannot, follow instructions is so great, and the consequences of failure so vital to the defendant, that the practical and human limitations of the jury system cannot be ignored. (citations omitted). Such a context is presented here, where the powerfully incriminating extrajudicial statements of a codefendant, who stands accused side-by-side with the defendant, are deliberately spread before the jury in a joint trial. Not only are the incriminations devastating to the defendant but their credibility is inevitably suspect, a fact recognized when accomplices do take the stand and the jury is instructed to weigh their testimony carefully given the recognized motivation to shift blame onto others. The unreliability of such evidence is intolerably compounded when the alleged accomplice, as here, does not testify and cannot be tested by cross-examination.

20. In Illinois, Non-Testifying Accomplice's Statement Implicating Defendant Is Inadmissible Even If Defendant's Trial Is Separate from Accomplice's Trial
People v. Johnson, 116 Ill. 2d 13 (1987)

Defendant was convicted of murder, conspiracy and attempted armed robbery after he attempted to rob a home and fired a shotgun that killed a 10-year-old occupant in the home. The state introduced in evidence statements by two accomplices who did not testify at defendant's trial because they invoked the fifth amendment privilege against self-incrimination. Two police officers testified as to the accomplices' statements which indicated that the defendant was the gunman. Defendant denied that he was the gunman and argued that admissibility of these statements violated his right to confront witnesses against him. The state argued that the evidence introduced via the police officers' testimony merely explained the procedures the police followed, but the Illinois Supreme Court disagreed, noting that

> [a]lthough a police officer's testimony recounting steps taken in the course of an investigation may be admissible without violating a defendant's confrontation rights, even though the officer's description of the progress of the case might suggest that non-testifying witnesses implicated the defendant (*see* People v. Holman, 103 Ill. 2d 133, 149 (1984); *see also* People v. Johnson, 114 Ill. 2d 170, 194 (1986)), the testimony presented here went beyond that. The detectives did more than simply recount what had been done; their testimony regarding the statements of [the accomplices] directly implicated the defendant in these crimes. [. . .] We conclude that the substantive use of the evidence violated the defendant's confrontation rights under the Federal and State constitutions. [citations omitted].
>
> ***
>
> Confrontation errors, though constitutional violations, do not automatically warrant reversal (*see* Lee v. Illinois, 476 U.S. 530 (1986); Delaware v. Van Arsdall, 475 U.S. 673 (1986); Schneble v. Florida, 405 U.S. 427 (1972), and the defendant's convictions may therefore be affirmed if we are able to conclude that the error was harmless beyond a reasonable doubt. *See* Chapman v. California, 386 U.S. 18 (1967). The error in admitting the evidence was repeated rather than isolated. The prosecutors referred at length to [the accomplices'] statements implicating the defendant, through the examination of the two detectives, and they stressed the information in closing argument [. . .]. Moreover, the defendant did not confess to the crime, and there was no physical evidence connecting him to the occurrence [. . .]. [The accomplices'] out-of-court accusations against the defendant went to the central issue at trial-whether the defendant was the gunman-and we cannot say that the error in presenting that information as substantive, and therefore hearsay, evidence of the defendant's guilt was harmless beyond a reasonable doubt. *See* People v. Smith, 38 Ill. 2d 13 (1967).

21. Limiting Instruction Directing Jury to Not Use Non-Testifying Co-Defendant's Confession Against Defendant Is Proper to Safeguard Defendant's Rights Where Confession Was Redacted to Eliminate All References to the Defendant

Richardson v. Marsh, 481 U.S. 200 (1987)

Defendant and two other individuals were implicated in robbery and multiple murders. Defendant and co-defendant were charged with murder, robbery and assault and were tried together, while the third individual remained at large. A police officer testified that co-defendant confessed to the crime. In his confession the co-defendant indicated that on the way to the victims' home, the third individual told him that he would have to kill the victims after robbing them. The co-defendant did not testify and the confession was redacted so that it contained no mention of the defendant and no indication that anyone other than co-defendant and the third individual participated in the crime. Defendant testified at trial that she did not plan to rob or kill anyone and that she did not know the other persons with her were armed and intended to kill the victims. She also claimed that she could not hear co-defendant and the third individual discussing their plans in the car because she sat in the back seat and the music was too loud to allow her to hear. Although the state warned the jury not to use the co-defendant's confession against defendant in the closing argument, it later linked co-defendant's statement regarding his conversation in the car to defendant.

The United States Supreme Court distinguished this case from *Bruton*, noting that in this case defendant was not "expressly implicated" in the crime by co-defendant's confession.

> By contrast, in this case the confession was not incriminating on its face, and became so only when linked with evidence introduced later at trial (the defendant's own testimony). [. . .] Where the necessity of such linkage is involved, it is a less valid generalization that the jury will not likely obey the instruction to disregard the evidence.
>
> ***
>
> We hold that the Confrontation Clause is not violated by the admission of a nontestifying codefendant's confession with a proper limiting instruction when, as here, the confession is redacted to eliminate not only the defendant's name, but any reference to his or her existence.

22. Evidence of Co-Conspirator's Admission Does Not Violate Sixth Amendment Confrontation Clause

People v. Schmitt, 131 Ill. 2d 128 (1989)

Defendant and co-defendant were initially tried in a joint bench trial for unlawful delivery of a controlled substance, but later requested that their trials be severed. Both parties agreed that the trials would be conducted simultaneously but as separate bench trials. Law enforcement agents testified at defendant's trial about circumstantial evidence that implicated him in the charged crime. The agents stated that they arrested co-defendant after one undercover officer bought cocaine from him. Co-defendant then agreed to call his "source" to come pick up the money from the transaction. The "source" agreed to come over to co-defendant's home. When the "source" arrived, the agents hidden inside within earshot heard him make several incriminating statements to co-defendant, and later identified the "source" as the defendant. The agents heard defendant counting the money and arrested him as he was leaving. Defendant argued that co-defendant's statement identifying him as the "source" of the drugs was erroneously admitted against him as a co-conspirator's admission and that it violated his right to confront witnesses against him. The Illinois Supreme Court explained that the statement was properly admitted and that it did

> not violate the confrontation clause of the sixth amendment and [was] reliable because (1) the statement was not an assertion about a past fact, (2) abundant evidence showed that declarant had personal knowledge of the incident, (3) it was unlikely that the declarant's statement was founded upon faulty recollection, (4) the statement made was spontaneous and against the declarant's penal interest, (5) the statement was not crucial or devastating, and (6) defendant was able to cross-examine the person who contended the statement was made. Dutton v. Evans, 400 U.S. 74, 87-89 (1970); People v. Goodman, 81 Ill. 2d 278 (1980).

23. Limiting Instruction Is Insufficient to Cure Prejudice of Non-Testifying Co-Defendant's Statement Implicating Defendant Where Statements Were Not Cleansed of All References to Non-Declaring Defendant
People v. Williams, 182 Ill. 2d 171 (1998)

Three defendants were charged with the shooting deaths of five victims. Defendant and one co-defendant were tried jointly and were convicted. Defendant contended on appeal that the trial court improperly admitted co-defendant's statements which implicated him. Several witnesses testified that co-defendant told them about the crime. Defense counsel objected to some of the testimony claiming that it was not "cleansed" of all references to the defendant, but the trial court overruled the objection. At the urging of both parties, the trial court instructed the jury the next day that the evidence was to be considered only against co-defendant. In closing arguments, the prosecutor "addressed the connection" between defendant's and co-defendant's statements. State argued that the statements were properly admitted because defendant was never mentioned by name or nickname. The Supreme Court disagreed, indicating that it is enough to "clearly imply the defendant's guilt." In this case, the Supreme Court observed that the "nature" of the statements and the "context of the joint trial" made it "impossible for the jury to conclude that the other person" implicated by co-defendant's statements was anyone other than defendant. State further contended that the trial court's limiting instructions were sufficient to protect the defendant's rights because the prosecutor did not urge the jury to use co-defendant's statements against the defendant. The Supreme Court rejected this argument as well, explaining that

> [h]ere, the limiting instructions were not proper. Despite a timely request, the limiting instructions were not given contemporaneously with any of the disputed witnesses' testimony; the jury was not instructed regarding the disputed witnesses until the day after they all finished testifying. *See* People v. Duncan, 124 Ill. 2d 400, 411 (1988).
>
> Furthermore, and contrary to the State's assertion, the prosecution did encourage the jurors to consider [co-defendant's] admissions against [defendant]. Such actions erased any possibility that the jury would be able to follow the mandate of the limiting instructions.
>
> ***
>
> The Supreme Court has recognized that it is error for a prosecutor to attempt to negate the court's limiting instruction by encouraging the jury to use a codefendant's statements in evaluating a defendant's case. *See* Richardson v. Marsh, 481 U.S. 200, 211 (1987). The prosecution's attempts during closing arguments to connect [defendant] to [co-defendant's] statements was a "constitutionally unacceptable attempt *** to circumvent the strictures of *Bruton* and the confrontation clause." People v. Cruz, 121 Ill. 2d 321, 333 (1988). Moreover, the admission of [co-defendant's] statements "at a joint trial, absent a total deletion of all references to defendant, violated established Illinois case law that is independent of *Bruton-Richardson* constitutional doctrine." People v. Duncan, 124 Ill. 2d 400, 415 (1988).

The Supreme Court concluded that the error in admitting the statements against defendant was not harmless beyond a reasonable doubt because the evidence of guilt was not overwhelming.

24. Accomplice's Confession Is Admissible for the Non-Hearsay Purpose of Rebutting Defendant's Testimony That His or Her Own Confession Was Coerced
Tennessee v. Street, 471 U.S. 409 (1985)

The United States Supreme Court held that a defendant's rights under the confrontation clause of the sixth amendment are not violated by the introduction of a confession of an accomplice for the non-hearsay purpose of rebutting the defendant's testimony that his own confession was coercively obtained. In defendant's separate murder trial, the state relied on his confession that he made to a sheriff. At trial, defendant claimed his confession was coercively obtained when the sheriff read him his accomplice's confession and instructed him to say the same thing. The sheriff testified that the defendant was never read the accomplice's confession. The accomplice's confession was admitted at trial for rebuttal. The Supreme Court explained that the

> [s]tate's most important piece of substantive evidence was [defendant's] confession. When [defendant] testified that his confession was a coerced imitation, therefore, the focus turned to the State's ability to rebut [his] testimony. Had the prosecutor been denied the opportunity to present [the accomplice's] confession in rebuttal so as to enable the jury to make the relevant comparison, the jury would have been impeded in its task of evaluating the truth of [defendant's] testimony and handicapped in weighing the reliability of his confession. Such a result would have been at odds with the Confrontation Clause's very mission—to advance "the accuracy of the truth-determining process in criminal trials." [. . .]
>
> The State introduced [the accomplice's] confession for the legitimate, nonhearsay purpose of rebutting [defendant's] testimony that his own confession was a coerced "copy" of [the accomplice's] statement. The jury's attention was directed to this distinctive and limited purpose by the prosecutor's questions and closing argument. In this context, we hold that the trial judge's instructions were the appropriate way to limit the jury's use of that evidence in a manner consistent with the Confrontation Clause.

See also People v. Caffey, 205 Ill. 2d 52 (2001) (finding that a statement by a third party inculpating someone other than defendant made to police officers during interrogation is not admissible because of the possible self-serving nature of such statement).

25. Marital Privilege Does Not Defeat Defendant's Right to Confrontation of Witnesses
People v. Foskey, 136 Ill. 2d 66 (1990)

In addition to the statutory exceptions, the marital privilege, which protects the disclosure of confidential communication, may not defeat a defendant's constitutional right to confront and cross-examine witnesses. Here, the Illinois Supreme Court held that the defendant's sixth amendment right to confront witnesses superseded his wife's marital privilege during cross-examination of her as a prosecution witness. The court stated that the marital privilege may yield to constitutional rights where the challenged evidence is critical and the purposes underlying the privilege would not be served. Here, the public policy for the privilege—marital harmony—had already been defeated by the wife's cooperation with the police and her testimony against the husband at trial. In this prosecution for possession of heroin with the intent to deliver, the wife was an important witness whose credibility was extremely important. Consequently, the court held that the accused could use evidence of letters and conversations, in which she allegedly admitted that she had had fabricated a story of conspiracy to murder police officers, in his cross-examination of his wife, notwithstanding the fact he was already allowed to cross-examine his wife as to bias and drug use.

See also People v. Sandoval, 135 Ill. 2d 159 (1990) (holding that right to confrontation is not violated where accused is prevented under Illinois rape shield law from inquiring about victim's prior sexual conduct with another person).

26. Confrontation Clause Applies Only to Criminal Proceedings
People v. Waid, 221 Ill. 2d 464 (2006)

The state charged the defendant with various drug and alcohol related offenses in four separate cases. A jury found the defendant unfit to stand trial and the trial judge found that there was no substantial probability that he would attain fitness in one year. The state moved for a discharge hearing to determine the sufficiency of the evidence against the defendant. A discharge hearing determines whether or not the state has sufficient evidence against the defendant. The discharge hearing is conducted by the court without a jury. Pursuant to 725 ILCS 5/104-25(a), the state moved for the admissibility of hearsay and affidavit evidence, including police reports, evidence logs, and state police lab reports regarding the chemical composition of the substances recovered from the defendant. The defendant argued that to allow the hearsay evidence without "accompanying testimony" would violate his right under the confrontation clause. The trial court agreed with the defendant and declared 725 ILCS 5/104-25(a) unconstitutional. The trial court recognized that although a discharge hearing is "apparently" a civil proceeding, "a finding of no acquittal (not not guilty) could result in the loss of defendant's freedom . . . if he were to be hospitalized or placed in facility of some sort."

On direct appeal to the Illinois Supreme Court, the state argued that the statute is constitutional, claiming that the confrontation clause applies only to criminal proceedings and a discharge hearing is akin to a civil proceeding rather than a criminal trial. Furthermore, the state argued that a discharge hearing is not a criminal prosecution. It is instead an "innocence only" proceeding that results in a final adjudication of charges only if the evidence fails to establish guilt beyond a reasonable doubt, resulting in an acquittal, or the defendant is found not guilty by reason of insanity. Should the evidence be found to be sufficient to establish the defendant's guilt, no conviction results. Instead, the defendant is found not not guilty and may be held for treatment. The defendant argued that a discharge hearing is comparable to a criminal proceeding because he could lose his freedom if found not not guilty. Additionally, the defendant argued that a discharge hearing is more criminal than civil in nature. Under section 104-25, a defendant who is found not not guilty is subject to an initial period of treatment, which may be followed by civil commitment. The defendant analogized the period of treatment and possible civil commitment to incarceration that results from a criminal conviction. A discharge hearing, he argued, is meant to determine whether a defendant is guilty and to impose punishment.

The Illinois Supreme Court agreed with the state that a discharge hearing is a civil proceeding. The court noted that a discharge hearing is an "innocence only" hearing, where the defendant may be acquitted but may not be found guilty. The court also acknowledged that the purpose of a discharge hearing is not to impose punishment, rather a discharge hearing enables an unfit defendant to have charges dismissed if the state cannot prove guilt beyond a reasonable doubt. According to the Supreme Court, "[t]he only possible final outcome is one that is favorable to the defendant: a determination that he is not guilty or not guilty by reason of insanity." Therefore, the court concluded that a discharge hearing is a civil proceeding. The statute that permits hearsay evidence did not violate the confrontation clause because the confrontation clause applies only to criminal proceedings. The Supreme Court determined that reliable hearsay of the type specified in 725 ILCS 5/104-25(a) is admissible at a discharge hearing, and it validated the constitutionality of the statute.

27. Defense Counsel May Waive Defendant's Right of Confrontation by Stipulating to Unavailable Witness' Out-of-Court Statement as a Matter of Trial Strategy as Long as Defendant Does Not Object

People v. Campbell, 208 Ill. 2d 203 (2003)

Defendant was charged with burglary after he entered a house occupied by two college roommates. The roommates were going out of town later that day for the spring break. A police officer testified at trial that burglaries increase significantly during times like spring break when most students leave town. On the day in question one occupant of the roommates' house was upstairs and the other was asleep on the couch downstairs. Defendant loudly knocked on the door for about two minutes. The upstairs occupant eventually came downstairs and saw defendant leaving the house. The state intended to call both roommates to testify at defendant's trial, but the roommate who was downstairs during the incident was unavailable. His testimony was material to the state's case because only he saw the defendant walk into his house and could testify as to whether defendant entered "without authority." State offered to stipulate to the unavailable witness' testimony and defense counsel agreed. The witness' stipulated testimony was that on the day in question he was asleep on the couch of his living room. He was awakened by loud knocking on the front door. He then heard the front door open and saw the defendant walk into the house. The defendant asked the witness if he had a room available for rent, after which the witness called the police and identified the defendant as the individual who entered his house without permission.

On appeal, defendant claimed that his attorney stipulated to the unavailable witness' testimony without his knowing consent and denied him the right to confront witnesses against him. In agreement with a majority of federal and state courts, the Illinois Supreme Court held that

> counsel in a criminal case may waive his client's sixth amendment right of confrontation by stipulating to the admission of evidence as long as the defendant does not object to or dissent from his attorney's decision, and where the decision to stipulate is a matter of legitimate trial tactics or prudent trial strategy. Where the stipulation includes a statement that the evidence is sufficient to convict the defendant or where the State's entire case is to be presented by stipulation, we find that a defendant must be personally admonished about the stipulation and must personally agree to the stipulation.

Defendant argued that without his attorney's stipulation to the key witness' testimony he could not have been convicted of the charged offense. Specifically, he argued that "defense counsel cannot stipulate to facts which establish the guilt of the accused because the constitutional right implicated in that situation is the right of a defendant in a criminal case to plead not guilty." The Supreme Court disagreed, noting that

> defense counsel can stipulate to prosecution testimony without a defendant's knowing consent because the decision to stipulate is a matter of trial strategy within defense counsel's sound judgment. [citation omitted]. The appellate court recognized two exceptions to its holding: (1) when the State's entire case is to be presented by stipulation; and (2) when the stipulation includes a statement that the evidence is sufficient to convict the defendant. [citation omitted]. In those situations, "the stipulation is tantamount to a guilty plea," so a defendant must be admonished about the stipulation and must agree to the stipulation before the court can accept such a stipulation. [citation omitted].

The Supreme Court did not find that the stipulation impacted defendant's fundamental rights or that it established defendant's guilt. Rather, it found that defense counsel used the stipulation strategically to explain that defendant's mindset was innocent when he entered the house because he was looking for a room to rent. The Supreme Court concluded that without the stipulation the defendant lacked an innocent explanation for his entry into the house and that defense counsel's decision to stipulate to the evidence was therefore a matter of trial strategy.

28. Where Defendant Fails to Object to a Stipulation and Defense Counsel Stipulates as a Matter of Trial Strategy, Defendant's Right to Confrontation Is Not Violated
People v. Phillips, 217 Ill. 2d 270 (2005)

A jury convicted the defendant of possession of a controlled substance with intent to deliver, unlawful possession of a controlled substance, unlawful possession of cannabis, and driving with a suspended license. The charges stemmed from a police officer recovering 25 individual bags containing a substance that appeared to be crack cocaine under the driver's side seat in the defendant's automobile. The officer pulled the defendant over and placed her under arrest for driving while her license was suspended. While conducting a search of the vehicle, the officer found the contraband. The officer questioned the passengers of the car regarding the suspicious items, and they denied having knowledge that the contraband was in the automobile. At trial, the defendant denied having knowledge of the cocaine that was found in the vehicle. She argued that the cocaine belonged to one of the passengers in the vehicle who was left unsupervised while the officer placed the defendant in his squad car. At the trial, the defendant stipulated as to the chain of custody and the chemical composition of the substance confiscated from her vehicle. On appeal, she argued that the stipulation violated her right under the confrontation clause because the record did not show that she had knowingly and voluntarily entered into the stipulation. The appellate court agreed with the defendant and reversed the trial court's judgment.

The Illinois Supreme Court discussed its holding in People v. Campbell, 208 Ill. 2d 203 (2003), which recognized that defense counsel may waive the defendant's right of confrontation when the accused fails to object to the stipulation and that defense counsel's decision to stipulate is a matter of trial tactics and strategy. In *Campbell*, the Supreme Court also recognized that the defendant must personally waive his confrontation rights "when the State's entire case is to be presented by stipulation and the defendant does not present or preserve a defense . . . or where the stipulation includes a statement that the evidence is sufficient to convict the defendant." The Supreme Court held that unless the stipulation is tantamount to a guilty plea there is no obligation on the trial court or counsel to admonish the defendant or to make a record of such advisement.

Here, the defendant presented a defense that she did not knowingly possess the substance but she did not object to the stipulation at trial. The court reasoned that the stipulation was a matter of trial strategy because it allowed the jury to focus its attention on the critical issue of whether the defendant had knowingly possessed the cocaine. Therefore, the Illinois Supreme Court reversed the appellate court and reinstated the conviction.

29. Where a Stipulation Is Tantamount to a Guilty Plea, Defendant Must Receive Personal Admonishment and Must Indicate That He or She Agrees to Its Entry
People v. Clendenin, 238 Ill. 2d 302 (2010)

Defendant was charged with unlawful possession of child pornography after his girlfriend found computer disks containing what she believed was child pornography at his home and turned them over to the police. The parties agreed to a stipulated bench trial. They entered a stipulation that in response to a police officer's question about how many disks contained child pornography, defendant responded "not many." Defendant did not stipulate to the sufficiency of the evidence and indeed objected to it twice and filed a motion to suppress evidence seized from his home and the statements he gave to the police. The stipulation "explicitly stated that it did not concede the sufficiency of the evidence to support a conviction." The trial court found defendant guilty and he appealed his conviction. Defendant contended that the stipulation amounted to a guilty plea and that he should have received personal admonishment and agreed to its entry. The Illinois Supreme Court disagreed, noting that

> this case does not present the circumstance where the stipulation was tantamount to a guilty plea, which would remove it from the ambit of the [People v. Campbell, 208 Ill. 2d 203 (2003)], general rule. As we have repeatedly held, a stipulation is tantamount to a guilty plea—and therefore requires a defendant's personal admonishment and agreement—in only two instances: (1) the State's entire case is to be presented by stipulation and the defendant does not present or preserve a defense; or (2) the stipulation includes a statement that the evidence is sufficient to convict the defendant. [citation omitted].
>
> Applying this rule to the instant appeal, it is clear that neither instance is met. Although the State's entire case was presented by stipulation, defense counsel adequately preserved a defense by preserving the suppression issue for appellate review. The stipulation twice objected to evidence and testimony "on the same grounds presented" in the earlier suppression motion, twice requested the circuit court to reverse its denial of the suppression motion, and objected to all evidence seized from defendant's home and his statements to police "as the illegal fruit of the unlawful search and seizure of the computer disk delivered to the police by [defendant's girlfriend]." Moreover, the stipulation explicitly stated that it did not concede the sufficiency of the evidence to support a conviction. Accordingly, the stipulation was not tantamount to a guilty plea requiring that defendant receive personal admonishments and that he agree to its entry.

The Supreme Court concluded that the defense counsel validly waived defendant's right to confrontation by entering into the stipulation as a matter of trial strategy and that defendant did not object to the stipulation.

30. Expert Testimony That Relies on Reliable Hearsay Is Nonetheless Proper to Explain Basis of Opinion
People v. Lovejoy, 235 Ill. 2d 97 (2009)

The Illinois Supreme Court held that a medical examiner's testimony as to toxicology testing performed by someone else did not violate Crawford v. Washington, 541 U.S. 36 (2004). The United States Supreme Court in Crawford held that testimonial out-of-court statements are barred unless the out-of-court declarant is unavailable as a witness and defendant had a prior opportunity to cross-examine him or her. The Illinois Supreme Court reasoned that the evidence was not admitted to prove the truth of the matter asserted but was instead used to explain the steps that the expert took in formulating his opinion. The Supreme Court observed that

> [t]his court has long held that prohibitions against the admission of hearsay do not apply when an expert testifies to underlying facts and data, not admitted into evidence, for the purpose of explaining the basis of his opinion. People v. Nieves, 193 Ill. 2d 513, 528 (2000); Sutherland, 223 Ill. 2d 187 (2006).

31. Analyst Report That a Substance Seized from Defendant Is a Controlled Substance Contains Testimonial Statements Requiring Analyst Who Generated the Report to Testify at Trial to Comport with the Sixth Amendment Right to Confrontation
Melendez-Diaz v. Massachusetts, 129 S. Ct. 2527 (2009)

The United States Supreme Court held that defendant was entitled to confront the analysts who generated reports introduced at trial attesting that a recovered substance was cocaine. The United States Supreme Court noted that the analysts' reports contained testimonial statements for purposes of defendant's sixth amendment right to be confronted with witnesses against him. If analysts were unavailable, the reports would be admissible only if defendant had a prior opportunity to cross-examine the analysts. State argued that the analysts' reports were admissible under the official and business records exception to the hearsay rule. The Supreme Court disagreed, explaining that

> the affidavits do not qualify as traditional official or business records, and even if they did, their authors would be subject to confrontation nonetheless. Documents kept in the regular course of business may ordinarily be admitted at trial despite their hearsay status. *See* FED. RULE EVID. 803(6). But that is not the case if the regularly conducted business activity is the production of evidence for use at trial. [. . .] Business and public records are generally admissible absent confrontation [. . .] because—having been created for the administration of an entity's affairs and not for the purpose of establishing or proving some fact at trial—they are not testimonial. Whether or not they qualify as business or official records, the analysts' statements here—prepared specifically for use at petitioner's trial—were testimony against petitioner, and the analysts were subject to confrontation under the Sixth Amendment.

32. Blood-Alcohol Analysis Report May Not Be Introduced Against the Accused at Trial Unless the Witness Who Made the Report Is Unavailable and Accused Had a Prior Opportunity to Cross-Examine Him or Her
Bullcoming v. New Mexico, 131 S. Ct. 2705 (2011)

Defendant was arrested for driving while intoxicated. State offered a forensic laboratory report that indicated his blood-alcohol level was above the threshold levels required for an aggravated DWI conviction. The analyst who signed the report did not testify at trial because he had recently been put on unpaid leave, but another analyst "familiar with the laboratory's testing procedures" testified. State offered the report in evidence as a business record. Defense counsel objected to the admissibility of this evidence, contending that it violated defendant's right to be confronted with witnesses against him. Trial court overruled the objection.

The United States Supreme Court followed its precedent in Melendez-Diaz v. Massachusetts, 129 S. Ct. 2527 (2009) and noted that the forensic laboratory report was not a business record because it was "prepared in connection with a criminal investigation or prosecution" and its primary purpose was to serve "as a substitute for trial testimony," making the report testimonial. The Supreme Court noted that the state failed to show that the analyst on unpaid leave was unavailable and no evidence existed that defendant had a prior opportunity to cross-examine him. The Supreme Court therefore held that "if an out-of-court statement is testimonial in nature, it may not be introduced against the accused at trial unless the witness who made the statement is unavailable and the accused has had a prior opportunity to confront that witness."

33. Statute Permitting State in Drug Prosecutions to Use Lab Reports in Lieu of Actual Testimony as *Prima Facie* Evidence of Contents of Substance at Issue Violates the Confrontation Clause
People v. McClanahan, 191 Ill. 2d 127 (2000)

Defendant was charged with the unlawful possession of less than 15 grams of cocaine. He challenged the constitutionality of 725 ILCS 5/115-15 that allows admissibility of laboratory reports without the testimony of the laboratory technician who conducted the analysis of the illegal substance. The Illinois Supreme Court found 725 ILCS 5/115-15 unconstitutional. Section 115-15 allows the state, in prosecutions under the Cannabis Control Act or the Illinois Controlled Substances Act, to "use lab reports in lieu of actual testimony as *prima facie* evidence of the contents, identification and weight of the substance at issue unless the defendant files a demand for the testimony of the witness who prepared the report" within seven days from receipt of the report.

On appeal, the defendant argued that section 115-15 violated the confrontation clause since it did not fit within any of the recognized hearsay exceptions. The Supreme Court agreed, finding that lab reports prepared for litigation do not fall within any recognized hearsay exception. Additionally, defendant challenged the seven day notice requirement, arguing that section 115-15(c) "impermissibly requires defendants to take an affirmative step to secure their confrontation rights or be deemed to have waived them, and that it fails to contain sufficient procedural safeguards to ensure that any such waiver is knowing and voluntary." The court again agreed with defendant's claim because it found that the statute did not require the state to show how the analysis was conducted or the qualifications of the technician who conducted the analysis. Moreover, the statute placed the burden of requesting the technician to testify on defendant within a specified amount of time and therefore required defendant to take affirmative steps to safeguard his or her confrontation rights. The Supreme Court explained that

> [t]he right of a defendant to be confronted with the witnesses against him is guaranteed by the Constitution and arises automatically at the initiation of the adversary process. Taylor v. Illinois, 484 U.S. 400, 410 (1988). Subsection (c) of section 115-15 impermissibly requires the defendant to take affirmative action to secure a right that he has already been constitutionally guaranteed or be deemed to have waived that right. We are unaware of any authority that permits the legislature to make a defendant's confrontation rights contingent upon action by the defendant, and the State has not argued that such authority exists.

34. Expert May Testify About Non-Testifying Third Party's Findings to Form Opinions

Williams v. Illinois, 132 S. Ct. 2221 (2012)

Defendant was charged with aggravated criminal sexual assault, aggravated kidnapping, and aggravated robbery. A sample of semen was recovered from the victim and was submitted for analysis to a laboratory. The laboratory examined that sample and generated a report. The report was not introduced in evidence at trial, but a forensic biologist relied on the report during her testimony as an expert. She compared the DNA profile analyzed by the laboratory to a sample of the defendant's blood. The prosecutor asked the expert whether the two samples matched, but the defendant objected to this line of questioning. Defendant contended that the expert was not permitted to rely on the DNA testing performed by another laboratory technician. The trial court, however, permitted the expert to answer the question. The expert concluded that the DNA sample from the victim matched that taken from the defendant. After the expert concluded her testimony, defendant sought to strike the evidence arguing that the state failed to establish proper foundation for the evidence and that it violated his sixth amendment right to confront witnesses against him. The Illinois Supreme Court disagreed.

The Illinois Supreme Court observed that there was sufficient evidence showing that the laboratory report was reliable and that sufficient foundation had been established for its use in the expert's testimony. The Supreme Court noted that the expert did not merely accept the laboratory's results but rather that she considered those results and drew her own conclusion while conducting an "independent evaluation of data." Moreover, the expert testified that she developed guidelines in addition to those employed by the laboratory to further safeguard the integrity of the process. The Supreme Court reasoned that the defendant had sufficient opportunity to cross-examine the expert, and that her reliance on the laboratory report "went to the weight of her opinion and not its admissibility."

With respect to the defendant's sixth amendment argument, the Supreme Court explained that "it is well established that an expert may testify about the findings and conclusions of a nontestifying expert that he used in forming his opinions." Defendant contended that the laboratory report relied upon by the expert was hearsay because the expert needed it to establish truth of the matter asserted—that defendant's DNA was a match to the sample recovered from the victim and analyzed by the laboratory. The Supreme Court disagreed, explaining that "the only statement that the prosecution offered for the truth of the matter asserted was [the expert's] own opinion." The Supreme Court distinguished Melendez-Diaz v. Massachusetts, 129 S. Ct. 2527 (2009). The Illinois Supreme Court explained the difference between the two cases as follows:

> We find that *Melendez-Diaz* does not change our determination. In *Melendez-Diaz*, the disputed evidence was a "bare-bones statement" that the substance was cocaine, and the defendant "did not know what tests the analysts performed, whether those tests were routine, and whether interpreting their results required the exercise of judgment or the use of skills that the analysts may not have possessed." *Melendez-Diaz*, 557 U.S. at ——, 129 S. Ct. at 2537. Here, [the expert] testified about her own expertise, judgment, and skill at interpretation of the specific alleles at the 13 loci, and confirmed her general knowledge of the protocols and procedures of [the laboratory]. [The expert] also conducted her own statistical analysis of the DNA match. She did not simply read to the judge, sitting as a fact finder, from [the] report. This [report] did not include any comparative analysis of the electropherograms or DNA profiles and was not introduced into evidence . . . [but] rather, was part of the process used by [the expert] in rendering her opinion concluding that the profiles matched. Thus, [the expert's] opinion is categorically different from the certificate in *Melendez-Diaz*.

The United States Supreme Court granted a writ of certiorari and affirmed the Illinois Supreme Court. The U.S. Supreme Court held that the expert's evidence did not violate the confrontation clause even though the expert lacked personal knowledge as to whether the DNA profile produced by Cellmark was based on the vaginal swabs of the victim. The Court found that the evidence was not offered for the truth of the matter asserted, and that there was no danger that during the bench trial the judge had considered the evidence substantively.

See also People v. Leach, 405 Ill. App. 3d 297 (1st Dist. 2010) *appeal allowed*, 239 Ill. 2d 572 (2011) (finding that autopsy reports, as "historically nontestimonial" business records may be admitted in evidence as *prima facie* proof of the cause of death under the public records exception to the hearsay rule).

Chapter 8

Chapter 8

Article IX – Authentication and Identification

Rule 901. Requirement of Authentication or Identification

(a) General Provision. The requirement of authentication or identification as a condition precedent to admissibility is satisfied by evidence sufficient to support a finding that the matter in question is what its proponent claims.

(b) Illustrations. By way of illustration only, and not by way of limitation, the following are examples of authentication or identification conforming with the requirements of this rule:

(1) **Testimony of Witness With Knowledge.** Testimony that a matter is what it is claimed to be.

(2) **Nonexpert Opinion on Handwriting.** Nonexpert opinion as to the genuineness of handwriting, based upon familiarity not acquired for purposes of the litigation.

(3) **Comparison by Trier or Expert Witness.** Comparison by the trier of fact or by expert witnesses with specimens which have been authenticated.

(4) **Distinctive Characteristics and the Like.** Appearance, contents, substance, internal patterns, or other distinctive characteristics, taken in conjunction with circumstances.

(5) **Voice Identification.** Identification of a voice, whether heard firsthand or through mechanical or electronic transmission or recording, by opinion based upon hearing the voice at any time under circumstances connecting it with the alleged speaker.

(6) **Telephone Conversations.** Telephone conversations, by evidence that a call was made to the number assigned at the time by the telephone company to a particular person or business, if (A) in the case of a person, circumstances, including self-identification, show the person answering to be the one called, or (B) in the case of a business, the call was made to a place of business and the conversation related to business reasonably transacted over the telephone.

(7) **Public Records or Reports.** Evidence that a writing authorized by law to be recorded or filed and in fact recorded or filed in a public office, or a purported public record, report, statement, or data compilation, in any form, is from the public office where items of this nature are kept.

(8) **Ancient Documents or Data Compilation.** Evidence that a document or data compilation, in any form, (A) is in such condition as to create no suspicion concerning its authenticity, (B) was in a place where it, if authentic, would likely be, and (C) has been in existence 20 years or more at the time it is offered.

(9) **Process or System.** Evidence describing a process or system used to produce a result and showing that the process or system produces an accurate result.

(10) **Methods Provided by Statute or Rule.** Any method of authentication or identification provided by statute or by other rules prescribed by the Supreme Court.

Adopted September 27, 2010, eff. January 1, 2011.

Committee Commentary

(3) Modernization: Where there was no conflict with statutes or recent Illinois Supreme Court or Illinois Appellate Court decisions, and where it was determined to be beneficial and uniformly or almost uniformly accepted elsewhere, the Committee incorporated into the Illinois Rules of Evidence uncontroversial developments with respect to the law of evidence as reflected in the Federal Rules of Evidence and the 44 surveyed jurisdictions. [One of t]he 14 instances of modernization of note [is] as follows:

***

> **(9) Rules 803(16) and 901(b)(8).** Statements in Ancient Documents. The 30-year limitation to real property, Reuter v. Stuckart, 181 Ill. 529, 54 N.E. 1014 (1899), is relaxed in favor of 20 years without subject matter restriction.

ILL. R. EVID. Committee Commentary § 3, pg. 2.

AUTHOR'S COMMENTARY

The new Illinois Rule of Evidence 901 has codified the Illinois common law rule that requires as a condition of admissibility the authentication or identification of evidence. People v. Greer, 28 Ill. 2d 107 (1963). The proponent must establish a foundation for the admissibility of the evidence. The foundation for the introduction of physical evidence may be established either through identification by a witness who is familiar with the item or by showing a chain of custody for it. People v. Woods, 214 Ill. 2d 455 (2005). If the opponent of the evidence wishes to challenge its authenticity, the proponent must demonstrate that the evidence, with reasonable probability, was not altered. People v. Alsup, 241 Ill. 2d 266 (2011). The proponent of the evidence need not establish both identification and a chain of custody, since a dual requirement would impose an unnecessary burden and not necessarily ensure a more fair trial. If an item is not readily identifiable or if it is susceptible to alteration by tampering or contamination, it must be authenticated by the chain of custody method. *Woods*, 214 Ill. 2d 455. This method requires that persons who had custody of the evidence testify that the possession was continuous and that the evidence remained in substantially the same condition during each person's possession. *Id.*; People v. Alsup, 241 Ill. 2d 266 (2011). A sufficient chain of custody does not require that every person involved in the chain testify. *Woods*, 214 Ill. 2d 455. Where one link of the chain is missing, the evidence may nonetheless satisfy the authentication process if a witness describes the condition of the evidence on its delivery and when it was examined. *Id.*

Illinois Rule of Evidence 901 mirrors the Federal Rule of Evidence 901, effective prior to its stylistic amendment on December 1, 2011, except that Illinois Rule of Evidence 901(b)(10) does not contain a reference to "Act of Congress" and omits the last four words ("pursuant to statutory authority"), of the federal rule. Gino L. DiVito, *The Illinois Rules of Evidence: A Color-Coded Guide Containing the New Rules, the Committee's General and Specific Comments, a Comparison with the Federal Rules of Evidence, and Additional Commentary* (*Including the Federal Rules of Evidence as Amended Effective December 1, 2011*) (Jan. 1, 2012), at 135, http://www.tdrlawfirm.com/assets/downloads/Illinois_Rules_of_Evidence_Color-Coded_Guide.pdf.

Pursuant to Illinois common law and now under Illinois Rule of Evidence 901(b)(1), foundation by identification is established by a witness familiar with the exhibit who identifies it in court. People *ex rel.* Sherman v. Cryns, 203 Ill. 2d 264 (2003).

Under prior Illinois common law and now under Rule 901(b)(2), a nonexpert witness may give an opinion authenticating a handwriting or signature if he or she is sufficiently familiar with the handwriting of the writer. The witness may testify to the authenticity of the writing or signature if it is shown that he or she had seen the person write on other occasions or had seen other writings that the author previously admitted to be in his or her handwriting. Authentication by circumstantial evidence is also permissible. A nonexpert witness may not testify about familiarity with handwriting that he or she gained after a litigation-triggering event. Board of Trustees v. Misenheimer, 78 Ill. 22 (1875). An expert witness, on the other hand, may authenticate a handwriting by comparing the exhibit with a previously authenticated sample per Illinois Rule of Evidence 901(b)(3). Pursuant to 735 ILCS 5/8-1501, jurors may examine the sample and the authenticated exhibit. Prior to the enactment of the Illinois Rules of Evidence, several Illinois appellate decisions cited Federal Rule of Evidence 901(b)(4) with approval and favored the rule's "liberality and flexibility" in its standard for authenticating a private writing. People v. Munoz, 70 Ill. App. 3d 76 (1st Dist. 1979); *see also* People v. Williams, 274 Ill. App. 3d 598 (1st Dist. 1995); People v. Chromik, 408 Ill. App. 3d 1028 (3d Dist. 2011). Under Illinois Rule of Evidence 901(b)(4) and under prior Illinois common law, an exhibit may be authenticated on the basis of its appearance, contents, substance, or other distinctive characteristics in conjunction with circumstantial evidence. People v. Munoz, 70 Ill. App. 3d 76 (1st Dist. 1979). The proponent need not disprove the possibility that someone other than the accused authored the writing. The writing may be authenticated merely by proving that the author was one of a small group of individuals that includes the accused.

Under Illinois Rule of Evidence 901(b)(3) and prior Illinois common law, an expert witness may authenticate evidence by comparing the exhibit with a previously authenticated exemplar. This method of authentication is commonly used in the authentication of bullets to show that a particular bullet was fired from a specific weapon. By comparing a bullet with one that is known to have been fired from a particular gun, the expert witness can determine whether the exhibit had the same source. The key to this method is that the exhibit shares common characteristics with an exemplar that comes from a known source. Before a comparison can be made, the proponent must establish that the control evidence is genuine. This may also be shown by stipulation.

Under prior Illinois common law and now under Illinois Rule of Evidence 901(b)(5), a voice may be authenticated by identification testimony of a person who states that he or she can identify the speaker, and is familiar with and could recognize the speaker's voice. People v. Harris, 17 Ill. 2d 446 (1959).

Under Illinois Rule of Evidence 901(b)(6), and under prior Illinois common law, voice identification of telephone conversations may be made by direct or circumstantial evidence. To lay a proper foundation for the admissibility of voice recordings of telephone conversations, "a witness to the conversation" must testify that the recording "as presented in court, accurately portrays the conversation in question." People v. Griffin, 148 Ill. 2d 45, 56 (1992). When a person calls a place of business for purposes relating to the business, the call is authenticated by testimony indicating that a phone call was made to a number assigned to a business, and that "the conversation related to business reasonably transacted over the telephone." ILL. R. EVID. 901(b)(6). The rationale for this rule is that a business "invites communication" and there is regularity of incoming calls and answers. Godair v. Ham Nat. Bank, 225 Ill. 572, 575 (1907).

Pursuant to Illinois Rule of Evidence 901(b)(7) and under prior Illinois common law, an official document or a public record must be authenticated as genuine before it may be admitted. People v. Halpin, 276 Ill. 363 (1916). It may be authenticated by proof that it is a public record, is authorized by law, and is kept by a public office. ILL. R. EVID. 901(b)(7).

Illinois Rule of Evidence 901(b)(8) has altered the prior Illinois common law rule which allowed statements in ancient documents in evidence if the documents pertained to real property and were in existence for 30 years or more. Gino L. DiVito, *The Illinois Rules of Evidence: A Color-Coded Guide Containing the New Rules, the Committee's General and Specific Comments, a Comparison with the Federal Rules of Evidence, and Additional Commentary* (*Including the Federal Rules of Evidence as Amended Effective December 1, 2011*) (Jan. 1, 2012), at 114, http://www.tdrlawfirm.com/assets/downloads/Illinois_Rules_of_Evidence_Color-Coded_Guide.pdf; *see* Johnston v. Masterson, 397 Ill. 168, 171 (1947); *and see* Reuter v. Stuckart, 181 Ill. 529 (1899). The "30-year limitation [has been] relaxed in favor of 20 years without subject matter restriction." ILL. R. EVID. Committee Commentary § 3, pg. 2.

Under prior Illinois common law and now under Illinois Rule of Evidence 901(b)(9), results or products of a process or system may be authenticated and admitted in evidence by a showing that the process or system produces an accurate result when properly operated and that it was in fact properly operated at the time the product or the process was generated. People v. Hanna, 207 Ill. 2d 486 (2003).

Photographs and videotapes may be admitted without witness testimony as to the accuracy of images depicted if the accuracy of the process that produced the evidence is established with sufficient foundation. People v. Taylor, 2011 IL 110067. A witness who has personal knowledge that the photograph is a correct portrayal of certain facts that existed when the photograph was taken must identify the photograph. People v. Cheek, 93 Ill. 2d 82 (1982). The witness need not be the photographer or have personal knowledge of the time or circumstances of the taking of the photograph, but the witness must have personal knowledge of the scene or of the object portrayed in the photograph and testify that the photograph correctly portrays it. Before a photograph may be admitted, the opponent is entitled to cross-examine the foundation witness. People v. King, 29 Ill. 2d 150 (1963). Photographs that may confuse or mislead the jury should be excluded. When a photograph portrays a crime scene but the conditions in the photograph differ from the conditions that existed when the crime was committed, it should not be admitted unless the changes in the conditions can be explained in a way that does not confuse or mislead the jury. However, the prosecutor, as the proponent of the photograph, does not have to prove that an unsecured crime scene was not altered between the time of the crime and the time that the photograph was taken. People v. West, 294 Ill. App. 3d 939 (5th Dist. 1998). The possibility that the condition of the scene may have changed goes to the weight of the evidence, not to its admissibility. *Id.*

A recent Illinois Supreme Court decision set forth the standards for the admissibility of a surveillance videotape under the new Illinois Rules of Evidence. The Supreme Court in People v. Taylor, 2011 IL 110067, held that the state established proper foundation for the admissibility of a surveillance videotape. The Supreme Court evaluated the following non-exhaustive factors:

> (1) the device's capability for recording and general reliability; (2) competency of the operator; (3) proper operation of the device; (4) showing the manner in which the recording was preserved (chain of custody); (5) identification of the persons, locale, or objects depicted; and (6) explanation of any copying or duplication process.

The Supreme Court emphasized that courts should evaluate these factors on a case-by-case basis and should primarily remain focused on the "accuracy and reliability of the process that produced the recording" *Id.* at 439.

Illinois Rule of Evidence 901(b) provides that methods of authentication and identification enumerated in sections (b)(1) through (b)(10) are not exhaustive and section (b)(10) indicates that methods provided by statute "or by other rules prescribed by the Supreme Court" are also proper.

Relevant Statutory Authority

Prosecutions for Theft, Retail Theft, Deceptive Practice, etc.; Evidence: 725 ILCS 5/115-9

§ 115-9. (a) In a prosecution for theft, retail theft, deceptive practice, robbery, armed robbery, burglary or residential burglary, the court shall receive as competent evidence, a photograph of property over which the accused is alleged to have exerted unauthorized control or to have otherwise obtained unlawfully, if the photograph:

(1) will serve the purpose of demonstrating the nature of the property; and
(2) is otherwise admissible into evidence under all other rules of law governing the admissibility of photographs into evidence. The fact that it is impractical to introduce into evidence the actual property for any reason, including its size, weight, or unavailability, need not be established for the court to find a photograph of that property to be competent evidence. If a photograph is found to be competent evidence under this subsection, it is admissible into evidence in place of the property and to the same extent as the property itself.

(b) A law enforcement agency that is holding as evidence property over which a person is alleged to have exerted unauthorized control or to have otherwise obtained unlawfully, shall return that property to its owner if:

(1) the property has been photographed in a manner that will serve the purpose of demonstrating the nature of the property, and if these photographs are filed with or retained by the law enforcement agency in place of the property;
(2) receipt for the property is obtained from the owner upon delivery by the law enforcement agency;
(3) the prosecuting attorney who is prosecuting a case that involves the property furnishes the law enforcement agency with a written request for return of the property to its owner; and (4) the property may be lawfully possessed by the owner.

(c) Notwithstanding the provisions of subsection (b) of this Section a court may, if a motion so requesting is filed by defendant before expiration of the time period specified in subsection (d) of this Section, order the law enforcement agency to hold such property as evidence pending completion of trial.

(d) The time period during which the defendant may file a motion with the court for retention of the property as evidence shall be as follows:

(1) if the property was being displayed, held, stored or offered for sale to the public by a person or entity holding a Retailers Occupation Tax Number issued by the State of Illinois, the time period shall expire 14 days after the arrest of the defendant;
(2) for all other property, the time period shall expire 30 days after the filing of an information or indictment, or in the case of misdemeanor charges within 30 days after the filing of a complaint.
Effective September 11, 1984.

Comparison: 735 ILCS 5/8-1501

§ 8-1501. Comparison. In all courts of this State it shall be lawful to prove handwriting by comparison made by the witness or jury with writings properly in the files of records of the case, admitted in evidence or treated as genuine or admitted to be genuine, by the party against whom the evidence is offered, or proved to be genuine to the satisfaction of the court.

Effective July 1, 1982.

Tests to Determine Inherited Characteristics: 750 ILCS 45/11

§ 11. Tests to determine inherited characteristics.

(a) In any action brought under Section 7 to determine the existence of the father and child relationship or to declare the non-existence of the parent and child relationship, the court or Administrative Hearing Officer in an Expedited Child Support System shall, prior to the entry of a judgment in the case, advise the respondent who appears of the right to request an order that the parties and the child submit to deoxyribonucleic acid (DNA) tests to determine inherited characteristics. The advisement shall be noted in the record. As soon as practicable, the court or Administrative Hearing Officer in an Expedited Child Support System may, and upon request of a party shall, order or direct the mother, child and alleged father to submit to deoxyribonucleic acid (DNA) tests to determine inherited characteristics. If any party refuses to submit to the tests, the court may resolve the question of paternity against that party or enforce its order if the rights of others and the interests of justice so require.

(b) The tests shall be conducted by an expert qualified as an examiner of blood or tissue types and appointed by the court. The expert shall determine the testing procedures. However, any interested party, for good cause shown, in advance of the scheduled tests, may request a hearing to object to the qualifications of the expert or the testing procedures. The expert appointed by the court shall testify at the pre-test hearing at the expense of the party requesting the hearing, except as provided in subsection (h) of this Section for an indigent party. An expert not appointed by the court shall testify at the pre-test hearing at the expense of the party retaining the expert. Inquiry into an expert's qualifications at the pre-test hearing shall not affect either parties' right to have the expert qualified at trial.

(b-1) Genetic testing must be of a type reasonably relied upon by experts in the field of genetic testing and performed in a testing laboratory accredited by the American Association of Blood Banks, or a successor to its functions.

(b-2) A specimen used in genetic testing may consist of one or more samples, or a combination of samples, of blood, buccal cells, bone, hair, or other body tissue or fluid.

(b-3) The testing laboratory shall determine the databases from which to select frequencies for use in calculation of the probability of paternity based on the ethnic or racial group of an individual. If there is disagreement as to the testing laboratory's choice, the following procedures apply:

(1) The individual objecting may require the testing laboratory, within 30 days after receipt of the report of the test, to recalculate the probability of paternity using an ethnic or racial group different from that used by the laboratory.

(2) The individual objecting to the testing laboratory's initial choice shall:

(A) if the frequencies are not available to the testing laboratory for the ethnic or racial group requested, provide the requested frequencies compiled in a manner recognized by accrediting bodies; or

(B) engage another testing laboratory to perform the calculations.

(b-4) If, after recalculation using a different ethnic or racial group, genetic testing does not rebuttably identify a man as the father of a child, an individual who has been tested may be required to submit to additional genetic testing.

(c) The expert shall prepare a written report of the test results. If the test results show that the alleged father is not excluded, the report shall contain statistics based upon the statistical formula of Combined Paternity Index (CPI) and the Probability of Paternity as determined by the probability of exclusion (Random Man Not Excluded = RMNE). The expert may be called by the court as a witness to testify to his or her findings and, if called, shall be subject to cross-examination by the parties. If the test results show that the alleged father is not excluded, any party may demand that other experts, qualified as examiners of blood or tissue types, perform independent tests under order of court, including, but not limited to, blood types or other tests of genetic markers. The results of the tests may be offered into evidence. The number and qualifications of the experts shall be determined by the court.

(d) Documentation of the chain of custody of the blood or tissue samples, accompanied by an affidavit or certification in accordance with Section 1-109 of the Code of Civil Procedure, is competent evidence to establish the chain of custody.

(e) The report of the test results prepared by the appointed expert shall be made by affidavit or by certification as provided in Section 1-109 of the Code of Civil Procedure and shall be mailed to all parties. A proof of service shall be filed with the court. The verified report shall be admitted into evidence at trial without foundation testimony or other proof of authenticity or accuracy, unless a written motion challenging the admissibility of the report is filed by either party within 28 days of receipt of the report, in which case expert testimony shall be required. A party may not file such a motion challenging the admissibility of the report later than 28 days before commencement of trial. Before trial, the court shall determine whether the motion is sufficient to deny admission of the report by verification. Failure to make that timely motion constitutes a waiver of the right to object to admission by verification and shall not be grounds for a continuance of the hearing to determine paternity.

(f) Tests taken pursuant to this Section shall have the following effect:

(1) If the court finds that the conclusion of the expert or experts, as disclosed by the evidence based upon the tests, is that the alleged father is not the parent of the child, the question of paternity shall be resolved accordingly.
(2) If the experts disagree in their findings or conclusions, the question shall be weighed with other competent evidence of paternity.
(3) If the tests show that the alleged father is not excluded and that the combined paternity index is at least 1,000 to 1, and there is at least a 99.9 percent probability of paternity, the alleged father is presumed to be the father, and this evidence shall be admitted.
(4) A man identified under paragraph (3) of subsection (f) as the father of the child may rebut the genetic testing results by other genetic testing satisfying the requirements of this Act which:

(A) excludes the man as a genetic father of the child; or
(B) identifies another man as the possible father of the child.

(5) Except as otherwise provided in this Act, if more than one man is identified by genetic testing as the possible father of the child, the court shall order them to submit to further genetic testing to identify the genetic father.

(g) (Blank).

(h) The expense of the tests shall be paid by the party who requests the tests, except that the court may apportion the costs between the parties, upon request. Where the tests are requested by the party seeking to establish paternity and that party is found to be indigent by the court, the expense shall be paid by the public agency providing representation; except that where a public agency is not providing representation, the expense shall be paid by the county in which the action is brought. Where the tests are ordered by the court on its own motion or are requested by the alleged or presumed father and that father is found to be indigent by the court, the expense shall be paid by the county in which the action is brought. Any part of the expense may be taxed as costs in the action, except that no costs may be taxed against a public agency that has not requested the tests.

(i) The compensation of each expert witness appointed by the court shall be paid as provided in subsection (h) of this Section. Any part of the payment may be taxed as costs in the action, except that no costs may be taxed against a public agency that has not requested the services of the expert witness.

(j) Nothing in this Section shall prevent any party from obtaining tests of his or her own blood or tissue independent of those ordered by the court or from presenting expert testimony interpreting those tests or any other blood tests ordered pursuant to this Section. Reports of all the independent tests, accompanied by affidavit or certification pursuant to Section 1-109 of the Code of Civil Procedure, and notice of any expert witnesses to be called to testify to the results of those tests shall be submitted to all parties at least 30 days before any hearing set to determine the issue of parentage.

Effective January 1, 2011.

Illinois Case Law Under the New Illinois Rules of Evidence

Photographs and Videotapes May Be Admitted Under the "Silent Witness Theory" of Admissibility Without Witness Testimony If Accuracy of the Process That Produced the Evidence Is Established with Sufficient Foundation

People v. Taylor, 2011 IL 110067

Defendant was caught stealing money out of a high school principal's office after a police officer installed a surveillance camera there. The police officer testified at defendant's bench trial about the surveillance equipment. He conceded that he "only recently begun using such equipment" and that he set the camera up according to instructions supplied by the camera's manufacturer. After the camera recorded defendant's actions, the officer copied the content of the video surveillance onto a VHS tape and locked it in his office desk. Defendant filed a motion *in limine* to exclude evidence of the tape. Defendant argued that the tape should be excluded because it contained a "30-second skip." The trial court denied the motion. At trial, defendant objected to the insufficiency of the foundation for the admissibility of the video, but ultimately the trial court found that the state had laid sufficient foundation and admitted the tape in evidence. The first segment of the video showed a man enter the principal's office, open a desk drawer and remove a pouch containing money. The second segment, recorded 30 seconds after the first segment had ended, showed the man still crouched behind the desk and then leaving. Defense counsel again objected, noting that the state failed to explain the 30-second skip on the tape. The officer explained that the camera stops recording when it does not sense motion and then starts recording again as soon as it senses motion. The trial court convicted defendant of misdemeanor theft and subsequently denied his motion to reconsider. The appellate court found that the copying process was insufficiently explained and that therefore the tape was inadmissible. The appellate court found that the state failed to establish proper foundation because it did not

> establish the reliability of the process that produced the tape. Specifically, according to the court, the State failed to establish a proper chain of custody, failed to establish that the camera

> was working properly and the original DVR recording had been preserved, and failed to give an explanation of the process of copying the recording on the DVR to the VHS tape. As such, the appellate court found that the State failed to establish even the probability that the VHS tape had not been tampered with.

The Illinois Supreme Court reversed the appellate court's judgment and affirmed defendant's conviction. In considering the admissibility of the tape, the Supreme Court noted that

> [m]ost jurisdictions now allow photographs and videotapes to be introduced as substantive evidence so long as a proper foundation is laid. Such evidence is generally admitted under the "silent witness" theory. (citation omitted). Under this theory, a witness need not testify to the accuracy of the image depicted in the photographic or videotape evidence if the accuracy of the process that produced the evidence is established with an adequate foundation. In such a case, the evidence is "received as a so-called silent witness or as a witness which 'speaks for itself.'" The silent witness theory was originally utilized in Illinois and elsewhere in connection with the admissibility of X rays. *See* Stevens v. Illinois Central R.R. Co., 306 Ill. 370, 375 (1922). The majority of cases now involve automatic cameras or surveillance systems where videotapes, CDs or DVDs are made from the system and sought to be admitted.
>
> ***
>
> Most jurisdictions point out that the circumstances of each case and, thus, the requirements to guarantee the genuineness of the evidence, will always differ. [. . .] Thus, while most courts set forth various factors to consider when assessing the process that produced the recording, these factors are not deemed exclusive foundation requirements.

The Supreme Court indicated that the appellate court considered six different factors, including the device's capability to record, the operator's ability, proper operation of the device, chain of custody, identification of what the tape depicted and explanation of the copying process. The Supreme Court emphasized that although these factors may be relevant, each case must be approached on an individual basis with the "dispositive issue in every case [being] the accuracy and reliability of the process that produced the recording." Specifically, the Supreme Court observed that the appellate court erred in not considering a police report that discussed the copying process. The Supreme Court explained that

> [i]t is widely recognized that when the trial court addresses preliminary questions, like the admissibility of evidence, it is not constrained by the usual rules of evidence. RALPH RUEBNER, ILLINOIS CRIMINAL TRIAL EVIDENCE 3 (4th ed. 2001); 11 ILL. PRAC., COURTROOM HANDBOOK ON ILLINOIS EVIDENCE § 104.1 (2001). *See also* ILL. R. EVID. 104(a) ("Preliminary questions concerning *** the admissibility of evidence shall be determined by the court, subject to the provisions of subdivision (b). In making its determination, the court is not bound by the rules of evidence except those with respect to privileges."). What this means is: "the court may consider hearsay or other evidence that would not be admissible if offered to the jury." Lorraine v. Markel Am. Ins. Co., 241 F.R.D. 534, 539 (D. Md. 2007); JACK B. WEINSTEIN & MARGARET A. BERGER, WEINSTEIN'S FEDERAL EVIDENCE § 901.06(1)(c)(iii) (2d ed. 1997) ("Rule 104(a) provides that inadmissible evidence may be considered in determining preliminary questions of admissibility"). Thus, the appellate court should have considered the report in determining the admissibility of the videotape and erred when it said there was no explanation of the copying process.

The Supreme Court concluded that the totality of circumstances indicated that the state established sufficient foundation for admissibility of the tape by showing that the camera was capable to record and that it was operating properly.

See also People v. Kladis, 2011 IL 110920 (holding that video recording of a traffic stop is relevant evidence and discoverable in misdemeanor DUI prosecutions).

Prior Illinois Case Law

1. Evidence Is Admissible Without Foundation If It Is Clear That the Matter in Question Is What the Proponent Claims It Is

People v. Normand, 215 Ill. 2d 539 (2005)

The Illinois Supreme Court found that photographs depicting pornographic images of children were "themselves the evidence of defendant's offense" in a child pornography prosecution. State introduced in evidence the photographs seized from defendant's home that depicted pornographic images of children. The state offered no other evidence supporting or explaining these photographs. Defendant was convicted. Defendant argued on appeal that if the photographs were sufficient evidence to sustain his conviction, then it was improper for the trial court to admit them without requiring authentication showing that they were a fair and accurate depiction of actual children. Defendant contended that the state did not prove that actual children were used in making the computer images. The appellate court rejected defendant's argument, finding that the state was not required to show that "the image is not something other than it plainly appears to be through some means other than an examination of the image itself." The Supreme Court also disagreed with the defendant and affirmed the appellate court, finding that the trier of fact was "capable of determining whether real children were used in pornographic images simply by viewing the images themselves." The court held that "any trier of fact could [have] conclude[d] beyond a reasonable doubt that the photographs depicted actual children, and that defendant knowingly possessed the images."

2. To Introduce an Object in Evidence, State Must Lay Adequate Foundation Either Through Identification Witnesses or Chain of Possession, Depending on the Character of the Item

People v. Woods, 214 Ill. 2d 455 (2005)

Defendant was charged with possession of a controlled substance with intent to deliver. In a bench trial, a police officer testified that he had observed a man, later identified as co-defendant, yelling "blows," a street term for heroin, to passing vehicles. The police officer observed one vehicle stop. He then saw the person driving the vehicle engage in a conversation with the co-defendant. The co-defendant directed the individual to the defendant. The individual exited the vehicle and walked over to the defendant. Defendant then accepted money from the individual, went to a parked van, retrieved an object underneath the vehicle and handed it to the individual. The police officer approached the defendant and placed him under arrest. The officer found no narcotics on his person but recovered three zip-lock packets from under the van. The defendant entered a stipulation regarding the chain of custody and a forensic chemist's opinion regarding the chemical composition of the zip-lock packets. The trial court found the defendant guilty of simple possession. In an unpublished opinion, pursuant to Supreme Court Rule 23, the appellate court reversed the conviction because the state did not establish a sufficient chain of custody for the physical evidence and a proper foundation for the testimony of the forensic chemist as an expert.

The state appealed to the Illinois Supreme Court. It argued that the defendant had waived his chain of custody claim because he failed to object to it at trial or raise it in a post-trial motion. Additionally, the state argued that the appellate court had erred in holding that the prosecution did not establish a proper chain of custody because the defendant did not allege any tampering of the contraband and had in fact stipulated to the chemical composition of the substance. The Illinois Supreme Court reversed the appellate court, explaining that

> [w]hen the State seeks to introduce an object into evidence, the State must lay an adequate foundation either "through its identification by witnesses or through a chain of possession." People v. Stewart, 105 Ill. 2d 22, 59 (1984); People v. Kabala, 225 Ill. App. 3d 301, 305 (1st Dist. 1992). The character of the item sought to be introduced into evidence determines which method of establishing a foundation must be employed. People v. Irpino, 122 Ill. App. 3d 767, 773 (2d Dist. 1984); People v. Graves, 107 Ill. App. 3d 449, 454 (1st Dist. 1982). For example, where an item has readily identifiable and unique characteristics, and its composition is not easily subject to change, an adequate foundation is laid by testimony that the item sought to be admitted is the same item recovered and is in substantially the same condition as when it was recovered. *Irpino*, 122 Ill. App. 3d at 773; People v. Gilbert, 58 Ill. App. 3d 387, 390 (1st Dist. 1978).
>
> However, in cases, such as that at bar, where a defendant is accused of a narcotics violation, the physical evidence is often not readily identifiable or may be susceptible to tampering, contamination or exchange. In such instances, the State is required to establish a chain of custody. *See* People v. Bynum, 257 Ill. App. 3d 502, 510 (1st Dist. 1994); People v. Hominick, 177 Ill. App. 3d 18, 29 (2d Dist. 1988). The State bears the burden to establish a custody chain that is sufficiently complete to make it improbable that the evidence has been subject to tampering or accidental substitution. People v. Harris, 352 Ill. App. 3d 63, 68 (1st Dist. 2004); *see also* People v. Whirl, 351 Ill. App. 3d 464, 471 (2d Dist. 2004); People v. Winters, 97 Ill. App. 3d 288, 289-90 (1st Dist. 1981). The State must show that the police took reasonable protective measures to ensure that the substance recovered from the defendant was the same substance tested by the forensic chemist. People v. Ryan, 129 Ill. App. 3d 915, 919 (1st Dist. 1984). Unless the defendant produces evidence of actual tampering, substitution or contamination, a sufficiently complete chain of custody does not require that every person in the chain testify, nor must the State exclude every possibility of tampering or contamination; the State must demonstrate, however, that reasonable measures were employed to protect the evidence from the time that it was seized and that it was unlikely that the evidence has been altered. *Harris*, 352 Ill. App. 3d at 68-69; *Bynum*, 257 Ill. App. 3d at 510; People v. Reed, 243 Ill. App. 3d 598, 604 (1st Dist. 1993); People v. Pettis, 184 Ill. App. 3d 743, 753 (2d Dist. 1989).
>
> "Once the State has established the probability that the evidence was not compromised, and unless the defendant shows actual evidence of tampering or substitution, deficiencies in the chain of custody go to the weight, not admissibility, of the evidence." *Bynum*, 257 Ill. App. 3d at 510; *Reed*, 243 Ill. App. 3d at 604; People v. Tsombanidis, 235 Ill. App. 3d 823, 833 (1st Dist. 1992). Even where the chain of custody has a missing link, "trial courts have properly admitted evidence where there was testimony which sufficiently described the condition of the evidence when delivered which matched the description of the evidence when examined." *Bynum*, 257 Ill. App. 3d at 510; *Pettis*, 184 Ill. App. 3d at 754; *Irpino*, 122 Ill. App. 3d at 775.

The Supreme Court determined that the state introduced evidence that linked the substance seized at the time of the arrest to the substance tested by the forensic chemist. It therefore concluded that the state had established its *prima facie* case showing that the evidence had not been compromised. Subsequently, the Supreme Court noted that the burden would shift

> to the defendant to produce evidence of actual tampering, alteration or substitution. Upon the defendant making such a showing, the burden again shifts to the State to rebut the defendant's claim. Under this scheme, a defendant is not required to show evidence of actual tampering or

> substitution unless the State has first established its *prima facie* showing that it is improbable that the evidence was compromised.

The Supreme Court then explained that a defendant may waive the requirement that the prosecution show a sufficient chain of custody "by entering into a stipulation with respect to the evidence." The state contended that defendant had waived his claim because he had failed to object to the chain of custody at trial and had stipulated to the chain of custody as well as to the chemist's analysis of the contraband. The Illinois Supreme Court agreed with the state and rejected the defendant's request to consider his claim under plain error. The Supreme Court recognized that a chain of custody attack may be raised for the first time on appeal under the plain error doctrine

> in those rare instances where a complete breakdown in the chain of custody occurs—e.g., the inventory number or description of the recovered and tested items do not match-raising the probability that the evidence sought to be introduced at trial was not the same substance recovered from defendant, a challenge to the chain of custody may be brought under the plain error doctrine. When there is a complete failure of proof, there is no link between the substance tested by the chemist and the substance recovered at the time of the defendant's arrest. In turn, no link is established between the defendant and the substance. In such a case, a failure to present a sufficient chain of custody would lead to the conclusion that the State could not prove an element of the offense: the element of possession. However, in the instant matter we are not faced with a situation that requires preservation of defendant's right to challenge the State's chain of custody for the first time on appeal.

The Supreme Court found that the state satisfied its burden to establish that reasonable protective measures were employed to protect the evidence and that it was unlikely that the evidence had been tampered with, substituted, or altered between the time of its seizure and the forensic testing. Regarding the defendant's argument that the state did not lay a proper foundation for the expert testimony, the Supreme Court held that by stipulating to the chemist's report and not objecting to the chain of custody at trial, the defendant had waived the claim for review because the stipulation informed the prosecution that the chain of custody was not an issue. The stipulation prevented the state from correcting a potential missing link in the chain of custody at trial.

3. Evidence May Be Authenticated by a Witness Who Has Personal Knowledge and Can Testify That Evidence Fully Represents What It Purports to Portray

People *ex rel.* Sherman v. Cryns, 203 Ill. 2d 264 (2003)

The defendant, a lay midwife, appealed a finding that she had violated provisions of the Nursing and Advanced Practice Nursing Act when she participated in the birth of a baby who died after a breech birth. The Director of the Illinois Department of Professional Regulation (hereinafter Department), filed a petition for injunctive relief against the defendant, alleging that her actions during the birth constituted practice of professional nursing and advanced practice nursing without a license. The parents of the baby engaged defendant to work with them in an at-home water birth. The birth was videotaped by two video cameras. One was mounted on a tripod and the other held by a friend. The baby's father testified that on the evening before giving his testimony, a police officer brought a videotape to his home. "Upon viewing the videotape, [the father] realized that the one tape contained the video recordings from both cameras present during the birth . . . [and] although he did not know who combined the two videotapes together, the videotape he viewed on the evening prior to his testimony truly and accurately reflected the events which transpired at his home on [the night of the birth]." The trial court admitted the tape in evidence over a foundation objection. The court did not at any time view the videotape during the proceedings, nor was the tape ever played in court. After the Department rested its case, defendant moved for a directed verdict, arguing that the Department failed to present evidence that "any of the acts performed by [defendant] during the birth . . . constituted acts of nursing or advanced practice nursing." The trial court granted the motion and denied the Department's petition for a preliminary injunction. The appellate court vacated the order, stating that the trial judge abused his discretion in ruling on the Department's request for a preliminary injunction without first viewing the videotape. On remand, the trial court reaffirmed its decision after viewing the videotape, stating that "there is no evidence in the record [. . .] from which this court could conclude that the activities of [defendant] constituted the practice of nursing or [m]idwifery." The appellate court reversed, holding that the father's testimony and the events depicted in the videotape established a *prima facie* case that defendant was practicing nursing or midwifery without a license at the time of the birth.

On appeal to the Illinois Supreme Court, defendant raised, *inter alia*, an evidentiary claim with respect to the videotape. The Supreme Court explained that

> [a] videotape may be admitted as demonstrative evidence when it is properly authenticated and is relevant to a particular issue in the case. Cisarik v. Palos Community Hospital, 144 Ill. 2d 339, 341-42 (1991). First, a foundation must be laid, by someone having personal knowledge of the filmed object, that the film is an accurate portrayal of what it purports to show. *Cisarik*, 144 Ill. 2d at 342. "Verification may be furnished by the testimony of any competent witness who has sufficient knowledge to testify that the videotape fully represents what it purports to portray." [citation omitted] Second, a videotape will be considered relevant only as long as its probative value is not substantially outweighed by the danger of unfair prejudice. *Cisarik*, 144 Ill. 2d at 342. The admission of a videotape into evidence is within the sound discretion of the circuit court and will not be disturbed absent an abuse of discretion.

Defendant asserted that "although [the father] stated that the videotape he viewed in his home the evening before his court testimony was an accurate portrayal of the events that occurred during his son's birth, this testimony was inadequate support for the admission of the videotape that was actually admitted into evidence." The Supreme Court agreed, stating that the Department proffered no testimony that the videotape that was actually admitted in evidence was the same tape the father had viewed at home and, therefore, his testimony with respect to the tape was insufficient to establish a foundation for the tape that was admitted. The court held that the circuit court abused its discretion when it admitted the videotape with insufficient foundation. Nevertheless, the court affirmed the order against the defendant based on the other *prima facie* evidence presented by the Department.

4. The Chain of Custody Method of Authentication Requires the Proponent of the Evidence to Establish That Is Improbable That the Evidence Had Been Subjected to Tampering or Accidental Substitution

People v. Alsup, 241 Ill. 2d 266 (2011)

Defendant was convicted of possession of a controlled substance with intent to deliver. Police officers participating in surveillance observed defendant standing in an alley alone. A man approached defendant and gave him money. Defendant then walked over to a row of garbage cans, leaned down, and picked up a small item. He then gave the item to the man. Defendant had two more transactions with two unknown men. The officers observing defendant called in an enforcement team. Members of the enforcement team arrested defendant and found a ziplock bag filled with 10 smaller ziplock bags and five tinfoil packets behind the garbage cans. The 10 ziplock bags weighed 1.05 grams, and the tinfoil packets weighed less than 0.1 grams. The police determined that the bags contained cocaine and packets contained heroin.

One police officer testified at trial that he transported the heroin to the police station where he turned the evidence over to an officer assigned to inventories. The officer assigned to inventories then labeled the evidence with a unique inventory number and entered it into a computer database. The officer then placed the evidence into a clear plastic bag labeled with information pertaining to the case and handed it over to the sergeant on duty. The sergeant then placed the narcotics into the narcotics vault. Following this testimony, the parties entered a stipulation as to expert testimony pertaining to the fact that the controlled substances recovered were cocaine and heroin, that the expert tested 9 items of heroin and 10 items of cocaine, and that a proper chain of custody of the substances was maintained.

The appellate court observed that there was a discrepancy between the number of items recovered from defendant and the number tested by the expert. The police recovered 5 bags containing heroin but the stipulation stated that the expert tested 9 bags containing heroin. Defendant argued that the state failed to prove him guilty of possession of heroin with intent to deliver because it did not establish a sufficient chain of custody for the items. The appellate court rejected his contention. Defendant filed a petition for rehearing. The appellate court granted the petition for rehearing and found that state had failed to establish a chain of custody. State appealed. The Illinois Supreme Court reversed, explaining that

> [i]n cases involving controlled substances, the rules of evidence require that before the State can introduce results of chemical testing of a purported controlled substance, it must provide a foundation for its admission by showing the police took reasonable protective measures to ensure that the substance recovered from the defendant was the same substance tested by the forensic chemist. People v. Woods, 214 Ill. 2d 455, 466 (2005). The trial court must determine whether the State has met its "burden to establish a custody chain that is sufficiently complete to make it improbable that the evidence has been subject to tampering or accidental substitution." *Id.* at 467. Once the State has established this *prima facie* case, the burden then shifts to the defendant to show actual evidence of tampering, alteration or substitution. *Id.* at 468.
>
> In the absence of such evidence from defendant, a sufficiently complete chain of custody does not require that every person in the chain testify, nor must the State exclude every possibility of tampering or contamination. *Id.* at 467. It is not erroneous to admit evidence even where the chain of custody has a missing link if there was testimony which sufficiently described the condition of the evidence when delivered which matched the description of the evidence when examined. *Id.* at 467-68247. At this point, deficiencies in the chain of custody go to the weight, not admissibility, of the evidence. *Id.* at 467.
>
> The chain of custody establishes a foundation for such evidence as reliable and admissible; it does not function as proof of the existence of an element of the crime of possession of a controlled substance. *Id.* at 473. Accordingly, a challenge to the chain of custody does not serve as a challenge to the sufficiency of the evidence to support a conviction and is not exempt from forfeiture. *Id.* Rather, such a challenge is considered an attack on the admissibility of the evidence and is thus subject to the ordinary rules of forfeiture. *Id.*; *see also* People v. Blair, 215 Ill. 2d 427 (2005) (discussing waiver and forfeiture).

The Supreme Court found that the state established a *prima facie* case as to the chain of custody by the stipulation and testimony of police officers, indicating that the items recovered by police were the same ones tested by the expert. The Supreme Court determined that defendant failed to satisfy his burden of proof because he did not present evidence showing that the evidence had been altered, tampered with, or substituted. The court concluded that any deficiencies in the chain of custody were relevant in considering the weight of the evidence rather than its admissibility. The Supreme Court observed that, unlike in People v.

Woods, 214 Ill. 2d 455 (2005), where there were missing links in the chain of custody and no witnesses who could testify to explain the lack of links, the evidence here was presented after the prosecution established a chain of custody. The court found that plain error review was not available to the defendant because he had "not established that 'rare' case where a 'complete breakdown' in the chain of custody occurred permitting him to raise a challenge to the discrepancy for the first time on appeal."

See also People v. Williams, 238 Ill. 2d 125 (2010), *aff'd* Williams v. Illinois, 132 S. Ct. 2221 (2012) (finding that to establish foundation for expert testimony pertaining to DNA testing performed by a non-testifying third party, it is sufficient to show that the testifying expert is qualified and based opinion on information reasonably relied upon by experts in the field).

5. Results or Products of a Process May Be Authenticated and Admitted in Evidence by a Showing That the Process Produces an Accurate Result When Properly Operated and That It Was in Fact Properly Operated

People v. Hanna, 207 Ill. 2d 486 (2003)

The Illinois Supreme Court held that the Department of Public Health was not required to repeat each test performed by the National Highway Traffic Safety Administration (NHTSA) on the breath analysis instruments used to test alcohol level in order to maintain the standards adopted by the NHTSA. In other words, the results of breath tests were not invalid, for purposes of DUI charges, because the testing devices were not maintained in accordance with NHTSA standards. Uncontradicted and undisputed "real-world" testimony of an expert witness for the state indicated that the Department did not have the equipment to conduct the tests and that the breath testing devices were all kept in a stable environment of a police station and, therefore, were not exposed to power fluctuations, vibrations, or temperature extremes.

6. To Establish Foundation for the Admissibility of Computer-Generated Business Records, Proponent Must Show That the Equipment Is Standard, Entries Were Made in the Regular Course of Business Near Time of Event and There Are Sufficient Indicia of Trustworthiness

People v. Hagan, 145 Ill. 2d 287 (1991)

Defendant was convicted of forgery and attempted theft by deception of over $100,000. He sought to lease commercial space from a firm. The firm requested that he submit a summary of his bank accounts. Defendant requested such a summary from his banker. The banker indicated that his bank accounts contained very low sums of money. She then wrote and signed a letter that did not contain defendant's account balances and included a separate note that provided the balance. Defendant took the letter that did not contain the balances and added information pertaining to his balances that was much higher than the actual amount in his bank accounts. Defendant then faxed the letter containing the banker's signature to the firm from Mailboxes, Etc. store. Employee of Mailboxes who was in charge of the facsimile machine testified at trial that she saw defendant fax various documents at the store. She noted that the store's facsimile machine "timely" records the dates and times it prints on documents it faxes. Defendant argued on appeal that he was prejudiced by the admissibility of the faxed letter because its authenticity had not been established and it was inadmissible hearsay. In determining whether the faxed letter had been authenticated, the Illinois Supreme Court looked to the

> guidelines for determining the admissibility of computer printouts of business records stored on electronic computing equipment. [S]uch printouts are admissible where it is shown that:

> (1) the electronic computing equipment is recognized as standard equipment;
>
> (2) the entries are made in the regular course of business at or reasonably near the time of the occurrence of the event recorded; and
>
> (3) the foundation testimony satisfies the court that the sources of information, method and time of preparation indicated its trustworthiness and justify its admission.
>
> We are concerned here with the third prong of the test [. . .] because defendant's objection is based on the foundation requirement. Accordingly, it was necessary that the sources of information, method and time of preparation indicated the trustworthiness and justify the admission of the "faxed" letter. Evidence which can establish the foundation requirement, by establishing the trustworthiness of such a document, includes testimony by a person who can explain a business' procedures for compiling information and methods for checking for mechanical and human error; explain the operation of the machine and testify that the machine properly did what it was supposed to do; and testify as to the mechanical reliability of the machine.

The Supreme Court observed that state fulfilled the foundation requirements for the facsimile document. The Mailboxes employee testified in detail about the store's procedures for faxing documents and that the machine was programmed to indicate the date, time and store's name on each document sent. The Supreme Court also rejected defendant's argument that the faxed letter and transmittal sheet were inadmissible hearsay, finding that defendant failed to preserve this issue for appeal.

Rule 902. Self-Authentication

Extrinsic evidence of authenticity as a condition precedent to admissibility is not required with respect to the following:

(1) Domestic Public Documents Under Seal. A document bearing a seal purporting to be that of the United States, or of any State, district, Commonwealth, territory, or insular possession thereof, or the Panama Canal Zone, or the Trust Territory of the Pacific Islands, or of a political subdivision, department, officer, or agency thereof, and a signature purporting to be an attestation or execution.

(2) Domestic Public Documents Not Under Seal. A document purporting to bear the signature in the official capacity of an officer or employee of any entity included in paragraph (1) hereof, having no seal, if a public officer having a seal and having official duties in the district or political subdivision of the officer or employee certifies under seal that the signer has the official capacity and that the signature is genuine.

(3) Foreign Public Documents. A document purporting to be executed or attested in an official capacity by a person authorized by the laws of a foreign country to make the execution or attestation, and accompanied by a final certification as to the genuineness of the signature and official position (A) of the executing or attesting person, or (B) of any foreign official whose certificate of genuineness of signature and official position relates to the execution or attestation or is in a chain of certificates of genuineness of signature and official position relating to the execution or attestation. A final certification may be made by a secretary of an embassy or legation, consul general, consul, vice consul, or consular agent of the United States, or a diplomatic or consular official of the foreign country assigned or accredited to the United States. If reasonable opportunity has been given to all parties to investigate the authenticity and accuracy of official documents, the court may, for good cause shown, order that they be treated as presumptively authentic without final certification or permit them to be evidenced by an attested summary with or without final certification.

(4) Certified Copies of Public Records. A copy of an official record or report or entry therein, or of a document authorized by law to be recorded or filed and actually recorded or filed in a public office, including data compilations in any form, certified as correct by the custodian or other person authorized to make the certification, by certificate complying with paragraph (1), (2), or (3) of this rule or complying with any statute or rule prescribed by the Supreme Court.

(5) Official Publications. Books, pamphlets, or other publications purporting to be issued by public authority.

(6) Newspapers and Periodicals. Printed materials purporting to be newspapers or periodicals.

(7) Trade Inscriptions and the Like. Inscriptions, signs, tags, or labels purporting to have been affixed in the course of business and indicating ownership, control, content, ingredients, or origin.

(8) Acknowledged Documents. Documents accompanied by a certificate of acknowledgment executed in the manner provided by law by a notary public or other officer authorized by law to take acknowledgments.

(9) Commercial Paper and Related Documents. Commercial paper, signatures thereon, and documents relating thereto to the extent provided by general commercial law.

(10) Presumptions Under Statutes. Any signature, document, or other matter declared by statutes to be presumptively or *prima facie* genuine or authentic.

(11) Certified Records of Regularly Conducted Activity. The original or a duplicate of a record of regularly conducted activity that would be admissible under Rule 803(6) if accompanied by a written certification of its custodian or other qualified person that the record

(A) was made at or near the time of the occurrence of the matters set forth by, or from information transmitted by, a person with knowledge of these matters;
(B) was kept in the course of the regularly conducted activity; and
(C) was made by the regularly conducted activity as a regular practice.

The word "certification" as used in this subsection means with respect to a domestic record, a written declaration under oath subject to the penalty of perjury and, with respect to a record maintained or located in a foreign country, a written declaration signed in a country which, if falsely made, would subject the maker to criminal penalty under the laws of the country. A party intending to offer a record into evidence under this paragraph must provide written notice of that intention to all adverse parties, and must make the record and certification available for inspection sufficiently in advance of their offer into evidence to provide an adverse party with a fair opportunity to challenge them.

Adopted September 27, 2010, eff. January 1, 2011.

Committee Commentary

(3) Modernization: Where there was no conflict with statutes or recent Illinois Supreme Court or Illinois Appellate Court decisions, and where it was determined to be beneficial and uniformly or almost uniformly accepted elsewhere, the Committee incorporated into the Illinois Rules of Evidence uncontroversial developments with respect to the law of evidence as reflected in the Federal Rules of Evidence and the 44 surveyed jurisdictions. [One of t]he 14 instances of modernization of note [is] as follows: ***

> **(12) Rule 902(11)**. Certified Records of Regularly Conducted Activity. Self-authentication of business records is provided by Rule 902(11), following the model of FED. R. EVID. 902(11) and 902(12) and 18 U.S.C. 3505. ILL. R. EVID. Committee Commentary § 3, pg. 2-3.

AUTHOR'S COMMENTARY

Illinois Rule of Evidence 902(1) Domestic Public Documents Under Seal

Certain types of evidence are inherently reliable and therefore need no independent basis for authentication. Consistent with prior Illinois common law, copies of domestic public documents under Illinois Rule of Evidence 902(1) are self-authenticating when accompanied by an official seal of the custodian of records. A certified copy or transcript of a public record may be introduced whenever the original would be admissible if the proponent can show that it is properly certified or otherwise authenticated as the original would have been. Court records may be authenticated by the signature of the court clerk and by affixing the court's seal. Illinois Rule of Evidence 902(1) has adopted Federal Rule of Evidence 902(1), in effect prior to its stylistic amendment on December 1, 2011. *See* Gino L. DiVito, *The Illinois Rules of Evidence: A Color-Coded Guide Containing the New Rules, the Committee's General and Specific Comments, a Comparison with the Federal Rules of Evidence, and Additional Commentary* (*Including the Federal Rules of Evidence as Amended Effective December 1, 2011*) (Jan. 1, 2012), at 136, http://www.tdrlawfirm.com /assets/downloads/Illinois_Rules_of_Evidence_Color-Coded_Guide.pdf; *see also* FED. R. EVID. 902, Federal Advisory Committee Notes (2011 Amendments) (noting that "changes are intended to be stylistic only"). The Federal Advisory Committee Notes to Federal Rule of Evidence 902(1) explain that

> [t]he acceptance of documents bearing a public seal and signature, most often encountered in practice in the form of acknowledgments or certificates authenticating copies of public records, is actually of broad application. Whether theoretically based in whole or in part upon judicial notice, the practical underlying considerations are that forgery is a crime and detection is fairly easy and certain. 7 WIGMORE § 2161, p. 638; CALIFORNIA EVIDENCE CODE § 1452.
>
> FED. R. EVID. 902, Federal Advisory Committee Notes (1972 Proposed Rules, Note to Paragraph (1)).

Illinois Rule of Evidence 902(2) Domestic Public Documents Not Under Seal

Illinois Rule of Evidence 902(2) has adopted Federal Rule of Evidence 902(2), in effect prior to its stylistic amendment on December 1, 2011. *See* Gino L. DiVito, *The Illinois Rules of Evidence: A Color-Coded Guide Containing the New Rules, the Committee's General and Specific Comments, a Comparison with the Federal Rules of Evidence, and Additional Commentary* (*Including the Federal Rules of Evidence as Amended Effective December 1, 2011*) (Jan. 1, 2012), at 137, http://www.tdrlawfirm.com/assets/downloads/ Illinois_Rules_of_Evidence_Color-Coded_Guide.pdf. The Federal Advisory Committee Notes to Federal Rule of Evidence 902(2) explain that

> [w]hile statutes are found which raise a presumption of genuineness of purported official signatures in the absence of an official seal, 7 WIGMORE § 2167; California Evidence Code § 1453, the greater ease of effecting a forgery under these circumstances is apparent. Hence this paragraph of the rule calls for authentication by an officer who has a seal.
>
> FED. R. EVID. 902, Federal Advisory Committee Notes (1972 Proposed Rules, Note to Paragraph (2)).

In Illinois, statutes provide for the self-authentication of court records (735 ILCS 5/8-1202), municipal records (735 ILCS 5/8-1203), and corporate records (735 ILCS 5/8-1204), which require the attachment of a corporate or a private seal if a corporation or an entity has one.

Illinois Rule of Evidence 902(3) Foreign Public Documents
Pursuant to prior Illinois common law rule, and now under new Illinois Rule of Evidence 902(3), public documents of foreign countries are self-authenticating provided they are certified by the appropriate authority in accordance with the laws of that country. *See In re* Ersch's Estate, 29 Ill. 2d 572 (1963). Illinois Rule of Evidence 902(3) mirrors Federal Rule of Evidence 902(3), in effect prior to its stylistic amendment on December 1, 2011. *See* Gino L. DiVito, *The Illinois Rules of Evidence: A Color-Coded Guide Containing the New Rules, the Committee's General and Specific Comments, a Comparison with the Federal Rules of Evidence, and Additional Commentary (Including the Federal Rules of Evidence as Amended Effective December 1, 2011)* (Jan. 1, 2012), at 137-38, http://www.tdrlawfirm.com/assets/downloads/Illinois_Rules_of_Evidence_Color-Coded_Guide.pdf.

Illinois Rule of Evidence 902(4) Certified Copies of Public Records
Illinois Rule of Evidence 902(4) follows the model of Federal Rule of Evidence 902(4), in effect prior to its stylistic amendment on December 1, 2011, but it has substituted the word "statute" in the place of an "Act of Congress." *See* Gino L. DiVito, *The Illinois Rules of Evidence: A Color-Coded Guide Containing the New Rules, the Committee's General and Specific Comments, a Comparison with the Federal Rules of Evidence, and Additional Commentary (Including the Federal Rules of Evidence as Amended Effective December 1, 2011)* (Jan. 1, 2012), at 139, http://www.tdrlawfirm.com/assets/downloads/Illinois_Rules_of_Evidence_Color-Coded_Guide.pdf. It provides for the admissibility of public records if they are certified by the custodian of the records or another authorized person, by a certificate complying with Illinois Rules of Evidence 902(1), 902(2) and 902(3), or any statute or a Supreme Court Rule. ILL. R. EVID. 902(4). The new Illinois Rule of Evidence 902(4) is consistent with prior Illinois common law. *See e.g.*, People v. Smith, 113 Ill. App. 3d 101 (4th Dist. 1983) (noting that "Rule 902(4) of the Federal Rules of Evidence . . . permits proof of public records by copy certified by the custodian or other person authorized to make the certificate. The rule makes no limitation upon the use of such certified copies against an accused in a criminal case."). The commentary to Federal Rule of Evidence 902(4) warns, however, that

> the certification procedure here provided extends only to public records, reports, and recorded documents, all including data compilations, and does not apply to public documents generally. Hence documents provable when presented in original form under paragraphs (1), (2), or (3) may not be provable by certified copy under paragraph (4).
>
> FED. R. EVID. 902, Federal Advisory Committee Notes (1972 Proposed Rules, Note to Paragraph (4)).

The certification procedure under Illinois Rule of Evidence 902(4), like the procedure under Federal Rule of Evidence 902(4), does not extend to "public documents generally." FED. R. EVID. 902, Federal Advisory Committee Notes (1972 Proposed Rules, Note to Paragraph (4)).

Illinois Rule of Evidence 902(5) Official Publications
Pursuant to prior Illinois common law, and now under Illinois Rule of Evidence 902(5), official documents, books, or publications issued by a public authority are self-authenticating on the basis of the presumed validity of their source. Illinois Cent. R. Co. v. Warriner, 229 Ill. 91 (1907). Illinois Rule of Evidence 902(5) mirrors Federal Rule of Evidence 902(5), in effect prior to its stylistic amendment on December 1, 2011. *See* Gino

L. DiVito, *The Illinois Rules of Evidence: A Color-Coded Guide Containing the New Rules, the Committee's General and Specific Comments, a Comparison with the Federal Rules of Evidence, and Additional Commentary (Including the Federal Rules of Evidence as Amended Effective December 1, 2011)* (Jan. 1, 2012), at 139, http://www.tdrlawfirm.com/assets/downloads/Illinois_Rules_of_Evidence_Color-Coded_Guide.pdf.

Illinois Rule of Evidence 902(6) Newspapers and Periodicals
Printed materials such as newspapers or periodicals are self-authenticating because of the unlikelihood that they are false. The Federal Advisory Committee Notes to Federal Rule of Evidence 902(6) note that "[t]he likelihood of forgery of newspapers or periodicals is slight indeed. Hence no danger is apparent in receiving them." FED. R. EVID. 902, Federal Advisory Committee Notes (1972 Proposed Rules, Note to Paragraph (6)). Illinois Rule of Evidence 902(6) mirrors Federal Rule of Evidence 902(6), in effect prior to its stylistic amendment on December 1, 2011. *See* Gino L. DiVito, *The Illinois Rules of Evidence: A Color-Coded Guide Containing the New Rules, the Committee's General and Specific Comments, a Comparison with the Federal Rules of Evidence, and Additional Commentary (Including the Federal Rules of Evidence as Amended Effective December 1, 2011)* (Jan. 1, 2012), at 139, http://www.tdrlawfirm.com/assets/downloads/Illinois_Rules_of_Evidence_Color-Coded_Guide.pdf.

Illinois Rule of Evidence 902(7) Trade Inscriptions and the Like
Under prior Illinois common law rule, and now under Illinois Rule of Evidence 902(7), trade inscriptions, brand names, or labels used in the business world are self-authenticating because accuracy promotes business interests. *See e.g.*, People v. Shevock, 335 Ill. App. 3d 1031 (4th Dist. 2003). Illinois Rule of Evidence 902(7) is modeled on Federal Rule of Evidence 902(7), but it has added that labels "indicating [. . .] content [and] ingredients," are also self-authenticating, in addition to inscriptions specifying "ownership, control [. . .] or origin," per Federal Rule of Evidence 902(7). *See* Gino L. DiVito, *The Illinois Rules of Evidence: A Color-Coded Guide Containing the New Rules, the Committee's General and Specific Comments, a Comparison with the Federal Rules of Evidence, and Additional Commentary (Including the Federal Rules of Evidence as Amended Effective December 1, 2011)* (Jan. 1, 2012), at 139, http://www.tdrlawfirm.com/assets/downloads/Illinois_Rules_of_Evidence_Color-Coded_Guide.pdf. Justice DiVito notes that this change to Illinois Rule of Evidence 902(7) was made to "codify Illinois common law." *Id.*; *see e.g.*, People v. Shevock, 335 Ill. App. 3d 1031 (4th Dist. 2003) (finding that an ingredients label on a medicine container is a self-authenticating trade inscription).

Illinois Rule of Evidence 902(8) Acknowledged Documents
Consistent with Federal Rule of Evidence 902(8), in effect prior to its stylistic amendment on December 1, 2011, Illinois Rule of Evidence 902(8) provides for the self-authentication of acknowledged documents. *See* Gino L. DiVito, *The Illinois Rules of Evidence: A Color-Coded Guide Containing the New Rules, the Committee's General and Specific Comments, a Comparison with the Federal Rules of Evidence, and Additional Commentary (Including the Federal Rules of Evidence as Amended Effective December 1, 2011)* (Jan. 1, 2012), at 140, http://www.tdrlawfirm.com/assets/downloads/Illinois_Rules_of_Evidence_Color-Coded_Guide.pdf. Statutes such as the Uniform Recognition of Acknowledgments Act, 765 ILCS 30/1 *et seq.*, and the Conveyances Act, 765 ILCS 5/0.01 *et seq.*, provide procedures for self-authentication of deeds, mortgages, powers of attorney, conveyances or other documents.

Illinois Rule of Evidence 902(9) Commercial Paper and Related Documents
Pursuant to Illinois Rule of Evidence 902(9), which is based on Federal Rule of Evidence 902(9), in effect prior to its stylistic amendment on December 1, 2011, commercial paper

and related documents are self-authenticating pursuant to "general commercial law" such as the Illinois Uniform Commercial Code, 810 ILCS 5/1-202. *See* Gino L. DiVito, *The Illinois Rules of Evidence: A Color-Coded Guide Containing the New Rules, the Committee's General and Specific Comments, a Comparison with the Federal Rules of Evidence, and Additional Commentary (Including the Federal Rules of Evidence as Amended Effective December 1, 2011)* (Jan. 1, 2012), at 140, http://www.tdrlawfirm.com/assets/downloads/Illinois_Rules_of_Evidence_Color-Coded_Guide.pdf.

Illinois Rule of Evidence 902(10) Presumptions Under Statutes

Illinois Rule of Evidence 902(10) is based on Federal Rule of Evidence 902(10), in effect prior to its stylistic amendment on December 1, 2011, although it has substituted the word "statutes" for "Acts of Congress" to make it Illinois-specific. *See* Gino L. DiVito, *The Illinois Rules of Evidence: A Color-Coded Guide Containing the New Rules, the Committee's General and Specific Comments, a Comparison with the Federal Rules of Evidence, and Additional Commentary (Including the Federal Rules of Evidence as Amended Effective December 1, 2011)* (Jan. 1, 2012), at 141, http://www.tdrlawfirm.com/assets/downloads/Illinois_Rules_of_Evidence_Color-Coded_Guide.pdf. It provides for self-authentication of signatures, documents or other matters that are under a statute "presumptively or *prima facie* genuine or authentic." Some examples of such statutes include 65 ILCS 5/1-2-6, which provides that published municipal ordinances are *prima facie* evidence of their contents; and 810 ILCS 5/8-114, which creates a presumption that signatures on securities certificates are "genuine and authorized."

Illinois Rule of Evidence 902(11) Certified Records of Regularly Conducted Activity

Illinois Rule of Evidence 902(11) "follow[s] the model of FED. R. EVID. 902(11) and 902(12) and 18 U.S.C. 3505." ILL. R. EVID. Committee Commentary § 3, pg. 4. It provides that an "original or a duplicate of a record of regularly conducted activity that would be admissible under [Illinois] Rule [of Evidence] 803(6)" is self-authenticating "if accompanied by a written certification of its custodian or other qualified person." ILL. R. EVID. 902(11). The record is properly certified if certain requirements previously codified in 725 ILCS 5/115-5 and regulated by Illinois Supreme Court Rule 236 are met. *See* Gino L. DiVito, *The Illinois Rules of Evidence: A Color-Coded Guide Containing the New Rules, the Committee's General and Specific Comments, a Comparison with the Federal Rules of Evidence, and Additional Commentary (Including the Federal Rules of Evidence as Amended Effective December 1, 2011)* (Jan. 1, 2012), at 139, http://www.tdrlawfirm.com/assets/downloads/Illinois_Rules_of_Evidence_Color-Coded_Guide.pdf. These requirements are now also stated in Illinois Rule of Evidence 902(11), which provides that a qualified individual must certify "that the record

A. was made at or near the time of the occurrence of the matters set forth by, or from information transmitted by, a person with knowledge of these matters;
B. was kept in the course of the regularly conducted activity; and
C. was made by the regularly conducted activity as a regular practice."

Illinois Rule of Evidence 902(11) differs from Federal Rule of Evidence 902(11) in that it provides for certification of domestic as well as foreign records. Federal Rule of Evidence 902(11) only provides for certification procedures of domestic records, while Federal Rule of Evidence 902(12) provides for such procedures where foreign records must be certified. *See* DiVito, *Color-Coded Guide* at 141-42. Illinois has not adopted Federal Rule of Evidence 902(12) as a separate rule, but rather it has incorporated its content in Illinois Rule of Evidence 902(11). *Id.* at 142-43.

Relevant Statutory Authority

Court Records: 735 ILCS 5/8-1202

§ 8-1202. Court records. The papers, entries and records of courts may be proved by a copy thereof certified under the signature of the clerk having the custody thereof, and the seal of the court, or by the judge of the court if there is no clerk.

Effective September 23, 1983.

Municipal Records: 735 ILCS 5/8-1203

§ 8-1203. Municipal records. The papers, entries, records and ordinances, or parts thereof, of any city, village, town or county, may be proved by a copy thereof, certified under the signature of the clerk or the keeper thereof, and the corporate seal, if there is any; if not, under his or her signature and private seal.

Effective September 23, 1983.

Corporate Records: 735 ILCS 5/8-1204

§ 8-1204. Corporate records. The papers, entries and records of any corporation or incorporated association may be proved by a copy thereof, certified under the signature of the secretary, clerk, cashier or other keeper of the same. If the corporation or incorporated association has a seal, the same shall be affixed to such certificate.

Effective July 1, 1982.

Authentication of Authority of Officer: 765 ILCS 30/3

§ 3. Authentication of authority of officer. (a) If the notarial act is performed by any of the persons described in paragraphs 1 to 4, inclusive of Section 2, other than a person authorized to perform notarial acts by the laws or regulations of a foreign country, the signature, rank, or title and serial number, if any, of the person are sufficient proof of the authority of a holder of that rank or title to perform the act. Further proof of his authority is not required.

(b) If the notarial act is performed by a person authorized by the laws or regulations of a foreign country to perform the act, there is sufficient proof of the authority of that person to act if:

(1) either a foreign service officer of the United States resident in the country in which the act is performed or a diplomatic or consular officer of the foreign country resident in the United States certifies that a person holding that office is authorized to perform the act;

(2) the official seal of the person performing the notarial act is affixed to the document; or (3) the title and indication of authority to perform notarial acts of the person appears either in a digest of foreign law or in a list customarily used as a source of such information.

(c) If the notarial act is performed by a person other than one described in subsections (a) and (b), there is sufficient proof of the authority of that person to act if the clerk of a court of record in the place in which the notarial act is performed certifies to the official character of that person and to his authority to perform the notarial act.

(d) The signature and title of the person performing the act are *prima facie* evidence that he is a person with the designated title and that the signature is genuine.

Effective January 1, 1970.

Certificate of Acknowledgment: 765 ILCS 30/6

§ 6. Certificate of acknowledgment. The words "acknowledged before me" means

(1) that the person acknowledging appeared before the person taking the acknowledgment, (2) that he acknowledged he executed the instrument, (3) that, in the case of:

(i) a natural person, he executed the instrument for the purposes therein stated;
(ii) a corporation, the officer or agent acknowledged he held the position or title set forth in the instrument and certificate, he signed the instrument on behalf of the corporation by proper authority, and the instrument was the act of the corporation for the purpose therein stated;
(iii) a partnership, the partner or agent acknowledged he signed the instrument on behalf of the partnership by proper authority and he executed the instrument as the act of the partnership for the purposes therein stated;
(iv) a person acknowledging as principal by an attorney in fact, he executed the instrument by proper authority as the act of the principal for the purposes therein stated;
(v) a person acknowledging as a public officer, trustee, administrator, guardian, or other representative, he signed the instrument by proper authority and he executed the instrument in the capacity and for the purposes therein stated; and

(4) that the person taking the acknowledgment either knew or had satisfactory evidence that the person acknowledging was the person named in the instrument or certificate.

Effective January 1, 1970.

Rights Saved, Deeds, Limitation: 5 ILCS 85/2

§ 2. The repeal of the acts and parts of acts mentioned in the preceding section shall not affect suits pending or rights existing at the time this act takes effect, and as to all corporations, municipal or private, heretofore formed under any act of incorporation mentioned in the preceding section, such act of incorporation, and all amendments thereof, shall continue in force to the same extent and with like effect as if the same had not been repealed by this act, nor shall such repeal, as above mentioned, be taken, construed or held to avoid or impair any grant made or right acquired, or cause of action now existing under any such acts or the amendments thereto, but as to all grants made or rights acquired or causes of action now existing, said laws shall be continued in full force and effect. *And all deeds or other instruments of writing affecting real estate, which have been proved or acknowledged according to any law in force at the time such proof or acknowledgment was made, may be recorded, and the same or a certified copy of the record thereof be read in evidence,* notwithstanding the repeal of such laws by this or any other act of this or the twenty-seventh General Assembly. And when any limitation law has been revised by this or the twenty-seventh General Assembly, and the former limitation law repealed, such repeal shall not be construed so as to stop the running of any statute, but the time shall be construed as if such repeal had not been made. [emphasis added].

Effective July 1, 1874.

Foreign Acknowledgment; Certificate of Conformity: 765 ILCS 5/22

§ 22. Where any deed, conveyance or power of attorney has been or may be acknowledged or proved in any foreign state, kingdom, empire or country, the certificate of any consul or minister of the United States in said country, under his official seal, that the said deed, conveyance, or power of attorney is executed in conformity with such foreign law *shall be deemed and taken as prima facie evidence thereof*. Provided, that any other legal mode of proving that the same is executed in conformity with such foreign law may be resorted to in any court in which the question of such execution or acknowledgment may arise. [emphasis added]

Certified Copies Recorded; Evidence: 765 ILCS 5/29

§ 29. Where an original deed, mortgage or other instrument relating to or affecting the title to real estate, having tracts of land therein described lying in different counties, has been or may hereafter be recorded in any of such counties, it shall be lawful to record a certified copy of such deed or other instrument in counties where the original has not been recorded; and the recording of such certified copy heretofore or hereafter shall be notice in the same manner that the filing and the recording of the original would be, and copies from *such records shall be prima facie evidence to the same extent as if the original had been so recorded.* [emphasis added]

Deeds and Other Writings; Record or Copy as Evidence; Presumption of Recital of Seal: 765 ILCS 5/35

§ 35. Every deed, mortgage, power or attorney, conveyance, or other writing, of or concerning any lands, tenements or hereditaments, which, by virtue of this act, shall be required or entitled to be recorded as aforesaid, being acknowledged or proved according to the provisions of this act, whether the same be recorded or not, may be read in evidence without any further proof of the execution thereof; and if it shall appear to the satisfaction of the court that the original deed, so acknowledged or proved and recorded, is lost or not in the power of the party wishing to use it, the record, or a transcript thereof, certified by the recorder in whose office the same may be recorded, may be read in evidence, in any court of this state, without further proof thereof; provided that if said deed, mortgage, power of attorney, conveyance, or other writing, or the acknowledgment thereto shall recite that the grantors therein sealed said instrument but the record of such instrument in the recorder's office fails to show the seal of said grantors, *it will be presumed that said instrument was properly sealed and that the omission of such seal arose in the transcription thereof in the recorder's office*. [emphasis added].

Effective July 15, 1941.

Illinois Uniform Commercial Code: 810 ILCS 5/1-202

§ 1-202. Notice; knowledge.

(a) Subject to subsection (f), a person has "notice" of a fact if the person:

(1) has actual knowledge of it;
(2) has received a notice or notification of it; or
(3) from all the facts and circumstances known to the person at the time in question, has reason to know that it exists.

(b) "Knowledge" means actual knowledge. "Knows" has a corresponding meaning.

(c) "Discover", "learn", or words of similar import refer to knowledge rather than reason to know.

(d) A person "notifies" or "gives" a notice or notification to another person by taking such steps as may be reasonably required to inform the other person in ordinary course, whether or not the other person actually comes to know of it.

(e) Subject to subsection (f), a person "receives" a notice or notification when:

(1) it comes to that person's attention; or
(2) it is duly delivered in a form reasonable under the circumstances at the place of business through which the contract was made or at another location held out by that person as the place for receipt of such communications.

(f) Notice, knowledge, or a notice or notification received by an organization is effective for a particular transaction from the time it is brought to the attention of the individual conducting that transaction and, in any event, from the time it would have been brought to the individual's attention if the organization had exercised due diligence. An organization exercises due diligence if it maintains reasonable routines for communicating significant information to the person conducting the transaction and there is reasonable compliance with the routines. Due diligence does not require an individual acting for the organization to communicate information unless the communication is part of the individual's regular duties or the individual has reason to know of the transaction and that the transaction would be materially affected by the information.

Effective January 1, 2009.

UNIFORM COMMERCIAL CODE COMMENT

* * * Purposes:

1. This section is designed to supply judicial recognition for documents which have traditionally been relied upon as trustworthy by commercial men.

2. This section is concerned only with documents which have been given a preferred status by the parties themselves who have required their procurement in the agreement and for this reason the applicability of the section is limited to actions arising out of the contract which authorized or required the document. The documents listed are intended to be illustrative and not all inclusive.

3. The provisions of this section go no further than establishing the documents in question as *prima facie* evidence and leave to the court the ultimate determination of the facts where the accuracy or authenticity of the documents is questioned. In this connection the section calls for a commercially reasonable interpretation.

Evidentiary Rules Concerning Certificated Securities: 810 ILCS 5/8-114

§ 8-114. Evidentiary rules concerning certificated securities.

The following rules apply in an action on a certificated security against the issuer:

(1) Unless specifically denied in the pleadings, each signature on a security certificate or in a necessary indorsement is admitted.

(2) If the effectiveness of a signature is put in issue, the burden of establishing effectiveness is on the party claiming under the signature, but *the signature is presumed to be genuine or authorized.*

(3) If signatures on a security certificate are admitted or established, production of the certificate entitles a holder to recover on it unless the defendant establishes a defense or a defect going to the validity of the security.

(4) If it is shown that a defense or defect exists, the plaintiff has the burden of establishing that the plaintiff or some person under whom the plaintiff claims is a person against whom the defense or defect cannot be asserted. [emphasis added].

Effective January 1, 1996.

Proof of Ordinances; Book or Pamphlet as *Prima Facie* Evidence: 65 ILCS 5/1-2-6

§ 1-2-6. The contents of all municipal ordinances, the date of passage, and the date of publication or posting, where required, may be proved by the certificate of the municipal clerk, under the seal of the corporation.

Whenever municipal ordinances are printed in book or pamphlet form, and purport to be published by authority of the corporate authorities, such book or pamphlet shall be *prima facie* evidence of the contents, passage, and legal publication of such ordinances, as of the dates mentioned in such book or pamphlet, in all courts and administrative tribunals.

Effective July 1961.

ILLINOIS CASE LAW UNDER THE NEW ILLINOIS RULES OF EVIDENCE

Domestic Documents Are Certified by a Written Declaration Under Oath Subject to the Penalty of Perjury Pursuant to Illinois Rule of Evidence 902(11)

Ulm v. Mem'l Med. Ctr., 2012 IL App (4th) 110421

Plaintiff sued her former employer, a hospital, for retaliatory discharge and violation of the Whistleblower Act (740 ILCS 174/1 through 35). She had worked for her employer's information management department. Whenever the department received a subpoena for medical records, "it was customary for an employee within the department to include with the record a certification stating the record was complete and accurate and had been prepared in the regular course of defendant's business." Plaintiff carried out this task until she became aware that she could not legally certify the documents because the electronic system was not in compliance with legal and accreditation standards. She brought her concerns to defendant and was subsequently fired. The trial court entered summary judgment for defendant and plaintiff appealed. The appellate court affirmed the trial court, noting that

> [a]ssuming *arguendo* that defendant fired plaintiff in retaliation for her refusal to sign these certifications, plaintiff fails to persuade us defendant breached the Whistleblower Act because she cites no law, rule, or regulation which she would have violated by participating in the refused activity. In her initial brief, plaintiff contends signing such certifications would have violated the Federal Rules of Evidence related to self-authenticating documents. Specifically, plaintiff claims that her certification of medical records she suspected were tainted by defendant's inadequate record-keeping system would have run afoul of Rule 902(11), which provides for self-authentication of domestic records of regularly conducted business activity (authentication being a prerequisite to admissibility). FED. R. EVID. 902(11). That rule provides, in pertinent part, that an otherwise admissible business record is self-authenticating if accompanied by a certification by the record's custodian that it (1) "was made at or near the time of the occurrence of the matters set forth by, or from information transmitted by, a person with knowledge of those matters"; (2) "was kept in the course of the regularly conducted activity"; and (3) "was made by the regularly conducted activity as a regular practice." FED. R. EVID. 902(11). The rule further provides that "[a] party intending to offer a record into evidence under this paragraph *** must make the record and declaration [(certification)] available for inspection sufficiently in advance of their offer into evidence to provide an adverse party with a fair opportunity to challenge them." FED. R. EVID. 902(11).
>
> Rule 902(11) provides no support for plaintiff's claim that certifying a business record for self-authentication under the Federal Rules of Evidence may violate a law, rule, or regulation if the certification's maker knows or suspects that the business record may be inaccurate due to the business's noncompliance with record-maintenance principles. Nevertheless, plaintiff purports to quote from the same rule as follows: " 'The word "certification" as used in this subsection means with respect to a domestic record . . . if falsely made, would subject the maker to criminal penalty under the laws of the country.' " This erroneous quotation apparently was derived from Rule 902(12), regarding self-authentication of foreign business records, which provides, in relevant part: "The declaration must be signed in a manner that, if falsely made, would subject the maker to criminal penalty under the laws of the country where the declaration is signed." FED. R. EVID. 902(12). This provision is irrelevant to the self-authentication of the regularly kept records of an American business and does not itself establish penalties for untruthful certifications accompanying self-authenticating business records.

> Rule 902(11) says nothing about the accuracy or genuineness of a certification. In fact, Rule 902(11) provides a means for an adverse party to oppose self-authentication where the certification accompanying the record may be spurious. False certifications were, thus, apparently contemplated by the drafters of the rule. Further, it is unclear defendant's medical records would be self-authenticating under Rule 902(11) as the form of defendant's certifications does not track the essential language of that rule.
>
> This conclusion finds additional support in Illinois Rule of Evidence 902(11), which our supreme court adapted from Federal Rule 902(11). Illinois Rule of Evidence 902(11) defines a qualifying certification with respect to a domestic record, in part, as "a written declaration under oath subject to the penalty of perjury." Plaintiff has not claimed the certifications defendant issued with subpoenaed medical records were made under oath subject to the penalty of perjury. Accordingly, the relevance of these rules on self-authenticating documents to plaintiff's Whistleblower Act claim is dubious.

PRIOR ILLINOIS CASE LAW

1. Certified Copy of Secretary of State's Order Revoking Defendant's Driving Privileges Is Admissible in the Same Manner as the Original

People v. Smith, 162 Ill. App. 3d 739 (5th Dist. 1987)

Defendant was convicted of driving with a revoked license. He had previously been convicted of driving while intoxicated, a conviction that also served to revoke his license. Defendant argued on appeal that the state failed to prove him guilty beyond a reasonable doubt because the prior conviction was an element of the charged offense and the state failed to introduce an authenticated copy of the record. At trial, state introduced only a certified copy of an order of revocation. The appellate court rejected defendant's claim, noting that section 2-108 of the Motor Vehicle Code provided that certified copies of records under the seal of the Secretary of State were "admissible in any proceeding in any court in like manner as the original." The appellate court therefore found that a certified copy of an order of revocation that stated "the reason for such revocation [. . . was] sufficient evidence to prove the previous DUI conviction."

2. Foreign Certified Public Documents Are Self-Authenticating If an Authorized Person Certifies the Genuineness of the Records

In re Ersch's Estate, 29 Ill. 2d 572 (1963)

The Illinois Supreme Court considered the sufficiency of the foundation for the introduction of documents recording births, deaths, and marriages that took place in Poland. The proponent of the evidence introduced certified copies of the originals and the opponent claimed that there was no showing that the individual who certified the records had a duty to maintain the records. The Supreme Court disagreed, noting that the officer who certified the records indicated that he was "the keeper of the records of vital statistics" for the relevant region in Poland and that he attested to the fact that the "document [was] a true, perfect and complete copy of the record kept" by the office of vital statistics. The Supreme Court observed that the records were sealed and signed by the chairman of the office and that the American consul in Poland certified the chairman as a legal custodian of such records. The Supreme Court explained that

> [t]hese authentications, when coupled with the testimony of the witnesses as to the manner in which these records came into the custody of the certifying officer, are, in our judgment, sufficient to warrant their admission into evidence. (People *ex rel.* Wenzel v. Chicago and

> Northwestern Railway Company, 28 Ill. 2d 205 (1963); 5 WIGMORE ON EVIDENCE, 3rd ed., sec. 1632, et sub.) This court recognizes the common-law exception to the hearsay rule, and, as we said in *Wenzel* (28 Ill. 2d p. 212): '*** records kept by persons in public office, which they are required either by statute or the nature of their office to maintain in connection with the performance of their official duties, are admissible in evidence and are evidence of those matters which are properly required to be maintained and recorded therein.'

3. Certified Copy of a Record of Conviction Under Seal Is Sufficiently Authenticated
People v. Funk, 325 Ill. 57 (1927)

Defendant was convicted of armed robbery of a bank. The state introduced a certified copy of defendant's prior conviction for burglary and larceny that occurred in another state. Defendant contended that the certified copy of his prior conviction was erroneously admitted in evidence because it was not properly authenticated. The Illinois Supreme Court disagreed, finding that a certified copy of a record of conviction under seal from another state was sufficiently authenticated to be admitted in evidence. It explained that

> [t]he certified copy of the transcript of the record, offered and admitted in evidence, is certified by the clerk of the circuit court of Audrain county, Mo., under the seal of the court, as 'a full, true and complete copy of all proceedings in the case of State of Missouri v. Harry Funk, as the same remains on file and of record in my office in record book No. 38, at page 248.' There appear also the certificate of the judge of the court as to the form of the attestation, and that the clerk is the duly authorized clerk of that court, and a like certificate of the clerk as to the authority of the judge. The Evidence Act (Smith-Hurd Rev. St. 1925, c. 51) does not apply to the admission in evidence of copies of records of courts of foreign jurisdiction in criminal cases, but the authority for the introduction of such a record is derived from an act of Congress, under the so-called 'full faith and credit' clause (article 4, § 1) of the federal Constitution. That act provides:
>
> > 'The records and judicial proceedings of the courts of any state or territory, or of any such country, shall be proved or admitted in any other court within the United States, by the attestation of the clerk, and the seal of the court annexed, if there be a seal, together with a certificate of the judge, Chief Justice, or presiding magistrate, that the said attestation is in due form,' etc. U. S. Comp. Stat. 1916, p. 2431, § 1519.
>
> The attestation of this record complies with the requirement of the act of Congress and it was properly admitted in evidence. McMillan v. Lovejoy, 115 Ill. 498 (1886).

4. Official Publications Are Self-Authenticating
Illinois Cent. R. Co. v. Warriner, 229 Ill. 91 (1907)

A child was struck and killed by a train. At trial, the plaintiffs introduced an ordinance that "prohibit[ed] a greater rate of speed than 10 miles an hour" in the village where the child was killed. Defendant contended that the printed pamphlet containing the ordinance was inadmissible at trial. The Illinois Supreme Court noted that the ordinance was

> contained in a printed pamphlet, the cover of which was partly torn off so as to show only the first half of the title. The cover did not show what the pamphlet contained, but the first page was entitled, 'The Revised Ordinances of the Village of Peotone,' and on the last page there was what purported to be a printed copy of a certificate of the president of the board of trustees and the clerk of the village certifying to the ordinances as true copies of the revised ordinances of said village, and it was therein stated that they were printed and published by the authority of the president and board of trustees of the said village. The ordinance was objected to because the memorandum at the foot of the ordinance showed that it was passed on August 19,

> 1890, and approved August 20, 1890, while the copy of the certificate stated that the ordinances contained in the pamphlet were passed and approved on August 19, 1890. The ordinance was printed, with other ordinances, in pamphlet form, and was admissible in evidence under the statute, not by virtue of the printed copy of a certificate, but on the ground that the ordinance purported to be published in that pamphlet by authority of the president and board of trustees.

After consideration of this evidence, the Supreme Court concluded that

> [a]ll that was necessary to authorize the admission of the pamphlet in evidence was the fact that it purported to be published by such authority, and the statute made it evidence of the passage and legal publication of the ordinances contained in it as of the dates mentioned in the pamphlet. Eagan v. Connelly, 107 Ill. 458; McCraney v. Glos, 222 Ill. 628; Chicago & Alton Railroad Co. v. Wilson, 225 Ill. 50. The printed copy of the certificate had no legal effect as a certificate, and did not affect the ordinance. The further objection was made that the certificate did not show where the publication was made. If it had any effect at all, it showed that the publication was made in that pamphlet, and neither objection had any force. The court did not err in admitting the ordinance in evidence.

5. Printed Newspapers or Periodicals Are Self-Authenticating
Alimissis v. Nanos, 171 Ill. App. 3d 1005 (1st Dist. 1988)

Defendant contended that evidence of stock quotations was inadmissible to prove damages in a breach of contract case because it was not sufficiently authenticated. The Illinois Appellate Court for the First District disagreed, noting that

> the fact that the stock quotations here were submitted in an uncertified photocopy does not in itself make the evidence inadmissible. (See Curran v. Unis (Tex. App. 1986), 711 S.W.2d 290, 294 (authentic photocopies of business records admissible over objections that they did not satisfy the best evidence rule).) Further, in Virginia v. West Virginia, 238 U.S. 202 (1915), the United States Supreme Court stated: "It is unquestioned that, in proving the fact of market value, accredited price-current lists and market reports, including those published in trade journals or newspapers which are accepted as trustworthy, are admissible in evidence." *Virginia*, 238 U.S. 202, 212. The Illinois Supreme Court has held that the closing stock market quotations from the previous day are admissible as proof of market value. Nash v. Classen, 163 Ill. 409 (1896). It is, thus, within the trial court's discretion to determine the admissibility of the stock market quotations as evidence within this exception to the hearsay rule. 29 Am. Jur. 2d Evidence § 893 (1967). Hence, the defendant's contention that the evidence here was not the best evidence available and was incompetent to prove the plaintiff's damages is without merit.

6. Ingredients Label on a Medicine Container Is a Self-Authenticating Trade Inscription
People v. Shevock, 335 Ill. App. 3d 1031 (4th Dist. 2003)

The appellate court affirmed a jury verdict finding the defendant guilty of unlawful possession of a methamphetamine manufacturing chemical with the intent to manufacture methamphetamine. Among the many items found in the defendant's lab, a motel room, were 23 boxes of Sudafed antihistamine medication. The police also found a chunky substance wrapped in tinfoil, later identified as methamphetamine. A state police special agent testified that the amount of Sudafed in the defendant's possession would yield between 33 and 51 grams of methamphetamine. The label of a box of Sudafed, stating its active ingredient was pseudoephedrine, was admitted over the defendant's objection. On appeal, the defendant argued that the trial judge erred in admitting the box label as proof that Sudafed actually contained ephedrine or pseudoephedrine because it was so stated on the label. Ultimately, the evidence was used to prove that the defendant possessed 5,520 milligrams of ephedrine or pseudoephedrine. The defendant argued that the label on the box constituted hearsay and did not fit under the business records exception or any other recognized exception to the rule against hearsay. He also argued that the state failed to present any witness to authenticate the pills, interpret the labels, or testify that Sudafed pills were a necessary ingredient of a methamphetamine recipe.

The appellate court allowed the label as a trade inscription exception to the hearsay rule. The state argued that this case was analogous to a Second District case, *In re* T.D., 115 Ill. App. 3d 872 (2d Dist. 1983). In that case, the appellate court allowed the use of a label on a glue container to prove the glue contained a chemical that was a hazardous substance. There, the court found that the container did not fit the business records exception to the hearsay rule because no one identified the label, nor was there testimony that the label was produced in the routine course of business. However, the court found the label admissible because it was sufficiently reliable and trustworthy—reliability or trustworthiness was derived from state and federal laws that require such a label, subject to penalty, because the chemical in question was hazardous. Moreover, since the product had been purchased by the defendant and it was in its original package, there was a reduced opportunity for tampering or adulteration.

Here, the appellate court applied the rationale adopted in *In re* T.D. The court first determined that because the Sudafed boxes were unopened when they were confiscated from the defendant, the opportunity for tampering or adulteration was reduced. The court further relied on the Illinois Food, Drug and Cosmetic Act (410 ILCS 620/15(e)(1)(A)(ii) (West 2000)), which requires that drugs with more than two ingredients must list each active ingredient, subject to penalty.

7. Acknowledged Documents Are Self-Authenticating
Zilvitis v. Szczudlo, 409 Ill. 252 (1951)

A brother claimed that a deed from his mother to his sister was void because it had not been acknowledged. The Illinois Supreme Court disagreed, noting that

> an acknowledgment is not necessary for the validity of a deed, and it will properly pass title without being acknowledged. Acknowledgment goes only to the proof, which permits the deed being offered in evidence without further showing as to its genuineness. Robinson v. Robinson, 116 Ill. 250 (1886); Shadden v. Zimmerlee, 401 Ill. 118 (1948); Lucas v. Westray, 408 Ill. 243 (1951).

See also People v. Boening, 68 Ill. App. 2d 1 (1st Dist. 1966) (noting that an unacknowledged deed is not void).

8. Any Document That Is by a Statutory Presumption *Prima Facie* Genuine Is Self-Authenticating
Fish v. Walsh, 323 Ill. 359 (1926)

Neighboring property owners brought suit to enjoin defendant from building a gas station on his property pursuant to a municipal ordinance that prohibits such construction on a mostly residential block. Defendant contended that the statute had been repealed and not re-enacted, and had been inadvertently included in the municipal code. The Illinois Supreme Court agreed with the defendant, noting that

> a printed book of ordinances shall be received as the evidence of the passage and legal publication thereof. Cahill's Stat. 1925, c. 24, par. 68. Such evidence is *prima facie* only of the validity of the ordinances, and the records of the city council and the manner of the passage of

> the ordinances may be resorted to for the purpose of overcoming such *prima facie* evidence. Illinois Central Railroad Co. v. People, 143 Ill. 434, 33 N.E. 173, 19 L. R. A. 119; People v. Hatch, 33 Ill. 9.
>
> The assistant corporation counsel testified that the 'around the block ordinance' was included in the Code through inadvertence, and such is not denied. There is no proof that it was ever re-enacted after its repeal in 1915. This being true, there was no ordinance in the city of Chicago governing the licensing of filling stations at the time the permit was issued, and appellant has complied with the law regulating the placing of tanks containing gasoline and other inflammable liquids. It was error, therefore, to grant the relief prayed in the bill.

Rule 903. Subscribing Witness' Testimony Unnecessary

The testimony of a subscribing witness is not necessary to authenticate a writing unless required by the laws of the jurisdiction whose laws govern the validity of the writing.

Adopted September 27, 2010, eff. January 1, 2011.

AUTHOR'S COMMENTARY

Illinois Rule of Evidence 903 has adopted Federal Rule of Evidence 903, in effect prior to its stylistic amendment on December 1, 2011. Gino L. DiVito, *The Illinois Rules of Evidence: A Color-Coded Guide Containing the New Rules, the Committee's General and Specific Comments, a Comparison with the Federal Rules of Evidence, and Additional Commentary (Including the Federal Rules of Evidence as Amended Effective December 1, 2011)* (Jan. 1, 2012), at 144, http://www.tdrlawfirm.com/assets/downloads/Illinois_Rules_of_Evidence_Color-Coded_Guide.pdf. Federal Rule of Evidence 903 has changed the common law rule that required a witness to first authenticate a writing before it could be admitted in evidence. The Federal Advisory Committee Notes indicate that

> [t]he common law required that attesting witnesses be produced or accounted for. Today the requirement has generally been abolished except with respect to documents which must be attested to be valid, e.g. wills in some states. MCCORMICK § 188. Uniform Rule 71; California Evidence Code § 1411; Kansas Code of Civil Procedure § 60-468; New Jersey Evidence Rule 71; New York CPLR Rule 4537.
>
> FED. R. EVID. 903, Advisory Committee Notes (1972 Proposed Rules).

The new Illinois Rule of Evidence 903 has adopted the modern view and no longer requires "the testimony of a subscribing witness [. . .] to authenticate a writing unless required by the laws of the jurisdiction whose laws govern the validity of the writing." For example, pursuant to 735 ILCS 5/8-1601, the execution of a deed, mortgage or other such writing pertaining to the disposition of real estate does not require the testimony of a subscribing witness and proof of "the execution of such instrument may be proved by secondary evidence without producing or accounting for the absence of the subscribing witness or witnesses." Note that admissibility of wills to probate is governed by the provisions of 755 ILCS 5/6-4, which require a witness to prove the existence of a will by

> (1) testimony before the court, (2) an attestation clause signed by the witness and forming a part of or attached to the will or (3) an affidavit which is signed by the witness at or after the time of attestation and which forms part of the will or is attached to the will or to an accurate facsimile of the will.

RELEVANT STATUTORY AUTHORITY

Execution of Deed: 735 ILCS 5/8-1601

§ 8-1601. Execution of deed. Whenever any deed, mortgage, conveyance, release, power of attorney or other writing of, or relating to the sale, conveyance or other disposition of real estate, or any interest therein, or any other instrument in writing not required by law to be attested by a subscribing witness, may be offered in evidence in any action pending in any court of this state, and the same appears to have been so attested, and it becomes necessary to prove the execution of such deed or other writing otherwise than as now provided by law, *it shall not be necessary to prove the execution of the same by a subscribing witness to the exclusion of other evidence, but the execution of such instrument may be proved by secondary evidence without producing or accounting for the absence of the subscribing witness or witnesses* (emphasis added).

Effective July 1, 1982.

Admission of a Will to Probate: 755 ILCS 5/6-4

§ 6-4. Admission of will to probate—Testimony or affidavit of witnesses. (a) When each of 2 attesting witnesses to a will states that (1) he was present and saw the testator or some person in his presence and by his direction sign the will in the presence of the witness or the testator acknowledged it to the witness as his act, (2) the will was attested by the witness in the presence of the testator and (3) he believed the testator to be of sound mind and memory at the time of signing or acknowledging the will, the execution of the will is sufficiently proved to admit it to probate, unless there is proof of fraud, forgery, compulsion or other improper conduct which in the opinion of the court is deemed sufficient to invalidate or destroy the will. The proponent may also introduce any other evidence competent to establish a will. If the proponent establishes the will by sufficient competent evidence, it shall be admitted to probate, unless there is proof of fraud, forgery, compulsion or other improper conduct which in the opinion of the court is deemed sufficient to invalidate or destroy the will.

(b) The statements of a witness to prove the will under subsection 6-4(a) may be made by (1) testimony before the court, (2) an attestation clause signed by the witness and forming a part of or attached to the will or (3) an affidavit which is signed by the witness at or after the time of attestation and which forms part of the will or is attached to the will or to an accurate facsimile of the will.

Effective January 1, 1980.

PRIOR ILLINOIS CASE LAW

Testimony of Subscribing Witnesses Is Necessary to Admit Will to Probate

In re Walsh's Estate, 400 Ill. 454 (1948)

The proponent of a will introduced in evidence an authenticated transcript of the testimony of the subscribing witnesses who testified earlier at a will probate hearing where they stated that the testator was of sound mind when the will was executed. The probate judge

> admitted the instrument to probate. An appeal was perfected by [the opponent of the will] and others from the order of the probate court to the circuit court of Cook County. From an order of the circuit court admitting the instrument to probate and remanding cause with directions to admit the instrument, [the opponent] and others appeal[ed] to the Supreme Court.

The proponent of the will called the subscribing witnesses and they testified in the circuit court that they "gave it no thought" whether the testator was of sound mind at the time he signed the will. The circuit court admitted the instrument to probate and the Illinois Supreme Court affirmed, explaining that

[i]t is apparent [. . .] that *prima facie* case was made in the circuit court of Cook County, entitling the will to admission in the absence of any testimony which the contestants offered to invalidate or destroy it. The will appears regular on its face and the signatures of the testator, and of the subscribing witnesses who testified in probate court, are admittedly genuine. This transcript constituted proponent's case. The contestants produced the subscribing witnesses in the circuit court and interrogated them principally concerning what belief, if any, they had at the time of signing the will as to the sanity of the testator.

***

[T]he proponent of the will made out the case in the probate court, and that upon appeal to the circuit court a *prima facie* case was likewise made out by the introduction in evidence of the certified copy of the testimony given by the witnesses in the probate court.

As we have heretofore pointed out, section 71 of the Probate Act provides that at the hearing on an appeal the proponents may introduce an authenticated transcript of the testimony of the attesting witnesses and the contestant may introduce any competent evidence of fraud, forgery, compulsion or other improper conduct; and that, 'If the proponent establishes the will by sufficient competent evidence it shall be admitted to probate unless there is proof of fraud, forgery, compulsion or other improper conduct which in the opinion of the court is deemed sufficient to invalidate or destroy the will.' Here the *prima facie* case was made by the introduction in evidence of the authenticated transcript of the testimony taken in the probate court. This testimony shows upon its face that the attesting witnesses were of the belief, at the time they signed as witnesses, that the testator was of sound mind and memory. This was sufficient in the circuit court to establish a *prima facie* case. As was said in the case of Shepherd v. Yokum, 323 Ill. 328, 154 N.E. 156, what the witnesses may have believed afterwards is a matter of no consequence.

Article X – Contents of Writings, Recordings, and Photographs

Rule 1001. Definitions

For purposes of this article the following definitions are applicable:

(1) Writings and Recordings. "Writings" and "recordings" consist of letters, words, sounds, or numbers, or their equivalent, set down by handwriting, typewriting, printing, photostating, photographing, magnetic impulse, mechanical or electronic recording, or other form of data compilation.

(2) Photographs. "Photographs" include still photographs, X-ray films, video tapes, motion pictures and similar or other products or processes which produce recorded images.

(3) Original. An "original" of a writing or recording is the writing or recording itself or any counterpart intended to have the same effect by a person executing or issuing it. An "original" of a photograph includes the negative or any print therefrom. If data are stored in a computer or similar device, any printout or other output readable by sight, shown to reflect the data accurately, is an "original."

(4) Duplicate. A "duplicate" is a counterpart produced by the same impression as the original, or from the same matrix, or by means of photography, including enlargements and miniatures, or by mechanical or electronic rerecording, or by chemical reproduction, or by other equivalent techniques which accurately reproduces the original.

Adopted September 27, 2010, eff. January 1, 2011.

AUTHOR'S COMMENTARY

Illinois Rule of Evidence 1001(1) provides a definition for writings and recordings and mirrors Federal Rule of Evidence 1001, in effect until its stylistic amendment on December 1, 2011, except that it has added "sounds" to the definition. *See* Gino L. DiVito, *The Illinois Rules of Evidence: A Color-Coded Guide Containing the New Rules, the Committee's General and Specific Comments, a Comparison with the Federal Rules of Evidence, and Additional Commentary (Including the Federal Rules of Evidence as Amended Effective December 1, 2011)* (Jan. 1, 2012), at 145, http://www.tdrlawfirm.com/assets/downloads/Illinois_Rules_of_Evidence_Color-Coded_Guide.pdf [hereinafter DiVito, *Color-Coded Guide*].

Illinois Rule of Evidence 1001(2) is modeled after Federal Rule of Evidence 1001(2), in effect prior to its stylistic amendment on December 1, 2011, but it contains additional language, noting that "other products and processes which produce recorded images" may be included in the definition of photographs, along with X-ray films, videotapes and "motion pictures." DiVito, *Color-Coded Guide* at 145 (citing People v. Taylor, 2011 IL 110067).

Illinois Rule of Evidence 1001(3) mirrors Federal Rule of Evidence 1001(3), in effect prior to its stylistic amendment on December 1, 2011. *See* DiVito, *Color-Coded Guide* at 146. Federal Rule of Evidence 1001(3) has since been re-numbered as 1001(d). *Id.*

Illinois Rule of Evidence 1001(4) provides a definition of a "duplicate" and is modeled on Federal Rule of Evidence 1001(4), in effect until its stylistic amendment on December 1, 2011. *Id.* Federal Rule of Evidence 1001(4) has been re-numbered as 1001(e). *Id.*

ILLINOIS CASE LAW UNDER THE NEW ILLINOIS RULES OF EVIDENCE

An Original of a Writing or Recording Consists of the Writing or Recording Itself or Any Counterpart Intended to Have the Same Effect

People v. Taylor, 2011 IL 110067

Defendant was caught stealing money out of a high school principal's office after a police officer installed a surveillance camera there. The police officer testified at defendant's bench trial regarding the surveillance equipment. He conceded that he "only recently begun using such equipment" and that he set the camera up according to instructions supplied by the camera's manufacturer. After the camera recorded defendant's actions, the officer copied the content of the video surveillance onto a VHS tape and locked it in his office desk. The Supreme Court noted that

> "[w]ritings" and "recordings" are commonly identified as "letters, words, or numbers, or their equivalent, set down by handwriting, typewriting, printing, photostating, photographing, magnetic impulse, mechanical or electronic recording, or other form of data compilation."[citation omitted]. "Photographs" include "still photographs, x-ray films, video tapes, and motion pictures." [citation omitted]. *See also* ILL. R. EVID. 1001(2) (including "similar or other products or processes which produce recorded images"). An "original" of a "writing" or "recording" consists of "the writing or recording itself or any counterpart intended to have the same effect by a person executing or issuing it. An 'original' of a photograph includes the negative or any print therefrom. If data are stored in a computer or similar device, any printout or other output readable by sight, shown to reflect the data accurately, is an 'original.' " [citation omitted].
>
> ***
>
> [. . .] The VHS tape was made by copying the data stored on the hard drive of the DVR and, therefore, satisfies the definition of "original." See Commonwealth v. Leneski, 66 Mass. App. Ct. 291 (2006) (videotapes, like photographs, are not subject to the best evidence rule and the

same is true for digital images placed and stored on a hard drive and transferred to a CD; thus, a CD would be an original).

PRIOR ILLINOIS CASE LAW

Accurately Reproduced Duplicate of the Original Is Competent Evidence

People v. Hauke, 335 Ill. 217 (1929)

Defendant was convicted of murder and contended on appeal that the trial court erroneously admitted a copy of his confession because there was no evidence that the original of the statement had been lost. The Illinois Supreme Court found that

> [t]he statement as shown by the witness [officer] was a carbon copy of the original, made at the same time and by one impression of a typewriter. Under the law, such carbon copy is an original, and is competent as evidence. People v. Chicago, Rock Island & Pacific Railway Co., 329 Ill. 467 (1928).

Rule 1002. Requirement of Original

To prove the content of a writing, recording, or photograph, the original writing, recording, or photograph is required, except as otherwise provided in these rules or by statute.

Adopted September 27, 2010, eff. January 1, 2011.

AUTHOR'S COMMENTARY

Illinois Rule of Evidence 1002 codifies the so-called "best evidence rule" which is a rule of preference for the production of the original of a writing when the purpose of the evidence is to prove its contents. The best evidence rule is intended to bar the introduction of secondary evidence when the proponent has more direct, positive, and conclusive evidence—namely, the original. *See, e.g.*, People v. Taylor, 2011 IL 110067 (noting that a VHS copy from a hard drive of a DVR qualified as an "original").

Illinois Rule of Evidence 1002 "is identical" to Federal Rule of Evidence 1002, in effect until its stylistic amendment on December 1, 2011. *See* DiVito, *The Illinois Rules of Evidence: A Color-Coded Guide Containing the New Rules, the Committee's General and Specific Comments, a Comparison with the Federal Rules of Evidence, and Additional Commentary* (*Including the Federal Rules of Evidence as Amended Effective December 1, 2011*) (Jan. 1, 2012), at 147, http://www.tdrlawfirm.com/assets/downloads/Illinois_Rules_of_Evidence_Color-Coded_Guide.pdf. The best evidence rule applies only to documentary evidence and does not require the production of the original of physical evidence. Testimony that describes physical evidence or photographs portraying physical evidence are exempted.

ILLINOIS CASE LAW UNDER THE NEW ILLINOIS RULES OF EVIDENCE

A Copy of a Videotape from the Hard Drive of a Digital Video Recording Qualifies as an Original

People v. Taylor, 2011 IL 110067

Defendant was caught stealing money out of a high school principal's office after a police officer installed a surveillance camera there. After the camera recorded defendant's actions, the officer copied the content of the video surveillance onto a VHS tape and locked it in his office desk. The appellate court concluded that the VHS tape was inadmissible because "the state failed to preserve the original DVR recording." The Illinois Supreme Court disagreed, noting that

> [t]here are several problems with the appellate court's analysis and conclusion with respect to preservation of the "original." "[W]ritings" and "recordings" are commonly identified as "letters, words, or numbers, or their equivalent, set down by handwriting, typewriting, printing, photostating, photographing, magnetic impulse, mechanical or electronic recording, or other form of data compilation." [citation omitted]. "Photographs" include "still photographs, x-ray films, video tapes, and motion pictures." [citation omitted]. *See also* I ILL. R. EVID. 1001(2) (including "similar or other products or processes which produce recorded images"). An "original" of a "writing" or "recording" consists of "the writing or recording itself or any counterpart intended to have the same effect by a person executing or issuing it. An 'original' of a photograph includes the negative or any print therefrom. If data are stored in a computer or similar device, any printout or other output readable by sight, shown to reflect the data accurately, is an 'original.'" [citation omitted].

A finding that the VHS tape was not an original cannot be reconciled with these definitions. The VHS tape was made by copying the data stored on the hard drive of the DVR and, therefore, satisfies the definition of "original." See Commonwealth v. Leneski, 66 Mass. App. Ct. 291 (2006) (videotapes, like photographs, are not subject to the best evidence rule and the same is true for digital images placed and stored on a hard drive and transferred to a CD; thus, a CD would be an original). The State was not required to bring the DVR system into court to show the surveillance video.\

PRIOR ILLINOIS CASE LAW

1. Best Evidence Rule Does Not Require Production of the Strongest Proof Available

People v. Ristau, 363 Ill. 583 (1936)

Defendant was convicted of assault with intent to commit rape. He alleged on appeal that the trial court erroneously allowed the victim's aunt to testify about the condition of her niece's clothing after the assault. Defendant alleged that the clothes should have been introduced in evidence because they represented "the best evidence." The Illinois Supreme Court disagreed, noting that

> the best evidence rule does not prevent proof as to the condition of the prosecutrix' clothing, shortly after the rape, by description rather than by producing such clothing before a jury. The best evidence rule is not infringed by a selection of weaker instead of stronger proof, or by an omission to supply all the proof capable of being produced. 10 R.C.L. 903.

See also People v. Tharpe-Williams, 286 Ill. App. 3d 605 (2d Dist. 1997) (noting that the best evidence rule does not require that a party "produce the best evidence that the nature of the case permits").

2. Failure to Introduce a Card from Which Defendant's *Miranda* Warnings Were Read Did Not Violate the Best Evidence Rule Where the Accused Did Not Request the Card's Production and the Same Warnings Appeared in a Confession Signed by Defendant

People v. Pittman, 55 Ill. 2d 39 (1973)

Defendant and two other individuals were convicted of murder and sentenced to death. Defendant provided a written confession to the police which was admitted in evidence. The confession was transcribed on a standard police statement form which included "a paragraph detailing the *Miranda* warnings" and contained defendant's signature underneath the warnings. Defendant argued on appeal "that the card from which his *Miranda* warnings were read" should have been introduced in evidence pursuant to the best evidence rule. The Illinois

Supreme Court disagreed, noting that an officer "had this card with him at the time of the hearing and no defense request for its introduction into evidence was presented. Moreover, [another officer] stated the same warnings which appeared on the card were contained in the first paragraph of the statement forms." The Supreme Court concluded that there was "no merit to the argument that the card containing the *Miranda* warnings should have been placed in evidence."

3. Where Witness Admits to Having Made a Contradictory Statement, the Statement Need Not Be Introduced in Evidence to Satisfy the Best Evidence Rule
People v. Pelegri, 39 Ill. 2d 568 (1968)

Defendant was convicted of murder after he was involved in a fight with the victim. At trial, defendant claimed self-defense. An eyewitness testified that he saw a knife in the victim's hand while he was struggling with defendant. The state impeached the witness with his earlier statement to the police which he had made shortly after the incident, indicating that he saw defendant with a knife in his hand during the fight. The witness conceded that he had made the earlier statement to the police. Although the witness' earlier statement was also recorded in writing, the state did not introduce it in evidence. Defendant contended that the state violated the best evidence rule when it failed to introduce the earlier statement in evidence. The Illinois Supreme Court disagreed, explaining that

> defendant's best-evidence argument fail[ed] because where a witness admits having made the contradictory statement, the statement itself is not required to be introduced into evidence. 3 WIGMORE ON EVIDENCE 268 (1964 Supp.); Rau v. First National Stores, 97 N.H. 490 (1952); *see also* People v. McCrimmon, 37 Ill. 2d 40, 46-47 (1967).

Rule 1003. Admissibility of Duplicates

A duplicate is admissible to the same extent as an original unless (1) a genuine question is raised as to the authenticity of the original or (2) in the circumstances it would be unfair to admit the duplicate in lieu of the original.

Adopted September 27, 2010, eff. January 1, 2011.

AUTHOR'S COMMENTARY

Illinois Rule of Evidence 1003 is modeled after Federal Rule of Evidence 1003, in effect prior to its stylistic amendment on December 1, 2011. *See* Gino L. DiVito, *The Illinois Rules of Evidence: A Color-Coded Guide Containing the New Rules, the Committee's General and Specific Comments, a Comparison with the Federal Rules of Evidence, and Additional Commentary (Including the Federal Rules of Evidence as Amended Effective December 1, 2011)* (Jan. 1, 2012), at 148, http://www.tdrlawfirm.com/assets/downloads/Illinois_Rules_of_Evidence_Color-Coded_Guide.pdf. Historically, admissibility of a duplicate required a showing that

> the person to whose possession it was last traced must be produced unless this is shown to be impossible, in which case search among his papers must be proven if that can be done. In all events search must be made for the paper with the utmost good faith and the search must be as thorough and diligent as if the rule were that all benefit of the paper would be lost unless it be found.
>
> People v. Wells, 380 Ill. 347, 355 (1942).

Later Illinois decisions relaxed this requirement and allowed admissibility of a duplicate if a party demonstrated:

1. the prior existence of the original;

2. its loss, destruction, or unavailability;
3. the authenticity of the substitute; and
4. party's diligence in attempting to procure the original.

See People v. Carter, 39 Ill. 2d 31 (1968); *and* People v. Baptist, 76 Ill. 2d 19 (1979); People v. Bowman, 95 Ill. App. 3d 1137 (5th Dist. 1981). The sufficiency of a preliminary showing depended on the particular circumstances of each case and the admissibility of secondary evidence was a matter of discretion for the trial judge. *See* People v. Baptist, 76 Ill. 2d 19, 27 (1979).

Under the new Illinois Rule of Evidence 1003, a "duplicate is admissible to the same extent as an original" unless its authenticity is challenged or its admissibility would be unfair. There is evidence that this has been the rule recognized in some Illinois appellate decisions prior to the enactment of the Illinois Rules of Evidence. *See e.g.*, People v. Bowman, 95 Ill. App. 3d 1137 (5th Dist. 1981) (noting that "the current trend of the law of evidence [is] away from strict adherence to . . . 'lengthy and laborious' foundation requirements" for the admissibility of photocopied documents); Law Offices of Colleen M. McLaughlin v. First Star Fin. Corp., 2011 IL App (1st) 101849 (noting that the court "long ago adopted the Federal Rule of Evidence [1003]"). The primary concern under the new Illinois Rule of Evidence 1003 is the "authenticity of the original" where photocopies of an original document are offered in evidence. People v. Bowman, 95 Ill. App. 3d 1137 (5th Dist. 1981). Pursuant to 725 ILCS 5/115-5, Illinois provides for the admissibility of copies of business records whether or not the originals exist.

Illinois Case Law Under the New Illinois Rules of Evidence

1. Duplicates Are Admissible to the Same Extent as Originals Under Prior Illinois Common Law and Now Pursuant to Illinois Rule of Evidence 1003

Law Offices of Colleen M. McLaughlin v. First Star Fin. Corp., 2011 IL App (1st) 101849

An attorney brought suit to recover attorney fees from a settlement agreement she helped reach between her client and a defendant corporation. The trial court admitted a photocopy of the settlement agreement in evidence. Defendants argued that the trial court erred in admitting a copy of the agreement in evidence because plaintiff failed to establish sufficient foundation for the document's introduction. The appellate court disagreed, noting that

> this court long ago adopted the Federal Rule of Evidence on the issue (Fed. R. Evid. 1003) and held that "a duplicate of a document should be admissible in Illinois to the same extent as an original unless a genuine issue is raised as to the authenticity of the original or unless it would be unfair to admit the duplicate as an original under the circumstances present in the case where the document was offered into evidence." People v. Bowman, 95 Ill. App. 3d 1137, 1143 (1981). In *Bowman*, we stated our recognition "that the accuracy of a duplicate resulting from the reproduction of the contents of an original is in most cases no longer a significant issue." *Bowman*, 95 Ill. App. 3d at 1143. We note also that this rule as set forth in *Bowman* was recently codified in the Illinois Rules of Evidence. *See* Ill. R. Evid. 1003 (eff. Jan. 1, 2011) ("A duplicate is admissible to the same extent as an original unless (1) a genuine question is raised as to the authenticity of the original or (2) in the circumstances it would be unfair to admit the duplicate in lieu of the original." (Emphasis added.)). Although there are very few citations to *Bowman* in subsequent authority, the rule is part of our common law evidentiary rules, which applied at the time of trial in this case.
>
> Under the evidentiary rule on duplicates as adopted in *Bowman*, the admission of the photocopy of the settlement agreement in this case was proper. Here, defendants raised no

issue as to the authenticity of the original settlement agreement, either below or on appeal. They do not claim that the photocopy was not an accurate duplicate of the original agreement, and they make no argument that the content and terms of the original settlement agreement are at issue. *See* Indian Valley Golf Club, Inc. v. Village of Long Grove, 173 Ill. App. 3d 909, 920 (1988) (rejecting the defendant's best evidence objection where the defendant raised no issue as to the authenticity of the original deeds in the case other than objecting on a purely technical basis). Also, defendants fail to make a showing that admission of the copy of the settlement agreement was unfair. Thus, under our common law evidentiary rules, the admission of the copy of the settlement agreement was proper.

PRIOR ILLINOIS CASE LAW

1. A Duplicate Is Admissible to the Same Extent as an Original Unless Authenticity of the Original Is Challenged or It Would Be Unfair to Admit the Duplicate

People v. Bowman, 95 Ill. App. 3d 1137 (5th Dist. 1981)

Defendant was convicted of burglary and argued on appeal that the trial court improperly admitted a photocopy of his written confession. A detective testified at trial that the original copy of defendant's confession was missing, but stated that the copy presented at trial was an accurate representation of the original. Defendant contended that the state was required to show the foundation requirements established in People v. Wells, 380 Ill. 347 (1942), where the Illinois Supreme Court stated that

> to let in secondary evidence of contents of a written instrument, the person to whose possession it was last traced must be produced unless this is shown to be impossible, in which case search among his papers must be proven if that can be done. In all events search must be made for the paper with the utmost good faith and the search must be as thorough and diligent as if the rule were that all benefit of the paper would be lost unless it be found. *Wells*, 380 Ill. at 355.

The appellate court disagreed with defendant's contention, noting that

> [l]ater authorities indicate that the foundation described in *Wells* has not consistently been applied. It is now accepted that the sufficiency of a foundation for admission of secondary evidence of the contents of a writing "depends upon the circumstances of each case and is, to some degree, within the discretion of the trial court." People v. Baptist, 76 Ill. 2d 19, 27 (1979). Where a duplicate of a confession is involved, such as that in the instant case, the foundation described in *Wells* has not been required. In discussing a similar controversy, the court in People v. Carter, 39 Ill. 2d 31 (1968), stated:
>
>> The defendant next charges that the State violated the best evidence rule when it introduced into evidence, over objection, a multilith copy of his confession. It appears from the record that the confession was typed by a stenographer and was signed by the defendant. Copies of the confession were then made from the original by an offset duplicating process, and it was one of these copies which was introduced into evidence by the State. Upon demand by defense counsel that the original be produced, the State's Attorney explained to the court that the original was destroyed after the copies from it had been made. The original, according to the State, does 'not hold up very long, it is not kept.'
>>
>> 'Where the destruction or loss of an original document is claimed, the circumstances should be shown, so as to rebut any inference of fraudulent design by the party seeking to introduce a copy or parol evidence or, to show that the original was not initially concealed, destroyed or disposed of for the purpose of introducing a copy.' (4 Callaghan's Evidence 186, sec. 6.19.) In view of the circumstances and the explanation offered by the State, we are of the opinion that the absence of the original confession was adequately explained and that sufficient foundation was laid for the introduction of the multilith copy. 39 Ill. 2d at 36.

A similar conclusion was reached in People v. Taylor, 40 Ill. 2d 569 (1968).

Left unspoken in *Carter* and *Taylor* is the foundation rule which replaced the rationale of *Wells*. This standard requires that a party prove the following: (1) the prior existence of the original; (2) its loss, destruction, or unavailability; (3) the authenticity of the substitute; and (4) the party's own diligence in attempting to procure the original. (Gillson v. Gulf Mobile and Ohio Railroad Co. (1969), 42 Ill. 2d 193, 246 N.E.2d 269; People v. Baptist (1979), 76 Ill. 2d 19, 27 Ill. Dec. 792, 389 N.E.2d 1200.) The foundation required by these cases was established in the instant case. Detective [. . .] testified as to the existence of the original confession, which he typed from the defendant's narrative. He also testified as to its unavailability, noting that he did now know the location of the original and was surprised at its absence from the file. The authenticity of the copy was established by [the] testimony that it fairly and accurately reflected the original. Furthermore, the officer's expressed surprise at the absence of the original served to rebut any inference of fraudulent design on behalf of the prosecution. In view of the circumstances, sufficient foundation was laid for the introduction of the photocopy.

We also note the current trend of the law of evidence away from strict adherence to "best evidence" foundation requirements where photocopies and other duplicates of original written instruments are involved. Such "lengthy and laborious" foundation requirements as that established in *People v. Wells* have been criticized as "ill-judged expenditures of effort" in light of the accuracy and reliability of modern methods of information storage and retrieval. (*See* 4 WIGMORE, EVIDENCE § 1195.) In recognition of these technological changes, the Federal Rules of Evidence provide:

> "A 'duplicate' is a counterpart produced by the same impression as the original, or from the same matrix, or by means of photography, including enlargements and miniatures, or by mechanical or electronic re-recording or by chemical reproduction, or by other equivalent techniques which accurately reproduces the original. (FED. R. EV. RULE 1001(4).)
>
> "A duplicate is admissible to the same extent as an original unless (1) a genuine question is raised as to the authenticity of the original or (2) in the circumstances it would be unfair to admit the duplicate in lieu of the original. (FED. R. EV. RULE 1003.)"

The substance of the Federal Rules of Evidence has been adopted by a number of states. For example, Indiana has concluded that a duplicate of a document is admissible "to the same extent as an original unless a genuine issue is raised as to the authenticity of the original, or under the circumstances existing it would be unfair to admit the duplicate as an original." (Brandon v. State (Ind. 1979), 396 N.E.2d 365, 370; *see also* Cooper v. State (1979), 41 Md. App. 392, 397 A.2d 245; State v. Demouchet (La. 1977), 353 So. 2d 1025; State v. White (1970), 4 Or. App. 151, 477 P.2d 917.) These cases express what implicitly has been recognized in Illinois in *People v. Carter* and *People v. Taylor* that the accuracy of a duplicate resulting from the reproduction of the contents of an original is in most cases no longer a significant issue. The inquiry instead is directed to the authenticity of the original, unless circumstances suggest that further inquiry is required. In the instant case, defendant does not question the authenticity of the wording of the original of his purported confession. In fact, he identified the copy of the signature on the document as being his signature. His only objection was that the contents thereof were obtained by coercion.

*** We therefore believe that a duplicate of a document should be admissible in Illinois to the same extent as an original unless a genuine issue is raised as to the authenticity of the original or unless it would be unfair to admit the duplicate as an original under the circumstances present in the case where the document was offered into evidence.

> In the instant case, the admission of the photocopy of the confession was not error. There was no showing fraudulent design in the disappearance of the original, and the prosecution established a foundation for admission of the duplicate which comports with the standard established in *People v. Carter*. Accordingly, defendant's conviction is hereby affirmed.

2. Destruction or Loss of the Original May Excuse Its Production If Proponent Establishes That Destruction Was Not Intentional and Trial Court Determines That Loss Was Not Fraudulently Designed by the Proponent of the Evidence
People v. Carter, 39 Ill. 2d 31 (1968)

Defendant was convicted of armed robbery and contended on appeal that the trial court violated the best evidence rule by allowing the introduction of a multilith copy of his written confession. The Illinois Supreme Court disagreed, observing that

> the confession was typed by a stenographer and was signed by the defendant. Copies of the confession were then made from the original by an offset duplicating process, and it was one of these copies which was introduced into evidence by the State. Upon demand by defense counsel that the original be produced, the State's Attorney explained to the court that the original was destroyed after the copies from it had been made. The original, according to the State, does 'not hold up very long, it is not kept.'
>
> 'Where the destruction or loss of an original document is claimed, the circumstances should be shown, so as to rebut any inference of fraudulent design by the party seeking to introduce a copy or parol evidence or, to show that the original was not initially concealed, destroyed or disposed of for the purpose of introducing a copy.' (4 CALLAGHAN'S EVIDENCE 186, sec. 6.19.) In view of the circumstances and the explanation offered by the State, we are of the opinion that the absence of the original confession was adequately explained and that sufficient foundation was laid for the introduction of the multilith copy.

Rule 1004. Admissibility of Other Evidence of Contents

The original is not required and other evidence of the contents of a writing, recording, or photograph is admissible if-

(1) Originals Lost or Destroyed. All originals are lost or have been destroyed, unless the proponent lost or destroyed them in bad faith; or

(2) Original Not Obtainable. No original can be obtained by any available judicial process or procedure; or

(3) Original in Possession of Opponent. At a time when an original was under the control of the party against whom offered, that party was put on notice, by the pleadings or otherwise, that the contents would be a subject of proof at the hearing; or

(4) Collateral Matters. The writing, recording, or photograph is not closely related to a controlling issue.

Adopted September 27, 2010, eff. January 1, 2011.

Committee Commentary
(3) Modernization: Where there was no conflict with statutes or recent Illinois Supreme Court or Illinois Appellate Court decisions, and where it was determined to be beneficial and uniformly or almost uniformly accepted elsewhere, the Committee incorporated into the Illinois Rules of Evidence uncontroversial developments with respect to the law of evidence as reflected in the Federal Rules of Evidence and the 44 surveyed jurisdictions. [One of t]he 14 instances of modernization of note [is] as follows:

(13) **Rule 1004.** Admissibility of Other Evidence of Contents. Rule 1004 does not recognize degrees of secondary evidence previously recognized in Illinois. Illinois Land & Loan Co. v. Bonner, 75 Ill. 315 (1874). In addition, it is no longer necessary to show that reasonable efforts were employed beyond available judicial process or procedure to obtain an original possessed by a third party. Prussing v. Jackson, 208 Ill. 85, 69 N.E. 771 (1904). ILL. R. EVID. Committee Commentary § 4, pg. 2-4.

AUTHOR'S COMMENTARY

Illinois Rule of Evidence 1004 is modeled on Federal Rule of Evidence 1004, in effect prior to its stylistic amendment on December 1, 2011. *See* Gino L. DiVito, *The Illinois Rules of Evidence: A Color-Coded Guide Containing the New Rules, the Committee's General and Specific Comments, a Comparison with the Federal Rules of Evidence, and Additional Commentary* (*Including the Federal Rules of Evidence as Amended Effective December 1, 2011*) (Jan. 1, 2012), at 149, http://www.tdrlawfirm.com/assets/downloads/Illinois_Rules_of_Evidence_Color-Coded_Guide.pdf [hereinafter DiVito, Color-Coded Guide]. Illinois Rule of Evidence 1004 "eases Illinois' recognition of degrees of secondary evidence and provides the same circumstances as do the federal rules under which the requirement of the original of a document is relaxed." DiVito, *Color-Coded Guide* at 148. The Committee Commentary states that Illinois Rule of Evidence 1004 no longer

> [r]ecognize[s] degrees of secondary evidence previously recognized in Illinois. Illinois Land & Loan Co. v. Bonner, 75 Ill. 315 (1874). In addition, it is no longer necessary to show that reasonable efforts were employed beyond available judicial process or procedure to obtain an original possessed by a third party. Prussing v. Jackson, 208 Ill. 85, 69 N.E. 771 (1904). ILL. R. EVID. Committee Commentary § 4, pg. 2-4.

The rule stated in Prussing v. Jackson, 208 Ill. 85, 69 N.E. 771 (1904), which no longer represents the law in Illinois, required that

> in order to let in secondary evidence of the contents of a written instrument, the person in whose possession it was last traced must be produced, unless shown to be impossible, in which case search among his papers must be proved, if that can be done. In all events, search must be made for the paper with the utmost good faith, and be as thorough and vigilant as if the rule were that all benefit of the paper would be lost unless it be found.

Pursuant to Illinois Rule of Evidence 1004 and under the prior Illinois common law rule, the proponent of documentary evidence is usually required to produce an original, however, the destruction or loss of the original of a writing may excuse its production. Only then may the proponent prove its contents by a copy or parol testimony. The proponent must first establish that he or she did not intentionally destroy or conceal the original, and the trial judge must be convinced that the destruction or loss was not fraudulently designed by the party seeking the admissibility of secondary evidence. People v. Carter, 39 Ill. 2d 31 (1968).

An accused who has been charged with a felony offense has the right to be informed of evidence as provided by Illinois Supreme Court Rule 412(c). *See* ILL. S. CT. R. 412; ILL. S. CT. R. 411 (noting that "[t]hese rules shall be applied in all criminal cases wherein the accused is charged with a felony . . ."). The sanctions for the prosecution's failure to disclose are provided in Illinois Supreme Court Rule 415(g)(i). An accused charged with a felony offense is entitled to the production of names and addresses of witnesses and their statements; statements by the accused; grand jury transcripts of potential witnesses; expert reports; prior convictions; and any tangible items belonging to the accused the prosecution intends to use.

ILL. S. CT. R. 412. Although an accused charged with a misdemeanor driving under the influence offense is not entitled to the "broader discovery available for felony cases" under Supreme Court Rule 411, he or she is entitled to the production of relevant evidence, including a list of witnesses, exculpatory evidence, any confession by the defendant, police reports and any video recording of the arrest. People v. Kladis, 2011 IL 110920.

The right of an accused to be informed of exculpatory evidence is separately guaranteed by the due process clause of the fourteenth amendment of the United States Constitution. When the prosecutor or the prosecutor's agent acts in good faith and in conformity with routine procedures and practices, destruction of potentially useful evidence does not constitute an impermissible infringement of the defendant's right to due process. Arizona v. Youngblood, 488 U.S. 51 (1988). However, a due process violation occurs when the prosecution fails to disclose material exculpatory evidence, regardless of the good or bad faith on the part of the prosecution. Illinois v. Fisher, 540 U.S. 544 (2004); Brady v. Maryland, 373 U.S. 83 (1963).

RELEVANT ILLINOIS SUPREME COURT RULES

Illinois Supreme Court Rule 411. Applicability of Discovery Rules

These rules shall be applied in all criminal cases wherein the accused is charged with a felony, and all juvenile delinquency cases wherein the accused is charged with an offense that would be a felony if committed by an adult. They shall become applicable following indictment or information or petition for adjudication of wardship and shall not be operative prior to or in the course of any preliminary hearing.

Effective October 1, 1971; amended March 1, 2001, effective immediately, except when in the opinion of the trial, Appellate, or Supreme Court the application of the amended provisions in a particular case pending at the time the amendment becomes effective would not be feasible or would work an injustice, in which case former procedures would apply; amended December 9, 2011, effective immediately.

Committee Comments
Special Supreme Court Committee on Capital Cases
March 1, 2001
Rule 411, as amended, makes criminal discovery rules applicable to the sentencing hearing in a capital case. A capital sentencing hearing is a unique and complex proceeding, which often takes place immediately following trial on the merits. Allowing pretrial discovery for capital sentencing will assist counsel in preparing for this critical stage of a capital trial and prevent delay and disruption of the sentencing hearing. *See also* Rule 416(c) (pretrial notice of aggravating factors the State will rely upon in sentencing).

The amendment to Rule 411 does not create new forms of discovery. Instead, the amendment extends the application of existing discovery methods to capital sentencing hearings. The committee notes that any discovery rule that requires disclosure by the defense is subject to constitutional limitations and limitations based on attorney-client or other privilege. Existing discovery rules expressly mention constitutional limitations on defense disclosures (see, e.g., Rule 413) and provide that attorney work product is not subject to disclosure by the State or the defense (Rule 412(j)).

The committee found that the existing discovery rules and associated case law would adequately address constitutional and privilege-based objections to pretrial disclosure of sentencing information by the defense. However, constitutional and privilege-based limitations on discovery do not preclude the possibility that pretrial disclosure of defense sentencing information could directly or indirectly aid the State's case on the merits. The extension of discovery procedures to capital sentencing is not intended to provide such an advantage to the State.

In the event the defense objects to disclosure of specific sentencing information on the ground that disclosure would harm the defense case on the merits, the trial court should take any action necessary to prevent that harm. Options available to the trial court include excision of objectionable material pursuant to Rule 415(e) and the use of protective orders to defer disclosure or restrict the use of information disclosed (Rule 415(d)). *In camera* review of a claim of potential harm from disclosure of sentencing information (Rule 415(f)) may be appropriate to prevent disclosure of defense theories or strategy, or where the identity of a defense sentencing witness is unknown to the State.

Committee Comments
To avoid confusion, the committee rejected the ABA standard which called for the application of discovery rules in "all serious criminal cases." No such standard exists in Illinois, and the application of the discovery rules is extended to all offenses carrying a possible penalty of penitentiary imprisonment. The use of the extensive discovery procedures prescribed in these rules at preliminary stages of the criminal trial would serve no valid purpose, and their use is confined to post-indictment procedures. The committee considered but unanimously declined to make the rules applicable in juvenile court proceedings since the nature of such proceedings generally does not require discovery rules. However, if such proceedings become more adversary in nature, it may be desirable or necessary to apply the rules to them at some future date. In any event, the requirements of *In re* Gault (1967), 387 U.S. 1, must be met.

Illinois Supreme Court Rule 412. Disclosure to Accused

(a) Except as is otherwise provided in these rules as to matters not subject to disclosure and protective orders, the State shall, upon written motion of defense counsel, disclose to defense counsel the following material and information within its possession or control:

(i) the names and last known addresses of persons whom the State intends to call as witnesses, together with their relevant written or recorded statements, memoranda containing substantially verbatim reports of their oral statements, and a list of memoranda reporting or summarizing their oral statements. Upon written motion of defense counsel memoranda reporting or summarizing oral statements shall be examined by the court *in camera* and if found to be substantially verbatim reports of oral statements shall be disclosed to defense counsel;

(ii) any written or recorded statements and the substance of any oral statements made by the accused or by a codefendant, and a list of witnesses to the making and acknowledgment of such statements;

(iii) a transcript of those portions of grand jury minutes containing testimony of the accused and relevant testimony of persons whom the prosecuting attorney intends to call as witnesses at the hearing or trial;

(iv) any reports or statements of experts, made in connection with the particular case, including results of physical or mental examinations and of scientific tests, experiments, or comparisons, and a statement of qualifications of the expert;

(v) any books, papers, documents, photographs or tangible objects which the prosecuting attorney intends to use in the hearing or trial or which were obtained from or belong to the accused; and

(vi) any record of prior criminal convictions, which may be used for impeachment, of persons whom the State intends to call as witnesses at the hearing or trial.

If the State has obtained from the defendant, pursuant to Rule 413(d), information regarding defenses the defendant intends to make, it shall provide to defendant not less than 7 days before the date set for the hearing or trial, or at such other time as the court may direct, the names and addresses of witnesses the State intends to call in rebuttal, together with the information required to be disclosed in connection with other witnesses by subdivisions (i), (iii), and (vi), above, and a specific statement as to the substance of the testimony such witnesses will give at the trial of the cause.

(b) The State shall inform defense counsel if there has been any electronic surveillance (including wiretapping) of conversations to which the accused was a party, or of his premises.

(c) Except as is otherwise provided in these rules as to protective orders, the State shall disclose to defense counsel any material or information within its possession or control which tends to negate the guilt of the accused as to the offense charged or which would tend to reduce his punishment therefor. The State shall make a good-faith effort to specifically identify by description or otherwise any material disclosed pursuant to this section based upon the information available to the State at the time the material is disclosed to the defense. At trial, the defendant may not offer evidence or otherwise communicate to the trier of fact the State's identification of any material or information as tending to negate the guilt of the accused or reduce his punishment. ***

Committee Comments
Special Supreme Court Committee on Capital Cases
March 1, 2001
*** The amendment to paragraph (c) requires a "good-faith" effort to specifically identify exculpatory and mitigating materials "based on information available to the State at the time the material is disclosed to the defense." Thus, the duty to specifically identify is not as broad as the duty to disclose under Rule 412(c). See Rule 416(g), committee comments. The good-faith standard is intended to avoid creating an impossible burden for the prosecution. A "good-faith" effort by prosecutors would include the specific identification of information that clearly tends to be exculpatory or mitigating. The amended rule is not intended to require that prosecutors specifically identify materials with remote or speculative exculpatory or mitigating value. The need to specifically identify materials falling between the extremes will depend upon the facts of the case.

The language stating that the duty to identify exculpatory or mitigating information must be viewed in light of the information available to the State when the material is disclosed to the defense is significant for several reasons. First, the information available to the State when disclosure is made will guide the determination of whether the State has made a good-faith effort to specifically identify exculpatory or mitigating information. Failure to identify information that can be characterized as exculpatory or mitigating only when viewed in light of the defense's theory of the case cannot be seen as evidence of failure to comply with the rule when the State was not aware of the defense theory. Second, placing the focus of the inquiry regarding compliance with the rule on information available at the time of disclosure to the defense is intended to avoid a standard based on hindsight evaluation of the exculpatory or mitigating value of information. Thus, a prosecutor's failure to identify information should not be second-guessed based on defense theories revealed after the information has been disclosed, unexpected events at trial, or new theories suggested after the trial.

The committee notes that in light of new evidence received or events at trial, materials that had no exculpatory value when initially disclosed could be viewed as exculpatory later in the trial process. The committee did not intend that the duty to specifically identify exculpatory or mitigating information would be subject to continuous updating.

The specific identification of potentially exculpatory or mitigating material by the prosecution pursuant to paragraph (c) is not an admission by the State for any purpose. Neither the terms or manner of the specific identification by the prosecution nor the fact that the prosecution has made the specific identification are relevant or admissible for the purposes of trial on the merits or sentencing. In addition, specific identification of materials pursuant to paragraph (c) does not imply that the material will be admissible as evidence.

Committee Comments

***

Paragraph (c) is included to comply with the constitutional requirement that the prosecution disclose, "evidence favorable to an accused *** where the evidence is material either to guilt or to punishment." (Brady v. Maryland, 373 U.S. 83, 87, 10 L. Ed. 2d 215, 218, 83 S. Ct. 1194, 1196-97 (1963).) Although the pretrial disclosure of such material is now not constitutionally required, it is clear that, if a conviction is to be valid, the material must be disclosed so that the defense can make use of it. In providing for pretrial disclosure, this paragraph permits adequate preparation for, and minimizes interruptions of, a trial, and assures informed pleas by the accused. ***

Illinois Supreme Court Rule 415

Regulation of Discovery

(a) Investigations Not to Be Impeded. Except as is otherwise provided as to matters not subject to disclosure and protective orders, neither the counsel for the parties nor other prosecution or defense personnel shall advise persons having relevant material or information (except the accused) to refrain from discussing the case with opposing counsel or showing opposing counsel any relevant material, nor shall they otherwise impede opposing counsel's investigation of the case.

(b) Continuing Duty to Disclose. If, subsequent to compliance with these rules or orders pursuant thereto, a party discovers additional material or information which is subject to disclosure, he shall promptly notify the other party or his counsel of the existence of such additional material, and if the additional material or information is discovered during trial, the court shall also be notified.

(c) Custody of Materials. Any materials furnished to an attorney pursuant to these rules shall remain in his exclusive custody and be used only for the purposes of conducting his side of the case, and shall be subject to such other terms and conditions as the court may provide.

(d) Protective Orders. Upon a showing of cause, the court may at any time order that specified disclosures be restricted or deferred, or make such other order as is appropriate, provided that all material and information to which a party is entitled must be disclosed in time to permit counsel to make beneficial use thereof.

(e) **Excision.** When some parts of certain material are discoverable under these rules, and other parts not discoverable, as much of the material should be disclosed as is consistent with the rules. Excision of certain material and disclosure of the balance is preferable to withholding the whole. Material excised pursuant to judicial order shall be sealed, impounded and preserved in the records of the court, to be made available to the reviewing court in the event of an appeal.

(f) *In Camera* Proceedings. Upon request of any person, the court may permit any showing of cause for denial or regulation of disclosures, or portion of such showing, to be made *in camera*. A record shall be made of such proceedings. If the court enters an order granting relief following a showing *in camera*, the entire record of such showing shall be sealed, impounded, and preserved in the records of the court, to be made available to the reviewing court in the event of an appeal.

(g) Sanctions.

(i) If at any time during the course of the proceedings it is brought to the attention of the court that a party has failed to comply with an applicable discovery rule or an order issued pursuant thereto, the court may order such party to permit the discovery of material and information not previously disclosed, grant a continuance, exclude such evidence, or enter such other order as it deems just under the circumstances.

(ii) Wilful violation by counsel of an applicable discovery rule or an order issued pursuant thereto may subject counsel to appropriate sanctions by the court.

Effective October 1, 1971.

Committee Comments

Paragraph (a). One barrier to pretrial investigation and meaningful discovery procedures is the practice of some attorneys of advising witnesses not to cooperate with opposing counsel. This paragraph is included to provide that discovery shall not be frustrated by improper conduct of counsel or the various agents of counsel.

Paragraph (b) is modeled after Federal Rule of Criminal Procedure 16(c). This paragraph is intended to permit thorough preparation and to minimize paperwork and delay. After discovery has been conducted as provided, any additional material or information acquired by either side which is subject to disclosure should be automatically and promptly disclosed. The notification required by this paragraph is intended to make such disclosures as simple and easy as possible.

Paragraph (c). If the materials to be provided were to become, in effect, matters of public availability once they had been turned over to counsel for the limited purposes which pretrial disclosures are designed to serve, the administration of criminal justice would likely be prejudiced. Accordingly, this paragraph establishes a mandatory requirement in every case that the material which an attorney receives shall remain in his exclusive custody. While he will undoubtedly have to show it to, or at least discuss it with, others, he is not permitted to furnish them with copies or let them take it from his office. It should be noted that this paragraph also applies to the State. Nothing in this paragraph should be interpreted to prevent counsel from having tests performed by experts on materials furnished by opposing counsel or from having experts examine reports received from opposing counsel. Tangible objects, such as guns, knives, clothing, not subject to duplication but furnished for purposes of testing, etc., should be returned to the furnishing party when such testing or inspection is completed. If not returned routinely the last phrase permits the court to so order, in addition to any other terms and conditions provided.

Paragraph (d). In order that legitimate needs of exceptional cases will not shape discovery policy and result in denial of discovery in all cases, this paragraph is designed to provide sufficient flexibility to meet such exceptional needs. This paragraph, adapted from Federal Rule of Criminal Procedure 16(e), permits application by the party concerned to the court for a protective order adjusting the time, place, recipient, or use of the disclosures as are necessary in a particular case. It is anticipated that it will ordinarily be needed with respect to those matters for which discovery is mandatory, rather than matters where the court has discretion in allowing discovery under Rule 412(h). While the protective order is designed to permit flexibility, it is to be used under a policy of as full and as early discovery as possible; it is not intended to permit denial of disclosure, although it may result in deferral until a later time. The disclosure must be made in time for a party to make beneficial use of it. Normal use of the protective order will be made when there is substantial risk to any person of physical harm, intimidation, bribery, or economic reprisals which outweigh any usefulness of disclosure to the defendant or State.

Paragraph (e). Occasions will arise when material will contain information which is both discoverable and nondiscoverable. This paragraph recognizes the right of a party to excise, or have excised, the nondiscoverable portion. The procedure under this paragraph is different from that under the Jencks Act, 18 U.S.C. § 3500(c), and under present Illinois practice, only in giving approval to a party excising portions of material without court supervision. Approval of counsel's independent conduct is consistent with the purpose of expediting the discovery process, but it is expected that in many cases counsel will seek a decision by the court, and that, in any event, he will be held accountable for excisions, if they are challenged by opposing counsel. The only change from the ABA standards is the requirement that the material excised pursuant to a judicial order not only be sealed, but also impounded and preserved.

Paragraph (f) provides for preserving the confidentiality of material at such times as the trial court is called upon to decide whether to require its disclosure. In issuing protective orders under paragraph (d), allowing excision of portions of material under paragraph (e), or in otherwise deciding that certain material is not subject to disclosure, the trial court must have an opportunity to examine, in private, the particular material as well as the reasons for nondisclosure. The purpose of issuing such rulings would often be defeated if the hearing were to be held in open court. To protect the litigants from error by the trial court, provision is made for the making and preserving of a record of all such proceedings for purposes of appeal.

Through paragraph (g), the committee intended to emphasize that these discovery rules must be enforced. Rather than attempt to provide specific sanctions for specific violations, the committee deemed it wise to leave the sanctions to the discretion of the trial court. This paragraph does contain one provision not present in the ABA standards. If justified under the circumstances, the court may exclude evidence which a party has failed to disclose under applicable discovery rules. The committee felt that such a device is a useful sanction, and that even though some problems may arise in applying it against the accused, the sanction can be applied in some situations. In this regard this paragraph conforms to Federal Rule of Criminal Procedure 16(g), and further guarantees the expedition of the discovery process. The sanctions listed are not exclusive.

Illinois Case Law Under the New Illinois Rules of Evidence

An Accused Charged with a Misdemeanor DUI Offense Is Entitled to the Disclosure of Relevant Evidence Such as a Video Recording of a Routine Traffic Stop

People v. Kladis, 2011 IL 110920

Defendant was arrested for a misdemeanor DUI offense. Prior to trial she requested that the state produce the arresting officer and any video tapes taken of her while she was in custody. The state produced the officer at the first hearing but did not produce a copy of the videotape from the arresting officer's car. The state promised to have the videotape ready at the next court date. Instead of producing the videotape at the next court date, the state indicated that the video recording had been destroyed by the police department prior to the defendant's first hearing pursuant to a departmental policy. The trial court imposed sanctions on the state and prohibited it from introducing evidence pertaining to the event that had been recorded on the destroyed videotape. The trial court, however, allowed testimony about the defendant's conduct before the video recording equipment started its recording and after it had stopped. The state contended on appeal that the trial court's ruling "substantially impaired its ability to prosecute defendant," but the appellate court affirmed the trial court's decision. On review to the Illinois Supreme Court, the state claimed that it had no obligation to tender the video recording and that the trial court had erred in imposing sanctions. The state relied on People v. Schmidt, 56 Ill. 2d 572 (1974), arguing that video recordings are not discoverable because the Supreme Court in *Schmidt* set out a "rigid list" of items that are discoverable, including a list of witnesses, exculpatory evidence, any confession by the defendant and a "Driving While Intoxicated Arrest Report" in a misdemeanor DUI case. The Supreme Court rejected the state's argument and explained that the state had interpreted *Schmidt* too narrowly, stating that

> pretrial discovery "presupposes a range of relevance and materiality which includes not only what is admissible at the trial, but also that which leads to what is admissible." Krupp v. Chicago Transit Authority, 8 Ill. 2d 37, 41, (1956). The State overlooks the nature and relevancy of these discovery items, instead focusing on the incorrect concept that *Schmidt* set forth a rigid list which it believes should remain static and not take into account the fundamental changes which have occurred in law and society since that ruling.
>
> Relevancy is "determined by reference to the issues, for generally, something is relevant if it tends to prove or disprove something in issue." Bauter v. Reding, 68 Ill. App. 3d 171, 175, (1979). In the nearly four decades since we decided *Schmidt*, video recordings made by in-squad car cameras in misdemeanor DUI cases have become as relevant to the issue of proving or disproving guilt as the materials specifically mentioned in *Schmidt*. As such, allowing their discovery furthers the objectives of pretrial discovery to "enhance the truth-seeking process, to enable attorneys to better prepare for trial, to eliminate surprise and to promote an expeditious and final determination of controversies in accordance with the substantive rights of the parties." D.C. v. S.A., 178 Ill. 2d 551, 561 (1997).
>
> Since the time of *Schmidt*, the use of video recordings as evidence at trial has become a common practice to allow a defendant the opportunity to present an effective defense and to further the truth-seeking process. We recently reaffirmed the general admissibility of such evidence (People v. Taylor, 353 Ill. Dec. 569, 956 N.E.2d 431 (Ill. 2011)), and courts across the country are increasingly relying on video recordings to present an objective view of the facts in a case.

***

> In sum, we conclude that the routine video recording of traffic stops has now become an integral part of those encounters, objectively documenting what takes place by capturing the conduct and the words of both parties. We therefore hold that this important and relevant evidence falls within the scope of materials held to be discoverable under *Schmidt*. We therefore clarify that under *Schmidt*, these video recordings are discoverable in misdemeanor DUI cases.

The state argued that making video recordings discoverable in misdemeanor DUI prosecutions would be "unduly burdensome" and "delay the judicial process." The Illinois Supreme Court disagreed, noting that

> [t]he video recording is relevant and admissible evidence because it reveals what transpired during the traffic stop which serves to further the truth-seeking function of a trial. This evidence may be helpful to both the defendant and the State. Indeed, the flow of cases actually going to trial may be eased upon allowing defendants and their counsel to review these recordings: those which reflect events favorable to the State may result in defendants willing to enter pleas which they otherwise may not have contemplated. This also advances the purpose of our DUI statutes to ensure that our roads remain safe from impaired drivers.
>
> ***
>
> In sum, we hold that the trial court did not abuse its discretion in finding that the video recording of defendant's stop and arrest was subject to discovery in her misdemeanor DUI case and that the State committed a discovery violation by allowing the destruction of the recording.

PRIOR ILLINOIS CASE LAW

1. Duplicate of the Original Is Admissible If Proponent Shows Prior Existence of the Original and Explains Its Unavailability

People v. Baptist, 76 Ill. 2d 19 (1979)

Defendant was convicted of murder and attempted armed robbery. The appellate court reversed defendant's conviction finding that the trial court erroneously admitted testimony of a state's witness about the contents of a letter that had not been introduced in evidence. The witness was a sister of an eyewitness to the crime who also testified for the state. She testified that she had received a letter from defendant threatening that if her brother testified about the shooting, he would harm her family. The witness stated when she received the letter; noted that it bore a return name and address; described the signature of the sender; and explained that the original was not available because a fire had destroyed her house and its contents. The Illinois Supreme Court determined that the state had established a sufficient foundation for the admissibility of parol testimony about the contents of the letter, noting that

> the appellate court's ruling regarding the letter was based on the so-called "best evidence" rule. The appellate court held that [the witness'] explanation that the letter had been destroyed was insufficient to serve as a basis for allowing her to testify to the letter's contents. To introduce secondary evidence of the letter, it was incumbent upon the State to prove the prior existence of the original and also its unavailability. Gillson v. Gulf, Mobile & Ohio R. R. Co., 42 Ill. 2d 193, 199 (1969). Here, the State presented the testimony of [. . .] the purported recipient and custodian of the letter, who stated approximately when she received it, described the return name and address, and described the signature. She further testified to the reason for the letter's unavailability, namely, its destruction by fire. Defense counsel offered nothing on cross-examination or rebuttal to contravene [her] testimony, nor did he suggest to the trial court what more, if anything, should have been required by the State. When a party seeks to

> introduce secondary evidence of a writing, the sufficiency of the evidence showing that it is not within the offering party's power to produce the original depends upon the circumstances of each case and is, to some degree, within the discretion of the trial court. Maxcy-Barton Organ Co. v. Glen Building Co., 355 Ill. 228, 238 (1934). In our opinion, under the circumstances of this case a sufficient foundation was laid to permit the introduction of parol evidence of the contents of the letter. *See generally* People v. Carter, 39 Ill. 2d 31, 36-37 (1968) (sufficient foundation was laid for the introduction of a multilith copy of defendant's typed confession where the prosecution stated that the original was destroyed after copies had been made because an original does not hold up very long); Felix v. Caldwell, 235 Ill. 159 (1908); Forsyth v. Vehmeyer, 176 Ill. 359, 361-63 (1898), Aff'd (1900), 177 U.S. 177, 20 S. Ct. 623 (parol evidence of the contents of court records allowed where the records were destroyed by fire).

2. Party Who Offers Testimony About an Amount on a Receipt Must Either Produce the Receipt or Demonstrate That the Original Is Missing
People v. Furby, 138 Ill. 2d 434 (1990)

Defendants, two brothers, were convicted of theft of property worth more than $300. They allegedly stole money from a restaurant where they both worked. The owner of the restaurant testified that

> the cash register tape showed that the restaurant's receipts for November 7 had amounted to $658. In response to the trial judge's inquiry, [the owner] stated that when he left the restaurant during the afternoon of November 7, his desk drawer contained "just under $200" in petty cash and an additional $200 in a bank of rolled coins and currency. [The owner] thus believed that some $1,058 in cash should have been in his office desk when the restaurant closed on November 7. The money was never recovered, but the missing payroll book was later found in a dumpster behind the building.

Defendant objected to the testimony based on a lack of foundation but the trial court overruled the objection. The appellate court held that the trial court improperly allowed the owner's testimony about the amount of sales for the day of the theft. The Illinois Supreme Court reversed, noting that defendant had waived his objection by not raising it at trial and in a post-trial motion. The Supreme Court, however, noted that

> the evidence concerning the cash register readout was vulnerable to two separate objections. First, [the owner's] testimony concerning the figure was not in conformity with the original writing, or best evidence, rule, and no attempt was made to demonstrate that the original document was missing. Second, the figure shown on the register readout itself would be hearsay (see People v. Holowko (1985), 109 Ill. 2d 187), and its admission would then depend on compliance with the business records exception to the hearsay rule (see ILL. REV. STAT. 1987, ch. 38, par. 115-5). These are distinct objections: production of an original writing does not guarantee the document's admission if some further evidentiary hurdle must be overcome, and a writing that is itself hearsay will be inadmissible unless a hearsay exception is also satisfied. (M. GRAHAM, CLEARY & GRAHAM'S HANDBOOK OF ILLINOIS EVIDENCE § 1001.1, at 743 (5th ed. 1990); see Kerbis v. Kerbis (1976), 38 Ill. App. 3d 866, 872, 350 N.E.2d 1 (party's objection to admission of slip of paper as violation of original writing rule not sufficient to also raise noncompliance with business records exception).) In the present case, although defense counsel's objection did correctly intimate that appropriate grounds for admission of the testimony were missing, counsel's objection on foundation grounds failed to pinpoint either of the two defects we have discussed.

3. Failure of Police to Preserve Potentially Useful Evidence Is Not Denial of Defendant's Due Process Absent Showing of Bad Faith on the Part of the Police

Arizona v. Youngblood, 488 U.S. 51 (1988)

The United States Supreme Court held that the defendant was not denied due process of law when the police officers, who investigated the sexual assault of a 10-year-old boy, had failed to refrigerate the boy's clothing and perform tests on semen samples. The Supreme Court reasoned that the "fundamental fairness" requirement of the fourteenth amendment due process clause does not mandate that law enforcement retain or preserve "all material that might be of conceivable evidentiary significance." The Supreme Court explained that

> [t]he Due Process Clause of the Fourteenth Amendment, as interpreted in Brady [v. Maryland, 373 U.S. 83 (1963)], makes the good or bad faith of the State irrelevant when the State fails to disclose to the defendant material exculpatory evidence. But we think the Due Process Clause requires a different result when we deal with the failure of the State to preserve evidentiary material of which no more can be said than that it could have been subjected to tests, the results of which might have exonerated the defendant. Part of the reason for the difference in treatment is found in the observation made by the Court in California v. Trombetta, 467 U.S. 479, at 486 (1984), that "[w]henever potentially exculpatory evidence is permanently lost, courts face the treacherous task of divining the import of materials whose contents are unknown and, very often, disputed." Part of it stems from our unwillingness to read the "fundamental fairness" requirement of the Due Process Clause, [citation omitted], as imposing on the police an undifferentiated and absolute duty to retain and to preserve all material that might be of conceivable evidentiary significance in a particular prosecution. We think that requiring a defendant to show bad faith on the part of the police both limits the extent of the police's obligation to preserve evidence to reasonable bounds and confines it to that class of cases where the interests of justice most clearly require it, i.e., those cases in which the police themselves by their conduct indicate that the evidence could form a basis for exonerating the defendant. We therefore hold that unless a criminal defendant can show bad faith on the part of the police, failure to preserve potentially useful evidence does not constitute a denial of due process of law.
>
> In this case, the police collected the rectal swab and clothing on the night of the crime; respondent was not taken into custody until six weeks later. The failure of the police to refrigerate the clothing and to perform tests on the semen samples can at worst be described as negligent. None of this information was concealed from respondent at trial, and the evidence—such as it was—was made available to respondent's expert who declined to perform any tests on the samples.

4. A Due Process Violation Occurs When Prosecution Suppresses or Fails to Disclose Material Exculpatory Evidence Regardless of Good or Bad Faith on Part of the Prosecution

Illinois v. Fisher, 540 U.S. 544 (2004)

The defendant was arrested in September 1988 and the police seized a plastic bag containing a white powdery substance. Four tests were conducted on the substance and all showed that the bag contained cocaine. Although the defendant had filed a motion for discovery in October 1988, in July 1989 he failed to appear in court and an arrest warrant was issued. Thereafter, the defendant remained a fugitive for 10 years. When defendant was finally caught, the state reinstated the 1988 cocaine-possession charge. Prior to trial, after the state had informed the defendant the police had destroyed the substance seized from him, the defendant filed a motion to dismiss the charge based on the destruction. The trial court denied the motion and the defendant was thereafter convicted and sentenced to one year in prison. The Illinois Appellate Court reversed the conviction. The appellate court concluded that the charges against the defendant had to be dismissed because the police, although acting in good faith and according to normal police procedure, had destroyed the substance that the defendant had requested more than 10 years earlier in discovery, and that the destruction of the evidence violated the defendant's due process rights. The appellate court distinguished Arizona v. Youngblood, 488 U.S. 51 (1988), noting that "the police in *Youngblood* did not destroy evidence subsequent to a discovery motion by the defendant." The Illinois Supreme Court denied leave to appeal.

The United States Supreme Court granted the state's petition for a writ of certiorari. The Supreme Court first noted that "when the State suppresses or fails to disclose material exculpatory evidence, the good or bad faith of the prosecution is irrelevant: a due process violation occurs whenever such evidence is withheld." However, in *Youngblood*, the Supreme Court concluded that a different result must be had when dealing with the state's failure to "preserve evidentiary material of which no more can be said than that it could had been subjected to tests, the results of which might have exonerated the defendant." In these situations, where the evidence is only "potentially useful," a due process violation does not occur "unless a criminal defendant can show bad faith on the part of the police."

Here, the Supreme Court concluded that the evidence which defendant sought was "plainly" the sort of "potentially useful evidence" recognized by *Youngblood*, and was not "material exculpatory evidence" because the chemical testing of the substance inculpated defendant. Since defendant did not allege that the police acted in bad faith and, to the contrary, the evidence demonstrated that they acted in good faith and followed normal procedures, the Supreme Court concluded that pursuant to *Youngblood*, defendant had failed to demonstrate a due process violation.

The Supreme Court noted that it had never held that a "pending discovery request" eliminated the requirement that the defendant must demonstrate that the police acted in bad faith. The Supreme Court further disagreed that

> *Youngblood* does not apply whenever the contested evidence provides a defendant's "only hope for exoneration" and is "'essential to and determinative of the outcome of the case.' " [citation omitted] In *Youngblood*, the Arizona Court of Appeals said that the destroyed evidence "could [have] eliminate[d] the defendant as the perpetrator." 488 U.S., at 54 (quotation marks and citations omitted). Similarly here, an additional test might have provided the defendant with an opportunity to show that the police tests were mistaken. It is thus difficult to distinguish the two cases on this basis. But in any event, the applicability of the bad-faith requirement in *Youngblood* depended not on the centrality of the contested evidence to the prosecution's case or the defendant's defense, but on the distinction between "material exculpatory" evidence and "potentially useful" evidence. 488 U.S., at 57-58. As we have held, [citation omitted], the substance destroyed here was, at best, "potentially useful" evidence, and therefore *Youngblood*'s bad-faith requirement applies.

5. Defendant Should Not Be Rewarded for the Inadvertent Loss of a Piece of Evidence Where Other Evidence Sufficient to Support His or Her Conviction Remains

People v. Sutherland, 223 Ill. 2d 187 (2006)

The defendant appealed convictions by a jury of first degree murder, aggravated kidnapping, and aggravated criminal sexual assault, arguing that the state had violated his due process right when it failed to produce a vehicle seized in Montana pursuant to his discovery request. After conducting a thorough search of the vehicle, the state had disposed of it.

The Illinois Supreme Court held that unless the accused can show bad faith on the part of the police, failure to preserve evidence that may be potentially useful is not a denial of due process. The Illinois Supreme Court observed that

> [d]efendant liken[ed] the loss or destruction of the vehicle in this case to the improper suppression of material evidence by the State under Brady v. Maryland, 373 U.S. 83 (1963). In *Brady*, the United States Supreme Court held "that the suppression by the prosecution of evidence favorable to an accused upon request violates due process where the evidence is material either to guilt or to punishment, irrespective of the good faith or bad faith of the prosecution." *Brady*, 373 U.S. at 87; *see also* United States v. Agurs, 427 U.S. 97, 110-11 (1976) (expanding *Brady* by recognizing a constitutional duty on the part of the State to disclose exculpatory evidence to the defendant, irrespective of whether the defendant makes a specific request).
>
> This court has recognized that the *Brady* analysis is "ill-suited" in cases where, as here, the evidence has been lost or destroyed. *In re* C.J., 166 Ill. 2d 264, 272, 209 Ill. Dec. 775 (1995), citing People v. Hobley, 159 Ill. 2d 272, 307 (1994). This court instead has applied the analysis in Arizona v. Youngblood, 488 U.S. 51 (1988). *See* [citations omitted] People v. Ward, 154 Ill. 2d 272, 298 (1992).

The Illinois Supreme Court considered and articulated the "underlying policy considerations" enumerated by the United States Supreme Court in the *Youngblood* case:

> In order to promote the preservation of exculpatory evidence, there must be the possibility of a sanction where evidence is lost or destroyed. On the other hand, a defendant should not be rewarded for the inadvertent loss of a piece of evidence where other evidence sufficient to support his conviction remains. The proper balance between these competing interests can be accomplished through careful consideration of (1) the degree of negligence or bad faith by the State in losing the evidence, and (2) the importance of the lost evidence relative to the evidence presented against the defendant at trial. People v. Hobley, 159 Ill. 2d 272, 307 (1994).

The court concluded that the loss of the vehicle was not a denial of due process because the defendant failed to show that the state acted in bad faith when it destroyed the vehicle. The court also found that there was no evidence that the vehicle itself was pivotal or probative because the critical evidence against him was not the vehicle but all of the physical evidence that was taken from the vehicle.

Rule 1005. Public Records

The contents of an official record, or of a document authorized to be recorded or filed and actually recorded or filed, including data compilations in any form, if otherwise admissible, may be proved by copy, certified as correct in accordance with Rule 902 or testified to be correct by a witness who has compared it with the original. If a copy which complies with the foregoing cannot be obtained by the exercise of reasonable diligence, then other evidence of the contents may be given.

Adopted September 27, 2010, eff. January 1, 2011.

AUTHOR'S COMMENTARY

Illinois Rule of Evidence 1005 is modeled on Federal Rule of Evidence 1005, in effect prior to its stylistic amendment on December 1, 2011. Gino L. DiVito, *The Illinois Rules of Evidence: A Color-Coded Guide Containing the New Rules, the Committee's General and Specific Comments, a Comparison with the Federal Rules of Evidence, and Additional Commentary* (*Including the Federal Rules of Evidence as Amended Effective December 1, 2011*) (Jan. 1, 2012), at 150, http://www.tdrlawfirm.com/assets/downloads/Illinois_Rules_of_Evidence_Color-Coded_Guide.pdf.

Relevant Illinois Supreme Court Rules

Illinois Supreme Court Rule 216. Admission of Fact or of Genuineness of Documents

(a) Request for Admission of Fact. A party may serve on any other party a written request for the admission by the latter of the truth of any specified relevant fact set forth in the request.

(b) Request for Admission of Genuineness of Document. A party may serve on any other party a written request for admission of the genuineness of any relevant documents described in the request. Copies of the documents shall be served with the request unless copies have already been furnished.

(c) Admission in the Absence of Denial. Each of the matters of fact and the genuineness of each document of which admission is requested is admitted unless, within 28 days after service thereof, the party to whom the request is directed serves upon the party requesting the admission either (1) a sworn statement denying specifically the matters of which admission is requested or setting forth in detail the reasons why he cannot truthfully admit or deny those matters or (2) written objections on the ground that some or all of the requested admissions are privileged or irrelevant or that the request is otherwise improper in whole or in part. If written objections to a part of the request are made, the remainder of the request shall be answered within the period designated in the request. A denial shall fairly meet the substance of the requested admission. If good faith requires that a party deny only a part, or requires qualification, of a matter of which an admission is requested, he shall specify so much of it as is true and deny only the remainder. Any objection to a request or to an answer shall be heard by the court upon prompt notice and motion of the party making the request.

(d) Public Records. If any public records are to be used as evidence, the party intending to use them may prepare a copy of them insofar as they are to be used, and may seasonably present the copy to the adverse party by notice in writing, and the copy shall thereupon be admissible in evidence as admitted facts in the case if otherwise admissible, except insofar as its inaccuracy is pointed out under oath by the adverse party in an affidavit filed and served within 14 days after service of the notice.

(e) Effect of Admission. Any admission made by a party pursuant to request under this rule is for the purpose of the pending action and any action commenced pursuant to the authority of section 13-217 of the Code of Civil Procedure (735 ILCS 5/13-217) only. It does not constitute an admission by him for any other purpose and may not be used against him in any other proceeding.

(f) Number of Requests. The maximum number of requests for admission a party may serve on another party is 30, unless a higher number is agreed to by the parties or ordered by the court for good cause shown. If a request has subparts, each subpart counts as a separate request.

(g) Special Requirements. A party must: (1) prepare a separate paper which contains only the requests and the documents required for genuine document requests; (2) serve this paper separate from other papers; and (3) put the following warning in a prominent place on the first page in 12-point or larger boldface type: "WARNING: If you fail to serve the response required by Rule 216 within 28 days after you are served with this paper, all the facts set forth in the requests will be deemed true and all the documents described in the requests will be deemed genuine."

Amended July 1, 1985, effective August 1, 1985; amended May 30, 2008, effective immediately; amended October 1, 2010, effective January 1, 2011.

Committee Comment
(October 1, 2010)
Paragraphs (f) and (g) are designed to address certain problems with Rule 216, including the service of hundreds of requests for admission. For the vast majority of cases, the limitation to 30 requests now found in paragraph (f) will eliminate this abusive practice. Other noted problems include the bundling of discovery requests to form a single document into which the requests to admit were intermingled. This practice worked to the disadvantage of certain litigants, particularly pro se litigants, who do not understand that failure to respond within the time allowed results in the requests being deemed admitted. Paragraph (g) provides for requests to be contained in a separate paper containing a boldface warning regarding the effect of the failure to respond within 28 days. Consistent with Vision Point of Sale Inc. v. Haas, 226 Ill. 2d 334 (2007), trial courts are vested with discretion with respect to requests for admission.

RELEVANT STATUTORY AUTHORITY

Sworn Copies: 735 ILCS 5/8-1206

§ 8-1206. Sworn copies. Any such papers, entries, records and ordinances may be proved by copies examined and sworn to by credible witnesses.

Effective July 1, 1982.

PRIOR ILLINOIS CASE LAW

Oral Testimony About the Contents of Lost or Destroyed Public Records Will Be Allowed Where the Existence of Such Records Is Shown, Their Loss or Destruction Is Alleged, and It Is Not Possible to Produce Them

Forsyth v. Vehmeyer, 176 Ill. 359 (1898) *aff'd*, 177 U.S. 177 (1900)

The Illinois Supreme Court noted that the rule

> in respect to judicial records is that, before inferior evidence can be received of their contents, the loss of their existence must be clearly accounted for. It must be shown that there was such a record; that it has been lost or destroyed, or is otherwise incapable of being produced, or that its mutilation from time or accident has made it illegible.

See also People *ex rel.* Adams Elec. Co-op. v. Vill. of Camp Point, 286 Ill. App. 3d 247 (4th Dist. 1997) (finding that oral testimony may be used to prove the contents of a lost or destroyed public record).

Rule 1006. Summaries

The contents of voluminous writings, recordings, or photographs which cannot conveniently be examined in court may be presented in the form of a chart, summary, or calculation. The originals, or duplicates, shall be made available for examination or copying, or both, by other parties at reasonable time and place. The court may order that they be produced in court.

Adopted September 27, 2010, eff. January 1, 2011.

Author's Commentary

Illinois Rule of Evidence 1006 codifies prior Illinois common law and allows the contents of voluminous documents to be presented in the form of a chart, summary or a calculation. *See e.g.*, People v. Moone, 334 Ill. 590 (1929). It is modeled on Federal Rule of Evidence 1006, in effect prior to its stylistic amendment on December 1, 2011. Gino L. DiVito, *The Illinois Rules of Evidence: A Color-Coded Guide Containing the New Rules, the Committee's General and Specific Comments, a Comparison with the Federal Rules of Evidence, and Additional Commentary (Including the Federal Rules of Evidence as Amended Effective December 1, 2011)* (Jan. 1, 2012), at 151, http://www.tdrlawfirm.com/assets/downloads/Illinois_Rules_of_Evidence_Color-Coded_Guide.pdf.

Prior Illinois Case Law

1. Contents of Voluminous Documents May Be Presented in the Form of a Chart, Summary, or a Calculation

People v. Moone, 334 Ill. 590 (1929)

Defendant, an accountant for a partnership, was charged with forgery. He claimed on appeal that the summaries of a certified public accountant who performed an audit for the partnership were improperly admitted at trial. Defendant argued that there was no foundation laid for the admissibility of this evidence because the materials were "so voluminous as to warrant the testimony as to the result of their examination." The Illinois Supreme Court disagreed, noting that

> [i]t sufficiently appears from the record that so many items in accounts, papers, and documents were examined in making the reports that their introduction would have been a source of confusion to the jury without expert guidance in the matter of what they showed. It is well established that when the originals consist of numerous documents, books, papers, or records which cannot be examined in court and the fact to be proved is the general result of the examination of the whole collection, evidence may be given as to such result by any competent person who examined the documents, provided the result is capable of being ascertained by calculation. People v. Gerold, 265 Ill. 448, 107 N.E. 165, Ann. Cas. 1916A, 636. The production of the originals, of course, may be required in order that the adverse party may use them for cross-examination. People v. Sawhill, 299 Ill. 393, 132 N.E. 477; Welsh v. Shumway, 232 Ill. 54, 83 N.E. 549. In this case the court did require the state to produce all of the records and papers of [the partnership] that were used by the accountants in making their audits.

2. Originals or Duplicates of the Voluminous Documents Must Be Made Available to the Adverse Party

People v. Sawhill, 299 Ill. 393 (1921)

Defendant, a stock broker, established a corporation through which he allegedly obtained funds from various individuals under false pretenses. State introduced testimony of an expert who examined the books of defendant's corporation. Defendant argued that he should have been allowed to cross-examine the expert by using the original documents. The Illinois Supreme Court found that the trial court erred in not allowing defendant to examine the expert about the contents of the originals, noting that

> where the originals consist of numerous documents, books, papers, or records which cannot conveniently be examined in court, and the fact to be proved is the general result of an examination of the whole collection, evidence may be given as to such result by any competent person who has examined the documents, provided the result is capable of being ascertained by

calculation. It would be impossible for the jury to carry the numerous figures in their minds if merely read off to them by the witness, and it would be impracticable for the jurors to transcribe them for the purpose of adding them up themselves during the trial. It has therefore been held that it is in the discretion of the court to admit such statements or schedules of figures or the results of the examination of numerous documents or account books to be introduced in evidence, such statements, schedules, or results to be verified by the testimony of the witness by whom they were prepared, allowing the adverse party an opportunity to examine them before they are admitted in evidence and to cross-examine the witness from the original books, where such books are accessible. People v. Gerold, 265 Ill. 448, 107 N.E. 165, Ann. Cas. 1916A, 636; Lynn v. Cumberland, 77 Md. 449, 26 Atl. 1001; 22 Corpus Juris, 1017, and cases there cited; Jones on Evidence (2d Ed.) § 206; 1 GREENLEAF ON EVIDENCE (16th Ed.) § 563h; 2 WIGMORE ON EVIDENCE, § 1230; 2 ENCY. OF EVIDENCE, 690; 3 CHAMBERLAYNE ON MODERN LAW OF EVIDENCE, § 1841, and cases cited; Burton v. Driggs, 87 U.S. (20 Wall.) 125, 22 L. Ed. 299; Elmira Roofing Co. v. Gould, 71 Conn. 629, 42 Atl. 1002. Many of these authorities state directly that the books of account must ordinarily be introduced for inspection or for the purpose of cross-examination if requested by the opposite party, and none of them intimate that, if the books are accessible and can be brought into court, opposing counsel shall not have every reasonable opportunity of examining them and cross-examining the expert who has prepared the schedules or statements therefrom in order to ascertain the correctness of his conclusions. Indeed, the weight of authority appears to be that the books themselves may properly be introduced in evidence, and that the only purpose of the expert witness in testifying to the schedule or a synopsis of their contents is to make such contents readily intelligible to the jury, and that the statements made by the expert witness as to the synopsis or the conclusions reached by them are not necessarily binding on the jury; that the jury may make their own calculations from the books and papers in evidence, regardless of the statements of the expert witness. 22 Corpus Juris, 1017. This was the holding of this court in Welsh v. Shumway, 232 Ill. 54, 83 N.E. 549.

Rule 1007. Testimony or Written Admission of Party

Contents of writings, recordings, or photographs may be proved by the testimony or deposition of the party against whom offered or by that party's written admission, without accounting for the nonproduction of the original.

Adopted September 27, 2010, eff. January 1, 2011.

Committee Commentary

(3) Modernization: Where there was no conflict with statutes or recent Illinois Supreme Court or Illinois Appellate Court decisions, and where it was determined to be beneficial and uniformly or almost uniformly accepted elsewhere, the Committee incorporated into the Illinois Rules of Evidence uncontroversial developments with respect to the law of evidence as reflected in the Federal Rules of Evidence and the 44 surveyed jurisdictions. [One of t]he 14 instances of modernization of note [is] as follows:

> **(14) Rule 1007.** Testimony or Written Admission of Party. The Rule 1007 provision that testimony or a written admission maybe employed to prove the contents of a document appears never before to have been the law in Illinois. Bryan v. Smith, 3 Ill. 47 (1839).

ILL. R. EVID. Committee Commentary § 4, pg. 2-4.

AUTHOR'S COMMENTARY

Illinois Rule of Evidence 1007 is "identical" to Federal Rule of Evidence 1007, in effect prior to its stylistic amendment on December 1, 2011. Gino L. DiVito, *The Illinois Rules of*

Evidence: A Color-Coded Guide Containing the New Rules, the Committee's General and Specific Comments, a Comparison with the Federal Rules of Evidence, and Additional Commentary (Including the Federal Rules of Evidence as Amended Effective December 1, 2011) (Jan. 1, 2012), at 151, http://www.tdrlawfirm.com/assets/downloads/Illinois_Rules_of_Evidence_Color-Coded_Guide.pdf. Adoption of Federal Rule of Evidence 1007 represents a change to the Illinois common law. The Committee Commentary to the Illinois Rules of Evidence states that the "provision that testimony or a written admission maybe employed to prove the contents of a document appears never before to have been the law in Illinois. Bryan v. Smith, 3 Ill. 47 (1839)." ILL. R. EVID. Committee Commentary § 4, pg. 2-4.

PRIOR ILLINOIS CASE LAW

1. Historically, a Party Was Required to Produce an Original Document and Could Not Use an Admission of Its Opponent to Prove the Content of the Document

Bryan v. Smith, 3 Ill. 47 (1839)

The Illinois Supreme Court held that it was improper for plaintiffs to use defendants' admission to prove that they were tenants in common instead of producing the title to the lands. The Supreme Court noted that the plaintiffs used

> the admission by defendants, [that they were] tenants in common in the lands for which they ask them to account for the rents and profits. On this point we have no doubt the circuit court decided correctly. It was inadmissible for the plaintiffs to show title to the lands, by parol admissions, while paper title existed; upon the acknowledged principle that there was higher, better, and more certain testimony resting in record evidence, of their title, which was within their power to produce, the production of which would subject them to no possible inconvenience, if they were tenants in common, of the lands stated in the declaration.

Table of Cases

Index to Federal Rules of Evidence

Index to Illinois Statutes

Index to Illinois Supreme Court Rules

Index to Table of Authorities

Index

www.ingramcontent.com/pod-product-compliance
Lightning Source LLC
LaVergne TN
LVHW062243200926
848484LV00006B/1601
9781600421839